FOURTH EDITION

Literacy Development in the Early Years

Helping Children Read and Write

Lesley Mandel Morrow

Rutgers, The State University of New Jersey

Allyn and Bacon

Boston ■ London ■ Toronto ■ Sydney ■ Tokyo ■ Singapore

Editor: Arnis Burvikovs
Editorial Assistant: Patrice Mailloux
Marketing Manager: Kathleen Morgan
Editorial-Production Administrator: Deborah Brown
Editorial-Production Service: P. M. Gordon Associates
Composition Buyer: Linda Cox
Manufacturing Buyer: Julie O'Neill
Cover Administrator: Linda Knowles
Text Designer: Carol Somberg, Omegatype

A Pearson Education Company
160 Gould Street
Needham Heights, MA 02494

Internet: www.abacon.com

Library of Congress Cataloging-in-Publication Data

Morrow, Lesley Mandel.
Literacy development in the early years : helping children read and write / Lesley Mandel Morrow.—4th ed.
p. cm.
Includes bibliographical references (p.) and index.
ISBN 0-205-30589-X
1. Language arts (Preschool)—United States. 2. Reading (Preschool)—United States. 3. Children—Books and reading—United States. I. Title.

LB1140.5.L3 M66 2001
372.6'0973—dc21 00-020251

Printed in the United States of America

10 9 8 7 6 5 4 3 2 1 05 04 03 02 01 00

Photographs: Lenore Arone, Susan Arone, Joyce Caponigro, Deborah Hanna, Lori Harrje, Katherine Heiss, Pam Kelliher, Danielle Lynch, Mary Jane Kurabinski, Milton E. Mandel, Howard Manson, Franklin A. Morrow, Lesley Mandel Morrow, Dana Pilla, Andrea Shane

To Mary, Milton, Frank, Stephanie, and Douglas
my very special parents,
my very special husband,
and my very special daughter and son-in-law

Contents

chapter 5 *How Young Children Learn to Read and Write* 127

chapter 6 *Motivating Reading and Writing with Children's Literature: Using Children's Literature in Classrooms* 161

Foreword

Dramatic changes in our understanding of early literacy development have occurred during the past two decades. We once thought that children learned to speak and listen during their early years and later learned to read and write at five or six years. We now know that they begin to develop early forms of language and literacy ability concurrently and from the day they are born.

We also have discovered that the conditions that promote first language learning are the same conditions that promote total literacy development. These conditions, created in the social context surrounding a child, involve immersion, direct instruction, opportunity to practice, modeling by teachers, and feedback.

Lesley Mandel Morrow demonstrates the value of involving children in many types of language and literacy experiences. She provides numerous examples of children's approximations of writing and reading as she establishes the necessity of giving them unlimited opportunities to practice. Further, she illustrates the ways adults provide models, direct instruction, and feedback for young learners as they attempt to read and write. Dr. Morrow takes a balanced perspective toward literacy instruction by selecting the best techniques from learning theory, such as a constructivist model or problem-solving approach to more direct explicit instruction.

Children's literature plays an important role in Morrow's literacy environment. Literature serves as a model for language learning and provides strong motivation for learning to read and write. It is a springboard for many literacy-related activities. Most important, literature is a way of knowing. It is shaped around story—a primary act of human minds. Morrow is also aware that in early literacy development materials designed for instructional purposes are necessary for skill development and to accomplish national, state, and local standards for literacy learning.

Dr. Morrow recognizes the importance of parents, siblings, grandparents, and other caregivers reading to children and enjoying the wealth of books. She shows how reading to babies influences their grasp of language and story patterns that serve them well as they learn to read and write. She illustrates how children learn concepts about print, book handling, and conventions of stories as they interact with books. Morrow establishes that adults teach by example as they enjoy shared reading and shared writing with children. She shows the impact of having a literacy center in a classroom and the effects of storybook reading aloud by a teacher. She shows that when children know authors and illustrators as real people, they want to read their works and write in a manner similar to them. Morrow states that storytelling is similar to reading aloud in its impact on children. She also recognizes the necessity of skills that involve learning concepts about print and books. For example, children need to develop phonemic awareness, alphabetic principles, and phonics for reading success. They also must learn to construct meaning from text by learning strategies for comprehension. Speaking from her own experiences as a teacher, researcher, and parent, Morrow charts a path that leads to successful literacy learning.

Lesley Mandel Morrow has taken a long view of literacy development in the early years, showing its historical roots. She also knows and draws on the research of today's leaders because she is a member of that research community. She succinctly summarizes language theories and relates current research to shape sound practices. She has conducted much of the original research herself, testimony to the fact that she can bridge the gap among theory, research, and practice. Her examples are anchored in real classroom experiences—her own and those of other teachers with whom she works collaboratively. The examples are authentic and add credibility to her argument.

Dr. Morrow's treatment of literacy development is on the cutting edge of current knowledge. She is well informed about her subject and makes connections among all aspects of literacy learning. She is a sensitive observer and writer as she lets children and teachers speak for themselves through their work.

Dr. Morrow states that few children learn to love books by themselves. Someone must lure them into the joys of the printed word and the wonderful world of stories. She shows us how to do that and enriches our lives and the lives of children through her work. Her contribution to the literacy development of young children is a lasting one.

Bernice E. Cullinan
Professor of Early Childhood Education and Elementary Education
New York University

Preface

Literacy Development in the Early Years, Fourth Edition, is for teachers, reading specialists, administrators, students in teacher education programs, and parents. It is appropriate for graduate, undergraduate, and staff development courses in early literacy, and it complements texts on teaching reading in the elementary school, child development, the early childhood curriculum, teaching language arts in the elementary school, and children's literature.

I wrote the book because of my special interest in literacy development in early childhood. I taught in preschools, kindergartens, and in the primary grades; I was a reading specialist; and then I taught early childhood curriculum and literacy courses at the university level. My research has focused on instructional strategies in early literacy. A wealth of research information has been created in this area over the past several years. That research has generated new theory and given new strength to certain older theories of learning. It has implications for new instructional strategies and reinforces older practices that had little or no research to establish their validity. The book describes a program that nurtures literacy development from birth to third grade.

Although this book is about early literacy, its content has strong ramifications for reading instruction in the elementary grades. The fundamental ideas presented in this volume are applicable for literacy instruction in elementary grade classrooms. In many respects, some parts of this book may sound like some of the earliest volumes on early literacy because much of what we know is still valid. We do, however, have new research to shape our teaching, and the old research needs to be refined, reorganized, and verified.

This book does not provide a prescription. The ideas presented here have been tried and they have worked, but not all are appropriate for all teachers or all children. The good teacher functions most effectively with strategies he or she feels most comfortable with. The teacher needs to be a decision maker who thinks critically about the design of his or her literacy program and the selection of materials. Children should be included in some of the decision making. Children come to school with diverse cultural backgrounds, experiences, exposures to literacy, and abilities. Instructional programs can differ in different parts of the country, in different localities, and for different children in the same classroom.

Underlying this book is the merging of the art and the science of teaching. The science involves theories based on research findings that have generated instructional strategies. This book contains descriptions of strategies and steps for carrying them out. But, the scientific research does not necessarily take into account individual differences among teachers and children. The art of teaching concentrates on those human variables. This book provides a *balanced approach* to early literacy instruction. It discusses research that tested successful instructional strategies based on several learning theories. A blend of constructivist ideas that involve problem-solving techniques with some explicit direct instruction approaches are presented so that teachers can decide what works best for the children they teach.

Chapter 1 provides a framework of theory and research, past and current, that has influenced strategies for developing early literacy.

Chapter 2 covers the important issues of assessment and children with special needs—those children from diverse cultural backgrounds as well as children with special learning needs. This chapter introduces assessment concepts; practical strategies for assessment are integrated into all chapters. In addition to the focus on meeting individual needs in all chapters, issues of individual differences are discussed particularly in Chapters 1, 3, and 10.

Chapter 3 discusses the strong influence of the home on the development of literacy, especially in a child's earliest years. It discusses broad perspectives concerning family literacy such as integrated home/school programs, intergenerational programs, and sensitivity to cultural differences to provide programs that are not intrusive but build on the strengths of the families being served.

Chapters 4 through 9 deal with areas of language and literacy development, oral language, reading, and writing. These chapters discuss theory and research, specifically, developmental trends, instructional strategies, and methods for assessment. The book views the development of literacy skills (reading, writing, and oral language) as concurrent and interrelated: The development of one enhances the development of the others. Furthermore, the theories, stages, acquisition, and strategies associated with each are similar, and it is difficult to separate them entirely. To make the volume more readable, however, I have treated the different areas of literacy in different chapters.

Chapter 10 discusses the preparation and management of the components presented in the book that are organized to create a successful program. This chapter emphasizes the interrelatedness of the areas of literacy and describes how they can be integrated into the entire school day within content areas.

Each chapter begins with questions to focus on while reading the text. Each chapter ends with suggested activities, questions, an idea for the classroom from the classroom, and case study activities to be used by preservice and inservice teachers. The appendixes list materials that teachers use in carrying out a successful program to develop early literacy. Key words dealing with early literacy development are defined in the glossary at the end of the book.

Acknowledgments

I want to thank many individuals who helped in the preparation of the first, second, third, and fourth editions of this book. Students who helped in the past were Patricia Addonizio, Mary Belchik, Susan Burks, Kathleen Cunningham, Katie Farrell, Donna Fino Nagi, Mary Ann Gavin, Laura Babarca, Tricia Lyons, Melody Murray Olsen, Michele Preole, Mary Joyce Santoloci, Sari Schnipper, and Karen Szabo. Students who helped with this edition include Patricia DeWitt, Erica Erlanger, Michael Gravois, Katherine Heiss, Pamela Kelliher, Lisa Lozak, Stacey Rog, Monica Saraiya, Amy Sass, and Connie Zauderer.

Thank you to the teachers and administrators who helped with past editions and this present edition: Stephanie Adams, Ellen Abere, Maxine Bell, Karen Buda, Pat Burton, Barbara Callister, Jennifer Castio, Mehzga Colucci, Tom DelCasale, Fran Diamente, Tami-Lyn Eisen, Arlene Hall, David Harris, Lori Harrje, Catherine Hickey, Noreen Johnson, Linda Keefe, Sheryl King, Penelope Lattimer, Gail Martinez, Nancy Mason, Joyce McGee, Carna Meechem, Dennis Monaghan, Stephanie Moretti, Joyce Ng, Susan Nitto, Ellen O'Connor, Lucy Oman, Barbara Oxfeld, Mary Payton, Tammye Pelovitz, Cynthia Peters, John Quintaglie, Robert Rosado, Sonia Satterwhite, Joyce Schenkman, Linda Schifflette, Patty Thaxton, and Margaret Youssef.

Thank you to Andrea Shane, Milton Mandel, and Howard Manson for many of the photographs, and to Pamela Cromey and Michael Gravois for many of the illustrations. Thank you to Amy Sass and Jordan Ullman for proofreading the page proofs.

Major portions of the appendixes were prepared by Patricia DeWitt, Erica Erlanger, Gina Goble, Katherine Heiss, Pamela Kelliher, Joy Lesnick, Tricia Lyons, Melissa Marley, Dana Pilla, Stacey Rog, and Mary Joyce Santoloci. Thank you to my students who helped prepare lesson plans for the supplement and to Elizabeth Asbury for organizing this material.

Thank you to Arnis Burvikovs, Virginia Lanigan, Bridget Keane, and Deborah Brown from Allyn and Bacon, and Joan Saidel from P. M. Gordon Associates for supporting the concept of a fourth edition of this book and for the guidance they offered during the revision process. I am grateful to Chris Kempers for her editorial expertise.

Thank you, in particular, to the children I have taught, my college students, and the excellent teachers I have observed and from whom I've learned so much. Thank you to the researchers in early literacy who have provided exciting information in the field. I consider this book a cooperative effort as a result of the contributions of so many in both direct and indirect ways.

Thank you to those who reviewed the fourth edition of the book including Katharine G. Fralick, Plymouth State College of New Hampshire; Nancy L. Peterson, Utah Valley State College; Nancy Ratcliff, University of South Florida; and Elizabeth Rowell, Rhode Island College; and to the many college professors, college students, teachers, and parents who purchased the book and demonstrated their support for the publication. The fourth edition was made possible by you.

Thank you to my parents, Mary and Milton Mandel, who provided a rich literacy environment for me; thank you to Frank Morrow, my companion and computer consultant; and thank you to Stephanie Morrow Bushell, my daughter and friend, for demonstrating the validity of many of the concepts expressed in the book.

L.M.M.

chapter 1

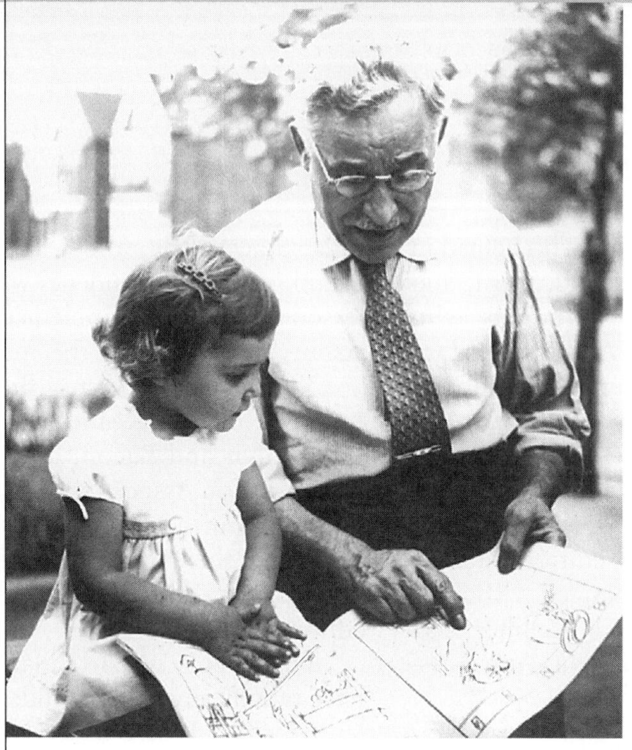

Foundations of Early Literacy Development

Surveying the Past to the Present

What a dangerous activity reading is: teaching is. All this plastering of foreign stuff. Why plaster on at all when there's so much inside already? So much locked in? If only I could draw it out and use it as working material. And not draw it out either. If I had a light enough touch, it would just come out under its own volcanic power.

—Sylvia Ashton-Warner
Spinster

Focus Questions

- Which educators, theorists, philosophers, and psychologists influenced early childhood education, and what was each one's unique contribution to instructional strategies used in classrooms for young children?
- What have been different approaches to literacy learning from the early 1900s to the present?
- What practical applications has the research on oral language, beginning early reading and writing, and rich literacy environments at home had on early literacy instruction in the classroom?
- What concepts reflect the whole language orientation?
- Describe what is meant by integrating the language arts with thematic instruction.
- What characteristics describe the explicit skills approach?
- What do we mean when we speak of a balanced perspective to literacy instruction?
- What knowledge about child development is important to literacy learning and why?

Four-year-old Darren and his mother were driving in the car to do some errands. As they approached the mall, Darren said, "Look Mommy, I can read those letters. M . . . A . . . C . . . Y . . . S. Those letters spell Sears." Darren's mother smiled and praised him. "That was great, Darren. You got every letter right. Now I'll read the sign for you; it says Macy's. This is another department store like Sears. You did some good thinking when you tried to read that word."

Not too long ago we would have chuckled at Darren's remarks as cute but incorrect. Today, we realize that he is demonstrating a great deal of literacy knowledge that needs to be recognized. First, he knows what letters are, and he can identify the ones in the sign. Next, he knows that letters spell words. He knows that words are read and have meaning. Although he did not read the word correctly, he made an informed guess. Darren was aware that this building was a department store, but even though he had never been to this one, he called the new store by a store name he knew. He was trying some of his literacy knowledge out on an adult whom he knew was interested and willing to interact positively with him. His mother offered positive reinforcement for what he did know and support by modeling the correct response when he needed some help.

Babies begin to acquire information about literacy from the moment they are born. They continue to build on their knowledge of oral language, reading, and writing as they go through early childhood and beyond. A great deal of attention is now being focused on literacy development in early childhood, an area somewhat neglected in the past. Teachers, parents, and administrators did not perceive preschoolers as readers or writers. Their emphasis was on oral language development and preparation for reading. Because of increased research, thinking about early literacy has changed: Very young children are now viewed as individuals with literacy skills. Although the literacy skills of preschoolers and kindergartners are not the same as older children or adults, they must be acknowledged because they have implications for instructional practice.

Over the past few years, research on literacy development in early childhood has burgeoned. That research not only has introduced new information, it also has raised concerns about certain common practices in early childhood literacy instruction and an awareness of the need for change. Like a child's first words and first steps, learning to read and write should be an exciting, fulfilling, and rewarding experience. This book draws on current research and blends it with theory and practice that have proved successful. It presents a program for developing literacy in children from birth to eight years. It is based on the following rationale drawn from the joint position statement of the International Reading Association and the National Association for the Education of Young Children entitled *Learning to Read and Write: Developmentally Appropriate Practices for Young Children* (1998). The joint statement was based on other versions written by the International Reading Association in 1985 and revised in 1990 and 1998.

1. Literacy learning begins in infancy.
2. Parents need to provide a literacy-rich environment and literacy experiences at home to help children acquire skills. Parents need to be actively involved in their children's literacy learning when they enter school.

3. School personnel must be aware that children come to school with prior knowledge about reading and writing and that this knowledge is different from one child to the next.
4. Children need to continue to develop reading and writing skills through experiences at school that build on their existing knowledge.
5. Literacy learning requires a supportive environment that builds positive feelings about self and literacy activities.
6. Learning requires a rich literacy environment with accessible materials and varied experiences.
7. Adults must serve as models for literacy behavior by demonstrating strategies to be learned and showing their interest in books and print.
8. During their literacy experiences children should interact within a social context to share information, which motivates them to learn from one another.
9. Early reading and writing experiences should be meaningful and concrete and actively engage children in both problem-solving experiences and explicit direct instruction of skills.
10. A literacy development program should focus on using functional and explicit instruction experiences that include oral language development and experiences with listening, reading, writing, spelling, and viewing.
11. Diversity in cultural and language backgrounds must be acknowledged and addressed in early literacy development.
12. Differences in literacy development will vary in children and individual needs must be met. Struggling readers, for example, must be provided for in inclusion-based classroom programs and in early intervention programs.
13. Assessment of achievement should be frequent, match instructional strategies, and use multiple formats for evaluating student behavior.
14. Standards for early literacy grade-level benchmarks should be tied to instruction and assessment and used as a means for reaching goals for all children to read fluently by the fourth grade. The standards are only benchmarks and may not be achieved by all children at a particular time.
15. Programs should be designed with the concept of developmentally appropriate practice in mind, that is, with high expectations for performance that are achievable.

This book incorporates the work of philosophers, educators, psychologists, and researchers who have described how young children learn. It builds on the implications their work holds for instruction and reflects a balanced approach toward literacy development in early childhood. The main emphasis of the book is development of literacy through teaching language and listening, reading, and writing in coordination with other content areas across the curriculum. Though some chapters concentrate on language, reading, or writing, an important concern at all times is the integration of all four dimensions of literacy.

Literacy development early in life must focus on both learning and teaching. The teacher prepares an environment rich in literacy materials and activities from which children can choose; the children are encouraged to be actively involved in learning with other children, with materials, and with the teacher. Another major focus of the book is how to provide an environment that will encourage children to take an interest in reading, to associate it with pleasure, and ultimately to read by choice.

Learning Theories That Have Shaped Practices

Several important philosophers, theorists, educators, and psychologists have addressed learning in early childhood, including the issue of appropriate educational practice. These ideas represent varying responses to the question of whether learning is primarily a matter of the *nature* or the *nurture* of the child.

Theory and Philosophy from the 1700s and 1800s

ROUSSEAU. Jean-Jacques Rousseau (1762) strongly suggested that a child's early education be natural. That is, children should not be forced to learn things for which they are not developmentally ready. Rousseau advocated abandoning the contrived imposition of instruction on children and instead allowing children to grow and learn with the freedom to be themselves. Education follows the child's own development and readiness for learning. According to Rousseau, children learn through curiosity; forcing education on them interferes with their learning and development. He believed that individual children have particular ways of learning, ways that formal instruction should not tamper with. Rousseau's philosophy suggests that the role of the educator is to use strategies that mesh with the child's readiness to learn and that require as little intervention by an adult as possible.

PESTALOZZI. Johann Heinrich Pestalozzi (Rusk & Scotland, 1979) was influenced by Rousseau's emphasis on natural learning, but he added a dimension to it. He started his own school and developed principles for learning that combined natural elements with informal instruction. He found it unrealistic to expect children to learn totally on their own initiative. Although Pestalozzi felt that children may be able to teach themselves to read, for example, he also felt that it was necessary for teachers or parents to create the conditions in which the reading process grows. The natural potential of a child develops, he believed, through sensory manipulative experiences, so he designed lessons that involved manipulating objects and learning about them through touch, smell, language, size, and shape.

FROEBEL. Friedrich Froebel's (1974) approach was similar in some ways to those of his predecessors. Like Rousseau, he believed that the adult responsible for the education of a child needs to be concerned with the child's natural unfolding. He also followed Pestalozzi's ideas and provided plans for instructing young children. But he is best known for emphasizing the importance of play in learning. He specified, however, that realizing the fullest benefits of playing-to-learn requires adult guidance and direction and a planned environment. Froebel saw the teacher as a designer of activities and experiences that facilitate learning. On this premise he designed a systematic curriculum for young children involving objects and materials that he called *gifts* and *occupations*. In handling and playing with these objects and materials, children not only use psychomotor skills but also learn about shape, color, size, measurement, and comparison. It was Froebel who coined the word *kindergarten,* which means "children's garden." The phrase illustrates his basic philosophy that children, like plants, will grow to fruition only if they are tended to and cared for. He often referred to the child as the seed being cared for by the gardener, or teacher.

Froebel was the first educator to design an organized curriculum for young children, and many of his strategies are evident in preschools and kindergartens today. Significant among his strategies were his emphasis on guided play as a method for learning, the learning of certain concepts through manipulative materials that use the senses, and *circle time*—an opportunity to sing songs and learn new ideas through discussion.

Moving into the Twentieth Century

DEWEY. John Dewey's (1966) views in the twentieth century were not unlike Froebel's. His philosophy of early childhood education led to the concept of the child-centered curriculum, or progressive education as it was often called. Dewey believed that the curriculum should be built around the interests of children. He agreed with Froebel that children learn best through play and in real life settings. He maintained that social interactions encourage learning and that interests are the vehicles for learning information and skills. Dewey rejected the idea of teaching skills as an end unto themselves. He also believed that learning is maximized through integrating content areas.

Froebel and Dewey have significantly influenced programs in American preschools and kindergartens throughout the twentieth century, especially from the 1920s through the 1950s. During those decades, preschools and kindergartens typically had different areas for different activities. Shelves in a "block corner" held various sizes and shapes of blocks, small cars, trucks, and wooden figures of people. An art area contained easels with watercolors, crayons, paper, paste, scissors, construction paper, clay, and scraps of interesting materials such as fabric, plastic foam, and pipe cleaners for making collages. The dramatic-play corner was set up like a kitchen, with sink, oven, refrigerator, empty food boxes, table and chairs, telephone, mirror, dolls, and some clothing for dressing up. Still another area held manipulative toys that teach concepts about color, shape, and size. A science area revealed a water-play table, shells, interesting rocks, plants, a class animal, magnets, and magnifying glasses. The music area usually had a piano, rhythm instruments, and a record player. Sometimes there was a rug for children to sit on when they came to sing by the piano. One corner of the room had a shelf of children's literature and, depending on the teacher, soft pillows to lie on when looking at books.

The daily routine was similar in most of these settings. As children entered the classroom, they played with quiet toys. The teacher then called them to circle time to talk about the weather and the calendar. Conversation soon focused on a topic in social studies or science—animals or community helpers, for instance—with perhaps a song in keeping with the theme. Circle time was commonly followed by a long period called free play in which children could use the materials in the different areas of the room. There was minimal guidance during free play; children could explore and experiment with the materials. A snack, sometimes followed by a rest period, was an integral part of the daily routine.

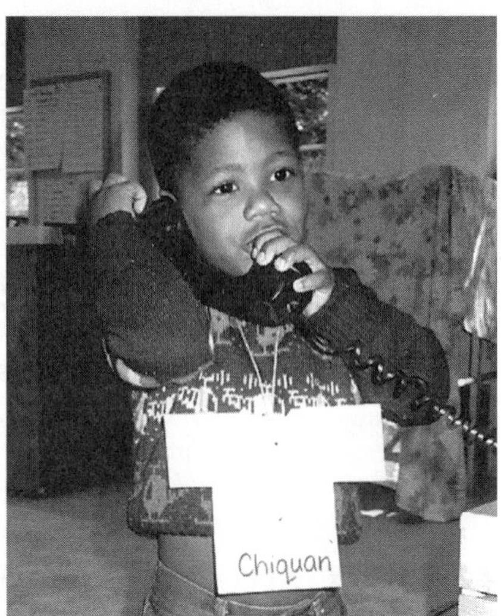

According to Pestalozzi, Froebel, Dewey, Piaget, Vygotsky, and other philosophers and theorists, learning in early childhood occurs when youngsters have the opportunity to explore, experiment, play at real-life experiences, and manipulate materials.

The day might also include a special lesson in art, social studies, or science appropriate to the unit being studied. Outdoor play allowed children to run, climb, play in sandboxes, and use riding toys. The teacher read a story daily, probably at the end of the day, often relating it to the topic being studied.

Reading and mathematics were not taught formally or as isolated skills. Instead, the teacher might ask a child to count out enough cookies for all the children in the class, to name the date on the calendar, or to compare the sizes of different children. There were no workbooks or commercial reading materials. Teachers led some informal activities that could eventually lead to reading, but they did not attempt to teach children to read. The letters of the alphabet might be found strung across the wall, the days of the week pointed out on a calendar, children's names written on their cubbies, and some other items in the room labeled with words. The general atmosphere was relaxed. The goal was to accustom children to school routines and make them comfortable in the school environment. The focus was on social, emotional, and physical development. There was no place in these programs for formal reading and writing instruction.

MONTESSORI. Maria Montessori (1965) departed from the educators and philosophers mentioned thus far. Although she believed in the use of the senses to promote learning, her emphasis on the senses was not based on the natural unfolding of the child, the child's interests, or play. Believing that children needed early, orderly, systematic training in mastering one skill after another, she supplied her teaching environment with materials for learning specific concepts in order to meet specific objectives. The materials provided the source of learning for the child. Children educated themselves by using these manipulatives, and because the materials were self-correcting, the children could determine their own errors and make corrections independently.

Montessori referred to this type of learning as *auto-education.* Like Froebel and Pestalozzi, she spoke of *sensitive periods,* when children are better able to learn certain things than at other times. It is the role of the parent or teacher to watch for these periods and take advantage of them by preparing the environment with appropriate materials and experiences for learning. In short, according to Montessori, the teacher is a guide who prepares an environment for learning. But unlike the educators already discussed, Montessori carefully designed learning materials to teach specific skills. In Montessori's curriculum, children's natural curiosity and their propensity for exploration are of less concern than their ability to work with specific materials to achieve a specific goal. Play is not as important as work because it might waste precious opportunities for goal achievement during sensitive periods for learning. Some of Montessori's ideas are not relevant to the new thrust in early literacy, her emphasis on learning rather than teaching; her concerns about independent learning, sensitive periods for learning, and respect for the child; and her insistence on organization and a prepared environment hold implications for today's instruction.

PIAGET. Jean Piaget's theory (Piaget & Inhelder, 1969) of cognitive development has had a particularly strong impact on early childhood education. In describing the stages of cognitive development, he recognized that children at certain stages are capable of only certain types of intellectual endeavors. Trying to involve children in abstract experiences during the preoperational stages of their early childhood, for instance, is considered inappropriate. Piaget did not advocate Montessori's systematic approach, nor did he believe in maturation as a completely natural unfolding. He believed, rather, that a child acquires knowledge by interacting with the world. Educators who have applied his theories involve children in natural problem-solving situations where they

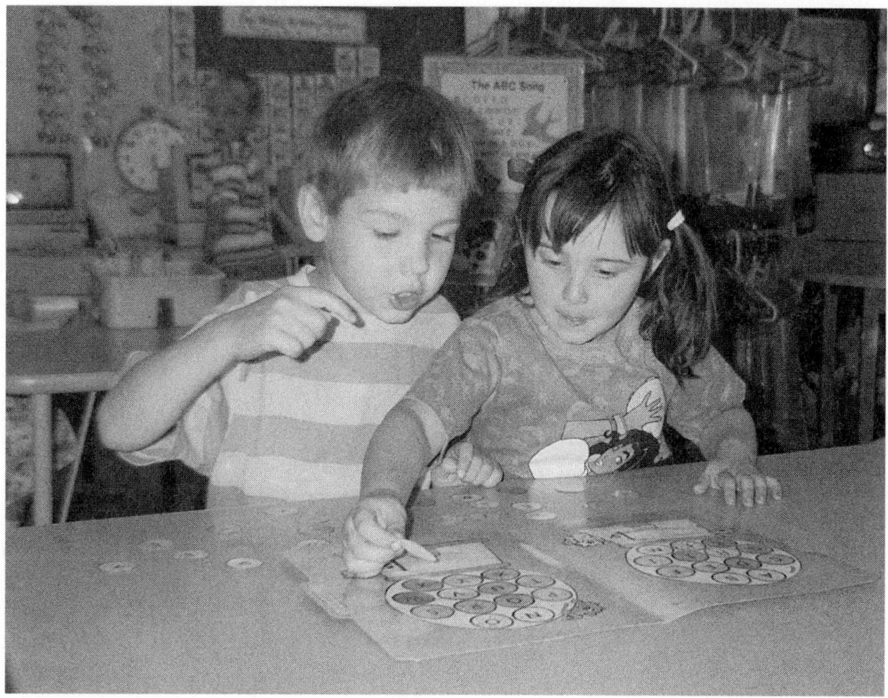

Piaget stressed that learning occurs when children interact with peers and adults in a social setting as they act upon the environment.

can assimilate new experiences into their existing knowledge. Children are active participants in their own learning, constantly changing and reorganizing their own knowledge.

Piaget stressed that learning occurs when children interact with peers and adults in a social setting as they act upon the environment. Educators who have incorporated Piaget's theories in curricula for early childhood education have designed programs that look very much like what Pestalozzi or Froebel might have created: a setting with many real-life materials, including the opportunity to play, explore, and experiment. Piaget agreed that young children should use their curiosity, inquisitiveness, and spontaneity to help themselves learn. In addition, a Piagetian preschool curriculum emphasizes decision making, problem solving, using self-discipline, goal setting, planning one's own activities, and cooperating with teachers and peers in evaluating learning.

VYGOTSKY. Lev S. Vygotsky's (1981) general theory of intellectual development also has implications for learning in early childhood. Vygotsky believes that mental functions are acquired through social relationships. Children learn by internalizing activities in the world around them. Children emulate behaviors and incorporate them into their existing structure of knowledge when they are exposed to new situations in which they can actively interact with others.

The learning theories of the individuals discussed have contributed to the way we look at literacy development in early childhood education. Their ideas are the basis for early literacy instruction as it is described in this book. Particularly applicable among their concepts are these:

1. Concern for a child's level of development—physical, social, emotional, and intellectual—when preparing a learning environment for that child
2. Concern for prepared environments in which learning can take place
3. Emphasis on learning rather than teaching
4. The learner's need for social interaction with supportive adults and other children
5. Focus on learning through real experiences in meaningful and natural settings rather than by imposed, contrived objectives or techniques
6. An awareness that children must actively participate in their own learning by engaging in manipulative experiences that are both functional and interesting

Practices in the Past: Early 1900s to the 1950s

Judging from the professional literature of the early 1900s, little attention was paid to a child's literacy development before he or she entered school. It was generally assumed that literacy began with formal instruction in first grade. A strong influence on reading instruction came from developmental psychologists such as Gesell (1925) who advocated maturation as the most important factor in learning to read. Reading instruction was not given until the child was ready to read. Preschool and kindergarten teachers generally ignored or avoided reading instruction. But they did follow some of the teachings of Pestalozzi and Froebel. Typically, they read to children often; encouraged play, exploration, and problem solving; and led songs and discussions in circle times. Methods were child centered, teaching units were interdisciplinary, and learning environments and instructional strategies were appropriate to the child's development.

Influenced by the climate of the times, Morphett and Washburne (1931) supported the postponement of reading instruction until a child was developmentally "old enough." Their study concluded that children with a mental age of six years six months made better progress on a test of reading achievement than younger children. But although many educators believed that natural maturation was the precursor to literacy, others grew uncomfortable with simply waiting for children to become ready to read. They did not advocate formal reading instruction in early childhood, but they did begin to provide experiences that they believed would help children become ready for reading.

The growing popularity of testing during the 1930s and 1940s helped educators in this effort and affected the next several decades of early childhood reading instruction. Generally, the standardized tests served the prevailing concept of maturation by indicating if a child had reached the maturity he or she needed to be able to learn to read. The tests usually included sections on specific skills. Unfortunately, those skills came to be seen as elements on which to base experiences that would help children become ready to read. The term ***reading readiness*** came into popular use during these decades. Instead of waiting for a child's natural maturation to unfold, educators focused on nurturing that maturation through instruction in a set of skills identified as prerequisites for reading. The concept gained strength when publishers of basal readers capitalized on the idea of readiness skills and began to prepare materials for preschool and kindergarten that would make children ready to read. Skills associated with reading readiness include *auditory discrimination,* the ability to identify and differentiate familiar sounds, similar sounds, rhyming words, and the sounds of letters; *visual discrimination,* including color recognition, shape, and letter identification; *left to right eye progression* and *visual motor skills,* such as cutting on a line with scissors and coloring within the lines of a picture; and such *large motor abilities* as skipping, hopping, and walking on a line.

Early childhood literacy instruction based on the reading readiness model implies that one prepares for literacy by acquiring a set of prescribed skills. These skills are taught systematically on the assumption that all children are at a fairly similar level of development when they come to preschool or kindergarten. The system does not consider experiences or information that a child may already have about literacy, and it focuses on a set of skills perceived as those needed for learning to read. (See Chapter 5 for more discussion about the reading readiness approach.)

Research Brings Change: 1960s to the 1980s

Research findings about early childhood literacy challenged the deep-rooted practices in reading readiness that had been evident since the 1950s. Teale

(1982) argued that the typical literacy curriculum with its progression from part to whole and its hierarchy of "skills" did not reflect the way children learn to read:

> The belief is that literacy development is a case of building competencies in certain cognitive operations with letters, words, sentences, and texts, competencies which can be applied in a variety of situations. A critical mistake here is that the motives, goals, and conditions have been abstracted away from the activity in the belief that this enables the student to "get down to" working on the essential processes of reading and writing. But . . . these features are critical aspects of the reading and writing themselves. By organizing instruction which omits them, the teacher ignores how literacy is practiced (and therefore learned) and thereby creates a situation in which the teaching is an inappropriate model for the learning. (p. 567)

I questioned the relevance of some of the readiness activities for young children when I was teaching kindergarten. The children were interested in looking at books, reading familiar words, and copying words that interested them. They approached the beginnings of literacy in ways that were meaningful, pleasurable, or functional. They carried out the reading readiness activities willingly, but it was obvious that they had no idea why they were doing them or how they were related to reading at all. This became even clearer to me in a conversation with Eric, who chose a worksheet identifying initial consonant sounds during one class:

> *"I see you are practicing your reading, Eric," I said.*
> *He looked up at me and said, "No, I'm not. I'm practicing my sounding."*
> *I then said, "Right, sounding is practicing reading."*
> *Eric looked up at me and said rather emphatically, "I'm not practicing reading, I am practicing sounding."*
> *"But Eric," I said, "sounding is a part of reading."*
> *Even more annoyed, Eric responded, "Now let's get this straight: reading is reading and sounding is sounding."*

This interchange left a strong impression on me and launched my general questioning of the reading readiness program. In my observations of early childhood classrooms, I found that many teachers no longer scheduled play time. Block corners and dramatic-play areas had disappeared from many rooms. Interdisciplinary units in social studies and science were replaced with units on skill instruction, such as learning the letter *t*. Classrooms were neither relaxed nor child centered. Children spent most of their time working on one skill worksheet after another. Social, emotional, and physical development were not a major concern. We seemed to have gone from one extreme to another.

Influences for Change in Early Literacy Practices

Researchers investigating early childhood literacy development have brought about changes in theory and practice. Generally, they base learning and instructional strategies on what is known about cognitive development. They use varied research methodologies for data collection, including interviews, observations, videotapes, and case studies in diverse cultural, racial, and socioeconomic settings. The research is field based, taking place in classrooms and homes rather than in laboratories as in the past.

Research on Oral Language Development

The first challenge to the attitudes rooted in the 1930s through the 1950s came in the 1960s and 1970s in studies of how children learn oral language. Although language acquisition is based somewhat on developmental maturity, much of the research concluded that children play an active role in their acquisition of language by constructing language. They imitate the language of adults and create their own when they do not have the conventional words they need to communicate their thoughts. Their first words are usually functional words, and they are motivated to continue generating language when their attempts are positively reinforced. Children who are constantly exposed to an environment rich in language and who interact with adults using language in a social context develop more facility with oral language than children lacking these opportunities (Bruner, 1975; Cazden, 1992; Chomsky, 1965; Halliday, 1975; McNeil, 1970; Menyuk, 1977). Findings from research on language acquisition motivated investigators to carry out similar studies of how reading and writing were acquired. Because reading and writing involve the use of language, many believed that the acquisition of oral language, reading, and writing might share some similarities.

For children whose primary language is not English, studies have demonstrated that a solid foundation in a first language supports academic achievement in a second language (Cummins, 1981). In this respect, students learning English as a second language are more likely to read and write English when they already have a firm foundation in the vocabulary and concepts of their primary language.

Research about Literacy Development in the Home

Other studies investigated homes in which children learned to read without direct instruction before coming to school (Durkin 1966; Heath, 1980; Holdaway, 1979; Morrow, 1983; Ninio & Bruner, 1978; Taylor, 1983; Teale, 1984). Such homes provide rich reading environments that include books and other reading materials. Family members serve as models of involvement in literacy activities. For example, they answer children's questions about books and print. They read to children frequently and reward them for participating in literacy activities. In addition, parents of successful readers most often are involved at school and seek information about their children's literacy development. The description of families and homes in which children learn to read naturally has implications for early literacy instruction in schools. (See also Chapter 3 for more information on family literacy.)

The phrase *learning to read naturally* is a bit misleading. It denotes a child suddenly picking up a book and reading it, with no instruction at all. Actually, a great deal happens in homes where children learn to read "naturally," without formal instruction. These homes are rich in the supportive and interactive behaviors conducive to learning to read. Specific studies of home storybook readings have provided information on the kinds of interaction that encourages literacy development. Analyses of the recorded questions and comments of children during shared book experiences at home, for example, provide information on what children already know about books and print and what they are interested in finding out (Flood, 1977; Heath, 1980; Morrow, 1988; Ninio & Bruner, 1978; Roser & Martinez, 1985; Yaden, 1985). They also illustrate the interaction and adult discussion that enrich the storybook reading experience. The results of these home studies hold strong implications for change in classroom instruction.

Research on the Development of Early Reading

In her research with preschool and kindergarten children, Goodman (1984) found that many already knew certain things necessary for reading. These children knew the difference between letter characters and pictures in books, how to handle a book, and how to turn pages. And they knew that books are sources of meaning through printed words. Her work also concerned children's awareness of environmental print in familiar contexts and suggested that literacy-rich environments can make learning to read as natural as language acquisition.

Other researchers have looked at the acquisition of reading in early childhood from a developmental point of view. They have studied children's knowledge and acquisition of the function, form, and structure of print (Ehri, 1979; Gibson & Levin, 1975; Mason, 1980, 1982; Mason & McCormick, 1981). The function of print refers to the first words children read and write, which have function and meaning for them. The form of print refers to letter names and sounds. The work of these researchers reinforces many of the ideas found in the studies of oral language and home literacy. These authors advocate early childhood reading instruction, but not instruction that emulates first-grade practice. Rather, they suggest more informal strategies similar to those discovered in homes where children learned to read without direct instruction. They also encourage activities that enhance language development and experiences in problem solving, listening to stories, and writing stories.

Research on Early Writing Development

Another area of research in early childhood literacy is writing. Studies of children's first attempts to make marks on paper have shown that youngsters try to communicate in writing at a very early age. Through sample analysis of children's first attempts at writing, it is clear that they have an interest in writing, that they model adult writing behaviors, and that their scribbles, drawings, random letters, and invented spellings are early forms of writing (Clay, 1975). Many researchers now prefer to speak of reading and writing development as one process. They view reading and writing as skills that build on each other. When they are cultivated concurrently, each adds to proficiency in the other. Traditionally, writing was perceived as developing after the ability to read and was not included in the early childhood curriculum. Research in early childhood writing has changed these attitudes, which has resulted in dramatic changes in classroom practice. Encouraging writing in preschool and kindergarten and praising children's first attempts to write have become standard practices in early childhood classrooms.

Tamika's early writing attempts, consisting of a mixture of letterlike forms and some real letters, need to be encouraged and positively reinforced.

The research and theories reviewed here enable us to understand better the processes involved in becoming literate. Certain levels of maturity are required for a child to reach specific levels of ability. To acquire skill in oral language, writing, and reading, children need models to emulate and the freedom to create their own forms of reading, writing, and speaking. They must be positively reinforced and guided so that they will continue in their development.

We have come to realize that literacy development does not begin with formal instruction when children enter school. When they enter school, children bring many concepts about literacy and certain competencies in oral language, writing, and reading. They have some command of language and have internalized many of its rules and some of the processes for learning more. Many children know the difference between drawing and writing and can imitate writing in invented ways. Many children have developed reading vocabularies from such environmental print sources as road signs, food packages, and store displays. Television and computer programs are a source for early literacy knowledge as well. Children know that books are for reading and expect that they will be able to read books in the early stages of schooling. We cannot, therefore, rationally view literacy in early childhood as something achieved by drilling children in specific contrived skills. Rather, we need to build on children's existing knowledge of literacy and help their literacy evolve.

Research tells us that children learn best in situations that are meaningful and functional. Children have developed their levels of literacy in social and cultural contexts and through interaction with adults and other children. The instruction they receive should reflect to a certain extent the natural and meaningful way in which they have learned what they already know and be sensitive to a child's stage of development socially, emotionally, physically, and intellectually. However, some systematic presentation of skills is necessary as well. The chapters that follow address each of the areas involved in the process of becoming literate. They reflect both old and new ideas that have made us aware of changes needed in our approaches to early literacy instruction. Based on theory derived from research, they focus on oral language, writing, and reading and on how these are acquired. They also reflect the development of the child.

Children need to be exposed to books and writing early in life. Early attempts at literacy should be encouraged and rewarded.

Recent Research and Practice: 1980s to the Present

The Whole Language Movement

One cannot review theory, philosophies, and research that have influenced changes in early literacy practices without a discussion of whole language. It is difficult to describe the whole language orientation because it has been defined in so many different ways and, therefore, there is the risk of misinterpreting one theorist's perception or leaving out some idea related to the concept. In spite of this, the whole language orientation has had a strong impact on early literacy instruction and throughout the grades. Many of its beliefs are drawn from the theorists of the past discussed in this chapter.

Whole language advocates support the natural approaches to learning fostered by Rousseau, Pestalozzi, and Froebel. Pestalozzi and Froebel added other dimensions with their concern for active learning through sensory experiences with materials. Dewey's progressive education contributed to the philosophy with its child-centered approach that integrated the learning of information and literacy skill development into content area themes that were of interest to children. The influence of Piaget and Vygotsky is also seen in whole language through its emphasis on active learning and the adult as a facilitator of learning by guiding experiences in a social context.

Definitions of Whole Language

From a content analysis of 64 professional articles related to whole language, Bergeron (1990) composed this definition:

> Whole language is a concept that embodies both a philosophy of language development as well as the instructional approaches embedded within, and supportive of, that philosophy. This concept includes the use of real literature and writing in the context of meaningful, functional, and cooperative experiences in order to develop in students motivation and interest in the process of learning. (p. 319)

Like many others, after reading the literature, I have formulated my own definition of whole language. The ideas presented here may not be shared by all. Whole language is a philosophy about how children learn, from which educators derive strategies for teaching. Some of its concepts and their implications for instruction follow.

Literacy learning is child centered because it is designed to be meaningful and functional for children. The function and meaning are drawn from the child's life experiences at home or those created in school. For example, if a beehive is discovered at school and removed by an exterminator, children may be interested in discussing, reading, or writing about bees. Although learning about bees is not built into the prescribed curriculum, the teacher allows children to pursue this spontaneous interest.

Literacy activities are purposefully integrated into the learning of content area subjects such as art, music, social studies, science, math, and play. The use of social studies and science themes, such as the study of ecology, links content areas and literacy experiences. Equal emphasis is placed on teaching reading, writing, listening, and oral language because all help create a literate individual. In the past, this has been referred to as an **integrated language arts approach.** Varied genres of children's literature are the main source of reading material for instruction. This is called **literature-based instruction.** Classrooms must be rich with literacy materials for reading and writing throughout the room and also housed in special literacy centers. This is often called the **rich literacy environment.**

In a classroom that uses holistic strategies, teachers place more emphasis on learning than on teaching. Learning is self-regulated and individualized, with self-selection and choices of literacy activities. Rather than give only lessons in literacy, teachers provide models of literacy activities for children to emulate. There is adult and peer interaction as children observe one another and adults engaged in literacy acts. There is opportunity for peer tutoring and collaboration with each other in active literacy experiences. Children also can learn through practice by engaging in long periods of independent reading and writing and sharing what is learned—by reading to others and presenting written pieces to an audience. Literacy learning is an active, interactive social process. A major objective for literacy instruction is the development of a desire to read and write.

In classrooms that use holistic approaches, skills are taught when they are relevant and meaningful—for example, when studying a theme such as dinosaurs, the teacher may focus on some letters and sounds in the initial consonants found in the names of dinosaurs. In early implementation of whole language programs, some thought that skills were not taught in any systematic way, and that children would acquire those that they needed by being immersed in experiences with reading children's literature and writing. Certainly skills are assimilated through this immersion, but specific skills such as how to use decoding strategies to approach unknown words may require some explicit instruction by the teacher. It is not realistic to assume that in natural settings the skills needed for developing competent readers and writers are acquired by children without some planned objectives. Although whole language strategies suggest authentic approaches for skill development, teachers need a planned set of objectives for ensuring that students have the opportunity to experience activities that will help develop skills necessary to become competent readers and writers. Occasionally, that means some traditional explicit instructional techniques.

In a whole language approach, assessment is continuous and takes many forms: Teachers collect daily performance samples of work; they observe and record children's behavior; they audio- and videotape them in different situations; and they build a portfolio filled with information about each youngster. The evaluation process is for both teacher and child, and conferences are held to discuss progress.

In a whole language orientation, teachers along with children are the decision makers about instructional strategies, the organization of instruction, and instructional materials used. Commercial materials do not dictate the instructional program although they may be used if desired. Literacy learning is consciously embedded throughout the curriculum in the whole school day. Large blocks of time are needed for process projects. There is whole-group, small-group, and individualized instruction, and children are able to have time to read and write independently for long periods of time.

Whole language can be implemented in many different ways, based on the needs and interests of those involved. There is no one right way because one program could not satisfy everyone's needs.

Integrating the Language Arts with Thematic Instruction

With whole language based strongly on authentic, meaningful, and functional learning, the integrated language arts concept combined with thematic instruction became important to the literacy curriculum. In classrooms that use an integrated language arts approach, literacy is not taught as a subject, but as a mechanism for learning in general. Literacy learning becomes meaningful when it is consciously embedded into the study of themes and content area subjects.

Thematic units vary, but the main goal is to teach literacy skills in an interesting way. Thematic units may revolve around the exposure to certain types of children's literature, such as the study of fables, fairy tales, informational books, and so on. In this type of unit, the teacher reads several samples of one type of genre or children read them to themselves if they are able. There are discussions about the style of the works, and children have the opportunity to engage in writing their own stories that follow the genre being discussed.

Another type of thematic unit involves selecting a topic that usually has a science or social studies thrust, such as the farm, and identifying several pieces of children's literature about the topic as the source of reading instruction. All writing activities revolve around the topic and are driven by the children's literature. There may be art and music activities as well, but they evolve from and revolve around the stories being read. For example, if the theme was the farm and one of the stories used in the unit was *The Little Red Hen,* some related activities might be to bake some bread, role-play the story, or write another version of the story in which the animals are all helpful in making the bread. One problem with using literature to drive the unit is that one piece may be overused for general activities and skill development. This practice could ruin the pleasure that can be received from the book. In addition, the literature often restricts the extension of ideas that could be generated.

The third type of thematic unit is one that uses a science or social studies topic and consciously integrates literacy into all content area lessons, including music, art, play, math, social studies, and science. Many selections of children's

Thematic units often use a science or social studies topic, and teachers integrate literacy activities into content-area lessons.

literature are used as a major part of the unit; however, the literature does not drive the unit—the topic of the unit is the main focus. In this type of unit, the classroom centers are filled with materials that relate to the topic, including literacy materials to encourage reading and writing. In all science and social studies lessons, reading and writing are purposefully incorporated. Skills are taught when they seem appropriate—for example, in the unit on the farm, when the class hatches baby chicks in an incubator, journals may be kept on the progress of the chicks, and the digraph *ch* could be emphasized. Unit topics are incorporated into the entire school day in all content areas. Topics may be predetermined by the teacher, selected by the children and teacher, or decided on spontaneously based on something of interest that occurs in the school, in someone's home, or in the world. Chapter 10 elaborates on the use of thematic units. A description of how units are implemented throughout the school day is also included. Appendix A provides a list of popular early childhood unit topics with related selections of children's literature to use when studying those topics.

Explicit Instruction and a Constructivist Approach: Phonics and Whole Language

Some problems evolved with the "whole language" movement. Schools did not provide adequate staff development, materials, and in-class support for the ambitious changes proposed in classrooms. Many misunderstood the philosophy and when interpreting it into strategies thought "whole language" meant that teaching children occurred only in whole groups. Thus, teachers stopped meeting with small groups of children for instruction to meet individual needs. Many thought that "whole language" meant that one could not teach phonics.

This was not the case at all: The manner in which phonics was to be taught involved immersion into literature and print and spontaneous and contextual teaching of skills. As a result of the misinterpretations, many children received little or no instruction in phonics. Many schools did not follow a scope or sequence of skills or did not monitor skill development. Although the strategies learned from the philosophy are excellent, because of misinformation, misinterpretation, and incorrect implementation, many children did not develop skills they needed to become fluent, independent readers.

Many placed the blame for these problems on the whole language philosophy. Researchers quoted from meaning-based whole language studies and phonics-based investigations to make a case for their point of view. Those advocating whole language suggested that rich literacy environments with immersion in literature not only helped children construct the meaning in the text but also developed positive attitudes toward reading to become lifelong voluntary readers (Anderson, Herbert, Scott, & Wilkinson, 1985).

Those who favored the more explicit approach to early literacy development with the use of phonics have cited many studies to substantiate their claims. According to Juel (1989), as children first begin to experiment with reading and writing, they need to focus on the sounds that make up words. Knowing that words are made up of individual sounds and the ability to segment those sounds out of the words and blend them together, is called phonemic awareness.

According to research, **phonemic awareness** instruction in preschool, kindergarten, and first grade strengthens reading achievement and is a precursor to phonics (Byrne & Fielding-Barnsley, 1993, 1995; Stanovich, 1986). With phonemic awareness, children can learn principles of phonics including: (1) alphabetic understanding (knowing that words are composed of letters), and (2) cryptoanalytic intent or sound–symbol relationships (knowing that there is a relationship between printed letters and spoken sound). Research also suggests that knowledge of sound–symbol relationships, or phonics, is necessary for success at learning to read and write (Adams, 1990; Juel, 1994). Some children need more instruction in phonemic awareness and phonics than others.

Although the evidence about the importance of instruction in phonemic awareness and phonics is important, it is only one piece of the complex act of learning to read. In addition, research has established that there is not one best method of instruction for all children. In fact, approaches that favor some type of well-organized phonics instruction along with meaningful, connected reading report superior progress in reading (Morrow & Tracey, 1997).

Concerns also were raised about the delivery of instruction in the whole language classroom. Questions were asked about whether we should teach with a direct transmission model in which teachers control instruction with explicit lessons and determined outcomes, or with a constructivist approach in which students problem solve and discover and teachers act as facilitators of learning. Many concerns came from those interested in what was called a balanced perspective to literacy instruction (Pressley, 1998).

A Balanced Approach to Literacy Instruction

A position statement by the International Reading Association, entitled *Using Multiple Methods of Beginning Reading Instruction* (1999), suggests there is no one single method or single combination of methods that can successfully teach all children to read. "Therefore, teachers must have a strong knowledge of multiple methods for teaching reading and a strong knowledge of the children in their care so they can create the appropriate balance of methods needed for the children they teach."

Another perspective for literacy instruction that emerged as a result of the whole language versus phonics discussion is a **balanced approach to literacy instruction.** A balanced perspective includes careful selection of the best theories available and use of learning strategies from those theories to match the learning styles of individual children to help them learn to read (Figure 1.1). This might mean the use of more skill-based explicit instruction or some holistic and constructivist ideas, which include problem-solving strategies. According to Pressley (1998), explicit teaching of skills is a good start for constructivist problem-solving activities, and constructivist activities permit consolidation and elaboration of skills. One method does not preclude or exclude the other.

A balanced perspective is not simply a combinaton of random strategies. A teacher may select strategies from different learning theories to provide balance.

Figure 1.1 *Strategies and Structures in a Balanced Literacy Program*

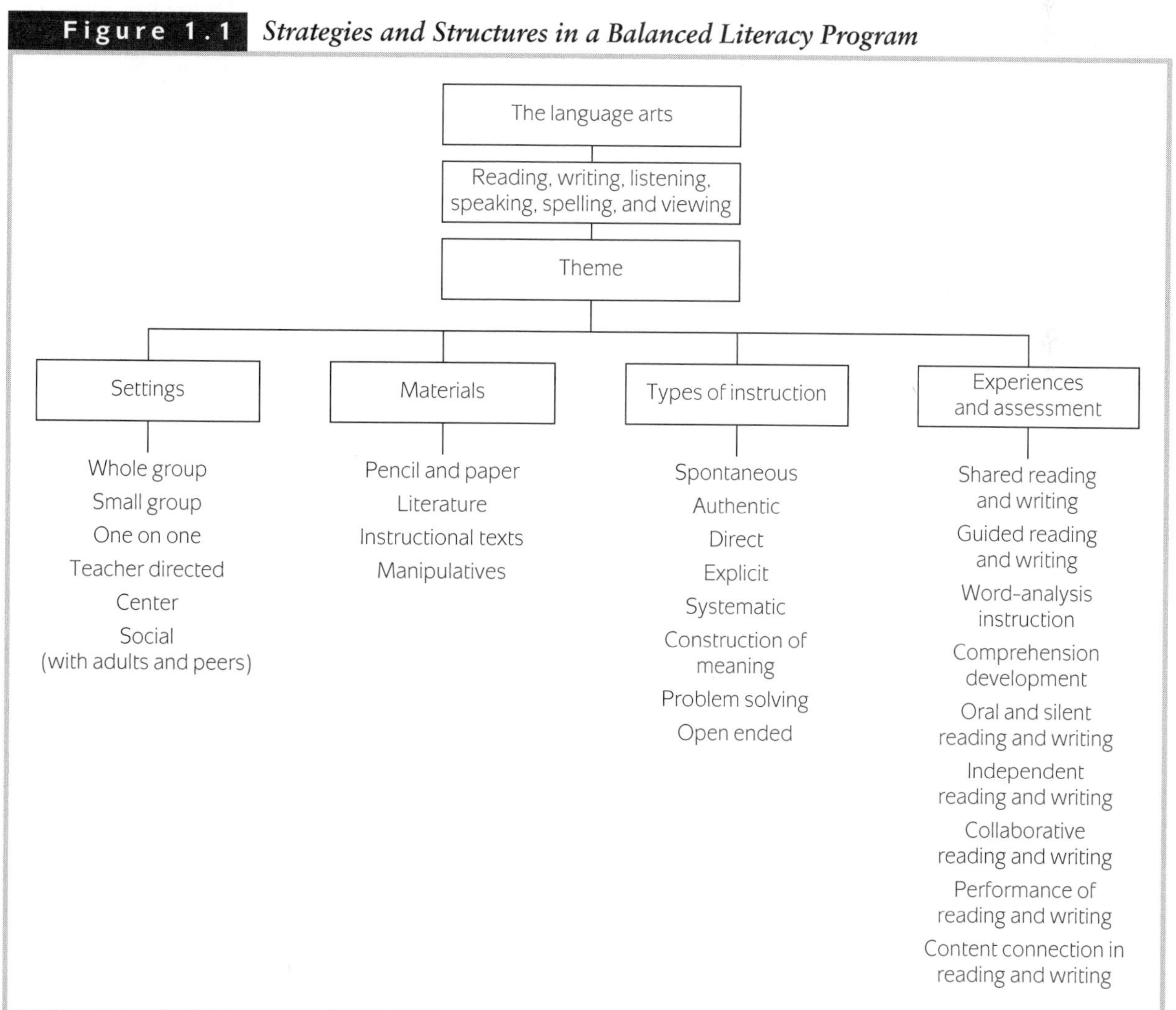

Source: Adapted from L. M. Morrow, D. S. Strickland, & D. G. Woo, 1998. In *Literacy Instruction in Half- and Whole-Day Kindergarten: Research to Practice* (Fig. 2, p. 76). Newark, DE: International Reading Association.

One child, for example, may be a visual learner and not benefit much from instruction in phonics; and another child's strength may be auditory learning and he or she will learn best from phonics instruction. The balanced approach is a thoughtful and mature approach. It focuses more on what is important for individual children than what the latest fad in literacy instruction is.

Balanced instruction is grounded in a rich model of literacy learning that encompasses both the elegance and the complexity of the reading and language arts processes. Such a model acknowledges the importance of both form (phonics, mechanics, etc.) and function (comprehension, purpose, meaning) of the literacy processes and recognizes that learning occurs most effectively in a whole-part-whole context. This type of instruction is characterized by meaningful literacy activities that provide children with both the skill and desire to become proficient and lifelong literacy learners. A balanced program includes the components in Figure 1.1.

A report by the National Reading Panel (2000) presents the most effective approaches to teaching children to read based on scientific research-based reading instructional practices used by teachers in classrooms across the country. The report discusses a balanced approach to reading instruction as it looks at the importance of phonemic awareness and phonics instruction, guided oral reading, comprehension strategies, vocabulary instruction, computer technology and reading instruction, and teacher education and reading instruction (National Reading Panel Report, 2000).

Stages of Child Development

The early childhood learning theories described were concerned about the physical, social, emotional, and cognitive development of the child. The curriculum emphasized all four areas equally. This early perspective, which remains with us today, makes it necessary to know what children are like developmentally, what they are capable of doing, and what they already know. This information is needed when preparing instructional environments. This knowledge also will help determine if children have special needs related to learning disabilities, giftedness, or communication disorders, for example. Considering the total development of the child and not just the cognitive has been and always should be a hallmark in early childhood education. The following description in Box 1.1 of developmental characteristics of children from birth through eight years (Seefeldt & Barbour, 1986, pp. 63–69) is provided to be used as a reference throughout this volume and in your teaching. A more complete description of language development is found in Chapter 4.

Box 1.1

Developmental Characteristics of Children

Infancy (birth through twelve months)

Physical

Develops rapidly.

Changes from waking because of hunger and distress to sleeping through the night with two naps during the day.

Changes eating patterns from every three hours to regular meals three times a day.

Develops control of muscles that hold up the head. By four months enjoys holding up head.

Focuses eyes and begins to explore the environment visually.
Begins to grasp objects at about sixteen weeks. Can grasp and let go by six months.
Rolls over intentionally (four to six months).
Holds own bottle (six to eight months).
Shows first tooth at about six months. Has about twelve teeth by age one.
Sits well alone, can turn and recover balance (six to eight months).
Raises body at nine months. May even pull self up to a standing position.
Starts to crawl at six months and to creep at nine or ten months.
May begin walking by age one.

Social

Begins to smile socially (four or five months).
Enjoys frolicking and being jostled.
Recognizes mother or other significant adult.
Notices hands and feet and plays with them.
By six months likes playing, alone or with company.
Begins to be wary of strangers.
Cooperates in games such as peekaboo and pat-a-cake.
Imitates actions of others.

Emotional

Differentiates crying according to specific discomforts, such as being hungry, cold, or wet.
Shows emotions by overall body movements such as kicking, arm waving, and facial expressions.
Begins to show pleasure when needs are being met.
By six months shows affection by kissing and hugging.
Shows signs of fearfulness.
Pushes away things not liked.

Cognitive

First discriminates mother from others; later, discriminates familiar faces from those of strangers.
Explores world through looking, mouthing, grasping.
Inspects things for long periods.
As a first sign of awareness, protests disappearance of objects.
Discovers how to make things happen and delights in doing so by repeating an action several times.
Between six and twelve months becomes aware of object permanency by recognizing that an object has been taken away and by looking for a hidden object.
Begins intentional actions by pulling at an object or removing an obstacle to get at an object.
Becomes increasingly curious about surroundings.

Toddlers (one and two years)

Physical

Begins to develop many motor skills.
Continues teething till about eighteen months; develops all twenty teeth by two years.
Develops large muscles. Crawls well, stands alone (at about a year), and pushes chair around.

(continued on next page)

Box 1.1 *(continued from previous page)*

Starts to walk at about fifteen months; may still be wobbly at eighteen months.
Places ball in and out of box.
Releases ball with thrust.
Creeps down stairs backwards.
Develops fine motor skills. Stacks two blocks, picks up a bean, and puts objects into a container. Starts to use spoon. Puts on simple things—for instance, an apron over the head.
By end of eighteen months, scribbles with a crayon in vertical or horizontal lines.
Turns pages of book.
During second year, walks without assistance.
Runs but often bumps into things.
Jumps up and down.
Walks up and down stairs with one foot forward.
Holds glass with one hand.
Stacks at least six blocks and strings beads.
Opens doors and cupboards.
Scribbles spirals, loops, and rough circles.
Starts to prefer one hand to the other.
Starts day control of elimination.

Social

At age one, differentiates meagerly between self and other.
Approaches mirror image socially.
By eighteen months, distinguishes between terms *you* and *me*.
Plays spontaneously; is self-absorbed but notices newcomers.
Imitates behavior more elaborately.
Identifies body parts.
Responds to music.
Develops socialization by age two. Is less interested in playing with parent and more interested in playing with a peer.
Begins parallel play, playing side by side, but without interaction.
By age two learns to distinguish strongly between self and others.
Is ambivalent about moving out and exploring.
Becomes aware of owning things and may become very possessive.

Emotional

At age one is amiable.
At eighteen months is resistant to change. Often suddenly—won't let mother out of sight.
Tends to rebel, resist, fight, run, hide.
Perceives emotions of others.
At age one, shows no sense of guilt. By age two, begins to experience guilt and shows beginnings of conscience.
Says no emphatically. Shows willfulness and negativism.
Laughs and jumps exuberantly.

Cognitive

Shows mental imagery: looks for things that are hidden, recalls and anticipates events, moves beyond here and now, begins temporal and spatial orientation.
Develops deductive reasoning: searches for things in more than one place.
Reveals memory: shows deferred imitation by seeing an event and imitating it later. Remembers names of objects.

Completes awareness of object permanence.
By age two or three distinguishes between black and white and may use names of colors.
Distinguishes one from many.
Says "one, two, three" in rote counting, but not often in rational counting.
Acts out utterances and talks about actions while carrying them out.
Takes things apart and tries to put them back together.
Shows sense of time by remembering events. Knows terms *today* and *tomorrow,* but mixes them up.

Preschoolers (three to four years)

Physical

Expands physical skills.
Rides a tricycle.
Pushes a wagon.
Runs smoothly and stops easily.
Climbs jungle gym ladder.
Walks stairs with alternating feet forward.
Jumps with two feet.
Shows high energy level.
By four can do a running broad jump.
Begins to skip, pushing one foot ahead of the other.
Can balance on one foot.
Keeps relatively good time in response to music.
Expands fine motor skills for dressing. Manipulates zippers, maybe even buttons.
Controls elimination at night.

Social

Becomes more social.
Moves from parallel play to early associative play. Joins others in activities.
Becomes aware of racial and sexual differences.
Begins independence.
By four shows growing sense of initiative and self-reliance.
Becomes aware of basic sex identity.
Not uncommonly develops imaginary playmates (a trait that may appear as early as two and a half).

Emotional

Begins enjoying humor. Laughs when adults laugh.
Develops inner control over behavior.
Shows less negativism.
Develops phobias and fears, which may continue until age five.
At four may begin intentional lying but is outraged by parents' white lies.

Cognitive

Begins problem-solving skills. Stacks blocks and may kick them down to see what happens.
Learns to use listening skills as a means of learning about the world.
Still draws in scribbles at age three, but in one direction and less repetitively.
At age four, drawings represent what child knows and thinks is important.
Is perceptually bound to one attribute and characteristic. "Why" questions abound.

(continued on next page)

Box 1.1 *(continued from previous page)*

Believes everything in the world has a reason, but the reason must accord with the child's own knowledge.
Persists in egocentric thinking.
Begins to sort out fantasy from reality.

Early Primary (five and six years)

Physical

Well controlled and constantly in motion.
Often rides a bicycle as well as a tricycle.
Can skip with alternating feet and hop.
Can control fine motor skills. Begins to use tools such as toothbrush, saw, scissors, pencil, hammer, needle for sewing.
Has established handedness well. Identifies hand used for writing or drawing.
Can dress self but may still have trouble tying shoelaces.
At age six begins to lose teeth.

Social

Becomes very social. Visits with friends independently.
Becomes very self-sufficient.
Persists longer at a task. Can plan and carry out activities and return to projects next day.
Plays with two or three friends, often for just a short time only, then switches play groups.
Begins to conform. Is very helpful.
By age six becomes very assertive, often bossy, dominating situations and ready with advice.
Needs to be first. Has difficulty listening.
Is possessive and boastful.
Craves affection. Often has a love–hate relationship with parents.
Refines sex roles. Has tendency to type by sex.
Becomes clothes-conscious.

Emotional

Continues to develop sense of humor.
Learns right from wrong.
At age five begins to control emotions and is able to express them in socially approved ways.
Quarrels frequently, but quarrels are of short duration.
At age six shifts emotions often and seems to be in emotional ferment.
New tensions appear as a result of attendance at school all day. Temper tantrums appear.
Giggles over bathroom words.
At age five develops a conscience, but sees actions as all good or all bad.
At age six accepts rules and often develops rigid insistence that they be obeyed.
May become a tattletale.

Cognitive

Begins to recognize conservation of amount and length.
Becomes interested in letters and numbers. May begin printing or copying letters and numbers. Counts.
Knows most colors.

Recognizes that one can get meaning from printed words.
Has a sense of time, but mainly personal time. Knows when events take place in his or her day or week.
Recognizes own space and can move about independently in familiar territory.

Late Primary (seven and eight years)

Physical

Great variation in height and weight, but rate of growth slows.
Masters physical skills for game playing and enjoys team sports.
Is willing to repeat a skill over and over to mastery.
Increases in fine-motor performance—can draw a diamond correctly and form letters well.
Has sudden spurts of energy.
Loss of baby teeth continues and permanent teeth appear.
Physique begins to change. Body more proportionately developed and facial structure changes.

Social

Beginning to prefer own sex—has less boy/girl interaction.
Peer groups begin to form.
Security in sex identification.
Self-absorption.
Begins to work and play independently.
Can be argumentative.
Seven still not a good loser and often a tattle teller.
By eight plays games better and not as intent on winning.
Conscientious—can take responsibility for routine chores.
Less selfish. Able to share. Wants to please.
Still enjoys and engages in fantasy play.

Emotional

Difficulty in starting things but will persist to end.
Worries that school might be too hard.
Beginning of empathy—sees other's viewpoint.
Sense of humor expressed in riddles, practical jokes, and nonsense words.
Discriminates between good and bad, but still immature.
Is sensitive and gets hurt easily.
Has sense of possession and takes care of possessions (makes collections).

Cognitive

Attention span is quite long.
Can plan and stay with a task or project over a long period.
Interested in conclusions and logical ends.
Aware of community and the world.
Expanding knowledge and interest.
Some sevens read well and by eight really enjoy reading.
Can tell time—aware of passage of time in months and years.
Interested in other time periods.
Conscious of other's work and their own. May comment "I'm good at art, but Sue is better at reading."
Differences in abilities widening.

Source: Reprinted by permission of Charles E. Merrill Publishing Co. Figure 2–1, pp. 63 to 69 in Seefeldt and Barbour, *Early Childhood Education: An Introduction.*

Professional Associations and Related Journals Dealing with Early Literacy

What we have learned over the years concerning learning theory and early literacy development is due to research by college professors and classroom teachers. Professional associations hold conferences and publish journals to inform and move the field forward. Following is a list of such groups and journals, along with other publications dealing with early literacy, for future study and reference.

American Library Association (ALA), 50 E. Huron Street, Chicago, IL 60611, www.ala.org

American Montessori Society, Inc. (AMS), 281 Park Avenue South, 6th Floor, New York, NY 10010, www.amshq.org

Association for Childhood Education International (ACEI), 17904 Georgia Avenue, Suite 215, Olney, MD 20832, www.acei.org
Journals: *Childhood Education; Journal of Research in Childhood Education*

Child Welfare League of America, Inc. (CWLA), 440 First Street NW, 3rd Floor, Washington, DC 20001, www.cwla.org
Journal: *Child Welfare*

Children's Bureau, Office of Child Development, U.S. Department of Health, Education and Welfare, Washington, DC 20201
Journal: *Children Today*

College Reading Association (CRA), Language, Reading, and Exceptional Department, College of Education, Appalachian State University, Boone, NC 28608
Journal: *Reading Research & Instruction*

The Education Center, Inc., 3515 West Market Street, Suite 200, Greensboro, NC 27403
Publication: *Learning* (www.learningmagazine.com)

Educational Resource Information Center/Elementary and Early Childhood Education (ERIC/EECE), University of Illinois at Urbana-Champaign, Children's Research Center, 51 Gerty Drive, Champaign, IL 61820, www.ericae.net

Gordon and Breach Science Publishers, Inc. P. O. Box 32160, Newark, NJ 07102
Journal: *Early Child Development and Care*

Highlights for Children, PO Box 269, Columbus, OH 43215-0269
Publication: *Teaching PreK–8* (www.teachingk-8.com)

International Reading Association (IRA), 800 Barksdale Road, PO Box 8139, Newark, DE 19711, www.reading.org
Journals: *The Reading Teacher; Reading Research Quarterly*
brochures, pamphlets, and monographs

National Association for the Education of Young Children (NAEYC), 1509 16th Street NW, Washington, DC 20036, www.naeyc.org

Journals: *Young Children; Early Childhood Research Quarterly*
pamphlets and monographs

National Council of Teachers of English (NCTE), 1111 Kenyon Road, Urbana, IL 61801, www.ncte.org
Journal: *Language Arts*
pamphlets and monographs

National Education Association (NEA), 1201 16th Street NW, Washington DC 20036, www.nea.org
Publication: *NEA Today*

National Reading Conference (NRC), 11 East Hubbard St., Chicago, IL 60603
Journal: *Journal of Literacy Research*

Scholastic, Inc., 555 Broadway, New York, NY 10012, www.scholastic.com
Publications: *Early Childhood Today; Instructor*

Society for Research in Child Development (SRCD), 5750 Ellis Avenue, Chicago, IL 60637, www.srcd.org
Journal: *Child Development*

An Idea for the Classroom from the Classroom

The following experience was created by an early childhood teacher for the children in her classroom. The ideas reflect theories discussed in this chapter. You may find them useful for your teaching.

Preschoolers Go Restaurant Hopping

As part of a unit dealing with nutrition, I have individual conferences with my preschoolers to help them create their own restaurant menus to be used during dramatic play. The children can write their menus themselves (any form of early writing will be accepted—from drawing a picture, scribble writing, to random letters), or they can dictate their menus and I will write them down. Their menus contain such savory items as fried chicken on the bone; apple juice; pink ice cream with sprinkles, whipped cream, and chocolate sauce; and cherry tacos. The children decorate covers for their menus and choose a name for their restaurant. The children have the opportunity to discuss and share their menus with the class during our "Morning Message" time.

The next step is to transform our housekeeping area into a restaurant. The play food and utensils are already there. We add items such as a tablecloth, serving trays, and small writing pads and pencils for taking orders. I've made large signs with every child's restaurant name on it. I rotate the names so that each child has a chance for his or her restaurant to be the restaurant of the day. When the children come to school, the first thing they do is rush over to the play area to see whose restaurant sign is posted.

During a typical play time, a great deal of literacy behavior occurs. Children read menus and take orders. They discuss the specials of the day and how the food tastes and pay the check. This science unit on good nutrition is conducive to providing meaningful literacy experiences for young readers and writers.

Meeting with each child individually in a conference allows me to identify and deal with his or her needs. The needs span from finding strategies for early reading and writing that suit his or her learning style to realizing that he or she can share his or her diverse background. For example, in addition to traditional hamburger and pizza places, we had a Japanese restaurant, one that featured Hispanic delicacies, and a Jewish deli.

Marcia Wesalo, Teacher
Play and Grow Nursery School, Somerset, New Jersey

Activities and Questions

1. Answer the focus questions at the beginning of the chapter.

2. Using one of the literacy skills (reading, writing, speaking, listening), create an experience for an early childhood classroom that reflects the doctrines of Piaget. Repeat for Froebel, Montessori, and Dewey. In other words, teach the same lesson four different ways.

3. In the section of the chapter entitled "Influences for Change in Early Literacy Practices," research and theory are described that have implications for

new strategies in early literacy. Most of this book is devoted to describing these strategies. Try to predict one strategy for each of the literacy areas discussed (oral language, reading, and writing) that reflects the theory described. After you have read the entire book, come back to your answer and see how well you did.

4. Observe an early childhood classroom (preschool through second grade). Decide which theoretical influences have determined the type of practices carried out. Document your findings with specific anecdotes illustrating the theory.

Case Study Activities

Case 1

Refer to "An Idea for the Classroom from the Classroom" to refresh your memory. Identify the theories and research discussed in the chapter that influenced the strategies used.

Case 2

Mr. Migel and Mrs. Colon are kindergarten teachers in an inner-city school district who teach in the same building. The children in their classrooms are mostly African American and Latino. Both teachers are very dedicated to their profession. They have created classroom settings that demonstrate their philosophy and theory about what they believe early childhood education should be like.

Mr. Migel has designed his room with content area centers, such as science, social studies, art, dramatic play, block play, and music. Each center reflects a theme the children are studying. For example, the children are studying spring, and there are plants in the science corner; tapes about spring in the music center; and books about plants, bugs, and new baby animals in the library corner. A zoo has been designed in the block center where baby gerbils have just been born, and a live hen is sitting on her eggs. There are tickets to buy to visit the zoo, signs on the real and play animal cages, and receipts for money spent.

In the morning when they arrive at school, the children and Mr. Migel sing songs about spring, talk about spring, and discuss what they are going to do in school. A good portion of the day is spent at centers with children working with each other, and with the manipulative materials. Often there is a lot of noise, and sometimes children are not productively engaged. Mr. Migel has no formal lessons for reading or writing. When children want to look at books, they are there for them. If children decide to write a story, there are materials for them to use, and Mr. Migel is always happy to help. Children are happy in his classroom. Mr. Migel is kind, supportive, warm, and caring. He believes that building a positive attitude about school and who they are is the most important part of the children's kindergarten experience. He emphasizes social, emotional, and physical development. He also believes that the children will learn reading and writing as a result of their exposure to books and print in a spontaneous way and that formal lessons in this area are inappropriate and unnecessary.

Mrs. Colon's classroom is different from Mr. Migel's. She too cares a great deal about the children. She is warm, kind, and supportive. She has organized the tables so that there is a definitive front of the room for her to carry out lessons. She feels that the children need to learn school behavior and be ready for first grade. According to Mrs. Colon, many of these children know almost nothing about reading and writing because their parents rarely work with them. She believes that they need to know the alphabet and be able to match sounds to their correct symbols as an aid to early literacy. She teaches a letter of the alphabet a week, and children use worksheets to reinforce what they have learned. The writing that takes place is mostly for the development of fine motor control to help the children learn to formulate letters, which they practice. Mrs. Colon's classroom is orderly, quiet, and organized, with specific objectives to be accomplished. Children do have the opportunity to play in her room. She views this not as a time to learn, but as a time to relax after they have done their work.

The reading specialist in the district is worried about both Mr. Migel and Mrs. Colon. She likes some of the things that both of them do, but feels that each is lacking some important classroom strategies. What theories do Mr. Migel and Mrs. Colon embrace, based on the descriptions given of their classrooms? Why do you feel the reading specialist is concerned about each? What do you suggest could be done in each classroom to improve instruction? If you feel strongly that one teacher or the other provides instruction in kindergarten as it should be, support your premise with the appropriate theory.

chapter 2

Observing and Assessing the Learning Needs of All Children

Bill of Rights for Children

Let me grow as I be
And try to understand
Why I want to grow like me
Not like my parents hope I will be
Or like my teacher thinks I should be,
Please try to understand and help me grow
Just like me.

—Gladys Andrews
Creative Rhythmic Movement for Children

Focus Questions

- Define authentic assessment and identify some measures.
- Describe the nature of standardized tests and standardized testing.
- What is meant by high-stakes assessment?
- What are the pros and cons of authentic assessment and standardized measurement?
- What do we mean when we speak about standards for early literacy development?
- How can we tie standards instruction and assessment together?
- Who are children with special needs? What implications for instruction do special needs children present in the classroom?
- What is meant by early intervention programs? What is meant by inclusion?
- How do we plan for early literacy instruction with children from diverse cultural backgrounds in our classrooms?

When the teacher passed out the standardized test booklets, Rosa was confused and frightened. She had limited English skills and had been in her present second grade for just four months. She had been learning English, but her ability was limited. She could read Spanish quite well and was capable of decoding printed English, but with little comprehension. As she looked at the test, she knew that she could not understand the questions or answers. She decided the only thing to do was to fill in the answers by marking an *X* in a box for each of the questions. She appeared busy at work filling in all the boxes without reading one question or answer. She felt better about doing this than letting the teacher know that she could not read the test.

In her book *First Grade Takes a Test,* Miriam Cohen describes the experience of a first-grade class taking a standardized test, and the consequences of the test results to the dynamics of the interpersonal relationships within the class. In one section of the story she writes:

> George looked at the test. It said: Rabbits eat
>
> ☐ lettuce ☐ dog food ☐ sandwiches
>
> He raised his hand. "Rabbits have to eat carrots or their teeth will get too long and stick into them," he said. The teacher nodded and smiled, but she put her finger to her lips. George carefully drew in a carrot so the test people would know. (1980, pp. 5–6)

In both of these incidents, children answered questions incorrectly on the standardized tests given to them but for different reasons. Rosa could not read the test because she was not able to read English. Although she was reading at grade level in Spanish, she was jeopardized due to her cultural background. George, relating his own experience to the question at hand, actually had a more sophisticated answer than those provided. His answer was marked incorrect because his background experience with rabbits was different from that of the person who wrote the test. In addition, George did not understand how to take the test, that is, to fill in the box beside the best answer provided.

In both incidents, children did not answer incorrectly because they did not know the answer. Rosa failed due to her limited language ability, which was not acknowledged when she was asked to take the test. George failed due to problems with the design of the test.

This chapter deals with critical issues facing early childhood educators today: recognizing and addressing special needs of children, and achieving standards by assessing the needs of children. The issues are different but have many things in common. Assessment must be sensitive to children's different backgrounds and abilities. Only when we recognize individual differences based on our assessment of special needs can appropriate instructional strategies be planned and standards be achieved.

I will address these topics as an introduction to the issues that surround them. The practical applications for addressing the individual needs of children from diverse cultures and having diverse abilities, as well as assessment of all children's performance, will be discussed in all chapters that deal with instructional strategies. These issues and the design of instruction to meet standards need to be integrated into discussions dealing with instruction. However, they need an introduction.

Assessing Early Literacy Development

Early literacy educators, with their concern for children's interests, learning styles, and individual levels of ability, have made us begin to take a closer look at our methods for assessing performance. It has become apparent that the same standardized group paper-and-pencil tests are not sensitive to strategies drawn from early literacy constructs. In addition, it has become clear that one measure cannot be the main source for evaluating a child's progress. Rather than testing children, we need to assess their performance for growth in many areas and under many conditions. Assessment should help the teacher, child, and parent determine a child's strengths and weaknesses and plan appropriate instructional strategies. Assessment should match educational goals and practices. To meet the needs of the different populations in our schools, assessment measures need to be diverse because there are children who perform better in some situations than in others.

The International Reading Association (IRA) and the National Association for the Education of Young Children's (NAEYC) joint position statement on learning to read and write (1998) makes the following recommendations: "Use evaluative procedures that are developmentally and culturally appropriate for the children being assessed. The selection of evaluative measures should be based on the objectives of the instructional program and should consider each child's total development and its effect on reading performance." Quality assessment should be drawn from real-life writing and reading tasks and should continuously follow a range of literacy activities.

The type of assessment referred to is often called ***authentic assessment.*** There are many definitions for the term, but one that seems to capture its essence is assessment activities that represent and reflect the actual learning and instructional activities of the classroom and out-of-school world. Several principles emerge from an authentic assessment perspective as outlined by Ruddell and Ruddell (1995):

1. Assessment should be based primarily on observations of children engaged in authentic classroom reading and writing tasks.
2. Assessment should focus on children's learning and the instructional goal of the curriculum.
3. Assessment should be continuous, based on observations over a substantial period.
4. Assessment should take into account the diversity of students' cultural, language, and special needs.
5. Assessment should be collaborative and include the active participation of children, parents, and teachers.
6. Assessment should recognize the importance of using a variety of observations rather than relying on one assessment approach.
7. Assessment must be knowledge based and reflect our most current understanding of reading and writing processes.

To accomplish these goals, assessment must be frequent and include many types. The main goal is to observe and record actual behavior that provides the broadest possible picture of a particular child. Every chapter in this book that deals with a specific area of literacy development contains a section with suggestions for collecting material related to assessment for that particular skill. A list of generic types of authentic assessment measures that will help paint a comprehensive picture of a child is provided here.

Generic Authentic Assessment Measures

- *Observation Forms.* Teachers create their own forms for observing and recording children's behavior. Observation forms usually have broad categories with large spaces for notes about children's activities. Goals for observing should be planned and forms designed to meet the goals.
- *Checklists.* Inventories including lists of behaviors or skills for students to accomplish are a common form of authentic assessment. The list is prepared based on objectives a teacher may have for instruction. Therefore the inventory is designed to determine if goals set forth have been accomplished.
- *Daily Performance Samples.* These are samples of the child's work in all content areas that are done on a daily basis. Various types of samples should be collected periodically. Samples of writing, artwork, and science and social studies reports can be collected throughout the school year (Figure 2.1).
- *Anecdotes of Observations.* Anecdotes of observations can be used for many different purposes. Teachers will want to write down interesting, humorous, and general comments about the child's behavior in the classroom. Observations should focus on one particular aspect of the child's performance, such as oral reading, silent reading, behavior while listening to stories, or writing. Within the descriptions of behavior dialogue is often included.

Figure 2.1

A Daily Performance Sample of Nicole's Writing at the End of Her Kindergarten Year

Dear m.rswilley
I thingk you are
The hisist tetcher in
The scool. I had a
Grat year in kindrgrdin.
I Like The serkis I LikT Dansing
Love Nicole E. oxoxoxo
Have a nice sum.er

■ *Audiotapes.* Audiotapes are another form of assessment that can be used to determine language development and to analyze progress in oral reading. They can also be used in discussion sessions related to responses to literature to help understand how youngsters function in a group, and the types of responses they offer.

■ *Videotapes.* Videotapes relate information similar to that in audiotapes with the additional data that can be gained by seeing the child in action. Because writing is not an auditory activity, videotapes of children in writing situations would be useful for assessment purposes. Audio- and videotapes are methods teachers can also use for assessing their own performance.

■ *Surveys.* Surveys can be prepared by teachers to assess children's attitudes about how they think they are learning or what they like or dislike in school. Surveys can be in the form of questionnaires or interviews with written or oral answers.

■ *Teacher-Prepared Pencil-and-Paper Tests.* These tests will probably match instruction better than measures designed by commercial companies; therefore, teachers need to provide this type of experience for children.

■ *Student Evaluation Forms.* Authentic assessment must involve the child. Forms are prepared for children to evaluate their own performance (see below).

Children's Self-Evaluation Form

Name ______________________________ **Date** ______________

1. I know all the letters of the alphabet. yes ☐ no ☐

2. I can write the letters. yes ☐ no ☐
   Here is a sample of some letters I can write:

3. I know letter sounds. yes ☐ no ☐
   Here are some letter sounds I know:

4. Things I need help with letters are:

---

1. I like to read: yes ☐ no ☐ Why?

2. Things I like to read are:

3. The things I do well in reading are:

4. The things I need to learn how to do better in reading are:

---

1. I like to write: yes ☐ no ☐ Why?

2. Things I like to write are:

3. The things I do well in writing are:

4. The things I need to learn how to do better in writing are:

Children should regularly evaluate their performance by collecting samples of their work, discussing them with the teacher and other children. Children are an integral part of the assessment process.

- *Parent Assessment Forms.* Authentic assessment also involves parents as evaluators of their children. Parents may be asked to collect work samples from home and to write anecdotes about behavior, for which they may be provided forms for observing and recording behavior. Children should talk about their work with their parents in the home. The parent is an important resource for providing more information about the child from the home perspective.
- *Conferences.* Conferences allow the teacher to meet with a child on a one-to-one basis to assess skills such as reading aloud, to discuss a child's progress, to talk about steps to improve, to instruct, and to prescribe activities. Children should take an active role in evaluating their progress and are equal partners in the assessment process. Parents also are involved in conferencing with teachers about their child's progress. They meet with teachers alone and with their child. They bring materials they have collected at home to add to the packet of information.

Informal Reading Inventories and Running Records

Informal Reading Inventories (IRI) are tests to determine a child's instructional level. IRIs consist of paragraphs of graded reading materials for children to read aloud. Errors are counted and an accuracy percentage calculated, which indicates if the child reads at the independent, instructional, or frustration level. Errors typically are not analyzed for type, for example, to determine if a child has a decoding problem or one that involves the use of context or meaning from text. IRIs do reveal the material that is suitable for a child's instructional level. For children who can read passages silently, there are checks for comprehension in this test.

Marie Clay (1993a) created **running records** for closely observing and recording children's oral reading behavior and for planning instruction. In the analysis, what a child can do and the types of errors he or she makes when reading, such as insertions, deletions, substitutions, or repetitions, are recorded. Self-corrections are recorded but are not considered errors. Running records also determine the appropriate material for instructional purposes and for independent reading. In addition, a student's frustration level will be identified. Determining the level of material for instruction and the types of strategies for instruction based on errors made is crucial for productive guidance in reading to occur. Running records spend more time indicating the types of errors students make in oral reading than evaluating their ability to comprehend text.

In taking a running record the child is asked to read a short passage of 100 to 200 words. Younger children have shorter passages and older children have longer ones. The teacher has a copy of the passage, and as the child reads the teacher uses the prescribed coding system to indicate on a running record form whether words are read correctly and what type of errors are made such, as an insertion of a word, a deletion, a repetition, or substitution (see Figures 2.2 and 2.3). As the child reads, the teacher records whether reading is accurate with checks over each word, or records the type of error. If a child reads 95 to 100 percent of the words correctly, the material is at his or her independent level; if 90 to 95 percent of the words are correct, the material is at the instructional level; less than 90 percent of the words read correctly suggests the

Figure 2.2

Running Record Form

Name ______________________ **Date** ______________

Book ______________________ **Book level** ______________

Words: **Error rate:** **Accuracy rate:**

Errors:

Self-correction rate:

			Cues used						
			E—errors			SC—self-correction			
E	SC	Text	M	S	V		M	S	V

M—meaning, S—structure, V—visual, E—error, SC—self- correction

Reading level

Independent: 95 to 100% accuracy

Instructional: 90 to 95% accuracy

Difficult (or Frustration): 89% or less accuracy

Reading proficiency: fluent ______ word by word ______ choppy ______

Retelling

Setting: characters ______ time ______ place ______

Theme: problem or goal ______

Events: number included ______

Resolution: solved problem ______ achieved goal ______ ending ______

Source: Adapted from M. Clay, 1985. In: *The Early Detection of Reading Difficulties (3rd edition)*. Portsmouth, NH: Heinemann.

child's frustration level. Calculations for running records for percent of accuracy rate follow:

1. Record the number of words in a testing passage (for example 70).
2. Count the number of errors made by the child and subtract that from the total number of passage words (for example, 5 errors minus 70 equals 65).
3. Divide that number (65) by the total words in the passage (70).
4. Multiply that by 100, which equals 90 percent or the percent of accuracy for the passage read.

Figure 2.3 *Running Record Coding System*

Type of error or miscue	Code	Description
Accurate reading	√√√√	For each word read correctly a check or dash is placed above the word. Some prefer no marking to mean accurate reading.
Self-correction (not counted as an error)	his | SC / her	Child reads the word incorrectly, pauses, and then corrects the error.
Substitution (counted as an error)	boat / barge	The student substitutes a real word that is incorrect.
Refusal to pronounce Told word (counted as an error)	— / table | T	The student neither pronounces the word nor attempts to do so. The teacher pronounces the word so that testing can continue.
Insertion (counted as an error)	at / —	The student inserts a word or a series of words that do not appear in the text.
Omission (counted as an error)	— / rat	The student omits a word or a continuous sequence of words in the text, but continues to read.
Repetition (not counted as an error)	← The horse ran away	The student repeats one or more words that have been read. Groups of adjacent words that are repeated count as one repetition.
Reversal	he said / was	The student reverses the order of words or letters.
Appeal for help (counted as an error)	--- | App / house | T	Child asks for help with a word he or she cannot read.

Source: Adapted from A. P. Shearer & S. P. Homan, 1994. In: *Linking Reading Assessment to Instruction*. New York: St. Martin's Press.

Another quick way to determine reading level is as follows: 0 to 3 errors in the passage is considered independent level; 4 to 10 errors instructional; 11 or more errors frustration. If a child is at the frustration level with the first book he or she tries, for kindergarten to first grade, stop testing. If the child is at the frustration level for grade 2–3 material, use K–1 material to test.

An important part of a running record is to analyze further why errors are being made. This is done by classifying them one step further as M for meaning, S for structure, or V for visual. To determine the type of error, go back to the text and look at the error and predict what it might be. Here are some examples:

1. A child makes a meaning error when the word read is incorrect but the meaning of the text is intact and makes sense. For example, if a child reads, "This is my house," instead of "This is my home," although the word is not correct the meaning is intact. That error should be marked with an M.
2. A child makes a structure error when the word in the sentence sounds correct in the sentence, but was not read correctly. For example, if a child reads, "I went to the zoo," instead of "I ran to the zoo," the English grammar or syntax is correct, but the word is not. Therefore the error is marked S for structure.

Running records document children's oral reading behavior and help teachers to plan instruction.

3. The last type of error is visual. Here the child might say "spilt" for "spill," because the words look similar and he or she is not looking carefully enough.

For kindergarten and first-grade children the running record can start with a letter-recognition test. This test simply has the letters of the alphabet printed out of order in upper and lower case. Children are asked to read the letter names one row at a time. The teacher records letters correct and incorrect. The test can go one step further to determine if students know sound–symbol correspondence by asking children if they know the sound that particular letters make, and a word that begins with that letter or sound, and recording their responses. In addition, high frequency word recognition assessment can be done. In Chapter 8 in Figure 8.1, a high frequency word list is presented. The list can be divided by grade level according to which words are considered most difficult. The teacher asks children to read words from the list beginning with what are considered to be the easiest first. If they are successful the next group of words for the next grade level are tried.

Running records should be done about once a month for all early childhood students. The teachers should talk to children about the types of errors they make in a running record to give them strategies such as listening to the meaning of a sentence and looking at the letters in the word to figure out a word.

There is place on the running record form to indicate if the child's reading was fluent, word by word, or choppy. Teachers can ask children to retell stories read to determine comprehension of text (Harp, 2000).

Portfolio Assessment

A portfolio provides a way for teachers, children, and parents to collect representative samples of children's work. The portfolio can include work in progress and completed samples. It provides a story of where children have been, and

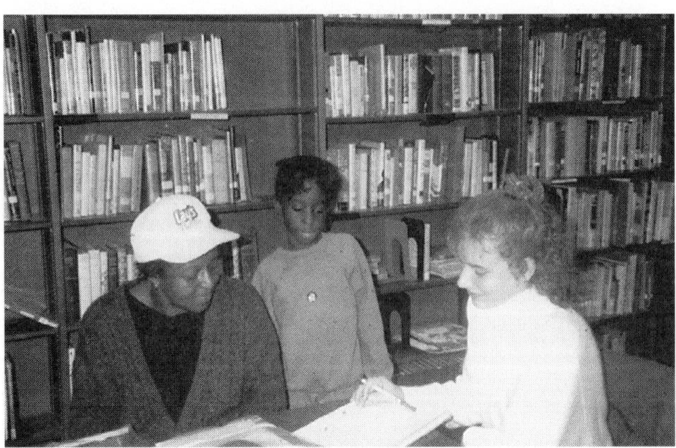

Conferences should include the teacher, parent, and child all taking an active role in assessing the student's progress.

what they are capable of doing now, to determine where they should go from this point forth. The teacher's portfolio should include work selected by the child, teacher, and parent. It should represent the best work that a child can produce and illustrate difficulties he or she may be experiencing. It should include many different types of work samples, and represent what the child has been learning.

The physical portfolio is often an accordion-type folder with several pockets to hold work. The folder can be personalized with a drawing by the child, a picture of the child, and his or her name. Because portfolios often are passed on to the next grade, the pieces collected need to be carefully selected to limit the size of the folder. The portfolio should include different samples representing different areas of literacy and the best work the child has to offer. Included, for example, should be daily work performance samples, anecdotes about behavior, audiotapes of oral reading, language samples, story retellings, checklists recording skill development over the course of a year, interviews, standardized test results, a child's self-assessment form, journals, expository and narrative writing samples, and artwork. Some schools have prepared formal schedules for collecting portfolios and administering tests (see Figure 2.4). A portfolio also should be prepared by the child with the teacher that he or she can keep and take home at the end of a school year (Valencia, Hiebert, & Afflerbach, 1994).

Throughout the chapters of this book, assessment will be discussed at the end of sections that deal with specific skill development. Multiple measures will be offered to include a portfolio of assessment materials for children. These materials should help teachers create appropriate instructional strategies, help parents understand their child's development, and make the child aware of his or her strengths and weaknesses and how he or she can improve.

Standardized Tests

Standardized tests measure what students have learned. They do not, however, concern themselves with how they learn. The product is more important than the process in standardized tests.

Standardized tests are prepared by publishers and are norm-referenced, that is, they are administered to large numbers of students in order to develop norms.

Figure 2.4 *Schedule for Collecting Portfolio Samples and Tests*

Student ______________________ Grade ______________

School ______________________ Teacher ______________

Tests are given in September (S), January (J), and May (A). Record the test when given in the space provided.

Grade	Sept. K	Jan. K	May K	Sept. 1	Jan. 1	May 1	Sept. 2	Jan. 2	May 2
1. Child interview									
2. Parent interview									
3. Self portrait									
4. Concepts about print test									
5. Story retelling									
6. Written retelling									
7. Free writing									
8. Letter recognition									
9. Running record									
10. High-frequency sight words									
11. Observation comments									

Source: Adapted from South Brunswick, New Jersey Public Schools Portfolio Assessment Strategies.

Norms are the average performance of students who are tested at a particular grade and age level. When selecting a standardized test, it is important to check its validity for your students. That is, does the test evaluate what it says it tests for and does it match the goals you have for your students? The reliability of the test is important as well. That is, are scores accurate and dependable?

Other features of standardized tests are as follows:

1. *Grade equivalent scores* are raw scores converted into grade level scores. For example if a child is in first grade and receives a grade equivalent score of 2.3, his performance would be considered above grade level.
2. *Percentile ranks* are raw scores converted into a percentile rank. They tell where the child ranked as compared to all children who took the test at his or her grade and age level. Therefore, if a youngster received a percentile rank of 80, it would mean that he or she scored better than or equal to 80 percent of those students taking the test at his or her grade and age level, and that 20 percent of the children taking the test scored better.

Although many criticisms are associated with standardized measures, they do present another source of information about a child's performance. Parents often like receiving the information from the test because it is concrete information regarding where their child ranks among others in the same grade. It must be realized, though, that it is just one type of information that is no more important than all of the other measures discussed earlier. Taking a standardized test does expose children to another type of literacy situation that they are likely to encounter in later years both in and out of school. Many question, however, whether it is necessary to use such a measure in the early childhood grades.

Problems Associated with Standardized Testing

There are a number of problems associated with standardized tests. First, we must recognize that they represent only one form of assessment; their use must be coordinated with that of other assessment measures. Second, some standardized tests for early literacy evaluate children on skills such as auditory memory, rhyme, letter recognition, visual matching, school language, and listening. By contrast, practices that nurture early literacy that may not be included in the test emphasize children's prior knowledge, book concepts, attitudes about reading, association of meaning with print, and characteristics of printed materials. One child might pass all portions of a standardized test yet not be able to begin to read, whereas a second child might not pass any portion of the test but may already be reading.

Some standardized tests do not match the instructional practices suggested by the latest research and theory on early literacy. This leads to a third problem. Unfortunately, because school districts are often evaluated on how well children perform on the standardized tests, teachers may feel pressured to teach for the test. This is often referred to as **high stakes assessment** because major decisions are being made from the results of one test score. Teachers who succumb to this temptation are likely to be using inappropriate strategies for teaching young children. In addition, such teachers spend an enormous amount of time preparing children for standardized tests by drilling them on sample tests similar to the real ones. The sample tests are graded, and instruction is geared to remedy student weaknesses indicated by the test. If teachers do not prepare children for the test with practice sessions, and do not teach to the test, their children may not score well. Aside from the content of the test, the knowledge of how to take the test is crucial for success. Thus, teachers may feel they are jeopardizing their own jobs if they refuse to teach to standardized tests. It is a frightening dilemma.

A fourth, higher-stakes issue with standardized tests is that the results of such tests are commonly used in placing children in specific classrooms and reading groups. Once placed, a child may never be moved to a different group. Yet, the standardized tests on which placement decisions are based can yield inaccurate information. Figure 2.5 illustrates hypothetical subscores and overall percentile ranks of three kindergarten children on a typical standardized reading readiness test.

Child A scored well in auditory and visual discrimination skills, and poorly in language skills. The child's overall score is at the 50th percentile. Child B has good auditory skills, poor visual skills, and good language skills and also scored overall at the 50th percentile. Child C scored fairly consistently across visual, auditory, and language skills and likewise scored overall at the 50th percentile.

Figure 2.5

Hypothetical Subtest Profiles on Three (3) Kindergarten Children Achieving about the Same Test Performance Rating

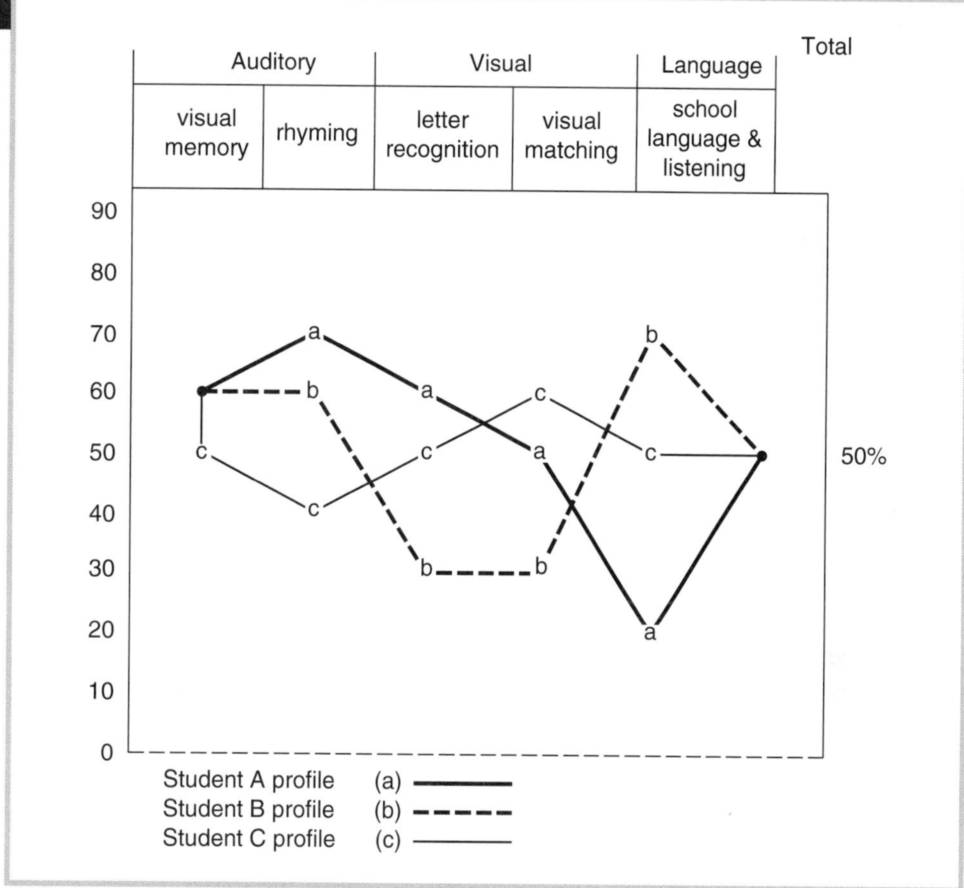

All three children will go to the first grade and could be placed in the same reading group, even though Child A has a possible language deficit and is missing one of the most important ingredients for reading success—a strong language base. These three children are quite different in ability yet have scored at the same overall percentile on a standardized test. It is very unlikely that the three will achieve similar success in reading, although they might be expected to on the basis of their test scores.

Another problem with standardized tests is bias. For example, standardized test scores are less reliable with younger children than with older children. Furthermore, some standardized tests are still biased in favor of white, middle-class children despite genuine attempts to alleviate the problem. Their use tends to place rural, African American, and bilingual youngsters at a disadvantage. Prior knowledge plays a large role in how well children will do on the test. Children from white, middle-class homes tend to have experiences that lead to better achievement on the tests. In addition, following test directions such as "Put your finger on the star" or "Circle the goat that is behind the tree" is often a problem for the young child. Children who have never seen a goat may not circle anything because the animal on the page might look like a dog to them.

The joint IRA/NAEYC position statement *Learning to Read and Write: Developmentally Appropriate Practices for Young Children* (1998) suggests that evaluative procedures used with young children be developmentally and culturally appropriate and that the selection of evaluative measures be based on the objectives of an instructional program and consider each child's total development and its effect on reading performance. Various steps can be taken to remedy the abuse of standardized testing in early childhood education. Administrators and teachers must understand the shortcomings of standardized tests and that the use of multiple assessment tools given frequently throughout the school year would tend to prevent undue emphasis on standardized test results.

Although standardized tests are problematic with young children, if they are used, teachers need to help youngsters learn about them. Children need to learn how to follow the directions and how to fill in the answers. Children must have the advantage of knowing what the test is like before they are faced with taking it.

Finding suitable tests is a difficult task. However, some test makers are becoming aware of the discrepancies between new instructional strategies and the design of the present tests. There are tools for assessing many aspects of early literacy that acknowledge and reflect the instructional strategies we evaluate today, specifically Clay's (1979) Concept about Print Test. This test evaluates what the child knows about print and how it is used in books. In addition to any standardized test, authentic assessment measures such as interviews, anecdotal records, collection of work samples, and others described throughout the book should be used frequently.

Standards and Standardized Tests for Reading and Writing

With the call for all children in the United States to be fluent readers by the end of third grade, professional literacy organizations and many states are outlining standards for achievement. **Standards** define what students should know about reading and writing and be able to do with reading and writing. The purpose of standards is to articulate what student need to learn at each grade level in the English language arts—reading, writing, listening, speaking, viewing, and visually representing.

Tests to determine whether children have become fluent readers are now being given at the fourth-grade level. These standardized tests could represent high-stakes assessment for school districts and children because the scores might indicate promotion decisions and ratings of districts, and could put jobs at risk for principals and teachers. One test should never be the determining factor for important decisions such as these. Nonetheless, to be successful in these tests, and more important to help students become fluent readers, schools must begin with a set of standards for children to achieve from kindergarten to the third grade. In reality the test is not a fourth-grade test, but rather an accumulation of specific behaviors learned from the beginning of a child's school experiences. The creation of standards helps develop fluent readers who will accomplish the goals.

The *Standards for the English Language Arts,* a project of the International Reading Association (IRA) and National Council of Teachers of English (NCTE)(1996), suggests that standards are needed to do the following:

1. Prepare students for literacy now and in the future with specific concerns about how technology will change the manner in which we deal with literacy in the future.

2. Ensure that students attain the vision of parents, teachers, and researchers about expectations for their achievement in the language arts.
3. Promote high expectations for literacy achievement among children and bridge inequities that exist in educational opportunities for all.

General standards were articulated by IRA and NCTE, and since this first endeavor, many states have adopted their own standards for the English language arts. These state standards and others being generated by various groups are extremely specific. They list expectations for reading and writing for every grade level. In addition, standards, instruction, and assessment are being linked to ensure accountability for achieving the goals that have been set forth.

The National Center on Education and the Economy (NCEE) and the University of Pittsburgh Learning Research and Development Center (LRDC) developed a document entitled *Reading and Writing Grade by Grade: Primary Literacy Standards for Kindergarten through Third Grade* (1999). There are a set of general standards for all grade levels and then specifics outlined for each level. For early literacy the standards are linked to instruction and assessment. In kindergarten, for example, one of the standards is the acquisition of phonemic awareness, more specifically the ability to segment and blend sounds. The standard is even more specific and suggests that it is expected that by the end of kindergarten children be able to do the following in the area of phonemic awareness:

- produce rhyming words and recognize pairs of rhyming words;
- isolate initial consonants in single-syllable words (for example, /t/ is the first sound in *top*);
- when a single-syllable word is pronounced (for example, *cat*), identify the **onset** (/c/) and the **rime** (-at) and begin to segment, or separate, the sounds (/c/-/a/-/t/) by saying each sound aloud; and
- **blend** onsets (/c/) and rimes (-at) to form words (*cat*) and begin to blend separately spoken phonemes to make a meaningful one-syllable word (for example, when the teacher says a word slowly, stretching it out as "mmm–ahhh–mmm," children can say that the word being stretched out is *mom*). (p. 54)

Instructional activities are being presented with standards to help teachers achieve these goals with children. In addition, a means for assessing the standard is provided. Standards may differ somewhat from one state to the other. However, there is a great deal of similarity among them as they are adopted throughout the country. The *Primary Literacy Standards* (NCEE/LRDC, 1999) mentioned suggest the areas for the development of literacy in grades K through 3. For the different areas specific expertise for each grade level is suggested. The following is the general outline for reading and writing:

Reading Standards

Print–Sound Code

- Knowledge of letters and their sounds
- Phonemic awareness: The ability to hear the different sound segments at the beginning, middle, and end of words and say, or blend, separate phonemes to make meaningful utterances.
- Reading words: The ability to figure out words from knowledge of the alphabetic principles and the ability to read words learned by sight.

Getting the Meaning

- Accuracy and fluency when reading: Accuracy is the ability to recognize words correctly. Fluency is the ability to read aloud with appropriate intonations and pauses indicating that students understand the meaning.
- Self-monitoring and self-correcting strategies
- Comprehension

Reading Habits

- Reads a lot
- Discusses books
- Has a large vocabulary

Writing Standards

Habits and Processes

Writing Purposes and Resulting Genres

- Sharing events, telling stories: narrative writing
- Informing others: report or informational writing
- Getting things done: functional writing
- Producing and responding to literature

Language Use and Conventions

- Style and syntax
- Vocabulary and word choice
- Spelling
- Punctuation, capitalization, and other conventions

In each of the chapters dealing with reading and writing, objectives for instruction will be listed that match standards.

Literacy and Diversity: Addressing Children's Individual Needs

Many of the theoretical, philosophical, and psychological perspectives presented in Chapter 1 discuss the necessity for meeting the individual needs of children. Early childhood education has always been child centered and concerned about the social, emotional, physical, and intellectual needs of children. In early childhood, every youngster is seen as a unique individual with his or her own special needs. There is, however, greater diversity than ever in classrooms today, and there are more and more individual needs to meet.

Frequently texts such as this devote a separate chapter to a discussion about meeting individual needs. In addition, special needs that deal with physical, social, intellectual, and emotional diversity are often separated from special needs associated with cultural and language diversity. Although these are very different concerns, for me they all fit under the heading of "Literacy and

Diversity: Understanding and Addressing Children's Individual Needs." Therefore, I address them together in this chapter, and instead of a separate chapter on each, I highlight them in most of the chapters because of their importance. We have become aware that appropriate instructional techniques for all children will probably be appropriate with some modifications for those with special needs.

Identifying special needs is the first step in dealing with them. Identification makes us more aware that they exist and then helps us determine the educational implications for instructional programs.

Children with Physical Impairments

Physical impairments refer to visual or hearing impairments, communication disorders, and orthopedic impairments. Children with minimal problems in these areas will be in the regular classroom. Others will be mainstreamed for portions of the day. ***Mainstreaming*** means that children who are in special classes will be integrated into regular classrooms for part of the school day.

Children with *visual impairments* are legally blind, have no useful vision, or have low vision with very limited sight. For these children, strategies that include auditory and tactile experiences are important. There are learning materials available in large print for low-vision children. Children with no vision must learn to read through the use of Braille, a system of reading for the blind consisting of characters represented by raised dots on paper. These materials are available in basal readers from the American Printing House for the Blind (Ward & McCormick, 1981). For the most part, only children with minimal visual problems will be present in the regular classroom.

Hearing impaired children are completely deaf or have some useful limited hearing. Some hearing impaired youngsters can be helped through the use of a hearing aid, which amplifies sounds for them. Hearing impaired children who are likely to be mainstreamed into regular classrooms or are in regular classrooms will be those with some hearing ability. Visual and tactile methods for learning are encouraged with these students. Those who are deaf or have very limited hearing may use sign language to communicate. Some knowledge of signing would be helpful for classroom teachers.

Mobility impairment in this context refers to handicaps that are often congenital or acquired during childhood through such diseases as cerebral palsy, muscular dystrophy, spina bifida, and rheumatoid arthritis. Children who suffer from these problems to a severe degree are not usually in regular classrooms; however, those with mild cases may be in the classroom or mainstreamed in. Children with these problems may have normal intelligence but often need help with mobility. Learning strategies will be similar to those used with all children. If the ability to use fine motor control is compromised, alternative methods for writing need to be found, such as using a computer or having a teacher or peer take dictation. Youngsters with diseases that cause mobility problems may need more time to complete assignments, not necessarily because of their intellectual ability, but because of motor coordination problems. Because their disability is more obvious than others, an important goal with these youngsters is helping non–special needs children feel more positively toward them so that all are comfortable in one another's presence. Discussing the problems, how they occurred, and how everyone feels about them will often help.

Children with *communication disorders* are likely to be a part of the regular classroom. These are children who have speech or language difficulties. Speech impairments include problems in articulation, voice disorders (abnormal loudness, pitch, or voice quality), and fluency disorders such as stuttering.

Children with *language disorders* have difficulty acquiring and using language. Delayed language children are significantly behind their peers in both the production and comprehension aspects of language development. These children will go to special classes for help with their problems. For the most part, strategies that are appropriate for all children will be appropriate for these youngsters in the regular classroom. Chapter 4, which deals with language development, discusses instructional contexts appropriate for children with minimal language problems.

The Gifted and the Learning Disabled

***Gifted** youngsters* are those who develop academic or other skills such as playing a musical instrument at an ability level far above that expected of a same-age child. These special talents need to be encouraged, but not at the expense of recognizing the social, emotional, and physical needs of the child. Differentiating assignments to make them more challenging for the ability levels of these children will accommodate their special talents.

***Learning disabled** youngsters* are those who perform at a level below what is expected for their age or grade. Children are learning disabled for a variety of reasons, including mental retardation, emotional problems, and neurological problems. These children are often easily distracted and have short attention spans. Techniques for instruction need to be concrete and include active involvement. Helping these youngsters stay on task is an important goal. Activities that will grasp their attention are those that are most likely to be successful. Working with them on an individual basis is crucial to finding out the best ways for these children to learn. As with the gifted child, differentiating regular classroom activities to meet their ability levels will accommodate their needs.

When trying to meet the special needs of children, focusing on the instructional goal rather than activities is important. A team of school personnel needs to be involved in preparing plans for disabled youngsters. This team needs to figure out how to help these children compensate for their disability and therefore be able to carry out activities successfully. For example, a child who has an attention deficit disorder and moves too quickly during independent center work from one task to the next can be paired with a peer who is known to be able to stay focused. This peer can read directions for the student who has the disability thus providing explicit instruction about the activity.

Parents can be an excellent resource for informing the teacher about a child's strengths, weaknesses, and interests. The collective guidance of other children, special education consultants, and aides also can help support the engagement of children with special needs.

All those involved in dealing with children with special needs must have tolerance for differences. Thinking of children with differences as less fortunate is not conducive to learning. The attitude must be, how do we help children compensate for their disabilities, so they can learn to function independently (Erickson & Koppenhaver, 1995).

Following are some instructional guidelines that can prove helpful when dealing with children who have physical impairments or developmental learning differences, whether they are learning disabled or gifted (Ruddell & Ruddell, 1995).

1. Observe students on a regular basis for indications that they may have some physical impairment or developmental learning differences. For example, a child who seems to have difficulty seeing the chalkboard, who copies things incorrectly, and who squints to see things may have a visual problem that needs attention.
2. Seek help from your district's support services with children you find are experiencing problems. Be sure you have suspected problems identified and appropriate assistance given to children in need.
3. When you find out the nature of the problem a child may be experiencing, become informed about it by discussing it with special education teachers and other staff members.
4. Use learning principles that are successful with all youngsters, such as encouragement, praise, and positive feedback.
5. Adapt instruction to meet special needs. Good strategies are often good for all children, with some adaptations to meet their individual differences.
6. Involve parents with children who have special needs. Discuss the help the school is providing, inform them of additional help they might seek outside the school environment, and enlist their help with activities they can do with their youngsters at home.

Multicultural Concerns: Addressing Needs in a Multicultural Society

The demographics of the United States population are becoming more racially and ethnically diverse. Current statistics show that one in every three children is from a different ethnic or racial minority group, and one in every seven children speaks English as a second language (Miramontes, Nadeau, & Commins, 1997).

Much of the research on the academic achievement in U.S. schools demonstrates that if English is not a child's first language, he or she is not likely to be successful (Rossi & Stringfield, 1995). Some reasons for this are that schools do not support the home culture, the complex nature of learning a second language,

Classroom strategies should enhance learning through understanding of cultural differences and their effect on lifestyles, values, and worldviews.

and the low socioeconomic status of many of the families who do not speak English as a first language (Banks & Banks, 1993; Connell, 1994; Garcia & McLaughlin, 1995).

In the past diversity was disregarded in the United States, and children were expected to ignore their cultural backgrounds and language differences and learn the English language and American customs. If we are to live in harmony in a pluralistic society, it is imperative that educational leaders accept the charge to provide a culturally relevant education for all students. We must be sensitive toward cultural and language differences and recognize that children can and should maintain their cultural heritage, and that they can still be considered American and learn English without abandoning their native language (Templeton, 1991).

The following sections discuss in more detail issues regarding children with cultural and language differences in the classroom.

Cultural Diversity

Multiculturalism is a complicated issue. Multiculturalism refers not only to race and ethnicity, but also to class, religion, sex, and age (Sue, Arredondo, & McDavis, 1992). The multiracial, multiethnic, multicultural, and multilingual nature of our dynamic society mandates that we teach tolerance and understanding of differences as an ongoing process involving self-reflection, self-awareness, increasing knowledge, and developing relevant skills (Pedersen, 1994). We need to welcome diversity in our schools. It adds a richness to the classroom and to topics of study. By recognizing students' diverse backgrounds, we will enhance their self-image. Differences can become the norm rather than the exception. Differences in cultural backgrounds often provide explanations of why children behave as they do. Behaviors that are acceptable in one culture might be thought of as disrespectful in another. Goals for classrooms in our multicultural society need to be as follows:

1. An improved understanding of cultural differences, and their effect on lifestyle, values, world view, and individual differences;
2. An increased awareness of how to develop strategies to enhance learning in a multicultural environment; and
3. A framework for conceptualizing ways to create a climate conducive to learning and development.

The goals we need to pursue for children in ethnically diverse classrooms and for children whose language is other than English are as follows:

1. Children need to learn to accept and be comfortable with their ethnic identities.
2. Children need to learn to function in other cultures, particularly in the dominant culture.
3. Children need to relate positively with individuals from varied ethnic backgrounds.
4. Children who do not speak English or standard English need to retain and value their first languages but learn English as well.

Teachers need to develop their own understanding of the multiethnic groups they serve. They must first recognize that the children they deal with are multiethnic. Teachers must also be aware of their own ethnic heritages, traditions, and beliefs. They must value and respect the ethnic identities, heritages, and traditions of others (Schickedanz, York, Stewart, & White, 1990).

Language Differences

Language differences vary. There are children who do not speak any English and are often classified as *English-as-a-second-language (ESL)* learners. These children come from homes where English is not spoken at all. There are children with very limited English proficiency who are often referred to as *bilingual.* The English proficiency of these youngsters varies. Many of them are more proficient in the home language than in English. The goal is for them to become truly bilingual—that is, equally proficient in English and the home language.

Children also come to school speaking different dialects. A *dialect* is an alternative form of one particular language used in different cultural, regional, or social groups (Leu & Kinzer, 1991). These differences can be so significant that an individual from a region with one English dialect may have difficulty understanding someone from another region because the pronunciation of letter sounds is so different. Dialects are not inherently superior to one another; however, one dialect typically emerges as the standard for a given language and is used by the more advantaged individuals of a society. Teachers must be aware of different dialects and help youngsters with the comprehension of standard dialects. Children are not to be degraded or viewed as less intelligent for speaking different dialects. Although it is important for children to achieve a level of standard English to help them succeed in society, emphasizing the need to become a standard English speaker before learning literacy is inappropriate and likely to create more difficulties for the children by slowing their literacy development. Chapter 4 discusses strategies for dealing with language differences and also provides an outline of language development from birth through eight years of age.

There are general strategies that will support the first language of students in regular classrooms. Although it is not necessary for the teacher to speak the first language of ESL students, it is helpful when there is another child or adult in the school who can speak the home language of ESL children to provide translation. The following strategies expose children in the class to other languages, thus creating an interest and appreciation for different backgrounds:

- Include print in the classroom that is from children's first language.
- Suggest that bilingual students create books in their first language and share their stories.
- Give children from different language backgrounds have the opportunity to read and write with others who speak their language, such as parents, aides, and other children in the school (Freeman & Freeman, 1993).

Along with the support of children's first language, it is also important to support the learning of English. As mentioned, Chapter 4 discusses activities for

English language development. A few strategies for learning English include the following:

- Allow children to talk.
- Have routine storytimes.
- Provide thematic instruction that elicits talk, reading, and writing, and heightens interests in exciting topics.
- Write charts based on talk about children's home life and experiences in school.
- Encourage children to copy experience charts, have them dictate their ideas for you to write, and encourage them to write themselves (Lindfors, 1989; Miramontes et al., 1997).

A variety of theoretical, educational, philosophical, and psychological perspectives for instruction have been presented in this chapter. Special needs are accommodated by finding a perspective that best suits a given problem and child. Classroom teachers must deal with children from diverse cultural and language backgrounds, students who have minimal learning disabilities and minimal physical impairments, as well as those who are gifted. Generally, good teaching strategies adapted to specific problems are those that work best. When appropriate, reference to youngsters with special problems with implications for instruction will appear throughout the book. Children's literature can be helpful in dealing with special needs, whether they be physical disabilities or cultural differences. Appendix A presents a list of books that deal with cultural diversity and lists books that discuss physical disabilities, learning disabilities, communication disorders, and the gifted.

Early Intervention

Meeting individual needs is a major concern. There are children with language differences and children who are considered "at risk" or are experiencing difficulty based on performance in kindergarten or first grade or on a test given by their school. There are many programs that have been used throughout the years to help these youngsters, and it has become apparent that meeting individual needs requires time with a teacher and child working together. Early intervention programs are based on the premise that more can be done and needs to be done in school to support young children's literacy learning. Many children, often from at-risk populations, could be more successful if early intervention were available (Hiebert & Taylor, 1994).

The term ***early intervention*** refers to programs in the primary grades that encourage instruction that is developmentally appropriate as far as reading and writing experiences are concerned. The purpose is to improve and enhance the literacy development of children entering school who have not achieved early literacy abilities similar to their peers. In programs that have been implemented, it has been found that children can be prevented from falling behind their peers and from experiencing failure (Slavin & Madden, 1989; Stanovich, 1986).

The difference between the newer early intervention programs and programs from the past with the same intention is the instructional focus. Head

Start, for example, has concentrated on social, physical, and emotional development. Direct instruction of skills was viewed as inappropriate (Spodek, 1988). Programs vary with many engaging children in activities such as reading stories aloud, writing, sharing books, and reading silently, to direct instruction of skills.

Another issue with early intervention is whether it is more appropriate for intervention to occur in the classroom with the support of special teachers who work with the classroom teacher, or whether **pull-out** programs are more successful, in which youngsters go to a special teacher to work on skill improvement. The ultimate goal of such programs is to provide supplemental instruction to accelerate literacy development with the use of quality instruction in reading and writing. There is a movement toward integrating the intervention into the regular classroom rather than taking children out of class. The rationale for this trend of **inclusion** is to limit the movement of children in and out of the classroom during the school day, and for the special instruction to be an integral part of the regular classroom instruction. In this way, children do not miss what is going on in the regular classroom. The instruction is coordinated with their classroom instruction. The stigma of being taken out for special help is eliminated, and the classroom teacher and special teacher work together toward helping children.

A well-known early intervention pull-out program is ***Reading Recovery,*** developed in New Zealand (Clay, 1987) and studied extensively at Ohio State University (Pinnell, Freid, & Estice, 1990). Reading Recovery is a program for young readers who are having problems in their first year of reading instruction. Children receive daily 30-minute one-to-one instructional sessions in addition to their regular classroom reading instruction. Reading Recovery lessons are tailored to the special needs of children and contain authentic literacy experiences that are collaborative and active between teacher and child, and also use specific skill instruction. Some Reading Recovery strategies within a lesson include the following:

1. The child reads a familiar story to enhance fluency and experience success.
2. The teacher introduces a new book and the teacher and the student walk through the book together, looking at the pictures predicting what the book is about.
3. The child reads the new book without assistance from the teacher.
4. The teacher takes a running record to check the child for types of errors made and comprehension through a retelling.
5. The teacher carries out a lesson that helps the child with word-analysis strategies looking at onsets of words and letter chunks or rimes at the end of words.

To make the experience more concrete, the teacher engages the child in the use of manipulating letters and chunks that are magnetic on a magnetic board. The child is asked to use words learned by writing them on a slate within a sentence. Also, sentences from the book are written on sentence strips for children to put into sequence, and sentences are cut into words for children to identify out of context and to sequence into context. These familiar activities are repeated in different lessons.

Teachers who participate in Reading Recovery receive special training to help develop their ability to observe and describe the behavior of children when they are engaged in literacy acts. Reading Recovery teacher training emphasizes how to respond to children with appropriate modeling and scaffolding to help them progress. Another feature of the program is the use of authentic literacy experiences balanced with skill development. Reading Recovery has demonstrated increased performance by at-risk children. In addition, Reading Recovery strategies have been adapted for small-group guided reading instruction within the classroom.

Many schools are creating their own early intervention programs with high-quality instructional strategies used to work with children who are not performing well. It is quite likely that if a teacher works with a student on a one-to-one basis using good strategies, the child should improve because of the extra and personal help received. A brief description of two intervention programs designed for at-risk children by school districts follows.

The *Early Intervention in Reading* program was designed for first-grade children in diverse communities. The purpose was to supplement instruction for groups of low-achieving students provided by their teachers. Teachers took 20 minutes a day to provide supplemental reading instruction to a group of five to seven children. Children in the program demonstrated improved literacy skills (Taylor, Strait, & Medo, 1994).

An early intervention program entitled *A Storybook Reading Program* was incorporated into a regular class for kindergarten children identified as at risk. In addition to traditional instruction with a skills-based program, the following were added to their literacy program: (1) directed listening and thinking activities when reading to children, (2) retelling of stories read to the children, (3) repeated readings of storybooks so that children could engage in attempted readings of these stories from hearing them frequently, (4) active discussions to construct meaning from stories read to the children, (5) provision for classroom reading and writing centers containing materials that encourage literacy activity, and (6) time for children to engage in periods of independent reading and writing to practice skills learned (Morrow & O'Connor, 1995). Work took place in whole-class, small-group, and one-to-one settings when teachers worked with children to discover their strengths and weaknesses. Basic skills teachers worked along with the classroom teachers in the room during the small-group and one-to-one periods to help with instruction. Students in this program made significant improvement over children also identified as at risk who did not have the advantage of the intervention described.

When deciding to implement intervention programs, consider the children involved, the resources you have, and how best to use the talent within your own school. Recognizing that special needs exist and what they are is the most important step for a teacher. Next is to respect and accept differences that exist in the children who you teach.

In a speech given at a National Reading Conference meeting, Lisa Delpit (1995) spoke about teaching "Other People's Children." She discussed general characteristics for a successful literacy program in urban school settings with children from diverse backgrounds and disadvantaged backgrounds. Some of the main points in her presentation were as follows:

1. Learn and respect the child's home culture.
2. Do not teach less content to children from disadvantaged backgrounds. They can learn as all other children learn. Teachers, parents, children, and the community should recognize children's ability and teach them accordingly.

3. Whatever instructional program or methodology is used, critical thinking should be a goal. Children achieve because of teachers who believe in them and have a vision for them. Poor children practice the use of critical skills on a regular basis because they have had to be independent and have many responsibilities at home.
4. All children must gain access to basic skills, the conventions and strategies that are essential to succeed in American education and life. Adults need to help children learn the skills they need to succeed outside of school.
5. Help children view themselves as competent and worthy.
6. Use familiar metaphors and experiences from children's lives to connect what they already know to school knowledge. If you cannot justify what you are teaching, you should not be teaching it.
7. Create a sense of family and caring in your classroom. Make the children your own while you have them. Tell them they are the smartest children in the world and expect them to be. Then they will learn for the teacher, not just from the teacher.
8. Monitor and assess needs and then address them with a wealth of diverse strategies.
9. Recognize and build on strengths that children and families already have.
10. Foster a connection between the child and the community so there is something greater than themselves to use for inspiration. Help them understand that they go to school for their community and predecessors. If they fail, they fail not only for themselves but for their community as well; if they succeed they succeed for everyone including themselves.

As mentioned, strategies described throughout this book will emphasize accommodations for children with diverse needs. For the most part, quality instruction is appropriate for all.

An Idea for the Classroom from the Classroom

The following experience, which reflects concerns for cultural diversity, was created by an early childhood teacher for the children in her classroom.

Where in the World Are You From?

At the beginning of the school year, I sent home a notice with the heading ***"Where in the World Are You From?"*** The parents were asked to fill in information on the heritage of their child. The responses were more than I anticipated. Parents were happy to cite the countries of origin and offered information about these lands. This exercise helped me begin my year with a clear view of the cultural diversity within my class.

From the information returned, I found that one of my students was related to Daniel Boone, and another had a grandfather who was one of the first African American pilots in the U.S. Air Force. One child, who was adopted from Peru, had an American father, his mother was German, and his brother, who was also adopted, was from Colombia. I received photographs and artifacts from the various countries as well. With this information, I was able to use books and activities in my classroom that represented the diversity within my class. I also had parents come to school to share information about their heritage.

We began a class book about the countries represented by the heritage of the children and called it *The Passport*. I met with all children on a one-to-one basis about their page in the book for which they could dictate things about their backgrounds. In addition, I featured one child a week on a small bulletin board where I placed a photograph of the child with information about his or her heritage. We tried to include things that are interesting to children such as food, stories, songs, dances, and clothing pertaining to the featured child's heritage. A map showing the country of origin was also included. Parents were invited to share their backgrounds.

This project gave me an immediate wealth of knowledge about my class and a glimpse into each child's background. It was a wonderful way to celebrate diversity, involve parents, read, write, and be involved with social studies within a meaningful context.

Katherine Heiss, Preschool Teacher
Summit Day Care Center, Summit, New Jersey

Activities and Questions

1. Answer the focus questions at the beginning of the chapter.

2. Begin a portfolio for yourself that will reflect the work you do in this course. Place in the portfolio pieces of work that you and your instructor would like to have there. Occasionally look over the materials, and at the end of the semester review them to help you remember things you have learned and to assess your own accomplishments.

3. Parents in your district are not pleased with the authentic measures for assessment being used. They want to know if their children are doing as well as others. Based on a test, they want to know if their child is above, below, or at grade level. You are convinced that authentic assessment is the right way to evaluate children. What can you do to help parents understand and accept the authentic assessment strategies?

4. Plan a parent workshop to inform them about standards and how you link your instruction and assessment to them.

5. The term *special needs* includes children with language differences (those who are non–English speaking or have limited English proficiency); children with learning differences (gifted, learning disabled); children with physical impairments (visual, hearing, mobility, communication disorders); and children from different cultural backgrounds. Select a special need and describe a theory that you feel has implications for instructional strategies appropriate for a child with that special need. Outline the strategies for learning.

6. Throughout the book, strategies will be presented for teaching literacy learning in classrooms. At all times have the interest of children with special needs in mind, and decide the strategies appropriate for these youngsters.

Case Study Activities

Case 1

Refer to "An Idea for the Classroom from the Classroom" to refresh your memory. Describe accommodations the teacher has made for meeting the special needs of the children in her classroom, that is, children from culturally diverse backgrounds, children with physical disabilities, etc. What other things might have been done to accommodate special needs in the activity described? What other special needs could be addressed in the situation described?

Case 2

Your district uses standardized tests in the early childhood grades, and all teachers keep portfolios on students with daily work samples, checklists of skills accomplished and those that still need improvement, anecdotes about the children, audiotapes of language and story retellings, and videotapes of the children working in social settings. The material on the standardized test does not completely reflect the teaching that is occurring in the classroom.

Mr. Manson is aware that standardized tests will be coming up soon. Although he uses an integrated language arts approach for literacy instruction most of the time, he also makes sure that his instruction reflects the contents of standardized tests, which he knows his students will be taking. About a month before the standardized tests, he stops much of his usual instruction and spends an hour a day preparing his children for the test. He gives them samples of test materials to teach them the content and format of the test. He spends practice time on how to fill in the correct box, how to press hard with the pencil, how to be sure to check the appropriate answer box for the particular question, how to make good guesses, what students should do if they cannot answer a question, how much time to spend on each question, etc. He checks the children's work and spends time helping those who are having difficulty.

Mrs. Kimmel uses an integrated language arts approach for teaching similar to Mr. Manson. She knows she must administer the standardized tests, but she does not pay much attention to them because she feels they are inappropriate for children in the early childhood grades. She also does not want to waste valuable instructional time preparing for them. The only preparation she offers her students for the test is a discussion a week before they are administered when she describes what they are like, tells how long they will take, and generally plays down their importance.

Mr. Manson's students score much better on the tests than Mrs. Kimmel's children, although on informal measures such as story retellings and rewritings the children do similarly.

There are concerns by parents and administrators about the approaches to testing taken by both teachers. What would your advice be to Mr. Manson and why? What would your advice be to Mrs. Kimmel and why? If you were a teacher in this school district, what would be your plan for assessment?

chapter 3

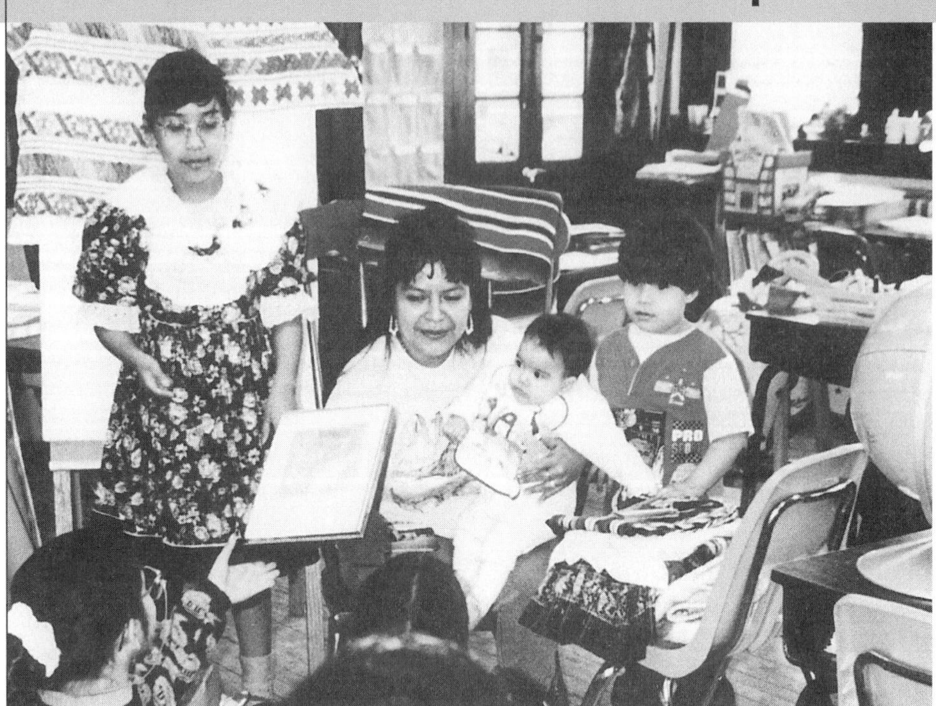

Family Literacy Partnerships

Home and School Working Together

You may have tangible wealth untold:
Caskets of jewels and coffers of gold.
Richer than I you can never be—
I had a Mother who read to me.

—Strickland Gillian "The Reading Mother"
from *Best Loved Poems of the American People*

Focus Questions

- Include descriptions of parent involvement and intergenerational family literacy programs.
- List and discuss factors described throughout the chapter that help promote rich family literacy environments in the home.
- What reading and writing materials should be present in a home, and where should they be placed to help promote children's literacy development?
- What reading and writing activities can families involve their children in to help promote literacy development?
- Define the term "family literacy."
- What are some concerns surrounding family literacy intervention programs with diverse, multicultural populations?
- What elements make for a successful family literacy program?
- What activities are successful in getting parents involved in literacy activities with their child at home and in school?

Mrs. Feller spread the newspaper on the floor as her two grandchildren (Adasha, 6, and Jonnelle, 4), started to put down the paint jars, water can, brushes, and paper to paint. She always used newspaper to protect the floor when the girls did something messy. As she spread the paper, she said, "Now let's see what section of the newspaper we have out on the floor today." "Oh look," said Adasha, "It's the sports section. Some team won that baseball game 7 points to 0." "That's right," said Mrs. Feller, "the Mets beat the Dodgers 7 to 0." Mrs. Feller always had the girls look at the contents of the newspaper on the floor. The children often would continue to investigate the newspaper and almost forget their clay or paint. Sometimes they would paint about what they had just read. Mrs. Feller was taking advantage of the print in her environment that was a familiar part of the children's lives and was making it a pleasurable experience that would enrich their literacy knowledge.

Roxana, a student in one of my graduate courses, said:

> *When I was young I don't remember being read to. What I do remember is storytelling. I remember listening to personal stories told over and over by my parents, grandparents, and relatives that had to do with funny, sad, but all real-life happenings about the family. Everyone took a part in telling the stories, adding parts they felt were missing. This was a special and favorite family tradition that took place every Sunday after church as we sat around the table having lunch in my grandmother's kitchen. I remember looking forward to it. The stories were often the same, but I wanted to hear them again and again.*

What Is Family Literacy?

The term family literacy is a complex concept. Here are some descriptions of family literacy in a brochure published by the International Reading Association entitled *Family Literacy: New Perspectives, New Opportunities* (Morrow, Paratore, & Tracey, 1994).

1. Family literacy encompasses the ways parents, children, and extended family members use literacy at home and in their community.
2. Family literacy occurs naturally during the routines of daily living and helps adults and children "get things done."
3. Examples of family literacy might include using drawings or writing to share ideas, composing notes or letters to communicate messages, keeping records, making lists, following written directions, or sharing stories and ideas through conversation, reading, and writing.
4. Family literacy may be initiated purposefully by a parent, or may occur spontaneously as parents and children go about the business of their daily lives.
5. Family literacy activities also may reflect the ethnic, racial, or cultural heritage of the families involved.
6. Family literacy activities may be initiated outside the home in institutions such as school or the public library. These activities are often intended to support the acquisition and development of school-like literacy behaviors of parents, children, and families.
7. Family literacy activities by outside institutions may include family storybook reading, completing homework assignments, or writing essays and reports.

Family Literacy: Why Is It Important?

Parents, or the family members who care for children, are children's first teachers. They are also children's teachers for the longest time. Beginning at birth, children's experiences affect their success in becoming literate. The success of the school literacy program frequently depends on the literacy environment at home. Studies carried out in homes have been a major catalyst for new early literacy strategies. Because many children come to school already reading and writing, apparently without formal instruction, investigators began to study the characteristics of those children and of their homes. Such children were said to have "learned to read naturally," a phrase that suggests that their ability to read developed similarly to their acquisition of language or their learning to walk.

This line of investigation has been extremely helpful from two points of view. First, the findings reveal home practices that could be successful in school settings. Second, they provide information on the crucial role a family plays in the development of children's literacy and on how they can help. The school can disseminate this information to parents. Additionally, the school must involve parents as an integral part of their literacy programs.

I can attest to the vital role of the home in the development of early literacy. From the day of our daughter Stephanie's birth, my husband and I read to her. I read to her daily while she sat on my lap, always in the same chair. We looked at books. I talked about the pictures and read the stories. By five months, Stephanie would listen as we read to her. We chose mostly cardboard picture storybooks with only a few words on each page. From time to time, her eyes focused intently on the brightly colored pictures. First she would be serious; next she would smile broadly. Sometimes she reached out to touch the book. Occasionally she made pleasant sounds that seemed attempts to imitate my reading voice. Because the experience was daily and positive, she became familiar with story readings and welcomed them.

As Stephanie grew older, her responses to the readings increased. Before she could talk, she pointed to pictures and made sounds as if naming objects or characters. As she acquired oral vocabulary, she labeled things in the book as I read. Naturally I responded with pleasure, reinforcing her attention and understanding of the concepts. Often I explained things beyond the words in the book. Both of us looked forward to these times we shared. They were relaxing, warm, and pleasurable. The practice has been referred to as the lap technique in story reading (McCracken & McCracken, 1972).

By the time she was 14 months old, Stephanie often could be found sitting on the floor reading a book—that is, reading as a 14-month-old child can. She knew how to hold the book right side up, she knew which was the beginning of the book and which was the end, and she knew how to turn the pages. She looked at the pictures and chanted in tones similar to the sound of my reading. Except for a few words, little of her language was understandable, but from a distance one might think that she was reading. Actually she was—not in the conventional manner, but by demonstrating early literacy behavior.

Books were all around the house. Stephanie had an accessible shelf of books in her room. We kept a crate of books with her toys on the floor of a closet, and she was free to use them at all times. There were books in the kitchen, the bathroom, and play areas. My husband and I had many books of our own, and we read a lot, both professional literature and recreational materials such as novels, magazines, and newspapers. Stephanie saw her parents reading frequently, and at times she joined us with her own books.

In addition to books, Stephanie had access to pencils, crayons, markers, and large supplies of different kinds of paper. Before three years, it was natural for her to pick up a pencil and a sheet of paper, sit down and draw a picture, and even write about it. I could not identify what Stephanie had drawn, but she would talk about it. She was well aware of the difference between drawing and writing, and the squiggles of "print" looked different from the scribbles of her drawing. Although not yet capable of either drawing or writing in the conventional sense, she attempted to do both and differentiated between them.

In the house and on trips to the supermarket or post office, environmental print surrounded her as it does other children. Cognizant of its importance in early literacy development, I pointed out STOP signs at street corners and asked her to name as many signs as she could as we drove along. At home we read cereal boxes, directions for assembling new toys, and letters that came in the mail. As a result, her awareness of the print around her and of its functions was heightened. She naturally learned to ask what labels said and looked to print for information.

When she was three and four, our story readings became more interactive. Stephanie asked questions and commented about pictures and episodes. I responded with answers and comments that expanded the discussion. She began to narrate familiar stories with me as I read. Occasionally she asked what certain words were as her attention focused more and more on print as well as on pictures.

One day, Stephanie was sitting in the back seat of the car on the way home from our weekly trip to the library. She was looking through one of the books she had selected and began reading it out loud. It was a humorous story called *Ten Apples Up on Top* (LeSieg, 1961). The book used a limited number of words, repetitive vocabulary, and rhyme. The attractive illustrations reflected the text. As she read, I first assumed that the book was one we had read together. Suddenly I realized it was not. I pulled to the side of the road and with great excitement confirmed what I thought was true. Stephanie was reading, actually reading on her own! She had made the transition from part-reading, part-narrating stories to reading each word.

Stephanie had reached this point in her literacy development gradually. I had offered school-like reading instruction, but not a great deal. Because of her constant exposure to books and print from birth, she had developed a large sight vocabulary and a number of reading skills. Her ability to read, in other words, did not just happen. Rather, it developed within a rich literacy environment and through the guidance, modeling, and encouragement of supportive adults.

Factors That Promote Literacy Development in the Home

The information that follows on the next few pages comes from the parent involvement framework, suggesting an American mainstream approach to family literacy. The constructs are appropriate in homes in which school-like literacy activities are a comfortable and natural part of the environment. It assumes that the parents have the literacy and language ability to share literacy experiences discussed; however, they would be appropriate if used in the native language of any family. After this initial presentation, which sets the groundwork for some basic ideas and strategies, a broader perspective will be discussed to take into consideration families who have limited literacy ability, speak a different language, and are not comfortable with typical school-like literacy activities.

According to Leichter (1984), families influence literacy development in three ways: (1) interpersonal interaction, (2) physical environment, and (3) emotional and motivational climate. *Interpersonal interaction* consists of the literacy experiences shared with a child by parents, siblings, and other individuals in the home. The *physical environment* includes the literacy materials available in the home. The *emotional and motivational climate* comprises the relationships among the individuals in a home, especially as reflected in the parents' attitudes toward literacy and their aspirations for their children's literacy achievement.

Various researchers have studied homes in which children read and write early without direct instruction (Morrow, 1983; Neuman, 1997; Teale, 1984). The results have consistently established that certain characteristics are common to these children and their homes. The IQ scores of early readers are not consistently high; they range from low-average to above average. Early readers can accomplish Piagetian concrete operational tasks and are interested in pencil-and-paper activities, letters, and words. Their parents read to them and readily help them with writing and reading. These parents, themselves also read a great variety of material, including novels, magazines, newspapers, and work-related information. They own or borrow books, both for themselves and for their children. Reading and writing materials can be found throughout their homes. Parents in these homes often take their children to libraries and bookstores (Morrow, 1983; Morrow, 1997; Neuman, 1997). The homes hold ample supplies of books and writing materials, and reading and writing are generally valued as important activities. Books are associated with pleasure, and literary activities are rewarded. The homes are well organized, with scheduled daily activities, rules, and designated responsibilities for family members. They provide a setting where interactions between adults and children are socially, emotionally, and intellectually conducive to literacy interest and growth (Holdaway, 1979).

The families of early readers and writers tend to be small. Many of the parents have college educations, but it is argued that it is a literacy-rich environment, not parents' education, occupation, or socioeconomic level, that correlates most highly with children's early literacy ability. Children with an early interest in reading and writing tend to spend playtime at home writing and drawing with

The interactive behavior between parent and child during storybook reading involves negotiating, mediating, and constructing meaning related to the print.

paper and crayons or looking at books. Parents in these homes enforce rules for selecting and limiting television viewing. These children are rated by their teachers as higher than average in social and emotional maturity, work habits, and general school achievement. They also perform well on standardized readiness tests (Applebee, Langer, & Mullis, 1988; Morrow, 1983; Sticht & McDonald, 1989).

Parents frequently ask teachers what they can do at home to help their children learn to read and write. When parents provide a rich literacy environment at home, teaching reading and writing becomes easier for both the teacher and the child at school. Because most children do not enter public school before age five and nursery school before age three, if at all, schools need to take responsibility for disseminating information in the community that parents can implement at home. The information that follows includes mainstream strategies and assumes that parents have the literacy ability and language ability to implement the suggestions offered. Although the suggestions are based on research, some children even in rich literacy environments may not learn to read easily.

Materials to Read in the Home

Researchers have found that books were readily accessible to children who read early (Applebee, Langer, & Mullis, 1988; Hannon, 1995; Sticht & McDonald, 1989). Parents can provide library corners for their children, preferably in their bedrooms. Books can be placed in a cardboard box or plastic crate to serve as a bookshelf. In addition, books can be made available all around the house. Kitchens and bathrooms are important, because children spend considerable time in both places. If there is a playroom or a place for toy storage, it should contain books. Every room can hold books that are visible and accessible. Before babies are crawling or walking, books can be brought to them in cribs and playpens; waterproof books are available for bathtubs.

A variety of books should be selected for the home. For babies up to 18 months, brightly colored concept books with cardboard, plastic, or cloth pages are appropriate. They must be safe, with rounded edges, and sturdy enough to withstand chewing and other rough treatment. As the child becomes a toddler, preschooler, and kindergartener, nursery rhymes, fairy tales, folktales, realistic literature, informational books, picture books, alphabet books, number books, poetry, books related to favorite television programs, and easy-to-read books (those with limited vocabularies, large print, and pictures closely associated with the text) should be made available. Children's magazines offer attractive print material for children and are a special treat if they come in the mail. In addition to children's literature, print material for adults, including books, magazines, newspapers, and work-related material, should be obvious in the home.

Reading as a Home Activity

Research indicates that children who are read to regularly by parents, siblings, or other individuals in the home, and who have parents who are habitual readers themselves, become early readers and show a natural interest in books (Teale, 1984). That is not surprising. Through frequent story readings, children become familiar with book language and realize the function of written language. Story

Print materials such as books and magazines need to be readily available for children to use at a very young age.

readings are almost always pleasurable, which builds a desire for and interest in reading (Cullinan, 1992; Huck, 1992). Continued exposure to books develops children's vocabularies and sense of story structure, both of which help them learn to read.

It is clear that verbal interaction between adult and child during story readings has a major influence on literacy development (Cochran-Smith, 1984; Ninio, 1980). Such interaction offers a direct channel of information for the child and thus enhances literacy development (Heath, 1982; Morrow, 1987a). It leads children to respond to story readings with questions and comments. These responses become more complex over time and demonstrate more sophisticated thinking about printed material. Research on home storybook readings has identified a number of interactive behaviors that affect the quality of read-aloud activities. Those behaviors include questioning, scaffolding (modeling dialogue and responses), praising, offering information, directing discussion, sharing personal reactions, and relating concepts to life experiences (Edwards,1995; Roser & Martinez, 1985; Taylor & Strickland, 1986).

The following transcription from the beginning of a story reading between a mother and her four-year-old son Ian illustrates how the adult invites and scaffolds responses, answers questions, offers positive reinforcement, and responds supportively to the child's questions and comments. As a result of the prompts, information, and support, Ian pursues his questions and receives additional information.

Mother: Are you ready for our story today, Ian? This is a new book. I've never read it to you before. It's about a mother and her baby bird.

Ian: (points to the title on the front cover) Hey, what's this for?

Mother: That's called a title. It says *"Are You My Mother?"* That's the name of the book. See, it's right here, too: *"Are You My Mother?"*

Ian: (long pause, then points to the words) *"Are You My Mother?"*

Mother: Right, you read it. See, you know how to read.

Ian: It says *"Are You My Mother?"* (points again with finger)

Mother: You read it again. Wow, you really know how to read!

Ian: Um, now read the book and I'll read it, too. (Morrow, 1986)

Ian's mother read the story. Each time they came to the words *Are You My Mother?,* she paused and looked at Ian, pointed to the words, and exaggerated her reading of the sentence. After two such episodes, Ian no longer needed prompting and simply read along each time they came to the phrase.

Research findings suggest that teachers should encourage parents to read to their children daily. Reading can begin the day a child is born. However, an infant's ability to listen attentively is generally limited and varies from one reading to the next. An infant may prefer to chew on the book or pound it rather than listen to it. However, babies read to from birth begin very early to be attentive in story reading situations.

One of my graduate students shared this story in his class journal about his first literacy experience with his new baby. She was born during the semester he was taking a course with me.

***Our First Literacy Experience* by John T. Shea**

When my wife and I packed for the trip to the hospital on the night before her scheduled caesarean procedure, one of the items that I included in my travel bag was my childhood copy of The Real Mother Goose, *a book my mother had given back to me when she learned that she was going to be a grandmother. I planned on reading some of this much treasured work to my child in a family literacy experience sometime after the birth procedure. My first literacy experience with Casey came much sooner than I had expected, and it happened in a rather unique, spontaneous, and intimate way.*

After she was born, Casey was taken to the nursery and placed under a heat device designed to help her body adjust to the change in temperature she experienced at birth. There were some chairs set up next to the heat devices for new fathers. As I sat beside my daughter and marvelled at her beauty, it suddenly occurred to me that I wanted to read to her at that very moment. I asked the nurse if I could take a book into the nursery to read to my child. The nurse smiled and said, "You're the first father in my 20 years as a maternity nurse to make such a request. I guess it's okay."

I was with Casey for the first hours of her life in the nursery, sitting by her side, listening to her breathe, and reading selections from The Real Mother Goose *to her. Prior to my reading she had been moving and crying, on and off. When I started reading she became very quiet and hardly stirred.*

By six months babies can be purposefully involved in story readings, pointing to pictures and demonstrating interest and pleasure.

Reading to Children at Home from Birth to Eight

From ***birth to three months,*** a child's attention to book reading is erratic. The baby who stares at the pictures and seems content and quiet can be considered receptive. If the baby wiggles, shows discomfort, or cries, the adult might just as well stop reading until the next time.

From ***three to six months,*** babies become more obviously involved in book readings. They begin to focus on pictures and to listen. Often, they will grab for a book, pound it, and try to put it in their mouths. As long as they seem content, they are probably involved with the reading.

Six- to nine-month-olds can be purposefully involved in story readings. They might try to turn pages. They might respond to changes in the reader's intonation or make sounds and movements to demonstrate involvement and pleasure. They sometimes begin to show preferences for books that have been read to them before.

One-year-old babies will show strong involvement in being read to. They might take a leadership role in turning pages, or babble along in tones that sound like reading. They actively look in the book for familiar things that they remember from other readings.

By ***15 months,*** babies who have been read to can tell which is the front and which is the back of a book, and if the book is right side up. They begin to identify and name characters in the book. They read along with the adult, verbalizing a great deal (Schickedanz, 1986).

Fathers, mothers, grandparents, babysitters, and older siblings should all read to younger children. Let reading become a ritual, done at the same time and in the same place each day. Bedtime is a favorite time and bedtime stories are a good reading habit to establish. Both child and parent look forward to it as a time to share at the end of the day. Reading before children go to sleep has a calming effect; it establishes a routine for the children, who will eventually read by themselves before going to bed.

Spontaneous readings are encouraged as well, and if a parent finds it easier to read at different times of the day, it is certainly more desirable to do this than

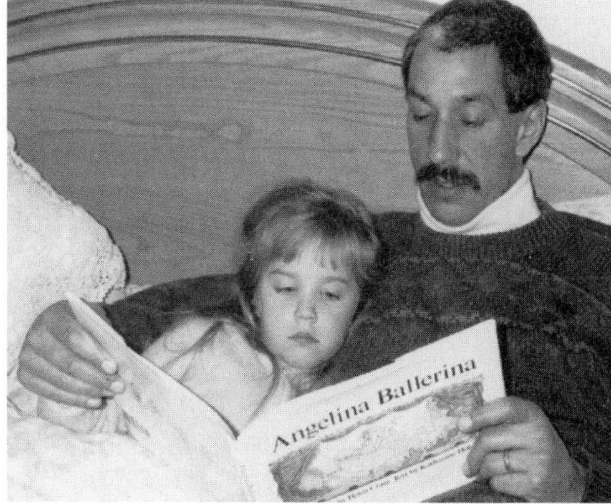

Fathers, mothers, babysitters, grandparents, and siblings should read together.

not to read at all. Reading to babies requires that the infant be held in the parent's arms. When the youngster is able to sit up alone, parent and child should be close to each other, preferably with the child on the adult's lap. The book with its pictures and print must be visible to the child. Children should be considered active participants in the story reading. Their comments and questions should be encouraged and acknowledged. Parents should relate comments about the story to life experiences whenever possible and question children about familiar things in a relaxed manner to encourage their involvement.

Reading to children does not end when they begin to read themselves. This is a crucial time to continue to support and guide them in this activity. When children are able to read, the bedtime story tradition can change to the child's reading to the parent. Or it can continue with the parent's reading books above the reading level of the child. ***Six- to eight-year-olds*** are often interested in books with chapters but are not yet ready to read them themselves. Parents can take this opportunity to share more grown-up pieces of literature with these youngsters to encourage their interest. Another important parent motivation is making sure that children have new material to read that is always accessible and of interest to them. Keep track of what your youngster has read. Sometimes we must continually put new books right in their hands even as they grow older and seem to have the reading habit established. As soon as we stop our interest in their reading, their reading interest is apt to wane.

In addition to reading to their children and reading themselves, parents should make a point of providing time for the family to read together. Sitting together around the kitchen table or in the living room, each member of the family reading his or her own book, makes for a pleasant, rich literacy activity. Talking about what each family member is reading is an important part of the experience.

Materials for Writing in the Home

Some of the researchers who reported characteristics of early readers also found that these children spend time on and show interest in pencil-and-paper activities (Morrow & Tracey, 1996). The parents of many such children reported that the interest in writing began with scribbling in babyhood. Certain scholars have suggested that writing develops naturally before reading. Many children, they point out, invent writing systems of their own that seem to have meaning for them. Whether reading comes before writing or writing before reading is an unsettled issue. What is known, however, is that learning to read is enhanced by concurrent experiences with writing and that the development of writing is facilitated by experiences with reading.

One implication of these findings is that writing materials should be made available for children at home. A variety of sizes of unlined white paper is preferable, especially for babies. As children become preschoolers, smaller sheets can be added to the household supply. A child approaching kindergarten might like lined paper as well. Pencils, crayons, colored pencils, a chalkboard and chalk, and markers are appropriate home writing tools. Manipulatives such as magnetic, felt, or wooden letters are also useful. Children should be exposed to them early and have free access to them. In addition, home computers encourage writing and are appropriate for preschoolers. (A list of computer software for young children can be found in Appendix C.)

As with book reading, youngsters need to see their parents involved in writing activities. Parents should communicate with their children through writing as often as possible. When children begin preschool, notes can be placed in lunch boxes that say simply, "Hi! Love, Mommy and Daddy." Notes on pillows can say "Good night" or "Good morning."

Parents also should make writing a family event whenever possible. Parents should ask children to help them write a thank-you note or a letter to his or her teacher. They can fill out school forms with children or make up the family grocery list together. Children will emulate parents who take opportunities to communicate through writing.

Responsive Adults Encourage Literacy

As mentioned, the parents of early readers answer their children's questions about books and print, offer information, provide experiences that enhance literacy development, and praise children for participating in literacy behaviors. Such channels of information and support systems in the home naturally encourage the development of reading. Durkin (1966) found that parents who attempted to teach children more formally were not as successful as parents who simply responded to children's requests for information about reading.

Responsiveness between parent and child needs to begin early and be cultivated. Language provides a primary opportunity for developing this behavior. Responsive adults not only answer questions, they initiate activities that promote literacy. While dressing, diapering, or feeding an infant, for instance, a parent can talk, sing, recite nursery rhymes, and tell stories. The baby responds by smiling, cooing, and moving, encouraging the parent to continue, and a cycle of mutual responsiveness develops.

Environmental print surrounds children and holds meaning for them. This natural source of reading material provides literacy experiences with items familiar to children (Neuman & Roskos, 1993, 1997). Children begin to read and ask about environmental print probably before they are interested in the print found in books. Parents who are aware of the importance of environmental print can point out familiar labels and other information on cereal boxes, vitamin bottles, detergent containers, and food packages. Children are naturally interested in telephone books, cookbooks, television guides, advertisements, and mail. They are particularly interested in personal letters, fliers, greeting cards, bills, catalogs, and magazines. The outside world presents a wealth of environmental print: road signs, street signs, and the names of fast food restaurants, gas stations, and other well-known chains. Parents note the environmental print that is meaningful to children and encourage children to do the same, pointing out specific letters in these familiar words and even sounding the letters. This gamelike involvement in skills has been found to promote early literacy.

In addition to responding to requests about books and print, parents of early readers generally respond to the need to provide varied experiences for their children. They take them to libraries and bookstores. They talk to them a great deal, which builds the children's vocabulary. Trips to zoos, fire stations, airports, and parks all foster literacy growth if they are accompanied by oral language and positive social interactions. It should be emphasized that a trip not only broadens a child's experience but also allows verbal interactions between parent and child before, during, and after. Those interactions include providing the child with background about the place to be visited and the things to be seen, answering questions about the experience, offering information, reading stories related to the experience, and discussing the trip afterward so that new ideas are absorbed. Suggesting that the child record the experience by drawing a picture about it and dictating a story for the parent to write will further expand literacy growth.

Television is part of our lives. To make the most of TV viewing, parents should watch some programs with their youngsters, posing questions, raising critical issues, and changing passive viewing into responsive interaction. They should also choose programs for which parallel books are available, such as "Sesame Street" and "Reading Rainbow." When specific stories are scheduled on television, such as *How the Grinch Stole Christmas* (Seuss, 1957a), parents can borrow the book from the library or purchase it.

In a series of informal interviews with parents whose children were early readers, it became apparent that literacy was embedded in daily activities that were meaningful, functional, and part of the mainstream of their lives. Various print materials were visible in the homes. Language was used interactively and frequently, in all its forms and in a positive emotional climate. There was praise for literacy activity and pleasure and joy in reading and writing. When asked what they believed helped their children become literate so early, the parents found it difficult to answer because they had not viewed the experiences they offered their children as attempts to promote reading and writing. Most of these activities had other functions, such as keeping the house running smoothly. Many of the experiences had social objectives—to promote positive interpersonal relationships and to teach responsibility and manners, for example. Here are some ideas related by these parents:

> *"I started a baby book for each of my children from the day they were born, with information about their weight and height, and I included pictures. I reported major events, such as first words, first steps, and events of interest to me. I looked at the book frequently and my toddler would snuggle beside me showing great interest. I've continued the books and as the children are getting older they add to them and read them over and over. They are without a doubt among their favorite books."*

> *"As a grandfather I don't get to see my grandchildren as frequently as I would like. In order to keep close contact, I often send them things through the mail. I'll enclose games cut from the children's section of the newspaper, which I'll ask them to complete. I send them pictures of famous people and ask them to call and tell me who they think they are, as well as questions to respond to me about."*

> *"From the time they were very young, my children were required to write thank-you notes for gifts received. At first they dictated them and I wrote down what they said. Later they were able to write simply 'thank you.' One good incentive for the task was to allow them to choose their own stationery for note writing."*

> *"The public library has provided many fine experiences for my children. One in particular is to help prepare them for experiences to come and allow them to relive experiences they have. Before we went to the circus, we took a cir-*

cus story out of the library in preparation for our trip. After seeing the circus we enjoyed another circus story from the library. Going to the public library for books is such a good habit to get into."

"I started leaving notes for my children in surprise places before they could read. Somehow they managed to find out what the notes said, even at the pre-reading stage. Now I put messages in their lunch boxes. The notes often just say 'hello.' Sometimes I'll write a riddle or a joke, and sometimes the note may require an answer. This has become a family tradition and lately I find surprise notes addressed to me left in the most unusual places."

"The amount of TV viewing by our three- and four-year-old children was a source of aggravation to us. To make the experience more meaningful, we read the television program guide to decide on what programs to watch and to limit the number of selections in one day. We try to watch some programs with them and ask who, what, when, *and* where *questions to elicit recall of facts. We also ask* why *questions to encourage more interpretive responses."*

"I've always kept a journal recording my daily experiences. My four-year-old found me writing in it one day and asked about what I was doing. She wanted to do the same thing, so we started a joint journal. I'd write things that happened to me during the day and she'd tell me what to write for her. Soon she was able to do her own writing. Sometimes I'd ask her questions about what she'd written. I did this by writing in the journal."

Researchers have found that home environments possessing the characteristics described here will generally instill in children an interest in reading and writing, a desire to read and write, and the ability to read and write early. However, there are children from homes that display all characteristics described who are not early readers and writers and have difficulty learning to read and write. There are also early readers and writers from environments lacking the characteristics described. Obviously there are factors other than the environment that affect successful literacy development. But it has been demonstrated that environmental factors do play a strong role in fostering literacy. A rich literacy environment at home gives children a better chance to learn to read and write easily and to enjoy reading and writing as well.

Parent Involvement in Your Literacy Program: What Teachers Can Do

Teachers need to view parents as partners in the development of literacy. Every teacher has the responsibility to inform parents about what is happening in school on a regular basis and how they can help their child, involve the parent in school activities during the day, and provide activities for parents to do at home. Parents should be made to feel that they are welcome in school, they should know what is happening there, and they should know how to help their youngster. Parents should be made to feel that they are partners with the school in the education of their child. They should be given the opportunity to offer input on what they would like their child to learn, to express how they feel about what happens in school, and to offer suggestions for change. Following are some suggestions on ways to make parents an integral part of the school.

1. At the beginning of the school year, send home the goals to be achieved for the grade level you teach for literacy development, in a format that can be understood by all.
2. With each new unit of instruction or concept being taught in literacy, send a newsletter to let parents know what you are studying and what they can do to help.
3. Invite parents to school for informational workshops, parent meetings about curriculum decisions, parent conferences, and school programs.
4. Invite parents to help with literacy activities in the classroom such as reading to children, helping with bookbinding, taking written dictation of stories, and supervising independent activities while teachers work with small groups and individual children.
5. Send home activities for parents and children to do together often. Require some feedback from the parents or child about working together. Include activities such as writing in journals together, reading together, visiting the library, recording print in the environment that they see, writing notes to each other, cooking together and following recipes, putting toys or household items together that require following directions, and watching and talking about specific programs on television. Participating in homework assignments is a must.
6. Invite parents to school to share special skills they may have, to talk about their cultural heritage, etc.
7. Send home notes when a child is doing well. Do not wait to send notes only for problems.
8. Provide lists of literature for parents to share with their children. Appendix A provides suggested books.
9. Parents should be invited to school to participate with their children in literacy activities. During periods of social-cooperative reading and writing, for

Parents should be invited to school to work together with their children on literacy projects regularly.

example, parents can read and write with their children, see what the literacy environment is like at school, and become an integral part of the child's literacy development at school.

10. Have parent and child meetings in which parents and children come to school to work together on projects.
11. Include parents in helping to assess their child's progress. Provide forms for them to fill out about their child's literacy activities and things they do with their child at home. Have them contribute information about their child's progress at parent conferences. Two forms that can be used for this process are "Guidelines: Promoting Early Literacy at Home" and "Checklist: Observing My Child's Literacy Growth."

The school needs to get information to homes about the need for rich literacy environments even before children enter school. Information can be disseminated at a special meeting for expectant parents, in hospital maternity wards, in obstetricians' and pediatricians' offices, and through churches, synagogues, and community agencies. A succinct handout such as "Guidelines: Promoting Early Literacy at Home" will be a helpful start and should be printed in languages commonly found in the community in which you live. Here it is provided in Spanish as well as English. (Booklets and pamphlets on the development of literacy at home can be found on page 85.)

Guidelines *Promoting Early Literacy at Home*

Your child's ability to read and write depends a lot on the things you do at home from the time he or she is born. The following list suggests materials, activities, and attitudes that are important in helping your child learn to read and write. Check off the things you already do. Try to do something on the list that you have not done before.

Materials

- ☐ 1. Have a space at home for books and magazines for your child.
- ☐ 2. If you can, subscribe to a magazine for your child.
- ☐ 3. Place some of your child's and some of your books, magazines, and newspapers in different parts of your home.
- ☐ 4. Provide materials that will encourage children to tell or create their own stories, such as puppets, dolls, and story tapes.
- ☐ 5. Provide materials for writing, such as crayons, markers, pencils, and paper in different sizes.

Activities

- ☐ 1. Read or look at books, magazines, or the newspaper with your child. Talk about what you looked at or read.
- ☐ 2. Visit the library and take out books and magazines to read at home.
- ☐ 3. Tell stories together about books, about your family, and about things that you do.
- ☐ 4. Look at and talk about written material you have such as catalogues, advertisements, work-related materials, and mail.

(continued on next page)

Guidelines *(continued from previous page)*

- ☐ 5. Provide a model for your child by reading and writing at a time when your child can see you.
- ☐ 6. Point to print outside, such as road signs and names of stores.
- ☐ 7. Write with your child and talk about what you write.
- ☐ 8. Point out print in your home such as words on food boxes or recipes, directions on medicine, or instructions on things that require assembly.
- ☐ 9. Visit the post office, supermarket, and zoo. Talk about what you saw and read. When you get home, draw and write about it.
- ☐ 10. Use print to talk to your child. Leave notes for each other. Make lists to do things, such as food lists, lists of errands, and lists for holiday shopping.

Foster Positive Attitudes toward Reading and Writing

- ☐ 1. Reward your child's attempts at reading and writing, even if they are not perfect, by offering praise. Say kind words like:

  "What nice work you do." "I'm happy to see you are reading."
  "I'm happy to see you are writing. Can I help you?"

- ☐ 2. Answer your child's questions about reading and writing.
- ☐ 3. Be sure that reading and writing are enjoyable experiences.
- ☐ 4. Display your child's work in your home.
- ☐ 5. Visit school when your child asks. Volunteer to help at school, attend programs in which your child is participating, attend parent conferences, and attend parent meetings. This lets your child know you care about him or her and school.

Visit School and Speak to Your Child's Teacher

- ☐ 1. If you want to volunteer help in any way.
- ☐ 2. If you want to visit your child's class during school hours.
- ☐ 3. If you have concerns about your child's reading and writing.
- ☐ 4. If you feel your child has problems with vision, hearing, or other things.
- ☐ 5. If you need help because the language you speak at home is not English.
- ☐ 6. If you need help with reading and writing yourself.
- ☐ 7. If you would like to know more about how you can help your child at home.
- ☐ 8. If you want to know more about what your child is learning at school.

Guía ***Fomentar en el hogar el desarrollo temprano de la capacidad de leer y de escribir***

La capacidad de su jovencito de leer y de escribir depende mucho de las cosas que hacen en casa desde el momento de su nacimiento. Usted puede hacer muchas cosas que no ocuparán mucho de su tiempo. La lista siguiente sugiere materiales, actividades, y actitudes que son importantes en ayudar a su hijo(a) a aprender, a leer y a escribir. Ponga una marca al lado de la sugerencia que usted ya practica en su casa. Procure hacer algo de la lista que no ha hecho antes.

Materiales

☐ 1. Prepare un lugar en su casa para poner libros y revistas para su hijo(a).

☐ 2. Si es posible, subscríbase a una revista para su hijo(a).

☐ 3. Coloque algunos de los libros de su hijo(a) y algunos de los suyos, incluyendo revistas y periódicos, en diferentes lugares en su casa.

☐ 4. Provea materiales, tales como títeres, muñecos, y cuentos grabados, que animarán a los niños a contar o a crear sus propios cuentos.

☐ 5. Provea materiales para escribir, tales como creyones, marcadores, lápices, y papel de various tamaños.

Actividades

☐ 1. Junto con su hijo(a), lean u hojeen libros, revistas o el periódico. Hablen sobre lo que hayan hojeado o leído.

☐ 2. Visiten la biblioteca y saquen algunos libros y algunas revistas para leer en casa.

☐ 3. Juntos, cuenten cuentos sobre libros, sobre su familia, y sobre las cosas que hacen.

☐ 4. Hojeen y hablen sobre el material escrito que tengan en su casa, tal como catálogos, anuncios, material relacionado con su trabajo, correo.

☐ 5. Sea un modelo para su hijo(a) leyendo y escribiendo en los momentos cuando él o ella le pueda observar.

☐ 6. Llame a la atención de su hijo(a) cosas impresas afuera, tales como letreros en la carretera y nombres de tiendas.

☐ 7. Escriba con su hijo(a) y hablen sobre lo que hayan escrito.

☐ 8. Indique palabras impresas en su casa, tales como las que están en cajas de comida, en recetas, en las instrucciones para medicinas, o en objetos que hay que armar.

☐ 9. Visiten la oficina de correos, el supermercado, el jardín zoológico. Hablen sobre lo que hayan visto y leído. Cuando regresen a su casa, hagan dibujos y escriban sobre estas experiencias.

☐ 10. Use la escritura para hablar con su hijo(a). Déjense notas el uno para el otro, hagan listas de cosas que hacer, tales como listas de comida para la compra, listas de tareas que hacer, listas de cosas que comprar para los días de fiesta.

Fomente actitudes positivas hacia la lectura y la escritura

☐ 1. Recompense con elogios los intentos de su hijo(a) por leer o escribir, aun cuando sus esfuerzos no sean perfectos. Use palabras bondadosas, tales como:
"¡Qué trabajo más bueno haces! Estoy muy contento(a) de ver que estás leyendo. Estoy muy contento(a) de ver que estás escribiendo. ¿Te puedo ayudar en algo?"

☐ 2. Responda a las preguntas de su hijo(a) sobre la lectura y la escritura.

☐ 3. Procure que el leer y el escribir sean experiencias agradables.

☐ 4. Exhiban el trabajo de sus hijos en la casa.

☐ 5. Visite la escuela cuando su hijo(a) se lo pida. Ofrezca su ayuda en la escuela, asista a los programas en los cuales su hijo(a) esté participando, asista a las conferencias y reuniones de padres. Esto permite que su hijo(a) se dé cuenta de que usted se interesa por él o por ella y por la escuela.

(continued on next page)

Guía *(continued from previous page)*

Visite la escuela y hable con el maestro o la maestra de su hijo(a)

- ☐ 1. . . . si usted quiere ayudar de alguna manera.
- ☐ 2. . . . si usted quiere visitar la clase de su hijo(a) durante las horas cuando la escuela está en sesión.
- ☐ 3. . . . si usted tiene dudas acerca del desarrollo do la lectura y la escritura en su hijo(a).
- ☐ 4. . . . si usted cree que su hijo(a) tiene problemas especiales con su visión, con su oído, o con cualquier otra cosa.
- ☐ 5. . . . si usted necesita ayuda porque el idioma que habla en casa no es el inglés.
- ☐ 6. . . . si usted necesita ayuda con sus propias habilidades de lectura y de escritura.
- ☐ 7. . . . si a usted le gustaría saber más sobre cómo puede ayudar a su hijo(a) en el hogar.
- ☐ 8. . . . si a usted le gustaría saber más y comprender mejor lo que su hijo(a) está aprendiendo en la escuela.

Checklist *Observing My Child's Literacy Growth*

Child's name ______________________ **Date** ____________

	Always	Sometimes	Never	Comments
1. My child asks to be read to.				
2. My child will read or look at a book alone.				
3. My child understands what is read to him/her, or what he/she reads to himself/herself.				
4. My child handles a book properly, knows how to turn pages, and knows that print is read from left to right.				
5. My child will pretend to read or read to me.				
6. My child participates in the reading of a story, with rhymes and repeated phrases.				
7. My child will write with me.				
8. My child will write alone.				
9. My child will talk about what he/she has written.				
10. My child reads print in the environment such as signs, and labels.				
11. My child likes school.				

Comments about Your Child:

Teachers should invite parents to school to share their cultural heritage. A father reads the Spanish version of *The Three Pigs* to his son's kindergarten class.

Multicultural Perspectives Concerning Parent Involvement and Family Literacy

In this chapter, family literacy has been approached from the perspective of parents helping children to support their reading and writing development on their own or as a result of involvement in literacy activities at school. In the United States, many families do not speak English and therefore are not able to help their children in the ways that schools may suggest. In addition, there are many parents who have limited literacy ability and although eager to help cannot do so in the mainstream approach. In some cases the parent is a teenager who has dropped out of school. Therefore, when we speak of family literacy, in many situations we need to recognize that it must be an intergenerational matter in which environments are created to enable adult learners to enhance their own literacy, and at the same time promote the literacy of their children. It has been generally accepted that poverty and illiteracy are linked. However, there is evidence that many low-income, minority, and immigrant families cultivate rich contexts for literacy development. Their efforts are, however, different from the school model we are accustomed to. We must learn from and respect parents and children from cultures in which books are not readily available although evidence of literacy activity, such as storytelling, exists (Morrow, 1995).

Research shows that the types and forms of literacy practiced in some homes are incongruent with those that children encounter in school (Auerbach, 1989; Heath, 1993; Taylor & Dorsey-Gaines, 1988). Although literacy activity is present in one form or another in most homes, the particular kinds of events that some parents or caregivers share with children may have little influence on school success. Conversely, the kinds of literacy practiced in classrooms may have little meaning for some children outside school. As mentioned, low-income, minority, and immigrant families cultivate rich contexts for literacy development and support family literacy with exceptional effort and imagination (Auerbach, 1989). Family literacy must be approached to avoid cultural bias, and intervention must be supportive rather than intrusive.

Family Literacy: What Is Being Done?

Based on work done by the Family Literacy Commission of the International Reading Association, three areas in which family literacy initiatives are taking place are as follows (Morrow, Paratore, & Tracey, 1994).

Studying the Ways Literacy Is Used by Families

Researchers are interested in advancing understanding of the ways in which literacy is used within families. In these studies, emphasis is placed on the richness of one's heritage and experiences rather than on perceived educational deficits. In some cases, researchers are exploring literacy events that occur naturally within diverse families. In other cases, researchers are describing the effects family literacy has on children's developing concepts about literacy. With the knowledge gained from such studies, educators can better understand the literacies that exist in diverse families and can help make literacy instruction in school more meaningful for both parents and children.

Delgado-Gaitan (1992) carried out a study to determine the attitudes of Mexican American families toward the education of their children and the roles played by these families. A major goal was to observe and describe the physical surroundings, emotional and motivational climates, and interpersonal interactions between parent and child.

Results of the study demonstrated that the Mexican American parents provided special areas for study for their children, in spite of space limitations. The parents wanted their children to succeed in school. Parents sought the help of friends, relatives, and others to assist them or their children with school-related matters. Parents punished their children for poor grades and rewarded them for doing well. Parents' attempts to help children with homework sometimes were fruitless, because they could not understand the directions and often misled their children. All parents believed that a person cannot be considered well educated through "book learning" alone but also must learn to be respectful, well mannered, and helpful to others. Family stories about life in Mexico guided the children's moral learning.

From the findings about these families, it seems that schools need to respond to Latinos' concerns that children learn good manners and respect in the curriculum. The schools need to be aware of and help with language problems that parents encounter when they want to help their children. They also need to incorporate oral history and storytelling into the curriculum because it is an important aspect of the Latino culture familiar to both parents and children.

Parent Involvement Initiatives

Parent involvement initiatives include programs that are designed to involve and inform parents about activities that will promote their children's literacy learning in school. Such programs involve parents as agents in supporting their child's literacy development and may originate from school, the library, or other community agencies. Often they are collaborative efforts among these agencies. A basic premise of parent involvement programs is that parents are both willing and committed to helping their families with literacy activities that will lead to improved school performance.

Running Start (RS) is an example of a parent involvement initiative. This school-based project created by Reading Is Fundamental (RIF) is designed to get books into the hands of first-grade children and to encourage and support family literacy. The goals of RS are (1) to increase first graders' motivation to read so they eagerly turn to books for both pleasure and information, (2) to involve parents in their children's literacy development, and (3) to support schools and teachers in their efforts to help children become successful readers. Participating classroom teachers are provided with funds to select and purchase high-quality fiction and informational books for their classroom libraries. Children are challenged to read (or have someone read to them) 21 books during the 10-week program. A Reading Rally is held to involve the community in supporting literacy development, and parents are encouraged to support their child in meeting the 21-book challenge by sharing books and stories with their children in a variety of ways. When a child meets the 21-book goal, he or she gets to select a book for his or her own personal library. Studies have demonstrated that first graders' reading motivation as well as parents' involvement in literacy activities in the home significantly increased in families that participated in the program (Gambrell, Almasi, Xie, & Heland, 1995).

Intergenerational Literacy Initiatives

Intergenerational literacy initiatives are specifically designed to improve the literacy development of both adults and children. These programs view parents and children as colearners, and are generally characterized by planned and systematic instruction for both adults and children. Instruction may occur when parents and children work in either collaborative or parallel settings. The instruction for adults is intended to improve their literacy skills while teaching them how to work with their children to aid their development.

Parents and Children Together is a nationwide intergenerational family literacy program established by the National Center for Family Literacy (NCFL) in Louisville, Kentucky. Parents who lack a high school diploma and their three- and four-year-old children attend school together between three to five days a week. An early childhood program is provided for the children, while the parents attend an adult education program to learn reading, math, and parenting skills.

In the adult education portion of the program, parents work on improving their reading and math skills, and are taught to set goals and collaborate with other parents in the program. "Parent Time" is a component of the program during which the adults discuss a variety of topics ranging from discipline to self-esteem. The last component of the program is "Parent and Child Together" time. During this hour, families play together. The activities are led by the children. Parents find they can learn both with and from their children (National Center for Family Literacy, 1993).

What Makes a Parent Involvement Literacy Program Successful?

Because no two communities are the same, family literacy programs need to be tailored to the needs of the individuals they serve. Here are some tested guidelines to follow that will help programs be successful.

- Respect and understand the diversity of the families you serve.
- Build on literacy behaviors already present in families. Although they may be different from conventional school-like literacy, most families use literacy in the routine of their daily lives. These behaviors should be identified, acknowledged, respected, preserved, and used in family literacy programs.
- Be aware of the home languages used within the community so that materials can be translated and understood.
- Family literacy programs should not take a "fix the family" attitude. Rather, they should view intervention as a supplement to the interactions that already exist.
- Hold meetings at varied times of the day and days of the week to accomodate all schedules (see posters in English and Spanish for *"Family Members Wanted").*
- Hold meetings in accessible locations that are friendly and nonthreatening. Transportation needs to be provided if no public transportation is available, or if parents do not have a way of getting to meetings.
- Provide childcare at meetings.
- Provide food and refreshments at meetings.
- Follow sound educational practices appropriate for literacy development of children and adults. Use varied strategies for literacy learning. Include writing together, reading together, and sharing materials that are fun and interesting for all.
- You may work with parents alone, children alone, and with parents and children together. There should be sharing times when both parents and children work together.
- Programs should provide support groups for parents to talk about helping their children and to find out what they want to know. Parent input is crucial.
- Family literacy programs seek not only to help with literacy development but to improve interactions between parents and children.
- Programs should provide parents with ideas and materials to use at home.
- Good programs provide functional literacy learning activities that parents consider useful such as talking and reading about child rearing concerns, community life problems, housing, applying for jobs and keeping them, and dealing with migration issues.
- Programs should include the opportunity for parental participation in school activities during school hours.
- Portions of school and home programs should parallel each other. Activities done in school should be the same as those sent home for parents to do with children. When this occurs parents can participate in their children's learning.

FAMILY MEMBERS WANTED

To Visit Your Child's Class

Dear Family Members,

Please come to school and be a part of our reading and writing time. On the form below list the types of things you can do when you visit. There is a space for you to let us know the time of day and dates that you can attend. We are flexible and will arrange our time when it is convenient for you. All family members are welcome—brothers and sisters, babies, grandparents, and of course parents. Please come and get involved in your child's education, and help us form a true home and school partnership.

Sincerely,

Mrs. Abere's second-grade class

Please fill out the following form and send it back to school with your child:

Your name ______________________________

Your child's name ______________________________

The days I can come during the week are ______________________________

The time of day I can come to school is ______________________________

When I come to school I would like to:

☐ 1. Watch what the children are doing.

☐ 2. Participate with the children.

☐ 3. Read to a small group of children.

☐ 4. Read to the whole class.

☐ 5. I am from another country and I would like to tell the children about my country and show them clothing, pictures, and books from there.

☐ 6. I have a hobby and would like to share it with the class.
My hobby is: ______________________________

☐ 7. I have a talent and would like to share it with the class.
My talent is: ______________________________

☐ 8. I'd like to tell the children about my job.
My job is: ______________________________

☐ 9. Other ideas you would like to do: ______________________________

☐ 10. Give children who need it some extra help.

☐ 11. I'd like some help in deciding what to do.

☐ 12. I would like to come on a regular basis to help.
I can come at the following times: ______________________________

SE BUSCAN MIEMBROS DE FAMILIA

Para Visitar la Clase de su Niño

Ayudenos Aprender–

Comparta sus Talentos y Envuélvase con Nuestra Clase:

Observe la clase y su niño

Cuente historias

Hable de su cultura

Lea libros

Comparta su pasatiempo favorito

Traiga su bebé o animal mimado

Explique su trabajo

Cocine o traiga dulces para la clase

Venga a cantarle a los niños

Comparta con nuestras actividades de "Highlights"

Por favor ponga los días, o día, que pueda venir a la clase:

Mes: Dia(s): Horas:

____

- -

Devuelva este papel a la maestra de su niño.

Nombre: _____________________________________.

Visitaré la clase en esta fecha ______________ y a esta hora ______________.

Me gustaría compartir: _____________________________________.

Models for family literacy programs must be developed in which family literacy activities are intended to promote parent/child interaction in a wide range of literacy events. Programs most view participating families from the perspective of the richness of their experiences and heritage, rather than from the perspective of their deficits and dilemmas.

Home school programs need to be easy to use. Materials sent home should be introduced to children in school first. For example, one program used

Successful family literacy programs respect and understand the diversity of the families they serve.

Highlights for Children Parent Involvement Program (Columbus, Ohio) as the home–school connection material. Teachers featured articles in the magazine at school and each child had a school copy. Another copy was sent home with activities for parents and children to do together that were similar to what was being done in school. The program was successful because children knew what to do with the materials. In addition, the magazine provided the following features that should be present in any home–school connection material: (1) multiple options for families to select activities from, (2) a nonthreatening format that is not school-like, (3) activities appropriate for many age levels and abilities, (4) culturally diverse content, (5) some activities that do not require the ability to read, and (6) activities that are fun and therefore engage parents and children in literacy together (Morrow, Scoblionko, & Shafer, 1995).

Following are comments by children, teachers, and parents concerning their participation in the family literacy program just discussed.

Children Said

"My mom could never work with me even though she wanted to 'cause she don't speak English. Well the magazine has Spanish things in it and you can do things in it that you don't need to read. You just look at the pictures. I teach her to read the English too. She's learning new words."

"When I work with my Mom and Dad at home, it makes you feel like a family and that's what families are supposed to do—sit and do things together."

"Working with my mom at home makes me feel happy, 'cause when your mom works and has lots of kids, you think she don't love you much or care about you, but when she does work with you, you feel special like you're the only one and you know she cares."

Teachers Said

"Parents who never work with their kids are doing so. It makes the children feel good."

"William is doing much better in school. He reads the magazine from cover to cover because he can take it home. There aren't any other reading materials for him there. His mother has worked with him once in a while, which is something she never did before. I notice a big difference in his reading."

Parents Said

"This is a good idea, sending the magazine home from school. I never knew what to do with Geremy, and this helps a lot. I don't like doing homework with him. But I don't mind working in the magazine."

"When we work in the magazine together my child helps me with my English. He can read it and he shows me. I can do some things since it has pictures. It makes me feel good that I can do school work with him."

Educators are recognizing that the family is the key to successful literacy development for both children and their parents. Policymakers from a wide range of agencies need to collaborate and form partnerships in their efforts to create and support effective family literacy programs. Literacy programs in school will be more successful if they have home support; therefore, family literacy programs are crucial.

Appendix A provides a bibliography of children's literature about families for teachers and parents to share with children. The books are representative of diverse cultural backgrounds. Each book illustrates some special relationship between family and extended family members. It could be parents, grandparents, an aunt or uncle, sisters or brothers, or a person who becomes like family although he or she is not actually related.

Learning More about Family Literacy

Agencies, associations, and organizations that deal with family literacy can be contacted for further information on ways to establish, administer, and evaluate family literacy programs. A few are listed here as a starting place.

The Barbara Bush Foundation for Family Literacy, 1112 16th Street, NW, Suite 340, Washington, DC 20036, www.barbarabushfoundation.com

Even Start Compensatory Education Programs, U.S. Department of Education, 400 Maryland Avenue, SW, Washington, DC 20202, www.evenstart.org

Highlights for Children Parent Involvement Program, 1800 Watermark Drive, Columbus, Ohio 43215.

International Reading Association, 800 Barksdale Road, PO Box 8139, Newark, DE 19714-8139, www.reading.org

National Center for Family Literacy, Waterfront Plaza, Suite 200, 325 West Main Street, Louisville, KY 40202-4251, www.famlit.org

Reading Is Fundamental (RIF), 600 Maryland Avenue, SW, Suite 600, Washington, DC 20024, www.rif.org

Resources for Parents

Beginning Literacy and Your Child: A Guide to Helping Your Baby or Preschooler Become a Reader

Make the Reading-Writing Connection: Tips for Parents of Young Learners

I Can Read and Write! How to encourage Your School-Aged Child's Literacy Development

*Explore the Playground of Books: Tips for Parents of Beginning Readers**

*Get Ready to Read! Tips for Parents of Young Children**

*Summer Reading Adventure! Tips for Parents of Young Readers**

*Library Safari: Tips for Parents of Young Readers and Explorers**

*Making the Most of Television: Tips for Parents of Young Viewers**

*See the World on the Internet: Tips for Parents of Young Readers—and Surfers**
(Booklets and brochures available from the International Reading Association, 800 Barksdale Road, PO Box 8139, Newark, DE 19714.)

Raising a Reader, Raising a Writer: How Parents Can Help
(Brochure available from the National Association for the Education of Young Children, 1509 16th Street, NW, Washington, DC 20036.)

Choosing a Children's Book
(Brochure available from the Children's Book Council, Inc., 568 Broadway, Suite 404, New York, NY 10012.)

*Also available in Spanish.

Ideas for the Classroom from the Classroom

A newsletter follows that is to be sent to parents describing a theme that their children are involved in entitled Life on the Farm. *A similar newsletter can be sent with every unit taught during the school year. This gives parents information about the theme and asks for their participation in working with their child at home and sending materials to school or coming to school to make presentations. This newsletter will heighten parents' awareness of activities to do at home that correspond with what their children are doing at school. It also makes parents active participants in school experiences.*

Life on the Farm Newsletter

MESSAGE TO PARENTS

Dear Parents:

This month your child is participating in a unit about farm life. This unit includes the study of people and the jobs they do on farms, farm animals and their babies, farm machinery, farm buildings, and products that come from farms.

The unit is organized so that all subject areas, social studies, science, math, art, play, reading, and writing, are incorporated within the farm theme. Reading and writing will have a special emphasis in all activities including those in art, music, and so on.

We would like to ask you to participate in the farm unit, and we feel that each and every one of you can help in some way. If you have any pictures, materials, or personal experiences to talk about related to the topic, please let me know and come to school to share them with us. There are a wide variety of topics dealing with the farm, and I'm sure each of you would have something to share. The following topics would be appropriate:

Jobs on the farm (growing plants, caring for animals, selling products, equipment), farm animals and their babies (cats, dogs, and their care, etc.), farm machinery (tractors, trucks, plows, etc.), farm buildings (barns, animal housing), the products that come from farms (corn, wheat, cotton, wool, fruit, vegetables, meat, milk, etc.), the preparation of food from farm products (apple pie, cheeses, etc.) and the preparation of other items from farm products (goose down pillows, wool sweaters, etc.). We always need help with projects so please volunteer to help at school whether you have a farm idea or not.

Featured Farm Activities in School

In school, your child will participate in the following experiences:

- In science, the children will learn to keep a journal to record the growth of their own lima bean plants.
- In social studies, we will discuss cooperation when we read and act out the story of *The Little Red Hen* (Galdone, 1973).
- In the dramatic-play area, we will learn about care of animals and the role of doctors and nurses by setting up a veterinarian's office that has prescription forms, books, and magazines in a waiting room, and stuffed animal patients. Materials in this area encourage reading and writing as children role-play.
- In the Library Corner, we will add books, poems, and songs about the farm to read to your children. Some of the titles are:
    1. *Petunia* by Roger Duvoisin
    2. *Over in the Meadow* by Ezra Jack Keats
    3. *Go Tell Aunt Rhody* by Aliki
    4. *Rosie's Walk* by Pat Hutchins

Things to Do at Home with Your Child about the Farm

- Ask your child about the activities he or she is doing in school. Some of them have been mentioned, and you can focus on those. Ask your child to draw a picture about the farm and write about it also.
- Try to get some of the books we are reading in school from your local library and reread the stories to your child. Ask your youngster to retell the story using the pictures if necessary. Talk about the issues discussed in the stories.
- The unit focuses on cooperating with others while doing a job. To reinforce this idea, encourage your child to help you with any household tasks or with the care of a pet or plant.
- When you prepare food at home, point out the products that come from the farm. Notice newspaper or magazine articles that relate to the farm and read and discuss them together.
- If possible, visit a farm, a petting zoo that has farm animals, a pet store, a plant nursery, or the supermarket where you can look at and talk about the products that come from the farm.

* * *

Thank you very much for your interest and enthusiasm which we and your child greatly appreciate.

I will be happy to answer any questions you may have about this unit and your child's development. I hope to hear from you.

Sincerely,

Susan Burks

Susan Burks, Teacher
North Plainfield, New Jersey

Highlighting Parent Involvement at School

Every month in Lincoln School several parent involvement activities occur. To emphasize the importance of them and others, teachers began a showcase called "Highlighting Parent Involvement." They keep cameras in school so when parents participate they take their pictures for the showcase. The following are the activities at school that help fill the showcase and bring parents to the building:

- *Theme Nights:* These are evenings devoted to different topics such as other countries where children and parents can learn together. Families share artifacts and then read, write, and do art projects about the theme.
- *Cooking Nights:* Families bring easy favorite recipes to share and make together. The best part is eating the goodies when the cooking is done.
- *Book Sharing Evenings:* Everyone brings a favorite book and reads or tells about their favorite part. The book can be in another language, and if necessary, a translator is used so everyone can participate.
- *Sharing Family Photos:* On this night we ask everyone to bring pictures they want to share about their families. We talk and write about them. Each family makes an album with the photos, and we encourage them to continue to fill the album they started at school.

Margaret Youssef, Teacher
New Brunswick, New Jersey

Activities and Questions

1. Answer the focus questions posed at the beginning of the chapter.

2. Interview members of your family or friends who are parents. Ask them to relate specific activities they have done with their children to promote literacy with natural events that arose from daily living. Collect ideas from all members of the class and put them together in a newsletter or pamphlet format to distribute to parents of early childhood youngsters.

3. Using the memories of your own home when you were a young child or the home of a friend or family member who is a parent of a young child, observe the physical characteristics and record activities done with children that promote literacy development. Determine elements that could improve the richness of the literacy environment you analyzed.

4. Select a child and his or her family to begin a portfolio of assessment materials to collect throughout the semester. Start a portfolio in a folder for the child that you will keep and provide a folder for the family. Make a copy of the "Guidelines: Promoting Early Literacy at Home" on pages 73–74 (or pages 74–76 for the Spanish version) for yourself and one for the family you will be working with. Ask a family member to fill out the form for themselves, and a copy for you. Provide the parent with two copies of the form entitled "Checklist: Observing My Child's Literacy Growth" on page 76. Have them fill it out at the beginning of the semester and at the end. Be sure to get a copy for your folder as well.

5. Create a family literacy program for a familiar community. If it is a community in which parents have literacy and English skills, you will probably want to develop a parent involvement program; if it is in a community where parents speak other languages, or have limited literacy ability, you may need to engage in an intergenerational program that involves development of literacy skills for parents as well as training them to help their children. Be sure that, whichever program you design, a portion of the home and school activities are similar to each other.

Case Study Activities

Case 1

Refer to the "Ideas for the Classroom from the Classroom" section. The newsletter in the first idea was created by an early childhood teacher for the parents in her classroom. After reading the newsletter, consider the following: David Hernandez will take the newsletter home to his mother who does not speak any English but is literate in Spanish, and Tiffany Jones will take the newsletter home to her mother who has minimal literacy skills. What is likely to be the response to the newsletter in each of these homes?

Critique the newsletter for parents and respond to these questions: What are the most important items in the newsletter? Present ideas you feel are missing. This newsletter was written for kindergartners or first graders. What changes would you make for second and third graders? What accommodations has this teacher made for meeting the needs of all the children and parents in her classroom? What else could she have included to accommodate special needs better?

Case 2

Mrs. Connor graciously accepts and solicits parent volunteers. She thinks it is very important to have parents involved in their children's education. When parents come to help out she has done the following:

Mr. Chan helps with photocopying activity sheets on Mondays. Mrs. De'Angelo works in the teachers' room on Tuesdays and makes materials that are needed for Mrs. Connor to use in the class. Mrs. Jones can't come to school because she has a baby at home so she does some typing for Mrs. Connor, which her daughter brings to school for her. Mrs. Gallagher collates and staples all of the extended reading activities needed for several days of the week.

Is Mrs. Connor using parent volunteers productively? What would you do differently? In what ways could the parents from different cultural backgrounds contribute to her class?

chapter 4

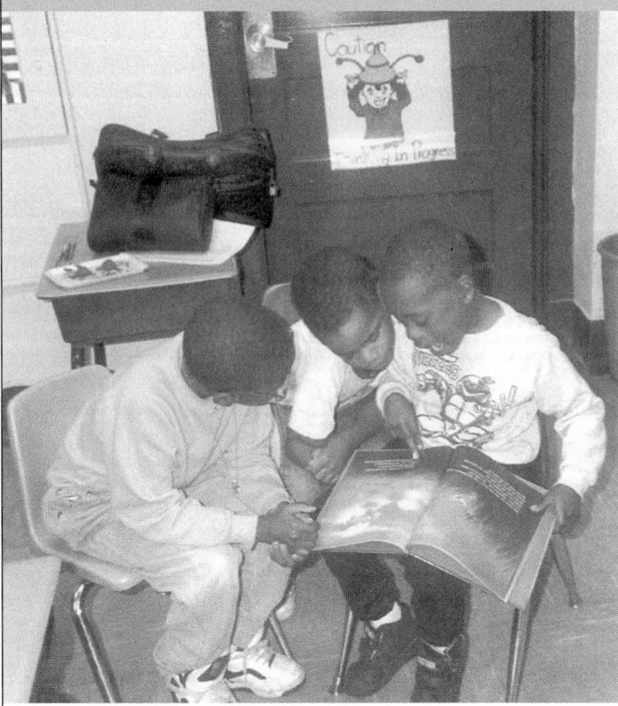

Language and Literacy Development

"The time has come," the Walrus said,
"To talk of many things:
Of shoes and ships and sealing-wax,
Of cabbages and kings. . . ."

—Lewis Carroll
"The Walrus and the Carpenter"

Focus Questions

- According to the different theorists described in the chapter, how is language acquired?
- What are the general stages of language development that a child progresses through from birth to age eight?
- What do we mean when we speak of children with language differences?
- What are the objectives for language development in early childhood?
- What strategies can teachers and parents carry out to encourage language development from birth to age two?
- What strategies can teachers and parents carry out to encourage language development from preschool through second grade?
- Describe specific strategies for building vocabulary and word meaning for second and third grade.
- What techniques can be used for a portfolio of materials that assesses children's language development?

From the moment of birth, the infant is surrounded by oral language. The development of language is one of the child's first steps toward becoming literate; it helps make reading and writing possible. Using newer research methods that involve close observation of children, investigators have been able to describe the strategies by which youngsters learn and use language. Among the many things these researchers have observed is that children are active participants in their learning of language. To learn, children involve themselves in problem solving, first creating hypotheses based on background information that they already have, and then interacting with those individuals around them who are generating language. These strategies have implications for initial instruction in early literacy.

A parent of a child in one of my kindergarten classes related a conversation she had had with her daughter Melody. Mrs. Tracey said they were outside looking at the sky one evening, and she noticed that the moon was full. She said to her daughter, "Look, Melody, the moon is full tonight." Melody looked up at the moon with a slightly confused expression on her face and said, "Why is it full, Mommy, did the moon eat too much for dinner?" Melody used her background language information to help her understand her mother. Until this time the word *full* meant filled up with food, and Melody made sense of the discussion with what she knew. Her mother explained what she meant by a full moon and that different words can have different meanings depending on the situation in which they are used.

Children do not learn language passively; they actually construct—or reconstruct—language as they learn. In another of my kindergarten classes, we were talking about what the children wanted to be when they grew up. It was Michael's turn. He started by telling us that his dad is a doctor and recently he had taken him to see the operating room where he works. Michael said, "I liked the people and all the machines that my daddy uses and so when I grow up, I want to be an *operator,* just like my daddy." Michael constructed a word for the situation that made wonderful sense under the circumstances.

The discoveries of how language is acquired laid the foundation for a new way of looking at how early reading develops. Researchers realized that, because reading is a language process, it must be closely associated with oral language.

Language Development and Reading

Now that language processes are commonly recognized as the basis for learning to read, *language learning* is considered an important part of *learning to read.* Ruddell and Ruddell (1995) define reading as the use of one's language ability to decode and comprehend text. Reading is the interaction between the reader and the written language. It is the attempt by a reader to reconstruct the author's message. The graphic sequences and patterns that appear as print represent the oral sequences of language. In the process of reading, we look and listen for recognizable grammatical sequences and patterns that trigger appropriate phrasing. Using what we already know of language structure, we then test how each word fits into the context of what we are reading. Lennenberg and Kaplan (1970) see the reader as continually assigning tentative interpretations to the text and then checking those interpretations. As readers, we use syntactic and semantic cues that enable us to predict what comes next. Our skill in processing semantics (meaning) and syntax (language structure) makes us more adept readers. The reader who encounters unfamiliar language structures and unfamiliar concepts in material to be read has difficulty understanding it. Familiarity with both syntax and semantics enables even very young readers to anticipate the format and content of sentences in print. Past theory held that it was our accumulation of letters and words that led to competent reading. Now we realize that our ability to understand what we are reading is based on our *reconstruction* of the meaning behind a printed word. Such reconstruction is based on our previous experience with the topic, our familiarity with its main concepts, and our general knowledge of how language works.

The relationship between reading and language is evident in studies of children who are early readers. It has been found, for instance, that early readers score higher on language screening tests than children who were not reading early. Early readers come from homes where rich language and a great deal of oral language are used (Dickinson & Tabors, 2000; Snow & Perlmann, 1985). When interviewed, parents of early readers revealed that their children tended to use very descriptive language and sophisticated language structures. The youngsters invented words, used humor, and talked a lot. The mother of a four-year-old early reader reported that while watching the first snowfall of the year, her youngster said, "The snow is swirling down and looks like fluffy marshmallows on the ground." One spring day a few months later, the same child noted, "Look, Mommy, the butterflies are fluttering around. They look like they are dancing with the flowers."

Halliday (1975) notes that, among other functions, language helps children learn how to ascertain meaning from the world around them. Early readers demonstrate an awareness of story language. They can retell stories using such literary conventions as "Once upon a time" and "They lived happily ever after." When telling stories they tend to use delivery and intonation like those of an adult reading aloud. This "book language" takes children beyond their own language patterns and is distinctively characteristic of early readers (Cazden, 1992; Snow, 1991).

How Children Acquire Language

Although we do not have all the answers about language acquisition, there are many theories that help explain how babies learn to speak. Knowing how language is acquired has strong implications for providing environments that promote language development. It also implies how reading and writing skills develop.

The Behaviorist Theory

The **behaviorists** have influenced our thinking about how language is acquired. Although behaviorism does not present the total picture, it still offers ideas about language acquisition that should be considered for instruction. Skinner (1957) defined language as the observed and produced speech that occurs in the interaction of speaker and listener. Thinking, he said, is the internal process of language; both language and thought are initiated through interactions in the environment—interactions such as those between a parent and a child, for instance. According to behaviorists, adults provide a language model that children learn through imitation. The child's acquisition of language is enhanced and encouraged by the positive reinforcement of an adult (Moerk, 1992).

It is evident that children imitate adult models and are motivated to continue using language because of positive reinforcement. Children surrounded by rich language begin to use the language they hear, even though imitation sometimes occurs with erroneous comprehension or no comprehension at all. A child can imitate the sounds of the "words" of a familiar song, for instance, with no concern for meaning. A three-year-old girl sang "My country 'tis of thee" as "My country tis a bee." A four-year-old sang "Torn between two lovers" as "Torn between two mothers." Both children were imitating what they heard and were thus acquiring language. But when they heard unfamiliar words in context, both substituted similar-sounding words that had meaning for them from their own experiences.

Social Interaction and Language Acquisition

Early attempts at language are often rewarded, which leads to additional responses by children. These attempts are also *interactive,* that is, the language is mediated by adults through interactions designed to elaborate and extend meaning (Neuman & Roskos, 1993). When newborns coo or make other verbal sounds, most parents are delighted and respond with gentle words of encouragement. The infant, in turn, responds to the positive reinforcement by repeating the cooing sounds. As babies become able to formulate consonant and vowel sounds, they try them out. It is not uncommon to hear a six-month-old playing with sounds such as *ba, ba, ba,* or *ma, ma, ma.* The responsive interactive parent perceives such sounds as the child's first words and assumes that the child's *ma-ma* means *mommy.* The delighted adult says more warm and loving things to the baby and adds hugs and kisses. The parent might say, "Come on, now say it again, *ma, ma, ma.*" The baby is pleased with the warm reception and tries to repeat the sounds to receive additional interaction and positive reinforcement.

As a child builds an oral vocabulary, he or she tries words more frequently. Children will point to a toy and name it. While playing with a ball, a child may say the word *ball* over and over again. The attentive parent now interacts with the child by expanding and extending the original language (Cazden, 1992). After the child says *ball,* the parent may say, "Yes, that is a nice, big, round, red ball." Through such *expansion* and reinforcement of words by the adult, the child acquires new language. The adult often *extends* upon the baby's words by asking questions, for instance, "Now what can you do with that nice red ball?" Such extension requires the child to think, understand, and act. Positive interactions encourage practice, which helps continue language development (Bohannon, 1993).

Unfortunately, the converse is also true. If a baby's babbling is considered annoying, if the parent is aggravated by the sound and responds with negative reinforcement by telling the baby in harsh tones, "Be quiet and stop making so much noise," the child is less likely to continue to explore the use of language.

The Nativist Theory

Chomsky (1965), Lennenberg (1967), and McNeil (1970) have described the **nativist** theory of language acquisition. They contend that language develops innately. Children figure out how language works by internalizing the rules of grammar, which enable them to produce an infinite number of sentences. They do so even without the practice, reinforcement, and modeling offered by adult language, which are considered necessary by the behaviorists. The ability to learn language must be innate to humans, the nativists believe, because almost all children develop and use language in the first few years of their lives. Language growth depends on maturation: As children mature, their language grows. Children learn new patterns of language and unconsciously generate new rules for new elements of language. The child's rule system increases in complexity as he or she generates more complex language. Lennenberg (1967), an extreme nativist, finds nothing in the child's environment to account for language development. Rather, language acquisition is motivated *inside* children; learning language is a natural ability (Pinker, 1994). Although maturation does play a role in language development, and it is innate to humans, newer theories offered by Piaget and Vygotsky have come to be the more accepted ideas concerning language acquisition.

Piagetian and Vygotskian Theory

Piaget's theory of *cognitive development* is built on the principle that children develop through their activities. Children's realization of the world is tied to their actions or their sensory experiences in the environment. According to this theory, children's first words are egocentric, or centered in their own actions. Children talk about themselves and what they do. Their early language and their general development relates to actions, objects, and events they have experienced through touching, hearing, seeing, tasting, and smelling (Piaget & Inhelder, 1969).

Vygotsky's theory of *basic learning* also has implications for language development. According to Vygotsky, children learn higher mental functions by internalizing social relationships. Adults initially provide children with names of things, for instance; they direct youngsters and make suggestions. Then, as children become more competent, the adults around them gradually withdraw the amount of help they need to give. Vygotsky (1978) describes a **zone of proximal development,** a range of social interaction between an adult and child. Theoretically, the child can perform within that range, but only with adult assistance.

Children learn language from social interaction with an adult who provides a language model and positive reinforcement for the child's early language attempts.

Proximal development ends when the child can function independently. The implications for language instruction are clear: To promote language development, adults need to interact with children by encouraging, motivating, and supporting them (Sulzby, 1986a).

The Constructivist Theory

The more contemporary perspective of language acquisition is the **constructivist** theory emerging from the work of Piaget and Vygotsky and described and supported by those who have studied language development (Brown, Cazden, & Bellugi-Klima, 1968; Halliday, 1975). Constructivists describe children as the creators of language on the basis of an innate set of rules or underlying concepts. They describe language as an active and social process. The child constructs language, often making errors. But making errors is a necessary part of learning how language works. We need to accept language errors in a child's first years.

The implications of the constructivist theory are important for early literacy development. Even though language development charts shows when to expect certain stages of development on average, we do not discipline babies who have not uttered their first words at eight months or their first complete sentences by two-and-a-half years. Sometimes we find their errors cute. We seem to respect their individuality and their right to grow at their own pace. Yet when children enter school, we neglect to recognize developmental differences; we prescribe tasks based on a curriculum, not on the child.

The process of acquiring language is continuous and interactive; it takes place in the social context of the child's interacting with others (Bohannan, 1993). Children also learn by playing with language themselves. They try out new words, involve themselves in monologues, and practice what they have learned. The acquisition of language varies from child to child, depending on his or her social and cultural background (Jagger, 1985). Children's remarks illustrate that they do not *simply* imitate adult language. It is as if children need to express themselves but do not have sufficient conventional language to draw upon, so they create their own based on their backgrounds and their awareness of semantics and syntax.

A three-year-old girl saw a freckled youngster for the first time and said, "Look, Mommy, that little girl has *sprinkles* on her nose." A four-year-old boy observed an elderly man with deep wrinkles and said, "I wonder why that man has *paths* all over his face." A father and his three-year-old daughter were toasting marshmallows; the little girl said, "Mmmm, I can smell the taste of them." After a quick summer rain, a three-year-old boy observed the sun returning to the sky and the water evaporating all around him. "The sun came out and ate up all the rain," he observed. Toward the end of the winter as the snow was melting, a four-year-old girl noted, "See how the grass is peeking out from underneath the snow."

Halliday's Theory of Language Development

Halliday (1975, p. 7) describes language development as a process by which children gradually "learn how to mean." According to his theory of developmental language, what a child can do during interactions with others has meaning and meaning can be turned into speech. In other words, children's initial language development is based on *function:* What can be said reflects what can be done. Language is learned when it is relevant and functional. The seven functions evident in the language of young children Halliday (1975, pp. 19–21) identifies are found in the following chart, with examples.

Halliday's Functions of Language

1. *Instrumental:* Children use language to satisfy a personal need and to get things done.
   Example: Cookie Mommy.
2. *Regulatory:* Children use language to control the behavior of others.
   Example: No sleep now.
3. *Interactional:* Children use language to get along with others.
   Example: You want to play?
4. *Personal:* Children use language to tell about themselves.
   Example: I'm running now.
5. *Heuristic:* Children use language to find out about things, to learn things.
   Example: What are cows for?
6. *Imaginative:* Children use language to pretend, to make believe.
   Example: Let's play space.
7. *Informative:* Children use language to communicate something for the information of others.
   Example: I'll tell you how this game works.

The theories just discussed explain how language is acquired. Each has something to offer but none by itself presents a complete picture. We *do* know, however, that children's language grows according to their need to use it, their interests, and the meaning it has for them. Children's language is acquired through exploration and invention and is controlled by their own maturity, the structure of the language, and its conventions. Language acquisition is fostered by positive interactions regarding language between the child and an adult.

Stages in Language Development

Children acquire language by moving through predictable stages. In doing so, they discover the rules that govern the structure of language—specifically, those of phonology (sound), syntax (grammar), and semantics (meaning).

There are 44 separate sounds, or *phonemes,* in English. With them we produce oral language. Children who grow up in a language-rich environment can learn these sounds quite easily. They learn appropriate articulation, pronunciation, and intonation. *Intonation* involves pitch, stress, and juncture. *Pitch* refers to how high or low a voice is when producing a sound, *stress* to how loud or soft it is, and *juncture* to the pauses or connections between words, phrases, and sentences (Berk, 1997).

Syntax refers to the rules that govern how words work together in phrases, clauses, and sentences. Internalizing the syntactic rules of language helps children understand what they hear and what they read. Syntax includes rules for forming basic sentence patterns, rules for transforming those patterns in order to generate new sentences, and rules for embedding, expanding, and combining sentences to make them more complex. Brief examples follow:

1. Some Basic Sentence Patterns
   a. Subject–verb: *The girl ran.*
   b. Subject–verb–object: *The girl ran the team.*
   c. Subject–verb–indirect object–direct object: *Susan gave Lynn a dime.*
   d. Subject–to be–noun or adjective or adverb complement: *Tom was the captain. He was happy. He was there.*
   e. Subject–linking verb–adjective: *Jane is tall.*
2. Some Basic Sentence Transformations
   a. Question
      (1) kernel: *Jim went to the store.*
      (2) transformation: *Did Jim go to the store?*
   b. Negative
      (1) kernel: *Jane is a cheerleader.*
      (2) transformation: *Jane is not a cheerleader.*
   c. Passive
      (1) kernel: *Jennifer gave Lisa some bubble gum.*
      (2) transformation: *Some bubble gum was given to Lisa by Jennifer.*
3. Some Embeddings (sentence expansion and combination)
   a. Adding modifiers (adjectives, adverbs, adverbial and adjective phrases)
      (1) kernel: *The boy played with friends.*
      (2) transformation: *The boy in the red pants played with three friends.*
   b. Compounding (combining words, phrases, or independent clauses to form compound subjects, verbs, etc.)
      (1) kernel: *Jane ran. Jane played. Jack ran. Jack played.*
      (2) transformation: *Jane and Jack ran and played.* (Morrow, 1978)

Semantics deals with the meaning that language communicates, both through content words and through function words. It largely governs vocabulary development. *Content words* carry meaning in themselves. *Function words* have no easily definable meanings in isolation, but they indicate relationships between other words in a sentence. Function words include prepositions, conjunctions, and determiners (Pflaum, 1986).

Although we have identified stages of language growth, the pace of development may differ from child to child. An individual child's language development also tends to progress and then regress, so that the stages of growth are not always easy to recognize. However, language development has been studied to the extent that it can be described generally.

From Birth to One Year

In the first few months of infancy, oral language consists of a child's experimenting or playing with sounds. Infants cry when they are uncomfortable and babble, gurgle, or coo when they are happy. Parents are able to distinguish cries. One cry is for hunger and another is for pain, for instance. Infants learn to communicate specific needs by producing different cries. They communicate nonverbally as well as by moving their arms and legs to express pleasure or pain.

When babies are about six months old, their babbling becomes more sophisticated. They are usually capable of combining a variety of consonant sounds with vowel sounds. They tend to repeat these combinations over and over. As mentioned, it is at this stage that parents sometimes think they are hearing their child's first words. The repeated consonant and vowel sounds, such as *da, da, da,* or *ma, ma, ma,* do sound like real words, ones that the parents are delighted to hear. Most parents reinforce the child's behavior positively at this stage. Repetition of specific sounds and continued reinforcement lead the child to associate the physical mechanics of making a particular sound with the meaning of the word the sound represents.

From eight to twelve months, children increase their comprehension of language dramatically; their understanding of language far exceeds their ability to produce it. They do, however, tend to speak their first words, usually those most familiar and meaningful to them in their daily lives: *Mommy, Daddy, bye-bye, baby, cookie, milk, juice,* and *no,* for instance. As they become experienced with their first words, children use holophrases—one-word utterances that express an entire sentence (Au, Depretto, & Song, 1994). For example, a baby might say "cookie," but mean "I want a cookie," "My cookie is on the floor," or "I'm done with this cookie."

From One to Two

A child's oral language grows a great deal between the ages of one and two. Along with one-word utterances, the child utters many sounds with adult intonation as if speaking in sentences. These utterances are not understandable to adults, however. Children begin to use telegraphic speech from 12 months on—the first evidence of their knowledge of syntax. Telegraphic speech uses content words, such as nouns and verbs, but omits function words, such as conjunctions and articles. In spite of the omissions, words are delivered in correct order, or syntax: "Daddy home" for "Daddy is coming home soon," or "Toy fall" for "My toy fell off the table."

Language grows tremendously once the child begins to combine words. By 18 months most children can pronounce four-fifths of the English phonemes and use 20 to 50 words (Bloom, 1990).

From Two to Three

The year between ages two and three is probably the most dramatic in terms of language development. Typically, a child's oral vocabulary grows from 300 words to 1000. The child can comprehend, but cannot yet use, 2000 to 3000 additional words. Telegraphic sentences of two or three words continue to be most frequent, but syntactic complexity continues to develop, and the child occasionally uses such functional words as pronouns, conjunctions, prepositions, articles, and possessives. As their language ability grows, children gain confidence. They actively play with language by repeating new words and phrases and making up nonsense words. They enjoy rhyme, patterns of language, and repetition (Bloom, 1990). Consider the following transcription of Jennifer's dialogue with her dog. Jennifer was two years ten months at the time. "Nice doggie, my doggie, white doggie, whitey, nicey doggie. Good doggie, my doggie, boggie, poggie. Kiss doggie, kiss me, doggie, good doggie." Jennifer's language is repetitive, playful, silly, and creative, demonstrating some of the characteristics of language production typical for a child her age.

From Three to Four

A child's vocabulary and knowledge of sentence structure continue to develop rapidly during the fourth year. Syntactic structures added to the child's repertoire include plurals and regular verbs. Indeed, children of this age are prone to overgeneralization in using these two structures, mainly because both plural formation and verb inflection are highly irregular in the English language (Jewell & Zintz, 1986). Four-year-old Jesse illustrated both problems when he had an accident in class and came running over very upset. He said, "Mrs. Morrow, hurry over, I knocked over the fishbowl and it broked and all the fishes are swimming on the floor." Jesse knew how to form the past tense of a verb by adding *ed*, but he did not know about irregular verbs such as *broke*. He also knew about adding an *s* to form a plural but again was unaware of irregular plural forms such as *fish*.

As they approach age four, children *seem* to have acquired all the elements of adult language. They can generate language and apply the basic rules that govern it. However, although their ability with language has grown enormously and they sound almost as if they are using adult speech, children have acquired only the basic foundations. Language continues to grow throughout our lives as we gain new experiences, acquire new vocabulary, and find new ways of putting words together to form sentences. At the age of three to four, children talk about what they do as they are doing it. They often talk to themselves or by themselves as they play. It seems as if they are trying to articulate their actions (Seefeldt & Barbour, 1986). While painting at an easel, four-year-old Christopher said to himself, "I'm making a nice picture. I'm making colors all over. I'm painting, pit, pat, pit, pat. I'm going back and forth and up and down. Now I'm jumping as I paint." As he talked and painted, he did exactly what he said, words and actions coinciding.

From Five to Six

Five- and six-year-olds sound very much like adults when they speak. Their vocabularies are always increasing, and so is the syntactic complexity of their language. They have vocabularies of approximately 2500 words, and they are extremely articulate. Many, however, still have difficulty pronouncing some sounds, especially *l*, *r*, and *sh* at the ends of words. They become aware that a word can have more than one meaning. When they are embarrassed or frustrated at misunderstanding things, they say something silly or try to be humorous. They also tend to be creative in using language. When they do not have a word for a particular situation, they supply their own. Adults often find the language used by children of this age to be amusing as well as delightful and interesting (Seefeldt & Barbour, 1986):

> *Benjamin ran into school very excited one morning. "Mrs. Morrow," he said, "you'll never believe it. My dog grew puppies last night!"*
>
> *My husband and I were going to a formal dance one evening. My five-year-old daughter had never seen us dressed up like this before. When I walked into the room wearing a long gown and asked Stephanie how I looked, she said, "Mommy, you look soooo pretty. What is Daddy's costume going to be like?"*
>
> *Escorted by her mother, Allison was on her way to her first day of kindergarten. She seemed a little nervous. When her mother asked her if she was okay, Allison replied, "Oh, I'm fine, Mommy. It's just that my stomach is very worried."*

There are other characteristics of kindergarteners' language. Kindergartners have discovered bathroom talk and curse words, and they enjoy shocking others by using them. They talk a lot and begin to use language to control situations. Their language reflects their movement from a world of fantasy to that of reality.

From Seven to Eight

By the time children are seven years of age, they have developed a grammar that is almost equivalent to that of adults. Of course they do not use the extensive numbers of grammatical transformations found in adult language nor do they have the extent of vocabulary found in adult speech. Seven- and eight-year-olds are good conversationalists who talk a lot about what they do.

Recognizing Language Differences in Young Children

A major instructional concern in early childhood literacy programs is the varied language backgrounds of the children who come to day-care centers, preschools, kindergartens, and first, second, and third grades. Any given group may contain children using words, syntax, and language patterns quite different from those of standard English. Particularly in the United States, there are many different forms of English usage. There are, for example, distinct grammars in rural New England, Appalachia, and some African American communities. There are children whose families have immigrated from Latin America, the Middle East, or Asia. In the United States about one in every three children is from an ethnic or racial minority group, and one in every seven children speaks a language other than English as their first language (Milamontes, Nadeau, & Commins, 1997). Foster (1982, p. 14) compiled the following six categories that represent the diverse language abilities of young children.

Diverse Language Abilities of Children

1. Recent immigrants with little or no English.
2. Children whose home language is something other than English, but who are themselves likely to know at least some English because of their experiences with television and their contacts outside the home.
3. Children who speak both English and another language fluently. Such children are usually easily assimilated into the majority group. Often English becomes the major language with which they communicate. They then risk losing the advantages that bilingualism gives them.
4. Children who speak mainly English but who have poor skills in their parents' or family's language. Often these children speak English at home, but their parents speak to them in another language. Children in this group sometimes deny their heritage and are ashamed of the cultural differences between themselves and their English-only-speaking classmates at school.
5. Children who speak nonstandard English because the English spoken at home is nonfluent or a dialect. Although they need to learn a more standard English at school, they must not be made to feel that their home language is inferior.

6. The majority of children, those who are monolingual in a pluralistic society. Their "understanding and appreciation of the various cultures in America," said Foster, "would be greatly enhanced through study in another language besides English."

All six categories represent major concerns because a firm base in oral language is strongly linked to literacy development. A child fluent in any form of nonstandard English may have difficulty reading and writing without some proficiency in standard English. Along with this concern for skill development are affective concerns. Unfortunately, we have often looked down on children with language differences and classified them as students with potential learning problems. We have come to realize, however, that differences do *not* mean deficits. Linguists have found, for example, that black English is a systematic, rule-governed dialect that can express all levels of thought. Teachers must be sensitive to the differences in language among youngsters in their classrooms. Children must not be embarrassed or made to feel inferior because they do not speak standard English. Teachers need to respect language differences and help children take pride in their backgrounds. Diversity in language and heritage should be shared in classrooms to enrich the classroom experience (Neuman & Reskos, 1994).

Children's Responses to Language Differences

Children tend to choose playmates who speak the same language, presumably because it is easier to communicate. They usually do not reject those who speak a different language, however, and will use gestures and other means of communication when interacting with them. Bilingual children will often act as interpreters for their parents and friends who are less skilled in the language of the classroom. Although children are curious about differences in speech and will often "correct" one another, they have not developed the biases that adults have toward nonstandard usage.

Children must become somewhat fluent in the language used at school in order to understand daily routines, directing, and so forth. And if they are expected to read standard English, they need a foundation in speaking standard English. According to Pflaum (1986), young children do not have much difficulty acquiring new language. She suggests that the typical preschool seems to provide a linguistic environment that enables young children to learn standard English if they are encouraged to speak it. An environment that provides varied experiences and opportunities to converse helps children acquire the ability to speak the language. Children who speak nonstandard dialects, such as black English, need the opportunity to use their own dialects in school during creative dramatics or in storytelling and discussions. Any child given the opportunity to use language frequently and effectively, even if it is not standard English, will be receptive to language learning in general (Robinson, Strickland, & Cullinan, 1977). Frequent opportunity to use language in varied situations will help children become more fluent. As Gonzales-Mena (1976, p. 14) has pointed out:

1. Children are eager to learn English or any other new language when there is an openness and an acceptance of them, their culture, and their native language.
2. Language should not be taught in isolation from any of the other basic school activities, but as a part of the total, integrated program, which in-

cludes a focus on language development. Listening, speaking, reading, and writing are all a part of math, social studies, art, and science.

3. Children learn through their senses, including their muscles. Concepts as well as new words and phrases are learned better when children can participate in some action. They need to examine and explore real objects and act out new expressions.

Younger children who do not speak English will acquire the language easily before age five, if they have good models of English and a sensitive teacher. To avoid inhibiting literacy development, however, it is recommended that schools have bilingual classrooms for primary-grade children. In bilingual classrooms, children learn to read and write in their first language while learning English. This type of learning setting promotes literacy development and supports children's family experiences as they acquire a new language (Ramirez, Yuen, Ramey, & Pasta, 1991; Delgado-Gaitan, 1992; Garcia & McLaughlin, 1995). It is crucial that children remain proficient in their first language as they learn English.

The strategies to help develop young children's language discussed on the following pages also will be successful with children who have language differences or special language needs.

Strategies for Language Development

The review of theory and research suggests how we can help children acquire and develop language pleasantly, productively, and appropriately. Children acquire language by emulating adult models, interacting with others when using language, and experiencing positive reinforcement for their efforts. If language is innate, it can develop naturally as individuals pass through common stages of development at certain times in their lives. As children mature, they become capable of generating ever more complex language structures. They learn language by doing, by acting on and within familiar environments. Their first spoken words are those that are meaningful for them within their own experiences. Their earliest language is an expression of needs. They learn language through social interaction with individuals more literate than they, whether adults or older children. Children also create their own language, play with it, and engage in monologues.

Using what we know of language acquisition and developmental stages as guidelines, we can begin to create appropriate materials, activities, and experiences in a suitable atmosphere to nurture children's language development. The following objectives are formulated for a program fostering language development in children from birth to age eight.

Objectives for Receptive Language Development

1. Provide children with an atmosphere in which they will hear language frequently.
2. Allow children the opportunity to associate the language that they hear with pleasure and enjoyment.
3. Give children the opportunity to discriminate and classify sounds they hear.
4. Expose children to a rich source of new words on a regular basis.

5. Offer children the opportunity to listen to others and demonstrate that they understand what is said.
6. Provide children with opportunities for following directions.
7. Provide children with good models of standard English, and allow them to hear their home language in school.

Objectives for Expressive Language Development

1. Give opportunities for children to use their own language freely at any stage of development. This could be a different dialect or mixtures of English and Spanish. Their desire to communicate should be encouraged, accepted, and respected.
2. Encourage children to pronounce words correctly.
3. Help children increase their speaking vocabularies.
4. Encourage children to speak in complete sentences at appropriate stages in their development.
5. Give children opportunities to expand their use of various syntactic structures, such as adjectives, adverbs, prepositional phrases, dependent clauses, plurals, past tense, and possessives.
6. Encourage children to communicate with others so that they can be understood.
7. Give children the opportunity to use language socially and psychologically by interpreting feelings, points of view, and motivation and by solving problems through generating hypotheses, summarizing events, and predicting outcomes.
8. Give children opportunities to develop language that involve mathematical and logical relations, such as describing size and amount, making comparisons, defining sets and classes, and reasoning deductively.
9. Provide children with the opportunity to talk in many different settings: in the whole group with the teacher leading the discussion, in teacher-led small groups, in child-directed groups for learning, or in conversation in social settings.

Providing children with rich sources of new words in storybook reading, for example, will develop receptive language and vocabulary.

Language is best learned when it is integrated with other communication skills and embedded within topics or content areas that have meaning for children. Approaching language development, reading, and writing as skills to be taught in isolation without meaning or function will not promote the development of lifelong literacy. Children are constructive learners; they are active meaning makers who are continuously interpreting and making sense of their world based on what they already know.

Language is the major system by which meanings are communicated and expressed in our world. Because language is used for various purposes, our meanings are expressed in various ways. Language cannot be understood or interpreted unless it is related to some meaningful context. Language is learned through use, as part of our daily social activities. In addition to being aware of all of the above, we need to accept language differences and help youngsters with special needs acquire skills and develop, enhance, and practice language. (Pappas, Kiefer, & Levstik, 1995).

Strategies for Language Development from Birth to Two

"Hi, Michael. How's my great big boy today? Let's change your diaper now, upsy-daisy. My goodness, you're getting heavy. Now I'll put you down right here on your dressing table and get a nice new diaper for you. Here, want this rubber ducky to hold while I change you? That's a good boy. You really like him. Let's clean you up now. This is the way we clean up Michael, clean up Michael, clean up Michael. This is the way we clean up Michael, so he'll feel so much better. You like that singing, don't you. I can tell. You're just smiling away, and cooing. Want to do that again? This is the way we clean up Michael, clean up Michael, clean up Michael. This is the way we clean up Michael, so he'll feel so much better. Wow, you were singing with me that time. That's right, ba-ba-ba-ba, now do it again. Mmmmm, doesn't that smell good? The baby powder is so nice and smooth."

DEVELOPING LANGUAGE IN THE CHILD'S FIRST YEAR. Michael was four months old when his mother's conversation with him was taped. Here in print, it reads like a monologue; in reality. Michael was a very active participant in the conversation. He stared intently at his mother's face. He cooed, he waved his arms, he smiled, and he became serious. His mother was providing a rich language environment for her baby. She encouraged his participation in the dialogue and acknowledged his responsiveness in a positive way. She provided him with the environmental stimuli necessary for his innate language ability to flourish. She engaged him in this type of conversation during feedings and while changing, bathing, and dressing him. She talked to him even when he was in his crib and she in another room, or while in the same room but involved in other things. The baby knew that communication was occurring because he responded to the talk with body movements, coos, babbles, and smiles. When he responded his mother responded in turn.

Surround Infants with Sounds. Infants need to be surrounded by the sounds of happy language. Whether from mother, father, caregiver at home, or teacher or aide in a day-care center, sounds and interaction should accompany all activities. Adults responsible for babies from birth through the first year need to know nursery rhymes, chants, finger plays, and songs. It is important for children simply to hear the *sounds* of language as well as the meanings. Thus, adults can make up their own chants to suit an occasion, as Michael's mother did when she spontaneously adapted "Here We Go Round the Mulberry Bush" to the situation at hand. Such experiences make the baby conscious of the sounds of language. Children learn that they can have control over language and that oral language can be a powerful tool as well as fun.

In addition to the conversation of nearby adults, infants should experience other sounds and other voices: soft music from a radio, record player, or music box. They need to hear the sounds of "book language," which differs in intonation, pitch, stress, juncture, and even syntax from normal conversation. They need familiarity with language in all its variety so they can learn to differentiate among its various conventions and patterns. Speaking to infants, singing to them, reading to them, and letting them hear the radio and television provide sources of language that help their own language grow. In addition, there are sounds in the immediate environment that need no preparation and are not the sounds of language but that provide practice in auditory discrimination—the doorbell ringing, the teapot hissing, the clock chiming, the vacuum cleaner humming, a dog barking, a bird singing, a car screeching, and so on. Bring them to the baby's attention, give them names, and heighten the child's sensitivity to them.

Surround Infants with Sensory Objects. In addition to hearing a variety of sounds, babies need objects to see, touch, smell, hear, and taste. Objects should be placed in the baby's immediate environment—the crib or playpen. They will stimulate the baby's activity and curiosity and become the meaningful things within the environment from which language evolves. Some of the objects should make sounds or music when pushed or touched. They can have different textures and smells. They should be easy to grab, push, kick, or pull. They can be placed so they are visible and within the child's reach, and at least one item should be suspended overhead: stuffed animals, rubber toys, music boxes made of soft material, plastic or wooden mobiles that can be kicked or grasped, mechanical mobiles that hang from the ceiling and rotate by themselves, and books with smooth edges. Books can be propped open against the side of the crib or playpen when the baby is lying on its back, or against the headboard when the baby is on its stomach. Certain familiar objects should always remain, and new objects frequently should be made available. In addition to allowing the child to play independently with these objects, the adults in charge need to talk about them, name them, occasionally join the child in playing with them, and discuss their characteristics.

From three to six months, the baby gurgles, coos, begins to laugh, and babbles. Adults or caregivers should recognize an infant's sounds as the beginning of language and reinforce the infant positively with responses aimed at encouraging the sounds. When the baby begins to put consonants and vowels together, again adults should reinforce the behavior, imitating what the baby has uttered and urging repetition. When the baby becomes aware of the ability to repeat sounds and control language output, he or she will do these things. Babies also will begin to understand adult language, so it is important to name objects, carry on conversations, and give the baby directions. At the end of its first year, assuming he or she has experienced appropriate sounds of language as well as encouragement and pleasant interaction, the baby will be on the verge of extensive language growth during its second year.

LANGUAGE DEVELOPMENT AT AGES ONE AND TWO. Through the second year of a child's life, the adults in charge need to continue the same kinds of stimulation suggested for developing oral language during the first year. However, because the baby is likely to develop a vocabulary of up to 150 words and to produce two- and possibly three-word sentences during the second year, additional techniques can be used to enhance language growth. As described earlier, one- and two-word utterances by children at this age usually represent sentences. When a 12-month-old points to a teddy bear and says "bear," the child probably means "I want my bear." Parents and caregivers at home or in day-care centers can begin to expand and extend the child's language at such times by helping increase the number of words the child is able to use in a sentence or by increasing the syntactic complexity of their own utterances.

Scaffolding to Help Language Develop. One method for helping a child develop language ability is a kind of modeling called *scaffolding* (Applebee & Langer, 1983). In scaffolding, an adult provides a verbal response for a baby who is not yet capable of making the response itself. In other words, the adult provides a language model. When the baby says "bear," for instance, the adult responds, "Do you want your teddy bear?" or "Here is your nice, soft, brown teddy bear." In addition to expanding on the child's language, the adult can extend it by asking the youngster to do something that demonstrates understanding and extends his or her thinking. For example, "Here is your nice, soft, brown teddy bear. Can you hug the teddy? Let me see you hug him." In addition to questions that require action, the adult can ask questions that require answers. Questions that require answers of more than one word are preferable—for example, "Tell me about the clothes your teddy is wearing." *How, why,* and *tell me* questions encourage the child to give more than a yes/no answer and more than a one-word response. *What, who, when,* and *where* questions, on the other hand, tend to elicit only one-word replies. As the child's language ability develops, the adult provides fewer and fewer such "scaffolds"; the child learns to build utterances along similar models.

New Experiences Help Develop Language. Adults should select songs, rhymes, and books for one- to two-year-olds that use language they can understand. They are capable of understanding a great deal of language by now, and the selections should help expand and extend their language. Both vocabulary and conceptual understanding are enhanced by experiences. For the one- to two-year-old, frequent outings such as visits to the post office, supermarket, dry cleaners, and park provide experiences to talk about and new concepts to explore. Household tasks taken for granted by adults are new experiences that enrich children's language. Involve them in activities. For example, an 18-month-old can put a piece of laundry into the washing machine or give one stir to the bowl of food being prepared. During such daily routines, adults should surround the activity with language, identifying new objects for the baby and asking for responses related to each activity (Schickedanz, York, Stewart, & White, 1990).

Overgeneralizations and Language Development. As children become more verbal, adults sometimes want to correct their mispronunciations or overgeneralization of grammatical rules. The child who says, "Me feeded fishes," for instance, has simply overgeneralized the rules for the following:

- forming most past tenses (*feeded* for *fed*)
- using pronouns (objective *me* for subjective *I*) and
- forming most plurals (*fishes* for *fish*)

Children also can overgeneralize concepts. A child who has learned to associate a bird with the word *bird* might see a butterfly for the first time and call it a bird, thinking that anything that flies is a bird. Correcting such an overgeneralization is best done positively rather than negatively. Instead of saying, "No, that's not a bird," it is better to refer to the butterfly as a *butterfly,* commenting on its beauty, perhaps, and thus expanding the child's verbal repertoire. Eventually, with positive reinforcement and proper role models in language, the child will differentiate between birds and butterflies as well as between regular and irregular grammatical conventions and forms.

Correcting overgeneralizations negatively as absolute error, alternatively, is not likely to help young children understand the error or use proper tense and plural forms. Rather, it is likely to inhibit the child from trying to use language. In learning, children need to take risks and make mistakes. Hearing good adult models will eventually enable them to internalize the rules of language and to correct their errors themselves. At least until age five, children should be allowed to experiment and play with language without direct concern for 100 percent correctness in syntax and pronunciation. The English language is extremely complex and irregular in many of its rules; in time, children will master these rules in all their complexity, if they have good adult models and plenty of verbal interaction. At the same time, encouraging "baby talk" simply because it is cute, for instance, is likely to inhibit growth because children will use whatever language they believe will please the adults around them.

Materials for Language Development at One and Two. Materials for the one- to two-year-old should be varied and more sophisticated than those in the first year. Now that the baby is mobile in the home or day-care center, books need to be easily accessible to the child. Toys should still include items of various textures, such as furry, stuffed animals and rubber balls. Other toys should require simple eye–hand coordination. Three-to-five–piece puzzles, trucks that can be pushed and pulled, dolls, a child-size set of table and chairs, crayons and large paper, and puppets are examples. Choose objects that require activity, for activity encourages exploration, use of the imagination, creation, and the need to communicate.

Strategies for Language Development in Early Childhood Classrooms

From ages three to seven a great deal of language development occurs. Children should continue to hear good models of language. They need constant opportunities to use language in social situations with adults and other children. Their oral language production must be reinforced positively. They must be actively involved in meaningful experiences that will expand their knowledge and interest in the world around them. Language should be purposeful and its development integrated with other subjects rather than taught separately.

To accomplish these continuing goals, early childhood teachers provide an environment in which language will flourish. They organize centers of learning, one for each content area, that include materials for encouraging language use. A science center, for instance, can include class pets such as a pair of gerbils. Gerbils are active, loving animals that are fun to watch and handle. Children surround the cage often and generate talk just from watching the animals. Gerbils reproduce in 28-day cycles. When litters arrive, the birth process can be observed. The new babies cause much excitement and generate questions, comments, and unlimited conversation.

In my own classroom, our parent gerbils reproduced a second litter 28 days after the first and before the first babies had been weaned. The mother looked tired and thin from feeding and caring for 10 baby gerbils. One morning one of the children noticed that the mother was not in the cage. We could not imagine what had happened to her. A few days later, we found her hiding behind the refrigerator in the teachers' room. We never figured out how she got out of the cage, but we hypothesized all kinds of possibilities, and there was lots of discussion about why she left. No teacher alone could provide a lesson in which language flourished and grew the way it did during that incident, simply because gerbils were part of the classroom.

CENTER MATERIALS FOR LANGUAGE DEVELOPMENT. Here are some examples of learning centers and appropriate materials in early childhood classrooms that will help generate language:

Science: aquarium, terrarium, plants, magnifying glass, class pet, magnets, thermometer, compass, prism, shells, rock collections, stethoscope, kaleidoscope, microscope, informational books and children's literature reflecting topics being studied, and blank journals for recording observations of experiments and scientific projects.

Social Studies: maps, a globe, flags, community figures, traffic signs, current events, artifacts from other countries, informational books and children's literature reflecting topics being studied, and writing materials to make class books or your own books about topics being studied.

Art: easels, watercolors, brushes, colored pencils, crayons, felt-tip markers, various kinds of paper, scissors, paste, pipe cleaners, scrap materials (bits of various fabrics, wool, string, and so forth), clay, play dough, food and detergent boxes for sculptures, books about famous artists, and books with directions for crafts.

Music: piano, record player and records, tape recorder with musical tapes, rhythm instruments, songbooks, and photocopies of sheet music for songs sung in class.

Varied art experiences with different media encourage descriptive language and develop the manual dexterity needed for writing.

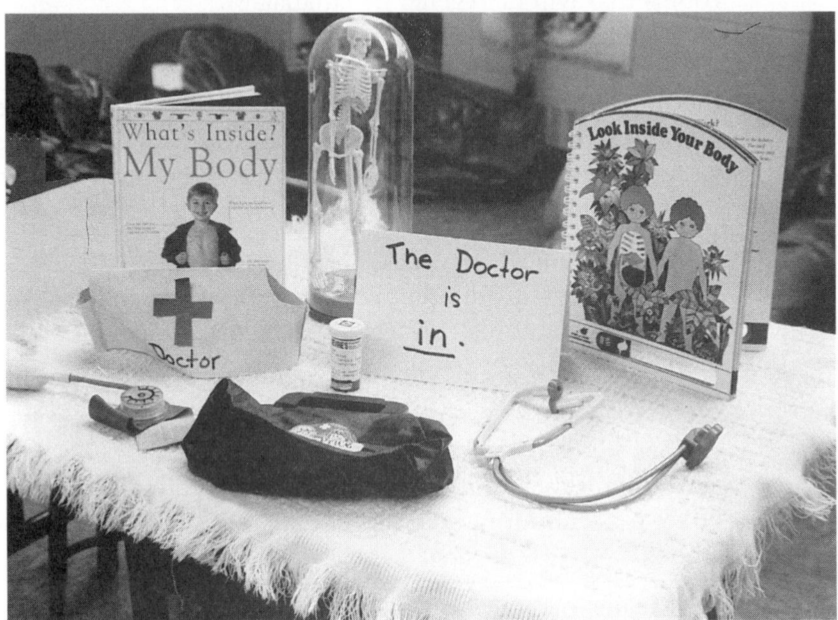

Experiences with science themes lead to new discoveries, new vocabulary, and reasons to talk and discuss.

Mathematics: scales, rulers, measuring cups, movable clocks, stopwatch, calendar, play money, cash register, calculator, dominoes, abacus, number line, height chart, hourglass, numbers (felt, wood, and magnetic), fraction puzzles, geometric shapes, math workbooks, children's literature about numbers and mathematics, writing materials for creating stories, and books related to mathematics.

Literacy: children's literature, tape recorder, headsets and taped stories, pencils, writing paper, stapler, construction paper, three-by-five cards for recording words, hole punch, letter stencils, typewriter, computer, puppets, storytelling devices such as felt-board and roll movies, stationery with envelopes, letters (felt, wood, and magnetic), sets of pictures for different units (Halloween, seasons, animals, and so on), rhyme games, color games, cards for associating sounds and symbols, alphabet cards, and pictures and words representing out-of-school environmental print. (The literacy center also includes a library corner, a writing center, oral language materials, and language arts manipulatives, all of which are described in later chapters.)

Dramatic Play: dolls, dress-ups, telephone, stuffed animals, mirror, food cartons, plates, silverware, newspapers, magazines, books, telephone book, class telephone book, cookbook, note pads, cameras and photo album, table and chairs, broom, dustpan, child-size kitchen furniture such as refrigerator, sink, ironing board, and storage shelves. (The dramatic-play area can be changed from a kitchen to a grocery store, beauty shop, gas station, business office, restaurant, etc., with the addition of materials for appropriate themes when they are studied.) Include appropriate materials for reading and writing related to the theme of the dramatic-play area.

Block Area: blocks of many different sizes and shapes and figures of people, animals, toy cars, trucks, items related to themes being studied, paper and pencils to prepare signs and notes, and reading materials related to themes.

Workbench: wood, hammer, screwdriver, saw, pliers, nails, and work table.

Outdoor Play: sand, water, pails, shovels, rakes, gardening area and gardening tools, climbing equipment, riding toys, crates, playhouse, balls, tires, and ropes.

Children need opportunities to use such areas for interacting with one another and the teacher. They should be given enough time to touch, smell, taste, listen, and talk about what they are doing. Exploring and experimenting with the materials in the centers are creative, imaginative, problem-solving, decision-making experiences in which children use language. The opportunity to *use* language is one of the key elements in language development.

Some materials remain permanently in the centers; others are replaced or supplemented occasionally so that new items of interest become available. Materials added to the centers are often coordinated with thematic units of instruction. For example, if a unit on Native Americans is introduced, Native American dolls and artifacts are added to the social studies center, and books about Native Americans to the literacy center. The different content-area centers provide sources for language use and development; the literacy center is devoted *primarily* to language development. Thematic units of instruction that integrate all areas make learning more meaningful and expand concepts. (Interdisciplinary instruction is described more fully in Chapter 10.)

DEVELOPING LANGUAGE WITH STRATEGIES USED IN THEMATIC UNITS. Each new unit of instruction offers specific language experiences that expand vocabulary, syntax, pronunciation, and the ability to understand others and be understood. Again, these experiences should incorporate all content areas and make use of the senses (Tompkins & Koskisson, 1995). The suggestions that follow can be used each time a new theme is initiated. They reflect or describe activities designed to aid language growth in early childhood classrooms. For purposes of illustration, assume that the topic throughout these suggestions is *winter.*

Discussion: Hold discussions about the unit topic. What is the weather like in winter? What kind of clothing do children need to wear in winter? What fun things can they do in winter that they can not do at other times of the year? What

Experiences related to themes generate oral language that can be written down and then read.

problems does winter bring? What is winter like in different parts of the country, for example, New York, Florida, and California?

Word Lists: Ask the children to name every word they can think of that makes them think of winter. Your list might eventually include *snow, ice, cold, white, wet, freezing, sleds, snowman, mittens, scarf, hat, slush, skiing, ice skating, snowballs, fireplace,* and *snowflakes.* Classify the words on the list into how winter feels, looks, smells, sounds, and tastes, or what you can and cannot do in winter. List the words on a chart, and hang the chart in the room. Leave the chart hanging when you go to the next unit. When the wall gets too crowded, compile the charts in a class book.

Pictures: Provide pictures of winter scenes for discussion, each depicting different information about the season.

Sharing Time (Show and Tell): Hold a sharing period during which children bring things from home related to the topic. Give all the children an opportunity to share if they wish, but assign different children for different days, because sharing by more than five or six children in one period can become tedious. Sharing objects from home is an important activity. It gives children confidence because they are talking about something from their own environment. Even the shyest children will speak in front of a group if they have the security of sharing something familiar from home. Encourage children to relate the items to the unit topic, if they can. Model language for children to encourage them to speak in sentences. Coordinate the activity with parents, informing them of their children's scheduled sharing and the general topic under discussion.

Experiments: Carry out a science experiment related to the topic being studied. Involve the children actively. Discuss the purpose and hypothesize what is likely to happen. Encourage children to discuss what they are doing while they are doing it. When the experiment is complete, discuss the results with the class. (Example: Allow water to freeze, then melt. In warm climates use the refrigerator for freezing the water.)

Art: Carry out an art activity related to the topic; the activity should be process oriented rather than teacher directed. Allow children to create their own work rather than making them follow specific directions that yield identical results from child to child. Discuss the project and the available materials before the activity. Provide interesting materials and encourage children to touch, describe, and compare them. While children are creating, it is natural for them to converse about what they are doing. Encourage such conversation. For example, provide blue construction paper, tin foil, white doilies, cotton, wool, tissue paper, and chalk for a winter collage. Discuss why these colors and objects were selected. What is there about them that makes people think of winter? Suggest creating a picture that makes someone think of winter. Discuss the textures of the materials and what can be done with them.

Music: Sing songs about winter, such as "It's a Marshmallow World in the Winter." Music is enjoyable and lyrics help build vocabulary and sensitivity to the sounds and meanings of words. Listen to music without words, music that creates images concerning the topic. Ask the children for words, sentences, or stories that the music brings to mind.

Food Preparation: Prepare food related to the unit. Make hot soup, flavored snowballs, or popcorn. Discuss food textures, smells, taste, and appearance. Follow directions and recipes, developing sequence as well as quantitative sense. Allow children to help prepare the food, then enjoy consuming it together, encouraging discussion and conversation throughout about the activity. Food

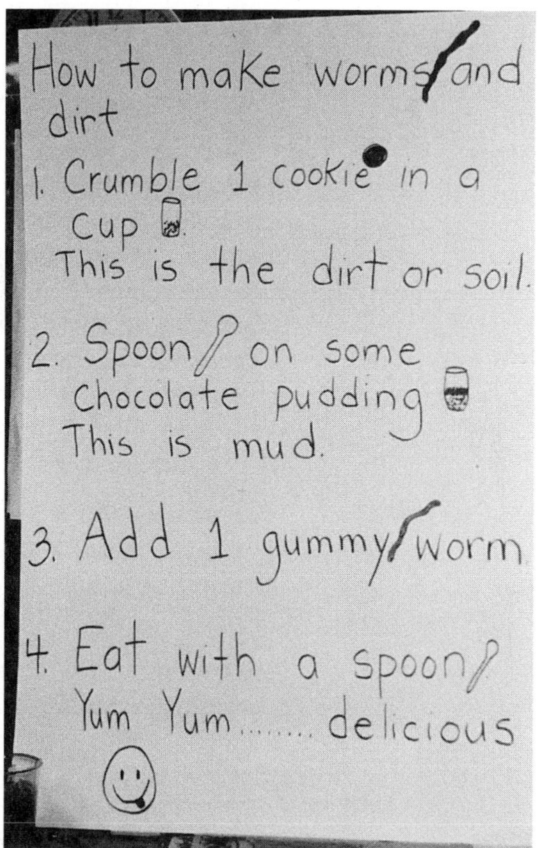

Children have fun with language and silly food preparation.

preparation can be a source of new vocabulary, especially because many of its terms take on special meanings—*stir, blend, boil, measure.*

Dramatic Play: Add items related to the topic to the dramatic-play area—mittens, hats, scarves, boots for dress-up—to encourage role-playing and language about winter. Introduce them by placing each in a separate bag and asking a child to reach in, describe what it feels like, and identify it without peeking. The sense of touch elicits descriptive language.

Outdoor Play: Encourage spontaneous language and frequent problem-solving situations during outdoor play. For example, provide snow shovels, sleds, pails, and cups during playtime in the snow. Discuss outdoor play before going out, and again after coming in.

Morning Message: Discuss weather and the calendar in a daily morning message. Encourage children to share news about themselves: a new pair of sneakers, a birthday. Make plans for the school day.

Class Trips: Take the class on a trip, bring in a guest speaker, or show a film. All three activities can generate language and encourage its use.

Read Stories: Read stories to the children about the topic under study. Books such as *Katy and the Big Snow* (Burton, 1943) enhance information and expand vocabulary.

Create Stories: Provide the children with a title, such as "The Big Winter Snowstorm," and let them think of a story about it.

Retell Stories: Ask children to retell stories. This activity encourages them to use book language and incorporate it into their own. Retelling is not always an easy task for young children, so props can be helpful—puppets, felt-boards and felt characters, roll movies, and pictures in a book. With these same props, children can make up their own stories as well.

Very Own Words: In any of these activities, children should be encouraged as often as possible to select their favorite Very Own Words about winter. Favorite Very Own Words can be selected from discussions, art lessons, science experiments, songs, books, poems, cooking experiences, or any other activity. After a particular experience, ask children to name a favorite word. Record children's favorite Very Own Words for them on three-by-five cards and store them in each child's own file box or on a binder ring. When children are capable of recording their own words, assist them with spelling when they ask for help. Favorite Very Own Words enhance vocabulary and are a source for reading and writing development.

Summary of the Day: Summarize the day's events at the end of the school day, encouraging children to tell what they liked, did not like, and want to do the next day in school.

CHILDREN'S LITERATURE AND LANGUAGE DEVELOPMENT. Among more general suggestions, select and offer children's literature that represents varieties of language and experience. Some children's books, such as *Too Much Noise* (McGovern, 1967), feature the sounds of language; they aid auditory discrimination or incorporate additional phonemes into a child's language repertoire. Others help develop the syntactic complexity of a child's language through embeddings and transformations and the use of numerous adjectives and adverbs—

A felt-board with story characters will help children use book language as they retell stories.

for example, *Swimmy* (Lionni, 1963). Craft books require children to follow directions. Wordless books encourage them to create their own stories from the pictures. Concept books feature words such as *up, down, in, out, near,* and *far,* or involve children in mathematical reasoning. Realistic literature deals with death, divorce, loneliness, fear, and daily problems; discussion of such themes leads to sociopsychological language, interpretation of feelings, sensitivity to others, and problem solving. Books of riddles, puns, jokes, and tongue twisters show children how language plays on meaning in certain situations. Poetry introduces children to rhyme, metaphor, simile, and onomatopoeia, and encourages them to recite and create poems. (Children's books are listed by these and other categories in Appendix A.) When children hear and discuss the language of books, they internalize what they have heard; the language soon becomes part of their own language. Research studies have found that children who are read to frequently develop more sophisticated language structures and increased vocabulary (Cohen, 1968; Lenz, 1992).

Two anecdotes illustrate how children incorporate into their own language the language of books that have been read to them. My kindergarten class was playing on the playground one early spring day. A few birds circled around several times. Melissa ran up to me and said, "Look, Mrs. Morrow, the birds are fluttering and flapping around the playground." Surprised at first by Melissa's descriptive and unusual choice of words, I thought for a moment, then remembered. The words that Melissa was using came directly from a picture storybook we had read shortly before, *Jenny's Hat* (Keats, 1966). In the book, birds *flutter* and *flap* around Jenny's hat. Melissa had internalized the language of the book and was able to use it in her own vocabulary.

One day after a big snowstorm, my daughter asked, "Mommy, can I go out and play? I want to build a smiling snowman." I was surprised and pleased with this sophisticated language being uttered by my four-year-old. *Smiling snowman,* after all, represents a participle in the adjective position, a syntactic structure usually not found in the language of children before the age of seven or eight. Then I noticed that Stephanie had a book in her hand, *The Snowy Day* (Keats, 1962). In it Peter goes outside and builds a *smiling snowman.* Stephanie had used the book's language and made it her own.

The activities just suggested can be repeated throughout the school year with each new theme that is studied. Such adaptation and repetition make it possible to introduce children to hundreds of new vocabulary words, concepts, and ideas. They will assure children of opportunities to participate in new kinds of spontaneous language as topics and structured experiences change. Word lists and other materials produced during each unit can be maintained and made available for review and reuse.

Most of the suggestions can be followed at home as well as at school. Parents should not be expected to create elaborate centers or carry out units of instruction. But daily living offers holidays, seasons, family events, and other topics and events of special interest. Parents can tap such meaningful occasions for their potential enhancement of language development. They can discuss events, list words, help children collect favorite Very Own Words, involve children in cooking and household chores, take trips, read stories, sing songs, and generally encourage the use of language as a pleasurable activity and a useful skill.

In the learning environment described throughout this chapter, language development is spontaneous and also encouraged. Modeling, scaffolding, and reinforcement make this environment interactive between child and adult, and they guide and nurture language development to an extent that children are not likely to achieve on their own. The strategies discussed are appropriate for children who have language differences and minimal language disorders. These youngsters, however, may need additional attention on a one-to-one basis from the classroom teacher or a resource room teacher.

Expanding Vocabulary and Word Meaning in Second and Third Grade

I have suggested many strategies to develop vocabulary for children from birth through the early childhood grades. Following are strategies for children in second and third grades to help them increase their vocabulary and make connections with the meaning of words when reading text. These strategies also should enhance vocabulary used in their writing.

Semantic Maps: Semantic maps are diagrams that help children see how words are related to one another (Johnson & Pearson, 1984). To enrich vocabulary development and the meaning of words try the following:

1. Choose a word related to a student's interests or a theme that is being studied.
2. Write the word in the middle of a chalkboard or on a piece of experience chart paper. (See Chapter 7 for diagram samples.)
3. Brainstorm other words that are related to the key word.
4. Create categories for the new words that emerge and classify them into those categories.
5. Use the words to create a story. (Cox, 1999)

Context Clues: Using clues from surrounding text is an important way of figuring out word meanings. Leaving blanks in sentences for children to determine the appropriate word is an activity that helps them understand how to use context to find word meanings. Students need to know that this is one of the best ways to learn new words because they are embedded in meaningful text. The clues they use are other words or phrases in the sentence that tell something about unknown words. Clues can be before or after the unknown word and are usually close to the word. They could also be in sentences before or after. Have students guess the meaning of the word from the clues, then discuss if the guesses are correct.

Word Parts: Learning word parts is a way for second and third graders to build vocabulary and meaning. Choose word parts that are well-known prefixes and suffixes and commonly used roots of words. With knowledge of a few of these, children can begin to build their own words. Teach children to talk through the use of word parts to get the meaning. For example, when students learn word part meanings they can talk through their word building as follows: "I know that the prefix *dis* means "not," and I also know that the word *content* means to be happy or pleased. If I add *dis* to the word *content* it would be *discontent.* Now it would mean that someone was not happy.

The Dictionary: Using the dictionary is another way to add to a students repertoire of strategies to find and check meanings. Students must learn that words have many meanings and they all may be listed in the dictionary. Therefore, when using the dictionary, they need to select the meaning for the word that makes sense in the context in which it occurs. Dictionaries prepared for young children should be used in the primary grades (Graves, Juel, & Graves, 1998).

Formats for Promoting Language in the Classroom

By the time children come to school, they have had varied opportunities for talk in their daily lives. Most of the talk is spontaneous and deals with real-life experiences. With their parents, talk has included questions and answers, with parents directing the discussion or the children playing a more active role. I have discussed strategies that initiate talk. Here I will offer organizational structures in classrooms that will provide different types of talk experiences. These include teacher-directed question and answer discussions, small-group conversations to give and receive information, and spontaneous discussions that are led by the teacher or children in social settings. In addition, conversations that include different types of talk will be described.

In ***structured question and answer discussions,*** teachers need to provide open-ended questions that will encourage talk such as: What would happen if? What would you do if? and Tell us why?

Conversations occur best in small-group settings that include three to six children. Any number beyond that can no longer be considered a conversation, but a large-group discussion. Guidelines, such as those on page 118, need to be established for conversation to be productive.

Guidelines *Small-Group Conversations with the Teacher*

1. **Children should listen to others during conversations.**
2. **Children need to take turns talking.**
3. **Students should raise hands, if necessary to ensure everyone gets a turn, and individuals do not interrupt each other.**
4. **Everyone should keep talk relevant to the topic of conversation.**
5. **Teachers need to help redirect conversation to its stated purpose, should it stray.**
6. **Teacher talk should be kept to a minimum as he or she becomes a participant. Teachers should follow the same rules as the children: Listen to others when they are talking, take turns, do not do all the talking, etc.**

Guidelines *Formal Conversations without the Teacher*

A group leader needs to be selected to help direct the conversation when children are in charge of their own discussion. All of the same guidelines for productive conversation when the teacher is present apply when children direct conversations themselves.

1. **Children should listen to others during conversations.**
2. **Children need to take turns talking.**
3. **Students should raise hands, if necessary.**
4. **Everyone should keep the talk relevant to the conversation's purpose.**

Informal Conversations without the Teacher

Children need time to talk without leaders or specific outcomes. This type of conversation is likely to occur during free-play periods, center time, or outdoor play. Although classrooms that encourage this type of talk can be noisy, it is important for children to have the opportunity to use language in social settings at school.

In addition to learning the types of organizational structures in which talk should take place, students need to engage in different types of talk including aesthetic talk, efferent talk, and talk in dramatic activities.

Aesthetic talk typically revolves around children's literature. In this talk children have the opportunity to interpret what they have read or listened to. Children can participate in aesthetic talk when discussing literature, telling stories, and participating in Readers Theatre. These activities will be discussed further in Chapter 6, which deals with using children's literature in the classroom.

Efferent talk is used to inform and persuade. Efferent talk occurs in discussion of themes being studied. It also occurs in situations such as show-and-tell, oral reports, interviews, and debates. These types of interchange are more formal than previously discussed and often require preparation on the part of the child.

Dramatic activities provide another avenue for different types of talk. When children participate in dramatic activities, they share experiences, explore their understanding of ideas, and interact with peers. Dramatic experiences can in-

Children should be encouraged to engage in conversation as they work together in small groups.

clude informal role playing in dramatic-play areas of the classroom. Use of props and puppets to act out stories provides another avenue for talk.

A teacher who uses these organizational frameworks for language and has children engage in the types of activities that motivate talk will be providing a classroom rich in experiences and topics to talk about. In turn, language development will be enhanced.

Assessment of Children's Language Development

It is important to assess children's language to determine if it follows expected stages of development. Assessment also determines how much a child has progressed. The word *assessment* suggests several rather frequent measures by which to judge progress. Assessment should reflect instructional objectives and strategies. It should include evaluation of a wide range of skills used in many contexts. A certain child, for example, may perform better in an interview than on a pencil-and-paper test. Both kinds of evaluation, therefore, should be used. Literacy includes a wide range of skills; it is important to evaluate a child for as many as possible to determine strengths and weaknesses. Unfortunately, many assessment instruments are quite narrow in scope and frequently do not measure a child's total abilities.

There are several ways to measure children's language development in early childhood, which are similar to these used for measuring literacy development described in Chapter 2. *Checklists* are practical because they provide concise outlines for teachers and appropriate slots for individual children. They are most effective if used periodically during the school year. Three to four evaluations during the year can provide sufficient data to determine progress. Program objectives offer criteria to include on checklists.

Checklist *Assessing Language Development*

Child's name ______________________ Date ____________

	Always	Sometimes	Never	Comments
Makes phoneme sounds				
Speaks in one-word sentences				
Speaks in two-word sentences				
Identifies familiar sounds				
Differentiates similar sounds				
Understands the language of others when spoken to				
Follows verbal directions				
Speaks to others freely				
Pronounces words correctly				
Has appropriate vocabulary for level of maturity				
Speaks in complete sentences				
Uses varied syntactic structures				
Can be understood by others				

Teacher Comments:

Anecdotal records are another form of language assessment. They tend to be time consuming but can reveal rich information. Loose-leaf notebooks and file cards offer two means for keeping anecdotal records. These records require no particular format. Rather, the teacher or parent simply writes down incidents or episodes on the days they occur. Samples of a child's language and situations involving language can be recorded. Like checklists, anecdotal samples are necessary periodically to determine growth over a school year.

Tape recordings are another means of evaluating language. The process can take the form of an open interview or a hidden recording. (Videotaping equipment can serve the same purpose but may not be readily available in most early childhood classrooms.) Children who are unaware that their conversation is being recorded are likely to be more spontaneous and uninhibited (Genishi & Dyson, 1984). It is often difficult, however, to place a tape recorder where it will record language clearly enough to transcribe and analyze. Interviews with children can be more natural when an adult familiar to the child does the interviewing. Or it is also helpful to allow the tape recorder to become such a familiar tool in the classroom that the child uses it often in the language arts center. Under such circumstances the machine is not threatening when used in an assessment interview.

To record samples of natural language, discuss the child's experiences. Ask about home, favorite games or toys, favorite TV programs, brothers and sisters, trips taken, or birthday parties recently attended. You should try to collect is a corpus of spontaneous language that provides a typical sample of the child's ability with language.

Tape assessment samples three or four times a year. Let children hear their own recorded voices and enjoy the experience. Then, for assessment purposes, transcribe the tapes and analyze them for such items as numbers of words uttered and numbers of words spoken in a single connected utterance (for example, "Tommy's cookie" or "Me want water"). The lengths of such utterances can be averaged to determine mean length. Length of utterance is considered a measure of complexity. When children begin to speak in conventional sentences, such as "That is my cookie," measure the length of the t-units. A **t-unit** is an independent clause with all its dependent clauses attached, assuming it has dependent clauses. It can be a simple or a complex sentence. Compound sentences are made up of two t-units. Length of t-units, like length of utterances, is a measure of language complexity. It typically increases with the user's age, and usually the more words per unit, the more complex the unit (Hunt, 1970).

Further analysis of taped utterances and t-units can determine which elements of language a child uses—number of adjectives, adverbs, dependent clauses, negatives, possessives, passives, plurals, and so on. The more complex the transformations, embeddings, and syntactic elements used, the more complex the language overall (Morrow, 1978). Data from several samples over a year can be most revealing.

The following is a verbatim transcription of a taped language sample from a seven-year-old boy in the second grade. The child was presented with a picture book and asked to tell a story from the pictures.

> *he's getting up in the morning and he's looking out the window with his cat and after he gets out of bed he brushes his teeth then when he gets done brushing his teeth, he eats he eats breakfast and then when he after he eats breakfast he he gets dressed to play some games then in the afternoon he plays with his toys then in the afternoon he plays doctor and early in the day he plays cowboys and Indians then when it's in the afternoon close to suppertime he plays cops and robbers when he's playing in his castle he likes to dream of a magic carpet he's driving his ship on the waves he's uh circus uh ringmaster he's lifting up a fat lady I mean a clown is standing on a horse a clown is on a high wire somebody fell and then hurt their head the cowboy is bringing some ice cream to the hurt man that night he goes in the bathroom and gets washed and then he goes to bed then he dreams I don't know what he's dreaming I will think of what he's dreaming he's dreaming of going to play and he's playing the same things over*

After the sample is transcribed, the language is segmented into t-units. Following is a sample of the segmented sample of t-units:

1. He's getting up in the morning.
2. And he's looking out the window with his cat.
3. And after he gets out of bed, he brushes his teeth.

4. Then when he gets done brushing his teeth, he eats.
5. He eats breakfast.
6. And then (when he) after he eats breakfast he (he) gets dressed to play some games.
7. Then in the afternoon he plays with his toys.
8. Then in the afternoon he plays doctor.
9. And early in the day he plays cowboys and Indians.
10. Then when it's in the afternoon close to suppertime he plays cops and robbers.
11. When he's playing in his castle he likes to dream of a magic carpet.
12. He's driving his ship on the waves.
13. He's (uh) circus (uh) ringmaster.
14. He's lifting up a fat lady.
15. I mean a clown is standing on a horse.
16. A clown is on a high wire.
17. Somebody fell and then hurt their head.
18. The cowboy is bringing some ice cream to the hurt man.
19. That night he goes in the bathroom and gets washed.
20. And then he goes to bed.
21. Then he dreams.
22. I don't know what he's dreaming.
23. I will think of what he's dreaming.
24. He's dreaming of going to play.
25. And he's playing the same things over.

I have discussed oral language separately from the other communication skills in this chapter in order to describe its developmental stages and the theories of how it is acquired. This separation is somewhat artificial, however, because oral language is as important to literacy development as are reading and writing. We know that communication skills develop concurrently, each helping the growth of the others. Coordination and integration of the several communication skills in a single program are described in Chapter 10.

An Idea for the Classroom from the Classroom

The following experience may be useful for your teaching.

The Five Senses and a Fall Theme Generate Language

My first-grade class had been studying the five senses. In October, I decided to associate the five senses with the fall season to generate vocabulary and increased language complexity. I asked the children to bring in fall things that one can taste, touch, smell, look at, and listen to. I told children to select a sense category, about five children to each, and asked their groups to discuss what each one might bring so as not to overlap. A great deal of excitement occurred within the groups as children collaborated with each other trying to figure out five different things that they could bring related to fall and to the sense they had selected. I also directed children to describe what they had brought, with as many interesting words as they could think of. They could tell how they decided what to bring and where they located their object.

On the day the materials were brought to school, the children were to have group meetings to show what they had brought and help one another with descriptions.

When we came together as a class, we wrote the names of the five senses, each on a separate piece of experience chart paper. The groups displayed their objects and talked about each item with as many descriptive words as possible. The items were listed on the appropriate sense chart with the descriptive words written under each.

Many rich ideas were generated about the fall materials and the five senses. The children talked about the sound of crunchy dry leaves that were crushed as they walked on them; they described the shape of acorns and how they looked like tiny elves with lumpy hats on their heads. They discussed the slimy texture of seeds inside the pumpkin and the stringy nature of its pulp. They took deep breaths as they discussed the fresh scent of pine cones, and their mouths watered as someone described juicy, tart apples that made their lips pucker.

Everyone in the class had an opportunity to describe what he or she had brought. I helped some children who were at a loss for words by scaffolding some descriptions to get them started. This form of the old show-and-tell format attached to themes that we were studying proved to be a rich source for language development.

Jane Roosa, First-Grade Teacher
MacAfee School, Franklin Township, New Jersey

Activities and Questions

1. Answer the focus questions at the beginning of the chapter.

2. Select an objective for language development listed in the chapter. Prepare a lesson that will help a child achieve the goal. Identify the theories of language acquisition used in your lesson.

3. Tape record children at play or working in a group. Identify which characteristics of their language can be described by various theories of language acquisition. For example, imitation could be explained by the behaviorist theory.

4. Begin a thematic unit that you will continue as you read this book. Select a social studies or science topic. Select three objectives for language development and describe three activities that will satisfy each of the objectives using your theme. An example follows:

Content Area: Science
Theme: Creatures That Live in the Sea
Objective for Language Development: Develop new vocabulary
Activity: Read *Swimmy* by Leo Lionni. Ask the children to remember two new words they hear in the story. After reading, list words that the children mention on a chart and discuss their meaning.

5. Observe a preschool, kindergarten, or first- or second-grade class for about three hours. Note the amount of time children are given to talk, the amount of time the teacher talks, and the amount of time during which there is no verbal interaction. Compare the three figures. Then classify talk in the classroom into the following categories:

a. Questions and answers
b. Whole-class discussion
c. Small-group discussion led by the teacher
d. Interactive discussion among children
e. Interactive discussion between teacher and children

Based on the results of this ministudy, determine how often we allow children to use language, and in how many different contexts or situations.

6. Plan an activity that will elicit aesthetic talk and one that will involve efferent talk. How is the language in each setting the same and how is it different?

7. Continue the collection of assessment materials for the child for which you began a portfolio in Chapter 2. Collect one language sample from a child age two through seven. Elicit the language by showing a picture to discuss or asking the child to talk about favorite TV shows, pets, friends, family members, or trips. Tape record the sample and transcribe it.

a. Check the characteristics of the child's language development according to the descriptions in this chapter and the checklist provided to decide if the child is above, below, or at a level appropriate to his or her age. Compare with other members of the class who have studied different age groups.
b. Divide your language sample into t-units and determine the average length per t-unit; then count the number and type of syntactic elements used. Compare your sample to someone else in the class who is working with a child of a different age.
c. Collect three additional language samples for the same child at different times in the year. Evaluate the new samples as you did the first time and check for growth.

Case Study Activities

Case 1

Refer to "An Idea for the Classroom from the Classroom." Read it again and identify the theories of language acquisition that the teacher is incorporating. Has she made any accommodations for children with language differences? If yes, how? If not, how could she do so?

Case 2

All port of entry kindergarten, first, second, and third graders in an urban school district with a large Latino population are separated into an English-as-a-Second-Language classroom. Children who speak both English and Spanish are in classrooms with standard English-speaking children. The rationale for separating the Latino children is to be able to instruct them in Spanish, so their skills continue to improve and grow, while teaching them English.

Mrs. Ruiz, the first-grade ESL teacher, works with her children as follows. In the morning when reading and math are taught, Spanish is used. In the afternoon, Mrs. Ruiz is supposed to teach in English. However, Mrs. Ruiz finds that many of the children refuse to speak English and, since she is fluent in Spanish, she often speaks in Spanish in the afternoons out of frustration. Instead of a half English, half Spanish day, the language being used in the classroom is mostly Spanish.

One child, Josef, was placed in a regular first grade by accident. He did not speak English at all. His teacher, Mrs. Mitchell, reported that after only one month in her class Josef was communicating in English. Because everyone was speaking English, he heard English more, and having a young child's natural ability to assimilate language, he was learning English.

Do you believe that children in the early childhood grades who have no English should be placed in separate programs? What alternative plan would you propose to solve the problem of helping children learn English while continuing to learn literacy skills?

chapter 5

How Young Children Learn to Read and Write

Thomas Jefferson articulated three fundamental beliefs about literacy and education that have become part of our national ethos: (1) the ability of every citizen to read is necessary to the practice of democracy, (2) it is therefore the duty of the general public to support the teaching of reading for all youngsters, and (3) reading should be taught during the earliest years of schooling. Among the reasons he cited, "none is more important, none more legitimate, than that of rendering the people safe, as they are the ultimate guardians of their own liberty."

—Thomas Jefferson
The Life and Selected Writings of Thomas Jefferson

Focus Questions

- How does the emergent literacy approach to literacy instruction differ from reading readiness?
- What are the ways in which reading and writing are acquired? Discuss how meaning, purpose, life experience, exposure to books, and decoding skills all play a role.
- What are the characteristics of an engaged reader and writer?
- Describe Holdaway's theory of developmental learning.
- Describe the importance and benefits of explicit small-group learning.
- What developmental trends do children go through as they learn to read and write?
- What are the major objectives for literacy development?
- What components are present in a guided reading lesson?
- How can technology and play help children learn to read and write?

Four-year-old Colleen was playing house in the dramatic-play area. She was the mommy and she asked Kevin to be the daddy. They had a doll in the cradle. Colleen got the book, *The Three Little Pigs* and sat in the rocking chair facing the doll and Kevin. She pretended to read as she rocked and turned the pages while telling the story.

Colleen was engaged in attempted reading behavior that she modeled or emulated after a real-life experience. She was read to regularly by her mother and father. In addition, she was read to daily in her preschool classroom. Because of these experiences, she was familiar with the act of reading; therefore, she found it natural to engage in the activity. It was a social activity with another child who took the role of the father.

Mrs. Schenkman created a restaurant in the dramatic-play area of her kindergarten with menus, play money, uniforms, a cash register, and an OPEN and CLOSED sign. Ricky turned the sign to read OPEN and began preparing burgers. Steven joined Ricky and seemed upset. He said, "See that sign, now that says OPEN." He flipped it over. "We're not opened. Now it says CLOSED. We need to clean up the place first before we can open."

The literacy that takes place in this socially interactive situation is functional. It is something that children had the opportunity to observe and then model. In this play situation, children are able to practice and perform literacy skills with one another—all a part of literacy learning.

The examples provided here represent developmentally appropriate practice for early literacy development. Teachers provided materials and modeled behavior for children to observe and emulate. In addition, they provided real-life situations to encourage literacy learning in a social and cooperative manner. This is one type of important literacy experience; there are other more explicit experiences as well.

How children acquire reading and writing is complex. Past research adds to our knowledge today. We must acknowledge that information and combine what is still relevant to new findings. After the following presentation about developmental trends, I discuss reading readiness and other early literacy approaches and concepts that have contributed to current research and practice.

Developmental Trends in Literacy Acquisition

Becoming literate is a process that begins at birth and continues throughout life. Children differ in their rates of literacy achievement; they must not be pressured into accomplishing tasks or placed on a predetermined time schedule. Certain traits of literacy are acquired by many youngsters before others, but the dividing lines among traits and among youngsters are not always distinct. Acquisition of reading, writing, and language does seem to follow a pattern, however: Children are more interested in the *functions* of literacy first, then the *form,* and later the *conventions.*

Researchers have found that children learn that print has *functions* as a first step in reading and writing (Goodman, 1984; Mason, 1980; Smith, 1971). The first words a child says, reads, and writes are those with meaning, purpose, and function in his or her life, such as family names, food labels, road signs, and names of fast food restaurants.

After function, the child becomes interested in the *forms* of print. Details about names, sound, and configurations of letters and words serve the child's learning more now than simple understanding of how print functions.

A child then learns the *conventions* of print. This involves recognition that we read and write from left to right, that punctuation serves a purpose in reading and writing, and that spaces demarcate letters and words. Although recognition of the function of print dominates the first stages of reading and writing development, children acquire an interest in and notions about the form and conventions of print at the same time, but to a lesser degree.

Sulzby (1986a) describes children's writing behavior that illustrates developmental trends as follows:

1. use of drawings for writing
2. scribble writing
3. use of letterlike forms
4. use of well-learned units or letter strings
5. use of invented spelling
6. writing conventionally

Sulzby warns, however, that children do not systematically go from one developmental stage to the next; for example, they often skip stages or go back to earlier stages.

In a study of what children know about reading and of their skill in letter and word recognition, McCormick and Mason (1981) established three developmental levels in word recognition. Children first identified words through context, then used letter-sound cues, and finally relied on sounding out words.

Studies of young children's responses to story readings also reveal developmental trends that follow McCormick and Mason's basic three-strand paradigm. Children's initial questions and comments during story readings are related to the pictures and the meanings of the stories. As they gain experience with story readings, their questions and comments begin to concern the names of letters, the reading of individual words, or attempts to sound out words (Morrow, 1987a; Roser & Martinez, 1985; Yaden, 1985). Again, the function of print dominates early responses; the form of print becomes more important in later responses.

Judging from the research, then, there are categories of literacy development in early childhood. Yet reading and writing are obviously complex processes, and individual case studies vary between children. One must never forget that each child is an individual developing at his or her own pace.

Reading Readiness

As noted in Chapter 1, early developmentalists believed in the natural unfolding of the child. At a certain level of maturity, they felt, a child was ready to read, instruction was then appropriate, and the child would learn to read. Some educators became impatient with the notion of simply waiting for maturation, even though they thought that certain levels of maturation were necessary before reading could be taught formally without detriment to the child. This attitude led to instructional programs in reading readiness.

In general, reading readiness programs viewed getting ready to read as a set of social, emotional, physical, and cognitive competencies. If a child possessed these competencies, adherents said formal reading instruction could take place. Conversely, a child who had not mastered particular tasks was not considered ready for reading instruction. Strategies for readiness instruction depended on lists of skills in the four areas of development. The skills list provided an outline of activities to be designed to help develop such skills. Typically, these lists included characteristics such as those listed on page 131, on which children were tested.

In programs that followed a ***reading readiness*** perspective, teachers prepared instruction to encourage social, emotional, physical, and intellectual development as outlined on the list and described following.

Social and emotional development is enhanced with periods of play during which children can select from materials placed in classroom centers. Centers may be for dramatic play, art, science, library, or outdoor play, and may contain blocks and manipulative toys. The main goal is for children to learn to share, cooperate, develop self-control and a good self-concept, and learn about appropriate school behavior. Discussions often will focus on the topic of sharing and getting along with others. There will almost always be a unit focused on "All About Me," which emphasizes building self-confidence and a positive self-esteem. Food plays an important role in the curriculum; a healthy snack is served daily and is considered a time to socialize and learn to get along with others.

Physical development of large and fine motor control is seen as a factor in literacy development. Teachers should have indoor and outdoor periods designed specifically to teach children to hop, skip, trot, gallop, jump, throw a ball, and walk a straight line. Often there is music to accompany these activities and specific pieces of equipment such as a balance beam.

To develop fine motor coordination, children can use clay and play with toys that require fitting pegs into holes or snapping things together. These activities supply strength little hands need to develop the coordination necessary to write letters. Teachers ask children to color pictures, stay within the lines, and trace around lines of a particular illustration to develop eye–hand motor control. Children also trace pictures and letters with their fingers and with tracing paper and a pencil. Children practice cutting on lines to enhance fine motor ability, which is needed to write letters.

Cognitive development is equally important to social, physical, and emotional development. In a reading readiness program, cognitive development meant developing auditory and visual discrimination skills in preparation for reading. To do this, children participated in **visual** and **auditory discrimination** activities.

Visual discrimination activities involve children in seeing likenesses and differences in shapes and pictures. Often worksheets are used to help children develop this skill. For example, a worksheet may picture a line of flowers that all look the same with one slightly different from the rest. Children are to find and circle or color the flower that is different. Another visual discrimination activity is color identification. Here children are asked to fill in pictures using specific colors, to classify objects into color groups, or to make a collage of pictures cut from a magazine that are all, for example, red, blue, or green. Identifying like and different shapes such as squares, circles, and rectangles is another activity provided on worksheets to develop visual discrimination. Finally, children are taught left to right eye progression because this is not a natural activity but is necessary for reading. After working with these visual discrimination skills, teachers ask children to identify letters of the alphabet. Children memorize the alphabet, trace and copy letters, and learn to identify upper and lower case letters. All of these activities are preparation for reading. The skills mentioned are still relevant, but the manner in which we engage children in learning them today is different.

Auditory discrimination prepares children for learning to use auditory decoding skills. Teachers ask children to identify sounds that are alike and different.

Checklist *Reading Readiness*

Child's name ______________________ **Date** ____________

Social and Emotional Development	Always	Sometimes	Never	Comments
Shares				
Cooperates with peers and adults				
Demonstrates confidence, self-control, and emotional stability				
Completes tasks				
Fulfills responsibilities				
Physical Development				
Demonstrates large motor control by being able to run, hop, skip, trot, gallop, jump, throw, and walk a straight line				
Demonstrates fine motor control by being able to hold a pencil properly, color within lines, and cut with scissors				
Demonstrates eye–hand coordination				
Can write name, copy letters, and draw a human figure				
Is generally healthy and vigorous				
Shows no visual or auditory defects				
Has established dominance (hand, eye, foot)				
Cognitive Development				
Demonstrates auditory discrimination by identifying familiar sounds, differentiating sounds, recognizing rhyming words, identifying initial and ending consonant sounds, and possessing an auditory memory				
Demonstrates visual discrimination by understanding left to right eye progression; recognizing likenesses and differences; identifying colors, shapes, letters, and words; possessing visual memory; and showing a sense of figure–ground perception				

Teacher Comments:

Pictures that represent animals, for example, may be used, with students asked to circle those that make different or like sounds. Listening to rhymes, identifying rhyming words, and creating rhyme word lists is another auditory discrimination activity. Again, worksheets with pictures of objects are provided, and children are asked to circle the ones that rhyme. From rhyme, the teacher progresses to associating letters with their sounds. They provide children with worksheets to circle pictures that begin with a specific letter; students collect objects that begin with the sound featured, and teachers may ask children to cut pictures from a magazine to make into a collage for the letter *M* for example. Figure 5.1 shows a typical reading readiness worksheet that asks the child to circle pictures that begin with consonant sounds *d, p,* and hard *c.* These worksheets can be confusing because the deer could be considered a moose or antelope, and the piano a baby grand or simply a piano. Based on their own experiences, children may identify an illustration as something different from what the artist had in mind and circle the wrong letter. Therefore if this type of activity is used, teachers *must* identify picture names for children.

The list of reading readiness skills can be very long. Previously it was assumed that a child must master all behaviors on the list before being given a book to read, or becoming engaged in what is called formal reading instruction. The activities associated with a reading readiness program do not really teach children much about the total act of reading. They engage them in a variety of abstract activities that are only a part of reading. There are many sad stories of kindergarten teachers who have retained children who were unable to master skipping, trotting, or galloping. Parents have become frantic and children have

Figure 5.1

Reading Readiness Worksheet for Sound–Symbol Relationships

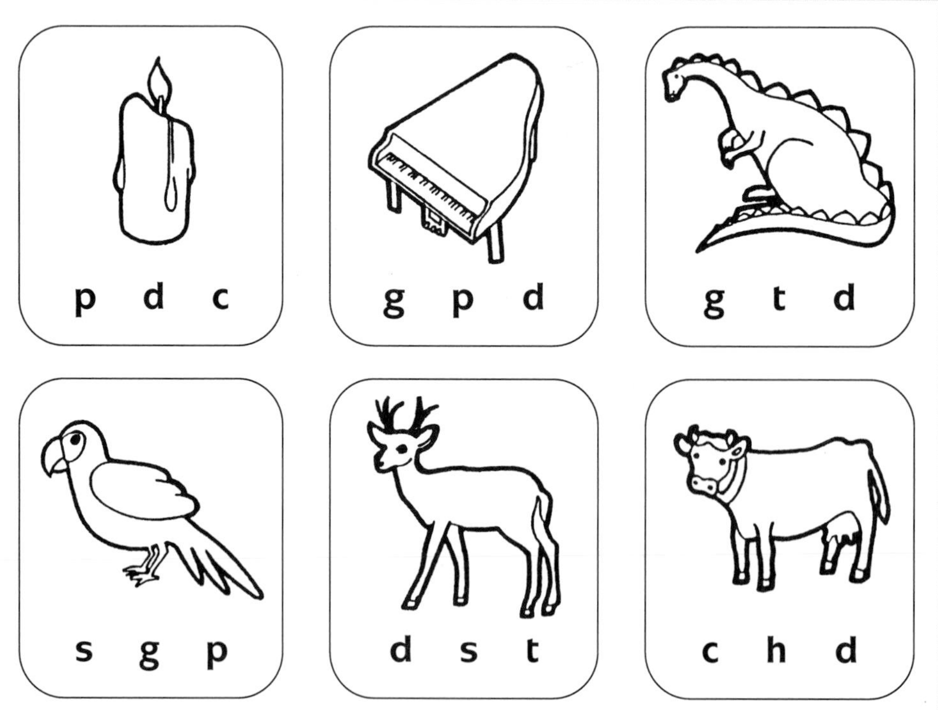

Directions: Circle the letter that each picture begins with, such as c as in candle, p as in piano, and d as in dragon.

been brought to tears by teachers' insistence on mastery of motor skills. It is still not uncommon to see classes of kindergarten children undergoing skipping lessons to the teacher's cadence of "step-hop, step-hop, step-hop, step-hop."

At least two misguided assumptions lie behind the reading readiness approach: (1) children know nothing about literacy before coming to school; and (2) they therefore need an instructional program in readiness. Reading readiness has not included writing and awareness of book and print characteristics that are necessary and important for reading. Instructional practices motivated by the readiness-skills approach abstract activities away from the total act of reading. There are children who have accomplished few of the tasks on a list of reading readiness skills but nonetheless are able to read. Their ability to read went unrecognized because reading readiness tests and activities never ask children to read. There are also children who can carry out the tasks on a list and experience difficulty learning to read. In today's classrooms, many readiness activities are still relevant. However, other experiences are also used to teach children about reading.

Emergent Literacy

Research concerning early readers and what they learn about books, print, and writing before going to school has changed attitudes and ideas about early childhood strategies for literacy development. In the past, reading, writing, listening, and speaking were thought of as separate skills taught independently of one another. We now realize, however, that literacy involves all of the communication skills and that each skill enhances the other as they are learned concurrently.

Although some of the skills associated with reading readiness are important to literacy learning, new concepts have broadened approaches to early literacy development. One such concept is ***emergent literacy,*** a phrase first used by Marie Clay (1966). Emergent literacy assumes that the child acquires some knowledge about language, reading, and writing before coming to school. Literacy development begins early in life and is ongoing. There is a dynamic relationship among the communication skills (reading, writing, oral language, and listening) because each influences the other in the course of development. Development occurs in everyday contexts of the home, community, and school through meaningful and functional experiences that require the use of literacy in natural settings. The settings for the acquisition of literacy are often social, with adults and children interacting through collaboration and tutoring. Literacy activities occur and are embedded purposefully within content areas such as art, music, play, social studies, and science, to ensure there is meaning involved. For example, in art, children should have a recipe to read in order to be able to make play dough.

Children at every age possess certain literacy skills, although these skills are not fully developed or conventional as we recognize mature reading and writing to be (Teale, 1986). Emergent literacy acknowledges as rudimentary writing a child's scribble marks on a page, even if not one letter is discernible. The child who knows the difference between such scribbles and drawings has some sense of the difference between writing and illustration. Similarly, when a child narrates a familiar storybook while looking at the pictures and print and gives the impression of reading, we acknowledge the activity as legitimate literacy behavior, even though it cannot be called reading in the conventional sense.

Emergent literacy constructs are sensitive to children with special needs because they look for youngsters' strengths rather than weaknesses. The emergent literacy perspective is sensitive to cultural diversity because children learn literacy skills through the study of themes that often focus on their heritage. Literacy development approached in this manner accepts children at whatever level of literacy they are functioning and provides a program for instruction based on individual needs. The emergent literary perspective is a child-centered approach with more emphasis on problem solving than on direct instruction of skills.

Holdaway's Theory of Literacy Development

Don Holdaway's (1979) theory of literacy development provides a summary concerning how reading and writing are acquired:

> The way in which supportive adults are induced by affection and common sense to intervene in the development of their children proves upon close examination to embody the most sound principles of teaching. Rather than provide verbal instructions about how a skill should be carried out, the parent sets up an emulative model of the skill in operation and induces activity in the child which approximates towards use of the skill. The first attempts of the child are to do something that is like the skill he wishes to emulate. This activity is then "shaped" or refined by immediate rewards. . . . From this point of view, so called "natural" learning is in fact supported by higher quality teaching intervention than is normally the case in the school setting. (p. 39)

Holdaway contends that this form of "developmental" teaching is appropriate for school-based literacy instruction. Characterized by self-regulated, individualized activities, frequent peer interaction, and an environment rich with materials, Holdaway's model is derived from observations of home environments where children have learned to read without direct instruction, such as those described in Chapter 3.

Holdaway (1986) explains four processes that enable children to acquire reading and writing ability. The first is *observation* of literacy behaviors—being read to, for example, or seeing adults reading and writing themselves. The second is *collaboration* with an individual who interacts with the child, providing encouragement, motivation, and help when necessary. The third process is *practice*. The learner tries out alone what has been learned, such as reading and writing activities—and experiments without direction or adult observation. Practice gives children opportunities to evaluate their performances, make corrections, and increase skills. In the fourth process, *performance*, the child shares what he or she has learned and seeks approval from adults who are supportive, interested, and encouraging. The ideas expressed by Holdaway (1986) are also articulated in work on literacy development by Calkins, 1983; Read, 1975; and Smith, 1983.

The Engagement Perspective and the Acquisition of Literacy

The engagement perspective defines the goals for literacy instruction. The perspective describes what readers and writers should be like when they reach their fullest potential (Figure 5.2). According to the National Reading Research Center (1991), engaged readers are *strategic* readers, who have word-analysis skills and can comprehend the meaning of printed materials. They possess multiple skills that enable them to read independently and comprehend what they read. Engaged readers are *knowledgeable* because they can read to learn with the

Figure 5.2

The Engagement Perspective

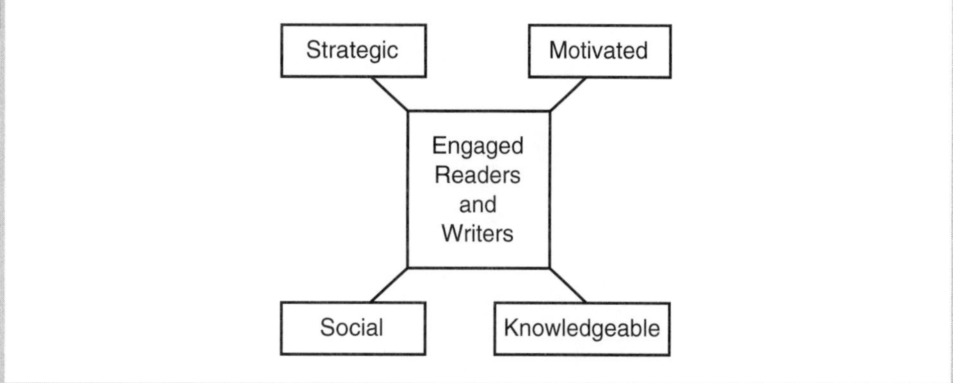

strategies they possess to read independently. Engaged readers are *motivated* to read voluntarily for pleasure and for information, and are *social* in their approach to learning and using literacy.

The engagement perspective is a guide for instructional settings for early literacy development. We need to teach strategies to create strategic readers and writers; we need to expose children to literature to gain information; and we need to provide instruction that will be challenging, offer children choices in literacy learning situations, and provide successful experiences. These are all elements that help motivate. Finally, we need to do these things in social settings so that children learn the social nature of reading and writing and approach literacy learning by interacting with others.

Reading and Writing Are Acquired through Social Collaborative Interaction

Teale (1982) views literacy as the result of children's involvement in reading and writing activities mediated by more literate others. It is the social, collaborative interaction accompanying these activities that makes them so significant to the child's development. Not only do interactive literacy events teach children the societal functions and conventions of reading, but they also link reading and writing with enjoyment and satisfaction and thus increase children's desire to engage in literacy activities. Teale's emphasis on the social aspects of literacy development reflects Vygotsky's (1981) more general theory of intellectual development. Vygotsky suggests that higher order thinking occurs as a result of social relationships that have been internalized. This movement from interpsychological learning to intrapsychological learning is apparent as children become increasingly able to engage independently in literacy activities that previously required interaction with more literate adults or children. As mentioned in Chapter 4, this time period has been referred to by Vygotsky as the *zone of proximal development.* It is that moment when the child becomes capable of participating in a particular literacy activity alone and adult assistance is no longer necessary.

Collaboration plays an important role in the acquisition of writing and reading among small groups of children in different settings. Studies dealing with student cooperation in academic tasks conclude that such cooperation promotes achievement and productivity and yields strong social and attitudinal benefits (Sharon, 1980; Yager, Johnson, & Johnson, 1985). Researchers propose that the positive effects observed are due to the dynamics of cooperative learning, which include a great deal of oral interaction among students and the heterogeneous

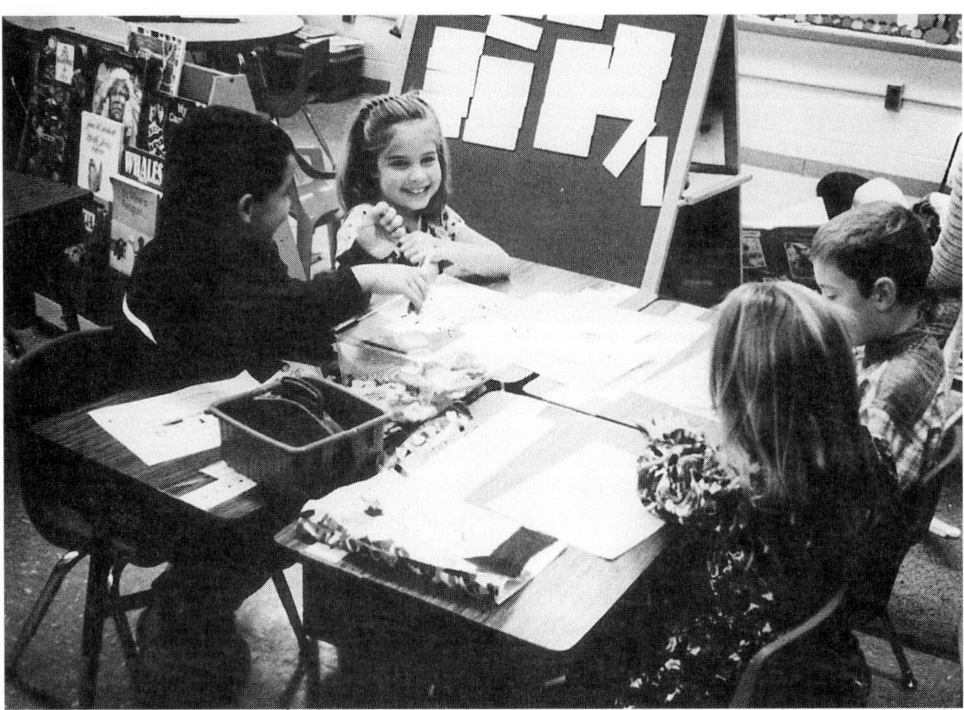

Reading and writing are acquired through social collaborative interaction.

nature of the groups. Yager, Johnson, and Johnson (1985) found that passive learners particularly benefit from small-group dialogue and interaction. They suggest that cooperative learning succeeds because it allows children to explain material to each other, to listen to each other's explanations, and to arrive at joint understandings of what has been shared. In addition, young children use language and nonverbal signals that other children understand easily.

Dewey (1966) argued that children who engage in task-oriented dialogue with peers can reach a higher level of understanding than that attained by students who listen to a teacher's didactic presentation of information. In addition, Piaget and Inhelder (1969) suggested that childhood peers can serve as resources for one another in their cognitive development.

Children Acquire the Ability to Read and Write as a Result of Life Experiences

Some children have considerable information about reading and writing before they enter school for formal instruction. Some are reading and writing before they come to school; others have had little exposure to literacy. Even though children's strengths in literacy vary, most children have a general command of language and a sizable vocabulary and have internalized rules of language. They know the difference between drawing and writing, and they associate books with reading. They can read environmental print, and they realize the functional purposes of reading and writing. Because their knowledge about literacy to this point is based on meaning and function, they expect that reading and writing will be activities that make sense.

Research since the 1960s has made us aware of early childhood competencies and literacy skills. As discussed in Chapter 3 studies have revealed that many children read early—that is, before starting school and without formal instruction. Investigations also have revealed how the environment supports literacy development. Children as young as three are able to read such common words in their environment as *Burger King, McDonald's, Exxon,* and *Sugar Pops* (Goodman & Altwerger, 1981; Hiebert, 1986; Mason, 1980). The results of these investigations indicate that very young children are aware of print, letters, and words, and that their ability to identify familiar printed symbols constitutes the beginning of reading. According to Goodman (1984), the "roots of literacy" are established in early childhood by most children in literate societies. Environmental print helps children discover how print is organized and used as well as what it is used for. Young children also demonstrate such knowledge of books and book handling as (1) where to begin reading, (2) the difference between pictures and print, (3) awareness of the left-to-right progression of print, (4) the difference between the beginning and the end of the book, and (5) how to turn pages. Efforts to expand children's reading abilities into reading fluency need to build on their strengths and on what they already know and expect of reading (Harste, Woodward, & Burke, 1984). Early writing, similar to early reading, is embedded in real-life experience. Many families do things together that involve meaningful literacy. They write each other notes, lists, holiday greetings, and directions.

Psycholinguistic Cueing Systems and the Acquisition of Language and Literacy

According to psycholinguistic theory, language and literacy are acquired as a result of children having the ability to use three cueing systems to figure out new and unknown words to grasp meaning.

1. *Syntactic cues:* Using the grammatical structure or syntax of language
2. *Semantic cues:* Using the meaning of words and sentences
3. *Graphophonic cues:* Using the visual cues of letters and print and associating them with letters, letter clusters, and corresponding sounds

Along with these cueing systems, the psycholinguistic definition of reading also recommends capitalizing on children's prior strengths, knowledge, and past experiences. Goodman (1967) described reading as a psycholinguistic "guessing game" in which the child attempts to reconstruct, in light of his or her own knowledge, what the author has to say. Young children bring to school concepts and understanding from past experiences. Their awareness and use of oral language are particularly helpful.

Reading is an active process. Therefore, when children try to read, they need to anticipate what the written message is likely to say. They need to search the printed page for cues based on what they already know. They need to use the three cueing systems.

- There are *syntactic* cues such as *The boy walked down the* ____________. The child's internalized knowledge of syntax indicates that the word to place in the blank must be a noun such as *hill, stairs,* or *street.* A verb would make no sense: *The boy walked down the jumped.*
- *Semantic* cues help children to determine which words make sense in a particular slot and which would not. Few would guess that the sentence reads, *The boy walked down the butter,* for example. It just doesn't make sense.

- *Graphophonic* cues enable the child to determine words by looking at the visual cues of letters and letter clusters, and associating them with their corresponding sounds.

Using the syntactic, semantic, and graphophonic cues, children can predict, guess, expect, make associations, and correct themselves to derive meaning from the printed page. The meaning comes from what they know about language and from their own experiences. Meaningful cues in whole pieces of print are often more useful in figuring out words than looking at an isolated word.

Children Acquire Literacy Skills That Have a Purpose

Children are likely to become involved in literacy activities if they view reading and writing as functional, purposeful, and useful. Studies of early reading and writing behaviors clearly illustrate that young children acquire their first information about reading and writing through their functional uses (Goodman, 1980; Mason & McCormick, 1981; Taylor, 1983). Grocery lists; directions on toys, packages, household equipment, and medicine containers; recipes; telephone messages; school-related notices; religious materials; menus; environmental print inside and outside the home; mail; magazines; newspapers; storybook readings; TV channels; telephone numbers; conversation among family members; and letters represent but a sample of the functional literacy information with which a child comes in contact daily. Children are familiar with such forms of literacy, they participate in them, they pretend to use them at play, and they understand their purposes. Parents and day-care, preschool, and kindergarten teachers need to provide experiences with reading similar to experiences children have already had.

Exposure to Books and Literacy Development

Being Read to Develops a Sense of Story Structure

Research indicates that reading to children benefits their acquisition of reading and writing. It enhances background information and sense of story structure, and familiarizes children with the language of books (Cullinan, 1992; Morrow, 1985). A well-structured story has a *setting* (a beginning, time, place, and introduction of characters), *theme* (the main character's problem or goal), *plot episodes* (a series of events in which the main character attempts to solve the problem or achieve the goal), and a *resolution* (the accomplishment of the goal or solving of the problem and an ending). From hearing many well-formed stories, children can predict what will happen next in an unfamiliar story on the basis of their awareness of its structure. Hearing stories with good plot structures also helps children write and tell their own stories (Morrow, 1985). The language of books is different from oral language and provides a model for their writing and speaking. The following sentences from two picture storybooks make this evident:

> One bad day a tuna fish, fierce, swift and very hungry, came darting through the waves. (Lionni, *Swimmy,* 1963)

> The wild things roared their terrible roars, gnashed their terrible teeth, and rolled their terrible eyes. (Sendak, *Where the Wild Things Are,* 1963)

This next piece is from E. B. White's *Charlotte's Web* (1952) and is appropriate to read to first and second graders.

> At last Wilbur saw the creature that had spoken to him in such a kindly way. Stretched across the upper part of the doorway was a big spiderweb, and hanging from the top of the web, head down, was a large grey spider. She was about the size of a gumdrop. She had eight legs, and she was waving one of them at Wilbur in friendly greeting. "See me now?" she asked.
>
> "Oh, yes indeed," said Wilbur. "Yes indeed! How are you? Good morning! Salutations! Very pleased to meet you. What is your name, please? May I have your name."
>
> "My name," said the spider, "is Charlotte."

Being Read to Enhances Comprehension and Knowledge about Books and Print

Children's comprehension skills are enhanced from their familiarity with vocabulary and syntactic structures in books that have been read to them. Children who have been read to frequently and early tend to read and write earlier than others and to learn to read more easily (Hiebert, 1981; Mason, 1980). Furthermore, reading to children at school or at home leads them to associate reading with pleasure and provides them with models for reading. In fact, when children begin to read on their own, they often choose books that have been read to them. After I read *The Little Engine That Could* (Piper, 1954) to a four-year-old, she said to me, "Show me where it says 'I think I can, I think I can.' I want to see it in the book." When I showed her the words, she repeated them while pointing to them and then asked to see them again in another part of the book. She proceeded to search through the rest of the book, reading with great enthusiasm each time she found the line "I think I can, I think I can."

Researchers have found that reading to children enhances the development of reading in many ways. Repeated reading of the same story is an important strategy as well (Morrow, 1986; Sulzby, 1985; Yaden, 1985). Smith (1978) suggests that reading to children gives them an understanding of the functions of print, a sense of how print is used and of what people are doing when they are reading. Children with storybook experience learn how to handle a book and are sensitive to its front-to-back progression; a story's beginning, middle, and end; and the concept of authorship. Mason (1980) found that reading to children contributes to their awareness of the functions, form, and conventions of print. It also develops metacognitive knowledge about how to approach reading tasks. *Metacognition* is one's own awareness of how learning is taking place; it thus nurtures ones own learning.

Being Read to Develops Positive Attitudes toward Reading and Writing

Children who are read to develop positive attitudes toward reading. The warmth that accompanies storybook readings by a caring adult lasts beyond the experience. It involves ritual, sharing, and mutual good feelings. Certain books take on special meanings between an adult and child through repetition or because they are favorites of the one or the other. My daughter and I have had a special relationship with the book *Alexander and the Terrible, Horrible, No Good, Very Bad Day* (Viorst, 1972). I first read it to Stephanie when she was four, and whenever

Being read to develops positive attitudes toward reading and writing.

things seemed to go wrong for her I found myself saying, "I guess you're having a terrible, horrible, no good, very bad day." Soon, when things were not going well for me, Stephanie would say the same thing to me.

When Stephanie was in the seventh grade, she came home from school one day, wearing only one sneaker, and looking generally distraught.

"What's the problem?" I asked.

"Someone stole one of my sneakers, I got yelled at for talking when my friend asked me a question in class and I answered her, I have tons of homework, and I lost my assignment notebook."

"I guess you're having a terrible, horrible, no good, very bad day," I said.

She smiled and said, "You're right. I think I'll go to Australia."

"Some days are like that, even in Australia," I replied.

We both laughed. The familiar words of a familiar book created a special ritual between us. Good feelings gained in story readings transfer to the act of reading itself (Hiebert, 1981; Taylor, 1983).

Interaction Is Important during Storybook Reading

Children who have been read to often begin to concern themselves with strategies for independent reading. It is not just the reading itself but the interaction between adult and child that motivates the interest. Studies carried out in school settings illustrate that active participation in literacy experiences enhances comprehension of story and sense of story structure. Role-playing stories they have heard, retelling them, and reconstructing them through pictures enable children to relate parts of a story, integrate information, and interact with teachers and other children (Morrow, 1985; Pellegrini & Galda, 1982).

Studies of home read-aloud sessions clearly illustrate that active social interaction between parents and children during these sessions is a major factor in literacy development. Initially, children are interested in the illustrations and label items pictured or repeat words said by the adult who is reading the story (Yaden, 1985). Such interactive behavior leads children to respond with questions and

Being read to and the interaction that occurs during reading play important roles in the acquisition of reading skills.

comments, which become more complex over time and demonstrate more sophisticated thinking about printed material. Eventually, children's remarks about story content reflect interests in interpretation, association, prediction, information, and elaboration. These remarks focus sometimes on title, setting, characters, and story events (Morrow, 1988; Roser & Martinez, 1985), and at other times on print characteristics, including names of letters, words, and sounds.

One of the primary goals of reading aloud is the reconstruction of meaning through the interaction between adult and child. The adult helps the child understand and make sense of the text through their cooperative personal interpretation of the written language based on their experiences and beliefs (Altwerger, Diehl-Faxon, & Dockstader-Anderson, 1985). Particularly helpful behavior includes prompting children to respond, scaffolding responses for children to model when they are unable to respond themselves, relating responses to real-life experiences, answering questions, and offering positive reinforcement for children's responses. We often stop reading to children as they begin to read themselves, usually during first grade. It is crucial to continue reading to children as they grow older because it continues to enhance skills already learned and to motivate interest in the books featured in the classroom.

Multiple Intelligences and Literacy Development

Howard Gardner (1993) has discussed the concept of multiple intelligences. His theory suggests that some people have all seven types of intelligences that he outlines and others have fewer. Gardner believes that most people can acquire a type of intelligence in which they may not be strong. Therefore, we need different learning experiences, some that foster our strengths and some that help us develop skills in other areas. Gardner's list of intelligences follows, along with types of activities that are appropriate for each of the intelligences (Armstrong, 1994).

Linguistic: lectures, discussions, word games, storytelling, choral reading, journal writing

Logical mathematical: brain teasers, problem solving, science experiments, mental calculations, number games, critical thinking

Spatial: visual presentations, art activities, imagination games, mind mapping, metaphor, visualization

Bodily kinesthetic: hands-on learning, drama, dance, sports that teach, tactile activities, relaxation exercises

Musical: rapping, songs that teach

Interpersonal: cooperative learning, peer tutoring, community involvement, social gatherings, simulations

Intrapersonal: individualized instruction, independent study, options in course of study, self-esteem building

When we teach children to read, we need to remember that not all children learn in the same way. We should, therefore, think about the different intelligences and provide many experiences to meet individual needs.

Phonemic Awareness and Phonics and Literacy Acquisition

Some research indicates that it is necessary to develop decoding skills for reading success. This area of literacy development has been of concern throughout the years: Should we teach these skills to preschoolers? Exactly what skills are necessary? How much time should be spent teaching them? How should they be taught? Despite these concerns, it has become apparent that we do need to deal with decoding skills in early literacy development. This section discusses the skills we should teach. A more in-depth presentation of the development of these skills is in Chapter 8, which deals specifically with the topic of word analysis.

A term that has caused much discussion among literacy educators and others is **phonemic awareness.** As mentioned in Chapter 1, phonemic awareness is the knowledge that words comprise individual sounds. Children who acquire this ability are able to hear rhyming words and can segment individual sounds out of words and blend them together again. Phonemic awareness is developed over time and through practice (Juel, 1991). When children are phonemically aware, they know that a word such as *bug* is composed of three sounds that can be segmented into those sounds */b/u/g/*. They also know that the sounds can be blended together again and the individual sounds make the spoken word, *bug*. Phonemic awareness does not involve associating the visual letter symbols with the sounds of the letters; it is simply hearing that there are different sounds in words and being able to segment the sounds, say them, and then blend them together. According to some researchers, phonemic awareness instruction strengthens reading achievement, is a precursor to phonics, and must be taught in preschool, kindergarten, and first grade (Byrne & Fielding-Barnsley, 1991, 1993, 1995; Foorman, Francis, Fletcher, Schatschneider, & Mehta, 1998; Lundberg, Frost, & Peterson, 1988; Stanovich, 1986).

We know it is important that young children learn phonemic awareness. There are many ways to teach this skill. Children can be taught phonemic awareness using linguistic games in which they manipulate speech segments (Byrne & Fielding-Barnsley, 1991; Lundberg, Frost, & Peterson, 1988). This type of training might not be developmentally appropriate for young children in preschool and kindergarten, and some recommend a less explicit and less formal approach. Researchers have suggested that children should study larger word units before learning about the more abstract segmenting and blending of sounds, and that some knowledge of letter units and sounds will enhance the development of phonemic awareness (Bryant, 1993; Moustafa, 1997).

Another skill crucial to literacy development is learning alphabetic principles. This is knowing that words are composed of letters and that there is a relationship between the printed letters and spoken sounds. Children who learn letter–sound relationships are better readers than children that do not (Adams, 1990; Baumann, 1984; Chall, Conrad, & Harris-Sharples, 1983). The International Reading Association (1998) reports that teaching phonics, more specifically the relationships of letters and sounds, is essential in the development of independent readers. However, phonics instruction should be meaningful and connected to reading in some way.

Guided Reading and Writing: A Means for Explicit Instruction of Skills

The whole language and emergent literacy perspectives emphasize that children learn through meaning and function and in settings that deal with real life. Skill instruction takes place when necessary and when spontaneous opportunities occur. Children are immersed in literacy activities and acquire skills from this rich exposure to books and print. Although skills are considered important, direct instruction of skills without a specific context is not advocated.

It is important to take into account that in natural settings for learning literacy, many children may require additional help with a particular skill, and opportunities may not occur spontaneously to teach all skills needed. Therefore, teachers should provide explicit instruction of skills for most youngsters. Explicit, or direct, instruction should be designed for the needs of individuals and handled in a manner that children will maintain their interest in reading. Direct instruction can take place in a whole group, in small groups, or on a one-to-one basis, although most often it occurs in small groups. Without the direct instruction component in literacy instruction, some children will miss learning many important skills. It is crucial that teachers be aware of the individual needs of their students and accommodate those needs with an appropriate balance of instructional strategies, both explicit and open ended.

Researchers have studied learning in small groups for the purpose of explicit instruction by a teacher. In small-group instruction teachers are better able to obtain and retain students' attention. The small group offers the opportunity for more student participation (Slavin, 1987; Sorenson & Hallinan, 1986). In addition, teachers can change instructional methods and materials to meet the needs of each student in small groups. When groups are homogeneous it is possible for teachers to provide more individualized instruction at the appropriate level (Slavin, 1987). In small groups, instruction can be paced for students' rate of learning, teaching styles can be modified to meet different learning styles, and students are easier to control (Hallinan & Sorenson, 1983).

There are some disadvantages of grouping. For example, children from minority backgrounds are often disproportionately placed in low ability groups. Groups can be inflexible and once a student is tracked in a particular group, that placement may never change throughout his or her school career. This affects self-esteem and the type of instruction a student receives (Slavin, 1987). Another disadvantage of grouping is that frequently only one measure determines a child's group placement. Often there are a set number of groups, such as three, in which all children must fit. In addition, teachers sometimes have low expectations for students in the low groups, which could lead to continued low performance for these students (Hallinan & Sorenson, 1983).

The whole language movement and emergent literacy perspective also have influenced a move away from small-group instruction to whole group. To have students benefit from the positive effects of grouping for literacy instruction, explicit instruction is characterized by small groups based on need, often called *guided reading groups*. Guided reading, which involves explicit instruction, can take place in a whole group, small groups or on a one-to-one basis, but is most often associated with small-group instruction. Fountas and Pinnell (1996) define guided reading lessons as follows:

> In guided reading a teacher works with a small group. Children in the group are similar in their development of the reading process and are able to read about the same level of text. Teachers introduce the stories and assist children's reading in ways that help to develop independent reading strategies. Each child reads the entire text. The goal is for children to read independently and silently. The emphasis is on reading increasingly challenging books. Children are grouped and regrouped in a dynamic process that involves ongoing observation and assessment (p. 4).

And, Spiegel (1992) writes,

> The overall purpose of guided reading is to enable children to read for meaning at all times. Guided reading instruction is systematic instruction with a scope of skills and objectives to accomplish. Activities are designed to meet the objectives. Skill instruction is not left to chance; it is assured. Although there is a systematic plan, guided reading instruction should allow for "teachable moments."

Teachers select the instructional materials for guided reading based on meeting the skill needs of the children. The texts can be any type, such as those from a reading program or children's literature; however, they must be at the instructional level of the child, neither too easy or too hard. Leveled reading books, often called "little books," are the most common materials used for guided reading. These books have been leveled for difficulty, which makes it easy for teachers to select those needed for particular groups. The texts also must be at the child's instructional reading level. This means that the child can read the text with 90 to 95 percent accuracy (Clay, 1993b). If the text is too easy there is not any opportunity to teach new strategies; if the book is too difficult, the child will not understand what he or she is reading, and the activity becomes an exercise in decoding words rather than trying to make meaning.

Objectives for each guided reading lesson should focus on strategies children are experiencing difficulty with and strategies they neglect to use. In the lesson many experiences are drawn upon to help children with phonograms, syntactic and semantic cues, and writing (Reutzel, 1997). The objectives for the lessons, like the selection of the text, depend on the students' reading ability and needs.

There are marked differences between guided reading groups and reading groups of the past. Guided reading groups are characterized by the following:

1. Children are assessed regularly so that their group placement is changed when their reading ability changes and they are not fixed in one group forever.
2. The teacher purposely uses other types of groups for instruction throughout the day so that students never associate themselves only with their guided reading group.

3. The number of groups formed is not set; it is determined by the number of different ability levels represented in a given classroom. Typically there are four groups.
4. Books selected for instruction meet the needs of the students regardless of their grade level.
5. Group activities are designed to provide children with strategies for becoming independent fluent readers.
6. Activities provided for children who are not in guided reading groups are often in centers. Children are actively engaged in interesting, productive work. (In the past the most commonly used method for occupying children was to provide them with workbook pages to fill in at their desks.)

A guided reading lesson can take most any form. The major concern is that it is designed to meet the needs of the children in the group. Some particular components are associated with the design of guided reading that follow a Reading Recovery lesson (Clay, 1991). The components are as follows:

1. The lesson begins with children reading something familiar that is easy. This creates fluent, smooth oral reading with good pronunciation, intonation, and flow.
2. The teacher introduces a new book to children by taking a "walk through the book" to build some background knowledge about it before it is read. This helps generate children's prior knowledge about the book's topic, which should help them comprehend what is read (Anderson & Pearson, 1984). Here are typical steps in the "walk through the book":
   a. Children are asked to make predictions about what they think might happen in the story.
   b. Children are asked to read the title, author's name, and illustrators' name.
   c. The teacher can give a short summary of the story.
   d. The teacher can introduce patterns in words.
3. With younger children the first reading of the book is done aloud. This is not round robin reading with different children taking turns, nor is it choral reading. Each child reads his or her copy of the text at his or her own pace.
4. While the children read, the teacher listens to provide guidance or scaffolding when a child cannot figure out a word. The teacher also takes notes about the children's reading strengths and weaknesses. He or she may have a different child from each group sit next to him or her during the lesson. This is the student she will take most notes about, which makes record keeping easier. The next day a different focus child will sit next to the teacher during guided reading.
5. After the first reading, children reread for fluency and comprehension, which is easier during the second reading because children are not concentrating on decoding as much. Multiple readings of the same text help students become better readers (Clay, 1991).
6. After the readings, the teacher selects specific skills to concentrate on, based on the needs of the group. He or she might select a word chunk from the text that occurs frequently, such as /og/ in the word *frog,* and build other words that use that chunk. The teacher provides several activities for learning this skill, such as having children generate new words as a whole group that end with the /og/ chunk, such as *log, fog, jog,* etc. The teacher also might

give students magnetic letters with the /og/ chunk and ask them to create /og/ words on their own small magnetic board. To further reinforce the concept, the teacher may ask children to select an /og/ word and write it in a sentence, paying attention to punctuation and spelling. The teacher then cuts each sentence into separate words for students to sequence and read for practice.

7. The teacher often writes notes to parents during the guided reading lesson for children to take home. The note suggests homework for the child and how parents can help.
8. The last component of a guided reading lesson is a running record. This is usually done on an individual basis. A child is asked to stay after the lesson and read a passage to determine progress. The teacher evaluates the child's reading needs and reading level, and determines if the child should remain in his or her present group or move to a group where the work is easier or at a more difficult level. A description of the administration and evaluation of a running record is in Chapter 2 with a sample evaluation form.

Throughout the following chapters on comprehension, writing, and word analysis different strategies are described that can be used in guided reading lessons.

Technology and Play: New and Old Resources for Helping Children Learn to Read and Write

Use of Technology for Literacy Development

Technology offers young children opportunities to develop literacy skills. Computers allow children to construct knowledge in social or independent literacy settings in which they deal with word study or with meaning of text (Labbo & Ash, 1998; Reinking, McKenna, Kuhn, & Phillips, 1996). For example, electronic books have been found to motivate children to read and enhance their achievement in analyzing words, recalling details of stories, and acquiring a sense of story structure (Kinzer & McKenna, 1999; Stine, 1993).

Computers today have huge storage capacities for sophisticated software. The Internet connects children to limitless sources of information from around the world. As teachers of young children, we need to be aware of what computers can do so that we can help our students use the technology to enhance their literacy development.

COMPUTER SOFTWARE. Software programs are one of the most common ways for teachers to use computers with children. Although it is not necessary to have elaborate computer equipment in the classroom, computers with a CD-ROM drive are necessary for some programs. Also, it is useful to have a TV monitor to project the software onto for an entire class to see.

The following general rules should be followed when selecting software for use (Wepner & Ray, 2000):

- Instructions for children are concise, clear, and easy to follow.
- The activities are engaging, promote active participation, and will hold the attention and interest of children.

Computers should be a part of early childhood equipment and provide a source for literacy development.

- The content matches and expands on what children are learning within their school curriculum.
- The program provides practice for concepts being learned.
- The text is narrated and highlighted for children to be able to deal with the activities independently.
- There is a guide for teachers for introducing and using the software.
- Assessment is provided.

Quality software is available for every type of literacy skill, such as the development of phonemic awareness, phonics, comprehension, writing, and vocabulary. According to Wepner and Ray (2000), the following criteria should be used to select quality software to develop reading skills such as phonics and phonemic awareness: (1) Skills are introduced in a predictable sequence; (2) Feedback is focused and immediate; (3) There is opportunity for repetitious feedback; and (4) Children are engaged in an active manner with the software.

Another type of software is the electronic book. Electronic books use the best children's literature and present stories to children in variety of ways. Images move on the screen, books are read aloud, and the text is clearly shown. Because these stories are animated, they are motivating to children. Another advantage to electronic books is that embedded in the book are skill development techniques such as K-W-L, emphasis on development of story structure, and the use of a Directed Reading and Thinking Activity format (Wepner & Ray, 2000).

Software to develop writing is helpful for beginning writers, children whose fine motor control is not well developed, and children with physical disabilities involving their hands. Quality software for writing development supports text that is generated by children and encourages students to expand on, revise, and edit what they have written.

When using software, be sure that you are familiar with it and that children know how to use the computer and the program. Software can be introduced to the whole class by projecting it onto a TV monitor that all can see. Your purpose will determine how you choose to use the software, but most of the time software is used for practicing skills already taught. The work is done alone or with a peer, independent of the teacher. Similar to a center activity, computer work is a perfect activity for children when teachers are engaged in guided reading groups for explicit instruction. There should be a time for students to discuss problems they may have with the software and to share accomplishments on the computer.

THE INTERNET. Another way to use the computer in the classroom is with the Internet, which has endless possibilities. Instead of corresponding with pen pals through regular mail, children now e-mail other students instantly all over the world. The World Wide Web is an unlimited resource for information related to whatever children are studying. For example, for a unit about space, the teacher can collect fiction and non-fiction books about space for the room and locate an appropriate Web site for children to use as a source for more information. There are sites for children on which to review books before reading them, review software they are using, and access electronic books. In addition, schools and classrooms can create their own Web sites for various reasons. Figure 5.3 is an example of a Web site prepared by a second-grade teacher to welcome her class at the beginning of the school year.

It is the teacher's responsibility to help students find Web sites that will be useful for them, and to help them learn how to find others on their own. A helpful reference book is *101 Best Web Sites for Kids* (Meers, 1999). When selecting Web sites for children, Wepner and Ray (2000) advise the following considerations:

- The Web site loads quickly.
- The title page presents a thorough overview of the contents.
- The contents of the Web site fit with your purpose.
- There are icons that link to pages on the site needed and possibly to other relevant sites.
- The graphics are attractive and enhance the concepts.
- The narration is clear and enhances the concepts to be learned.

The computer with software and the Internet with all of its capabilities for correspondence and retrieval of information must be included into daily routines for learning. Children will need to function with a computer on a daily basis. Appendix C provides a list of software and Web sites designated for specific skill development.

Use of Play for Literacy Development

A curriculum area we must continue to use is embedding literacy learning into play. In play settings, children interact and collaborate in small groups. When designed to promote literacy learning, the dramatic-play area is coordinated with a social studies or science theme that is being studied to bring meaning to the experience. Materials for reading and writing are provided to support the play

Figure 5.3

A Web Site Created by a Second-Grade Teacher

Welcome to Second Grade!

I Am So Excited to Begin Our Year Together!

We are going to have so much fun together! On our first day of school there will be many surprises for you! We have a special pet that can't wait to meet you! A yummy delicious treat will be on your desk! A bag of goodies will be waiting for you! I could go on and on, but I really want you to be surprised!

What Should You Bring On the First Day?

The first day is such a special day. It will be a day spent getting to know each other and the classroom. I thought that a fun way for us to get to know each other a little bit better is to make bags about ourselves. Let me explain. Take any bag that you have around your house. Fill it with things that would help us to get know you better. You might include a family picture, your favorite book, a special stuffed animal, or anything else that you dream up! We will each get a chance to share our special bags!

A Little Bit About Me

I have always wanted to be a teacher ever since I was in the second grade. I used to set up my dolls and pretend to teach them. Now I have real live students! (They are a lot more fun!) I am married and have three cats—Forest, Cleo, and Michina. I love to read, write my own stories, travel, cook, spend time with my family, go to the movies, rollerblade, and jog. I feel that I am the luckiest person in the world because I get to do my favorite thing every day—teach!

Source: McFadden, Loredana, 1999, second-grade teacher, Colts Neck, New Jersey.

theme, and during play children read, write, speak, and listen to one another using literacy in functional ways.

The use of play to promote literacy development is receiving recognition. Although early childhood educators have realized the value of play for social, emotional, and physical development, in the past it has not been viewed as a place or time to develop literacy. Recently, play has gained greater importance as a medium for literacy development because it provides meaningful, functional social settings. Literacy development involves a child's active engagement in cooperation and collaboration with peers, builds on what the child already knows, and thrives on the support and guidance of others. Play provides this setting. During observations of children at play, one can see the functional uses

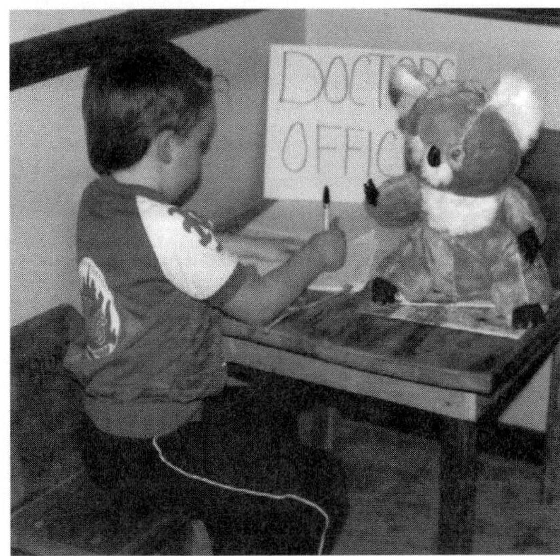

DOCTOR	SERVICE	ROOM

DATE	Note progress of case, complications, consultations, change in diagnosis, condition or discharge, instructions to patient.

After examining the stuffed bear, this young veterinarian in the dramatic-play center wrote: "This teddy bear's blood pressure is 29 points. He should take 62 pills an hour until he is better and keep warm and go to bed."

of literacy that children incorporate into their play themes. Children have been observed to engage in attempted and conventional reading and writing in collaboration with other youngsters (Morrow, 1990; Neuman & Roskos, 1990).

To demonstrate the importance of the social, collaborative, and interactive nature of literacy development, I take you into a classroom where the teacher, Mrs. Schifflette, has designed a veterinarian's office to go along with an animal theme with a concentration on pets. The dramatic-play area was designed with a waiting room; chairs; a table filled with magazines, books, and pamphlets about pet care; posters about pets; office hour notices; a "No Smoking" sign; and a sign advising visitors to "Check in with the nurse when arriving." A nurse's desk holds patient forms on clipboards, a telephone, an address and telephone book, appointment cards, a calendar, and a computer for recording appointments and patient records. Offices contain patient folders, prescription pads, white coats, masks, gloves, cotton swabs, a toy doctor's kit, and stuffed animals to serve as patients.

Mrs. Schifflette guides students in the use of the various materials in the veterinarian's office, for example, by reminding the children to read to pets in waiting areas, fill out forms with prescriptions or appointment times, or fill out forms with information about an animal's condition and treatment. In addition to giving directions, Mrs. Schifflette also models behaviors by participating in play with the children when the materials are first introduced.

The following anecdotes relate the type of behavior that was witnessed in this setting—a setting that provides a literacy-rich environment with books and writing materials; models reading and writing by teachers that children can observe and emulate; provides the opportunity to practice literacy in real-life situations that have meaning and function; and has children socially interacting, collaborating, and performing reading and writing with peers.

Jessica was waiting to see the doctor. She told her stuffed animal dog Sam not to worry, that the doctor wouldn't hurt him. She asked Jenny, who was waiting with her stuffed animal cat Muffin, what the kitten's problem was. The girls agonized over the ailments of their pets. After a while they stopped talking and Jessica picked up a book from the table and pretended to read Are You My Mother? *to her pet dog Sam. Jessica showed Sam the pictures as she read.*

Jennie ran into the doctor's office shouting "My dog got runned over by a car." The doctor bandaged the dog's leg; then the two children decided that the incident must be reported to the police. Before calling the police, they got out the telephone book and turned to a map to find the spot where the dog had been hit. Then they called the police on the toy phone to report the incident.

Preston examined Christopher's teddy bear and wrote out a report in the patient's folder. He read his scribble writing out loud and said, "This teddy bear's blood pressure is 29 points. He should take 62 pills an hour until he is better and keep warm and go to bed." While he read, he showed Christopher what he had written so he would understand what to do. He asked his nurse to type the notes into the computer.

Figure 5.4 shows forms that may be used in the dramatic-play center when it is designed as a veterinarian's office during a unit on animals.

Additional play settings that encourage reading and writing at different grade levels follow:

1. *Newspaper Office:* Includes telephones, directories, maps, computers, paper, pencils, and areas that focus on sports, travel, general news, and weather.
2. *Supermarket or Local Grocery Store:* Can include labeled shelves and sections, food containers with their labels left on, a cash register, telephone, computers, receipts, checkbooks, coupons, and promotional flyers.
3. *Post Office:* Can be used for mailing the children's letters and needs to include paper, envelopes, address books, pens, pencils, stamps, cash registers,

Figure 5.4 *Forms to write on for the Veterinarian's Office in the Dramatic-Play Center*

Appointment Card

Name: ______________________

Has an appointment on ______________

☐ Mon. ☐ Tues. ☐ Wed. ☐ Thurs. ☐ Fri. ☐ Sat.

Date ____________ at ________ a.m. p.m.

Prescription

Patient's Name:

Prescription:

Refills: Instructions:

Franklin A. Morrow, D.V.M.

Patient Record Form

Patient's Name: ______________ Type of animal: ______________

Owner's Name: ______________ Date of Visit: ______________

Address: ______________ Telephone Number: ______________

History and Physical Findings:	Treatment:

computers, and mailboxes. A mail carrier hat and bag are important for delivering the mail by reading names and addresses.

4. *Airport:* Can be created with signs posting arrivals and departures, tickets, boarding passes, luggage tags, magazines and books for the waiting area, safety messages on the plane, and name tags for the flight attendants. A computer is used to get onto the Internet to make plane reservations.
5. *Gas Station and Car Repair Shop:* Can be designed in the block area. Toy cars and trucks can be used for props. There can be receipts for sales, road maps to help with directions to different destinations, auto repair manuals for fixing cars and trucks, posters that advertise automobile equipment, and empty cans of different products that are sold in stations (Morrow & Rand, 1991).

For materials to be used for literacy to their fullest potential, teachers need to use props that are natural and from the child's environment. The materials in the setting created must serve a real function and be familiar to children. Do not set up several dramatic themes at once. Have the dramatic-play area match a theme being studied. Change the area when you begin to study a new theme. Teachers need to guide the use of materials initially. This is not a time for teaching specific skills but a time for literacy to be initiated by children naturally in the setting provided (Neuman & Roskos, 1993).

The materials in dramatic-play areas should be clearly marked and be accessible. All levels of literacy development should be accepted, and reading or writing attempts should be recognized as legitimate literacy behaviors. Teachers might find it useful to record anecdotes of literacy activities as an aid in assessing child development.

In the discussion of play, I have concentrated on cooperative learning to encourage literacy development. Play is typically thought of as a preschool and kindergarten activity; however, this type of setting could and should be used with first, second, and third grades as well. Older children engage in more sophisticated literacy behaviors when participating in play. For example, the Internet can be used in many play settings as a source of information, such as news stories, air travel routes, and so on.

Put Yourself in the Place of the Child

It is difficult for us as adults to understand and appreciate the various processes involved in learning to read and write because we have been doing it for many years. To understand better the nature of learning to read or write, put yourself in the place of the learner. With a contrived alphabet called the Confusabet, I have taken college students back to when they were five and six and first taught to read and write (Figure 5.5). Whole words are introduced in the unfamiliar alphabet, accompanied by picture clues and context clues. They are reinforced with worksheets. After being introduced to about 25 words, the students are given a book containing pictures and stories that use these words. They are called on to read just as they were in a reading group in an early childhood classroom. They are also asked to write one sentence about what they read in the Confusabet alphabet.

After the lesson we discuss how they have just learned to read and write with the Confusabet. Students consistently report similar strategies: They try to re-

Figure 5.5

Illustration of the Confusabet

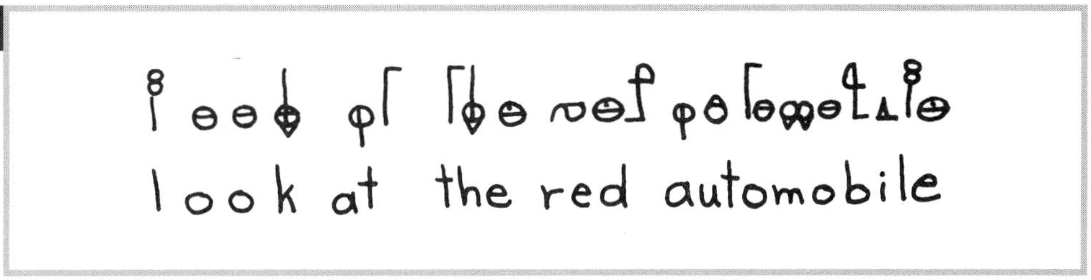

look at the red automobile

late information they already know about writing and reading to the situation. They realize quickly that Confusabet words have the same number of letters as words written in our regular alphabet, and their knowledge of words in general helps them make sense of Confusabet words. Certain similarities in letter forms help them figure out words. They use context and picture clues as much as possible. Their knowledge of syntax (language structures) and the meanings of words surrounding an unknown word helps them determine words they cannot otherwise identify. They skip around within a sentence looking for words they might know. Some rely on the first letter of a word to identify it. Many try to memorize words by the look–say method. Most agree that words with unusual shapes or lengths are easy to identify. They acknowledge that to learn they have to involve themselves actively in the reading process. In short, they guess, make mistakes, and correct themselves.

In addition to the strategies just described, my observations of the students' behavior during this class experience revealed another powerful strategy—the natural tendency to collaborate and cooperate with one another during learning. The students discussed successes and failures with those around them. They wanted to talk about the words they had figured out and share that excitement with others. They spontaneously expressed frustration when they experienced difficulty, and they sought help of those nearby. The room was noisy at times because of the social interaction of the literacy-learning experience. At times, two or three of them disagreed about a particular word, finally arriving at consensus. Sometimes problems were solved through peer tutoring, with one student helping another who was having trouble. They demonstrated a natural curiosity as they flipped eagerly through new materials.

All the students agreed that working together gave them a sense of security, provided easily accessible sources of information, and made the task more fun. They were almost unaware of their socially cooperative behavior until I pointed it out to them. Most commented that seeking and relying on social interaction when trying to learn to read with the Confusabet seemed to be a natural inclination.

In their descriptions of how they learned to read and write with the Confusabet, the students used emergent literacy and whole language perspectives. In all cases they sought meaning. They approached a printed message as a whole, and they drew on past experience as well as the help of one another. They guessed, predicted, and invented to construct meaning. They also used some traditional skill strategies such as trying to decode words by focusing on the first letter, using context clues, and using the sight word approach. Although these college students draw on many more experiences and associations with print and reading than the typical kindergarten or first-grade child can, this only indicates more emphatically how important it is for initial reading experiences to be based on meaning and function. (The Confusabet lesson can be found in Appendix D.)

Objectives for Literacy Development

According to Teale (1987), studies on emergent literacy suggest that to become literate young children must learn about the functions and uses of literacy, conventions of written language, decoding and encoding strategies, and comprehending and composing strategies. They also must develop positive attitudes toward reading and writing. From the theories on reading and writing acquisition and development, we can formulate objectives for beginning readers and writers from birth through seven:

1. Develop positive attitudes toward reading and writing.
2. Develop concepts about books.
3. Develop comprehension of story.
4. Develop phonemic awareness and alphabetic principles.
5. Develop the functions, forms, and conventions for writing and reading.

These objectives are intended simply as basic guidelines to help teachers design strategies for instruction. Another useful source that presents a continuum of children's development in early reading and writing is shown in Figure 5.6. This continuum is from the joint statement of the International Reading Association and the National Association for the Education of Young Children, *Learning to Read and Write: Developmentally Appropriate Practices for Young Children (1998).*

The instructional strategies described in the next four chapters are designed to serve these objectives. Chapter 6 emphasizes the uses of children's literature and concentrates on the first objective. Chapter 7 deals with the second and third objectives, Chapter 8 concentrates on objective four, and Chapter 9 with objectives one, four, and five. In all of the chapters, the strategies will be guided by the theories of how children learn to read and write that have just been discussed.

Figure 5.6 *Continuum of Children's Development in Early Reading and Writing*

Note: *This list intended to be illustrative, not exhaustive. Children at any grade level will function at a variety of phases along the reading/writing continuum.*

Phase 1: Awareness and exploration (goals for preschool)

Children explore their environment and build the foundations for learning to read and write.

Children can

- enjoy listening to and discussing storybooks
- understand that print carries a message
- engage in reading and writing attempts
- identify labels and signs in their environment
- participate in rhyming games
- identify some letters and make some letter-sound matches
- use known letters or approximations of letters to represent written language (especially meaningful words like their name and phrases such as "I love you")

What teachers do

- share books with children, including Big Books, and model reading behaviors
- talk about letters by name and sounds
- establish a literacy-rich environment
- reread favorite stories
- engage children in language games
- promote literacy-related play activities
- encourage children to experiment with writing

What parents and family members can do

- talk with children, engage them in conversation, give names of things, show interest in what a child says
- read and reread stories with predictable texts to children

- encourage children to recount experiences and describe ideas and events that are important to them
- visit the library regularly
- provide opportunities for children to draw and print, using markers, crayons, and pencils

Phase 2: Experimental reading and writing (goals for kindergarten)

Children develop basic concepts of print and begin to engage in and experiment with reading and writing.

Kindergartners can

- enjoy being read to and themselves retell simple narrative stories or informational texts
- use descriptive language to explain and explore
- recognize letters and letter-sound matches
- show familiarity with rhyming and beginning sounds
- understand left-to-right and top-to-bottom orientation and familiar concepts of print
- match spoken words with written ones
- begin to write letters of the alphabet and some high-frequency words

What teachers do

- encourage children to talk about reading and writing experiences
- provide many opportunities for children to explore and identify sound–symbol relationships in meaningful contexts
- help children to segment spoken words into individual sounds and blend the sounds into whole words (for example, by slowly writing a word and saying its sound)
- frequently read interesting and conceptually rich stories to children
- provide daily opportunities for children to write
- help children build a sight vocabulary
- create a literacy-rich environment for children to engage independently in reading and writing

What parents and family members can do

- daily read and reread narrative and informational stories to children
- encourage children's attempts at reading and writing
- allow children to participate in activities that involve writing and reading (for example, cooking, making grocery lists)
- play games that involve specific directions (such as "Simon Says")
- have conversations with children during mealtimes and throughout the day

Phase 3: Early reading and writing (goals for first grade)

Children begin to read simple stories and can write about a topic that is meaningful to them.

First graders can

- read and retell familiar stories
- use strategies (rereading, predicting, questioning, contextualizing) when comprehension breaks down
- use reading and writing for various purposes on their own initiative
- orally read with reasonable fluency
- use letter-sound associations, word parts, and context to identify new words
- identify an increasing number of words by sight
- sound out and represent all substantial sounds in spelling a word
- write about topics that are personally meaningful
- attempt to use some punctuation and capitalization

What teachers do

- support the development of vocabulary by reading daily to the children, transcribing their language, and selecting materials that expand children's knowledge and language development
- model strategies and provide practice for identifying unknown words
- give children opportunities for independent reading and writing practice
- read, write, and discuss a range of different text types (poems, informational books)
- introduce new words and teach strategies for learning to spell new words
- demonstrate and model strategies to use when comprehension breaks down
- help children build lists of commonly used words from their writing

What parents and family members can do

- talk about favorite storybooks
- read to children and encourage them to read to you
- suggest that children write to friends and relatives
- bring to a parent–teacher conference evidence of what your child can do in writing and reading
- encourage children to share what they have learned about their writing and reading

(continued on next page)

Figure 5.6 *(continued from previous page)*

Phase 4: Transitional reading and writing (goals for second grade)

Children begin to read more fluently and write various text forms using simple and more complex sentences.

Second graders can

- read with greater fluency
- use strategies more efficiently (rereading, questioning, and so on) when comprehension breaks down
- use word identification strategies with greater facility to unlock unknown words
- identify an increasing number of words by sight
- write about a range of topics to suit different audiences
- use common letter patterns and critical features to spell words
- punctuate simple sentences correctly and proofread their own work
- spend time reading daily and use reading to research topics

What teachers do

- create a climate that fosters analytic, evaluative, and reflective thinking
- teach children to write in multiple forms (stories, information, poems)
- ensure that children read a range of text for a variety of purposes
- teach revising, editing, and proofreading skills
- teach strategies for spelling new and difficult words
- model enjoyment of reading

What parents and family members can do

- continue to read to children and encourage them to read to you
- engage children in activities that require reading and writing
- become involved in school activities
- show children your interest in their learning by displaying their written work
- visit the library regularly
- support your child's specific hobby or interest with reading materials and references

Phase 5: Independent and productive reading and writing (goals for third grade)

Children continue to extend and refine their reading and writing to suit varying purposes and audiences.

Third graders can

- read fluently and enjoy reading
- use a range of strategies when drawing meaning from the text
- use word identification strategies appropriately and automatically when encountering unknown words
- recognize and discuss elements of different text structures
- make critical connections between texts
- write expressively in many different forms (stories, poems, reports)
- use a rich variety of vocabulary and sentences appropriate to text forms
- revise and edit their own writing during and after composing
- spell words correctly in final writing drafts

What teachers do

- provide opportunities daily for children to read, examine, and critically evaluate narrative and expository texts
- continue to create a climate that fosters critical reading and personal response
- teach children to examine ideas in texts
- encourage children to use writing as a tool for thinking and learning
- extend children's knowledge of the correct use of writing conventions
- emphasize the importance of correct spelling in finished written products
- create a climate that engages all children as a community of literacy learners

What parents and family members can do

- continue to support children's learning and interest by visiting the library and bookstores with them
- find ways to highlight children's progress in reading and writing
- stay in regular contact with your child's teachers about activities and progress in reading and writing
- encourage children to use and enjoy print for many purposes (such as recipes, directions, games, and sports)
- build a love of language in all its forms and engage children in conversation

Source: From *Learning to Read and Write: Developmentally Appropriate Practices for Young Children.* (1998). A joint position statement of the International Reading Association and National Association for the Education of Young Children.

An Idea for the Classroom from the Classroom

The following experience was created by an early childhood teacher. You may find this idea useful for your teaching.

A Bakery in the Dramatic-Play Area

In coordination with a unit on Community Helpers, we set up a bakery in the dramatic-play area. Materials included a baker's hat and apron, cookie cutter, rolling pin, mixing bowls, measuring spoons, and trays and boxes with labels for baked goods, such as donuts, cookies, cakes, and pies. Some classroom recipes that had already been made were hung in the area, and pens and pencils and books with recipes for baking were also placed in the area. A disk for the computer in the bakery has old recipes recorded. The Internet is consulted if a new recipe is needed.

For buying and selling baked goods, which were actually made, there were an ordering pad, a cash register, receipts for purchases, number tickets for standing in line, and name tags for the baker and salesperson.

To guide the children in their play, on different days, I modeled the behavior for a salesperson, a customer, and the baker. This was a popular play area in which a great deal of literacy behavior occurred. For example, the salesperson took orders on the phone and in person and wrote them down; the bakers followed recipes in the cookbook and on the wall; and the customers counted out money and read the labels naming the baked goods. Children participated in behaviors that I modeled and generated their own ideas when participating in play in the bakery.

Joyce C. Ng, First-Grade Teacher
Livingston, New Jersey

Activities and Questions

1. Answer the focus questions at the beginning of the chapter.

2. Describe how the approach to early literacy described is sensitive to children with special needs.

3. Reading and writing are acquired through (a) social and collaborative interaction with adults and other children, (b) association of print materials with real-life experiences, (c) awareness that there is a purpose for literacy, (d) the development of a desire to read and write that comes as a result of being read to, and (e) direct instruction of skills when additional help may be needed. Briefly discuss each of these five areas related to reading and writing acquisition. Then,

   a. Create a learning situation for each of the five categories mentioned.
   b. Observe a preschool, kindergarten, or first, second, or third grade and record literacy activities observed. Classify the literacy activities into the categories previously mentioned.

4. List components of a guided reading lesson and develop a lesson plan using leveled books as your source for reading for each element.

5. Observe a child between the ages of three and seven. Identify his or her beginning literacy behaviors.

6. Design a Web site for a primary classroom that will enhance literacy development.

7. You teach second grade and decide to design an area in your classroom for dramatic play as a source of literacy development. Because your students are studying different European countries, you decide to design a travel agency with books about countries being studied and posters about these lands and their languages, foods, customs, and clothing. During a center time, the children are encouraged to use the area to decide on trips they would like to take and do research about where they are going by using the Internet. They have to write itineraries about the places they will visit and include information about them. They pretend that they have taken the trip and share their experiences with their classmates through a written log that they read to their peers.

Parents are not particularly happy with the dramatic-play period. They do not think it is appropriate for second graders to be spending their time this way in school. Defend your principal's mandate for dramatic play, and how it theoretically and philosophically is good practice for literacy development.

Case Study Activities

Case 1

Review "An Idea for the Classroom from the Classroom" and identify the theories of literacy acquisition that exist in the learning setting described. Would this activity accommodate children with special needs? If yes, explain how; if no, suggest what might be done within this activity to accommodate such children better.

Case 2

Mr. Williams designed a dramatic-play area in his kindergarten classroom to stimulate natural literacy occurrences. He chose a pizzeria as the theme to match a unit the class was studying about nutrition. He was concerned about multicultural issues, so he decided that the type of restaurant would change occasionally to represent other cultural backgrounds.

He designed the pizzeria himself after the children had gone home from school. He included a telephone, pads for taking orders and reservations, aprons, pizza pans, a play oven, tables, and chairs. He made an OPEN and CLOSED sign for the restaurant, made menus, and placed a chalkboard on the wall for specials of the day. He also included a cash register, receipts, cookbooks, and a computer.

The next morning, Mr. Williams introduced the class to their pizzeria and suggested that, when they had free-play time, some of them could choose to play there.

After a week, Mr. Williams was thinking about dismantling the restaurant. Children were using the pizza pans as frisbees, and the order pad near the phone was unused, as were the other literacy materials. The only activity that was going on in the area was wild play.

Help Mr. Williams plan the dramatic-play area better so that it will bring about the literacy activity that he had hoped it would encourage. Use technology to accomplish the goal.

chapter 6

Motivating Reading and Writing with Children's Literature

Using Children's Literature in Classrooms

Children who read and write only when they have to are not being taught a love of reading. The best index of the success of literacy instruction is the eagerness with which children approach reading and writing.

Love of reading and writing is not taught, it is created.
Love of reading and writing is not required, it is inspired.
Love of reading and writing is not demanded, it is exemplified.
Love of reading and writing is not exacted, it is quickened.
Love of reading and writing is not solicited, it is activated.

—Russell Stauffer
Adapted from *Wilson Library Bulletin*

Focus Questions

- What does research have to say about the benefits of voluntary independent reading and writing?
- How do standards address the need for independent reading and writing?
- What are the physical characteristics of well-designed literacy centers and the benefits of having these centers in classrooms?
- Name and define different genres of children's literature.
- Describe strategies using children's literature that motivate interest in reading and writing.
- Describe activities in the literacy center and how they are organized to promote independent reading and writing.
- What characteristics of the literature experiences described in this chapter seem to be appropriate for children with special needs?
- What objectives help guide the development of positive attitudes toward literacy activities, thus motivating reading and writing?

During a social cooperative period for independent reading and writing, second graders Tesha and Jamin chose a felt story of the book *Are You My Mother?* (Eastman, 1960). The following transpired as they worked together reading the story and manipulating the felt characters:

Jamin: Can I read the story?

Tesha: OK.

Jamin: (He begins reading with enthusiasm as Tesha works the felt pieces on the board.) The baby bird asks the cow, "Are you my mother?"

Tesha: (She puts the cow on the felt-board.) Mooooooo.

Jamin: Moooooooo. (Jamin continues to read the book.)

Tesha: Look at this picture. (She points to the baby bird. Both start to giggle. They continue along in the story.)

Jamin: Here I am Mother! (He reads in a high-pitched voice.) Here comes the funny part. (He points to a picture of the mother bird in a red scarf and both children giggle. Jamin again does the bird-pitched voice.) Mother, mother, here I am!

Tesha: I like it when he says to the tractor, "You are my mother, Snort, Snort."

Jamin: Snort, Snort!

Tesha: Snort, Snort!

Jamin: I thought I had a mother. (He puts his hand to his head as he says this, using a baby bird voice and swaying back and forth pretending he is crying.)

Tesha: (She imitates Jamin by putting her hands on her hips.) I thought I had a mother!

Jamin: (He points to the felt-board.) Can I do this now and you read? (They trade places and Tesha starts reading. She speaks in a loud dramatic voice and has voices for the two birds. Tesha is reading the story too fast for Jamin to put the characters up on the board.)

Jamin: Wait, wait, will you wait a minute Tesha. (He puts the dog on the felt-board and Tesha continues.) Wait, Wait, Wait! (He puts the mother bird on the felt-board.)

The teacher asks everyone to put all work away because independent reading and writing time is over. Both children are disappointed and suggest they will continue tomorrow.

This dialogue was between two second-grade children engaged in an independent reading and writing period in which they had the opportunity to choose whom they would like to work with and what they would like to do that involves literacy behavior. The children have the opportunity to practice literacy to become proficient, the classroom atmosphere is relaxed, and a desire to read and write has been created through teacher modeling of pleasurable literacy activities. Because children can select what they want to do, and whom they do it with, the motivation and desire to read and/or write are high. The atmosphere promotes cooperative and collaborative behavior.

Two second graders reading and performing a felt story together.

The Extent of Voluntary Readers

Becoming a Nation of Readers (Anderson, Hiebert, Scott, & Wilkinson, 1985) states that learning to read requires (1) the motivation and desire to read, (2) practice to the point of proficiency, and (3) continuous and lifelong involvement so that fluency is maintained. One of the first goals in early literacy development is the nurturing of positive attitudes toward reading. Those attitudes usually result in voluntary readers. If children learn to read but have little desire to use their ability, we have not accomplished much. In a 1984 report to the U.S. Congress entitled *Books in Our Future,* Daniel Boorstin, then Librarian of Congress, warned that ***aliterates***—individuals who can read but choose not to—constitute as much of a threat to our democratic tradition as illiterates. Voluntary reading, or the lack of it, he wrote, "will determine the extent of self-improvement and enlightenment, the ability to share the wisdom and delights of our civilization, and our capacity for intelligent self-government" (p. iv).

Unfortunately, substantial numbers of children and adults read neither for pleasure nor for information. Surveys have found that about 20 percent of the adults in the United States who are able to read do so voluntarily on a regular basis. This means that of the four out of five Americans who can read, only one chooses to do so for pleasure or for information. Other surveys have indicated that after finishing school, about 60 percent of U.S. citizens never read a single book completely, and the rest read about one book a year (Woiwode, 1992). A reason suggested for these statistics is that schools do not deliberately and thoughtfully motivate children to acquire the reading habit.

Benefits Associated with Voluntary Reading

Apart from the common belief that voluntary reading is desirable, there is considerable empirical evidence that it correlates with success in school. Children identified as voluntary readers in elementary and middle grades demonstrated high levels of reading achievement in comprehension and in vocabulary development (Anderson, Wilson, & Fielding, 1985; Taylor, Frye, & Maruyama, 1990). Children who are introduced to literature at an early age tend to develop sophisticated language structures and vocabulary, which correlates with their subsequent success in learning to read. Both vocabulary and language structures can be improved significantly in youngsters by regular listening to stories read aloud. Children who experience literature early accumulate background knowledge, appreciate books, and show increased interest in learning to read. As discussed in previous chapters, they often begin to read early or learn to read more easily. Discussing books provides a foundation for comprehension skills because of the language development, background knowledge, and sense of story structure acquired thereby (Cambourne, 1987; Galda & Cullinan, 1991).

Researchers have repeatedly stressed the importance of providing children with daily opportunities to experience literature pleasurably; to discuss stories through literal, interpretive, and critical questioning; to relate literature activities to content-area learning; and to share the books they read or look at (Cullinan, 1987, 1989; Galda & Cullinan, 1991). Research has shown that children's use of literature increases dramatically when teachers incorporate enjoyable literature activities into the daily program and design attractive classroom library corners (Morrow, 1987b; Morrow & Weinstein, 1986).

The information in Chapter 3 for parents of infants and toddlers focuses on techniques and practices to develop positive attitudes toward books that are appropriate as well for aides and professionals in day-care centers. The discussion in this chapter focuses on techniques to use with two- to eight-year-olds (much of this information is applicable to younger children, too).

As you read the chapter, think about the characteristics of the strategies presented that would be particularly effective with children from diverse backgrounds.

Strategies for Motivating Reading and Writing

In a survey of classroom teachers concerning priorities for research, motivating children to want to read and write was ranked high on the list of suggestions (O'Flahavan, Gambrell, Guthrie, Stahl, & Alverman, 1992). Teachers recognize the importance of motivation in the development of children's literacy skills, and are interested in learning new ways to motivate their students.

Motivation is defined as initiating and sustaining a particular activity. It is considered the tendency to return to and continue working on a task with sustained engagement (Wittrock, 1986). A motivated reader chooses to read on a regular basis, and for many different reasons. Researchers have found that experiences that offer students (1) choice, (2) challenge, (3) social collaboration, and (4) success are likely to promote motivation.

Choice

Providing children with the opportunity to make *choices* about which literacy tasks they will participate in gives them responsibility and control over the situation. Choice needs to involve multiple modalities for learning; that is, developing literacy skills may combine traditional activities that use pencil and paper experiences with modalities that use technology, drama, or the visual arts. Choice instills intrinsic motivation (Lepper, 1988; Morrow, 1992; Turner, 1992).

Challenge

Students must perceive that there is some *challenge* to an activity, but that it is one that they can accomplish. That is, tasks should be perceived as not too hard but not too easy. When tasks are viewed as too easy, children become uninterested, whereas if tasks are too difficult, they become frustrated (Ford, 1992; Spaulding, 1992).

Social Collaboration

Motivation is increased through activities that offer opportunities for *social collaboration.* When children have the opportunity to learn in social situations involving collaboration with the teacher or peers, they are likely to get more done than they could do alone, and are more intrinsically motivated to participate than when they work alone (Brandt, 1990; Oldfather, 1993).

Success

When students complete a task they must consider it a *success.* Often children finish a task that is not completely correct, but if they perceive themselves as being successful, intrinsic motivation is enhanced (Turner, 1992). When a child has met with some but not total success, such as spelling the word *read* as *reed,* he or she should be acknowledged for the part of the spelling that is correct. After all, three of the four letters are right. In other words, the child's success should be noted at the same time he or she is helped with the conventional spelling of the word.

The information presented in this chapter is based on motivation theory, which offers children the experiences just outlined, and investigations revealing

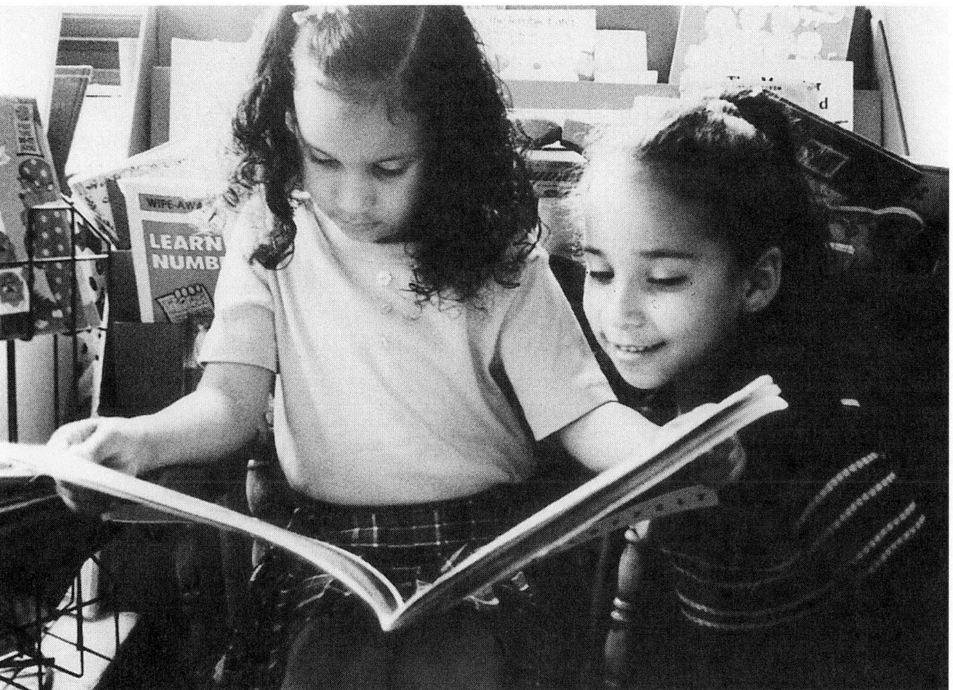

Children participate in independent reading with peers.

classroom practices that seem to promote children's voluntary reading. Investigators have observed and described such strategies, correlated use of literature to materials in classrooms and activities carried out by teachers, and intervened with programs to see if changes in attitudes toward reading, demonstrated by increased use of books, are possible. The programs or strategies are based on the following objectives to help motivate voluntary use of children's literature.

Objectives for Motivating Voluntary Reading and Writing with the Use of Literature

1. Children should be provided with an environment that is rich, with choices of literacy materials that are challenging but will bring success.
2. Teachers should provide models of literacy behavior for children to emulate.
3. Children need to be given the opportunity to participate in social collaborative settings during periods of independent reading and writing.
4. Children must be able to choose literacy activities in which to participate.
5. Children need to work in cooperative and collaborative settings as well as alone if they choose.
6. Children should have the opportunity to listen to stories read by their teachers and peers in a pleasant, relaxed atmosphere.
7. Teachers should allow for response to literature through discussion, role-playing, the use of puppets to retell stories, and so on.
8. Children need the opportunity to take books home from the classroom literacy center.
9. Children should experience varied genres of children's literature.
10. Teachers should help children enhance word-analysis skills and comprehension skills using children's literature.

Standards and Motivating Reading and Writing

Standards for literacy achievement generated by various groups, states, and school districts often appear to be skills based. However, most standards are concerned with developing readers and writers who do not learn just the skills of reading and writing, but also the joys of reading and writing. The focus is on the need for children to be motivated to read and write for pleasure and information. The standards in different states and from different groups have included in kindergarten through third grades sections about reading and writing habits and expectations for how students will acquire these habits. The following are standards for reading and writing habits from the National Center on Education and the Economy and the Learning Research and Development Center at the University of Pittsburgh (1999).

Reading Habits

Good reading habits will be established with children having opportunities to read independently often. Books should be read to children that are of high literary quality and interest, represent multiple genres, and are at a greater difficulty level than children could read on their own.

It is expected in the early childhood grades that to develop the reading habit, children will have the opportunity to

- read a lot independently
- read a wide range of genres in literature such as poems and stories, functional text (signs, messages, and labels), and narrative texts (expository text that is informational)
- choose reading during their free time at school and read several short books a day at school
- listen to books read to them each day at school and discuss the books
- listen and read books with parents

Writing Habits

Good writing habits will be established with children having opportunities to write independently often. Children should listen to each others' writing. Writing should occur in many different forms such as functional, informational, and narrative writing.

To develop good writing habits and thus enhance motivation to write, it is expected that in the early childhood grades children will

- write a lot and listen to what others write
- write a lot independently
- write in a wide range of genres such as poems and stories, functional text (signs, messages, and labels), and narrative texts (expository text that is informational)
- listen to others writing and discuss each others' work
- write at home

Standards for literacy achievement are important goals to attain. It is particularly important to include the standards just discussed so that we create students who not only can read but also who choose to read for pleasure and for information.

Preparing a Literacy-Rich Environment

Before planning instruction that will entice children to books, teachers must prepare appropriate materials and a physical setting that sets the stage for pleasurable literacy experiences. As Plato said, "What is honored in a country will be cultivated there." Teachers who honor the development of literacy demonstrate that attitude by providing within their classrooms a rich environment where the use of books can be cultivated. Their students honor literacy development by assimilating the attitudes and atmosphere presented by the teacher.

A classroom **literacy center** is essential for children's immediate access to literature. Children in classrooms with literature collections read and look at books 50 percent more often than children in classrooms without such collections. The efforts spent in creating an inviting atmosphere for a classroom literacy center are rewarded by increased interest in books (Morrow & Weinstein,

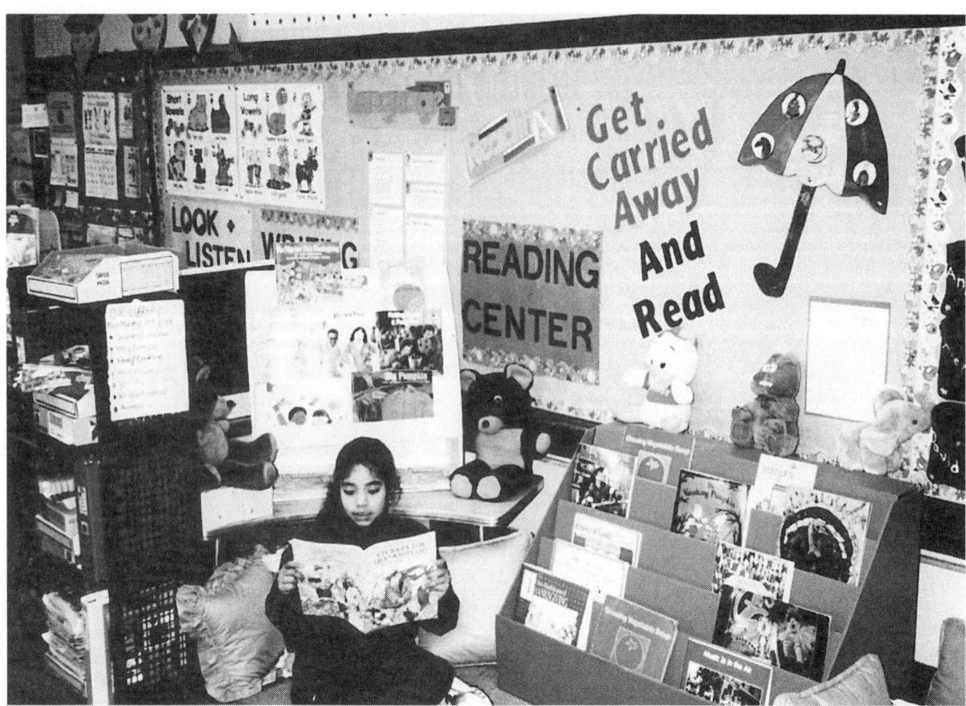

A classroom literacy center is crucial for children's immediate access to books.

1986). Morrow (1987b) found that well-designed classroom literacy centers significantly increased the number of children who chose to participate in literature activities during free-choice periods. Literacy centers in nursery schools, kindergartens, and first and second grades identified with having specific design characteristics correlated with children's use of the centers during free-choice periods. Conversely, poorly designed literacy centers were among the least popular areas during free-choice periods in early childhood rooms (Morrow, 1982). Suffice it to say, the physical features of a classroom literacy center can play an important role in enticing children to use the area voluntarily.

Features of Well-Designed Literacy Centers

Classrooms need multiple centers for children to practice skills learned and to work independently. Chapter 4 describes several content-area centers to meet this need. Classrooms should have literacy centers that include a library corner and writing area. In this chapter, the library corner portion of the literacy center will be described. In Chapter 9, the writing area is discussed in depth.

Physical Space

A classroom literacy center should be a focal area, immediately visible and inviting to anyone entering the classroom. To provide privacy and physical definition, it should be partitioned on two or three sides with bookshelves, a piano, file cabinets, or freestanding bulletin boards. The dimensions of the literacy center will vary with the size of the classroom. Generally, it should be large enough to accommodate five or six children comfortably (Figure 6.1).

Figure 6.1 *A Classroom Literacy Center*

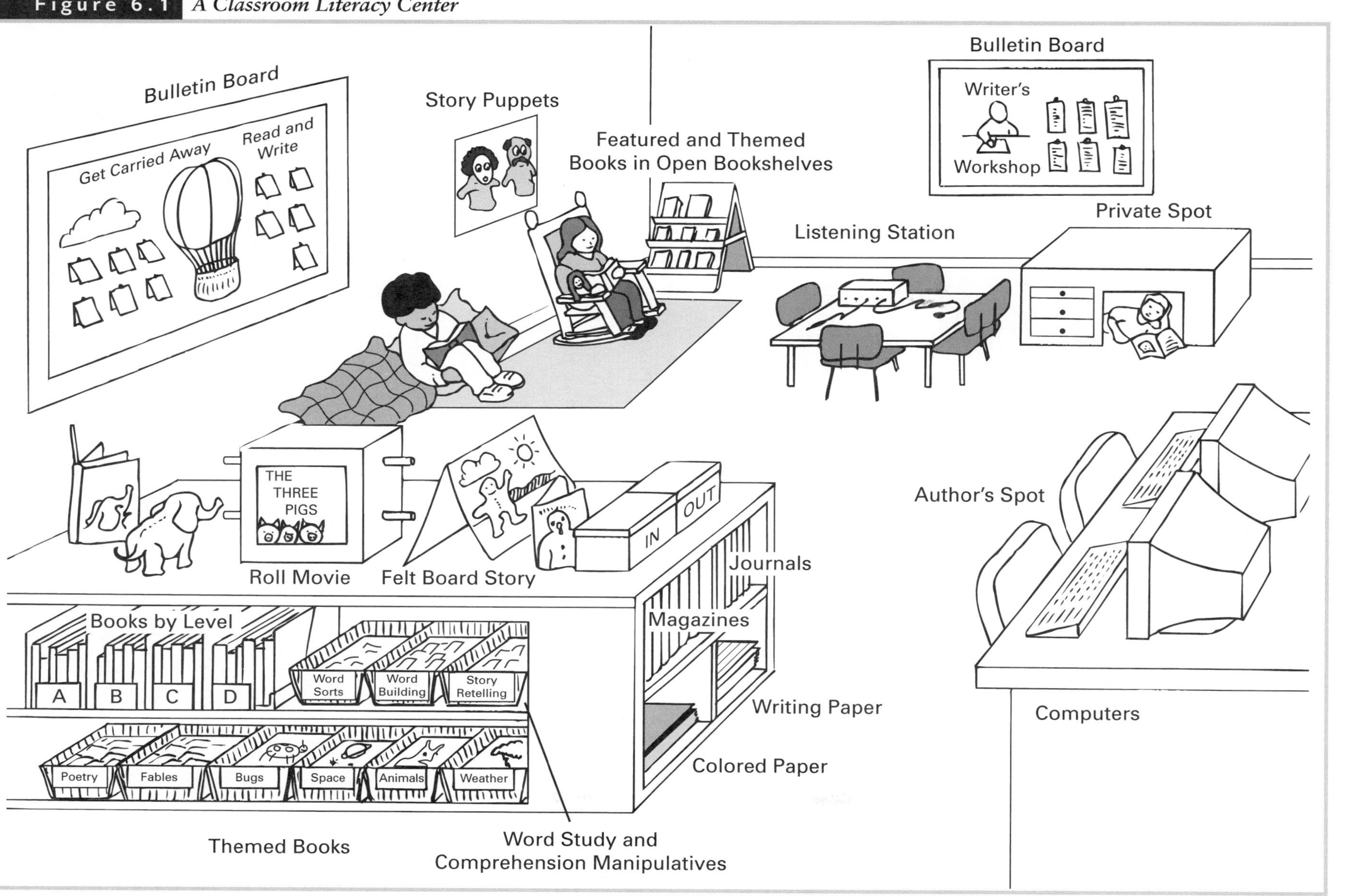

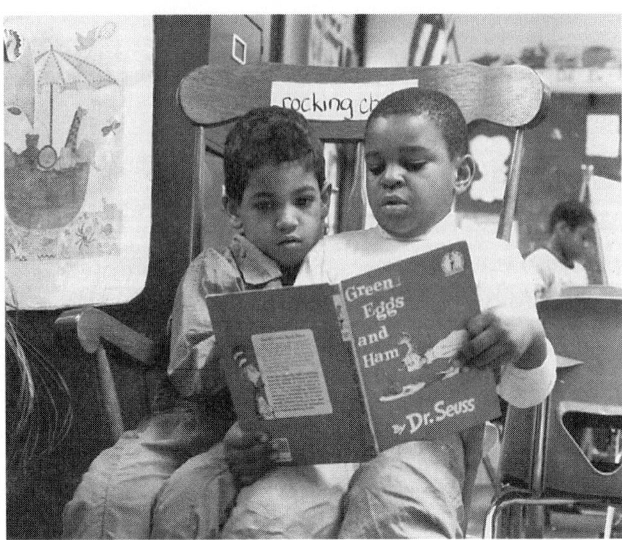

The rocking chair is the Literacy Chair of Honor.

The literacy center should be furnished with an area rug and pillows or beanbag chairs because much of the activity there takes place on the floor. If possible, it should also include a small table and chairs where children can use headsets to listen to taped stories and make their own books. A rocking chair allows comfortable reading: a place for teachers to read to children and children to read to their classmates. They read their original stories and present literacy projects to the group while sitting in the rocking chair. It is the chair that invited guests use to read or present other information to the class. The rocking chair is the Literacy Chair of Honor.

Children are given little privacy in the typical school. It has been found that many children relish privacy and sometimes read in coat closets and under shelves. Because it is partially partitioned from the rest of the room, the literacy center provides some privacy. Listening to recorded stories on headsets offers even more privacy, and an oversized carton, painted or covered with contact paper, makes a cozy separate reading room.

The Author's Spot is an integral part of the literacy center. It usually consists of a table and chairs with various writing materials available. There are colored felt-tip pens, crayons, and lined white paper ranging in size. It is necessary to include at least one computer in the Author's Spot. Materials for making books also should be present, including colored construction paper for covers, plain white paper for inside pages, a stapler, and scissors. (The Author's Spot will be described more thoroughly in Chapter 9.)

Children should be involved in the planning and design of a literacy center. They can develop rules for its use, be in charge of keeping it neat and orderly, and select a name for it, such as Book Nook.

The Library Corner

Well-designed library corners in literacy centers have several ways for storing books. One type houses the bulk of the books, which are shelved with the spines facing out. Another type is open faced, allowing the covers of the books to be seen, which is important for calling attention to special books. Featured books, changed regularly, are placed on the open-faced shelves for easy access. An alternative to open-faced shelving is the circular wire rack, commonly found in bookstores. These racks and open-faced shelving should highlight books with themes being studied. These books are changed with the theme and the shelving used to feature special new selections.

Books in the collection should be shelved by category. They can be color coded according to the type of book. Identify all animal books, for example, by placing a blue dot on their spines and clustering them on a shelf marked "Animals," with a blue dot next to the label. An even simpler method is to store genres in plastic crates or cardboard boxes, with labels on the front naming the types of books in the container.

About five to eight books per child is appropriate in a classroom library with three to four grade levels included. Some books can be storied by level of difficulty. For example, "A" would represent very easy books and "D" would be more difficult. If children want to read something very easy or something more challenging, leveling the books allows them to select on their own.

Books are not difficult to accumulate. They can be purchased inexpensively at yard sales or flea markets. Teachers can borrow up to 20 books a month from most public libraries, ask for book donations from parents, and hold fund raisers for book purchases. In addition, children's paperback book clubs offer inexpensive books and free bonus books for bulk purchases.

Children's magazines and newspapers belong in the classroom library, even if they are not current. For the cost of mailing and shipping, some publishers and local magazine agencies will donate outdated periodicals to schools.

To ensure continued interest, the teacher must introduce new books and materials and recirculate others in the library corner. Approximately 25 new books should be introduced every two weeks, replacing 25 that have been there for a while. In this way, "old" books will be greeted as new friends a few months later. Recirculation compensates limited budgets as well.

Books from the library corner should be available for students to check out and take home for a week at a time. The check-out system should be simple. At specified times during the school day, children might bring the books they want to borrow to the teacher, who notes the date, child's name, and book title. Some kindergarten children have been taught to check out books themselves by copying titles and recording dates on five-by-eight cards filed under their own names. Other youngsters enjoy keeping track of books borrowed by recording titles and dates on three-by-five cards hung on curtain-rod hooks or key rings mounted on a bulletin board, one hook or ring per child. Another method for checking out books is a loose-leaf notebook with a page for every child to record books taken out and returned. Figure 6.2 provides a sample check-out notebook page.

Books in the Library Corner

Books and other materials selected for the library corner should appeal to a variety of interests and span a range of grade levels. It is advisable to stock multiple copies of popular books. Children sometimes enjoy reading a book because a friend is reading it (Morrow, 1985). Several types of children's literature should be represented:

Picture concept books are appropriate for the very young child. Most picture concept books do not have story lines, though they often have themes, such

Figure 6.2

Looseleaf Notebook Page for Checking Out Books

Name Tamika Jones

Name of book	Date out	Date in
Green Eggs and Ham	Feb 10	Feb 17
Carrot Seed	Feb 20	Feb 26
Curious George	March 3	March 9
Where the Wild Things Are	March 15	March 21

as animals or toys. Each page usually carries a picture identified by a printed word. Many picture books are made of cardboard, cloth, or vinyl to withstand rigorous handling. Alphabet and number books are also considered picture concept books.

Traditional literature includes nursery rhymes and fairy tales, familiar stories that are part of our heritage and originated in the oral tradition of storytelling. We assume that children are familiar with *Goldilocks and the Three Bears* (Izawa, 1968a) and *The Three Little Pigs* (Brenner, 1972), yet many youngsters have not been exposed to these traditional stories. Children who *do* know the stories welcome them as old friends.

Picture storybooks are most familiar to us as children's literature. Their texts are closely associated with their illustrations. Picture storybooks are available on a wide range of topics, and many are known for their excellence. The Caldecott Medal is awarded annually to the author or illustrator of an outstanding picture storybook. Many of these books have become classics and their authors renowned—Dr. Seuss, Ezra Jack Keats, Tomie dePaola, Maurice Sendak, and Charlotte Zolotow, to name just a few. Every child should have the benefit of hearing some of these books read. However, emergent readers will often find the vocabulary and syntax too sophisticated to read on their own.

Realistic literature is a category within picture storybooks that deals with real-life issues. *Tight Times* (1983) by Barbara Hazen, for example, describes how a family handles the problems that arise when the father loses his job. He tries to explain the situation to his son so he will understand and calls it *Tight Times.* Books in this category deal with issues that many children face, such as fears a child has when it is time to go to sleep or problems that arise with a new baby in the house. Some touch on very sensitive issues, such as divorce, drugs, alcohol, and death. Many of these books can be read to the entire class if they address issues that all share. Teachers should use discretion as to what he or she reads to the whole class. Teachers also can recommend specific titles to parents and family members of children who face particular problems.

Easy-to-read books are designed to be read by emergent readers themselves. They have limited and repeated vocabularies, and many of them rhyme, which makes them predictable and aids independent reading. Because of their limited vocabulary, few easy-to-read books rate as quality literature, but many preschool and kindergarten children begin to read independently with them.

Fables and folktales retell many of the myths and traditional stories that are available in picture-book style for the younger child. Many of these stories originate in other countries and cultures and therefore broaden a child's experience and knowledge base.

Informational books or expository texts offer nonfiction for readers. There are books about holidays, plants, animals, foreign countries, communities, dinosaurs, and famous people. They broaden a child's background information, explore new ideas, and often stimulate deep interest in particular topics.

Wordless books carry definite story lines within pictures, but use no words. They are often thought appropriate for very young children and are confused with picture books. They are designed not for babies but for children three and older. The child creates the story by reading the pictures, some of which are intricate.

Poetry is too often forgotten in collections of children's literature at home and in school. Many themed anthologies have been compiled for young children, and they are an important part of the literacy center.

Novels are longer books with chapters. We can begin reading novels to young children to expose them to the genre. They are often quite attracted to them and eager to begin to read them. Children often call novels chapter books.

Biography is another genre appropriate for young children. There are simple biographies of historical figures, popular figures in sports, and on television.

Big Books are usually large versions of smaller picture storybooks. They can also be original stories. They are oversized books that rest on an easel in order to be read. The purpose of the Big Book is for children to be able to see the print as it is being read, to make the association between oral and written language, and to see how the print is read from left to right across the page.

In addition to these categories of books, young children enjoy joke and riddle books; craft books; cookbooks; participation books, which involve them in

Children's literature is stored by categories in baskets that are labeled for easy access.

touching, smelling, and manipulating; books in a series built around a single character; and books related to television programs appropriate for their age. As mentioned, magazines and newspapers also should be choices for reading in the library corner. They provide a nonthreatening format, diverse topics, and reading matter for diverse ability levels, and include multicultural material. Newspapers and magazines appeal to parents as well.

Children particularly enjoy literature that is predictable because it helps them understand the story line more easily and enables them to read along with the individual reading to them. Predictable literature contains rhyme; repetition; catch phrases; conversation; familiar sequences, such as days of the week or numbers; cumulative patterns, in which events are repeated or added on as the story continues; stories about familiar topics; familiar or popular stories; uncluttered illustrations that match the text; and stories that have well-developed story structures (setting, theme, plot, episodes, and resolution).

Listings of children's literature in several categories, including books for children with special needs and multicultural books, are in Appendix A. There is also a list of Web sites for locating children's books. Following are children's book clubs and children's book awards that provide additional literature resources.

Book Clubs

Scholastic Book Clubs, Inc., Firefly (preschool), SeeSaw (K–1), Lucky (2–3), 2931 East McCarty Street, PO Box 7503, Jefferson City, MO 65102–7503; 800-724-6527

Troll Book Club, #2 Lethbridge Plaza, Mahway, NJ 07430; 201-529-2210

Trumpet Book Club, PO Box 7511, Jefferson City, MO 65102

Children's Book Awards

Caldecott Medal. American Library Association, 50 East Huron Street, Chicago, IL 60611.

Children's Book Showcase. Children's Book Council, 568 Broadway, Suite 404, New York, NY 10012

Newbery Medal. American Library Association, 50 East Huron Street, Chicago, IL 60611

Other Materials in the Literacy Center

The literacy center needs to contain language arts materials for skill development. Manipulatives that help children learn letters of the alphabet, rhymes, and sound–symbol relationships of consonants, digraphs, long and short vowels should be included in a special section of the center. These manipulatives come in the form of magnetic letters and boards, puzzles, bingo games, and concentration and board games, to name a few. Teacher-made materials also can be used. (These types of materials will be described more in Chapter 8, which deals with skill development.) Materials to enhance comprehension must also be available in the literacy center. Techniques that will be described later, such as using the felt-board and story characters for storytelling and organizing puppet presentations, engage children in demonstrating knowledge of story sequence and structure, classifying details, predicting outcomes, and interpreting text—skills that develop and enhance comprehension of text.

The library corner invites children to read, and the Author's Spot provides accessible materials for writers.

Stuffed animals also belong in a library, especially if they are related to books available in the corner—a stuffed rabbit next to *The Tale of Peter Rabbit* (Potter, 1902), for instance. Children enjoy reading to stuffed animals or simply holding them as they look at books. A felt-board, with figures of story characters from favorite books, is one of the more frequently used materials in a literacy center, as are roll movies, puppets, and headsets with taped stories. A roll movie consists of a box with a picture window cut out that makes it look like a television. A dowel is inserted at the top and bottom of the box. Shelving paper is written on and illustrated and attached to the dowels for presentation (see photograph on page 191). The center also should include materials from which children can make their own books, felt stories, and roll movies. In addition, attractive posters that encourage reading are available from the Children's Book Council (568 Broadway, Suite 404, New York, NY 10012; www.cbcbooks.org) and the American Library Association (50 East Huron Street, Chicago, IL 60611; www.ala.org).

Reactions to Literacy Centers

Teachers and children had the following reactions to literacy centers I designed in their classrooms. Teachers said they were concerned that there was not enough space in their rooms for literacy centers and were surprised that all the materials could fit. Eventually, teachers themselves provided more space for the literacy centers. Teachers commented that the physical presence of the literacy center made a statement to the children that literacy was so valued that space was taken from the classroom to make room for the area. Teachers agreed that children were attracted to the area by the manipulative materials in the center, such as the felt-board stories and puppets. They found that the rocking chair, rug, pillows, and stuffed animals made the center relaxing and comfortable for reading:

> *The literacy center became a place where children of all reading and writing abilities mingled. . . . This social context seemed to provide an atmosphere for cooperative learning. The children looked forward to their time there each day.*

A child commented:

> *I liked to cuddle up on the pillows with a book, or crawl into a private spot, or rock in the rocking chair and read. You get to take books home right from the classroom center.*

Children referred to the center as a special place. They felt that the literacy center could be improved by adding more space, more books, and more time to use it. A child commented: "The only thing missing from the literacy center is a snack bar."

The Teacher as a Model to Motivate Interest

The teacher plays a critical role in influencing children's attitudes toward voluntary reading and literature.

> If children live in an environment that associates reading with pleasure and enjoyment, they are likely to become voluntary readers. How children live and learn at home and in the classroom ultimately determines whether they will live their lives as literate or alliterate individuals. (Morrow, 1985, p. 20)

Chapter 3 dealt with literacy activities appropriate for home use and was intended primarily to provide parental models for literacy behavior and to help children associate reading with pleasure. The school must follow a similar agenda.

> One of the clear points to emerge from research into reading failure is that there was no association between reading and pleasure. . . . The role of teachers in stimulating voluntary reading among children and young people is . . . potentially the most powerful of all adult influences upon the young. (Irving, 1980, p. 7)

Programs that incorporate pleasurable experiences with literature create interest in and enthusiasm for books that in turn increase children's voluntary use of books (Morrow, 1987b, 1992; Morrow & Weinstein, 1986). Among other specific activities in early childhood classrooms, teachers should read or tell stories to children daily. Interest heightens when stories are discussed both before and after being read, especially if they are related to issues that reflect children's real-life experiences or current school topics. Literal, inferential, and critical questions can be introduced even at the preschool level. Skill development can easily be incorporated into storybook reading activities in pleasurable and meaningful ways. The following example describes a discussion about *Goldilocks and the Three Bears* in which inferential and critical comprehension is being developed.

I recently led a discussion with four-year-olds after reading *Goldilocks and the Three Bears*. I asked who were the good and the bad characters. Hands waved in the air and Jennifer answered, "Goldilocks was good and the bears were bad." When I asked Jennifer why she thought that, she said, "Well, the bears scared Goldilocks."

Another hand went up and Tim said, "No, that's not right. The bears are good and Goldilocks is bad. Goldilocks went into the bears' house when they weren't home. She ate their food and didn't even ask."

"That's right," said Megan, "and she broke their chair and went to sleep in their bed and didn't even ask if it was okay."

Chris chimed in, "Yeah, Goldilocks was really bad. She did a lot of bad things because she didn't ask if she could."

"Would you go into a stranger's house and do the things Goldilocks did?" I asked. The whole group called out in unison "Nooooo." I asked why not. Sara answered, "Because that is bad. It's like stealing. She was naughty. If the cops found out, I bet they will arrest her."

Discussion about authors and illustrators also arouses interest. Reading different stories by the same author or a series of books about the same character, such as *Frog and Toad Are Friends* (Lobel, 1979) or *Amelia Bedelia* (Parish, 1970), increases interest as well. Read different kinds of literature to the class, and as often as possible coordinate stories with topics being discussed. If the topic is spring, bring a cocoon to class, discuss the life cycle of a butterfly, and follow the discussion with *The Very Hungry Caterpillar* (Carle, 1969), the story of the caterpillar's transformation to a butterfly. Read and recite poetry together regularly. Recruit older children, the principal, the custodian, the nurse, the librarian, parents, and grandparents to read to classes, to small groups, and to individuals. Encourage children to share books with one another. Books from home should be shared with the group and children encouraged to take books home from school.

Many popular folk songs have been made into picture storybooks, such as *Go Tell Aunt Rhody* (Quackenbush, 1973) and *Old MacDonald Had a Farm* (Quackenbush, 1972). These books are particularly good to read to children because the children are familiar with the words and want to pretend to read the books themselves and to another person. Cooking is another pleasurable activity that can be related to literature. Many picture storybooks feature food, such as *Bread and Jam for Frances* (Hoban, 1964). After reading the story the class can make bread and jam or whatever food is appropriate. *Art* activities also can be motivated by story readings. After reading *The Snowy Day* (Keats, 1962), have children create a winter collage from blue construction paper, white cotton, wool, doilies, chalk, and silver foil. After reading *Where the Wild Things Are* (Sendak, 1963), ask kindergarteners and first graders to think of a wild thing and draw a picture of it. Gather their pictures into a class book. Class books become favorites and are read frequently by children. Children also enjoy filmstrip and movie stories, which motivate their interest in reading the associated book.

Story Reading and Storytelling: Motivating Interest in Literacy

Making Story Reading Pleasurable

To make story reading as enjoyable and pleasurable as possible, select good pieces of literature—well-structured stories with well-delineated characters, clear and uncluttered illustrations, catch phrases, rhyme, and repetition. Read to youngsters in a relaxed atmosphere in a location designated for such readings. Each day let a different child sit close to you while you are reading, with the other children in a single or double semicircle. If you have a rocking chair, use it as the place where you sit when you read. Because children enjoy seeing illustrations in books during story reading, hold the book so it faces the group or turn the book at appropriate pauses so its pictures can be seen. Before reading a story to a group, practice reading it aloud to yourself.

Be expressive in your reading, change your voice when a different character speaks, and highlight special events. Use facial expressions. A story reading is like a dramatic presentation. Read slowly and with a great deal of animation. Record or videotape your readings to improve your technique. Begin a story with an introduction such as, "Today I'm going to read a story about a little girl who wanted to get a present for her mother's birthday. She can't think of anything and asks a rabbit to help her. The title of the story is *Mr. Rabbit and the Lovely Present* [Zolotow, 1962]. The author's name is Charlotte Zolotow and the illustrator is Maurice Sendak. While I read the story, think of which part of the present you like the best." When you have finished reading the story, begin a discussion with a question such as "Who would like to tell me which part of the present you liked best?"

Using Creative Storytelling Techniques

Storytelling strongly attracts children to books (Morrow & Weinstein, 1986). It has a power that reading stories does not, for it frees the storyteller to use creative techniques. It also has the advantage of keeping the storyteller close to the audience. Telling a story produces an immediate response from the audience and is one of the surest ways to establish rapport between the listeners and the storyteller. Long pieces of literature can be trimmed so that even very young children can hear whole stories in one sitting. Considered an art, storytelling can be mastered by most people.

It is not necessary to memorize a story, but be sure you know it well. Use all the catch phrases and quotes that are important to the story. Use expression in your presentation, but do not let your dramatic techniques overshadow the story itself. Look directly at your audience and take their attention into consideration. Storytelling allows you to shorten stories as you go if attention spans seem to be short. It is important to have the original book at hand when you have finished telling a story so that the children can see it and enjoy it again through its pictures and printed text.

Creative techniques help storytelling come alive. They excite the imagination, involve the listeners, and motivate children to try storytelling themselves and create their own techniques. Take clues for creative techniques from the story. Some stories lend themselves to the use of puppets, others are perfect for the felt-board, and still others can be worked up as chalk talks.

Felt-boards are a popular and important tool in a classroom. You can make characters or purchase them commercially. Prepare your own with construction paper covered with clear contact or laminate. Attach strips of felt or sandpaper to the backs of the cutouts so they cling to the felt-board. Stories that lend themselves to felt-board retelling are those with a limited number of characters who appear throughout the story.

Puppets are used with stories rich in dialogue. There are many kinds of puppets, including finger, hand, stick, and face puppets. Shy children often feel secure telling stories with puppets. Such stories as *The Gingerbread Boy* (Holdsworth, 1968) and *The Little Red Hen* (Izawa, 1968b) are appropriately told with puppets because they are short, have few characters, and repeat dialogue.

Sound-story techniques allow both audience and storyteller to provide sound effects when they are called for in a plot. The sounds can be made with voices, rhythm instruments, or music. When preparing to tell such a story, first select those parts of the story for which sound effects will be used. Then decide on each sound to be made and who will make it. As the story is told, students and storyteller chime in with their assigned sounds. Record the presentation, then leave the recording in the literacy center with the original book. Among books that adapt easily to sound-story techniques are *Too Much Noise* (McGovern, 1967) and *Mr. Brown Can Moo! Can You?* (Seuss, 1970).

Prop stories are easy to develop. Simply collect stuffed animals, toys, and other articles that represent characters and objects in a story. Display the props at appropriate times during the storytelling. Three stuffed bears and a yellow-haired doll aid in telling *Goldilocks and the Three Bears* (Izawa, 1968a), and several toy trains aid in *The Little Engine That Could* (Piper, 1954).

Chalk talks are another technique that attracts listeners. The storyteller draws the story while telling it. Chalk talks are most effective when done with a large chalkboard so that the story can keep going in sequence from beginning to end. The same technique can be carried out on mural paper hung across a wall; the storyteller simply uses crayons or felt-tip markers instead of chalk. The chalk-talk technique also can be adapted to easel and chart paper or an overhead projector. Choose a story with simple illustrations. Draw only a select few pictures as you tell the story. There are stories that have been written as chalk talks, including an entire series, *Harold and the Purple Crayon* (Johnson, 1955).

Headsets with taped stories are also popular materials in the literacy center. The stories are most often read but can be told on a tape for children to listen to and follow along in the text. They are helpful for second-language learners because they provide a model for good English. They are also good for struggling readers who can follow along in the text while listening to a fluent reader. Have parents, the principal, teachers, the nurse, the superintendent, and others record the tapes. Eventually children can make tapes for others as well.

Because there are numerous techniques for storytelling not mentioned, you can add to this list. All of the materials discussed need to be modeled for children who will then want to become storytellers themselves. After modeling children can do the following:

- Tell the story you modeled with one of the techniques you used.
- Select a piece of literature they know well, and create a technique for presenting it. When it is complete the children who worked on the project can present it to the class and leave it in the center for others to use.
- Write an original story, and create a technique for presentation. When it is complete the children who worked on the project can present it to the class and then place in the literacy center for others to use.

Storytelling activities involve children in literal comprehension because they must know the sequence, details, and elements of the story. They must problem solve as they create the materials, deciding what parts of the story to include or delete. They interpret voices of characters as they make a presentation of their finished project to the class.

The teaching of specific skills also can be embedded into teacher presentations of these storytelling techniques. For example, if you need to teach letter-writing skills, the story *A Letter to Amy* (Keats, 1968) is a perfect selection. The story is about a boy who wants to invite a girl to his birthday, but he worries that his friends might laugh. He sends her an invitation and wonders if she will come and what will happen. In the book there is a lot of discussion about the letter. A student of mine taught letter writing and introduced it by telling a feltboard version of *A Letter to Amy.* One of the items in the story for the feltboard was an envelope with a well-written letter having the appropriate heading, format, etc. Children used this model to write letters of invitation to others. Another story was used to reinforce the initial consonant "P." The teacher told the story *The Pigs' Picnic* (Kasza, 1988) using a chalk-talk technique and asked the children to be detectives and listen for all the words that started with the letter *"P."*

Practicing Story Reading and Storytelling

I had the opportunity to work with several first- and second-grade teachers who practiced sharing literature with children in pleasurable ways. The teachers read and told stories and made manipulatives for storytelling to use in their classrooms. These teachers incorporated many of the strategies discussed earlier, and one of them commented about their use:

> *The children enjoy being read to and they never grow tired of this activity. I thought that in second grade, reading to youngsters was not that important anymore; however, the benefits of read-aloud sessions became quite ev-*

ident as I involved my children in them more and more. The stories generated sophisticated discussion; we'd relate them to the students' own life experiences. We discussed authors, illustrations, and elements of story structure. Through these story readings and discussions, I found that my students seemed to appreciate literature more, they became more aware of the different genres of children's literature that exist, and vocabulary and comprehension were enhanced as well. I realized how important it was for me to model reading to children and in many different ways. I read using felt characters, roll movies, chalk talks, and so on. I learned how to make reading more appealing for the children. Consequently, I saw an increased desire in my children to read as they modeled my behavior in reading stories I had read to them and using the storytelling props.

Second graders who participated in the program were asked what they learned and liked. They commented:

I like it when the teacher reads to you. . . . She uses such good expression, you can learn to read better yourself by listening to her. . . . The teacher reads and tells stories in many different ways so it is always interesting, and you can learn to do it the way she does.

One day during a story reading session in a second-grade class with a focus on making comparisons between styles of illustrators, Ms. Payton told the children that she was going to read two picture storybooks that they had heard before. She asked the children to concentrate on the pictures or illustrations as she read the stories, to note their styles so they could describe them. After she read the stories, she asked if the children thought that the books were illustrated by the same individual. They all said no because they looked very different. Ms. Payton identified the illustrators of the books who were also the authors, Ezra Jack Keats for *Peter's Chair* and Dr. Seuss for *Green Eggs and Ham*. Then she asked the children to describe the illustrations for each book.

Tamika said, "Well in *Peter's Chair* the illustrations look like a painting. They are made like they are real. I think that Ezra Jack Keats is a very good drawer. I like the colors he uses."

Ms. Payton explained that not only does Mr. Keats paint his pictures but he uses collage as a technique. When you look closely at his illustrations, you see bits of wallpaper, newspaper, doilies, and so on blended into his pictures.

Ms. Payton asked if someone would like to describe the style of the other book. Marcel raised his hand. He said, "Dr. Seuss is very different from Keats; he uses lots of lines and sort of fantasy little shapes. He uses colors on people and things that aren't what we usually expect. His drawings look like cartoons and the other ones look like real things."

The discussion was followed by the children's illustrating stories they had written. They were told that their illustrations could be their own original styles or that they could use the style of an illustrator in a storybook that they knew. Ms. Payton walked around to talk about the work the children were doing. Magda decided to make her drawings similar to those of Dr. Seuss, and Ms. Payton said to her, "Magda, if Dr. Seuss came through our door he would think that he illustrated your story, your work looks so much like his." Magda is a child with limited English proficiency. The positive reinforcement in this situation started a conversation about her work with the teacher.

Additional Literature Activities Modeled and Initiated by Teachers

Literature activities need to be modeled and initiated by teachers to motivate children's interest. The following is a list of suggestions:

Carry Out on a Daily Basis

1. Read or tell stories to children.
2. Discuss stories read in many different ways. Discuss literal, interpretive, and critical issues.
3. Have a 30-minute independent reading and writing period (IRWP) three to five times a week, which includes the use of books and all other literature-related materials in the library corner and writing center.
4. During the IRWP, act as a model by reading.
5. Allow children to check books out of the classroom library.
6. Encourage children to read during their spare time.
7. Have children keep track of books read.
8. Have children keep the library corner neat and organized.

Carry Out Once a Week

1. Read poetry to the children.
2. Have the class recite poetry.
3. Allow for literature discussions with the whole class and in small groups.

Do Five of the Following Each Week

1. Have the principal, custodian, nurse, secretary, or a parent read to the children.
2. Discuss authors and illustrators.
3. Write to authors.
4. Have children read to younger children.
5. Have children read to each other.
6. Show filmstrips or movies of stories.
7. Use literature across the curriculum in content-area lessons.
8. Do art related to books (e.g., draw a mural of millions of cats related to the book of the same name or create a picture using the technique of a particular illustrator of children's books).
9. Tell stories using a creative storytelling technique such as one described earlier.
10. Have children tell stories with and without props.
11. Have children act out stories.
12. Prepare recipes related to stories (e.g., make stone soup after reading the story of the same name).
13. Read TV-related stories.
14. Make classbooks and individual books; bind them and store in the library corner.
15. Sing songs that have been made into books and have the book on hand (e.g., *I Know an Old Lady Who Swallowed a Fly*).

16. Make bulletin boards related to books.
17. Have children write advertisements for good books they have read.
18. Discuss proper ways to care for and handle books.

Carry Out on a Regular Basis

1. Feature new books on the open-faced bookshelves.
2. Introduce new books on the open-faced shelves.
3. Introduce new books added to the library corner.
4. Circulate 25 new books every two weeks.
5. Provide booklets for children and parents for selecting books to read in and out of school.
6. Have a bookstore in the school where children can buy books regularly.

Carry Out a Few Times a Year If Possible

1. Give bookmarks to children.
2. Give each child a book as a gift.
3. Have a young authors conference (share books children have written, bind books, invite authors).
4. Have a book fair for children to purchase books.
5. Have a book celebration day (e.g., dress up as book characters, tell stories to each other, show movie and filmstrip stories, have stories told creatively).
6. Take a field trip related to books (e.g., book binding factory, town library, publishing company).
7. Have children order books from a book club.

Activities for Parents Related to School Literature Program

1. Provide a newsletter a few times a year about book-related activities in school.
2. Ask parents to participate in some literature-related activity at school (e.g., reading to children, helping with book binding, raising money to buy books).
3. Have a workshop for parents that describes the importance, purpose, and activities of the school literature program.
4. Have a workshop for parents describing how they can participate in home recreational reading program.

Using the Literacy Center

The literacy center is an important part of the classroom. Centers have many purposes:

1. Centers can be used when children enter school in the morning so they are immediately involved in productive literacy activities.
2. Children can use centers when they finish their work before others to engage in interesting activities and reinforce strategies learned.

Children use the literacy center first thing in the morning when they arrive at school.

3. Centers engage students in productive independent work, which frees the teacher to work with small groups of students in guided reading instruction.
4. Centers allow students to select and enjoy literacy activities in a social setting during periods set aside to read and write for pleasure and for information. The purpose of these activities is to develop lifelong voluntary readers and writers.

The following sections discuss how literacy centers can be used to develop lifelong voluntary readers and writers. Research has shown that the amount of free reading done by children, both in and out of school, correlates with reading achievement (Anderson, Fielding, & Wilson, 1988; Taylor, Frye, & Maruyama, 1990). Children who read voluntarily develop lifelong, positive attitudes toward reading.

Independent Reading and Writing Periods

As discussed earlier in this chapter, elements that help motivate children include choice, social interaction, challenge, and success. Teachers can apply these elements to instructional settings by creating literacy centers in classrooms that provide children choice of activity, and modeling literacy activities that children find challenging to participate in. After the environment, materials, and activities are designed and modeled, children need time to look at books and become immersed in literature independently during the school day. Therefore, time should be provided for periods of independent reading and writing in social cooperative settings, with activities viewed as ones in which they can succeed. In the past, such periods have been called **sustained silent reading (SSR).**

Sustained silent reading has generally been defined as quiet time for children to engage in silent reading. Silent reading is important; it allows children to practice skills learned and to concentrate on understanding what is read. If we expect students to become interested in reading, young children (and perhaps older children as well) require more options and greater flexibility than have been characteristic of SSR periods. Setting aside 15 to 30 minutes three to five times a week for looking at books and engaging in other activities related to literature allows the variety, free choice, social interaction, and flexibility children need if they are to be enticed into voluntary reading. Research has indicated that children of different ability levels worked together well during independent reading and writing periods. It was also found that, although many options were available, including felt-boards, roll movies, and taped stories, 70 percent of the free-choice activities selected by children involved reading books. Other materials and options attract children into a free-choice literacy area, but they lead children to choose books (Morrow & Weinstein, 1986).

Following are descriptions of ways to help teachers and children function effectively during independent reading and writing periods, or literacy center time.

Organizing Independent Reading and Writing Periods: Literacy Center Time

In classrooms where teachers incorporate periods of social collaborative literacy activities, time is set aside three to five times a week for about 10 to 30-minutes. During literacy center time, children make decisions about what they will do and with whom they will work. Some guidelines for children to follow during this period are shown in Figure 6.3. These are posted in the classroom and reviewed before each session.

In addition to rules pertaining to use of materials, children are taught cooperative skills that are practiced and posted as shown in Figure 6.4. These include helpful things to say and to do for each other during literacy center time (Morrow, 1997).

Independent reading and writing periods can focus on a content-area theme or specific literacy skill to practice. If children are learning about animals, for example, they can focus their reading and writing activities on this topic. Likewise, if the teacher is featuring illustrators, children can think about the similarities and differences in style that characterize pictures in the books they read (Morrow, Pressley, Smith, & Smith, 1997).

Figure 6.3

Rules for Using Materials during Literacy Center Time

1. Decide with whom you will work or if you will work alone.
2. Choose a reading or writing activity from the literacy center.
3. Do only one or two activities.
4. Use the materials in or outside of the literacy center.
5. Handle the materials carefully.
6. Speak in soft voices; people are working.
7. Put materials back in their places before taking others.
8. Try activities you haven't done before.
9. Try working with people you haven't worked with before.
10. Be ready to share completed activities with the class.
11. Record completed tasks in your log.
12. Keep the literacy center neat.

Figure 6.4

Rules for Cooperating in Groups during Literacy Center Time

Helpful Things to Do When Working in Groups

- Select a leader to help the group get started.
- Give everyone a job.
- Share the materials and take turns talking.
- Listen to your friends when they talk.
- Stay with your group.

Helpful Things to Say When Working in Groups

- Can I help you?
- I like your work.
- You did a good job.

Check Your Work

- Did you say helpful things?
- Did you help each other?
- Did you share materials and take turns?
- Did you all have jobs?
- How well did your jobs get done?
- What can we do better next time?

When literacy center times are first initiated, some teachers assign children to groups, determine the activity in which they are to participate, and appoint a leader to organize the project. Other teachers have children decide on activities and groups before the period begins. As a result of participating in the assigned groups with assigned tasks, children eventually can make these decisions about what to do on their own. Children select others to work with, leaders of their groups, and tasks on which to work. To help children select activities, things to do during literacy center time are posted and reviewed, as illustrated in Figure 6.5. In addition, cards that explain how to use each activity are also posted (see Figure 6.6).

For children who are beginning readers, teachers often include pictures representing activities to help with reading rules and roles on the activity cards. However, it is important for teachers to review these lists, so children learn what they say and begin to read them.

The purpose of literacy center time is for children to read and write independently of the teacher in a social cooperative manner. Early in the program, some children do not stay on task for long and move from one activity to the next. Within a few weeks, most of the children stay with one or two activities throughout the entire period.

Children spend a great deal of time on projects during literacy center times, some extending over several days or weeks. When the period ends and a child has not completed an activity, a place is provided for projects to be stored and worked on in the next period. Each child fills in a log at the end of literacy center time to show what happened during that period (Figure 6.7).

It is helpful for teachers to share manipulative materials and books from other classrooms to increase their supply. The children also can be involved in making new materials for the literacy center. They can make taped stories, felt stories, and roll movies for others to use in the listening center. They can create original stories

Figure 6.5

Things to Do during Literacy Center Time

1. Read or look at a book, magazine, or newspaper.
2. Read to or share a book with a friend.
3. Listen to someone read to you.
4. Listen to a taped story and follow the words in the book.
5. Use the felt-board with a storybook and felt characters.
6. Use the roll movie with its storybook.
7. Write a story.
8. Draw a picture about a story you read.
9. Make a book for a story you wrote.
10. Make a felt story for a book you read or a story you wrote.
11. Write a puppet show and perform it for friends.
12. Make a taped story for a book you read or a story you wrote.
13. Check out books to take home and read.
14. Use activity cards with directions for the task you select.

Figure 6.6

Activity Card

Tell a Story Using the Felt-Board

1. Select a leader for your group.
2. Select a book and the matching felt-story characters.
3. Decide who will read or tell the story, and who will use the felt characters.
4. Take turns reading and placing the felt figures on the board.
5. Be ready to present the story to the class.
6. Record the activity in your log (see Figure 6.7 for a log sample).
7. Check your work:
   How well was the story presented?
   How well did the group work together?

and make them into books for the classroom library. Participation in these activities increases their feeling of ownership and respect for the area (Morrow, 1997).

The Teacher's Role during Literacy Center Time

Besides preparing the environment and modeling literacy activities, the teacher also plays an important role during literacy center time. The teacher interacts with the children in the following ways: (1) by facilitating or helping activities get started, (2) by scaffolding literacy behaviors when models are needed, (3) by participating along with the children in their activities, and (4) by modeling reading and writing for pleasure. The goal for this period, however, is for the children to be self-directed in the activities undertaken.

The effort to help children be independent during literacy center time will be extremely beneficial when teachers work with small groups for guided reading instruction. During guided reading instruction all children, except for a few who are working with the teacher, need to be productively involved in independent literacy activities. The center materials used during small-group guided reading instruction may need to be quieter and more skill oriented than during literacy center time, but the structure for working alone is much the same. This is important for what needs to be accomplished during that portion of language arts instruction.

Figure 6.7 *Log Sample*

Log: Circle, draw, or write about what you did during literacy center time

Name ______________________________

Activity ______________________________ **Date** ______________

Read by myself

Read to a friend

Told a roll movie

Listened to a taped story

Told a felt story

Wrote a story

Made a felt story, roll movie, or picture

Other

Write or draw what you did:

Source: Adapted from L. M. Morrow, 1997. In *The Literacy Center: Contexts for Reading and Writing.* York, ME: Stenhouse

Literacy Skills Developed during Literacy Center Time

The data collected in different research studies of students who participated in periods of independent reading and writing revealed that various literacy activities occurred during this time (Morrow, Sharkey, & Firestone, 1994). The activities were self-directed and involved the children in making decisions about what work to do and how to carry through with their plans. Children read books and wrote stories and also engaged in active manipulative projects, such as creating puppet presentations for pieces they had written or read. Most activities were done in groups of two to five and involved peer cooperation and peer tutoring. The groups were composed of single and mixed genders, and were generally friendly. Children took charge of their learning and demonstrated the use of oral reading, silent reading, and writing, while demonstrating their comprehension development in literal and inferential ways.

Literacy center time exposes children to reading and writing in many forms and gives them the opportunity to make choices. It is a positive approach toward activating interest in reading and writing, and is a time to practice and learn skills. As mentioned, it can be thought of as a variation of SSR, and what some have called **reading and writing workshop.** Because of the element of choice, there is something for everyone: gifted, average, and special needs children. Children from different backgrounds work together on similar interests. Children with language differences are welcomed as members of groups doing puppet shows and felt stories, and given roles in which they can participate.

I work with teachers regularly to implement programs with them similar to those described here. I visit the classrooms often. Mrs. Jacobs had a second-grade class in an inner-city district that I had been working with for an entire school year. I visited her room the last day of school to say good-bye to the children. Mrs. Jacobs and I shared a sense of pride while observing the children in their last IRWP for that school year. We saw some children curled up on a rug or leaning on pillows in the literacy center with books they had selected themselves. Louis and Ramon were squeezed tightly into a rocking chair, sharing a book. Marcel, Patrick, and Roseangela snuggled under a shelf—a "private spot" filled with stuffed animals. They took turns reading.

Tesha and Tiffany were on the floor with a felt-board and character cutouts from *The Gingerbread Boy,* alternately reading and manipulating the figures: "Run, run as fast as you can! You can't catch me, I'm the Gingerbread Man!"

Four children listened on headsets to tapes of Maurice Sendak's *Pierre* (1962), each child holding a copy of the book and chanting along with the narrator, "I don't care, I don't care." Yassin and Shawni were writing a story together and bouncing ideas back and forth.

Tyrone had a Big Book and gave several other children copies of the same story in smaller format. Role-playing a teacher, he read to the others, occasionally stopping to ask who would like to read.

Leon asked Tamaika if she would like to hear a story he had written. She agreed and he read it to her. When he finished, she suggested acting out Leon's story with puppets, which they did. Throughout the dramatization, Leon behaved like the director of a play. He knew his story and his characters and wanted them to act in a manner that reflected his intent.

Much of the information discussed here represents the results of studies that involved classroom observation and intervention in kindergarten through second grade. Children in these classrooms participated in literacy programs that included activities that have been described in this chapter. These youngsters scored significantly better on tests of reading comprehension, the ability to retell and rewrite stories, and the ability to create original oral and written stories by including elements of story structure than children in classrooms that did not participate in the program. Children in the treatment classrooms also showed significant improvement in use of vocabulary and language complexity (Morrow, 1990, 1992; Morrow, O'Connor, & Smith, 1990).

Teachers and children were interviewed to determine their attitudes toward the literacy center time and the program in general. Teachers commented that the children particularly like the literacy center time because they are able to

- choose activities they want to do
- choose the books they want to read
- choose to work alone or with others
- choose manipulatives such as puppets and roll movies

Teachers also said that children enjoyed the literacy center time because everyone participated, and there were few discipline problems.

Teachers said that children learned the following in the program:

- To work together and cooperate with each other
- To be independent and make decisions
- A sense of story structure from the stories they listened to and read, improved comprehension, and vocabulary development
- An appreciation for books and knowledge of different genres of children's literature
- The names of authors and illustrators and an increase in their general knowledge from the amount of reading done
- Their peers could teach them and were willing to do so
- To like to read and write

By participating in the program teachers said they learned that:

- The social family atmosphere created by the independent reading and writing period is conducive to learning.
- Children are capable of cooperating and collaborating independently in reading and writing activities and learning from each other.
- When there is choice of activity and person to work with, children of all ability levels choose to work together.
- There is something for everyone—advanced and slower children alike—in this program.
- The program made me more flexible and spontaneous and a facilitator of learning rather than always a teacher.
- Children who don't readily participate in reading and writing did so during literacy center time. I think it is because they are the ones making the decisions about what they do.

In the student interviews, children were asked what they learned in the literature program, and they answered:

- You learn that reading can be fun.
- You learn to read and write better because you read a lot and you read real books.
- You learn to understand what you are reading and you learn a lot of new words.

Headsets with taped stories and accompanying storybooks provide a good reading model for children.

During literacy center time, children may choose to tell a roll movie story or a felt-board story. All activities are literature related and are accompanied by the original book..

- You get to learn how to read better if you don't read real good because kids who know how to read good help you.
- You learn about authors and illustrators and that they are people like you and you think that you could be one.

What do you like about the literature program?

- It makes you want to read and write; it's fun and makes you feel happy.
- You can choose what you want to read, like long books or short books, or hard books or easy books.
- You can write stories.
- You can do felt stories, tape stories, chalk talks, and roll movies, which are all fun, and they have books with them too.
- During literacy center time, the teacher reads to you, and she never does in regular reading.
- During literacy center time, the teacher talks to you one at a time like a friend; in regular reading she talks to you all together (Morrow, 1992).

It became apparent when speaking with teachers that children's special needs were attended to in this program. Mrs. Nitto described an incident about a child who went to the resource room daily because her reading skills were far below grade level. According to Mrs. Nitto, Charlene never read aloud. One day Mrs. Nitto noticed her reading aloud to a rag doll as she sat in the rocking chair. Mrs. Nitto offered positive reinforcement to Charlene, and the reading aloud continued daily during independent reading and writing.

Mr. Abere described another situation with a bilingual youngster who had limited ability in English. This child would not speak in class at all. During an independent reading and writing period, Mr. Abere observed Tasha acting as a teacher with a group of children she had organized. She had each one taking turns reading.

Marcel was a gifted child in a classroom with mostly low achievers. He was alone all the time. About two months after independent reading and writing was initiated in his classroom, he was able to participate with other children in literacy activities. The first time I observed him with others, he was reading the newspaper and checking out the weather in other parts of the country.

Patrick asked Marcel if he could look too. Marcel was pleased and then David joined them. Together they read and discussed how hot and cold it was in Florida, Colorado, and so on.

There were numerous anecdotes from literacy center time describing how children were able to find a way to participate in spite of special problems. One teacher commented, "There seems to be something that every child can find to do during independent reading and writing and do it well." Center time also was an excellent time to invite parents to participate in the activities. We invited parents often and they were active participants.

The recommendations in this chapter for developing positive attitudes toward reading incorporate Holdaway's (1979) developmental approach to literacy. This approach highlights less teaching and more learning, learning that is self-regulated rather than regulated by adults. It has been suggested here that the teacher provide an environment rich with materials and activities from which children are invited to select, plus a social context in which children are actively involved with other children, with the teacher, and with materials. The environment is emulative rather than instructional, providing lively examples of reading skills in action. Teachers present themselves as models involved in literary activities. They serve as sources of support and positive reinforcement for appropriate behavior patterns in children. Through regularly scheduled literary activities and ready access to attractive and comfortable classroom literacy centers stocked with books and materials that inspire interest and active participation, children associate reading and writing with pleasure and develop an appreciation for books. Given time to use the literacy center and participate in independent reading and writing activities, children reinforce their learning of skills through enjoyable, self-selected practice. The outcome will be children who not only learn to read and write, but also choose to read and write voluntarily.

Assessing Independent Reading and Writing during Literacy Center Time

Assessing the success of a program that incorporates physical and social settings for literacy learning should be carried out on a regular basis. In the programs I helped implement, teachers often discussed literacy center time issues, such as helping children who were not on task, encouraging different children to work together, helping children try different activities, and seeing that everyone had a leadership role at some time. The opportunity for teachers to meet provided a support system for them. It helped teachers evaluate the program and build their confidence and skill levels as well.

During literacy center time, teachers observed their classes to notice which children were on task, which children needed help getting started, and what activities the children were choosing to participate in. They periodically made changes in the management of literacy center time to help enhance productivity.

Teachers recorded anecdotes of activities and collected writing samples. They made audiotapes and videotapes of the groups at work and of performances of completed tasks. Children were involved in evaluating their literacy center time activities. They discussed how they cooperated and the quality of their completed tasks. When completed activities were presented, peers offered constructive criticism. Children were asked about their suggestions for improving the program and identified materials and books they wanted added to the centers.

Teachers discussed literacy center designs and how they might be improved to increase student productivity. Teachers moved centers from one area of the room to another, because they found a space that was bigger, brighter, or quieter. They added books and manipulatives to provide more choices for children. The Literacy Corner Evaluation Form below provides a means for assessing available literacy center materials and those that are needed.

Literacy Corner Evaluation Form

	Yes	No
1. Children participate in some phase of the library corner design (develop rules, select a name for the area, develop materials, etc.).	☐	☐
2. The area is placed in a quiet section of the room.	☐	☐
3. The area is visually and physically accessible.	☐	☐
4. Part of the area is partitioned off from the rest of the room.	☐	☐
5. Bookshelves are available for storing books with spines facing outward.	☐	☐
6. There is an organizational system for shelving books (e.g., color coding for topic).	☐	☐
7. Open-faced bookshelves are available for new featured books.	☐	☐
8. Five to eight books are available per child.	☐	☐
9. Many books are available representing three to four grade levels and of the following types: a. picture books, b. picture story books, c. traditional literature, d. poetry, e. realistic literature, f. informational books, g. biographies, h. novels, i. easy to read books, j. riddle and joke books, k. participation books, l. series books, m. textless books, n. TV-related books, o. brochures, p. newspapers, q. magazines.	☐	☐
10. New books are circulated every two weeks.	☐	☐
11. There is a check-out/check-in system for children to check out books daily.	☐	☐
12. There is a rug.	☐	☐
13. There are throw pillows.	☐	☐
14. There is a rocking chair or bean bag chair.	☐	☐
15. There are headsets and taped stories.	☐	☐
16. There are posters about reading.	☐	☐
17. There are stuffed animals.	☐	☐
18. The area is labeled with a name selected by the class.	☐	☐
19. There is a felt-board and story characters and the related books.	☐	☐
20. There is a roll movie and related book.	☐	☐
21. There are materials for writing stories and making them into books.	☐	☐
22. There is a private spot in the corner such as a box to crawl into and read.	☐	☐
23. There is a system for children to keep track of books read.	☐	☐
24. The area occupies about 10% of the classroom space and five to six children can fit comfortably.	☐	☐

Assessing Children's Attitudes toward Books

Direct observation of children's behavior while they are listening to stories, reading, or looking at books independently is the most effective method for assessing their attitude toward books. How much attention do they give to the books they are looking at or reading? Do they simply browse? Do they flip through the pages quickly, paying little attention to print or pictures? Do they silently study the text, sustaining attention to pictures and print throughout (Martinez & Teale, 1988)? You should also note how frequently children select looking at books when faced with other options. In occasional interviews with individual children, asking what they like to do best in school and at home might reveal interest in reading. During conferences, ask parents if their children voluntarily look at books or pay close attention when they are read to. At the same time, ask parents how often they read to their children. Gather facts about the home literacy environment that will help you understand the child's attitude toward books.

A checklist for assessing attitudes toward reading and writing and a motivation interview for a child's portfolio of assessment materials (Figure 6.8) are provided on pages 194 and 195. They are useful tools concerning children's interest in reading and writing.

Checklist *Assessing Attitudes toward Reading and Writing and Amount of Voluntary Reading and Writing*

Child's name ______________________ **Date** ____________

	Always	Sometimes	Never	Comments
Voluntarily looks at or reads books at school				
Asks to be read to				
Listens attentively while being read to				
Responds during book discussions with questions and comments to stories read to him or her				
Takes books home to read voluntarily				
Writes voluntarily at home				
Writes voluntarily at school				

Teacher Comments:

Figure 6.8 *Motivation Interview*

Directions: Tell the child that you would like to find out more about what kids like to do and how they feel about reading and writing. Ask each question in the interview and read the multiple choice responses.

How often would you like your teacher to read to the class?

(2) every day	(1) almost every day	(0) not often

Do you like to read books by yourself?

(2) yes	(1) it's ok	(0) no

Which would you most like to have?

(2) a new book	(1) a new game	(0) new clothes

Do you tell your friends about books and stories you read?

(2) a lot	(1) sometimes	(0) never

How do you feel when you read out loud to someone?

(2) good	(1) ok	(0) bad

Do you like to read during your free time?

(2) yes	(1) it's ok	(0) I don't read in my free time

If someone gave you a book for a present, how would you feel?

(2) happy	(1) ok	(0) not very happy, disappointed

Do you take storybooks home from school to read?

(2) almost every day	(1) sometimes	(0) not often

Do you read books out loud to someone in your family?

(2) almost every day	(1) sometimes	(0) not often

What kind of reader are you?

(2) I'm a very good reader	(1) I'm ok	(0) I'm not very good

Learning to read is:

(2) easy	(1) a little hard	(0) really hard

Do you like to write?

(2) yes	(1) it's ok	(0) I'd rather do something else

Do you write in your free time?

(2) a lot	(1) a little	(0) not at all

What do you like to read best?

(2) books and magazines	(1) schoolwork	(0) nothing

Source: Adapted from L. B. Gambrell, *Me and My Reading Scale,* 1993. In *The Impact of Running Start on the Reading Motivation of and Behavior of First-Grade Children* (Research Report). College Park: University of Maryland, National Reading Research Center.

Ideas for the Classroom from the Classroom

I created the following experience when I was teaching children in a mixed-age grouping primary classroom. You may find this idea useful for your teaching.

Felt-Board Story

I wanted to introduce my children to the use of the felt-board as a means for retelling stories and creating their own original stories with characters. I selected a story that was easy to illustrate and a theme that would generate interpretive conversation, and I encouraged the opportunity to write additional episodes for it. The name of the story is *A Bunny Called Nat,* an anonymous tale. The story is about "a bunny named Nat, who was soft like a cat, and he could change his color, just like that." This is a repetitive rhyme in the story, and at the end of the rhyme fingers are snapped. The bunny in the story is a gray bunny who does not like his color because it is so plain. He is able to change his color, but each time he does, he has an unpleasant adventure.

When I introduced the story to the children, I asked them to listen for the different colors that Nat becomes and the problems he faces each time. I then told the story, using the different colored bunny characters on the felt-board to help. When the story was over we discussed Nat and his different colors. We also discussed the ending of the story and its meaning, trying to relate it to the experiences of the children. We discussed if they ever wanted to be anyone other than themselves and why, and would it really be better.

After the discussion, I asked the children to think of another color that Nat could become with an adventure attached to it as in the real story. I then asked them to write their story and draw and color a bunny to add to the felt story we already had. The bunnies were made of construction paper and felt strips were glued onto the back to make them stick to the felt-board.

Seven-year-old Lindsey wrote the following:

> *"I'm a bunny named Nat, I'm soft like a cat, and I can change my color just like that." And suddenly Nat was a red bunny. Red like an apple, red like a cherry, and red like a fire truck. Suddenly a group of bees was coming. They saw Nat in the red color and they were thinking that Nat was an apple. The group of bees was going where Nat was sitting, they wanted to eat him. Then Nat saw the bees. He ran and ran but the bees followed him. So he said as he ran, "Being red is not so good, but I'm a bunny called Nat, I am soft like a cat, and I can change my color, just like that."*

In this activity, children were given the opportunity to participate in a pleasurable experience with literature. They were actively involved in the discussion and the creation of a story, using the one that follows as a model. The underlying theme of this story concerning one's self-image is an important topic for conversation and can help children understand each other's strengths, weaknesses, and special needs.

The story of *A Bunny Called Nat* and a pattern for the bunny (Figure 6.9) follow:

Sample Felt-Board Story

A BUNNY CALLED NAT

(adapted version of an anonymous tale)

(As the story is being told, hold up and then place a new colored bunny on the felt-board as each bunny is named.)

Materials

Five bunny characters drawn identically but in the following colors: gray, blue, green, yellow, and orange. The bunny pattern is found at the end of the story.

Once upon a time there was a little gray rabbit and his name was Nat. One day he looked around and saw that all his brothers and sisters, cousins and friends were gray, too. He thought he would like to be different from them. So he said:

I'm a bunny called Nat,
I'm soft like a cat,
And I can change my color
Just like that. (Snap your fingers.)

And suddenly Nat was a blue bunny. He was blue like the sky and blue like the sea. He was blue like the twilight and blue like the dawn. It felt nice and cool to be blue. He decided to take a look at himself in the pond. He hurried to the edge and admired his reflection in the water. He leaned over so far that SPLASH! he fell into the pond. Nat fell deep into the blue water and he couldn't swim. He was frightened. He called for help. His friends heard him, but when they came to the pond they couldn't see him because he was blue just like the water. Fortunately a turtle swam by and helped Nat get safely to shore. Nat thanked the turtle. He decided that he didn't like being blue. So he said:

I'm a bunny called Nat,
I'm soft like a cat,
And I can change my color
Just like that. (Snap your fingers.)

And this time, what color did he change himself to? Yes, he was yellow—yellow like the sun, yellow like a daffodil, yellow like a canary bird. Yellow seemed like such a happy color to be. He was very proud of his new color, and he decided to take a walk through the jungle. Who do you think he met in the jungle? He met his cousins the lion and the tiger. The lion and the tiger looked at Nat's yellow fur and said, "What are you doing in that yellow coat? We are the only animals in this jungle that are supposed to be yellow." And they growled so fiercely that Nat the bunny was frightened and he ran all the way home. He said:

(Repeat bunny poem above.)

And this time what did he change his color to? Yes, he was green. He was green like the grass and green like the leaves of the trees. He was green like a grasshopper and green like the meadow. As a green bunny, Nat thought he'd be the envy of all the other bunnies. He wanted to play with his other bunny friends in the meadow. Since he was the color of the grass in the meadow, he could not be seen and his friends just ran and jumped about him not seeing him at all or mistaking him for a grasshopper. So Nat the bunny had no one to play with while he was green. Being green wasn't much fun. So he said:

(Repeat bunny poem above.)

Figure 6.9

Felt Figure for Story A Bunny Called Nat

And what color was he then? Right, he was orange. He was orange like a carrot, orange like a sunset, orange like a pumpkin—he was the brightest color of all. He decided he would go out and play with all his brothers and sisters and friends. But what do you suppose happened? When his friends saw him, they all stopped playing and started to laugh, "Ha-ha, whoever heard of an orange bunny?" No one wanted to play with him. He didn't want to be orange anymore. He didn't want to be a blue bunny because if he fell into the pond no one could see him to save him. He didn't want to be a yellow bunny and be frightened by the lion and the tiger. He didn't want to be a green bunny because then he was just like the meadow and none of his friends could see him. And so he said:

(Repeat bunny poem above.)

Do you know what color Nat the bunny changed himself into this time? Yes, you're right. He changed himself back to gray. And now that he was gray all of his friends played with him. No one growled or laughed at him. He was gray like a rain cloud, gray like an elephant, gray like pussy willows. It felt warm and comfortable being gray. From that time on, Nat the bunny was always happy being a gray bunny, and he decided that it's really best being just what you are.

A Fable Theme for Independent Reading and Writing Period

Mrs. Martinez assigns themes to periods of independent reading and writing. Following is an account of this when the theme was Fables.

During several literacy center periods over a few days, the theme for my second-grade class was writing fables. This activity inspired reading fable selections. Students selected particular animal characters and settings and wrote responses to the following questions in a prewriting activity:

1. What problem does one character have?
2. What happens?
3. What lesson might one character learn?

The students worked in groups and wrote original fables, accompanied by a moral. The morals were: "Think before you do something," "It's not fun to leave home," and "Never run away." After only one minilesson on fables followed by the opportunity to create during periods of independent reading and writing, I was amazed at how well the students understood the concept of a fable and incorporated the characters' dialogue and morals into their writing. The students prepared to present their fables in little plays. They worked together in groups during literacy center time, planning, writing, drawing, creating, rehearsing, and organizing their presentations.

We have a "Buddy" system with Mr. O'Leary's first-grade class, which gives the classes the opportunity to share literature experiences. My second graders were extremely proud to present their fables, which were well received by the first grade.

Gayle Martinez, Second-Grade Teacher
Judd School, North Brunswick, New Jersey

Activities and Questions

1. Answer the focus questions at the beginning of the chapter. Select a literacy skill to teach that is grade appropriate for you.

2. Select a literacy skill to teach that is grade appropriate for you. Select a piece of children's literature that provides an example of that skill and choose a creative storytelling technique that seems appropriate for the story and skill (e.g., felt characters, chalk talk, sound-story). Create materials for the story and tell it to a group of children or to your peers. Evaluate your performance according to the criteria for storytelling discussed in the chapter and how well the skill was taught.

3. Evaluate the literacy center in an early childhood classroom using the form on page 193. List all the characteristics of the center that reflect criteria described in this chapter. List items that need to be included.

4. Observe an early childhood classroom on three different occasions. List all the literacy activities carried out by the teacher that you believe contribute to developing positive attitudes toward reading.

5. Continue your portfolio assessment for the child you selected to assess. Observe the child using the assessment checklist provided in this chapter concerning the evaluation of his or her attitudes toward writing and reading. Interview the child using the motivation survey (Figure 6.8) on page 195.

6. Continue the thematic unit that you began in Chapter 4. Select three objectives for building positive attitudes toward reading and describe three activities using your theme that will satisfy each of the objectives.

Case Study Activity

Refer to "Ideas for the Classroom from the Classroom" about *A Bunny Called Nat*. Describe how you think it enhances a child's interest in books. Has the activity made accommodations for children with special needs? If yes, how? If not, how could the teacher do this? Has the teacher attempted to use the activity to build awareness of cultural diversity? How could he or she do this? Make a list of books that would help create interest in reading, addressing children with special needs and cultural diversity.

chapter 7

Developing Concepts about Books and Comprehension of Text

Few children learn to love books themselves. Someone must lure them into the wonderful world of the written word, someone must show them the way.

—Orville Prescott
A Father Reads to His Child

Focus Questions

- What are the concepts about books that are important for young children to know?
- What experiences enhance a child's concepts about books?
- What are the objectives for comprehension development for young children?
- Identify and describe strategies that develop comprehension such as directed reading and thinking activities, mapping, webbing, and story retellings.
- List and define the structural elements in a good story.
- List and describe strategies that develop aesthetic and efferent stance.

For several months, Mrs. Johnson has been discussing different authors and illustrators with the children in her first-grade class. The class has a chart on which their favorite authors and illustrators are listed. Today she asked them to add names to the list because they had recently read stories by authors and illustrators who were new to them. First she asked for authors and the following names were generated: Ezra Jack Keats, Leo Lionni, Tomie dePaola, and Arnold Lobel. Next she asked if they could name some illustrators, and the following names were mentioned and written next to the authors: Maurice Sendak, Dr. Seuss, Eric Carle, and Crockett Johnson. Jamie raised her hand and said, "Hey something weird just happened. I noticed that all of the authors named are also illustrators and all of the illustrators are all authors too." Christopher raised his hand and said, "That's not so weird, I know a bunch of people who are authors and illustrators at the same time. There's me, and Josh, Jennifer, and Patrick." Christopher was looking around the room and naming all the children in the class. When he finished naming his classmates, he continued, "We're all authors and illustrators. We all write books and illustrate them. They are published and they are in our classroom library. How could we forget that?"

Acquiring Concepts about Books and the Ability to Comprehend Text

Investigators have found a number of instructional strategies that nurture children's concepts about books and help them comprehend text. Those practices include children's role-playing, retelling, and reconstructing with pictures, stories that have been read to them. They also include discussions concerning the parts of books, how to handle books, and who authors and illustrators are. The involvement of children in experiences with literature enhances their comprehension of stories, their sense of story structure, and their language development. Through experiences with literature, young children integrate information and learn the connections among a story's various parts (Brown, 1975; Morrow, 1985; Pellegrini & Galda, 1982). The fact that interactive behavior plays a leading role in such learning reinforces a model of generative learning: The reader or listener understands prose by actively engaging in construction of and relationships with the textual information he or she hears or reads (Linden & Wittrock, 1981; Wittrock, 1974, 1986).

Teale (1984) has used Vygotsky's (1978) definition of higher mental functions as internalized social relationships and applied it to literacy. Literacy develops, according to Teale, from children's interactions with others in specific environments that involve reading and writing. Holdaway's (1979) model of developmental teaching, derived from observations of middle-class homes, indicates that a child benefits when early experiences with storybooks are mediated by an interactive adult who provides problem-solving situations. The child is asked to respond and the adult offers information when necessary. In such situations, children and adults interact to integrate, construct, and make relationships with printed text.

The many benefits of reading to children have been discussed throughout this volume. Strategies for reading to infants and toddlers that are applicable in the home and in day-care centers have been described, as have techniques for reading stories to children that will arouse their interest and entice them to books.

The following sections suggest strategies for using expository and narrative text to develop children's concepts about books and comprehension of books. The strategies described follow the theory, research, and models just outlined.

Concepts about Books

Developing children's concepts about books is an important step in their becoming literate individuals. The children in the opening vignette knew what an author and an illustrator are—two main objectives for developing concepts about books.

Objectives for Developing Concepts about Books

A child who has a good concept of books:

1. Knows that a book is for reading.
2. Can identify the front and the back of a book as well as the top and the bottom.
3. Can turn the pages of a book properly in the right direction.
4. Knows the difference between print and pictures.
5. Knows that pictures on a page are related to what the print says.
6. Knows where one begins reading on a page.
7. Knows what a title is.
8. Knows what an author is.
9. Knows what an illustrator is.

Activities That Develop Concepts about Books

Some adults assume that children know the concepts about books just outlined. However, to many two- to six-year-olds those concepts are totally unfamiliar. To help children master them, point them out at every opportunity when you read to children. You can introduce a story reading, for instance, by pointing appropriately as you say, "The title of the story that I'm going to read is *Mr. Rabbit and the Lovely Present* [Zolotow, 1962]. This is the title on the front of the book. The author of the book, the person who wrote it, is Charlotte Zolotow. Here is her name. And the illustrator, the person who drew the pictures, is Maurice Sendak. Here is his name. All books have titles and authors, and if they have pictures they also have illustrators. The next time you look at a book, see if you can find the title. It is always on the front cover."

The repetition of such dialogue familiarizes children with the concepts, which they assimilate easily. Similar dialogues explain other concepts. Point to a picture, then to print. Identify each, then ask, "Which do we read, the picture or the print?" As you get ready to read to them, ask children to point out the top and bottom of the book, the title, and where you should begin reading on a page. Not only will you give the children the opportunity to learn the concepts, but at the same time you can determine which children understand the concept and which need help. These activities and dialogues can be carried out during story readings to small groups or to individual students. A child's independent exploration of books will reinforce what you have pointed out or explained.

Big Books are an important part of early literacy instruction. They are oversized picture storybooks that measure from 14 × 20 inches up to 24 × 30 inches. Holdaway (1979) suggested that the enlarged print and pictures in these books help get children involved with concepts about books, print, and the meaning of text. Big Books are appropriate from preschool through third grade. Because these books are used in small and large group situations, active involvement by the group is encouraged. When using a Big Book, a teacher places it on a stand because it is difficult to handle otherwise. An easel is usually used for a Big Book stand and makes the print and pictures visible for the children. Class Big Books can be made as well as purchased. When they are made, children become even more aware of book concepts because they are engaged in creating a book. Figure 7.1 provides directions for making a Big Book.

Big Books are effective for developing concepts about books mainly because of their size. As the teacher reads the book and tracks the print from left to right across the page, children see that books are for reading and where one begins to read on a page. They also learn to differentiate the print from the pictures. The connection is made that the oral language they hear from their teacher is being read from the print on the page in the book. The correct way to turn pages is easy to see with Big Books because they are so enlarged. The title of the book is prominently displayed on the front of the book and on the title page, as is the name of the author and illustrator.

Figure 7.1

Instructions for Making a Big Book

Materials

- 2 pieces of oak tag for the cover (14″ × 20″ to 20″ × 30″)
- 10 pieces or more of tagboard or newsprint the same size as the oak tag used for the cover to be used for the pages in the book
- 6 looseleaf rings (1¼″)
- Holepunch

Directions

- Punch three sets of holes in top, middle, and bottom of the cover and paper that is to go inside of the book.
- Insert a looseleaf ring in each hole. The Big Book should have a minimum of 10 pages.
- Print should be 1½ to 2 inches high.

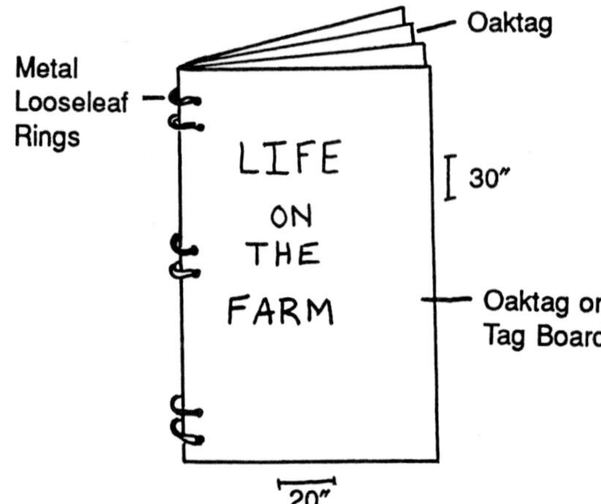

In addition to using Big Books to emphasize the concepts of author and illustrator, feature different authors and illustrators on a special bulletin board or in book displays. Carry out discussions about their work. In addition, remember to refer to the children in your class as authors and illustrators as they write stories and draw pictures about text.

In Mrs. Johnson's room, children are always encouraged to read the title of a book and the name of the author and illustrator before starting to read the text. One day during an independent reading and writing period, Damien placed the Big Book *Chicken Soup with Rice* (Sendak, 1962) on the Big Book stand. He had gathered three children to sit in front of him to read to. He started by saying, "The title of the book I'm going to read is *Chicken Soup with Rice.*" He turned the first page and began reading the text. Patrick popped up and said, "Damien, you can't read the book yet; you forgot to read who the author and illustrator are." Damien pounded his fist to his forehead, looked somewhat annoyed with himself, and said, "How could I forget that. Let's see, the author of this book is Maurice Sendak and he is the illustrator too."

Comprehension of Text

Understanding what is read, or comprehending text, is one of the major goals for reading instruction. The English poet Samuel Taylor Coleridge wrote the following short piece entitled *On Reading Comprehension*:

> *There are four kinds of readers. The first is like an hour glass, and their reading being as the sand, it runs out, and leaves not a vestige behind. A second is like the sponge, which imbibes everything and returns it in nearly the same state, only a little dirtier. The third is like a jelly bag, allowing all that is pure to pass away, and retaining only the refuse. And the fourth is like the workers in the diamond mines of Colconda, who cast aside all that is worthless and retain only pure gems.*

How do we get children to cast aside unnecessary information and retain only the pure gems when reading or listening to a passage?

Pressley and Afflerbach (1995) have outlined characteristics of the kind of skilled readers who comprehend well and we hope to create:

- Good comprehenders read materials from the beginning to end, and also jump around looking for information that might help with clarification.
- Good comprehenders slow down their reading when they come to information that is relevant to what they want to remember.
- Good comprehenders anticipate the content of the text based on prior knowledge about the topic.
- Good comprehenders reflect on ideas in the text by creating summaries about what they have read.
- Good comprehenders refer to the text about important information to clarify issues.

Definitions of comprehension emphasize that it is an active process. In this process, the reader or listener interprets and constructs meaning about what he or she reads or listens to based on prior knowledge about the topic, thereby making

Comprehension is an active process where readers and listeners interpret and construct meaning about what they read or listen to.

connections between the old and the new (Pearson & Johnson, 1978). This concept arises from research on schema theory that suggests that we have a schemata (background knowledge) for certain information based on prior experience with a given topic. That schemata is never complete because more can always be learned about a subject. For example, if someone told us something about the circus that would give us one bit of information, if we saw pictures of the circus we would have additional information, and if we went to see the circus we would know even more. Then when we read about the circus or listened to a story about it, the new information would expand and refine what we already know. Comprehension of a story or expository piece that is read or listened to involves a child's integration of his or her prior knowledge concerning a topic with the new text to create new knowledge (Pearson, Roehler, Dole, & Duffy, 1992).

Comprehension greatly depends on how the difficulty of the text matches the ability of the listener or reader. Therefore, it is important to keep in mind when reading to children, or when they read themselves, the following characteristics about the text that will determine how well they will comprehend:

- The familiarity of the content in the text,
- The background knowledge required to understand the text,
- The quality of the writing,
- How interesting the topic is to the listeners or readers,
- The syntactic complexity of the sentences,
- The amount and difficulty of vocabulary included, and
- The length of the piece to be listened to or read. (Graves, Juel, & Graves, 1998)

Objectives for Developing Comprehension of Text

A child is developing comprehension of narrative and informational text when he or she:

1. Attempts to read well-known storybooks that results in the telling of a well-formed story.

2. Participates in story reading by saying words and narrating stories as the teacher reads to him or her.
3. Retells and summarizes a story without referring to the book.
4. Includes elements of story structure in story retellings: setting (beginning, time, place, characters), theme (main character's problem or goal), plot episodes (events leading toward a solution of the main character's problem or attainment of his or her goal), and resolution (problem solution, goal achievement, ending).
5. Responds to discussing text after reading or listening with activities, questions, and comments that are factual, interpretive, and analytical. Responses also include evaluation of text, the author's purpose, and self-monitoring of one's own understanding of the material presented.
6. Learns meanings of new words and uses the new vocabulary learned in speaking and writing.
7. Uses reference and study skill materials such as the dictionary, encyclopedia, and magazines to find information; uses study aids in materials such as the table of contents, the index, titles, subtitles, charts, and so on.

In the past the categories most commonly used for classifying comprehension strategy development included literal, interpretive, and critical thought development. Regardless of the classification system, the types of thought processes we want children to engage in are the same. The list of cognitive skills usually starts with strategies that require lower level thought processes and progresses to the more sophisticated. The lower level thinking strategies have been considered to be for younger children, and the more sophisticated ones for older children. We have come to realize that, whether the child is an emergent or conventional reader, he or she can engage in many levels of thought from those considered lower level to higher level. They engage in these thought processes, however, at different levels of sophistication. The comprehension experiences we need to provide for young children are as follows:

1. Identify details, sequence events, follow directions, and find the main idea related to the text.
2. Classify ideas from different parts of the text, visualize episodes, paraphrase or retell, and focus on structural elements of text.
3. Predict outcomes, make associations, relate story episodes to their life experiences and background knowledge.
4. Put themselves in the place of different characters to determine how they feel and what they would do, to try to determine characters' motives as well as the author's purpose.
5. Compare and contrast, analyze, draw conclusions, apply information in other settings, and problem solve.
6. Evaluate passages and evaluate their own understanding of the text.

Items 1 and 2 would be considered literal skills, 3 and 4 interpretive thought development, and 5 and 6 critical or higher level cognitive processing.

Standards and Comprehension

The standards that deal with comprehension of text from the National Center on Education and the Economy and the Learning Research and Development Center at the University of Pittsburgh (1999) are referred to as "Getting Meaning from Text." When getting meaning from text, children are expected to have competence in self-monitoring and self-correcting strategies. When children self-monitor their reading:

- They notice when sentences or paragraphs are incomplete or when texts do not make sense.
- They use syntax to help figure out the meaning of new words.
- They raise questions about what the author was saying.

When children demonstrate comprehension:

- They can comprehend text when reading novels that have subplots as well as a main plot.
- They understand nonfiction that contains concepts with subordinate and coordinate structures presented in complex and compound sentences.
- They grasp meaning from figurative language such as similes and metaphors.
- They compare one text to another text they have read or heard.
- They explain motives of characters.

Strategies That Develop Comprehension of Text

The following sections describe several strategies to enhance children's comprehension development, which also include learning concepts about books and print. Most of these strategies are introduced in whole-group settings and used repeatedly with new materials. They are appropriate for small-group instruction, often referred to as guided reading groups, when explicit teaching takes place. Teachers decide which strategies to use in these reading groups that meet the needs of the children involved.

In many of the following activities, children play active roles as they respond to literature in different ways. Children's literature that includes both narrative and expository selections is especially appropriate for developing a child's sense that print conveys meaning. The stories or informational text are attractive, relate well to a child's real-life experiences, and are typically well structured. Narrative material contains clearly delineated settings, themes, episodes, and resolutions. Quality expository text is well organized and an important way of presenting nonfiction content-area information to children. Exposure to narrative and informational materials offers the opportunity for developing comprehension or cognitive instructional strategies.

Favorite Storybook Readings

To study emergent reading behaviors, Sulzby (1985) observed children from ages two to six attempt to read favorite storybooks. Although they were not yet readers in the conventional sense, the children were asked, "Read me your book." Sulzby found that, in their "reading," the children produced speech that could indeed be categorized as a first act of reading; that the speech they used as they "read" was clearly different in structure and intonation from their typical conversation; and that different developmental levels could be observed in these "oral readings."

From children's attempts at storybook reading, then, we can determine stages of development. Because the activity is developmental and leads to literacy, teachers should ask children to participate in it, either to evaluate their ability or simply to encourage their emergent literacy.

Sulzby's Simplified Classification Scheme for Children's Emergent Reading of Favorite Storybooks is found below.

Directed Listening and Thinking Activity and Directed Reading and Thinking Activity

When children read themselves or are read to, there should always be a purpose that complements content-area learning or develops specific concepts about what is being read. The format of the **directed listening and thinking activity** (DLTA) and the **directed reading and thinking activity** (DRTA) can be internalized with frequent use by the child and transferred when new material is presented (Morrow, 1984; Stauffer, 1980). Whatever a DLTA's or DRTA's

Emergent Reading Behaviors and Evaluation Form

1. *Attending to pictures but not forming stories.*
   The child "reads" by labeling and commenting on the pictures in the book but does not "weave a story" across the pages.

   yes ☐ no ☐

2. *Attending to pictures and forming oral stories.*
   The child "reads" by following the pictures but weaves a story across the pages through wording and intonation like those of someone telling a story. Often, however, the listener too must see the pictures in order to understand the story the child is "reading."

   yes ☐ no ☐

3. *Attending to a mix of pictures, reading, and storytelling.*
   The child "reads" by looking at the pictures. The majority of the child's "reading" fluctuates between the oral intonation of a storyteller and that of a reader.

   yes ☐ no ☐

4. *Attending to pictures but forming stories (Written-language–like).*
   The child "reads" by looking at the pictures. The child's speech sounds like reading, both in wording and intonation. The listener rarely needs to see the pictures in order to understand the story. With his or her eyes closed, the listener would think the child was reading print. The "reading" is similar to the story in print and sometimes follows it verbatim. There is some attention to print.

   yes ☐ no ☐

5. *Attending to print.*
   This category has two divisions:

   a. The child reads the story mostly by attending to print but occasionally refers to pictures and reverts to storytelling.

   b. The child reads in a conventional manner.

   a ☐ b ☐

Source: Adapted from E. Sulzby, 1985.

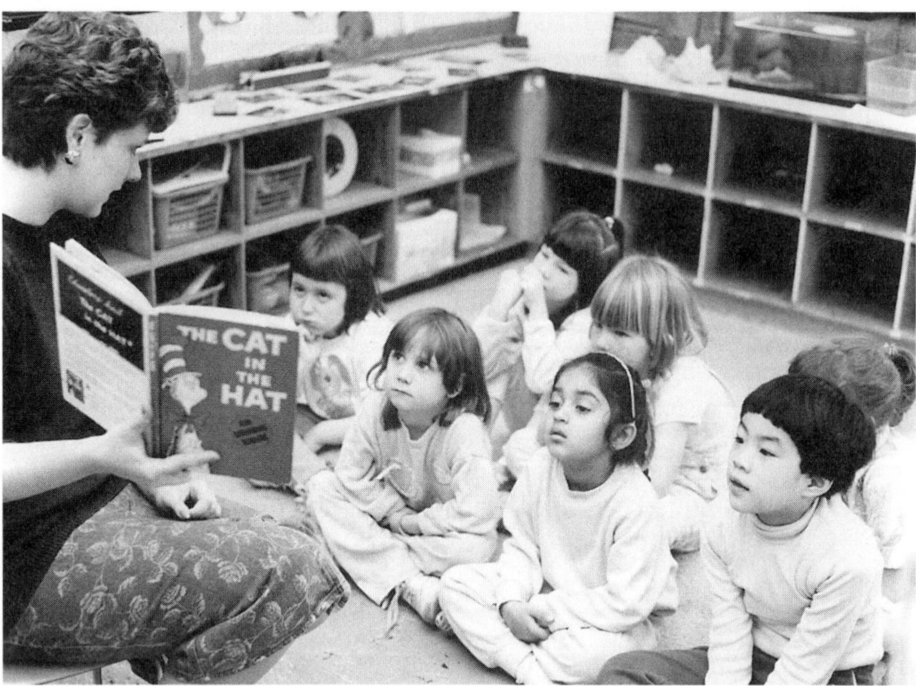

Directed listening and thinking activities set a purpose for reading or listening and help focus student's thoughts.

specific objective, its framework offers the listener or reader a direction and strategy for organizing and retrieving information from the text. In the following outline for *The Little Red Hen* (Izawa, 1968b), there are two main objectives: to emphasize the sequence of events and to involve children in making inferences and judgments from the text. The outline follows a DLTA or DRTA format. With the DLTA, the children listen to the story; with the DRTA, the children read the story.

Prepare for Listening or Reading with Prequestions and Discussion

1. Build a background by introducing the story: "Today I'm going to read a story (or, you will be reading a story) entitled *The Little Red Hen.* Let's look at the pictures to see if you can tell what the story is going to be about." Encourage children to respond as you turn the pages of the book. After they have offered their ideas say, "The story is about a hen who wants to bake some bread and asks her friends for some help." This activity has been referred to as a "walk through the book."

2. Ask prequestions that build additional background that sets a purpose for listening or reading. Relate the questions to real-life experiences whenever possible: "Have you ever asked people for help? What kind of help? Did they help you? Has anyone ever asked you for help? What kind of help? Were you able to help the person? How? While I'm reading (or, while you are reading), try to decide if you think the little red hen did the right thing with her bread at the end of the story, and why. Try also to remember what happened first, second, third, and at the end of the story."

3. When the children have gained enough experience with your prequestions, you can ask them to think of their own: "Now that I've told you a little

about the story, what do you want to find out when I read it to you (or, when you read it)?" When prequestioning, show the pictures in the book to the children as further preparation for their listening or reading.

Reading the Story

1. Be sure to show the children the pictures as you read the story. Stop a few times for reactions, comments, or questions from the children. If the children are reading the story, remind them to study the pictures. Model or scaffold responses to guide them in their thinking, keeping in mind the objectives for this particular DLTA or DRTA: "Can you remember what help the little red hen has asked for so far? How have the other animals acted about giving help?" If the children do not respond, scaffold or model responses by changing questions to statements: "These animals aren't very helpful to the little red hen. Each time the hen asks for their help, the animals all answer, 'Not I.' " Also ask for children's predictions of what will happen next. If the children are reading silently, assign stopping points for discussion. If there is oral reading, stop only in a few places.

Discussion after Reading

1. The postdiscussion should be guided by the objectives or purpose set for listening and reading: "What did the little red hen want help with first? second? and so on." Ask children to retell the story; retelling will demonstrate their knowledge of sequence. Allow children to use the pictures in the book to help them follow sequence. Finally, focus on the second goal, making inferences and judgments: "What would you have done if you were the little red hen? What lesson can we learn from this story?"

A DLTA or DRTA can have many different objectives. The framework, however, is always basically the same: (1) preparation for listening or reading—prequestions and discussion; (2) reading the story; and (3) discussion after reading. All three steps are focused on the DLTA's or DRTA's specific objectives. A DLTA or DRTA can focus on literal responses (such as recall of facts and sequencing), inferential responses (such as interpreting characters' feelings, predicting outcomes, and relating the story to real-life experiences), and critical responses (such as evaluating, problem solving, and making judgments). It can focus on elements of story structure, such as setting, theme, plot episodes, or resolution. It helps youngsters draw meaning from the print. Research has demonstrated that a DLTA can increase the story comprehension of young listeners (Morrow, 1984), just as a DRTA can increase the story comprehension of young readers (Baumann, 1992; Pearson et al., 1992).

K-W-L

K-W-L is a cognitive strategy to enhance comprehension that is used mainly with expository text, and can be adapted for use with stories. It shares some similarities to a DRTA and a DLTA. *K-W-L* stands for *What We **Know**, What We **Want** to Know,* and *What We **Learned*** (Ogle, 1986). With this technique students use prior knowledge to create interest about what is to be read. It helps set a purpose for reading to direct thinking, and it encourages sharing of ideas. The K-W-L chart (page 212), which lists items generated in a K-W-L discussion, is particularly useful when reading material for thematic instruction. The

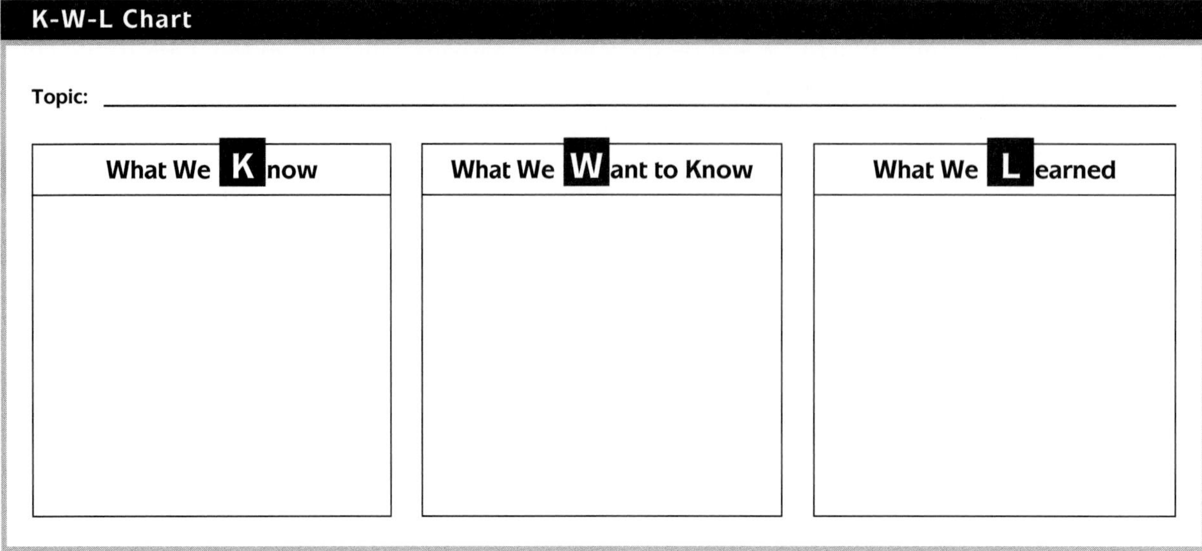

following are the steps involved in putting the strategy into practice. Before reading expository text:

1. Children brainstorm what they think they know about a topic. For example, if the book is about spiders a list of *What We **Know*** about spiders is created by the class.
2. Children list questions about *What We* **Want** *to Know* as a result of reading the book about spiders.
3. After reading the text, children make a list of *What We **Learned*** about spiders.

Finally children might compare information from the text that they already knew before reading the text, what they learned as a result of reading the text, and what is still on the list of what they would like to learn because it was not included in the book.

Productive Discussions

Productive Discussions are necessary to help develop comprehension. Discussion includes talking about what is read or listened to with children interacting with each other and the teacher. Discussions must include more than a few words by participants and include questions, clarification, explanations, predictions, and justifications. Discussion questions should reflect a teacher's interest in what children have to say and think rather than the correct answer. Questions should stimulate discussion and elicit responses that reflect what children think and feel about what has been read. These questions are asking for an aesthetic response because children have to synthesize ideas, sensations, feelings, and images. The following questions will enable children to give aesthetic responses:

- How did you feel about the story?
- What did this story mean to you?
- What questions do you have about the story?

- What did you learn from what you read?
- How will that information be useful to you?
- Do you agree with what the characters did in the story? Why? Why not? (Gambrell & Almasi, 1994)

The efferent stance is usually taken with expository text that offers content information. Questions that ask for an efferent response require students to remember and analyze details, main ideas, and cause and effect. Some questions that will elicit efferent responses (Rosenblatt, 1988) include the following:

- How would you describe the central character?
- What idea did you find most interesting?
- What new ideas did you learn?
- How could you find out more about these ideas?
- If you talked to the author, what would you like to ask?

Small-Group and One-to-One Story Readings

The importance and benefits of reading to small groups and to individuals must not be overlooked. Too often considered impractical in school settings, one-to-one and small-group readings yield such tremendous benefits that they must be incorporated into school programs. The most striking benefit of one-to-one story readings at home—often called the lap technique—is the interactive behavior it involves, along with the direct channels of information it gives the child. It also provides the adult with insight into what the child already knows and wants to know. In one study (Morrow, 1988), it was determined that one-to-one readings in a school setting had positive results with preschoolers from lower socioeconomic backgrounds, even though the youngsters had little previous experience interacting with adults. Teachers in the study practiced the same interactive behaviors identified by researchers who had studied home storybook readings (Applebee & Langer, 1983; Cochran-Smith, 1984; Roser & Martinez, 1985). These teacher behaviors included managing storybook reading by introducing the story and providing background information.

Frequent readings by teachers who followed the guidelines outlined on page 214 increased the number and complexity of the children's responses. The youngsters offered many questions and comments that focused on meaning. Initially, they labeled illustrations. Later, they gave increased attention to details, their comments and questions became interpretive and predictive, and they drew from their own experiences. They also began narrating—that is, "reading" or mouthing the story along with the teacher. As the program continued, some children focused on structural elements, remarking on titles, settings, characters, and story events. After many readings, the children began to focus on print, questioning names of words, letters, or sounds. They also began to recognize letters and words and read them as they were able (Morrow, 1987a). Compared with one-to-one readings, reading to small groups of children seems to encourage more and earlier responses. Children tend to repeat one another's remarks, and they are motivated to respond to and elaborate on what their peers have said.

The following segments from transcriptions of small-group story readings illustrate the various questions and comments children make when they are involved in the activity, and the wealth of knowledge and information they

Guidelines *Teacher Behavior during Storybook Reading*

1. Manage
a. Introduce story.
b. Provide background information about the book.
c. Redirect irrelevant discussion back to the story.

2. Prompt Responses
a. Invite children to ask questions or comment throughout the story when there are natural places to stop.
b. Scaffold responses for children to model if no responses are forthcoming. ("Those animals aren't very nice. They won't help the little red hen.")
c. Relate responses to real-life experiences. ("I needed help when I was preparing a party, and my family shared the work. Did you ever ask for help and couldn't find anyone to give it to you? What happened?")
d. When children do not respond, ask questions that require answers other than yes or no. ("What would you have done if you were the little red hen and no one helped you bake the bread?")

3. Support and Inform
a. Answer questions as they are asked.
b. React to comments.
c. Relate your responses to real-life experiences.
d. Provide positive reinforcement for children's responses.

Source: From Morrow, 1988.

receive from the responding adult. The transcriptions also illustrate what the children already know and what their interests are, which helps us design instruction.

Story: *The Very Hungry Caterpillar* (Carle, 1969) (questions about a part of the book)

Jerry: (He points to the picture on the front of the book.) Why does it have a picture on it?

Teacher: The cover of the book has a picture on it so you will know what the story is about. Look at the picture. Can you tell me what the book is about?

Jerry: Ummm, I think that's a caterpillar. Is it about a caterpillar?

Teacher: You're right, very good. The book is about a caterpillar, and the name of the story is *The Very Hungry Caterpillar.* When you look at the pictures in a book, they help you find out what the words say.

Story: *Caps for Sale* (Slobodkina, 1947) (asks for a definition)

Teacher: I'm going to read a story today called *Caps for Sale.*

Jamie: What are caps?

Teacher: A cap is a little hat that you put on your head. See, there is a cap in the picture.

Jamie: I never knew that before. I knew about hats, but I never heard about caps.

Small-group storybook reading with the teacher encourages interesting responses and elaboration of text by children.

Story: *Chicken Soup with Rice* (Sendak, 1962) (attends to print)

Chris: Wait, stop reading. Let me see this again. (He turns back to the page that talks about the month of June.) How come they're the same? (He refers to the words of *June* and *July.*)

Teacher: What do you mean?

Chris: Look at the letters, J–U, J–U . . . They look alike.

Teacher: Look more closely at the ends of the words. Are they the same?

Chris: Ohh, nooo, just the front part.

Story: *Caps for Sale* (Slobodkina, 1947) (predicts)

Colleen: I wonder why those monkeys took the caps?

Teacher: I don't know. Can you think why?

Colleen: Well, the peddler was sleeping and those monkeys looked at the caps, and maybe they think they're for them. Or, I know! Maybe they're cold so they want a cap.

Teacher: Those are good ideas, Colleen.

Story: *Madeline's Rescue* (Bemelmans, 1953) (relates to real-life experience)

Jamie: What's the policemen going to do?

Teacher: He's going to help Madeline. Policemen are nice; they always help us.

Jamie: Policemans aren't nice. See, my daddy beat up Dominic and the policeman came and took him away and put him in jail for no reason. And my Daddy cried. I don't like policemans. I don't think they are nice.

Segments such as these reveal children's understandings. Do their comments and questions relate to literal meanings? Do they raise interpretive and critical issues by associating the story with their own lives, make predictions of what will happen next in a story, or express judgments about characters' actions? Do comments or questions relate to matters of print, such as names of letters, words, and sounds? The same types of questions and comments occur when small groups of children read together without the presence of a teacher. Recording and then analyzing one-to-one and small-group story readings reveal what children know and want to know (Morrow, 1987a). The coding sheet in Figure 7.2 aids such analysis.

Figure 7.2

Coding Children's Responses during Story Readings

Child's name ______________________ **Date** __________

Name of story ______________________

(Read one story to one child or a small group of children. Encourage the children to respond with questions and comments. Tape record the session. Transcribe or listen to the tape, noting each child's responses by placing checks in the appropriate categories. A category may receive more than one check, and a single response may be credited to more than one category. Total the number of checks in each category.)

1. Focus on story structure ________
   a. setting (time, place) ________
   b. characters ________
   c. theme (problem or goal) ________
   d. plot episodes (events leading toward problem solution or goal attainment) ________
   e. resolution ________
2. Focus on meaning ________
   a. labeling ________
   b. detail ________
   c. interpreting (associations, elaborations) ________
   d. predicting ________
   e. drawing from one's experience ________
   f. seeking definitions of words ________
   g. using narrational behavior (reciting parts of the book along with the teacher) ________
3. Focus on print ________
   a. questions or comments about letters ________
   b. questions or comments about sounds ________
   c. questions or comments about words ________
   d. reads words ________
   e. reads sentences ________
4. Focus on illustrations ________
   a. responses and questions that are related to illustrations ________

Although whole-class readings are more practical and have tremendous value in simply exposing children to literature, the interactive behavior between adult and child in one-to-one readings and small-group readings does not occur in the large-group setting. If we review transcripts of story readings in all three settings, several things become apparent. In whole-group settings, a child cannot ask questions or comment repeatedly throughout the story without interfering with the story line for the other children. The teacher might never get through a coherent reading. Dialogue that does occur is managed by the teacher to such an extent that the teacher often says more than the children. A truly interactive situation does not exist because of the size of the group. In small-group and one-to-one readings, by contrast, a teacher initially may manage and prompt often, but only to encourage and model responses for children. In a short time the roles reverse: Most dialogue is initiated by children through questions and comments, and the teacher offers positive reinforcement and answers questions (Morrow, 1987a).

Children who do not experience one-to-one readings at home are at a disadvantage in their literacy development. It is necessary to carry out such strategies in school to compensate for what is not provided at home as well as to provide the other benefits. Gains in both literacy skills and positive attitudes toward books can occur. To learn to associate books with warmth and pleasure, children who have not had the benefit of the lap technique at home can experience it at school. It is difficult to provide one-to-one readings in school because of time limitations and the number of children, but asking aides, volunteers, and older children to do so helps solve the problem. Reading to small groups of youngsters from time to time, perhaps replacing some of the traditional instruction in reading groups, also helps. Many school districts have federal funding for work with young children identified as having potential learning problems. Ratios in such programs may be as low as five children per teacher. Those settings also allow one-to-one readings as part of a literacy development program.

Shared Book Experiences

The **shared book experience** (Holdaway, 1979) is usually a whole-group approach, although it may be carried out in small groups as well. Either way, it enables children to participate in the reading of a book. It also helps develop listening skills, for children must listen attentively to participate.

Predictable stories are ideal for shared book experiences because they allow children to guess what will come next, thereby encouraging participation. Predictability takes many forms. The use of catch phrases, such as " 'Not I,' said the dog," " 'Not I,' said the cat," and so on, in *The Little Red Hen* (Izawa, 1968b) encourages children to chant along. Predictable rhyme enables children to fill in words, as in *Green Eggs and Ham* (Seuss, 1960). Cumulative patterns contribute to predictability. For example, new events are added with each episode, then repeated in the next, as in *Drummer Hoff* (Emberley, 1967). *Are You My Mother?* (Eastman, 1960) repeats phrases and episode patterns as its central character, a baby bird, searches for his mother by approaching different animals and asking the same question. Conversation can contribute to predictability, as in *The Three Billy Goats Gruff* (Brown, 1957) or *The Three Little Pigs* (Brenner, 1972). All stories become predictable as children become familiar with them, so repeating stories builds a repertoire for shared book experiences. Fairy tales are already familiar to most children and therefore often predictable to a group. Books that carry familiar sequences, such as days of the week, months of the year, letters, and numbers, are predictable—*The Very Hungry Caterpillar* (Carle, 1969), for instance. Books gain predictability through good plot structures and topics familiar to children. Books in which pictures match text page by page tend to be predictable to children, especially if everyone in the group can see the pictures as the story is being read.

Predictable books are excellent for emergent and conventional readers in shared book experiences as well as in independent reading. They allow the child's first experience with reading to be enjoyable and successful with minimal effort. Such immediate success encourages the child to continue efforts at reading. (A list of predictable books is provided in Appendix A.)

One shared book technique involves reading from a Big Book or a similar book made by the class or the teacher. As mentioned, such a book is designed so that everyone in the group can see the pictures and the words of the story clearly while it is being read. If the book is a new one for the class, the children are asked to listen during the first reading. If it is being read for the second time or is already familiar, immediate participation is encouraged. Often the teacher uses a pointer during the reading to emphasize left-to-right progression and the correspondence of spoken and written words. The teacher encourages participation by stopping at predictable parts and asking children to fill in words and phrases. As the children become more familiar with the books, they begin to know them by memory. This enables the children to associate words as they say them with the printed words the teacher points to on the page. Big Books and regular-size copies of the same book should be available for children to use independently after a first Big Book reading.

Shared book experiences can involve children in dramatizations of a story, art activities, or other extended experiences after the story has been read. Shared book experiences can be recorded and made available in the listening station, as can tapes of teachers' readings and commercially recorded tapes. These will provide fluent models with good phrasing and intonation for children to emulate. Shared book experiences easily can be adapted to the DLTA format, if teachers emphasize that shared book experiences are to be pleasurable, relaxed, participatory, and enjoyable read-aloud events.

Shared book experiences involve the children in some way during the story reading. Often Big Books are used so that they can be seen easily by all and children can see the print as the teacher reads and points to it.

Repeated Story Readings

Children enjoy repetition, as we all do. Being familiar with an experience is comfortable, like singing a well-known song. Besides offering the pleasure of familiarity, a repeated story helps develop concepts about words, print, and books. One study compared responses of two groups of four-year-olds (Morrow, 1987a). One group listened to three readings of each of three stories, the other group a different story at each of nine sessions. The repeated-reading group increased the number and kind of responses, and their responses differed significantly from those of the different-story group. Their responses became more interpretive, and they began to predict outcomes and make associations, judgments, and elaborative comments.

They also began to narrate stories as the teacher read (their first attempts at reading) and to focus on elements of print, asking names of letters and words. Even children of low ability seem to make more responses with repeated readings than with a single reading (Roser & Martinez, 1985).

Repeated readings are important to youngsters because they engage in the activity frequently on their own. Children who are able to read themselves or engage in pretend reading behaviors often will select the same book to look at or read over and over again. This is an activity they enjoy and learn from and at which they succeed. Teachers should repeat readings of stories to children and encourage youngsters to read stories more than once and carry out discussions about books that have been read and discussed previously.

The following dialogue is from a transcription of a child's responses to a third reading of *The Little Red Hen.* This excerpt includes primarily the child's comments and questions and the teacher's responses; most of the story text has been omitted.

Teacher: Today I'm going to read the story, *The Little Red Hen.* It is about a hen who wanted some help when she baked some bread. (The teacher begins to read the story.) . . . Who will help me to cut this wheat?

Melony: "Not I," said the cat. "Not I," said the dog. "Not I," said the mouse.

Teacher: That was good, Melony. You are reading. (The teacher continues reading.) . . . Who will take this wheat to the mill to be ground into flour?

Melony: "Not I," said the cat. "Not I," said the dog. "Not I," said the mouse with the whiskers.

Teacher: Very nice, Melony. (The teacher continues to read.)

Melony: I want to read that part, but I don't know how.

Teacher: Go ahead and try. I bet you can. I'll help you: The cat smelled it.

Melony: The cat smelled it and she said *umm* that smells good, and the mouse smelled it, and it smelled good.

Teacher: (The teacher continues reading.) Who will eat this cake?

Melony: The mouse, the doggy, the kitty!

Teacher: You're right again, Melony. (The teacher reads to the end of the story.) Did you want to say anything else about the story?

Melony: He was bad so he couldn't have no cake. (Melony searches through the pages.) That's the wrong part.

Teacher: Show me the part you are talking about.

Melony: There it is, almost at the end. She's going to make a cake and she'll say who's going to bake this cake for me. And the cat says, "Not I," the dog says, "Not I," the mouse says, "Not I." And then when she's cooking it they smell a good thing and then they wanted some, too, but they didn't have any, 'cause they didn't plant the wheat.

Teacher: You're so right. They didn't help do the work, so they didn't get to eat the cake.

Melony: Where does it say "Not I"? Show me the words in the book.

Teacher: Here it is. Can you find it again?

Melony: (She flips through the pages.) I'm looking for where she bakes the cake. Here it is. Yea. And he smelled it. And he smelled it. And the mouse smelled it. (She turns pages.) They're going in the kitchen. And she said, "All by myself, I cut the wheat. All by myself, I took it to the mill to get it into flour. All by myself I baked the cake. All by myself I'm going to eat it."

Teacher: That's terrific, Melony. That's what the hen said.

Melony: (She points to the dog.) The dog was not happy. Where does it say *dog*?

Teacher: You're right. He doesn't look happy. Here is where it says dog (pointing).

Melony: There's the word, *dog, dog, dog*. How does that dog look?

Teacher: He looks hungry and mad because he can't have any bread.

Melony: You're right. But it's his fault. He didn't help. And that's the end. (Morrow, 1987a)

Besides illustrating the value of repeated readings in the responses generated by the child, this exchange demonstrates the encouragement, reinforcement, and rapport that can evolve from one-to-one storybook reading sessions.

Story Retelling and Rewriting

Letting a listener or reader retell or rewrite a story offers active participation in a literacy experience that helps develop language structures, comprehension, and sense of story structure (Morrow, 1985). Retelling, whether it is oral or written, engages children in holistic comprehension and organization of thought. It also allows for original thinking as children mesh their own life experiences into their retelling. Retelling contrasts with the more traditional piecemeal approach of teacher-posed questions that require children to recall bits of information (Gambrell, Pfeiffer, & Wilson, 1985). With practice in retelling, children come to assimilate the concept of story structure. They learn to introduce a story with its beginning and its setting. They recount its theme, plot episodes, and resolution. In retelling stories, children demonstrate their comprehension of story details and sequence, organizing them coherently. They also infer and interpret the sounds and expressions of characters' voices.

Retelling is not an easy task for children, but with practice they improve quickly. To help children develop the practice of retelling, tell them before they read or listen to a text or story that they will be asked to retell or rewrite it (Morrow, 1996). Further guidance depends on the teacher's specific purpose in the retelling. If the immediate intent is to teach or test sequence, for instance, instruct children to concentrate on what happened first, second, and so on. If the goal is to teach or assess the ability to integrate information and make inferences from text, instruct children to think of things that have happened to them like those that happen to characters in the story. Props such as felt-board characters or the pictures in the text can be used to help students retell the story. Pre- and post-discussion of the story help to improve retelling ability, as does the teacher's modeling a retelling for children. The procedure shown below is helpful in guiding a child's oral or written retelling. With written retellings, a teacher may prefer to have the child write the entire piece first and then conference with him or her afterward.

Retellings can be used to develop many types of comprehension. The prompts should match the goals. In addition to its usefulness as a learning technique, retelling also allows adults to evaluate children's progress. If you plan to evaluate a retelling, tell the child during your introduction of the story that he or she will be asked to retell it after the reading. During the evaluative retellings, do *not* offer prompts beyond general ones such as "Then what happened?" or "Can you think of anything else about the story?" Retellings commonly reveal a child's sense of story structure, focusing mostly on literal recall, but they also reflect a child's inferential and critical thinking ability. To assess the child's

Guidelines *Story Retelling*

1. Ask the child to retell the story. "A little while ago, I read the story [name the story]. Would you retell the story as if you were telling it to a friend who has never heard it before?"
2. Use the following prompts only if needed:
   a. If the child has difficulty beginning the retelling, suggest beginning with "Once upon a time," or "Once there was . . ."
   b. If the child stops retelling before the end of the story, encourage continuation by asking, "What comes next?" or "Then what happened?"
   c. If the child stops retelling and cannot continue with general prompts, ask a question that is relevant at the point in the story at which the child has paused. For example, "What was Jenny's problem in the story?"
3. When a child is unable to retell the story, or if the retelling lacks sequence and detail, prompt the retelling step by step. For example:
   a. "Once upon a time," or "Once there was . . ."
   b. "Who was the story about?"
   c. "When did the story happen?" (day, night, summer, winter?)
   d. "Where did the story happen?"
   e. "What was [the main character's] problem in the story?"
   f. "How did [he or she] try to solve the problem? What did [he or she] do first [second, next]?"
   g. "How was the problem solved?"
   h. "How did the story end?" (Morrow, 1996)

retelling for sense of story structure, first parse (divide) the events of the story into four categories—*setting, theme, plot episodes,* and *resolution.* Use a guide sheet (see Figure 7.3) and the outline of the parsed text to record the number of ideas and details the child includes within each category in the retelling, regardless of their order. *Do* credit the child for partial recall or for recounting the "gist" of a story event (Pellegrini & Galda, 1982). Evaluate the child's se-

Figure 7.3

Story Retelling and Rewriting Evaluation Guide Sheet: A Quantitative Analysis

Child's name Beth **Age** 5

Title of story Jenny Learns a Lesson **Date** ______

General directions: Give 1 point for each element included as well as for "gist." Give 1 point for each character named as well as for such words as *boy, girl,* or *dog.* Credit plurals (friends, for instance) with 2 points under characters.

Sense of Story Structure

Setting

a. Begins story with an introduction		1
b. Names main character		1
c. Number of other characters named	2	
d. Actual number of other characters	4	
e. Score for "other characters" (c/d):		.5
f. Includes statement about time or place		1

Theme

Refers to main character's primary goal or problem to be solved		1

Plot Episodes

a. Number of episodes recalled	4	
b. Number of episodes in story	5	
c. Score for "plot episodes" (a/b)		.8

Resolution

a. Names problem solution/goal attainment		1
b. Ends story		1

Sequence

Retells story in structural order: setting, theme, plot episodes, resolution. (Score 2 for proper, 1 for partial, 0 for no sequence evident.)		1

Highest score possible: 10 Child's score: 8.3

Source: From Morrow, 1996.

quencing ability by comparing the order of events in the child's retelling with the proper order of setting, theme, plot episodes, and resolution. The analysis indicates not only which elements the child includes or omits and how well the child sequences, but also where instruction might be focused. Comparing analyses of several retellings over a year will indicate the child's progress.

The following example uses a parsed outline of *Jenny Learns a Lesson* (Fujikawa, 1980). The parsed outline is accompanied by transcriptions of two children's retellings of the story. A retelling guidesheet follows with a quantitative analysis of the first transcription told by a child named Beth (Morrow, 1996).

Parsed Story

Setting

a. Once upon a time there was a girl who liked to play pretend.

b. Characters: Jenny (main character), Nicholas, Sam, Mei Su, and Shags, the dog.

Theme

Every time Jenny played with her friends, she bossed them.

Plot Episodes

First episode: Jenny decided to pretend to be a queen. She called her friends. They came to play. Jenny told them all what to do and was bossy. The friends became angry and left.

Second episode: Jenny decided to play dancer. She called her friends and they came to play. Jenny told them all what to do. The friends became angry and left.

Third episode: Jenny decided to play pirate. She called her friends and they came to play. Jenny told them all what to do. The friends became angry and left.

Fourth episode: Jenny decided to play duchess. She called her friends and they came to play. Jenny told them all what to do. The friends became angry and left.

Fifth episode: Jenny's friends refused to play with her because she was so bossy. Jenny became lonely and apologized to them for being bossy.

Resolution

a. The friends all played together and each person did what he or she wanted to do.

b. They all had a wonderful day and were so tired that they fell asleep.

Verbatim Transcriptions

(Beth, age five) Once upon a time there's a girl named Jenny and she called her friends over and they played queen and went to the palace. They had to . . . they had to do what she said and they didn't like it so then they went home and said that was boring. It's not fun playing queen and doing what

she says you have to. So they didn't play with her for seven days and she had . . . she had an idea that she was being selfish, so she went to find her friends and said, I'm sorry I was so mean. And said, let's play pirate, and they played pirate and they went onto the ropes. Then they played that she was a fancy lady playing house. And they have tea. And they played what they wanted and they were happy. The end.

This retelling by five-year-old Beth was transcribed when she was in the first part of her kindergarten year. To demonstrate how retellings can become more sophisticated and improve with practice and time, another retelling by this same child when she was at the end of her kindergarten year follows. The story is called *Under the Lemon Tree* (Hurd, 1980.) It is about a donkey who lives under a lemon tree on the farm and watches out for all the other animals. A fox comes in the night to steal a chicken or duck and the donkey hee-haws loudly to protect them. He scares the fox away but wakes the farmer and his wife who never see the fox. This happens frequently until the farmer can no longer take the noise and moves the donkey to a tree far from the farm house where he is very unhappy. The fox comes back and steals the farmer's prize red rooster. The other animals quack and cluck and finally wake up the farmer who chases after the fox. When the fox passes him, the donkey makes his loud noises again, frightening the fox, who drops the red rooster. The farmer realizes that the donkey has been protecting his animals and moves him back to the lemon tree where he is happy again.

Here is five-year-old Beth's retelling of *Under the Lemon Tree:*

Once upon a time there was a donkey, and he was in a farm. He lived under a lemon tree close to the animals on the farm. In the morning all the bees buzzed in the flowers under the lemon tree. He was next to the ducks, the chickens, and the roosters. It was night time. The red fox came into the farm to get something to eat. The donkey went "Hee-Haw, Hee-Haw" and then the chickens went "cluck, cluck" and the ducks went "quack-quack." . . . Then the farmer and his wife waked up and looked out the window and saw nothing. They didn't know what came into their farm that night. They said, "What a noisy donkey we have. When it gets dark we will bring him far away." So when it get darker and darker they brang the donkey over to a fig tree. And he had to stay there. He couldn't go to sleep alone. That night the red fox came into the farm again to try and get something to eat. All the ducks went quack-quack and the turkeys went gobble-gobble. The farmer and his wife woke up and said, "Is that noisy donkey back again?" They rushed to the window and saw the fox with their red rooster in his mouth and yelled, "Stop thief, come back." The fox passed the donkey and shouted "hee-haw, hee-haw." The red fox heard it and dropped the rooster and ran away. The farmer and his wife said, "Aren't we lucky to have the noisiest donkey in the whole world." And they picked up the rooster and put one hand around the donkey and they all went home together and tied the donkey under the lemon tree.

Retellings can be evaluated for many different comprehension tasks. The directions to students prior to retelling and the method of analysis should match the goal. Figure 7.4 provides an analysis form for evaluating oral and written retellings in which checks are used instead of numbers for a general sense of elements a child includes and to determine progress over time. Also provided in

Figure 7.4

A Qualitative Analysis of Story Retelling and Rewriting

Child's name ______________________ **Date** ____________

Name of story ______________________________

Setting	***Yes***	***No***
a. Begins story with an introduction	☐	☐
b. Names main character	☐	☐
c. List other characters named here: ____________ ____________		
d. Includes statement about time and place	☐	☐
Theme		
a. Refers to main character's primary goal or problem to be solved	☐	☐
Plot Episodes		
a. Episodes are recalled	☐	☐
b. List episodes recalled	☐	☐
Resolution		
a. Includes the solution to the problem or the attainment of the goal	☐	☐
b. Puts an ending on the story	☐	☐
Sequence		
a. Story is told in sequential order	☐	☐

Interpretive and Critical Comments: Read through the retelling or rewriting and list comments made or written by students that are of an interpretive or critical nature.

the form is a qualitative evaluation of interpretive and critical responses. Figure 7.5 provides a student evaluation form for oral and written retellings. Self-evaluation with a teacher, with a child, or alone is a crucial part of the learning process.

Webbing and Mapping

Webs and maps are graphic representations, or diagrams, for categorizing and structuring information. They help students see how words and ideas are related to one another. Webs tend to be drawn using a spider-like effect, and maps may have boxes with labels in them that connect in different places. **Webbing** and **mapping** strategies build on a child's prior knowledge and makes him or her become active in the reading process. They help the child retrieve what is known about a topic, expand his or her knowledge, and use the information in reading and listening to text. Research has demonstrated that the use of webbing and mapping strategies is successful in the development of vocabulary and comprehension. This research has also shown the effectiveness of the strategies with

Figure 7.5

Student Oral or Written Retelling Self-Evaluation Form

Name ______________________ Date ____________

Name of story ______________________

Setting	***Yes***	***No***
a. I began the story with an introduction.	☐	☐
b. I talked about the main character.	☐	☐
c. I talked about other characters.	☐	☐
d. I told when the story happened.	☐	☐
e. I told where the story happened.	☐	☐
Theme		
I told about the problem in the story or the main goal of the characters.	☐	☐
Plot Episodes		
a. I included episodes in the story.	☐	☐
Resolution		
a. I told how the problem was solved or goal achieved.	☐	☐
b. I had an ending on the story.	☐	☐
Sequence		
My story was retold or rewritten in proper order.	☐	☐

Comments for Improvement:

Next time I need to include in my retelling:

poor readers, minorities, and bilingual children (Pittelman, Levin, & Johnson, 1985; Pittelman, Heimlich, Berglund, & French, 1991).

When webbing or mapping is used to develop vocabulary concepts and definitions related to a word, the word is written on the board or chart paper. Children are asked to brainstorm ideas related to the word. For example, after reading *The Snowy Day* (Keats, 1962), the teacher asks the children to provide words that describe what snow is like. The word *snow* is written in the center of the chart or chalkboard, and the words given by the children are attached to it. A sample of a snow web done by a kindergarten class is shown in Figure 7.6.

Another web about the same story could be used to expand ideas about activities to do in the snow. In Figure 7.7 a first-grade class generated the things that Peter did in the snow in the story and then other things that we can do in the snow.

A map provides a different format for graphically presenting materials before and after listening to or reading a book. Maps deal with more complex rep-

Figure 7.6

A Web for Expanding Vocabulary

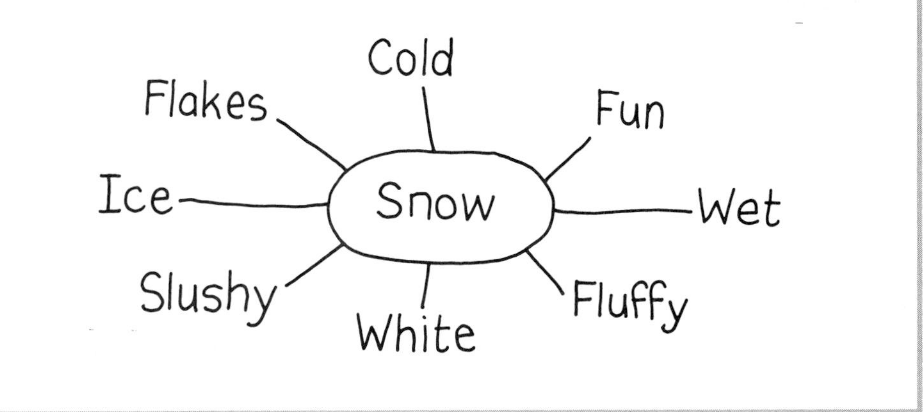

Figure 7.7

A Web for Expanding Ideas

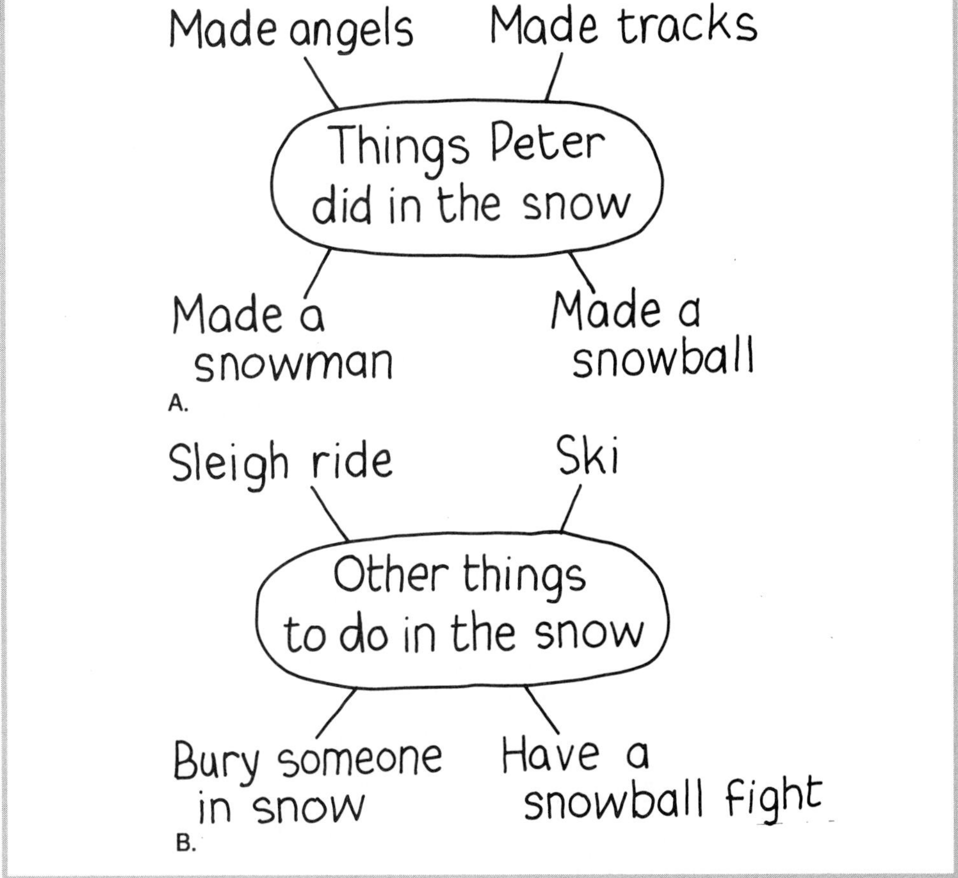

resentations; therefore, boxes for different categories are needed to present the ideas graphically. Story structures can be mapped to help children learn about the structural elements in the text. Sequence of events or studies of individual characters can be mapped also. Figure 7.8 is a map of the story *Mr. Rabbit and the Lovely Present* created by a second-grade class. That illustrates the structural elements in the story.

Figure 7.8

A Story Structure Map

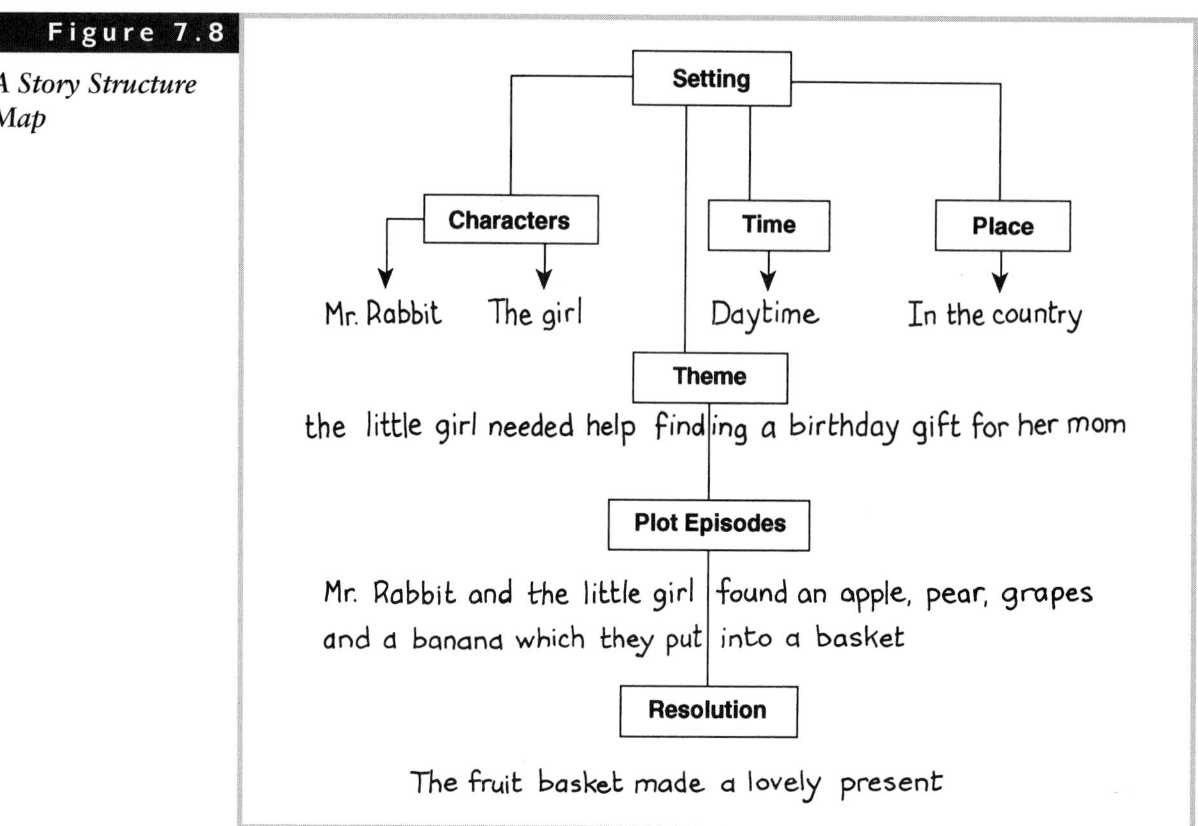

Collaborative Response Groups

Strategies discussed for enhancing comprehension thus far are done in whole-group, small-group, or one-to-one settings with the teacher as director. In the following strategies, students participate with one another, independent of the teacher. These strategies are often referred to as **"response groups."** Response groups have many different names and formats. However, they all enable children to engage in productive conversations about text independently, which elicits personal responses. Response groups allow students to exchange ideas, refine ideas, and to think critically about issues related to what they read or listened to. In these groups they learn to offer responses and to listen to what others have to say. Because young children need the teacher to model behavior for response groups before they are able to participate in them with peers, the groups are introduced in teacher-directed settings first. A brief description of types of response groups follows.

LITERATURE CIRCLES. *Literature circles* are formed for children to discuss books they have read with one another. Children can discuss the same book or different stories. Most often, however, the group discusses the same story. Teachers need to model literature circle activities so they can be carried out successfully. With young children, literature circles will be more successful if topics are raised for discussion, such as telling the parts of your story you liked best, the parts of the story you did not like, and how you might have ended the story if you were the author. Children can place sticky notes on pages to remember issues to discuss. They ask the group to turn to the page as they refer to it. Children can comment on an issue, ask a question of others, or ask for clarification to help them better understand. This type of exercise requires guidance from the teacher and practice on the part of children.

BUDDY READING. *Buddy reading* is usually a situation in which a child from an upper grade is paired with a child in kindergarten, or first or second grade. The child in the upper grade is instructed how to read to children. At specified times during the school week, buddies get together for storybook reading.

PARTNER READING. *Partner reading* involves peers reading together. This may mean simply mean that the children take turns reading to each other, or that they read sitting side by side. Teachers can structure partner reading similar to literature circles with topics posed for partners to discuss after reading to each other.

THINK, PAIR, SHARE. The *think, pair, share* strategy involves teacher-posed questions, which students are asked to *think* about before answering. Students are then *paired* with peers to discuss their answers to the questions. They then return to a larger group to *share* the answers they have discussed among themselves (Gambrell & Almasi, 1994).

MENTAL IMAGERY AND THINKALOUDS. *Mental imagery* and *thinkalouds* involve children in several strategies, alone, together, and with and without the teacher. Mental imagery asks children to visualize what they see after they have been read to or read a passage themselves. We ask children to "Make a picture in your minds to help you remember and understand what you read or what was read to you." After the mental imagery, we ask children to "thinkaloud" and talk about their images to peers or to the teacher. We also ask children to predict what will happen next in the story. We tell children to ask themselves questions about the story, and to reread when they need to clarify ideas or remember forgotten details. We often ask them to personalize the text by asking them if

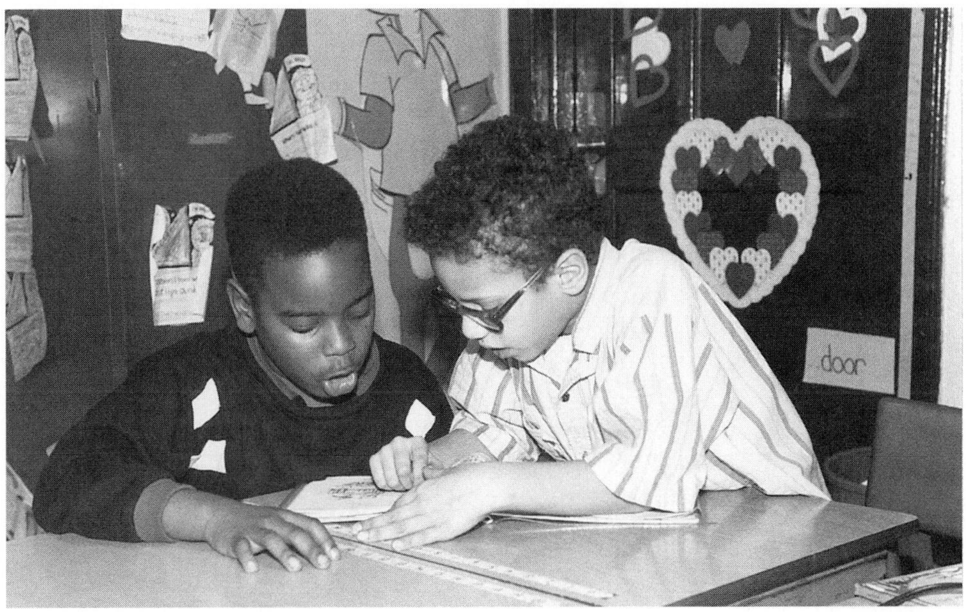

Buddy reading and retelling stories to each other enhance comprehension.

they have ever been in a similar situation as the main character and what did they do. Visualizing ideas, and relating those visualizations orally, helps clarify information and increase understanding (Brown & Lytle, 1988; Gambrell & Jawitz, 1993).

In this chapter, several strategies have been discussed for developing concepts about books and comprehension of text. The strategies are appropriate for both beginning and conventional readers. Most of them can be used with children aged two through eight; however, it is the manner in which they are implemented and the children's literature used that will determine the appropriate age group. With younger children, the teacher will have to do more modeling of strategies. In grades one, two, and three, children are able to participate in some of them more independently.

Strategies such as the DLTA and DRTA are appropriate with all ages. It is the objectives set for them that will make the difference. Whole-group, small-group, and one-to-one literature sessions are active procedures for preschool through third grade. Shared book experiences, in which a group participates in the story reading and repeated readings of books, are appropriate for all early childhood youngsters. Story retellings are one of the most effective procedures for developing comprehension skills and take many forms for children two through eight. There are oral or written retellings, retellings through dramatic role-playing organized by the children, puppet shows, roll movies, chalk talks, and felt-story presentations. When children engage in these types of retellings, they must know the setting, theme, plot episodes, resolution, and story sequence. They infer how characters feel, sound, and act as they take their parts in role-playing stories. They make judgments and decisions about the responsibilities of everyone participating to make the best presentation. With all of these strategies for comprehension development, including mapping, webbing, literature circles, buddy reading, partner reading, think-pair-share, mental imagery, thinkalouds, and discussions, children are active participants in their learning without the teacher's having to ask the typical comprehension questions, such as "How many pigs are in the story?" or "Which house did the wolf go to first, second, and third?" Children demonstrate knowledge as they are actively engaged in the strategies discussed.

All of the strategies discussed are often introduced to the whole class and reinforced in guided reading groups based on student need. In addition, independent activities can be created for many of the strategies to be done by children during center time or as independent work to practice skills when the teacher is working with guided reading groups. Teachers can create independent activities with instructions on activity cards for the following activities, skills, and strategies to enhance comprehension and concepts about books:

- Making a big book
- Independent reading using a directed reading and thinking activity format
- K-W-L activity with an informational book
- Story retelling activity
- Story rewriting activity
- Mapping and webbing activity
- Literature circle discussion group
- Partner reading activity
- Think, pair, share activity
- Mental imagery thinkalouds

Comprehension Strategies with Special Needs Children

Because many comprehension experiences involve the use of oral language, they are helpful in improving an ESL child's facility with English. The variety of strategies from which children and teachers can choose will accommodate different learning styles of students with learning difficulties. The participation required when involved in the activities discussed also addresses the special needs of children.

Assessment of Children's Concepts about Books and Comprehension of Text

The techniques described in this chapter are designed to develop concepts about books and comprehension of story through the use of expositery and narrative text. The skills listed below in the Checklist for Assessing Concepts about Books and Comprehension of Text can be developed and assessed by a broad range of strategies used in various contexts. To determine how much children know about books, such as their front, back, top, and bottom; which part is print and

Checklist *Assessing Concepts about Books and Comprehension of Text*

Child's name ______________________ **Date** __________

Concepts about Books	Always	Sometimes	Never	Comments
Knows a book is for reading				
Can identify the front, back, top, and bottom of a book				
Can turn the pages properly				
Knows the difference between the print and the pictures				
Knows that pictures on a page are related to what the print says				
Knows where to begin reading				
Knows what a title is				
Knows what an author is				
Knows what an illustrator is				

(continued on next page)

Checklist *(continued from previous page)*

Comprehension of Text	Always	Sometimes	Never	Comments
Attempts to read storybooks resulting in well-formed stories				
Participates in story reading by narrating as the teacher reads				
Retells stories				
Includes story structure elements in story retellings:				
Setting				
Theme				
Plot episodes				
Resolution				
Responds to text after reading or listening with literal comments or questions				
Responds to text after reading or listening with interpretive comments or questions				
Responds to text after reading or listening with critical comments or questions				

Participates and Responds during:	Always	Sometimes	Never	Comments
Partner reading				
Buddy reading				
Literature circles				
Mental imagery				
Thinkalouds				
Discussions				
Think, Pair, Share				

Vocabulary Development	Always	Sometimes	Never	Comments
Learns new words daily in oral language				
Uses new words in writing				

Teacher Comments:

which parts are pictures; how pages are turned; where reading begins; and what titles, authors, and illustrators are, one can observe regularly how youngsters handle books; hold one-to-one interviews with children; question and encourage response in whole-group, small-group, or individual interaction; or use any of the several other techniques described in this chapter. Children's responses can be literal, interpretive, or critical. They can reflect simple recall, detail, sequence, association, prediction, judgment, and evaluation. Children's comprehension of story can be demonstrated and evaluated through their story retelling, story rewriting, attempted reading of favorite storybooks, role-playing, picture sequencing, use of puppets or felt-boards to reenact stories, and their questions and comments during storybook reading. When possible, keep periodic performance samples of activities, such as a story rewriting and audio- or videotapes of retellings.

Throughout this chapter, assessment tools for evaluating strategies have been provided. These materials should be placed in a child's portfolio to evaluate his or her concepts about books and comprehension of text. Baseline data from children should be collected early in the school year with assessment measure repeated every six to eight weeks.

An Idea for the Classroom from the Classroom

The following experience was created by a second-grade teacher in an inner-city school. You may find it useful for your teaching.

Acting Out Stories Demonstrates Comprehension

The experience was motivated by my students' interest to create costumes they discovered in a craft book. I seized the opportunity to integrate my youngsters' desire to design costumes with a literature selection that I thought would work into a dramatization of a play. I had a collection of T. S. Eliot's poems in a picture storybook format. I decided to read *Growl Tiger's Last Stand* to them and suggested that this might be a poem they could create costumes for and act out because there were several unusual characters. Some of the vocabulary in the poem was difficult for the children, and as I read, I needed to stop occasionally to discuss the meaning of certain words. The children became very engrossed when I read that the tiger was missing an ear and an eye. They were sprawled on the floor listening, and they drew closer to me to see the pictures more clearly as the story ended.

Immediately following the story, two boys (Yassin and James) took the lead in motivating the rest of the class to act out the poem and make costumes. The children flipped through the pages to reread certain lines so that costumes would be accurate. Roseangela decided that Lady Grittlebone must have gloves because this was a ladylike thing to do. There was a long discussion of how to make a costume for Growl Tiger. A patch on one eye would be good for depicting the missing eye, but they couldn't figure out what to do about the ear.

I stayed close at hand to facilitate ideas when necessary or get the children back on track to help them accomplish their goal. Costumes were made and the poem dramatized. In this activity, I drew from the spontaneous interests of my children and created an experience that involved them in demonstrating literal, inferential, and critical comprehension skills. Youngsters had to know the details of the story to act it out and create costumes. They made many inferences about how the characters should act and sound. They engaged in critical thinking as they discussed costumes, roles, and scenery.

For this classroom activity, I used the interests of my children to create a learning experience. This was a comprehension activity in which youngsters were actively engaged, instead of a question-and-answer session without real child involvement.

Tammye Pelovitz, Second-Grade Teacher,
McKinley School, New Brunswick, New Jersey

Activities and Questions

1. Answer the focus questions at the beginning of the chapter.

2. Ask a two-, four-, and six-year-old to read his or her favorite storybook. Describe the reading behaviors they attempt. Are developmental differences evident among their performances?

3. Meet with a child between the ages of three and eight three-to-five times, each time letting the child practice retelling a story. Tape and transcribe each session. Using the forms provided in Figures 7.3 and 7.4, analyze the tapes for the elements of story structure, details, sequence, and so on that the child includes in retelling. Are there developmental changes in the child's performance from session to session? Have the child evaluate his or her story retelling and rewriting with the student evaluation form provided in Figure 7.5.

4. Select a piece of children's literature and prepare three literal, three interpretive, and three critical comprehension thinking questions to test a child's knowledge of that story. Then change those questions into activities (such as role-playing stories or creating chalk talks or felt stories) that enable children to demonstrate their comprehension of the story.

5. Prepare two different directed listening-thinking and directed reading-thinking activities, including pre- and postdiscussions. Select different objectives for each DLTA or DRTA. Use your plans with small groups of children.

6. Using another comprehension strategy discussed in the chapter, create a lesson to accompany the activity with a piece of children's literature you select. Use both expository and narrative texts.

7. Continue your portfolio assessment for the child you selected to assess for language development in Chapter 4. Observe the child using the assessment checklist provided in this chapter concerning the evaluation of concepts about books, comprehension of text, and other measures provided.

8. Continue the thematic unit that you began in Chapter 4. Select three objectives in the area of concepts about books and three in comprehension of text, and describe three activities that will satisfy each of the objectives using your theme.

Case Study Activities

Case 1

Two first-grade teachers have come to you as the reading specialist in the district for help with students who have limited English proficiency. You are concerned about improving their ability in English and are also aware that they must learn about book concepts and strategies for comprehending text. You prepare a workshop to share strategies to help these teachers with the students. You decide to use children's literature as a resource. Describe the strategies you will share with the teachers.

Case 2

The following passages describe reading lessons taught by three different second-grade teachers. Each uses strategies to promote comprehension. While reading these passages, think about the following questions:

1. Do the questions posed by the teachers foster factual or interpretive thought?
2. Is there an emphasis on specifics or understanding of issues raised?
3. Is the plan flexible or predetermined?
4. Is there time for problem solving, in an interactive manner with peers.
5. Is the atmosphere constricted, controlled, supportive, warm, or rewarding?
6. Can children raise questions?
7. Are students asked to predict and analyze?
8. Is there an emphasis on higher order thinking or literal levels of thought?

Read Teachers A and B and then answer the questions. If you had to select just one of these teachers to be, which one would you choose and why? After answering the questions, read Teacher C and then go back and answer all the questions again.

TEACHER A: READING LESSON #1

Teacher A begins her lesson by announcing that the class will be reading the story *Goldilocks and the Three Bears.* She introduces new vocabulary from the story such as "porridge" and "middle" by writing them on the chalkboard. The teacher calls on different children to read the story orally. To check their comprehension, the teacher stops after each child reads and asks factual questions about the text such as, Who are the main characters in the story? and What did Goldilocks do first when she got to the bears' house? She asks similar questions all the way through the passage. Occasionally, the teacher stops to emphasize the structure or spelling of a word. Throughout the story, the teacher pauses to discuss the pictures. Again, she asks very specific detail questions such as, Who is in the picture?

After reading the story, the children are given a worksheet to complete at their desks. The worksheet is designed to reinforce the details of the story and enhance vocabulary. It includes questions that require the children to circle the correct answer. When the children are finished with the worksheet, the lesson is over.

TEACHER B: READING LESSON #2

Teacher B begins her lesson by asking the students to share things they have done that they knew were wrong. After the children describe their experiences, the teacher asks why they did these things. She then tells the children that they are going to read the story *Goldilocks and the Three Bears*. Before reading, she has the children look at the pictures in the book to predict what the story is about. The teacher asks the class to think about who does bad things in the story while they read. The class then reads the story silently from beginning to end. Afterward, the teacher asks questions designed to elicit information about the students' comprehension of the story theme by asking, What are the main events in the story? Who are the good characters and who are the bad ones, and why? Why were they good or bad? Was it okay for Goldilocks to go in the bears' house uninvited? Why yes or why no? Children are asked to discuss favorite parts of the story and read these parts to the class. A discussion follows about the illustrations in the book. Are the pictures important to the story? Do they help tell parts of the story?

The teacher asks the students what types of extended activities they would like to do related to the story, for example, draw a picture or make a felt story. The children decide to act out the story. The teacher helps the children discuss what the major scenes are and who the main characters are. The children volunteer for roles. They follow the content of the story, but without using the book. The children act out the scenes spontaneously. The class is asked to return to their seats, illustrate their favorite part of the story, and rewrite it in their own words.

Reminder: **Answer the questions posed at the beginning of the case study activity and then read Teacher C.**

TEACHER C: READING LESSON #3

Teacher C begins his lesson by asking the students if they have any special personal things. He asks how they might feel if someone came and took their personal things without asking or used them and ruined them. He introduces the story *Goldilocks and the Three Bears* and asks the class to read the book silently and determine how Goldilocks intruded on the bears' personal things. He asks the class to discuss how they think the bears felt when they got home and found someone had been in their house. All suggestions are accepted as the teacher explains that there are no right or wrong answers; it is the judgments of the class regarding the situation that are of interest. Students select favorite parts of the story, which are reread and discussed in terms of content and style. Illustrations are discussed in terms of what feelings are being portrayed in the pictures.

As a related activity, rather than dramatize the story as it is written, the class creates an entirely new story about Goldilocks and the three bears or a new ending for the story. The teacher allows the children to decide with which students they would like to work. In small groups they create their new scenes independent of the teacher, and then act them out for the class. When all groups have made their presentations, the scenes are discussed.

Now answer the questions at the beginning of this case study activity for Teacher C, and decide which teacher you would like to be now that you have read Teachers A, B, and C. Support your answer.

chapter 8

Word-Study Skills

Phonemic Awareness and Phonics

First words must have an intense meaning.
First words must be already part of the dynamic life.
First books must be made of the stuff of the child himself, whatever and wherever the child.

—Sylvia Ashton-Warner
Teacher

Focus Questions

- What word-study skills are important for a young child to learn?
- Define and describe how the use of the following strategies enhances a child's knowledge about print: (1) environmental print, (2) Very Own Words, (3) language experience approach, (4) context and picture clues, and (5) high-frequency sight words.
- Define the following terms: (1) alphabetic understanding, (2) phonemic awareness, (3) phoneme–grapheme correspondence, (4) digraphs, (5) consonant blends, (6) long and short vowel sounds, (7) hard and soft consonant sounds, (8) diphthongs, (9) inflectional endings, and (10) phonics.
- Describe the characteristics of commercially prepared materials designed for literacy instruction.

Mrs. Abere's class was studying nutrition. The dramatic-play area was set up like a supermarket with products displayed separately into food groups: dairy products; breads and cereals; meat, poultry, and fish; and fruits and vegetables. To connect the learning of sound–symbol relationships and letter names with the unit, three letters were featured: *m* for meat, *f* for fish, and *d* for dairy. In addition to creating nonsense stories using the featured letters such as *Fanny the Fish was a Friendly Flounder who liked to Flip her Flippers as she Fluttered through the waves,* the children were to collect things that began with the featured letters and place them in boxes labeled with the appropriate symbol. These experiences caused them to talk about letters, sounds, and words in spontaneous play. Kathy and Kelly were pretending that they were shopping in the dramatic-play store. Kathy picked up a can of tuna fish and said, "Kelly, let's see how many foods we can find that begin with the letter *f*." They looked around and Kathy found a box of Frosted Flakes and some French Fries. Kelly found a can of Fruit Cocktail, Froot Loops cereal, and a container of Frozen Yogurt. The girls were excited when each found some food that began with the letter *f*. They said each word with a strong emphasis on the beginning *f* sound. Another activity the children were asked to do was to copy the names of the food that began with *f*. Mrs. Abere told them to do the same activities for the other featured letters in the unit, *m* for meat and *d* for dairy.

Word Study: Helping Children Figure Out Words

Word-study skills and knowledge about print involve learning strategies that will help children figure out words and become independent readers. Word-study skills for decoding words include the use of context and syntax, the development of a sight vocabulary, the use of the configuration or the shape of a word, and structural analysis (attending to different parts of words such as prefixes, suffixes, or the root). The most well known word-study strategy is the use of phonics, which involves learning letter sounds and combinations of letter sounds (referred to as phonemes) associated with their corresponding letter symbols (referred to as graphemes). One of the problems with phonics is that the English alphabet has at least 44 different sounds, and sound–symbol correspondence is not consistent—there are many irregularities and exceptions to many rules.

Phonemic awareness, described earlier in this book as the ability to recognize that words are made up of individual sounds that can be segmented from the rest of the word and blended together to form words, is considered to be a precursor to phonics or an important skill for learning phonics. Phonics has received much attention as an important skill for reading success to a greater and lesser extent over the years. There is no doubt that research has demonstrated its importance. However, it is the concurrent use of several of the word-study skills mentioned that creates a proficient reader.

Research concerning early literacy has demonstrated the importance of meaningful experiences in early literacy instruction (Goodman, 1984; Teale, 1982). When this research was new, word-analysis skill development with an emphasis on decoding was considered as a synthetic approach that lacked meaning for young children. However, research discussed in Chapter 6 demonstrates that to become a proficient reader, language codes need to be learned. This is true not only in English-speaking countries; there is considerable evidence from both experimental and longitudinal studies from many countries that phonemic awareness and knowledge of phonics are necessary for success in learning to read and write alphabetic languages (Adams, 1990; Juel, 1994). According to Juel (1989), a child needs to have the following in order to learn to read proficiently: (1) alphabetic understanding (knowing that words are composed of letters), (2) phonemic awareness, and (3) cryptoanalytic intent (knowing that there is a relationship between the printed letters and spoken sounds). These three elements are in some ways precursors to learning phonics.

Early literacy educators have some concerns about word study. They question exactly what skills should be taught, when to introduce them, how to teach them, and how much time to spend dealing with them. Although there are no definitive answers to all these questions, we have found that teaching word-study skills in a variety of ways seems to be the best approach. For example, there should be some explicit systematic instruction and spontaneous instruction, and teaching the skills and practicing them in meaningful contextually based settings.

Skills and Objectives for Word Study

The following are objectives for word study to enhance literacy development. The child should be able to:

1. Demonstrate that print is read from left to right.
2. Demonstrate that oral language can be written down and then read.
3. Demonstrate what a letter is and point to one on a printed page.
4. Demonstrate what a word is, point to one on a printed page, and know there are spaces between words.
5. Demonstrate that print in the environment has a message, and read some of this print on signs and logos.
6. Recognize high-frequency words and other words by sight.
7. Identify rhyming words he or she hears and make up a rhyme.
8. Identify and name upper- and lowercase letters of the alphabet.
9. Blend and segment phonemes in words.
10. Associate letters with their initial and final corresponding consonant sounds, including sounds of the same letter (Such as hard and soft *c*-cat, city; *g*-goat, George).
11. Associate letters with corresponding long and short vowel sounds (*a*-acorn, apple; *e*-eagle, egg; *i*-ice, igloo; *o*-oats, octopus; *u*-unicorn, umbrella).
12. Read fluently at instructional level.
13. Blend together consonant blends *bl, cr, dr, fl, gl, pr, st,* etc. (consonant blends are two or three letters that when placed together blend into one sound that represents the two or three letter sounds).

14. Identify consonant digraph sounds *ch, ph, sh, th,* and *wh* (digraphs are two letters that when placed together make a new sound unlike the sounds of either letter).
15. Use context, syntax, and semantics to identify words.
16. Divide words into syllables.
17. Attempt reading by attending to picture clues and to print.
18. Predict words based on a knowledge of phoneme–grapheme correspondence.
19. Identify different structural elements of words, such as prefixes, suffixes, and inflectional endings -ing, -ed, and -s at the end of a word.
20. Apply the following phonic generalizations:
    a. In a consonant–vowel–consonant pattern, the vowel sound is usually short (bat, bet, but, bit).
    b. In a vowel–consonant–e pattern, the vowel sound is usually long (cake, cute).
    c. When two vowels come together in a word, the first is usually long and the second is usually silent (train, receive, bean).
21. Identify common word families referred to also as rimes or phonograms, and build words by adding initial consonants (called onsets) to word families (*it, an, am, at, ite, ate,* and so on).

Standards and Word Study

State and U.S. national standards are concerned with word-study skills. Standards for kindergarten to third grade, as outlined by the National Center on Education and the Economy and the Learning Research and Development Center at the University of Pittsburgh (1999), talk about word study as *print-sound code*. In this area the standards are knowledge of letters and their sounds, phonemic awareness, and reading words.

Based on these standards, kindergarten through third grade children should be able to do the following related to word study:

- Have knowledge of letters and their sounds
- Segment and Blend Sounds (phonemic awareness)
- Read words with more than one syllable
- Recognize or figure out irregularly spelled words and patterns
- Read words based on their knowledge of letters and their sounds, and recognize a large number of high-frequency words
- Read text with accuracy and fluency at their own particular level. (Fluency suggests that reading is done in a smooth manner with appropriate intonation and pauses; accuracy refers to correct reading of words.)
- Have self-monitoring and self-correcting strategies. (This means that children recognize when they need help and ask for it. They recognize when they have made a mistake and use strategies learned to try to correct their errors.)

Chapter 9 on writing discusses the development of spelling. Spelling also is learned as sound–symbol relationship patterns are acquired. As you use the strategies discussed for the acquisition of phonics, have children practice these word patterns frequently by using them in their writing to help with spelling.

Teaching Strategies for Word-Study Skills

In the past, word-study skills were taught often through the use of worksheets that asked children for mechanical responses. It was believed that a child could not read until many of the beginning skills were mastered. However, not all skills are necessary for all children. There are many ways for this information to be learned that are meaningful for children, and less time is needed to deal with these skills than was thought in the past.

Instructional activities designed to help youngsters learn about the function, form, structure, and conventions of print should involve the same types of learning experiences as other skill areas dealt with in this book. Children need to be socially interactive when they are learning about print; they need models to emulate; and the learning must be through experiences that are meaningful and connected with real life and incorporate what children already know. If children see a need or usefulness attached to a reading skill, that skill probably will be learned without difficulty.

In the sections that follow, strategies are described to help children learn about print in meaningful and functional ways. Each strategy is appropriate for youngsters from preschool through third grade—the teacher simply adjusts the activity to the age group he or she is working with. Learning these skills should be connected to content-area material and functional activities. Activities such as reading to children; pointing out words in the environment; noting their letters and sounds; taking a child's dictation; encouraging children to write in their own way; allowing youngsters to see the print as it is read from a Big Book and tracked from left to right across the page; and using predictable books that rhyme or have patterned language and that allow children to guess and share in the reading all help youngsters learn about print (Juel, 1989). Through these experiences, children learn that print is read from left to right, that words in a book are oral language that has been written down and can be read, that letters have sounds, that letters make up words, that words have meaning, that pictures hold clues to what the print says, and that words can be predicted based on the meaning of the text. In addition, some direct instruction of phonemic awareness, phonics, and alphabetic knowledge is needed.

When direct instruction is used, lessons need to teach the skill as a strategy for children to use. In these lessons the teacher does the following:

1. Begins with an explanation and rationale for the children by letting them know what is being taught and why it is being taught.
2. Models and demonstrates how to use the skill and when to use the skill.
3. Gives students the opportunity to practice the skill taught.
4. Encourages students to apply the skills.

The use of an occasional worksheet will reinforce skills taught. Children can read several words and simple books through their knowledge of syntax, semantics, and acquired sight vocabulary before phonics is emphasized. When youngsters have experienced success with initial reading, they will seek information about the forms of print because they will want to read independently.

Using Environmental Print

Several researchers have found that children as young as two can read familiar environmental print (Goodman, 1980; Harste, Woodward, & Burke, 1984; Hiebert, 1978). Others, however, have shown that a child often is reading the sign rather than its print; when the print is separated from its familiar environmental context, the young child sometimes can no longer identify it (Mason, 1980). Even so, when very young children associate the McDonald's logo with the word *McDonald's* and try to read it, they are learning that a group of letters makes up a word that can be read and thus provides information. The ability to read environmental print also gives the child a sense of accomplishment and usually elicits positive reinforcement of the child's achievement by caring adults.

As noted earlier, parents can make children aware of environmental print from the first year of life. During daily routines, parents need to point out and read words and labels on food boxes, road signs, stores, and restaurants. The world is filled with environmental print. School, however, is not. With the exception of *Exit, Boys, Girls,* and special names such as *Library* and *Office,* few familiar words appear in the typical school building. Thus, environmental print needs to be brought into school from outside, and teachers need to label items within the walls of their own day-care centers, nursery schools, kindergartens, and first and second grades. The print should be traced and copied. Such print, once familiar, becomes part of a child's sight vocabulary.

The environmental print that children tend to know best appears on food containers, especially those for cereal, soup, milk, and cookies, and on detergent boxes and bottles. Among common signs, they recognize fast-food logos, road signs, traffic signals, and names of popular store chains, supermarkets, and service stations. Collect such logos and trade names and make them available in your classroom by posting them on charts, pasting them onto index cards, and creating looseleaf books of environmental print. Most firms distribute various printed materials free, complete with logos. Photograph examples of environmental print to bring to your classroom. Suggest that children read such words and copy them.

Fill your room with its own environmental print. Start at the beginning of a school year with only a few signs, such as children's names on their cubbies, and the word *Block Center* to identify that area of the room. Make labels with five-by-eight index cards and dark felt-tip markers. Begin each word with a capital letter and continue with lowercase manuscript, thus providing youngsters with configuration clues. Hang labels at heights easy for children to see. Point out the labels to the children, and suggest that they read them to friends and copy them. As the school year progresses, label new items that are added to the classroom. Refer to the labels as part of your normal routine so that they are used and will then add to the child's sight vocabulary. Label items because they are of interest to the class and serve a function such as identifying important classroom materials and learning centers. Use labels for relating messages such as *Wash Your Hands Before Snack*. Refer to the labels often so the children identify them as useful and functional.

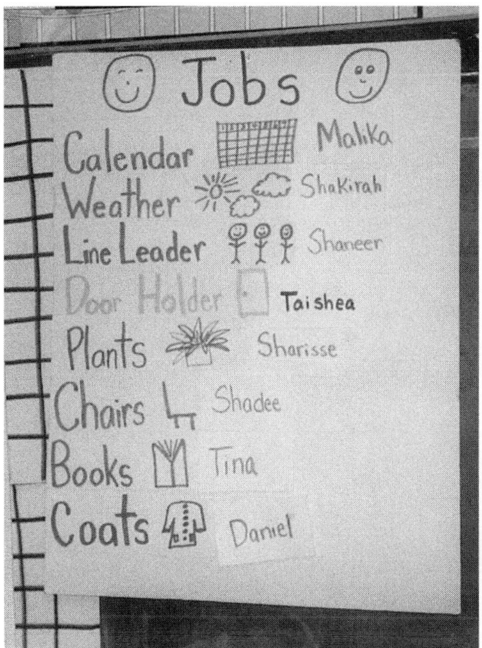

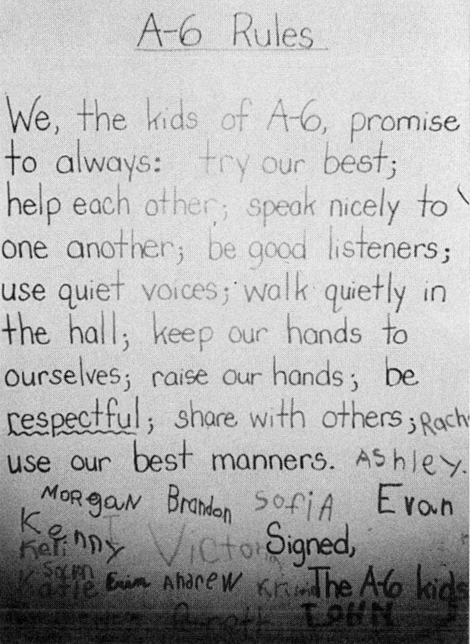

A chart with class jobs and a list of class rules provide important pieces of environmental print to early childhood rooms.

Label items related to content-area topics. If you are studying dinosaurs—a popular topic in early childhood—display model dinosaurs and label each with its name. Even long, difficult words such as *Brontosaurus* and *Tyrannosaurus* immediately become sight words for many early childhood youngsters. It is not uncommon to observe preschool, kindergarten, first-grade and second-grade children reading labels to themselves or to each other. I observed a kindergarten class after the teacher had posted two new labels in the science center, which featured a lesson on the sense of touch and focused on items that were hard and soft. I watched Josh take Jennifer by the hand and heard him say, "See, Jen. See this. This bunny is soft. This word says 'soft.'" Josh continued, "See this, Jen. This is a rock and this word says 'hard.' Touch it. It is hard." The two children stroked the bunny, pointed to the label, and said in unison, "soft"; they then touched the rock, pointed to the label, and said, "hard." They repeated the sequence several times.

THE MORNING MESSAGE. Another way to make print part of the classroom environment is to communicate with print, even with preschool children. Every day post messages and assignments for children. Select a permanent spot on the chalkboard or on chart paper. Use rebus or picture writing along with print to help children make sense of the message. Here are a few examples of appropriate messages:

Happy Birthday, Tyrone.

Happy Valentine's Day

Read a book to a friend.

We are going on a trip to the town library today.

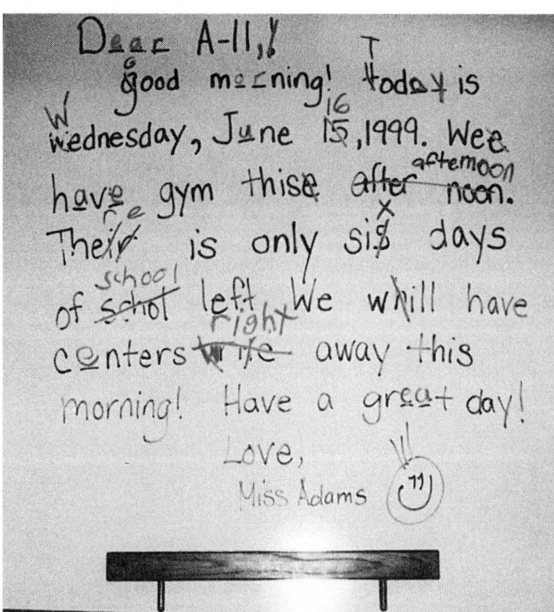

Miss Adams has made spelling, punctuation, and grammatical errors in her morning message. Her student detectives corrected all but one of the mistakes.

This routine will teach children to look automatically at the chalkboard each day for a special message. They will learn that print carries meaning that is interesting and useful. Some teachers refer to this practice as the ***morning message*** and have formalized it into a lesson when the school day begins (Stewart, Benjamin, & Mason, 1987). Continue to communicate in print throughout the day whenever the opportunity occurs. Write at least some of the message with the children watching, so that you provide a writing model for them. Use the message to develop various concepts about print. Emphasize specific words or letters, pursue questions about meaning, or let children add sentences to the original message.

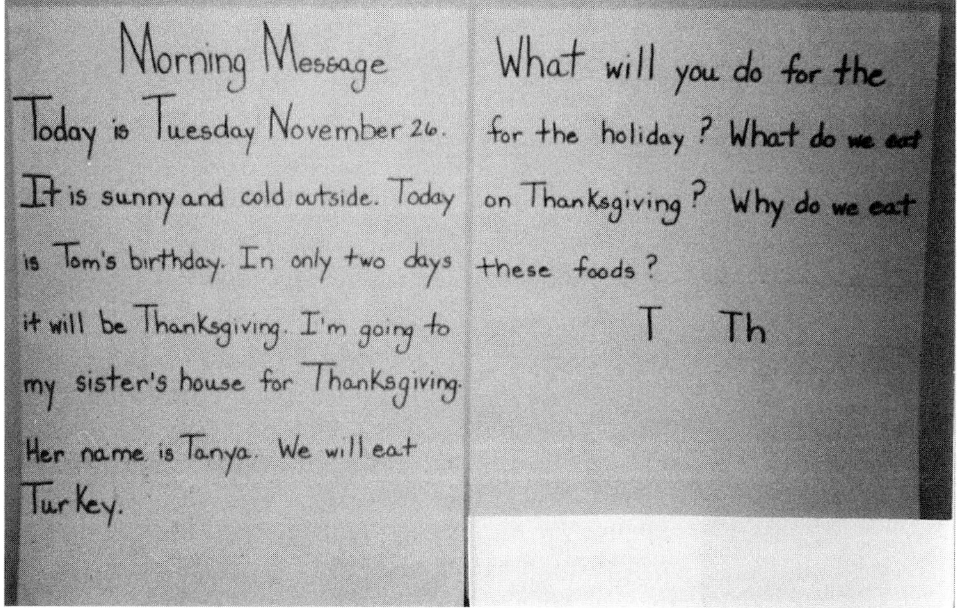

This morning message is used to talk about an upcoming holiday and point out the initial consonant *t* and digraph *th*.

When working with seven- and eight-year-olds, the contents of the morning message and the environmental print displayed in the room will be more sophisticated than when working with younger children. They can be used to point out sound–symbol relationships or phonic generalizations that are appropriate to deal with in first and second grade. For example a morning message such as the following is a perfect opportunity to the point out the *sh* digraph:

Shelly is wearing shiny new shoes that she bought today.

In another message, such as the following, there are five examples of the phonic generalization that, in a vowel–consonant–e pattern, the vowel is usually long.

Kate's birthday cake was made in the shape of a kite.

This is a perfect opportunity to observe and discuss this letter–sound pattern.

Teachers use morning messages to teach letter writing by writing some of the messages in the form of a letter and pointing out the elements of the format. Teachers also sometimes purposefully make spelling or punctution errors in messages and ask the children to find the mistakes. Letters of the alphabet can be left out of words to be filled in, or complete words can be left out for children to figure out from the context of the sentence. Some teachers embed the class spelling words into the message. Or, they include words that demonstrate skills being taught, such as words with long *a* sounds or short vowel sounds, or words with digraphs or blends. Children are asked to identify and circle the featured words, vowels, etc.

Developing Sight Vocabulary

In *Teacher* (1963), Sylvia Ashton-Warner described Very Own Words as a method for developing sight vocabulary. She encouraged children to write their favorite words from a story or content-area lesson on three-by-five cards, each word on a separate card. Very Own Words are often from a child's home life—*Mommy, Daddy, Grandpa, Grandma, birthday.* They also reflect emotional feelings—*naughty, nice, good, no, punish.* After Very Own Words are recorded on index cards, they are stored in a child's file box, in a coffee can, a plastic baggie, or on a loose-leaf ring hung on a bulletin board. Teachers have devised many other methods for storing Very Own Words.

Helping children start their collections of Very Own Words is an exciting experience in school. Before an activity or exercise, let them know that at its completion you will ask them to name their favorite words from the activity. The activity should be a pleasant one that produces interesting language, perhaps popping corn or making play dough. Children also can choose a favorite word in a storybook or words generated from the study of social studies and science units. Soon children will request their Very Own Words without being asked.

Encourage children to do things with their words—read them to friends or to themselves, copy them, dictate them to the teacher, and use them in sentences or stories. Because words are based on a child's expressed interests in situations at home and in school, the collection of Very Own Words is a powerful technique for developing sight vocabulary.

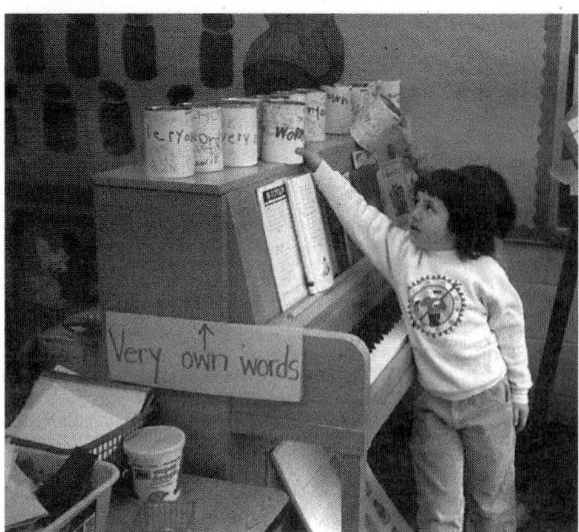

Very Own Words are a source for personal sight vocabulary. Teachers should encourage children to copy them, write them, and read them.

Seven- and eight-year-olds also enjoy and learn from collecting Very Own Words. They should alphabetize them and store them in a file box. Teachers can encourage children to study the letter patterns in their Very Own Words. They can discuss consonant and vowel sounds, blends, digraphs, and structural elements such as prefixes and suffixes, as well as phonic generalizations that may be evident. When a child studies letter patterns in words he or she has selected, it will mean more than doing the same task with words selected by the teacher or found in a textbook.

Very Own Words are also useful with bilingual children. The index card should include a child's Very Own Word in English and can have the word written in his or her native language as well.

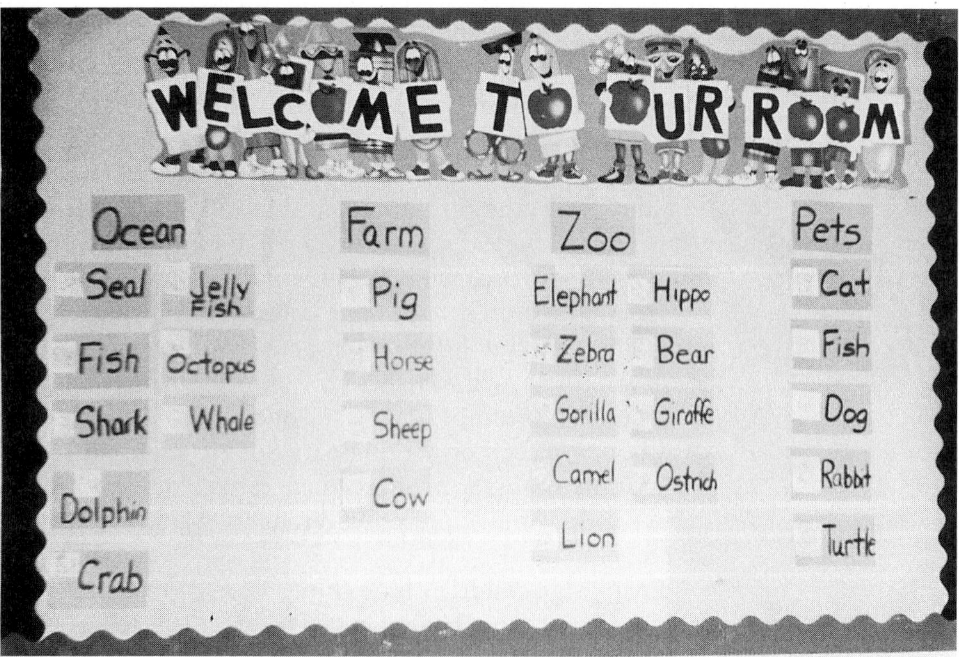

Very Own Words and sight words are generated from collections of theme-related words from specific units of study in science and social studies.

HIGH-FREQUENCY WORDS AS SIGHT WORDS. There are a group of words that are found frequently in reading materials for young children that need to be learned for quick recall. They are words that do not carry meaning but that hold sentences together. They are often difficult to decode because they have irregular patterns in their spelling. It is helpful for children if they do not have to spend time segmenting these words as they read; they should be able to read them easily because they have been learned by memory or sight.

Sight words are often taught in a systematic and explicit manner. The teacher selects a few of these words for the children to learn each week. To learn these words, the following activities are used:

- Words are said aloud and used in sentence.
- The sentence is written on a chalkboard or flip chart and the sight word is underlined.
- Features of each word such as the letters or its similarity to other words are discussed. The teacher also points out any regular or irregular patterns the word may have.
- Children are asked to spell the word aloud, spell the word with their finger in the air, and write the word on paper.
- Children chant the letters as they spell words.
- The words can be written on index cards similar to Very Own Words and stored with the child's other cards.

In Figure 8.1 is a list of **high-frequency words** (Fountas & Pinnell, 1996). According to Adams (1990), the following 13 words are 25 percent of the words children find in early literacy texts: a, and, for, he, in, is, it, of, that, the, to, was, you.

Figure 8.1

Frequently Used Words

a	came	her	look	people	too
after	can	here	looked	play	two
all	come	him	long	put	up
an	could	his	make	run	us
and	day	house	man	ran	very
are	did	how	mother	said	was
am	do	I	me	saw	we
as	don't	I'm	my	see	went
asked	down	if	no	she	were
at	for	in	not	so	what
away	from	into	now	some	when
back	get	is	of	that	where
be	go	it	old	the	will
because	going	just	on	then	with
before	good	keep	one	there	would
big	had	kind	or	they	you
boy	has	know	our	this	your
but	have	like	out	three	
by	he	little	over	to	

Source: Reprinted by permission of Irene Fountas and Gay Su Pinnell: *Guided Reading: Good First Teaching for All Children* (Heinemann, A division of Reed Elsevier, Inc., Portsmouth, NH, 1996).

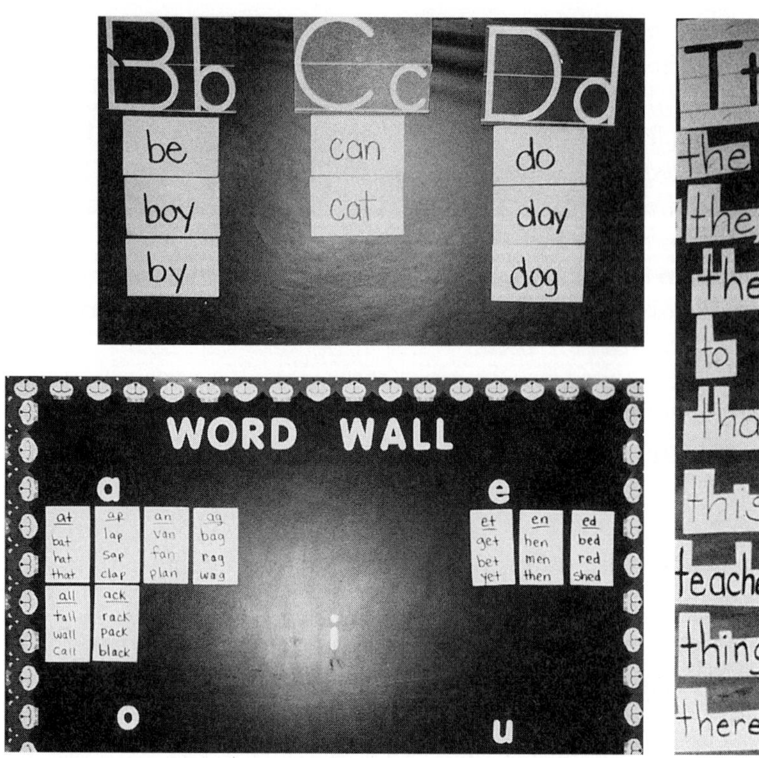

Word walls can feature high-frequency words or words with short vowel sounds. Some teachers cut high-frequency words to illustrate their shape or configuration to help children remember them better.

WORD WALLS TO TEACH HIGH-FREQUENCY AND OTHER WORDS. A **word wall** typically has the letters of the alphabet posted across the wall. As high-frequency words are featured they are pasted under the letter where they belong. The featured words are ones teachers select as being a priority to learn. Others may be ones that children are having difficulty with reading and spelling. The words are placed on index cards. Children are asked to spell each word out loud, trace it in the air, and copy it. Sometimes words are written and then cut out into the shape of the word providing more clues for remembering it.

The word wall can be used to play word-study games. For example, if the teacher wants to work with rhymes, he or she can point to a word such as *went* and say, "the word I am thinking of rhymes with *went,* but begins with a *b,*" or, "The word I am thinking of rhymes with *look* and begins with a *b.*" Word-wall words also can be sorted by word families, word endings, and so on by moving the words around the wall and working on a sheet of paper. Many different lessons and directions for using the wall independently can be provided (Cunningham, 1995; Moustafa, 1997).

To ensure that children are acquiring sight recognition of high-frequency words, they should be tested in their ability to read them. The teacher should ask them to identify the words with flash cards and find them in context within passages to read. This can be done several times during the school year.

Using the Language Experience Approach

The **Language Experience Approach** (LEA) has been used for many years in reading instruction. It can help children associate oral language with written language, teaching them specifically that what is said can be written down and read.

It illustrates the left-to-right progression of our written language. In practice, it demonstrates the formation of letters plus their combination into words; it helps build sight vocabulary; it is a source for meaningful teaching of phoneme–grapheme correspondence as well as other knowledge about print; and it is based on the child's interest and experiences.

Many educators have been associated with developing and articulating the Language Experience Approach, among them R. V. Allen (1976), M. A. Hall (1976), and J. Veatch et al. (1973). The LEA is based on the following premises, all from the learner's point of view:

What I think is important.

What I think, I can say.

What I say can be written down by me or by others.

What is written down can be read by me and by others.

The interests and experiences on which the LEA builds come from children's lives both at home and at school. Home experiences, of course, tend to be spontaneous. In school, the teacher needs to plan experiences—for example, class trips, cooking projects, use of puppets, guest speakers, class pets, holiday events—or the study of topics that are exciting to young children, such as dinosaurs, outer space, and other cultures. The language experience lesson is usually carried out with an entire class, but it also can take place with a small group or an individual child.

An LEA lesson begins with oral language. A discussion is usually generated from an interesting or exciting class experience—for instance, a recent trip to the zoo, Halloween costumes, or the pet gerbil's new litter. To begin the discussion, ask open-ended questions that will encourage descriptive responses rather than yes/no answers. For example, if the topic is a trip to the zoo, ask children to name their favorite animal. Why was it their favorite animal? What did the animal look like? What did the animal do while they were watching it at the zoo? It is important to accept all the children's responses. Accept nonstandard English without correction, but provide a language model by using standard English to paraphrase what the child has said.

After a discussion has generated several ideas, write them down. With a large group of children, write the ideas on a large sheet of paper (approximately 24 × 36 inches), which becomes an experience chart. It can be taped to the wall or mounted on an easel. Print with a dark felt-tip marker of medium thickness, allowing ample spacing between words and between lines so that the chart is very readable. Use manuscript in upper- and lower-case letters, following the conventions of regular print and thus giving configuration to words that the use of uppercase alone cannot give. Word configuration aids children in word identification.

In recording language on experience charts, teachers should write quickly and legibly, providing good manuscript samples for children to read and copy. As you write what children dictate, use their language unless it is difficult for others to understand. When dictation is difficult to understand, ask a child to restate an idea or, if necessary, help the child restate it. It is important to include the comments of as many children as possible. When creating a new chart, try to remember which children have not contributed in the past, and encourage them to contribute to the new chart. It is a good idea to identify who said what.

The chart is more interesting to youngsters whose names are included. For example: John said, "I liked the gorilla at the zoo. He jumped around and made funny faces." Jordanna said, "I liked the baby deer. They had big, bright, black eyes, wet black noses, and shiny brown fur." Try to accompany each sentence with an illustration; this will help children read the charts.

Experience charts should not be very long. Charts dictated by two- and three-year-olds can be simply lists of words, such as names of animals with illustrations next to them. Used occasionally, lists of words make appropriate charts for older children as well. They are a quick way to record and reinforce vocabulary associated with topics being studied. Small-group and individual dictations of experiences can be made into books by the teacher or the child. While writing a chart, take the opportunity to point out concepts about print: "Now I am writing the word 'gorilla'—g-o-r-i-l-l-a. See, it begins here with a *g* and ends here with an *a*." Mentally note which letters or sounds interest children. Ask children to point out on the chart where you should begin to write. Like directed listening (or reading) and thinking activities and the morning message, the LEA lesson can have a specific skill objective.

The last step in the LEA lesson is to read the chart to the class. Use a pointer to emphasize left-to-right progression. Let the class read the chart in unison, or ask individual children who contributed different sentences to read them. Leave the chart in a visible spot in the room and encourage the children to read it and copy parts of it, copy words they like, or add to their Very Own Word collection from the chart. Vocabulary charts and experience charts representing different topics discussed in school can be left hanging in the room if space permits, then made into Big Books for children to look at throughout the school year. If a laminating machine is available, it is wise to preserve charts. Children's dictated stories also can be placed in the class library for others to read, as can books made by the entire class. Those made by the class often become the most popular books in the room. Class books can be made by having each child draw and write directly onto a duplicating master. This method allows easy production of multiple copies, one for each child.

Pocket chart activities are associated with the Language Experience Approach. Words associated with experiences the class has had are featured in the chart. Short stories, poems, and songs also are printed on individual sentence strips that students chant together. The charts can be copied to practice writing. In addition, the sentence strips can be scrambled and sequenced into the pocket chart. Sentence strips are often cut up for students to work with on the word level, to help identify and practice new words and place them into sentences.

Experience charts, dictated by the children and written by the teacher, develop language and encourage reading and writing.

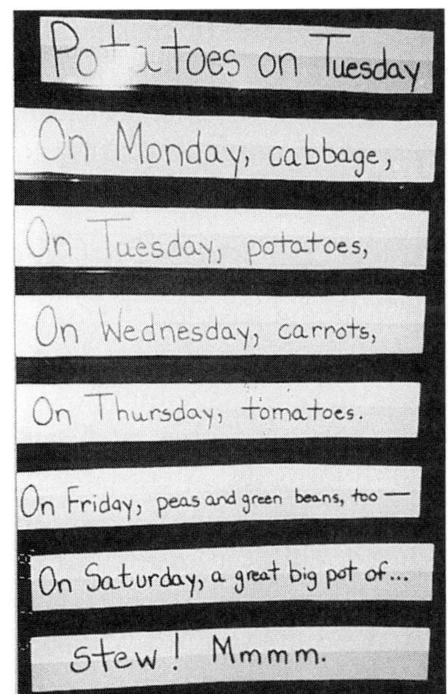

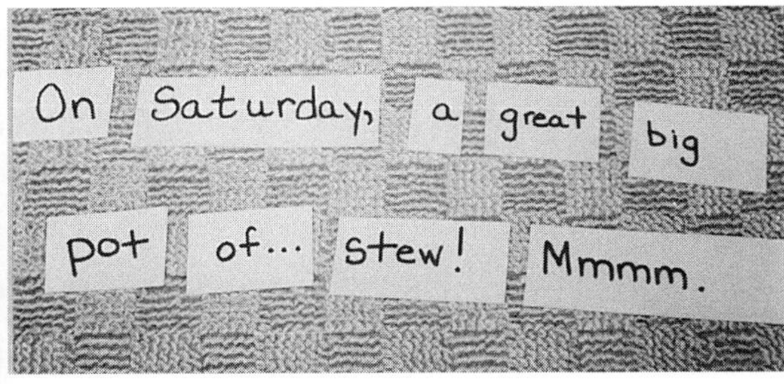

Ms. Asbury wrote the words to the little story on chart paper and then on sentence strips for children to sequence. She cut a second set of sentence strips into words for children to sequence.

When teaching a unit on food and featuring the consonant ***t*** in all parts of words, Ms. Asbury selected *Potatoes on Tuesday* (Lillegard & McPhail, 1993) to read to her kindergarten class to reinforce this skill. The text of the book is as follows:

> On Monday, cabbage,
> On Tuesday, potatoes,
> On Wednesday, carrots,
> On thursday, tomatoes;
> On Friday, peas and green beans, too—
> On Saturday, a great big pot of . . .
> Stew! Mmmm.
>
> *Source:* From *Potatoes on Tuesday* by Dee Lillegard. © 1995, 1993 by Scott, Foresman and Company. Published by Good Year Books. Used by permission.

Ms. Asbury wrote the words to the story on chart paper and then on sentence strips. She cut a second set of sentence strips into individual words. This provided the children with activities to practice sequencing whole sentences into a story, building sentences from individual words by using the syntax and semantics of the text, and identifying of the consonant ***t*** within the context of a story. Children also were able to practice new vocabulary that appeared in the story. Pocket chart activities are often used to practice new skills during independent center time.

The Language Experience Approach, which is appropriate throughout early childhood and beyond, can be used similarly to the morning message and Very Own Words for noticing phonic generalizations and sound–symbol correspondences. Learning about print in this situation is done with material that is familiar and meaningful. Occasionally prepare a chart in the language of bilingual children in your class. If necessary, solicit help from bilingual parents or colleagues. This strategy will guide bilingual youngsters in making connections between their language and English.

LEA materials are inexpensive and easy to use. They include chart paper, markers, colored construction paper, white paper, index cards, scissors, staplers, pencils, and crayons. With directions from the teacher, these simple classroom materials record the precious words and pictures created by children from their own meaningful, real-life experiences. The LEA should be central, not supplemental, to literacy instruction in early reading programs.

Using Context and Pictures to Figure Out Words

Experiences with literature can lead children to use contextual print and illustrations to recognize that words have meaning and help them decode written words. Again, those experiences can take place in whole-class, small-group, or one-to-one settings and through such techniques as directed listening (or reading) and thinking activities, shared book experiences, and repeated readings of stories. For example, select a story that is predictable, in which the text and illustrations are closely related. Ask children to look at the pictures on a page before reading it to them. Ask them what they think the words will say. Then read the page to demonstrate that print and illustration are closely related and that the pictures provide information that can help the children as they read the story.

The syntax and semantics of a sentence (its grammatical structure and meaning) also help children identify words. Encourage children to use these elements of written language by stopping your oral reading at predictable points in a story and asking them to fill in words. For example, when reading *The Little Engine That Could* (Piper, 1954), first read the complete repetitive phrase "I think I can," then, the second time say, "I think I _____," the next time "I think _____," and last "I _____." This technique is most effective with a Big Book because you can point to the words as the children say them. As the children begin to understand the concept of filling in words, choose more difficult passages for your pauses. Prepare charts and sheets with predictable text and leave out words to be filled in as you read. Children use their prior knowledge of syntax and context in predicting words. They assimilate and use the strategy when they read themselves.

In addition to these general suggestions, specific experiences to figure out words can be varied so that students have many different strategies for using context. A common way to determine words from context is through the meaning of the text. For example, in the sentence that follows, it is apparent that the missing word is *Queen*. We need to show children how to use the meaning of the text to figure out a word that might be unknown to them.

The King and ________ lived in the castle together.

Another context clue exercise involves a series of related words. To help with this exercise or other context clue exercises, the initial consonant can be included. For example:

My favorite kinds of fruit are apples, b_______, pears, and oranges.

A gamelike context clue activity involves the use of scrambled words, as in the following sentence:

I am always on time, but my sister is always__________ (alte).

When working with context clues, teachers can choose to omit all nouns, verbs, every fourth word, etc. There are endless ways to use this strategy, and each contributes to helping children figure out unknown words.

Identifying Letters of the Alphabet

Many young children who cannot yet identify individual letters of the alphabet are able to read. As noted, they read sight words from environmental print, from classroom labels, and from Very Own Words lists. They learn other sight words from repeated readings and shared book experiences. It is not necessary to be able to identify and name the letters of the alphabet in order to develop an initial sight-reading vocabulary. It is easier for a young child *initially* to learn whole words already familiar through oral language, rather than learn abstract letters. Familiar words carry meaning for them, whereas isolated letters do not.

Children of course, need to learn the alphabet to become independently fluent readers and writers. However, there is no evidence that alphabet identification should be treated as the first skill in early literacy; it makes more sense for children to learn to identify letters after they have learned several sight words. Traditionally, the alphabet has often been the first thing parents try to teach their children at home, and it is usually high on any list of reading readiness skills in preschool and kindergarten curricula. Because it is difficult to depart from deeply rooted tradition, learning the alphabet will always be prominent in early literacy programs.

Allow children to explore letters by using manipulative materials available in the literacy center. Be sure to include in the center alphabet puzzles, magnetic upper- and lowercase letters with an accompanying magnetic board, a set of wooden upper- and lowercase letters, tactile letters made of sandpaper, alphabet games, felt letters and an accompanying felt-board, letter stencils, alphabet flash cards, and a long alphabet chart posted along the wall of the classroom at the children's eye level. In addition to these materials, a large supply of alphabet books and taped songs about the alphabet should be in the classroom library. (See Appendix A for a list of alphabet books.) Encourage children to explore these materials, first through play. Later, they will begin to identify the letters they are playing with, and teach letters they know to other children. Provide chalk and a chalkboard so they can make letters themselves. Children also enjoy finger-painting letters, painting them on easels, shaping them out of clay, and eating them in alphabet soup or as cookies or pretzels. Shaping letters with their fingers and whole bodies is an activity often used in early childhood rooms.

Systematic teaching of the alphabet, one letter per week, is not as successful as teaching children letters that are meaningful to them. Many teachers help children identify the letters in their own names first. When teaching thematic units, select a few letters to feature that are used in the context of the theme. For example, in a unit on transportation, feature *b* for boat and *t* for train. When children have learned to identify several different letters, ask them to look for the same letters in other contexts, such as magazines, newspapers, and books. Check children individually by using flash cards to determine which letters they know and which they do not know. Ask children which letters they would like to learn next from their Very Own Words. Give children flash cards of the letters they choose to learn, and encourage them to use those letters in all the activities just mentioned. Letters also need to be practiced all year through.

Additional ideas for learning and reinforcing what is known about the alphabet include the following:

- Sing the alphabet song often and pointing to the letters on a poster as they are sung.
- Play letter Bingo, which involves cards filled with letters and markers to cover them. Call a letter and hold up a card with the letter on it to help children with letter identification. When a child covers one row of letters on the card, he or she gets Bingo.
- Provide children with alphabet journals. On each page is another letter of the alphabet. On the different letter pages children can trace the letter, write the letter, and find words in a magazine that use the letter and paste them on the page.
- Create an alphabet center with many different alphabet materials such as those already mentioned (magnetic letters, wooden letters, matching letter games, alphabet puzzles, alphabet books, alphabet stamps, alphabet flash cards). Children will identify this area with the alphabet and should be encouraged to use the materials often.

State standards expect that by the end of kindergarten, children are able to name and recognize the letters of the alphabet. Teachers need to check children's knowledge of the alphabet and provide instruction based on the findings. If more direct instruction is needed to help students, then it should be provided. The letters of the alphabet must be practiced regularly. Students should be exposed to letters on a daily basis and in different settings. Figure 8.2 illustrates a commonly used form to record children's letter knowledge.

Phonemic Awareness and Phonics

Chapter 5 discusses the importance of phonemic awareness and phonics instruction in early literacy as a way for students to become independent readers. The work in this area should be done concurrently with other strategies for learning to read such as acquiring sight words and learning how to use context clues and picture clues. Some knowledge about the act of reading is important when learning more abstract letter–sound associations. When children have some knowledge about books and print, they will want to try to decode unknown words independently.

As mentioned, phonemic awareness has been referred to as a precursor to phonics and necessary for children to learn in order to benefit from phonics instruction. Some educators disagree with this concept and feel that the concurrent instruction of phonemic awareness and phonics is more appropriate.

The simplest level of phonemic awareness is to understand that words are made up of sounds that we can hear, identify, and match to similar word patterns such as rhymes. As children gain this knowledge and perform these functions, they are developing auditory discrimination. One of the ways that young children acquire knowledge about the sounds in words is through exposure to rhymes and jingles. Reading books that contain rhyme such as *Green Eggs and Ham* (Seuss, 1960), *Goodnight Moon* (Brown, 1947), and *The Queen of Hearts*

Figure 8.2 *A Form to Record Children's Letter Knowledge*

Letter Identification Score Sheet

Child's name ______________________ **Age** ____________ **Date** ______________

Recorder ______________________ **Date of birth** ________

	A	IR		A	IR
A			a		
F			f		
K			k		
P			p		
W			w		
Z			z		
B			b		
H			h		
O			o		
J			j		
U			u		
C			c		
Y			y		
L			l		
Q			q		
M			m		
D			d		
N			n		
S			s		
X			x		
I			i		
E			e		
G			g		
R			r		
V			v		
T			t		

Confusions:

Letters unknown:

Comments:

A = Alphabet response: (✓); IR = Incorrect response: record what the child says.

Test Score: ☐

(Hennessy & Pearson, 1989) helps develop the skill. Teachers can recite rhyming and nonrhyming words from the books and ask children to differentiate between them. For additional practice with rhyme, children can do the following:

- Make up words that rhyme with their names.
- Sing songs that rhyme and separate out the rhyming words.
- Act out well-known nursery rhymes such as Jack and Jill or the Itsy Bitsy Spider.

Segmenting and blending words is more difficult for children. It is easier for a child to segment the beginning sound or onset, and then the ending chunk or rime. If this is done with the word *man,* the child should be guided to say *mmm* for the onset /m/ and then *annn* for the rime /an/. After segmenting the word, the child can blend it back together again to say the entire word *man.*

The goal is for children to be able to identify each sound within a word, know the number of sounds heard, and be able to blend the word back together again. The following are some activities that will help children learn to segment and blend:

- Sing the song Bingo. In the song each letter is chanted and then blended together. Change the words from "There was a farmer had a dog and Bingo was his name," to "There is a pretty girl (or handsome boy) that I know and Jenny was her name-o, J-e-n-n-y, J-e-n-n-y, J-e-n-n-y, and Jenny is her name-o."
- Play a riddle substitution of onsets game. Say, "I'm thinking of a word that sounds like *head,* but begins with the /b/ sound," or "I'm thinking of a word that sounds like *fat,* but has an /mmm/ sound at the beginning."
- Select and write words on a piece of paper. Draw square boxes next to each word. Have chips for students to put into the squares. Say the name of a word on the paper such as *tree* and have the children put the number of chips in the boxes that represent the number of sounds in the word. For the word *tree*, children would put three chips into the boxes because the second /e/ in the word is silent (Fitzpatrick, 1997; Johns, Lenski, & Elish-Piper, 1999) (see Figure 8.3).

Figure 8.3

Word-Study Game

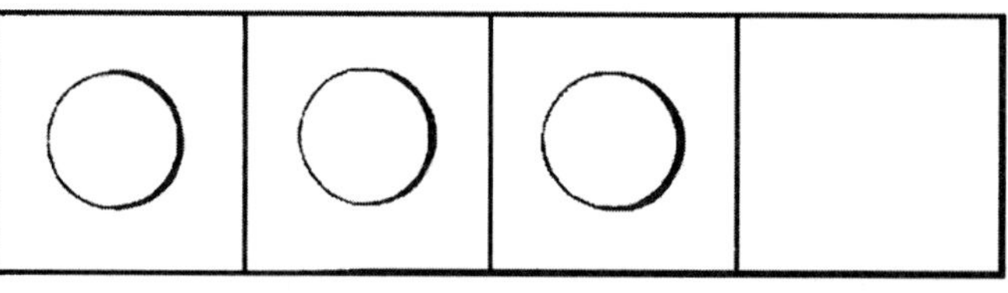

Directions: Let's figure out how many sounds in the word "bell." I'm going to say it again, B-E-LL. Put a chip in the squares for each sound you heard in the word BELL. How many chips did you use? Now look at the letters in the word BELL. How many do you count (4)? A word can have different numbers of letters and sounds.

Strategies for Teaching Phonics

There is a recommended sequence for teaching phonics. However, when teachable moments occur, teachers should take advantage of them whether or not they are within recommended sequences. We frequently begin teaching phonics with most commonly used initial consonant sounds such as *f, m, s, t, and h,* and then use these same sounds in ending word positions. The next set of initial and final consonant sounds usually taught are *l, d, c, n, g, w, p, r, k,* then *j, q, v, final x, initial y, and z.* Next we deal with short vowels, then long vowels, consonant blends, consonant digraphs, and some structural aspects of words. At each grade level, teachers should review what has been learned and add on medial consonant work, variant consonant sounds and blends, compound words, r-controlled vowels, y as a vowel, vowel pairs, vowel digraphs (two vowels together that make a new sound, which can be a long or short vowel sound or a new sound unlike the sound of either letter, such as *ea* in *head* or *seat*), and diphthongs (a combination of one or two vowels that form a new vowel sound representing a blend of the two to form a new vowel sound such as *oy* in toy and *oi* in oil), syllabication, contractions, prefixes, suffixes, synonyms, antonyms, and homonyms.

Earlier in the chapter I discussed the necessity for teaching phonics within meaningful contexts, along with some systematic and explicit presentation of skills. It is also important that children have continual practice to learn sound–symbol relationships; rarely is a single lesson sufficient. Therefore, teachers should provide several experiences with letter and letter–sound combinations, and review with children as often as possible.

Meaning-Based Strategies

How can we help children recognize the sound–symbol relationships of consonants and vowels in a meaningful context? Science and social studies themes lend themselves to featuring letters that appear in units. For example, when studying farm, pet, and zoo animals, feature the letter *p,* because it is used frequently with this context. The following types of activities can follow:

1. Read *The Pig's Picnic* (Kasza, 1988), *Pet Show* (Keats, 1974), and *The Tale of Peter Rabbit* (Potter, 1902) during the unit, and point out words that begin with the letter *p* in these books.
2. Make word charts using words from the books that begin with the letter *p.*
3. On a field trip, bring peanuts to the zoo to feed the animals.
4. Make lists of animals that begin with the letter *p.*
5. Read the book *Animalia* (Base, 1987) and point out the *p* page, which says "Proud Peacocks Preening Perfect Plumage."
6. Collect sensory items about animals that begin with the letter *p,* such as Puppy Chow to smell, peanuts to eat and to feed to elephants when you visit the zoo, peacock plumes to touch, a purring kitten to listen to, and the book *Petunia* (Duvoisin, 1950) to look at and read.
7. List words from the unit that begin with the lettter *p.*
8. Write an experience chart of activities carried out during the unit, and highlight the letter *p* when it appears in the chart.

9. Ask children to add to their Very Own Word collection with favorite words from the unit that begin with the letter *p*.
10. Make a collage of pictures featuring things from the unit, and mark those that begin with the letter *p*.
11. Print on a chart the song "Peter Cottontail." Sing the song and highlight the letter *p* when it appears.
12. Have children help you make up nonsense rhymes for featured letters and chant them, such as:

    My name is Penelope Pig.
    I pick petals *off of* petunias.
    I play patty *cake*
    and eat pretzels *with* pink punch.

13. Add a page for the letter *p* to a class Big Book entitled *Our Own Big Book of Letters, Sounds, and Words.* Have children draw pictures or paste in pictures of words that begin with the letter *p*. (Directions for making a Big Book are in Chapter 7, p. 204.)
14. Complete a worksheet for the letter *p* that requires students to trace the letter, write the letter, and circle pictures that begin with the letter *p,* such as *pig* and *popcorn*.
15. Encourage children to write about their experiences during the unit such as their visit to the zoo, the books they read, and the songs they sang. In their writing they will be using the letters emphasized, and, although their writing may not be conventional, through the use of their invented spellings they are indirectly enhancing their phonemic awareness. When children write, they have to face the problem of mapping spoken language into written language. This can lead to an understanding of the structure of spoken language. The more children write, the better they become at segmenting sounds in words. This is demonstrated in the following example of Zach's story about *The Pig's Picnic*. He wrote "Pig wanted the picnic to be perfect," as follows:

    Pg wtd tha pcnc to be prfkt

Children's literature is an excellent source for featuring letters attached to themes. Be careful not to abuse the stories by overemphasizing the sounds featured; however, do not pass up the opportunity to feature letters in this natural book setting. For example, in a unit on food, Ms. Fino, a first-grade teacher, featured the letter *b* and read *Blueberries for Sal* (McCloskey, 1948), *Bread and Jam for Frances* (Hoban, 1964), and *The Berenstain Bears and Too Much Birthday* (Berenstain, 1987).

These and similar activities can be carried out for any initial consonant. Whenever letters being featured in a thematic unit appear in a language experience chart or a piece of children's literature, point them out to the children. Alphabet books generally use sound–symbol relationships as they introduce each letter as do picture storybooks that use a particular letter prominently. (See Appendix A for children's literature for building sound–symbol relationships.)

When we read, we use several skills concurrently to decode and derive meaning from the printed page. We therefore need to encourage children to use multiple rather than isolated skills in their approach to reading. Children should be taught to use context clues and phonic clues simultaneously. One strategy that accomplishes this goal has already been suggested—reading a sentence in which you pause and leave a "blank" to be filled in by the child. For example, say, "The b_____ flew up to the tree and landed on a branch." Supplying the initial consonant for the word, either by sound or by sight, draws on a child's skills with phonics, context, syntax, and semantics.

Whenever possible take advantage of spontaneous situations to help children learn about print, such as the following example:

> *Christopher, a child in first grade, had just written his name on a picture he drew and exclaimed, "Wow, the word* STOP *is right in the middle of my name. See Chri*stop*her." He pointed to the letters in his name that spelled* STOP. *He continued, "But that doesn't make sense, then I should say my name Chri-*STOP*-her." The teacher immediately seized the opportunity to point out the ph digraph and explain to Christopher that the word* STOP *was in his name but when the letters* p *and* h *come together, they make a new sound as heard in Christopher, like the sound of* F. *She mentioned other words such as* photograph *and* ph*antom that illustrated the* ph *sound.*

Explicit Word-Study Activities

Based on research about how children learn and how the brain works, it is apparent that activities with word families, often referred to as *phonograms,* to build and sort words into different patterns help children learn letter–sound relationships and consequently how to decode unknown words. Word sorts and word building with *onsets* (the initial letter or letters before the first vowel) and *rimes* (the vowel and what follows), allow children to look at bigger chunks of words. When children learn some words and learn how to figure out new ones by using patterns in words, they develop a strategy to deal with other unknowns. According to research, the brain looks for known patterns when involved in learning. It takes what is known and tries to apply it to the unknown. Patterns such as familiar word endings help children deal with unknowns (Adams, 1990).

MAKING WORDS. Making words is a gamelike activity in which children learn to look for patterns in words and how to make new words by changing one letter or more. In this activity, the teacher asks children to make words from a real word selected from a story, new vocabulary, themed words, etc. The word can be scrambled or spelled correctly.

Another type of word-making activity uses onsets and rimes. With younger children, the teacher provides a few well-known rimes such *at, an,* or *in* and asks the children to make as many words with these endings as they can think of by adding different initial consonants or consonant blends to the beginning of the rimes. With the rime *at,* for example, children could create the following words: cat, sat, mat, rat, hat, fat, nat, pat, and bat.

WORD SORTS. After making words, they can be sorted in many different ways or teachers can provide words for sorting. For example, if children make words from the word *Thanksgiving*, such as thanks, giving, sing, sang, hang, king, thanking, and having, they can be asked to sort the words that all have the -ing ending, words that rhymed, words ending with the consonant *g,* words beginning with the consonant *s,* etc. Sorting words for blends, digraphs, and numbers of syllable are other ways to help students see patterns. Words also can be sorted for meaning by categories such as colors and types of food.

Children sort words and make words to learn about word patterns with manipulative materials.

Using phonograms, or rimes, is an important way for children to sort and make words. A list of the most commonly used rimes for children to learn is presented in the following chart (Wylie & Durrell, 1970):

Common Rimes Used in Early Literacy

ack	al	ain	ake	ale	ame	an	ank	up	ush
at	ate	aw	ay	ell	eat	est	ice	ick	ight
id	ill	in	ine	ing	ink	ip	ir	ock	oke
op	ore	or	uck	ug	ump	unk			

Centers for Word-Study Activities

A center that contains materials for word study is necessary in early childhood classrooms. The activities for making and sorting words discussed earlier can be gamelike if they are presented with interesting manipulative materials.

With onsets and rimes as well as scrambled words, teachers can have children use magnetic letters and a magnetic board for making words. Students can use wooden moveable letters, rubber foam letters, or flash cards with letters on them. Flash cards can have word endings on them or initial consonants or consonant blends. All onsets can be written in one color and rimes in another. The flash cards can be used to make words on a table or a pocket chart. To make this activity even more interesting, letter stamps and white slates with magic markers will work for making words. Some teachers make manipulatives such as moveable wheels for making words. Board games such as Bingo, Lotto, Concentration, and Candyland and card games can be constructed so that children have to make words within the rules of the game. Figure 8.4 illustrates some sample word-study games to place in centers.

Games for centers can be purchased from teacher stores and large school supply companies. Teachers also can create numerous word-study activities that children learn from, use to reinforce what they know, and use independently when teachers are engaged in small-group instruction. Teachers can make materials and seek the help of parents, aides, and upper-grade children to make materials. Following is a list of books that contain ideas for word-study center materials:

Bear, D. R., Invernizzi, M., Templeton, S., & Johnston, D. (1996). *Words their way.* Englewood Cliffs, NJ: Prentice Hall.

Cunningham, P. & Hall, D. (1994). *Making words.* Torrance, CA: Good Apple.

Cunningham, P. (1995). *Phonics they use.* New York: HarperCollins.

Hill, S. (1997). *Reading manipulatives.* Cypress, CA: Creative Teaching Press.

Marriott, D. (1997). *What are the other kids doing?* Cypress, CA: Creative Teaching Press.

Rosencrans, G. (1998). *The spelling book: Teaching children how to spell, not what to spell.* Newark, DE: International Reading Association.

USING A WORD-STUDY CENTER. From his rich collection of ideas and materials, Mr. Rosen assigned word-study activities for students to work on while he worked with small groups in guided reading instruction. The following explains the activities the children engaged in during center time.

Four children made as many words from the word *Thanksgiving* that they could. The letters of *Thanksgiving* had been cut up and placed in plastic baggies for each child. In addition to manipulating the letters to create words, the children wrote the words on an activity sheet.

With magnetic letters and their own individual magnetic slates children created word ladders. They started with one-letter words, then two, then three, and so on. Each child also had a 5 × 8 index card to write his or her word from the bottom of the card up the ladder. A partner checked the words.

Another group of four children worked with ending phonograms or chunks, as Mr. Rosen referred to them, by creating words with onsets or initial consonants. He had prepared sliders, which are oak tag circles that have ending phonograms, with a slide of onsets to create words. Children created words with the slider and wrote them down. They wrote additional words thought of as well.

Figure 8.4 *Word-Study Games*

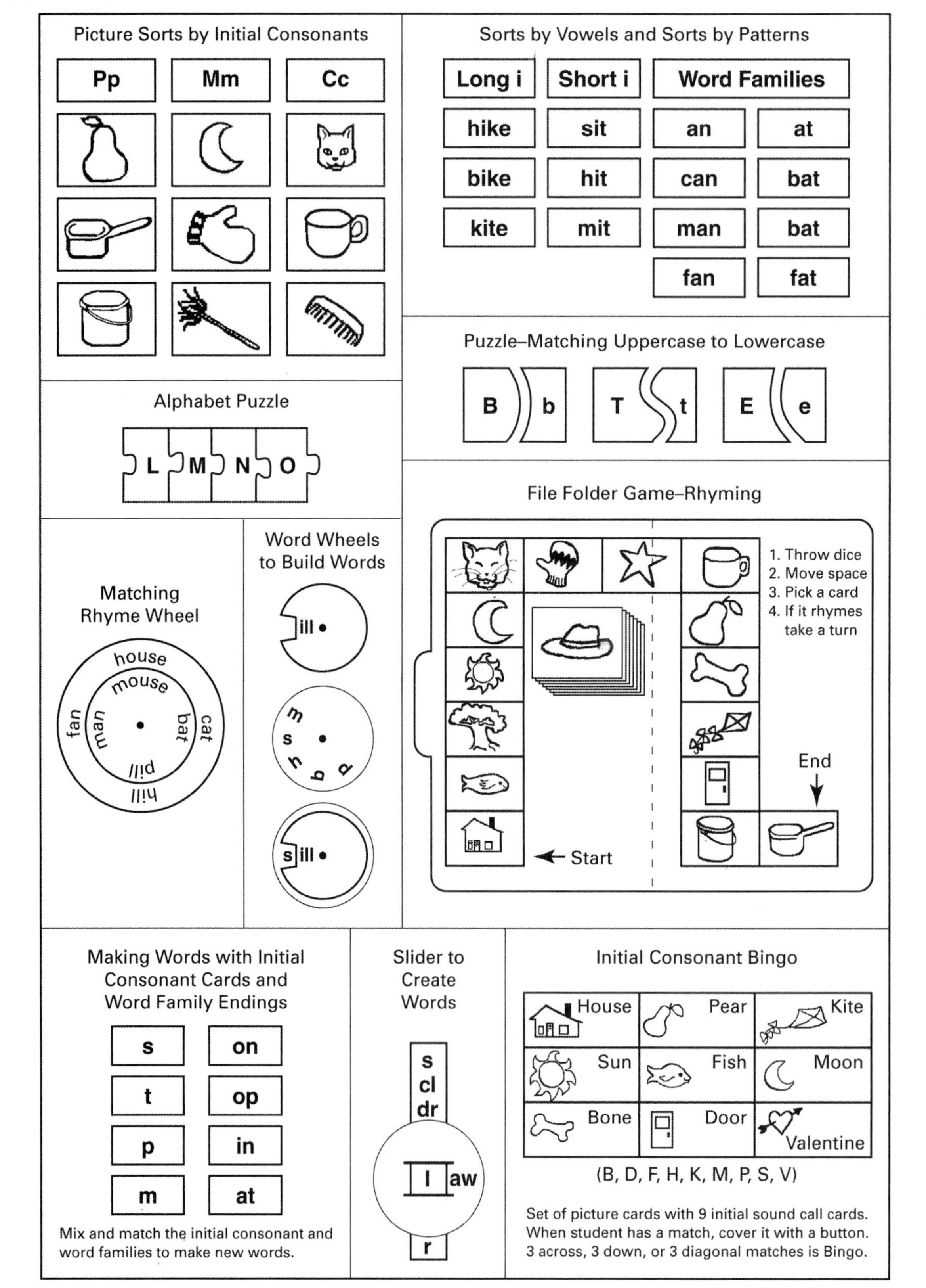

Source: Adapted from *Words Their Way* by D. R. Bear, M. Invernizzi, S. Templeton, & D. Johnston. © 1996 by Prentice Hall. Used by permission.

Finally children created sentences with letter and word stamps. The stamps had familiar words for the children to create into sentences.

All these activities were manipulative. They involved children working with words from individual letters, to letter chunks, beginning and ends of words, and total sentences. They also required children to work together, check each other's work, and collaborate. All children had the opportunity to use every material during this period.

Concerns about Phonics

There are several concerns about teaching phonics. A major problem is that so many rules for the English language have exceptions. For example, the sound of *k* in the word *k*ite is its usual sound, but when *k* is followed by *n* it becomes silent as in the word *k*not. I believe that we should teach fewer rather than more rules because the ability to apply them is so limited for young children. Many of the exceptions can wait to be taught until the children are older. Exceptions can be dealt with when they occur in print, or be treated as sight words when they are uncommon. In early childhood, our main concern should be with sound–symbol relationships and generalizations that rarely have exceptions.

Another problem when dealing with sound–symbol relationships is dialects. If a teacher from New York taught in the southern United States, he or she would teach long and short vowels with different sounds than those taught by a teacher who was from the South. Children in most parts of the United States live in communities comprising youngsters who speak many different dialects and attend the same school. These children may have difficulty dealing with sounds regardless of where their teacher is from.

In addition, there are different types of learners. There are auditory learners and visual learners. A child who is weak in auditory discrimination or has a learning problem is not likely to master phonics and is best taught to his or her strength rather than to a weakness. The skills a child acquires as a result of learning phonics are important for becoming a proficient reader; alternatively, it is just one strategy within the total picture of literacy development, and we need not overemphasize it.

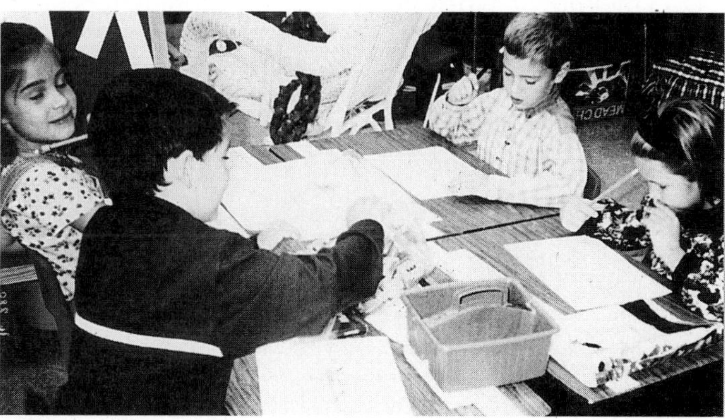

Children create words with letter cubes and write them down to account for what they have done.

Oral Reading

We ask children to read orally in early literacy classrooms for many reasons. We can determine their reading level, the types of strategies children have for decoding and comprehending text, the types of errors they make, and strategies they need to develop. Oral reading tells us about children's reading **fluency**, which is determined by the rate of reading, accuracy, expression used, and phrasing. Children who are fluent readers use verbal expression and intonation that conveys the meaning of the text, and they attend to punctuation. We have found that children who read fluently are able comprehend text. There seems to be a relationship between the two skills. With the information determined from a child's oral reading, we can plan appropriate instruction. Many well-known strategies help with fluency such as (1) children participating in repeated readings of stories, (2) children practicing reading with material that is easy, and (3) teachers modeling reading in read-aloud shared reading experiences.

The accuracy with which children read particular passages determines their reading level. Reading level indicates which materials should be used for instructional purposes, which for independent reading, and which materials will be too difficult. When children read orally, we can also find out if they self-monitor their own reading. For example, when they make an error, do they correct that error on their own? Do they search through the text to figure out words?

When we listen to children read, we can provide needed strategies for independent reading. The following are prompts for strategies students can use when they have difficulty decoding. The prompts should help children gain meaning from the text. These prompts are adapted from those presented by Fountas and Pinnell (1996).

Prompts to support the reader's use of sources of information:

- Check the pictures.
- Does that make sense?
- Does that word sound right?
- What's wrong with this? (Repeat what the child said.)
- Try that again and think of a word that makes sense.
- Do you know a word that starts with those letters?
- Do you know a word that ends with those letters?
- What can you do to help yourself?

Prompts to support the reader's use of self-monitoring or checking behavior:

- Were you right?
- Why did you stop?
- Would ________ fit here?
- Would ________ make sense?
- Check it. Does it look right and sound right to you?
- You almost got that. See if you can find what is wrong.
- Try that again.

Prompts to support the reader's self-correction behavior:

- I liked the way you worked that out.
- You made a mistake. Can you find it?
- You're nearly right. Try again.

Prompts to support phrased, fluent reading:

- Can you read this quickly?
- Put your words together so it sounds like talking.

Source: Adapted by permission of Irene Fountas and Gay Su Pinell: *Guided Reading: Good First Teaching for All Children* (Heinemann, A division of Reed Elsevier, Inc., Portsmouth, NH, 1996).

Published Materials for Literacy Instruction

When we discuss development of skills, it is natural to talk about published materials. Published materials have been available for many years and have played an important role in literacy instruction. The materials have been referred to as basal readers. In the early 1990s when whole language was the model for instruction and children's literature the main source for literacy development, basal readers were referred to as anthologies of children's literature. These prepared reading instructional materials have been more popular at some times than at others, depending on the focus for literacy instruction. The programs are used by most school districts, and probably will continue to be used because they provide a complete package of instructional materials and are revised to include new findings in early literacy development. Some general rules should be applied to the selection and use of materials.

- Study the objectives for the published program and determine if they incorporate the latest findings on strategies for nurturing early literacy.
- Determine if the program matches the goals for standards set forth by the district or state where the material will be used.
- Determine if the program includes developmentally appropriate practice as you view it in your district.
- Ensure that the materials suit the needs of the children you teach. Urban and rural children may need materials different from children in suburban settings. Are there materials suited for children who speak English as a second language?
- Examine the materials for clarity, appeal to children, and durability.
- Analyze the teacher's editions for clarity of objectives, descriptions of plans, suitability of lesson content, and flexibility for teachers in using the material. The program should put the teacher in charge of the materials; the materials should not dictate to the teacher.
- Ensure that leveled little books to match instruction to children's reading ability are included.

In addition, ask the following questions about the published materials:

- Are technology components available?
- Are there practice materials?
- Do the books have adequate multicultural representation?

- Are a variety of genres presented in stories?
- Do the stories link to other content areas?
- Are there manipulative independent activities for centers and independent work?
- Does the assessment component meet district's needs?
- Are there plans for organizing and managing the delivery of the program?
- Does the publishing company provide adequate staff development with the program?

Published materials have changed from contrived text to help children acquire specific skills to become fluent readers, to real literature to help children learn to read from authentic meaningful text. The issue of the type of text to use for literacy instruction has always been of concern. Contrived texts lack meaning and literary qualities, but they do provide a sequenced plan for helping young children understand text, with repeated vocabulary, limited vocabulary, phonetic elements, picture clues, etc. Another type of text proposed by some educators is called "decodable text," which has several definitions. Some suggest that with decodable text all skills needed to read are taught before giving a child the material to read. In this text about 75 percent of the words include letter–sound patterns that are familiar to children, and are taught until the text is given to the child to read. The main focus of the text is phonetically regular patterns. When introducing phonetic elements such as initial consonants ***D, R,*** and ***M,*** and the ***an*** phonogram, decodable text might read:

Dan ran after the man.

Before reading the text, the word ***the*** would be taught as a high-frequency word and the word ***after*** as a sight word.

Basal materials always have had grade designations. One of the problems with grade designations is that, although the material is probably appropriate for instructing most children in a particular grade, some students will be reading above the level or below the level of their designated grade. For instruction to be useful, the level of the material is critical.

Many teachers themselves figure out the difficulty level of books and level them to be sure they match the instructional level of the small groups they teach. Commercial publishers now also level their materials. The leveled books are typically little paperbacks. Publishers may designate the grade level, or simply give them a letter level such as A, B, or C books. The purpose of leveled little books is to disregard the grade assignment completely and to determine a child's level of reading and then select the appropriate level book for instruction. Books are leveled for difficulty based on the following factors (adapted from Fountas & Pinnell, 1996):

- The length of a book, including number of pages and words
- The size and layout of the print
- The patterns, predictability, and structure of language
- Text structures and genres used
- Phonetic patterns in the words
- How well the illustration supports the text

Teachers working together have leveled collections of their books based on the criteria outlined above. They test the books by having children read them to determine how difficult or easy they are to read. To enhance collections teachers use central areas for storing leveled books so they have access to those needed for their students.

Publishers also create sets of leveled books, which makes purchasing easier for teachers if funds are available. Publishers level books based on many different criteria. One publisher may level books with specific repeated vocabulary, introduction of specific phonetic elements, etc. Companies that are in the forefront with creating leveled books for instruction are listed following:

Benchmark Word I.D., 2107 N. Providence Road, Media, PA 19063

Rigby, 500 Coventry Lane, Suite 200, Crystal Lake, IL 60014

Scholastic, Inc., 555 Broadway, New York, NY 10012-3999

Scott Foresman, 1900 East Lake Avenue., Glenview, IL 60025

Sundance Publishers, 234 Taylor Street, Littleton, MA 01460

The Wright Group, 19201 120th Avenue NE, Bothell, WA 98011-9512

William H. Sadlier, 9 Pine Street, New York, NY 10005-1002

Selecting the appropriate book for instruction also can be done with the use of the running record described in Chapter 2. The test is administered with leveled material. When a child scores 90 to 95 percent with a particular book, the level of that book is his or her reading instructional level. If the child scores higher than a score 95 percent the book is for independent reading, and a score below 90 percent indicates the book is too difficult for the child to read.

Each teacher needs to make critical decisions about the use of materials in his or her instructional program. You should be in control of published materials and not allow the materials to dictate to you, as mentioned. For example, select sequences to use from the material that seem most appropriate. You need not start at the beginning of a book and follow it page by page to the end. Eliminate sections that you feel are inappropriate for your children. Repeat material when necessary. There is not one published program that will determine the success or failure of literacy development with young children. It is how you use the materials along with your basic philosophy and organization of the entire literacy program that will determine the success. Commercially prepared instructional materials are only one part of literacy development. Many school districts require the use of published materials, and many teachers depend on them as organizational tools. As a teacher you must decide on the design of your literacy instruction, the materials you use, and how you use them.

Assessing Knowledge of Word-Study Skills

There are numerous word-study skills discussed in this chapter. Initially, teachers should be concerned with a child's phonemic awareness. The Yopp-Singer Test of Phoneme Segmentation (1992), in Figure 8.5, is widely used to determine how well children can segment phonemes in words. The directions specify to

Figure 8.5 *Yopp-Singer Test of Phoneme Segmentation (1992)*

Child's name ______________________ **Date** ____________

Score (number correct) ______________________

Directions: Today we're going to play a word game. I'm going to say a word and I want you to break the word apart. You are going to tell me each sound in the word in order. For example, if I say "old," you should say /o/-/l/-/d/." (*Administrator: Be sure to say the sounds, not the letters, in the word.*) Let's try a few together.

Practice items: (*Assist the child in segmenting these items as necessary.*) ride, go, man

Test items: (*Circle those items that the student correctly segments; incorrect responses may be recorded on the blank line following the item.*)

1. dog ______	12. lay ______
2. keep ______	13. race ______
3. fine ______	14. zoo ______
4. no ______	15. three ______
5. she ______	16. job ______
6. wave ______	17. in ______
7. grew ______	18. ice ______
8. that ______	19. at ______
9. red ______	20. top ______
10. me ______	21. by ______
11. sat ______	22. do ______

Source: The author, Hallie Kay Yopp, California State University, Fullerton, grants permission for this test to be reproduced. The author acknowledges the contribution of the late Henry Singer to the development of this test.

ensure that the child says the sounds, not the letters in the word, because these are two different skills.

Fluency, self-monitoring, accuracy, level of text, knowledge of basic phonics when reading, and types of errors made all can be determined with the running record. A description of the purpose of a running record and how it is administered and scored is in Chapter 2.

In addition to daily performance samples of children's writing and activity sheets, observations and descriptions of children's reading behaviors should be included in word-study assessment. Checklists are also important materials for testing children on word-study skills. For example, to test for knowledge of the alphabet, the teacher can name particular letters and ask a child to circle them on a sheet of paper containing upper- and lowercase letters. Teachers can also use flash cards of letters for students to identify. Basic sight words are checked similarly to alphabetic knowledge on a sheet of paper to circle or with flash cards. To determine the ability to rhyme, the teacher says pairs of words and asks children to identify which do and which do not rhyme. Knowledge of phonetic sounds such as consonants are checked by having the child circle a picture that begins with a particular letter. Sometimes the teacher will say a word and ask the child to identify the letter it begins with. When asking children to determine the beginning letter of an object in a picture, ensure that the object is clear and easy to identify. For example, some children may mistake a donkey for a horse and choose the initial letter *h*, instead of *d*. Besides the assessments mentioned, some of the same gamelike activities used for instruction and practice materials for reinforcement are used for assessing children's knowledge of word-study skills.

✓ Checklist *Assessing Concepts about Print and Word Study*

Child's name ______________________ **Date** ____________

	Always	Sometimes	Never	Comments
Knows print is read from left to right				
Knows that oral language can be written and then read				
Knows what a letter is and can point one out on a page				
Knows what a word is and can point one out on a printed page				
Knows that there are spaces between words				
Reads environmental print				
Recognizes some words by sight and high-frequency sight words				
Can name and identify rhyming words				
Can identify and name upper- and lowercase letters of the alphabet				
Can blend phonemes in words				
Can segment phonemes in words				
Associates consonants and their initial and final sounds (including hard and soft *c* and *g*)				

(continued on next page)

Checklist *(continued from previous page)*

	Always	Sometimes	Never	Comments
Associates consonant blends with their sounds (*bl, cr, dr, fl, gl, pr, st*)				
Associates vowels with their corresponding long and short sounds (*a*—acorn, apple; *e*—eagle, egg; *i*—ice, igloo; *o*—oats, octopus; *u*—unicorn, umbrella)				
Knows the consonant digraph sounds (*ch, ph, sh, th, wh*)				
Uses context, syntax, and semantics to identify words				
Can count syllables in words				
Attempts reading by attending to picture clues and print				
Guesses and predicts words based on knowledge of sound–symbol correspondence				
Can identify structural elements of words such as prefixes & suffixes, and inflectional endings *-ing*, *-ed*, and *-s* and contractions				
Demonstrates knowledge of the following phonic generalizations:				
a. In a consonant–vowel–consonant pattern, the vowel sound is usually short				
b. In a vowel–consonant–*e* pattern, the vowel is usually long				
c. When two vowels come together in a word, the first is usually long and the second is silent (train, receive, bean)				
Uses word families often referred to as rimes and phonograms such as *an, at, it,* and *ot,* and initial consonants to build words, *eg, man, can, fan, ran.*				

Teacher Comments:

Ideas for the Classroom from the Classroom

I created the following experience to help teachers incorporate concepts about print into thematic units carried out in early childhood classrooms. The purpose was to connect knowledge about print with content-area learning to make the information about print more meaningful. This was also a way to be sure that all letters in the alphabet were highlighted at some given point in the school year. The order in which the units are studied is not important, and it would be expected that even though a particular letter was featured in a given unit, it would be reinforced in other units when appropriate. You may choose to study unit topics that are not suggested here. If that is the case, try to select appropriate letters to feature in other unit topics, making sure to include every letter in the alphabet as a featured letter at least once.

Refer to this chapter to include as many strategies as possible to use in meaningful ways to feature the letters mentioned.

■ Unit Topics with Featured Letters and Words

All about Me—*h* for home and *m* for mother

Fall—*a* for apples, *l* for leaves, *r* for raking leaves

Learning about Different Cultures—*ph* for photographs illustrating other lands, *f* for food represented in other cultures, *c* for clothing from different cultures

My Five Senses—*s* for sounds, *t* for touch, *q* for quiet

Animals—*p* for pets, *z* for zoo, *j* for jungle

Winter—*sh* for shoveling snow, *i* for ice, *g* for gloves

Jobs in the Community—*x* for X-ray, *n* for newspaper, *o* for office

Nutrition—*d* for dairy, *v* for vegetables, *e* for eggs

Spring—*y* for yellow flowers, *u* for umbrella, *k* for kite

Transportation—*w* for transportation that uses water, *b* for boats, *ch* for choo-choo

■ Using the Senses to Learn Letters and Sounds

We try to appeal to the different learning styles of our students. With each letter of the alphabet we focus on, we provide sensory experiences of sight, smell, touch, sound, and taste. Following is a list of words for the letters and sounds and their associated sensory ideas.

Sight	Smell	Touch	Sound	Taste
airplane	apple	acorn	ambulance	apricot
bicycle	bubble gum	blanket	bumble bee	banana
calculator	carnation	cotton	cuckoo clock	carrot
deer	daisy	denim	dog	doughnut
eagle	eggs	earmuff	elephant	eggplant
fork	fish	feather	fiddle	French fries
giraffe	grapefruit	gourd	goose	grapes

Sight	Smell	Touch	Sound	Taste
horse	hamburger	hair	harp	honey
igloo	incense	ice cube	insect	ice cream
jewelry	jelly	jacket	jingle bells	jello
kite	kiwi	kerchief	kids	ketchup
lion	lemon	lace	lullaby	lollipops
money	mustard	metal	music	milk
nest	nectarine	napkin	nightingale	nuts
octopus	onion	oil	owl	oatmeal
puzzle	peaches	paper	parrot	pears
quail	Quaker Oats	quilt	quiet	quiche
rain	raspberries	rock	rattlesnake	raisin
ship	syrup	satin	siren	soda
turtle	tulips	taffeta	turkey	tomato
unicorn		umbrella	ukulele	
volcano	vanilla	velvet	violin	vegetables
worm	wheat bread	water	weasel	watermelon
Xerox copy	Xmas tree	X-ray	xylophone	extracts
yo-yo	yogurt	yarn	yodel	yam
zebra	zinnia	zipper	zoo	zucchini

Erica Erlanger and Lisa Lozak
Rutgers University students

First-Grade Phonics Tied to Literature

In the beginning of first grade, I introduce the concept of word families and try to tie them in with authentic literature. The first family I do is the *at* family, and what better piece of literature to use than *The Cat in the Hat* by Dr. Seuss? We read the story, discuss the word family *at,* and brainstorm *at* words. The children draw a picture of themselves, like the cat in the hat, with their face, a hat, and bow tie like the cat in the story. They fill the tall hat with words in the *at* family such as pat, mat, sat, rat, cat see Figure 8.6. *Green Eggs with Ham* is good for introducing the *am, ould,* and *oat* word families.

Cindy Peters Healy, First-Grade Teacher
Harrison School, Livingston, New Jersey

Activities and Questions

1. Answer the focus questions at the beginning of the chapter.
2. Observe the environmental print in an early childhood classroom. Note what you think could be added to it, both from within the classroom and from the outside world.
3. Select three children from prekindergarten through second grade whose scores on standardized tests are available. Observe the children for oral language ability, competence in comprehension, and print knowledge. Compare what you observe concerning the children's literacy ability with their test results.
4. Write an experience chart dictated to you by children in an early childhood classroom. If you do not have access to children, do this in your college

Figure 8.6

Story Figures for Learning Phonics

classroom with your peers dictating the contents for the chart. Critique the appearance of your chart and note problems you encountered while writing it. Use your self-evaluation for ideas for improvement.

5. Select five children from an early childhood classroom in which the students have collected Very Own Words. List all the words in the children's collections. Compare the list with the words found in basal reading material for the age children you selected. How closely do the basal words and the children's Very Own Words match each other?

6. Select three initial consonants other than *p*. Design classroom experiences that will teach and reinforce the sound–symbol relationships of each. Connect the letters to a thematic topic that is commonly studied in science or social studies in early childhood classrooms. Use traditional and authentic experiences.

7. Create a lesson to teach high-frequency words using a word wall.

8. Create lessons to teach phonic skills using your morning message words. With a pocket chart and word cards, have children:

a. Make words from onsets and rimes
b. Sort words with similar patterns into piles
c. Make little words from a big word

9. Continue the portfolio assessment for the child you selected to assess for language development in Chapter 4. Observe the child using the assessment

checklist provided in this chapter concerning the evaluation of concepts about print. Check for phonemic awareness and reading level using a running record.

10. Continue the thematic unit that you began in Chapter 4. Select three objectives in the area of concepts about print, and describe three activities that will satisfy each of the objectives using your theme. (You dealt with sound–symbol associations earlier; select other concepts about print to emphasize.)

Case Study Activities

Case 1

Standardized testing and the use of commercially prepared basal reading instructional materials are of concern in your district. Two committees are formed to deal with both issues. Because you were recently promoted to the position of coordinator of language arts for the district, you are a member of both committees. The committee dealing with standardized tests is trying to decide whether to use them in early childhood classrooms. The committee is to write a statement supporting its position. If it decides to use standardized tests, the committee needs to continue that statement and describe how the results of the tests will be used.

The second committee is trying to decide which commercially prepared reading instructional programs for early literacy development to adopt. Describe criteria for the selection and use of these instructional materials.

Case 2

The following describes two first-grade teachers' approaches to teaching knowledge about print, specifically the sound–symbol relationship of the letter *s*. What are the pros and cons of each teacher's approach to teaching the alphabet sounds and symbols? What could each teacher do to improve her presentation? How could they attend to children with special needs?

Teacher A teaches reading in the morning from 9:00 to 10:30. She works on phonics during that time, and her approach is to teach a letter of the alphabet each week with the associated sound. She uses a commercially prepared program and follows it exactly the way the publisher has it outlined. This means that a letter is introduced through a little story provided by the publisher such as *Sam and the Big Snow Storm*. It is a short story with a lot of words that begin with *s*. After talking about the featured letter, there are worksheets showing pictures of items that begin with *s* such as *Sam, Snow,* and others in the story. Children are asked to circle the words that begin with *s*. Children are then asked to think of words they know that begin with *s*, and the teacher lists them on a chart. This same lesson is carried out for the next letter presented in the program.

Teacher B introduces letters spontaneously as they come up during the entire school day related to something that the children are studying. They are studying the ocean, and she reads the story *Swimmy* by Leo Lionni, about a fish who lives in the sea and his adventures there. She points out the letter *s* in the book and other words beginning with *s* such as sea, sand, swim, surf, sun, sailing, and snails. Children are asked if any of them have the letter *s* in their name, and it is written on a chart. Teacher B asks children if they know someone whose name has an *s* in it, or if they know of something in their home that has an *s* in it. After the wall chart is finished, the children sing a song about the sea, and the teacher mentions that the letter *s* is in several words in the song. She does not have a systematic plan for teaching letters of the alphabet. She says, "When they arise in context, I take the opportunity to feature them."

chapter 9

Writing and Literacy Development

Children want to write. They want to write the first day they attend school. This is no accident. Before they went to school they marked up walls, pavements, newspapers with crayons, chalk, pens or pencils . . . anything that makes a mark. The child's marks say, "I am."

—Donald Graves
Writing: Teachers and Children at Work

Focus Questions

- Describe theories concerning how early writing is acquired.
- Describe the categories that reflect children's early attempts at writing and compare them to the stages of spelling development.
- What objectives are appropriate for promoting writing development in early childhood?
- What strategies can be used for writing development from birth to two years of age?
- What strategies can be used for developing writing in preschool through third grade?
- What steps are involved in the process approach to writing?
- What mechanical aspects of writing are important for children to learn?
- What strategies will promote achievement in spelling?
- How can writing be assessed?

Mrs. Callister read the story *The Old Lady Who Swallowed a Fly.* It is a nonsense tale that is read and also sung. The story is composed of rhymes, and each segment is repeated to make it predictable. A portion of the story follows:

> I know an old lady who swallowed a fly,
> I don't know why she swallowed a fly, perhaps she'll die.
> I know an old lady who swallowed a spider
> That wiggled and giggled and tickled inside her,
> She swallowed the spider to catch the fly,
> I don't know why she swallowed the fly, perhaps she'll die.
> I know an old lady who swallowed a bird,
> How absurd to swallow a bird
> (the refrain is repeated)
> I know an old lady who swallowed a cat,
> Now fancy that she swallowed a cat
> (the refrain is repeated)
> I know an old lady who swallowed a dog,
> What a hog to swallow a dog
> (the refrain is repeated and additional verses are chanted).

After the story, Mrs. Callister suggested that the children think of additional rhymes for the story.

Tasha and Jason decided to work together. Tasha said, "I got one, I know an old lady who swallowed a snake, ummm, ummm, she got a big ache when she swallowed the snake." Jason said, "How about what a mistake to swallow a snake." Tasha agreed she liked that better. They tried another one. Jason said, "I know an old lady who swallowed a frog, what a hog to swallow a frog." Tasha said, "We can't do that, in the real story when she swallows a dog, they say what a hog to swallow a dog." Jason thought and said, "I know—she started to jog when she swallowed a frog." "That's great," said Tasha.

The class came together to see what they had come up with. Many of the rhymes were the same and many were different. There were about 10 to add to the story that they wrote out on an experience chart and then chanted together. When they were done, Michael said, "You know, I think what we wrote is better than the original one." Everyone nodded and agreed.

Children love to play. Through play they develop socially and intellectually in fundamental ways. Especially in literate societies, children's play can take the form of making marks on paper. Children enjoy the act of making the marks, the social relationships they develop in the process, the sense of accomplishment mark making brings, and the products of the action. By writing messages, children achieve a sense of identity in their own eyes and in the eyes of others. The continuum from playing with drawing and writing, to communicating through written messages, to writing narrative and expository text reflects the basic theories of early literacy development (Dyson, 1993; Halliday, 1975; Parker, 1983; Sulzby, 1986a).

Relationships between Reading and Writing

Readers and writers transform their experiences through verbal symbols. Writers reconstruct meanings by constructing texts; readers reconstruct texts by constructing anticipated meanings (Birnbaum & Emig, 1983).

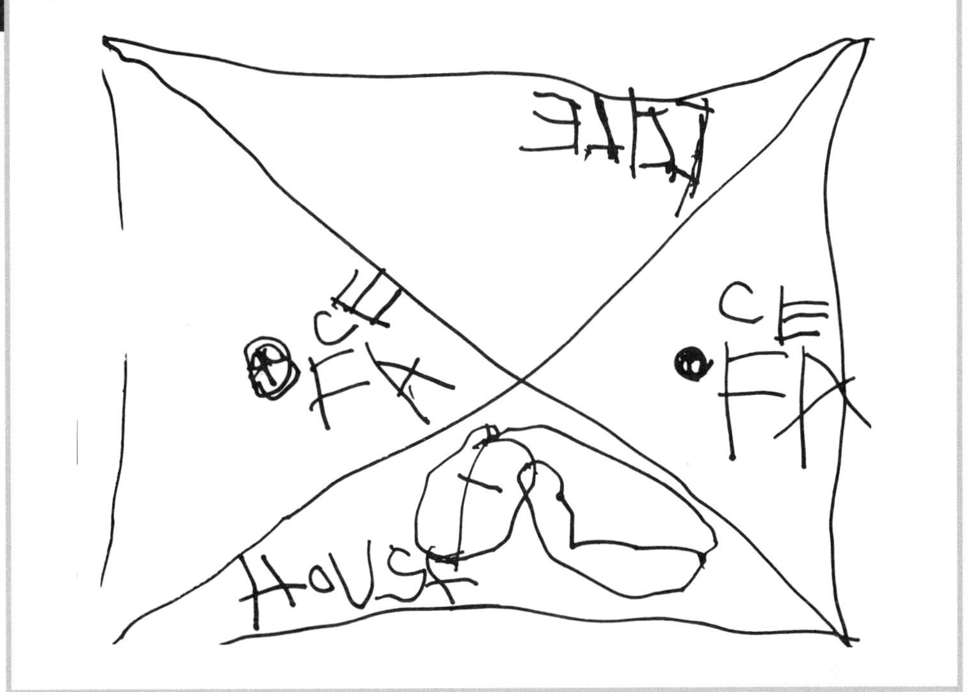

Figure 9.1

In this writing sample, Max, age five, uses his writing almost as a decoration for the drawing.

The parallels between writing and reading are obvious in young children. For example, children teach themselves to write in much the same way that they teach themselves to read: experimentally. Through personally motivated and directed trial and error—a necessary condition of their literacy development—they try out various aspects of the writing process. They invent and decorate letters, symbols, and words; they mix drawing and writing; they invent messages in various forms and shapes; and they often continue to use invented forms of writing after they have begun to master conventional ones (Figure 9.1).

How Early Writing Is Acquired

Children's early literacy experiences are embedded in the familiar situations and real-life experiences of family and community membership (Gundlach, McLane, Scott, & McNamee, 1985). In fact, ethnographic researchers have discovered that, because these literacy events are so natural, most parents simply do not know about many of their own children's writing and reading experiences until they are pointed out to them (Taylor, 1983). Many things that family members do, including the ways they relate to each other, involve literacy. They write each other notes, lists, holiday greetings, complaints, and directions. As Anderson and Stokes (1984) discovered in a study of working-class white, African American, and Latino families, early literacy experiences and learning are not confined to middle- and upper-class families, even though such experiences may differ greatly from one another. "Literacy," they concluded, "is influenced largely by social institutions and not cultural membership" (p. 35).

As a process, early writing development is characterized by children's moving from playfully making marks on paper, to communicating messages on paper, to creating texts. Children are at first unconcerned about the products of their "writing"; they lose interest in them almost immediately. However, once they begin to understand that the marks made can be meaningful and fun to produce, they are determined to learn how to write (Baghban, 1984).

Children learn the uses of written language before they learn the forms (Gundlach et al., 1985; Taylor, 1983). In observing children scribbling and inventing primitive "texts," researchers have noted that children seem to know what writing is *for* before they know much about how to write in correct forms. The letters to friends or relatives, the greeting cards, and the signs they produce hardly resemble conventional forms. Yet, the children seem impelled by an understanding of the function of written texts. Teale (1986) draws a similar conclusion: "The functions of literacy are as much a part of learning to read and write as are the formal aspects of written language" (p. 9). (See Figure 9.2.)

Children's writing develops through constant invention and reinvention of the forms of written language (Dyson, 1986; Graves, 1994). Children invent ways of making letters, words, and texts, moving from primitive forms through successively closer approximations of conventional forms. As they reconstruct their abilities to produce messages and texts, they simultaneously reconstruct their knowledge about written language (Hansen, 1987). Parents and teachers of preschool children who show great interest in writing typically accept and support their youngsters' production of the primitive forms. Just as children's early forms of oral language are sometimes called *proto-language,* their invented writing might be called *proto-writing.* No one teaches them the forms; they invent them from their observations of environmental print and their observing, modeling, and interacting with more literate individuals who write in their presence.

Children's involvement in written language, though typically embedded in social situations and interactions, is essentially self-initiated and self-directed. Most of the time, young children choose when to write, what to write, and how to do it. Parents, teachers, caregivers, other adults, or siblings may encourage them to write, and certain situations (such as playing restaurant or waitress) may require writing. Researchers such as Harste, Woodward, and Burke (1984) and Newman (1984) emphasize the importance of intent in children's early writing and learning. Children learn to expect written language to be meaningful, and they relate best to those situations in which writing occurs in that manner.

Figure 9.2

Jay, age five, attempts functional writing in a letter to his friend, Peter.

In writing, as in talking, story making is a primary impulse and activity. As humans, we share a deep and fundamental need to turn our experiences into stories. Story making is a fundamental means by which we learn and by which we shape our intellectual development. Making and telling stories play central roles in the development of literacy and the growth of children's minds. Children often surprise us with what they can do with written language and what they know about it (Britton, 1982). They seem to grasp important aspects of its functions and forms and produce primitive but extraordinary manifestations of language because they want to.

Children learn about writing through direction from teachers, by observing others more skilled than themselves, and by participating with others in literacy events. People who are more proficient writers play an important modeling role in children's writing development (Temple, Nathan, Burris, & Temple, 1988). Children need to observe adults participating in writing, and they must write having the guidance and support of adults.

Children need to work independently on the functions and form of writing that they have experienced through interactions with literate others. Teale (1986) calls these activities *explorations* and claims they make it possible for children's literacy to come to "complete fruition." They may involve practicing or rehearsing aspects of writing—letter formation and differentiation, similarities or differences between drawing and writing, spelling, punctuation, and so forth. They are apparently linked to children's evolving knowledge *about* language—their *metalinguistic knowledge.* When children explore their emergent knowledge and their skill in writing independently, they become more conscious of what they know and more explicit. They may even develop language to talk about it (Goodman, 1986). The more they make explicit their knowledge about language, the more children are able to use that explicit knowledge to direct and control their own attempts at writing, and thus the forms and functions of writing.

Two points are important here. First, children practice what they learn about writing, but such practice is most helpful when self-initiated. Second, self-initiated practice contributes to what children learn consciously about writing, an evolving phenomenon that plays a fundamental role in the development of their writing abilities. (See Figures 9.3 and 9.4.)

Figure 9.3

Three-year-old Robert separates his writing from his drawing by enclosing each in a circle during self-initiated practice

Figure 9.4

Jennifer, age three and a half, practices writing through the repetition of similar letter patterns from left to right across the page.

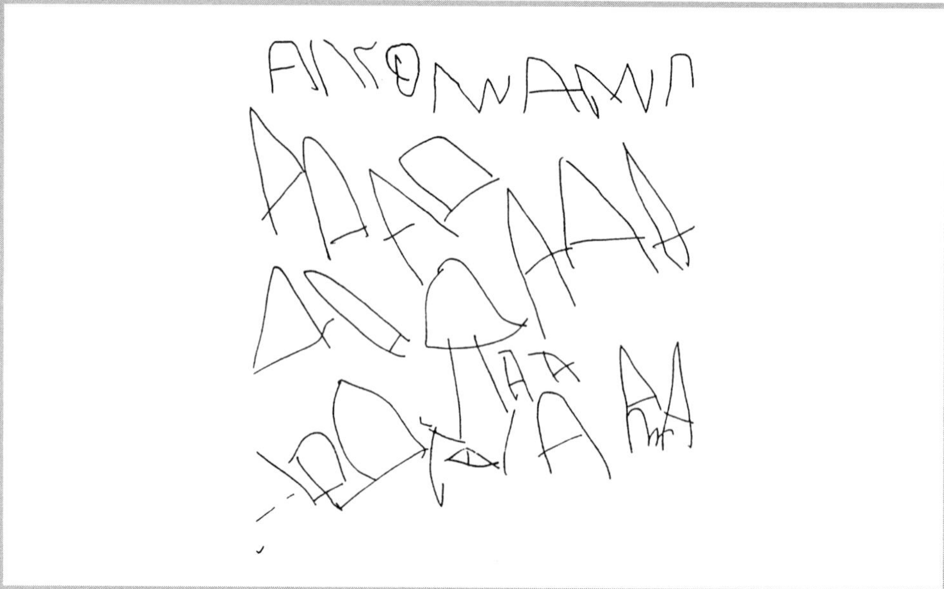

Theory of Early Writing Development

In the broadest sense, children's language development can be viewed as part of their process of learning to participate in sharing and making social meanings (Halliday, 1975). To achieve this participation, they learn to understand, use, and make various symbols. Though language is just one of the symbol systems used, it is the most important and pervasive one. Thus, as part of their broad process of symbol development, children learn to listen, talk, write, and read—that is, they develop language in all four of its uses. Their language learning begins in the prespeech communication that parents and infants construct, and it builds through listening to talking, to gesturing, to playing symbolically, to drawing, and to writing and reading (Vygotsky, 1978). Children's main resource for literacy learning is their knowledge of ways to symbolize experience and to communicate through those symbols in pre- and postspeech interactions.

This overall theoretical framework can be summarized as follows:

1. Literacy development is part of language development.
2. Language development is part of symbol development.
3. Symbol development is part of the development of social and cultural meanings.

For most children, the process occurs as a continuum. There are no sharp gaps or transitions from one aspect to another. Under normal circumstances, children's literacy development begins with the continual process of learning to communicate—first nonverbally, then by talking, next with symbolic play, and finally by drawing. Each new phase is rooted in earlier phases and forms a new network of communication resources and potential.

Further, literacy learning occurs naturally in the interactions of family and community life. In the process, children move from playing with written language to using it to communicate. They invent and reinvent forms. When children first begin making marks on paper, most do so with no knowledge of the alphabetic nature of the written language's symbol system. Initially, they do not conceive of writing as a means of encoding speech (Dyson, 1985; Ferreiro & Teberosky, 1982). Shortly thereafter, they view letters as referring to actual people or things, though they still believe that writing, like drawing, encodes or reflects only specific objects, not "filler" words such as articles or adjectives. Only later do children realize that writing represents language.

The Development of Writing Ability

Researchers have recorded varied descriptions of developmental stages of writing in early childhood (Dyson, 1985; Sulzby, 1986b; Teale, 1986). Most agree, though, that if there are stages, they are not well defined or necessarily sequential. Dyson (1986) describes children's writing development as having two broad phases. From birth to about age three, children begin to explore the form of writing by scribbling. Then, as children progress from three to six, their "controlled scribbling gradually develops into recognizable objects which they name, and similarly, the scribbling gradually acquires the characteristics of print, including linearity, horizontal orientation, and the arrangement of letterlike forms . . . " (p. 118). In fact, as noted, children may initially attempt to encode objects directly, as in drawing, and only later attempt to encode language.

Sulzby (1985) identified six broad categories of writing in kindergarten children, cautioning that these should not be considered a reflection of developmental ordering. They do however, describe children's early attempts at writing.

1. *Writing via Drawing.* The child will use drawing to stand for writing. The child is working out the relationship between drawing and writing, not confusing the two. The child sees drawing/writing as communication of a specific and purposeful message. Children who participate in writing via drawing will read their drawings as if there is writing on them (Figure 9.5).

2. *Writing via Scribbling.* The child scribbles but intends it as writing. Often the child appears to be writing and scribbles from left to right. The child moves the pencil as an adult does, and the pencil makes writing-like sounds. The scribble resembles writing (Figure 9.6).

Figure 9.5

Writing via drawing: When asked to write something, Brad (age four) drew a picture. The same request over time yielded the same response, a drawing for writing.

Figure 9.6

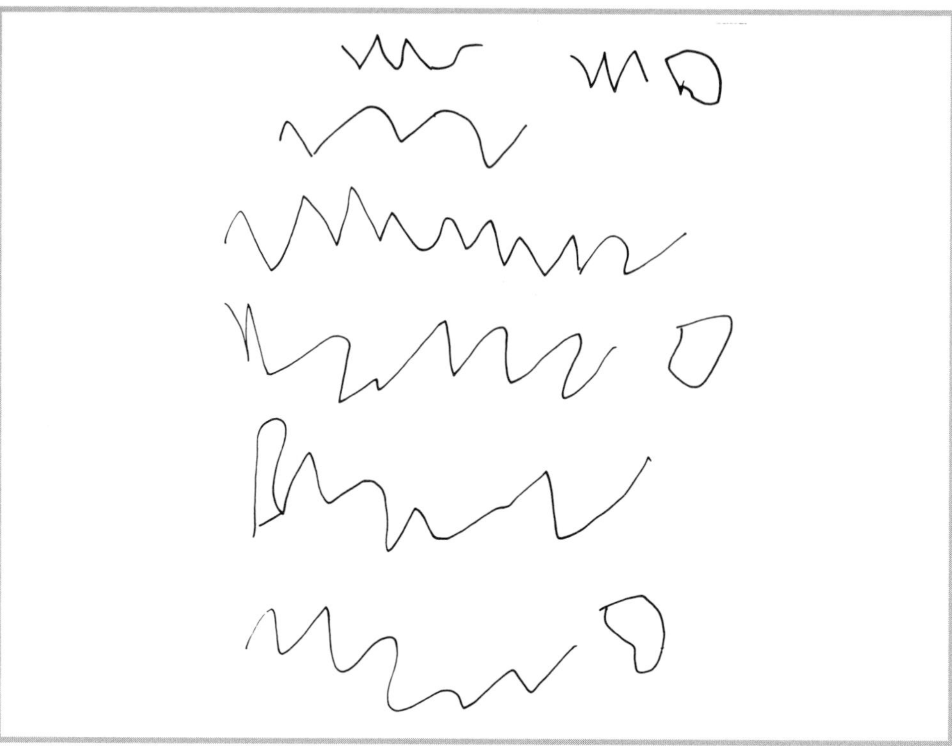

Writing via scribbling: When asked to write, Katie (age three) scribbled randomly. She eventually progressed to a left-to-right scribble and then purposeful marks that could be periods to end the sentence.

3. *Writing via Making Letterlike Forms.* At a glance, shapes in the child's writing resemble letters. However, close observation reveals that they only look like letters. They are not just poorly formed letters, though, they are creations (Figure 9.7).

4. *Writing via Reproducing Well-Learned Units or Letter Strings.* The child uses letter sequences learned from such sources as his or her own name. The child sometimes changes the order of the letters, writing the same ones many different ways, or reproduces letters in long strings or in random order (Figure 9.8).

Figure 9.7

Writing via making letterlike forms: Olivia (age four) wrote letterlike forms from left to right.

Figure 9.8

Writing via reproducing well-learned units or letter strings: Written by Brian (age four) these letters go from left to right across the page.

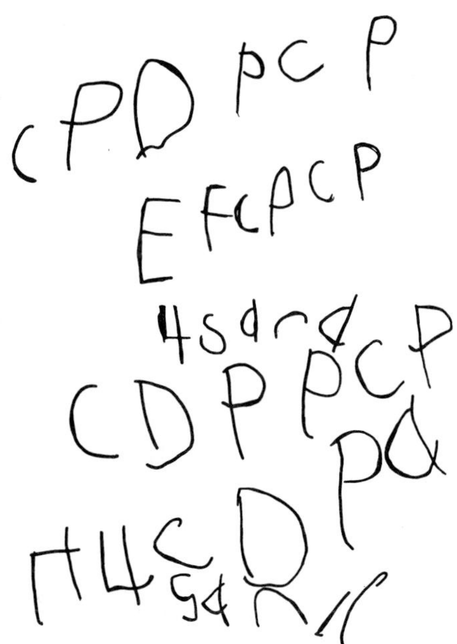

5. *Writing via Invented Spelling.* Many varieties and levels of ***invented spelling*** are demonstrated by children. Basically, children create their own spelling for words when they do not know the conventional spellings. In invented spelling, one letter may represent an entire syllable and words sometimes overlap and are not properly spaced. As the child's writing matures, the words look more like conventional writing, with perhaps only one letter invented or left out (Figure 9.9).

6. *Writing via Conventional Spelling.* The child's writing resembles adult writing (Figure 9.10).

Figure 9.9

Writing via invented spelling: "I love cats because they are so pretty and I like other animals too. I love my family and they love me back." This was written by Jenny in the spring of her kindergarten year.

I Love cat's Bcuz Thea are
So To. Prety and I lik uTher anmlz
I Love mi famle and Thea Love
me bac.

Figure 9.10

Conventional spelling: This story was written by Kevin, who was in third grade.

Little Red Riding hood

Once upon a time there
was a little girl named
little red riding hood.
No one knew why she always
walked, she should be riding
something. The next morning
Mrs. Shobert asked little Red
riding hood why are you always
walking? Then she walked
away and she was thinking
"hmm" that gave her an idea
to buy something. She went to
a toyota deler, she didn't like
anything. Then she went to
a bike place and said, "I
think I like that one." Now
Red riding hood rides.

Sulzby's general description of early writing is helpful for parents and teachers when they are observing and describing children's writing. As noted, however, Sulzby emphasizes that these categories are not necessarily developmental or sequentially invariant.

Objectives for Promoting Writing Development

Parents and teachers can use various strategies to encourage and respond to children's self-initiated writing efforts. They can create situations that will engage children in producing and learning about written language. These situations reflect our growing understanding that children's literacy develops within the context of family and community events that involve writing and reading.

Of all the ideas, theories, and strategies concerning early literacy, the way in which we think about writing represents the most obvious break with tradition. We have allowed children to use crayons and paper to encourage development of motor coordination in preparation for writing, but we never thought of writing to convey meaning as being an integral part of an early literacy program for children as young as two. We now integrate strategies for writing into the daily routines of babies, toddlers, preschoolers, kindergartners, and first graders. We consider even the youngest child's marks on paper as early attempts at writing, rather than as random marks. This perception is necessary in programs for early literacy development.

Generally, the best way to assist children in language and literacy development is to create situations for meaningful use in addition to offering direct instruction. This principle applies equally in the home, day-care center, nursery, kindergarten, and first, second, or third grade. The following objectives for promoting language and literacy development are posed from the perspective that children learn language, including writing and reading, by using it purposefully in many situations (for example, in playing or communicating).

1. Children will be provided with an environment in which they are regularly exposed to many kinds of print.
2. Children will experience print as a source of pleasure and enjoyment.
3. Children will regularly observe adults writing, both for work and for leisure.
4. Children will be given opportunities and materials for writing themselves.
5. Children will be assisted in deciding what to write about, but left alone to make such decisions.
6. Children's attempts at writing, whatever the form, will be responded to as meaningful communication (e.g., scribble writing, letterlike forms, random letters, invented spelling).
7. Children will be encouraged to use writing for a wide range of individual and social purposes, such as making lists, cards, letters, signs, announcements, stories, expository pieces, and books.
8. Children will be read stories in a variety of styles, which may serve as eventual models for their writing.
9. The use of writing will be integrated throughout the curriculum.
10. Teachers will take the opportunity through children's writing to point out sound–symbol correspondences as the spoken word is transformed into the written.
11. Children will be exposed to the appropriate way to write letters in manuscript.
12. Children will be exposed to the use of some aspects of punctuation: periods, commas, and quotation marks.
13. Children's invented spelling will be accepted and, as they make the transition to more conventional writing, there will be instruction for spelling.
14. Students will participate in evaluating their own work.
15. Experiences in writing from a constructivist perspective will be balanced with explicit instruction of skills.

Strategies for Writing Development from Birth to Two

Earlier chapters have described strategies that parents can use to help children with oral language development and early reading. Some of those strategies can be applied directly to children's early writing development; others can be adapted. Some strategies are helpful specifically with writing development. It is crucial to remember, though, that speaking, reading, and writing are dynamically linked in children's development. When we help children with oral language, we also contribute indirectly to their literacy development by increasing their language experience. Similarly, reading development contributes to speaking and writing, and writing to speaking and reading. This understanding forms the basis for the integrated language arts approach.

In a detailed case study, Baghban (1984) describes observations of her daughter Giti's writing development from 18 months, when Giti first began marking on paper, to 24 months. When Giti began scribbling, her productions sprawled all over the page. By 19 months she had begun to make dots and her sprawl was noticeably less extreme. By 20 months she had added circles and wavy lines to her repertoire. When she wrote after watching one of her parents write, her productions "more closely resembled English script" (p. 48). At 23 months she averaged 10 minutes per writing session, and at 24 months she began babbling over her own writing. She also attempted to write her first letter, *M* for *McDonald's* and for *Marcia,* her mother's first name. Throughout the period, and later as well, Giti's parents followed her literacy experiences and efforts attentively. Such attentiveness is important for all parents and primary caregivers to adopt.

As suggested in earlier chapters, another important way that we can support children's writing development is to become more aware of their experiences with environmental print, including print they see on television, in religious environments, on food cans and boxes, on signs, and in stores. Not only can we become more aware of the variety and frequency of children's experiences with environmental print, but also we can talk with them about these experiences, commenting, asking questions, and encouraging them to identify and remember signs, letters, and bits of print out of their normal contexts (for instance, an *M* used somewhere other than in a *McDonald's* sign). If we interact with children in this way, especially from their second year on, we are ready to support them when, as a part of their scribble writing, they try to write one or more of these environmentally learned letters. In fact, some children may make their first attempts to do this between 18 and 24 months, though most children will not begin until 24 to 36 months.

We also can assist children in their first attempts to make marks on paper. Often, when children begin scribbling (some at 18 months), they bang on the paper with their writing implements. Only a later do they begin using smoother, more deliberate, more coordinated movements to make their marks. When children are in their first, primitive stages of scribbling, we can show them how to hold markers or crayons. We can guide their hands to paper, not making marks for them but helping them understand that the paper is the place for writing.

Our responses to children's early scribbling are important. It is better not to urge children to write particular things. They should make marks spontaneously and decide for themselves when these marks are intended to represent something. It is important not to press them to tell us what their marks mean or represent. It is better to say, "I like that," than to ask, "What is it?" "Can you write some more?" is also a helpful response, but do not insist if the child says no. Expressing genuine pleasure in children's early markings, whether they resemble writing or not, and seeing them as an important step in a long developmental process are positive responses that will encourage children to continue. By continuing their "writing," they will incorporate in it what they are learning about print from daily literacy events.

Beyond responding supportively to children, we can model writing for them. We can let them see us writing letters, lists, and notes and filling out forms and bills, and we can interact with them about what we are doing. For example: "I'm writing a letter to Grandma and Grandpa. I'm telling them that we miss them. Do you want to tell them something? Do you want to write something on the paper to them?" When writing, invite the youngsters to sit with you, watch you, ask questions, and try their own hand at writing. This gives children opportunities to see how we go about writing and to begin to understand that the marks we make convey meaning.

Junk mail is a form of environmental print that can arouse interest in writing. Children enjoy writing or making marks on flyers, brochures, ads, announcements, and forms. They will write over the print and in the blank spaces. Apparently, the look and arrangement of the print give them the model and inspiration to make their own marks.

Repeating rhymes and singing songs also can contribute to children's early writing. So can using hand puppets and playing with toys and games, such as puzzles that can be taken apart and put back together. Manipulative toys that require dexterity help with the motor development needed to shape letters. Playing with clay or play dough, finger painting, using chalkboards, and painting on easels help build motor coordination as well. Of course, reading to children not only develops oral language and promotes early reading attempts, as discussed earlier, it also can motivate children to emulate the writing or to make their own books, no matter how crude the first attempts. Parents and caregivers in day-care centers can display children's early writings on walls, doors, and appliances, to be enjoyed and not judged or corrected.

Homes as well as day-care centers should provide environments for writing—comfortable spots with rugs and child-size tables and chairs—and storage for writing materials. The latter should include felt-tip markers, pencils, crayons, and chalk. There should be ample supplies and varied sizes of large unlined paper (newsprint works well) and a chalkboard. Materials should be stored consistently in the place provided for writing so that the child can learn how to select materials and put them away independently.

Standards for Writing in Kindergarten through Third Grade

As mentioned in earlier chapters, policy makers, educators, and others are concerned about expectations for children to accomplish specific goals at specific grade levels. The International Reading Association/National Council of Teachers of English *Standards for the English Language Arts* (1996) outline the following general standards for writing that are not grade level specific:

> Students employ a wide range of strategies as they write and use different writing process elements appropriately to communicate with different audiences for a variety of purposes.
>
> Students apply knowledge of language structure and language conventions (e.g., conventions, style, vocabulary) to communicate effectively with a variety of audiences and for different purposes. (p. 3)

Throughout this book I have referred to the *Primary Literacy Standards for Kindergarten Through Third Grade* (1999) prepared by the National Center on Education and the Economy and the Learning Research and Development

Center at the University of Pittsburgh. In the standards for writing in this document, each grade has similar headings. The outcomes for the grade levels, however, increase with difficulty.

The first standard listed for writing in the primary grades is called *Writing Habits and Processes.* This standard provides for children's exploration and experimentation. It suggests that students write daily in kindergarten through grade three to develop the desire and need to write regularly. Children should be given the opportunity to select their own topics and experiment with writing.

The next standard in the document involves *Writing Purposes and Resulting Genres.* It notes purposes for young children's writing such as telling stories through narrative writing, informing others with information reports, using functional writing, and responding to literature.

The third standard discusses *Language Use and Conventions.* It concerns style of writing and syntax, vocabulary and word choice, spelling, punctuation, capitalization, and other conventions.

These standards suggest some explicit and systematic instruction for the specific outcomes desired. The following section outlines strategies that can be used to accomplish these outcomes.

Strategies for Writing and Spelling Development in Early Childhood Classrooms

Parents and teachers can expect to see rapid development in writing in children from two to eight years of age. As we have seen, it is during this period that most children move from scribbling to producing random letters, to writing letters, to writing words with invented spellings, to beginning to use conventional writing. They will begin to space properly between words and use some marks of punctuation. They tend to write longer pieces, and their productions often represent wider ranges of functions and forms. This is a time when children show intense bursts of writing activity, perhaps alternating these with intense bursts of reading activity. It is important, therefore, that teachers have a sense of children's writing needs and interests at this time and know how to interact with them to support their efforts, learning, and growth.

Like younger children, preschoolers and kindergarteners take more pleasure in the *process* of writing than in its *products.* The act of writing is their center of interest, although they gradually develop concern for the products. When they play waiter or waitress, for example, and take an "order," they may be concerned that others can "read" it. The same thing might happen with notes or greeting cards sent to relatives or friends. Children begin to evidence concern that recipients are able to read their messages—perhaps so they can write back. Children who have had little experience pretending to write might be reluctant to make marks on paper even by kindergarten age, possibly because they have become aware that their marks are not conventional writing and thus might not be accepted. It is important to let them know that writing that is not conventional will be accepted. Some children may request conventional spellings and will not write unless they know it is correct. They should be given the help they request.

We must realize that what young children write about and how they approach writing is more important initially than their mechanics of writing (spelling, handwriting, punctuation, and spacing). Learning to write involves learning to compose texts that convey meaning. As children gain experience with writing, they will learn the skills and mechanics of writing through practice and instruction.

When children are free to write in unconventional ways, such as using invented spellings as illustrated in Figure 9.9, they are enhancing phonemic awareness and eventually knowledge of phonics. When children write, they have to transform the spoken word into written language. This fosters understanding of the structure of spoken language and how it is related to written language. The more children write, the better they become at segmenting sounds and blending them into words, which develops not only their ability to write, but also their ability to read independently.

Young children choose to write if a situation has meaning for them. If we impose upon them our selection of what they should write about all the time, we are not likely to see positive results. With these basic ideas in mind, we can create strategies and appropriate environments for helping children write.

The Writing Center

The literacy area in the classroom should include a place designated for writing. It should be easily accessible, attractive, and inviting. This area can be a part of the library corner. It should be furnished with a table and chairs, plus a rug for youngsters who want to stretch out and write on the floor. Writing implements should include plenty of colored felt-tip marking pens, large and small crayons, large and small pencils (both regular and colored), and chalk and a chalkboard. Various types of paper should be available, lined and unlined, plain white or newsprint, ranging from 8½ × 11 inches to 24 × 36 inches.

Index cards for recording Very Own Words should be stored in the writing area, as should the children's collections of Very Own Words. Each child should have a writing folder to collect samples of his or her written work during the school year. Several computers for word processing are also necessary. Materials for making books should be available, including colored construction paper for covers, plain white paper for inside pages, a stapler, and scissors. Teachers can prepare blank books, keyed to special occasions, for children to use. For example, a blank Valentine's Day book shaped like a heart and made of red construction paper with five or six sheets of plain white paper stapled inside provides inviting space that children can fill with their written greetings. (See Figures 9.11, 9.12, and 9.13 on preparing blank books.) Stock *bare books* (books with hard

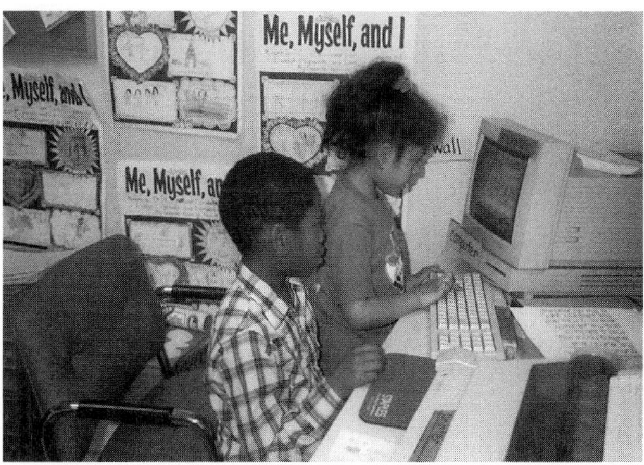

The computer allows young children to communicate thoughts. Early introduction to the computer will make it part of the child's life.

Figure 9.11

Stapled book. Cut colored construction paper and white writing paper into a desired shape. Staple at the side.

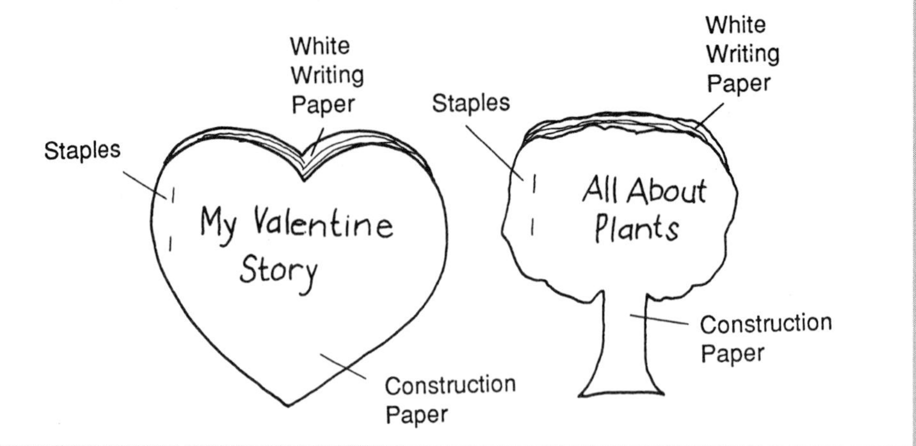

Figure 9.12

Folded, Stitched, and Glued Book

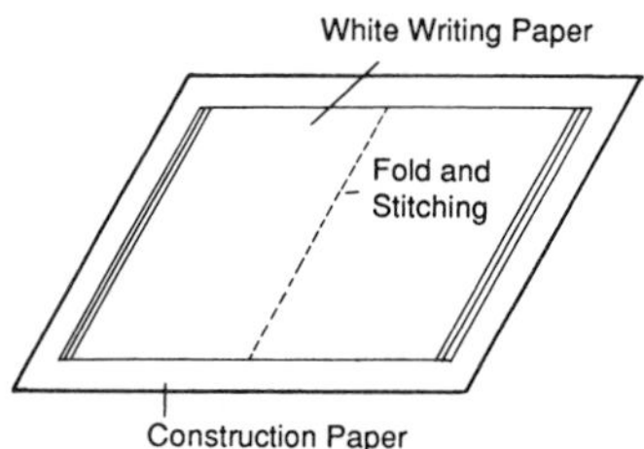

a. Sew a running stitch down the center of eight to ten sheets of eight-and-a-half-by-eleven plain white writing paper backed with a piece of nine-by-twelve colored construction paper.

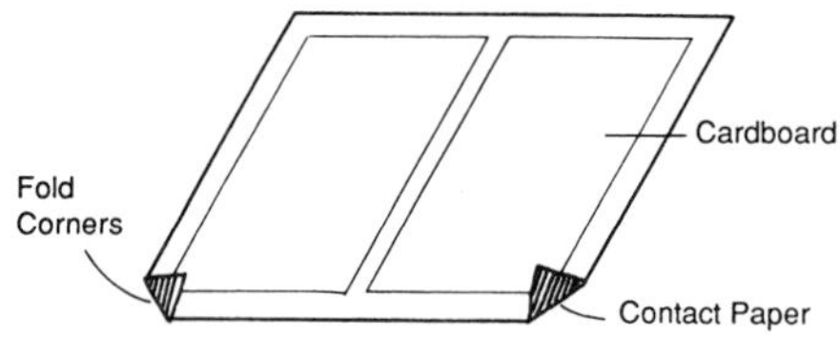

b. Place an eleven-by-fourteen piece of contact paper or wallpaper face down. Paste two pieces of six-by-nine oaktag or cardboard on the peeled contact paper a quarter inch apart, leaving about a one-inch border. Fold each corner of the contact paper onto the oaktag to form a triangle (glue if using wallpaper).

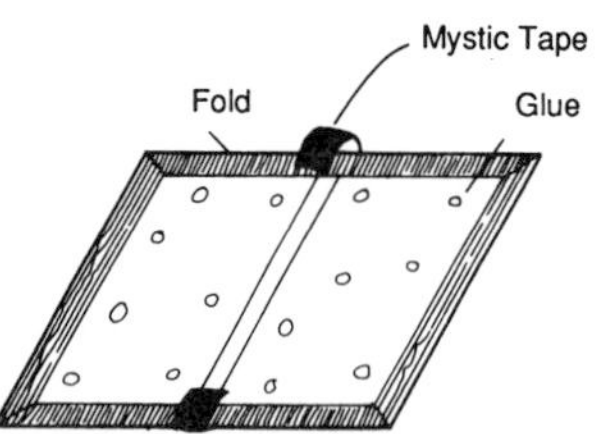

c. Fold the edges of the contact paper onto the oaktag (paste down if using wallpaper). Place a twelve-inch piece of Mystic Tape down the center of the contact paper and over its edges. Put glue on the two exposed pieces of oaktag and on the quarter-inch space between them.

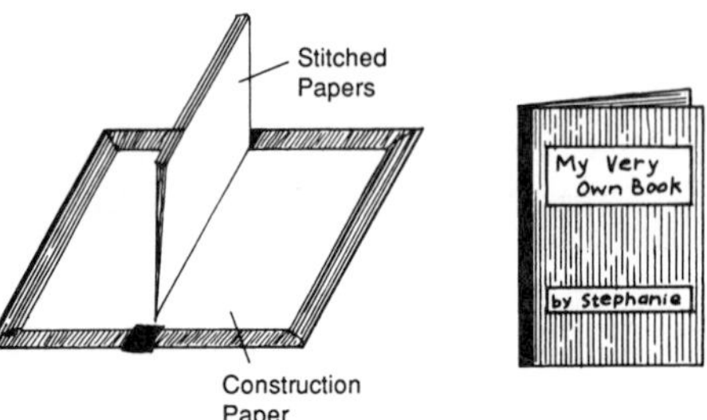

d. Place the folded and stitched edge of the construction paper and plain white paper in the quarter-inch glued space. Paste the construction paper onto the oaktag and over the contact-paper border to make the inside covers.

Figure 9.13

Sewn book. Punch holes into oak tag and white writing paper. Sew together with yarn.

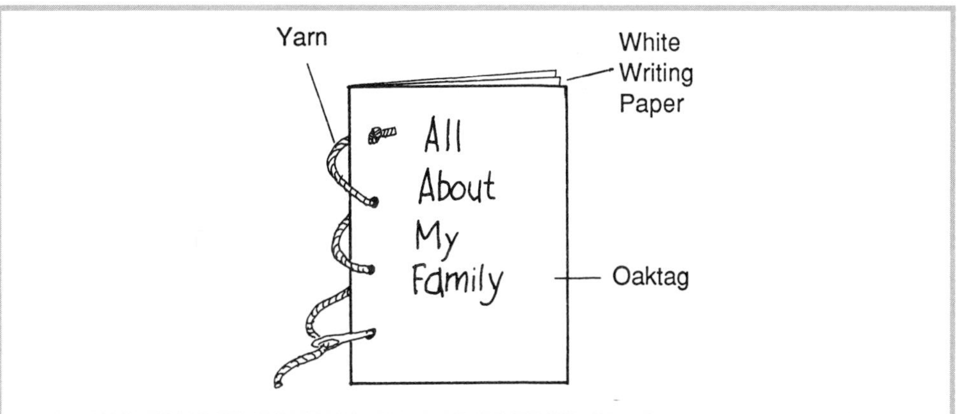

covers but no print inside) for special projects and blue books used for examinations are perfect for young children's writing. They can be purchased inexpensively from school supply companies. They come with 12 or 16 pages, which is usually just right for an original story by a young child. Try to purchase blue books with the name of a University or College on them. It makes children feel special about writing in them. Keep a supply of interesting pictures, posters, magazines, and newspapers; these can stimulate, decorate, or illustrate children's writing.

An alphabet chart in easy view helps children identify and shape letters they may need while writing. Tactile plastic, magnetic, wooden, and felt letters should be among the language arts manipulatives. These help develop motor dexterity for the act of writing and aid in letter recognition and formation. Small white slates are good for practicing new words learned and writing sentences that feature these words. A bulletin board should be available for children to display their own writing with a space for posting notices or sending and receiving private messages. "Mailboxes" for youngsters' incoming and outgoing "mail" can be placed in the writing center. The mailboxes for a pen pal program are discussed later in the functional writing section. The writing center should be labeled with a sign that says "Author's Spot" or whatever name is selected by the children.

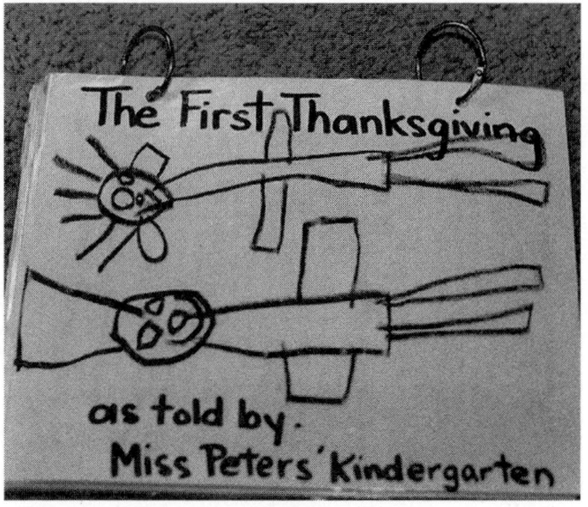

Allison adds her page to the class book at the writing table in the writing center.

Basic implements and supplies for writing should be stocked in every other learning center in the room as well. The accessibility of these materials will encourage writing (Morrow, 1990). A child might want to record the outside temperature on a chart in the science center, protect a construction of blocks with a "Do Not Touch" sign or copy a Very Own Word in the social studies or science area. A group might decide to turn the dramatic-play corner into a dentist's office, including in it an appointment book for recording dates, times, and patients' names; appointment cards; patients' records; and a prescription pad for medication.

The activities described for the writing center should be introduced to the entire group. They are used during writing workshop, for independent writing, and as center activities when the teacher works with guided reading groups.

In all the activities, children should write independently according to function and interest. The teacher has prepared the environment in which such writing can occur and has introduced the materials and made suggestions to the children. With this preparation, children look naturally to writing as a means of communication.

Independent Writing

Chapter 6 discussed the independent reading and writing period, which gives children the opportunity to participate in literacy activities. Children choose what to do based on several options, and they choose to work alone or collaboratively with others. Chapter 6 emphasized pleasurable experiences with reading, and collecting anecdotes concerning reading behaviors during this time. It is difficult to separate reading and writing, especially during this independent time when children direct their own behavior. However, it is interesting to note when observing children during independent reading and writing periods that equal time is spent at reading and writing. When children decide to engage in writing, it often is a cooperative effort. During this period, children have the opportunity to select from a list of literacy activities, such as the following:

Read a book, magazine, or newspaper alone or with a friend.

Listen to a story on the headsets at the listening station.

Read or tell a story using a felt-board and story characters.

Read or tell a story using a roll movie.

Read or tell a story using the chalk talk technique.

Read or tell a story using puppets.

Prepare a tape story by recording your reading of a book.

Write a story alone or with a friend.

Write a story and make it into a felt story.

Write a story and record it for the listening station.

Write a story and perform it as a puppet show.

Write a story and make it into a roll movie.

Write a story and present it as a chalk talk.

Present a play based on a story you wrote or read.

Bind a story you've written into a book and place it in the library corner for others to read.

Participate in content-area activities that involve reading and writing.

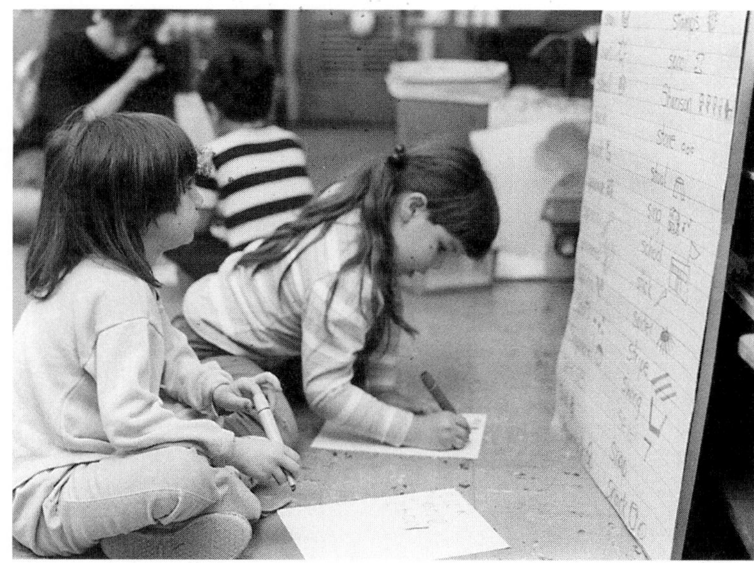

During independent writing, the girls are copying words from a thematic unit chart they need to use in an original story to be written.

The following anecdotes describe the writing that took place during my observations of independent reading and writing periods in a second-grade classroom. It is evident how closely reading and writing are linked. So many of the things children chose to do were motivated by what they had read or what was read to them. When writing, they often looked for additional information by reading more in other sources.

After listening to the teacher read *The Magic School Bus Inside the Earth* (Cole, 1987) Stephanie, Jason, Kevin, and Nicky decided to make a poster about the book that showed key pictures with captions for each picture. The children delegated responsibilities. They made up a title for the poster and called it, *Scenes from the Magic School Bus Inside the Earth.* They drew episodes from the story and wrote their own captions for the pictures. The poster took several days to complete. (One of the characteristics of independent reading and writing is that projects can be worked on over a long period.) When the poster was complete, the children presented their work to the class. Stephanie and Jason held the poster and Kevin and Nicky were the spokespersons. Kevin explained how the group wanted to illustrate the story in an unusual way and decided on a poster. Kevin and Nicky took turns pointing to the pictures they had all drawn and reading the captions they had written for each.

Heather, Kim, and Tina read a biography about a baseball hero. They decided to make a roll movie about the book. They wrote dialogue for the pictures they drew. Heather was concerned that they might need more information about the hero and suggested they look in the dictionary. Kim told Heather that dictionaries are for finding out how to spell words and getting their definitions and encyclopedias were for finding out information. The girls found additional information in the encyclopedia, copied it, and continued with their work.

Motivated by a story about magic, Zarah and Shakiera decided to write their own about a magical fish called Alexander. Shakiera asked Zarah to write the story, and Shakiera suggested that she would draw the pictures. Shakiera also offered to help think of the words to write. Zarah began to write the first line: "A fish called Alexander was a talking fish." Shakiera told Zarah to add to the sentence, "and he had magic."

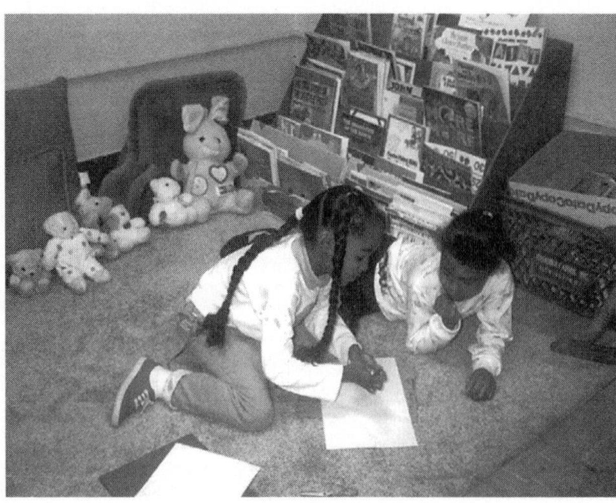

Second-grade girls engage in a cooperative writing experience.

Zarah said, "Magic, I don't know if that's the right word. I think he had powers." Shakiera said, "I think that magic and power are the same thing." The girls agreed and went on to write the rest of the story.

Television shows, rock stars, and current events also motivated writing during independent reading and writing. Three girls created a roll movie that included biographies of each member of a rock singing group. Another group made a felt story for an original episode they created for a popular television program.

Current events along with books children read motivated writing. Joey was reading a book about the U.S. Civil War. He asked the teacher to read it to the class, which she did. Joey decided to write his own book about the Civil War, and Christopher joined him. Christopher called the book "U.S. Saratoga." As they were drawing pictures, they made bombing sounds. Suddenly Joey said, "Wait a minute, this is weird. We're making airplane carriers fighting in the Civil War." The two boys changed their minds and decided to do a book about a war that could be happening now.

Julia and Katie wrote a script for a play they were going to have some children act out. It was a wedding ceremony, and their text is reproduced in Figure 9.14.

These episodes during independent reading and writing reveal a wide variety of topics that children focused on. Many of them we would never think to ask children to write about. If we did, they probably would never have the enthusiasm they demonstrated because they had not selected them themselves.

Figure 9.14

A Play Written by Julia and Katie during an Independent Writing Period

We are gathd her today to jon thes two wondrfal pepel in holey matramony. Silvea Do you tak Gim to be yor offl weded hasbind, I do. Gim do you tak Silvea to be yr offel weded wife. I do. Ma we have the rins. Silvea pot this ring on Gims Finger. Gim pot this ring on Silveas finger. I now prnawns you man and wife. Yo may now kis the brid

Melissa pretends to be a nurse and writes down an appointment in the dramatic-play center designed to be a doctor's office when the class was involved in a thematic unit about good health.

We also do not know all the interests of students. Some of the topics are much more sophisticated than one might have thought would interest children in grades one and two. Children have original ideas that they can draw from their varied and rich life experiences. The topics they select have meaning and function for them, and therefore they write freely and enthusiastically about them.

Independent writing activities can be adapted for children with special needs. Children can write to other youngsters who may share their problems. As teachers have said, "There is something for everyone during independent reading and writing, the gifted, the child who attends basic skills classes, and youngsters for bilingual backgrounds."

Children need to participate in many types of writing experiences. Center time when children write independent of the teacher alone or with peers is an important experience for practicing writing skills learned. Children practice different types of writing such as functional writing, journal writing, writing related to a theme being studied, responses to narrative and expository text, and using the process approach to writing in some of the activities mentioned. Before children engage in any type writing, the teacher should introduce them to the mechanics of writing, such as handwriting, punctuation, and spelling. This usually happens in what is referred to as ***The Writing Workshop.*** Here the teacher uses explicit instruction about a type of writing, and holds individual conferences with students to discuss their writing attempts when using the new skill learned.

The Writing Workshop

Many different terms used in literacy instruction often have different definitions depending on the author. *Writing Workshop* is one of those terms. It is described here as follows.

The teacher holds a whole-class or small-group minilesson to teach a particular type of writing, such as journal or letter writing. The children are then given an assignment to do independently or with a peer, to carry out writing that reflects what was taught. The teacher meets with each child for a conference about the writing they are doing to help with the new skill learned. When working with a peer, children are encouraged to conference with each other about their work and share their pieces of writing.

Writing workshop may end with children turning in a written product, sharing their finished work with each other, or sharing a piece of writing with the class based on the new skill learned.

Teachers may hold writing workshops with small groups of children based on need for the development of different writing skills. This type of arrangement is similar to guided reading lessons described in Chapter 2 and will be discussed further in Chapter 10.

Following are descriptions of different types of writing that need a formal introduction and initial support from the teacher.

Functional Writing

Children need to see purpose before they write. Class writing projects that are particularly purposeful include *greeting cards* for birthdays, holidays, and other occasions to parents, grandparents, sisters, brothers, friends, and relatives. Write *thank-you notes* to guest speakers who come to class, to adults who help on class trips, to the director of the zoo you visited, or to the librarian who spent time with the class at the public library. Prepare lists of things to remember to do in preparing a party, a special program, or a class trip. Make *address and telephone books* with entries from class members. Write notes to parents about activities in school. Encourage individual children to write to their parents about specific things they are doing in school.

Collecting and using Very Own Words offer opportunities for writing and copying and so does using classroom environmental print in one's own writing. Some preschools and kindergartens, as well as elementary classrooms, have established *mail service* and *pen pal* programs (Green, 1985; Martinez & Teale, 1987; Mason, 1986). Children are offered pen pals to write to regularly (once a week is reasonable). Teachers or aides may have to help children write their letters or take dictation. Encourage children to use what writing capabilities they have, even if they cannot produce conventional writing. Teachers also may have to read the incoming letters to students who cannot yet read conventionally.

The use of e-mail for pen pals (called "key pals") is another way for children to communicate with others for functional reasons. E-mail gives children the opportunity to write to others around the world, and sending and receiving messages are almost immediate.

A *notice board* for exchanging messages also motivates functional writing (Newman, 1984). Children can tack up pictures for each other as beginning messages. The teacher needs to provide a model by leaving messages for individuals and for the entire class. Notices about school or class events are appropriate. It is important to draw attention to the board when posting a class message or when leaving messages for individuals, so children get into the habit of looking for messages and leaving them themselves. There also needs to be a place for private messages. These can be posted on the notice board in an envelope or in student mailboxes. Some teachers have taped brown bags to each child's desk for them to receive private messages. Occasionally, the teacher should check the messages to see that children are writing. One teacher found the note in Figure 9.15, written by Asia, a first-grade girl, to Andra who is a boy in first grade.

Figure 9.15

This is a private message sent by a first-grade girl to a first-grade boy.

Dear Andra
look I am triing
to make this
relashtoin ship work.
I no that you are
mad at me but I
did not do anything
to you. All I did was
trie to take the
paper away from
you and you ript
it and you no that
you did. And if you
didthn wi did you
blame it all on me. Love Asia

Journal Writing

Journal writing can be carried out successfully in early childhood rooms, with entries made daily or at least several times a week. Journals can be written in notebooks or pages stapled together to create a book. Children are encouraged to write anything they want in their journals and to write at their own developmental levels. Thus, some children's journals might include only pictures, scribble writing, random letters, or invented spelling. The teacher models journal writing, perhaps with a personal message such as, "I'm very excited today. My daughter is going to be in a play tonight, and I'm going to watch her." By example children are given an idea about the kinds of entries that are appropriate. Some children draw or write stories in their journals; others write about personal experiences. Journals entries can be related to topics studied such as recording the growth of a seed that was planted, charting daily temperature, or reacting to a story that was read. From time to time the journal also can take on dialogue form, the teacher responding to a child's journal entry with a comment. If the child writes, "I had a picnic," the teacher might respond, "That sounds like fun. What did you eat?" The length and fluency of children's journal entries show great gains when the activity is continued regularly throughout a school year (Routman, 1991).

Juan keeps a learning log about a science experiment he is doing.

Because there are different names for journals, it often becomes confusing as to which one should be used. It is the concept of journal writing that is important, that is, putting one's thoughts and early writing attempts down on paper without concern for the mechanics of writing. To help differentiate the different uses of journals, several are mentioned here.

Personal journals are private journals in which children write about their lives or topics of special interest to them. These are shared only if a child chooses to do so. These are never subject to correction for spelling, punctuation, and so on.

Dialogue journals are similar to personal journals, but they are shared with teachers or peers who respond to what they have read. They are similar to a conversation, only the conversation is done in writing instead of by speaking. This provides students with feedback about their thoughts.

Reading response journals are those in which children respond to narrative or informational text read. They write their feelings concerning responses to the story or information. In these response logs they may even record vocabulary learned. Teachers do read response journals.

Learning logs and research writing usually involve other content areas, such as social studies or science. Children record information being learned, such as charting the growth of a plant or the progress of a setting hen's eggs. Children may want to learn more about science and social studies themes they study and record this information. Trade books that include minimal print and many pictures can be used as sources of information for young children's research.

There are many other titles for journals. As with terminology in the integrated language arts, different titles are associated with different and similar tasks. Journal writing has been found to be productive for students in helping them become more fluent writers, choose topics to develop, learn the mechanics of writing, reflect on ideas, and articulate them. Whatever they are called, some journal experiences should include private reflections about the life of the child, others should include responses to a child's journal writing by the teacher or peers, some should be written in response to literature, and some should be written in relation to information learned.

Children's Literature and Writing

Children's literature is as natural a medium for encouraging writing as it is for encouraging oral language and reading (Routman, 1991). Reading several books by the same author or illustrator can prompt a class letter asking the author how he or she gets ideas to write or asking the illustrator what kind of art materials he or she uses. It is best to identify authors or illustrators who are likely to respond, for it is important to receive a response, even if it comes from a publisher's representative.

Old favorites and series books—those that use the same character in several different books, such as *Madeline* (Bemelmans, 1939), *Curious George* (Rey, 1941), and *Harold and the Purple Crayon* (Johnson, 1955)—can motivate children to write their own books or a class book about the character. Books such as *Swimmy* (Lionni, 1963) and *Alexander and the Terrible, Horrible, No Good, Very Bad Day* (Viorst, 1972) involve the main character in a series of adventures or incidents as the story proceeds. Children can be asked to write still another episode or adventure for the character. Some stories, such as *Alexander and the Terrible, Horrible, No Good, Very Bad Day,* lend themselves to writing about personal experiences. (Figure 9.16 illustrates one child's response to this task.) Shared book experiences, directed listening/reading and thinking activities, and one-to-one and small-group story readings (described in Chapter 7) all can lead to writing experiences. Predictable books provide patterns that children can imitate in their own writing through cumulative patterns, as in *I Know an Old Lady* (Westcott, 1980); repetitive language, as in *Are You My Mother?* (Eastman, 1960); familiar sequences, as in *The Very Hungry Caterpillar* (Carle, 1969); or catch-phrases, as in *Horton Hatches the Egg* (Seuss, 1940). (See Appendix A for a list of such books.)

Children need to share their writing with an audience. When they know they will be sharing their work, they will write for that audience and have a greater

Figure 9.16

An example of writing motivated by children's literature.

purpose for writing. At a designated time during the day, usually at the end when the class gets together to review the day's happenings, a child can be selected as Author of the Day to share something that he or she has written (Graves & Hansen, 1983). More than one piece can be read and more than one child can be Author of the Day. Those authors who read their writings in a particular week should display them on a bulletin board in the writing center along with photographs of themselves. When sharing work, the child can sit in a chair marked "Author's Chair." Children in the audience should be encouraged to comment about their friends' work with such statements as "I like what you wrote" or "I fell and cut my knee once, too." Because at first the children may not comment readily, the teacher needs to model comments for the audience, whose young members will soon emulate the behavior.

It was Steven's turn in the Author's Chair. He sat down, organized his materials, and said,

> *I've been working on a series of stories. They are all about the same character and in each one he had another adventure. It is sort of like the books about* Clifford the Big Red Dog. *My stories are about a cat and the first one is called* The Cat Named Buster. *I call that Part I; I already have Part II and Part III. Part II is called* Buster Meets Pretzel. *Pretzel is a dog. Part III is called* Buster Gets Lost. *I'll read Part I to you.*

After reading Part I of his stories, Philip said, "Can I read one?" Steven replied, "Sure but you should read all of them. They go together." Philip continued, "I just want to read the first one now." Steven said, "OK, but you don't know what you're missing."

Children's work should be published. "Why publish?" almost answers the question "Why write?" "Writing is a public act, meant to be shared with many audiences" (Graves, 1983, p. 54). When children know their work will be published, they write for a defined purpose. When work is to be published, it becomes special; it needs to be done carefully. Children can publish their work in many ways. The most popular is to bind writings into books, which are placed in the literacy center and featured on open bookshelves for others to read. Other means of publishing include creating felt-board stories or roll movies, telling stories to classmates, role-playing what has been written, or presenting the story in a puppet show. A computer can be used to type, save, and print original material.

The Process Approach to Writing in Early Childhood

For experienced early writers, publishing can be the motivation for beginning the **process approach to writing.** The process approach makes children realize that writing involves thinking, organizing, and rewriting before a piece is complete. They become aware that a first writing rarely constitutes a finished product. Typical steps in this approach include prewriting, drafting, conferencing, revising, and editing (Calkins, 1986). *Prewriting* involves some brainstorming related to the topic. Brainstorming can take place with the entire class, a friend, the teacher, or alone. If the topic is the writer's favorite food, brainstorming might include listing the characteristics of the food, the different ways the writer likes it prepared, and what in particular he or she likes about it. Prewriting activities help generate ideas and organize thoughts prior to writing. Prewriting ideas made into an outline help determine what to write about first, second, and so on. *Drafting* is the second part in the process. The author makes a first attempt at writing the piece by getting the words down on paper. The lists prepared in the prewriting phase are used as a guide. The *conference,* which is next, can be done with a teacher or a friend. This is a time to reflect on what has been written to see if changes are needed. It is preferable to reflect with someone else but a child can also do it alone. The fourth step in the process approach to writing is *revising*. During the conference, suggestions for change may arise, and this is the time to make those changes. When the revision is made, the author goes on to the fifth step, which is called *editing*. Editing requires minor changes to the piece, mostly attending to mechanics such as as punctuation, grammatical corrections, and spelling.

The process approach should be used cautiously and only occasionally with children in the early childhood years. The prewriting phase may be accomplished through discussion and word lists. Drafting or initial writing can be carried out, but the teacher must be sensitive to the child's attempted writing behavior. The teacher then asks the child if he or she can think of any changes to be made or other ideas to be added. This is the revision stage. The final task is editing, and with young children this means copying the work over. If the child is publishing a book, it might mean copying it into a bound book. (Three ways of making a book are illustrated earlier in this chapter in Figures 9.11 to 9.13).

Some children may be frustrated by revisions and editing, particularly by having to copy their work over. Be selective in choosing students with whom to use the process approach. Involve only those who seem capable of handling it. Try only one or two of the steps in the process in writing experiences. As children increase their skills, more of the steps can be used.

Writing conferences between a teacher and a child are times to discuss what the child has written, to encourage the child in writing, and to assess progress

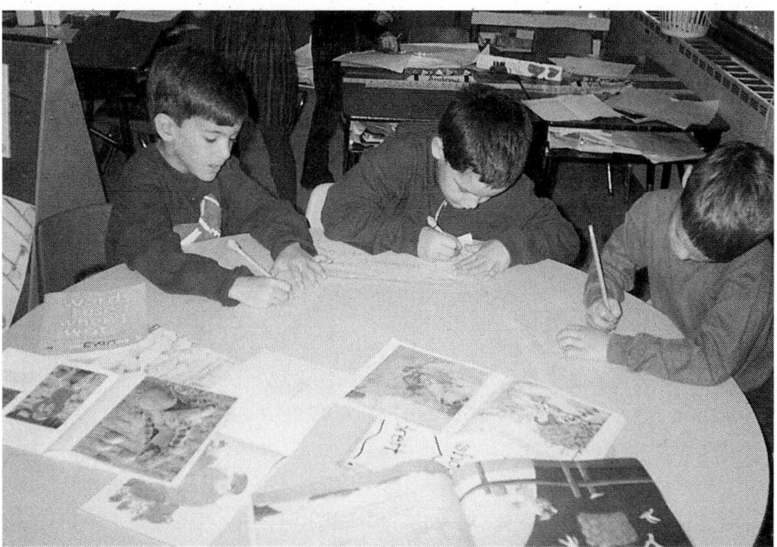

These first-grade boys are editing a book they have written together before publishing it into a bound book.

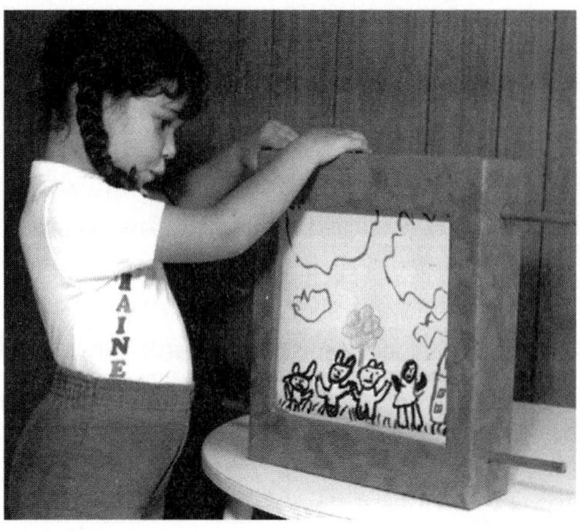

Stephanie created her story into a roll movie.

Stephanie puts the finishing touches on the cover of a book she has written.

by observing and reviewing the writing products gathered in the child's folder. During the conference the teacher can take dictation or help the child with a word, a caption, a picture, or a publishing activity. This is an especially good time to work with those students capable of dealing with any of the steps in process writing and to encourage reluctant writers.

Writing programs in early childhood should be initiated at the beginning of the school year. Teachers should refer to children as authors and writers so that they perceive themselves as such. Teachers need to model writing through messages on the message board, notes to parents, thank-you notes to children, and experience charts dictated by the class. They must be supportive when working with young writers. Reluctant writers need to be encouraged to write in "their very own way" (Martinez & Teale, 1987; Sulzby, 1986b). Youngsters need to know that their work does not have to look like adult writing. Showing them samples of other children's writing, including drawings, scribble writing, and random letters, helps them see that they can do the same thing. Adults need to facilitate young writers' attempts by taking dictation if children cannot or will not write themselves, spelling words, showing children how to form letters when asked, and answering questions that arise during writing. Like other areas of literacy, writing requires social interaction if it is to promote development. Therefore, teachers need to offer young writers feedback, encouragement, and positive reinforcement.

Taking Dictation

Taking dictation from children was a common language experience approach strategy used before we realized that young children could and should write in their own unconventional way. Taking dictation however does play an important role in writing development. We model reading for children by reading to them before they read conventionally; we should also model writing for them by taking dictation some of the time. When teachers take dictation, children have the opportunity to grow more in their writing ability as they

Teachers may need to take dictation for journal writing, for writing to pen pals, etc. Eventually children should be encouraged to do their own writing.

watch an adult model. The following ideas are important when teachers take dictation:

1. Begin with discussion to encourage ideas.
2. Write exactly what the child says, using standard spelling.
3. Make sure the child can see you write.
4. Write legibly.
5. Read the dictation back to the child when finished, tracking the print as you read it.
6. Encourage the child to read the dictation by themselves, to another child, or to an adult.

The Mechanics of Writing: Spelling and Punctuation

Thus far this chapter has emphasized the importance of promoting children's interest in writing and giving them opportunities to write that will prove to be enjoyable. This section deals with the **mechanics of writing.**

Writing requires dexterity. Although it is unnecessary and often unwise to teach preschoolers and kindergarteners the particulars of proper letter formation, they can be encouraged to use manipulatives such as puzzles and sewing cards that strengthen their fine motor coordination. In the earlier discussion of the literacy center, other materials that help with writing and identifying letters were mentioned, including magnetic letters, letter forms to trace and copy, and little chalkboards or whiteboard slates to practice writing letters, words, and sentences. The letters of the alphabet should be displayed at eye level for children, and the teacher can model the correct formation of upper- and lowercase manuscript (Figure 9.17). Legibility needs to be the main goal for handwriting. Learning about spaces between words is important so that words will not run into each other.

Figure 9.17

Forming the Letters of the Alphabet

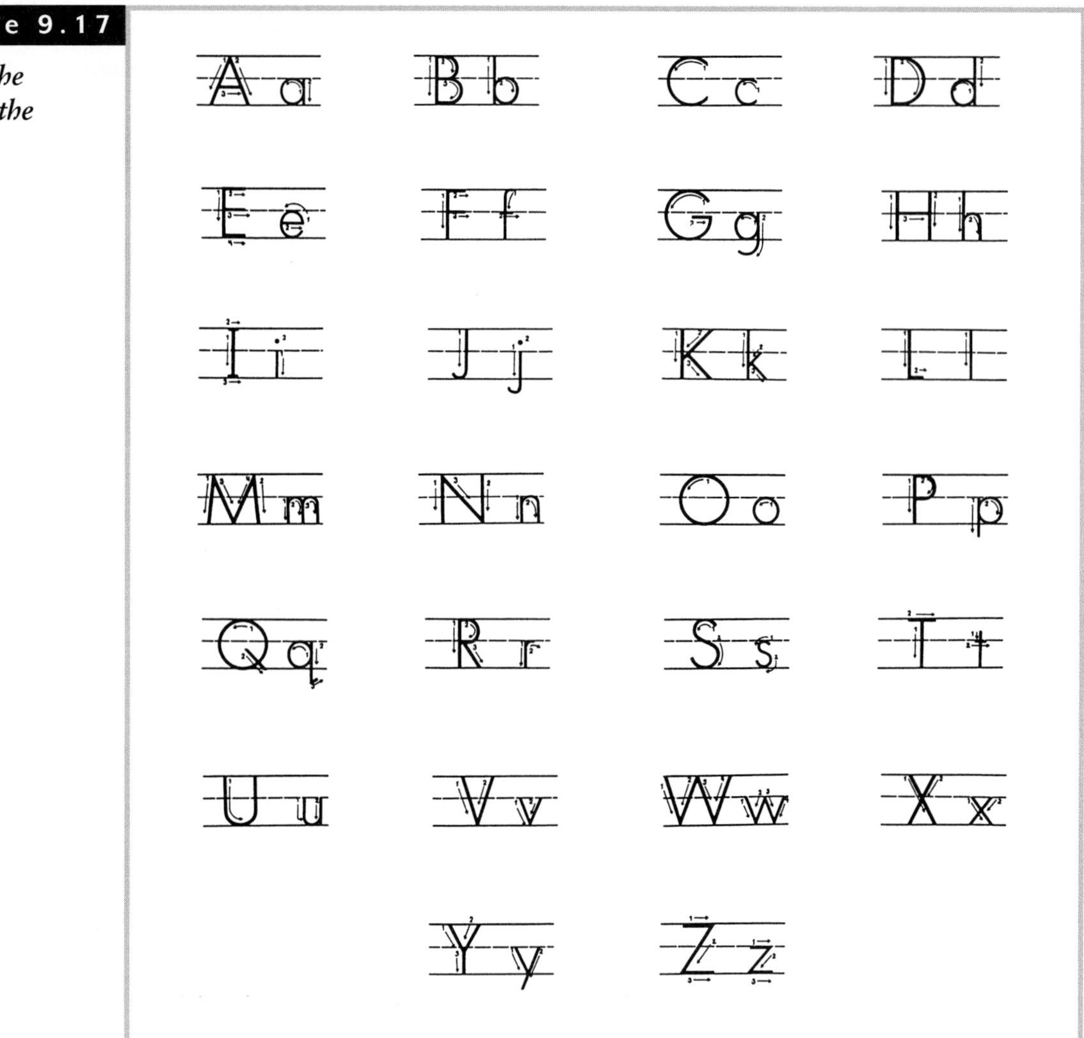

Punctuation and capitalization should be taught when the need arises, and in a systematic fashion during minilessons. Opportunities for dealing with commas, question marks, periods, and capital letters occur when reading a morning message, for example, and the mechanics of writing are discussed in a natural setting. Teachers will need to use direct instruction when dealing with these skills, but whenever possible, they should be handled when opportunities arise to discuss them in the print used in the classroom.

Spelling and punctuation have become areas of concern with the acceptance for example of invented spelling in the early stages of writing. Many teachers are not sure when to begin formal teaching of spelling and punctuation and to begin correcting invented forms. Children should be encouraged to write in any way that they can in their first attempts. However, they need to know that it is "a child's way of writing and not grown-up writing." When children are comfortable writing, and do so freely in their own style of early attempts, teachers should begin to point out elements of spelling and punctuation that will help them make the transition from invented spelling and punctuation to conventional forms. Figure 9.18 outlines stages of spelling development.

Figure 9.18

Stages of Spelling Development

Precommunicative spelling

- Children use scribbles.
- Children are developing a sense of directionality with scribbles.
- Children write some letters.
- Children write random strings of letters and numbers mixed with no association of the letters, marks, or numbers to sounds (e.g., L4TZMP for house).

Semiphonetic Spelling

- Consonants begin to represent words and are related to the sounds of the words (e.g., TIMGTAK—Today I am going to the Park.).
- Beginning and ending consonant sounds may be included (b for bug; bd for bed).
- One or two sounds maybe correct in a word.

Phonetic Spelling

Children spell words as they sound (e.g., sokar for soccer).

Transitional Spelling

Children use a high percentage of correctly spelled words, and the remaining words are spelled using some type of spelling generalization (e.g., Afternewn for afternoon).

Conventional Spelling

Children apply the basic rules of English to spelling and correctly spell 90% of the words they write.

Source: Adapted from Johns, Lenski, and Elish-Piper, 1999, p. 139–140.

The following are some suggestions for encouraging conventional forms of spelling and punctuation:

- When you take dictation from a child you can comment on the spelling of some unusual words and appropriate punctuation.
- When children use certain consistent invented forms of spelling and punctuation in their writing, put the correct form on a 3 × 5 Very Own Word card for them to copy the next time they use that word or punctuation. Get children in the habit of asking for words they do not know how to spell on index cards to help them develop their own spelling word list.
- When using Big Books, and tracking print, emphasize the spelling of words or types of punctuation that you feel are important.
- Use the **morning message** for teaching spelling and punctuation. Write new spelling words in the message for children to copy in their writing. Leave blanks for children to fill in words from a choice of the new spelling words for the week. You also can use incorrect spelling and punctuation so children act as detectives to correct the errors. Or, a message can be written in all lowercase letters for children to correct with appropriate capitals put in the right place. Use incorrect spacing between words and sentences to provide for conversation about these mechanics of writing. This leaves the opportunity for you to help children with spacing in their own writing by telling them how one finger space is used between words and two finger spaces between sentences.

- Encourage children to do free writing, which will result in improved spelling and punctuation.
- Phonic lessons which teach about word families and sound–symbol relationships will help with spelling. Make children aware that they should be using their knowledge of sound–symbol relationships when they spell words, and phonograms or chunks such as ch, sh are spelling patterns to learn.
- In writing conferences with children, take the opportunity to make them aware of editing, which includes correct spelling.
- Make children aware of spelling resources, such as the dictionary, and help them learn how to use them.
- Use word lists of common but difficult words to spell, such as *the, this,* and *but,* for children to memorize. A few words a week should be part of a spelling list to learn. The older the children, the more words can be assigned per week. (Figure 8.1 in Chapter 8, is a list of high-frequency words.)
- Add words from theme units to spelling lists.
- Encourage children to help each other with spelling words and punctuation.

As mentioned, it is important to free children to write their thoughts on paper without concern for the mechanics of writing. When they are ready, it is also important to make them aware of writing that is mechanically correct. There are times for free writing and times for edited pieces. Children should know that each type of writing is acceptable, but they occur in different settings. The word-study discussion in Chapter 8 about phonics provides activities that will help with spelling through word building. The following are some spelling games that are easy to use in the classroom to reinforce spelling words being taught.

Letter Box: Put five or six letters that make up the week's spelling words in a box. Students will arrange letters to make spelling words.

Mixed-Up Scrambled Word: Write spelling words with the letters mixed-up, and ask children to write each word correctly.

Spelling Collage: Ask children to write their spelling words randomly on a 9 × 12 paper covering as much an area as possible with the words. With markers and crayons have the students trace over the spelling words in different colors in a decorative manner. Display the spelling collages on a bulletin board.

Spelling Detectives: In various communications such as on word walls, morning messages, center activity directions, or job descriptions, make errors in spelling words. It is the children's job to find the errors daily.

Word Hunt: Have students look regularly for spelling words that appear in all that they do at school and at home, for example, in a math book, a science book, the newspaper, a book they are reading for pleasure, on food lists at home, etc.

Trace a Word: Have students "write" spelling words on a partner's back using their pointer finger. The partner has to guess the word.

Hidden Words: Prepare a list of spelling words that are surrounded by other letters. Have students circle or color the spelling words embedded within (example: ov**is**rm mx**the**uv qr**but**zi).

Transitions

Throughout this chapter theories and strategies for helping children develop the desire to write have been discussed. All the strategies are appropriate for preschool through third grade, with adaptations based on the particular age group. Teachers often want to know how children move from one level of writing ability to another or from unconventional writing to conventional. It is somewhat individual for every child, but trends do emerge. First and foremost we want to provide an atmosphere in which children will write. Children who are reluctant to write, because they think they can't, can be shown work done by others of their own age so that they see that unconventional writing is acceptable. We foster acceptance so that children will attempt writing. As youngsters learn more about phoneme–grapheme correspondence, they begin to realize that their invented spelling is not conventional spelling. At this point, they begin to ask for correct spelling as they move into the conventional stage of writing. It may seem as if they are taking a step backward because suddenly they will not be writing as much or spontaneously as they did in the past. Their concern for writing correctly has that effect on their performance. This will last for a short time as their spelling vocabulary increases, they learn to use the dictionary, and they seek help from friends and the teacher. Conventional writing is a gradual process in which a child often goes back and forth from conventional to unconventional writing until sufficient proficiency is gained for the writing to be considered completely conventional.

Assessment of Children's Writing Development and the Writing Environment

As in other areas of literacy, assessment of a child's writing should take place throughout the school year. That way the teacher can determine a child's level of development, monitor progress, and plan programs accordingly. Teachers also need to assess the classroom writing environment. The checklists on pages 312 and 313 provide a resource for the teacher to evaluate characteristics of a child's writing development and the classroom writing environment.

The assessment checklist is used to analyze individual writing samples collected through the school year for the specific characteristics outlined in the measure. Figure 9.19 provides another means of evaluating children's written original stories and oral dictations of stories for sense of story structure as well as the inclusion of interpretive and critical thoughts. Qualitative and quantitative assessment measures for story rewriting after reading or listening to a story read are found in Chapter 7 in Figures 7.3 and 7.4.

The measures for evaluating writing and the checklists in this chapter, along with the assessment tools in Chapter 7, provide the teacher with information about the language the child uses, the concepts included in the writing, the purpose for writing, and the writing mechanics used. The checklists provide information about the conventions of writing. They will indicate the stage of writing or spelling that a student is demonstrating, and the mechanics of writing used such as capitalization and punctuation. The measures for story rewriting and writing of original story will determine how well the child uses meaning and structure in his or her writing. All these assessment tools will help determine appropriate instruction and practice a child needs in order to progress in writing development.

✓ Checklist *Assessing Writing Development*

Child's name ______________________ **Date** ______________

	Always	Sometimes	Never	Comments
Explores with writing materials				
Dictates stories, sentences, or words he or she wants written down				
Copies letters and words				
Independently attempts writing to convey meaning, regardless of writing level				
Can write his or her name				
Collaborates with others in writing experience				
Writes in varied genres:				
narrative (stories)				
expository (personal and informational reports)				
Writes for functional purposes				
Check (√) the level or levels at which the child is writing				
_____ uses drawing for writing and drawing				
_____ differentiates between writing and drawing				
_____ uses scribble writing for writing				
_____ uses letterlike forms for writing				
_____ uses learned letters in random fashion for writing				
_____ uses invented spelling for writing				
_____ writes conventionally with conventional spelling				

Mechanics for Writing

	Always	Sometimes	Never	Comments
Forms uppercase letters legibly				
Forms lowercase letters legibly				
Writes from left to right				
Leaves spaces between words				
Uses capital letters when necessary				

	Always	Sometimes	Never	Comments
Uses periods in appropriate places				
Uses commas in appropriate places				

Spelling Development

	Always	Sometimes	Never	Comments
Check (√) the level or levels at which the child is spelling				
_______ precommunicative spelling				
_______ semiphonetic spelling				
_______ phonetic spelling				
_______ transitional spelling				
_______ conventional spelling				

Teacher Comments:

Checklist *Assessing the Classroom Writing Environment*

	Yes	No
Space provided for a writing center		
Tables and chairs included in center		
Writing posters and bulletin boards for children to display their writing themselves		
Writing utensils (pens, pencils, crayons, magic markers, colored pencils, etc.)		
Typewriter and/or a computer		
Writing materials (many varieties of paper in all sizes, booklets, pads)		
A message board or private message area for children to leave messages for the teacher and other members of the class		
A place to store Very Own Words		
Folders for children to place samples of their writing		
Materials to make books		

Figure 9.19

Evaluating Oral and Written Original Stories

Child's name ______________________ Date ____________

Name of Story ______________________________

Setting	***Yes***	***No***
a. The story begins with an introduction.	☐	☐
b. One or more main characters emerge.	☐	☐
c. Other characters are talked about.	☐	☐
d. The time of the story is mentioned.	☐	☐
e. Where the story takes place is mentioned.	☐	☐
Theme		
a. A beginning event occurs that causes a problem for the main character or goal to be achieved.	☐	☐
b. The main character reacts to the problem.	☐	☐
Plot Episodes		
An event or series of events is mentioned that relates to the main character solving the problem or attaining the goal.	☐	☐
Resolution		
a. The main character solves the problem or achieves the goal.	☐	☐
b. The story ends with a closing statement.	☐	☐
Sequence		
The four categories of story structure are presented in typical sequential order (setting, theme, plot episodes, resolution).	☐	☐

Interpretive and Critical Comments

Read through the oral taped story and the written original story and record comments and responses that demonstrate interpretive and critical thought.

Teachers should maintain a portfolio of materials related to a child's writing development, such as observation notes as the child writes, samples of the child's writing over a period of time, notes from conferences with the child, notes from conferences with the child's parents, and completed checklists. The portfolio should include the best of the child's work and samples showing need for improvement as well. The portfolio can be used during parent conferences and can accompany a child to his or her next teacher. Children should have their own writing folders in which they keep samples of their writing throughout the year. They also should be involved in the assessment process by participating in parent and teacher conferences, and in conferences with the teacher alone. Assessment should be kept as informal as possible based on children's self-initiated activities and on teachers' observations of and interactions with them. Figure 9.20 provides a means for children to assess their own writing interest and

Figure 9.20

Self-Assessment about Writing for Children

Name ______________________________

The good things about what I wrote are:

The things I don't like about what I wrote are:

I could make this writing better if I:

I used correct spelling:

I used my best handwriting:

Is writing hard or easy for me?

For me writing is (a) fun, (b) not so much fun.

Writing could be better if:

Next time I write something, I will try to do the following things to make it better:

ability. All of these suggestions support the purpose of assessment to (1) enhance the teacher's understanding of children's writing ability, (2) aid in program planning, and (3) help children and parents understand a child's progress and the processes involved to help gain more competence in writing.

An Idea for the Classroom from the Classroom

Preschool and First-Grade Pen Pals

Children from a nearby preschool wrote to my first graders to find out what the elementary school was like. We wrote a class letter back answering their questions and included our pictures. One week later, we received a response. Now we had established a letter writing routine. The children in my class took turns writing parts of each letter on chart paper. We went through the writing process steps of brainstorming, revising, editing, and rewriting for our new audience. Three children acted as scribes, while the rest of the class developed the letter. Later, three new children were chosen to revise and edit. Finally, three more children rewrote the letter. We also used e-mail to send messages to pen pals that need quick responses. Being pen pals became a part of our writing curriculum. We invited the preschoolers for a snack and a paired-reading session, and to our end-of-the-year play. In turn, the preschoolers invited our class for a picnic at the preschool. We developed a friendship with the younger students, and our first-grade class learned the purposeful and very rewarding skill of letter writing. In addition, the preschoolers became familiar with our school, which most of them would be entering soon.

Donna M. Ngai, First-Grade Teacher
Basking Ridge, New Jersey

Activities and Questions

1. Answer the focus questions at the beginning of the chapter.
2. Ask three children of different ages, for example, three, five, and seven, to write about their favorite food, television show, storybook, or game. Take notes on their behavior during writing, and analyze the sample of their writing to determine each child's writing developmental level.
3. Many functional and meaningful writing experiences are related in this chapter. Try to think of writing experiences not dealt with in the chapter that you could suggest for children to participate in.
4. Think of several dramatic-play themes that you could create in an early childhood classroom, such as a restaurant. For each theme, think of the writing materials you could provide for that play area for children to use.
5. Continue the portfolio assessment for the child you selected to assess for language development in Chapter 4. Observe the child using the assessment checklist provided in this chapter concerning the evaluation of writing development. Collect writing samples from the child over the course of several months. Evaluate them to determine the child's development in writing over time.
6. Continue the thematic unit that you began in Chapter 4. Select three objectives in the area of writing development and describe three activities that will satisfy each of the objectives using your theme. Be sure that your activities reflect functional and meaningful writing tasks.
7. Create an activity to enhance spelling and punctuation for young children.

Case Study Activities

■ Case 1

First-grade teacher Janice Bradley has students with many and different special needs. There are several children who have limited facility with English because it is their second language. There is a large group identified as "at risk" due to poor scores on tests that are used in the district. She also has a group of youngsters classified as gifted. She is very aware of the importance of writing experiences for children and the need for guided writing, shared writing, independent writing, and collaborative writing. With such a diverse group of children, she feels that she cannot allow independent writing or collaborative writing and confines the experiences to guided writing in whole-group lessons, and some sharing of finished products for the entire group. She is concerned that children will not get the skills needed in collaborative groups and independent periods of writing.

Do you feel Janice has made the correct decisions? If not why? If so, why? If you answered no, describe how she might better support the special needs of the children in her class.

Case 2

You have been assigned the responsibility to do a workshop for a group of irate parents who do not understand the concept of invented spelling. They feel that the school is teaching the children how to spell incorrectly and that undoing what is incorrect is much harder than learning the right way first. Describe what you will do in the workshop to convince the parents that allowing children to use invented spelling in preschool, kindergarten, and first and second grades is an important aspect of developing fluent writers.

chapter 10

Organizing and Managing the School Learning Environment for Literacy Development

"What is honored in a country will be cultivated there." In classrooms in which teachers honor literacy development, it will be cultivated as an integral part of the school curriculum.

—Plato

Focus Questions

- Describe classroom environments that are rich in literacy materials and support optimal literacy instruction.
- What is meant by integrating literacy learning into content areas through the use of themed units?
- How can literacy development be integrated into the following content areas: art, music, math, science, social studies, and play?
- Identify different grouping methods, or organizational arrangements, for working with children to meet their individual needs.
- Describe a language arts block that incorporates all aspects of a balanced literacy program.
- How can literacy learning be integrated into activities throughout an entire school day?

Mrs. Youssef wanted to integrate literacy activities in content-area subjects. Her second-grade students often found science boring with only the textbook, because it did not feature real-life situations. She decided to use selections of children's literature that related to different topics in science to make them more relevant.

The children were learning about "The Changes in our Earth," a unit that focused on topics such as hurricanes, glaciers, and the composition of the earth. Mrs. Youssef found several excellent selections of children's literature for this unit. Two of them were *How to Dig a Hole to the Other Side of the World* (McNulty, 1979) and *The Magic School Bus Inside the Earth* (Cole, 1987). Both books combined good literature with factual information about the topic. These books motivated a great deal of enthusiasm and discussion in class. Mrs. Youssef asked the children to write a science story—one that told a story, but included many science facts they had learned. This proved to be a difficult task for the children. Most of them wrote expository pieces that gave facts about the composition of the inside of the earth and what a volcano is and does. Those who wrote stories did not include very many science facts. Mrs. Youssef decided to have the children write a whole-class science story by having the students generate science vocabulary and concepts they learned and use those ideas to write the story together. The story they wrote follows.

Our Class Adventure

One sunny day in Sacramento, California, our class went on a camping trip to a mountain. We put down all our bags and set up the tents. Kevin, Alex, Jason, and Keri went to the stream to catch fish for lunch. Antoinette and Emily went to get wood for a fire since it was cold on the top of the mountain. While the other kids were setting up their tents, a bear came out. The bear saw the fish, ate them and went away. Two hours later, our class decided to go for a hike. Along the way we saw a river and rocks that were weathered. We also saw two glaciers which were blocking a river. Suddenly, everything started to rumble and shake and everyone fell to the ground. Little and big rocks tumbled down the mountain. Smoke started coming out of the mountain and everyone started to yell. Amber started running around in circles. Then what we thought was just a mountain blew its top. Lava started coming down out of the volcano and an earthquake started. It was a good thing we brought our earthquake survival kits. We all ran to our camp for cover, but the camp was destroyed. The survival kits were fireproof and lava proof, so they were okay. Inside there were tools which we used to fix up the camp. We fixed it up so well that it looked like new.

The success of any program depends to a large extent on how it is organized, designed, and managed. Even creative and knowledgeable teachers have difficulty without careful planning, preparation of the environment, organization of lessons, and management of daily routines. This chapter ties together the prerequisites for successful implementation of the ideas described earlier in this book. Specifically, it focuses on (1) preparation of the physical environment, including selection of materials and their placement in the classroom; (2) integration of literacy activities throughout the school day in all content areas; (3) grouping practices to meet individual needs; and (4) a suggested outline for a school day that provides literacy experiences throughout.

This chapter is concerned with the teaching of children from two-and-a-half to eight—preschoolers, kindergartners, first, second, and third graders. (Chapter 3 addressed home literacy environments and daily routines appropriate for infants and toddlers. Day-care centers for children of that age need to organize rich literacy environments, routines, programs, and activities similar to those described for homes.)

Preparation of the Physical Environment

The physical design of a classroom has been found to affect the choices children make among activities (Morrow & Tracey, 1996; Morrow & Weinstein, 1986). The design of the room should accommodate the organization and strategies of the teaching that occurs there. Programs that nourish early literacy require a literacy-rich environment, an interdisciplinary approach to the development of literacy, and recognition of individual differences and levels of development.

The following example shows children participating in functional literacy activities in a classroom environment prepared with materials and space that stimulated reading and writing.

Mrs. Shafer's kindergarten is learning about workers in the community. While discussing news reporters, the children decided they would like to have a news office in the dramatic-play area where they could publish their own newspaper. Their teacher helped create the center where they placed writing paper, telephones, phone directories, a typewriter, and a computer. There were pamphlets, maps, and other appropriate reading materials for the different sections of the newspaper, such as sports, travel, weather, and general daily news. The class completed their first newspaper, and Yassin was in charge of delivering the paper the first month. He had a newspaper delivery bag, and each paper had the name of a child on it. As the delivery person, Yassin had to match the names on the papers to the names on the children's cubbies. Later, when the kindergartners read their newspapers, they shared them with great enthusiasm. Each child had contributed something to the paper, for example, a drawing, a story, or a group poem.

Research Concerning Literacy-Rich Physical Environments That Motivate Reading and Writing

Historically, theorists and philosophers who studied early childhood development emphasized the importance of the physical environment in learning and literacy development. Pestalozzi (Rusk & Scotland, 1979) and Froebel (1974) described real-life environments in which young children's learning could flourish. Both described the preparation of manipulative materials that would foster literacy development. Montessori (1965) depicted a carefully prepared classroom environment intended to promote independent learning, and she recommended that every material in the environment have a specific learning objective.

Piaget (Piaget & Inhelder, 1969) found that children acquire knowledge by interacting with the world or the environment. Ideal settings are oriented to real-life situations, and materials are chosen to provide opportunities for children to explore and experiment. Dewey (1966) believed in an interdisciplinary approach. In other words, learning takes place through the integration of content areas. He believed that storing materials in subject-area centers encouraged interest and learning.

Based on these discussions, any classroom designed to provide a literacy-rich environment and optimum literacy development will offer an abundant supply of materials for reading, writing, and oral language. These materials will be housed in a literacy center. Literacy development will be integrated with content-area teaching reflected in materials provided in content-area learning centers. Materials and settings throughout the classroom will be designed to emulate real-life experiences and make literacy meaningful to children. They will be based on information children already possess, and will be functional so that children see a need and purpose for using literacy. Careful attention to a classroom's visual and physical design contributes to the success of an instructional program. Preparing a classroom's physical environment is often overlooked in planning instruction. Teachers and curriculum developers tend to concentrate on pedagogical and interpersonal factors, but give little consideration to the visual and spatial context in which teaching and learning occur. They direct their energies toward varying teaching strategies while the classroom setting remains relatively unchanged. When program and environment are not coordinated, "setting deprivation" often results, a situation in which the physical environment fails to support the activities and needs of students (Spivak, 1973).

When purposefully arranging the environment, teachers acknowledge the physical setting as an active and pervasive influence on their own activities and attitudes, as well as those of the children in their classroom. Appropriate physical arrangement of furniture, selection of materials, and the visual aesthetic quality of a room contribute to teaching and learning (Loughlin & Martin, 1987; Morrow, 1990; Morrow & Tracey, 1996; Morrow & Weinstein, 1986). For example, design of spatial arrangements alone affects children's behavior in the classroom. Field (1980) observed that rooms partitioned into smaller spaces facilitated such behaviors among peers as verbal interaction, fantasy, and cooperative play more than did rooms with large open spaces. Nash (1981) and Moore (1986) found that children in carefully arranged rooms showed more creative productivity and greater use of language-related activities than did children in randomly arranged rooms.

Studies that investigated the role of literacy-enriched dramatic-play areas based on themes being used in the classroom found they stimulated increased language and literacy activity and also enhanced literacy skills (Morrow, 1990; Neuman & Roskos, 1990, 1992). These researchers also have found that dramatic play with story props improves story production and comprehension, including recall of details and ability to sequence and interpret.

Preparing Literacy-Rich Physical Environments That Motivate Reading and Writing

Research that has investigated the physical design of classrooms strongly suggests that, by purposefully arranging the space and materials, teachers can create physical environments that exert an active, positive, and pervasive influence on instruction. Educators must think of their classrooms as places to project a visual atmosphere that communicates a definitive message. The following sections describe the visual presentation of a literacy-rich physical environment to motivate reading and writing based on the research discussed in previous chapters.

ENVIRONMENTAL PRINT IN YOUR CLASSROOM. Literacy-rich classrooms are filled with visually prominent functional print—labels on classroom items and areas; signs communicating functional information and directions, such as *Quiet Please* and *Please Put Materials Away After Using Them;* and charts labeled *Helpers, Daily Routines, Attendances,* and *Calendar* to name a few (Schickedanz, 1993). Labels identify learning centers and each child's cubby. A notice board placed prominently in the room can be used to communicate with the children in writing. Experience charts and morning messages are used to display new words generated from themes, recipes used in the classroom, and science experiments conducted. Word walls display high-frequency words learned, new spelling words, and words that feature phonics elements being taught. Teachers discuss and use the environmental print with the children to ensure it is noticed. Children are encouraged to read, copy, and use words from the print in their writing.

The outdoor environment also should accommodate literacy development. In addition to the usual playground equipment, new materials that reflect unit instruction add to the interest of outdoor play. Where climates are seasonal,

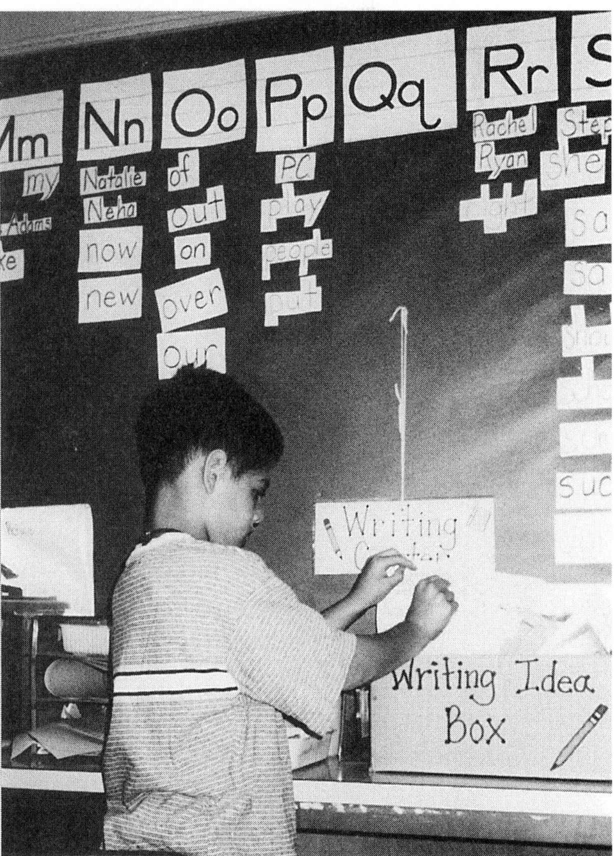

A word wall with high-frequency words and a writing center with ideas for writing activities provide a rich source of environmental print.

for example, flowers should be planted in the spring; rakes provided in the fall for leaf gathering; and pails, shovels, and other digging and building equipment provided in winter for snow play. Creative materials such as crates, boxes, plastic containers, boards, ropes, and balls give children incentives to play creatively. The materials generate language during play and in class discussions, and provide information for writing experience charts and class books.

THE CLASSROOM LITERACY CENTER. The literacy center, which includes the library corner and a writing area, should be the focal point in a classroom. Children's immediate access to literature and writing materials increases the number of children who participate in literacy activities during the school day. Both areas in the literacy center need to be obvious and inviting but also should afford privacy and be clearly defined. The areas should accommodate four to five children comfortably. The center says to children that as teachers we value literacy by making it an important part of our classroom. The materials range in difficulty to meet individual needs and the different developmental levels of the children. Each set of materials has its own place and is to be respected. The literacy center includes materials for reading, writing, oral language development, and developing word-study skills. The different parts of the center have already been discussed in other chapters (the library corner in Chapter 6, the writing center in Chapter 9, oral language center materials in Chapter 4, and materials to develop word study in Chapter 8). The library corner and writing center will be described again here to pull the entire area together.

The Library Corner. The library corner should house books on traditional shelves with only their spines showing. Shelve books by category and use some sort of coding system. Coding introduces the idea that books in regular libraries are organized systematically for easy access. Other shelves should be open faced to display full covers, thus calling attention to them. Use the open-faced shelving to feature books about themes being studied, and rotate new books in every few weeks. To ensure there is something for everyone in the center, include five to eight books per child at three or four grade levels representing different genres of children's literature. Stock multiple copies of popular stories. Children enjoy reading the same book together.

Furnish the area with a rug and pillows. Include a rocking chair representing the Literacy Chair of Honor, where the teacher and others read to the children. This area is where children read for pleasure, read to other children, or present stories to the class that they have written. Provide a cozy private spot for reading. Teachers have used large cartons from household appliances, painted or covered with contact paper, where children can crawl inside and read.

Posters and bulletin boards that celebrate reading should be used to decorate the area. Devise a method for checking books out of the classroom library to take home and read. Provide materials for active involvement in storybook reading and storytelling, with storytelling manipulatives such as a felt-board with story characters, roll movies, puppets, and headsets for listening to taped stories. These materials deal mostly with language and comprehension skills. Provide manipulative word-study games and activities that include making words and sorting words based on letter patterns to help build independent readers.

The Writing Area. The writing area requires a table and chairs, plus colored felt-tipped markers, large and small crayons, pencils (both regular and colored), chalk, a chalkboard, and paper in a variety of sizes, kinds, and colors. Include unlined plain paper or newsprint of many different sizes. Have index cards available to record children's Very Own Words, high-frequency words, or word patterns they may need to practice. A writing folder for each child can be kept in a large box. Computers must be in the writing area as well. Book-making materials include paper, a hole punch, a stapler, and construction paper. Blank books prepared by the teacher and children can be keyed to special occasions and completed by youngsters. Display children's writing on a bulletin board. Equally valuable are *notice boards* on which messages can be exchanged among classmates or between teacher and students.

Involve children in designing and managing the literacy center. They can help develop rules for its use and keep it neat and orderly.

DESIGNING CONTENT-AREA CENTERS TO ACCOMMODATE INDIVIDUAL NEEDS. Programs that motivate early literacy development require literacy-rich environments that recognize the need for an integrated approach to literacy learning and awareness of individual differences and developmental levels. These classrooms are arranged in centers designed for particular content areas. Centers contain materials specific to topics currently under study and general supplies and resources. The materials are usually manipulative and activity oriented. They are also designed such that children use them independently or in small groups. Centers are partially separated from each other by furniture that houses their materials. Centers should be labeled and their materials stored on tables, on shelves, in boxes, or on a bulletin board. Each piece of equipment in a center should have its own designated spot so that teachers can direct children to it and children can find and return it easily. Early in a school year, a center need hold only a small number of items; new materials are gradually added as the year progresses. The teacher should introduce the purpose, use, and placement of each item added.

Content-area centers are dedicated to social studies, science, art, music, math, literacy, dramatic play, and block play. Centers contain materials pertinent to the content area, and materials are added that are specific to themes being studied such as nutrition or animals. Each subject-specific center includes literacy materials as well: things to read, materials with which to write, things to listen to, and things to talk about. These materials create interest, new vocabulary and concepts, and a reason for participating in literacy activities. With each new theme studied, additional books, posters, artifacts, music, art projects, dramatic-play materials, and scientific objects can be added to create new interest. Chapter 4 describes general materials for each content-area center, and then discusses additions made for the study of a particular theme. The classroom floorplans in Figures 10.1 and 10.2 illustrate this type of learning environment from preschool through fifth grade.

Notice in Figure 10.1, in the preschool through first-grade floorplan, that the art center is placed by the sink for easy access to water. In this same area are children's cubbies for storing individual work. Because the working needs of early childhood classrooms are better met by table surfaces than by desks, children should be provided with these storage areas. The contents of the various centers diagramed in the figure have been described in Chapter 4. In addition to all the materials available in them, it is important that each has books and writing materials. The music center, for example, can include picture

Figure 10.1

Classroom Floorplan for Prekindergarten through First Grade

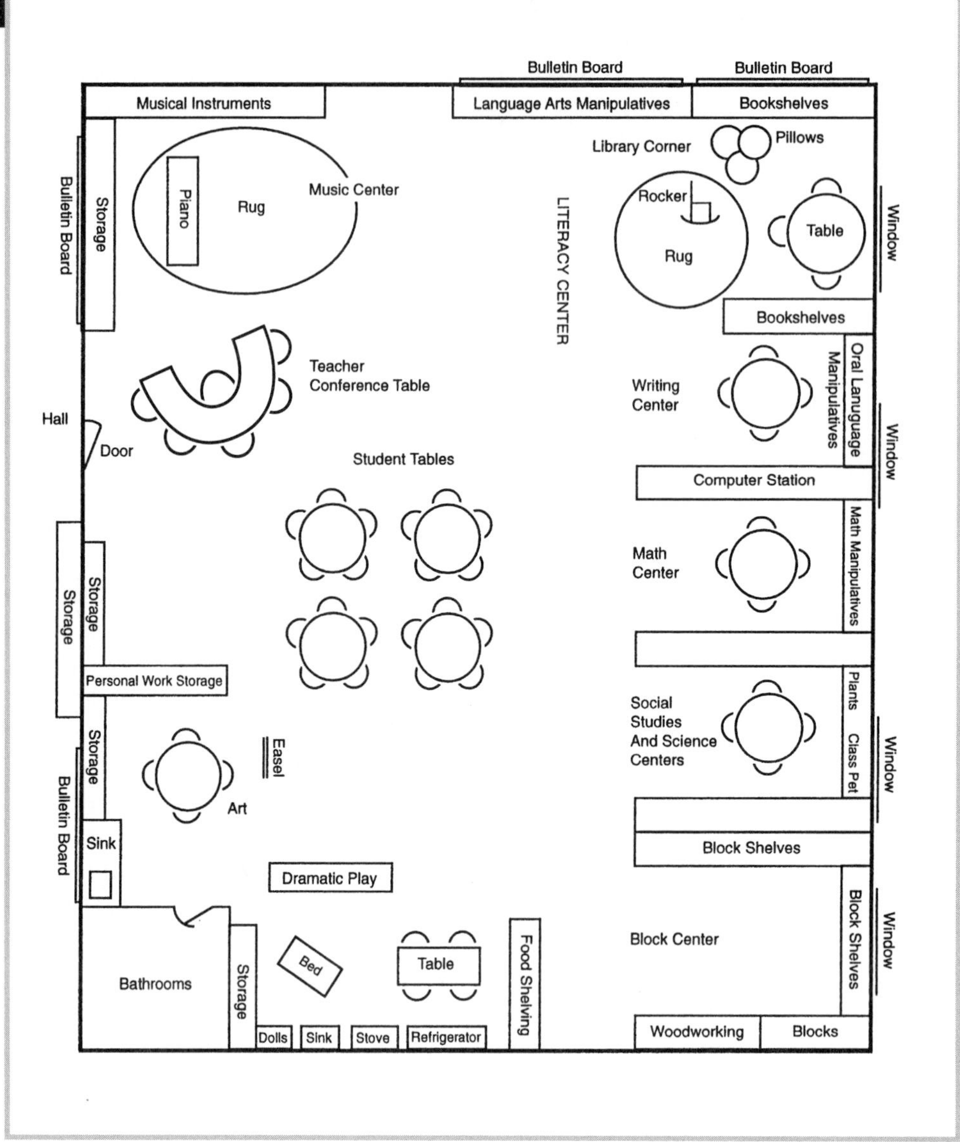

storybooks adapted from songs, such as Ezra Jack Keats's *Over in the Meadow* (1971). In addition to looking at the book, children may choose to copy words from the story. Certainly social studies and science centers should hold informational books and children's literature that relate to topics being studied. The art center might have books with craft ideas, including directions and diagrams. Books are appropriate as well in the dramatic-play area. If the class is discussing space, the area should have books about space and space stories for pretend caregivers to read to their "children." The block center can contain books that help develop ideas for building. Books that contain maps or plans of communities might motivate children to create such communities in their block play.

In addition to generating a rich literacy atmosphere and an interdisciplinary approach, the room is designed to cater to different teaching methods, organizational strategies, and grouping procedures so that the differences among the

Figure 10.2

Classroom Floorplan for Second through Fifth Grade

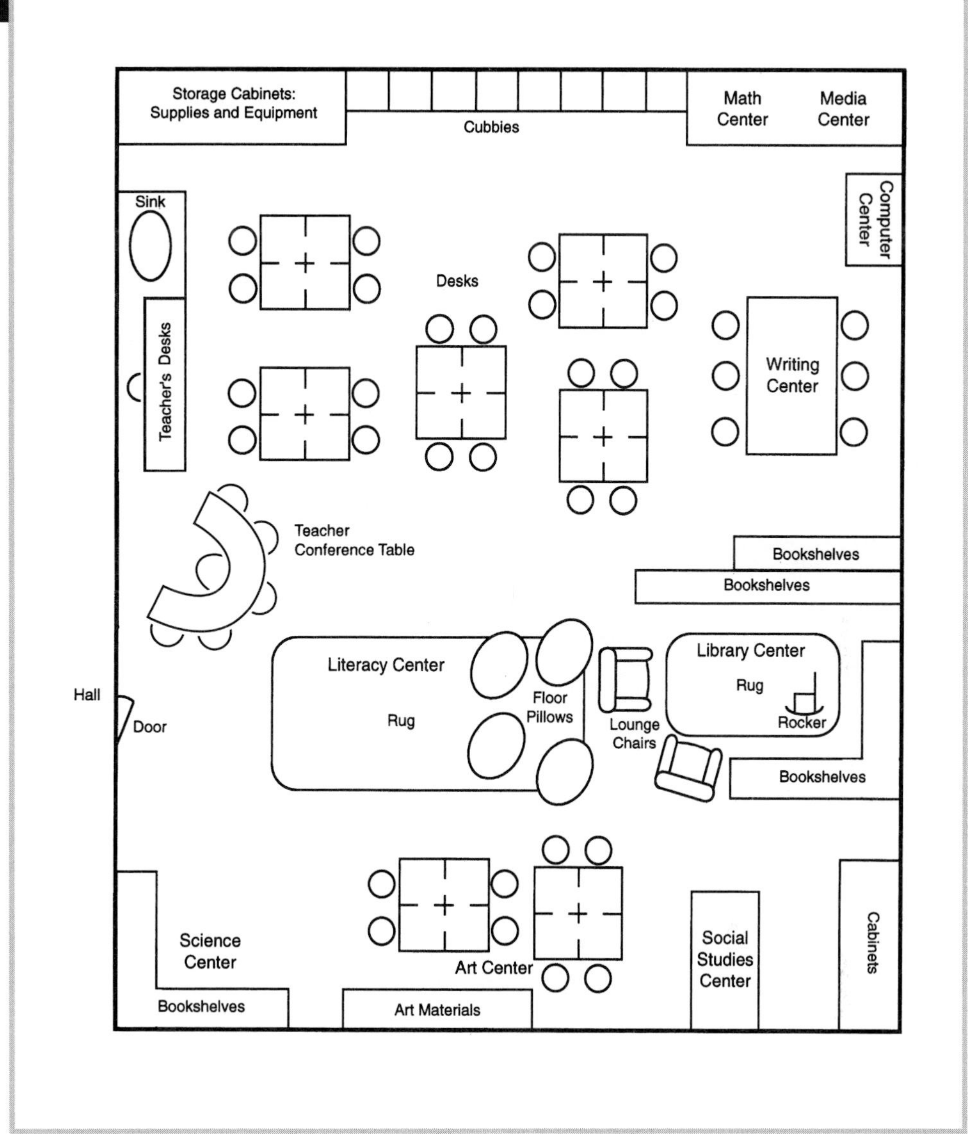

children can be accommodated. The centers provide space for independent or social learning, exploration, and self-direction. The tables illustrated in the classroom floorplan (Figure 10.1) provide a place for whole-class instruction, as does the open area in the music center with the rug on which children can sit. The teacher's conference table is a place for individual learning or small-group lessons. All furniture is, of course, movable so that any other needed teaching arrangement can be accommodated. The centers are located to create both quiet, relatively academic areas and places for more active play. The literacy center, for example, which houses the library corner, writing, and oral language areas, is next to the math center. Because these areas generally house activities that require relative quiet, they are in close proximity. Alternatively, dramatic play, woodworking, and block play tend to be noisier activities, so they are placed at the opposite end of the room from the quiet areas. The art center can also be a noisy area and is set aside from the quieter sections of the room. The teacher's conference table is situated in a quiet area yet allows the teacher a view of the rest of the classroom. While the teacher is involved in small-group or individualized instruction at the conference table, the rest of the class is working independently. The table's location allows the teacher to see all the children even while working with just a few.

The plan for the physical environment is used in many nursery schools and kindergartens, and some first and second grades. The assumption is that it is for younger children. Teachers in first and second grade should consider these designs because they encourage literacy learning. Figure 10.3 is a map for you to fill in the general materials for your centers and materials to add that are specific to a particular theme. Evaluate the richness of your literacy environment using the checklist on pages 329–330.

Figure 10.3

General Center Materials and Center Theme Materials

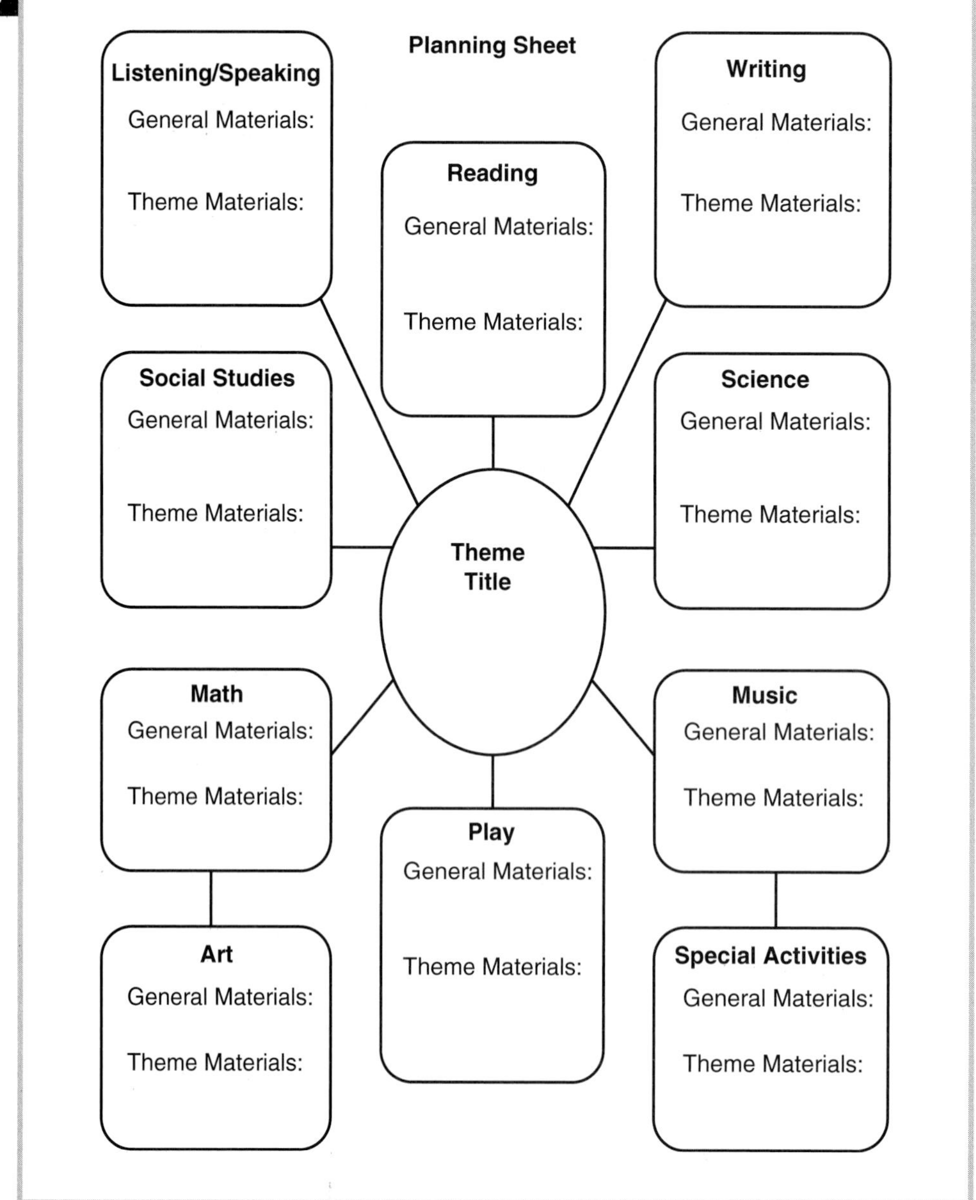

Checklist *Evaluating and Improving the Literacy Environment*

The Literacy Center

	Yes	No
Children participate in designing the center (e.g., develop rules, select a name for center, develop materials).		
Area is placed in a quiet section of the room.		
Area is visually and physically accessible, yet partitioned from the rest of the room.		
There are a rug, throw pillows, rocking chair, bean bag chair, and stuffed animals.		
There is a private spot in the corner such as a box to crawl into and read.		
The center uses about 10% of the classroom space and fits five to six children.		

The Library Corner

	Yes	No
Bookshelves for storing books with spines facing outward		
Organizational system for shelving books		
a. books shelved by genre	a.	
b. books shelved by reading level	b.	
Open-faced bookshelves for featured books		
Five to eight books per child		
Books represent three to four grade levels of the following types: (a) picture books, (b) picture story books, (c) traditional literature, (d) poetry, (e) realistic literature, (f) informational books, (g) biographies, (h) chapter books, (i) easy to read books, (j) riddle and joke books, (k) participation books, (l) series books, (m) textless books, (n) TV-related books, (o) brochures, (p) magazines, (q) newspapers.		
Twenty new books circulated every two weeks		
Check-out/check-in system for children to take books out daily		
Head sets and taped stories		
Felt-board and story characters with related books		
Materials for constructing felt stories		
Other story manipulatives (e.g., roll movie, puppets, with related books)		
System for recording books read		
Multiple copies of the same book		

(continued on next page)

Checklist *(continued from previous page)*

The Writing Center (The Author's Spot)	Yes	No
Tables and chairs		
Writing posters and bulletin board for children to display their writing themselves		
Writing utensils (e.g., pens, pencils, crayons, magic markers, colored pencils)		
Writing materials (many varieties of paper in all sizes, booklets, pads)		
Computers		
Materials for writing stories and making them into books		
A message board for children to post messages for the teacher and students		
A place to store Very Own Words		
Folders for children to place samples of their writing		
A place for children to send private messages to each other		

Literacy-Rich Environment for the Rest of the Classroom	Yes	No
The classroom should include literacy materials in all centers. Materials should be changed often to reflect the unit being studied—for example, in the science center there should be books on the unit topic, and in the music area posters of songs related to themes. Play areas should reflect units with themed play and literacy materials. All centers should contain the following:		
Environmental print, such as signs related to themes studied, directions, rules, functional messages		
A calendar		
A current events board		
Appropriate books, magazines, and newspapers		
Writing utensils		
Varied types of paper		
A place for children to display their literacy work		
A place for teachers and children to leave messages for each other		
A word wall		
Print representative of multicultural groups present in the classroom		

Content-area centers present are:

Circle centers

music art science social studies math dramatic play

Thematic Units: Integrating Literacy Learning into Content Areas

Dewey (1966) was largely responsible for bringing the concept of an interdisciplinary approach to teaching to educators' attention. This interdisciplinary approach, or the integrated school day, teaches skills from all content areas, within the context of a topic or theme being studied. The themes that are studied at school derive from children's real-life experiences and topics that they demonstrate an interest in. Learning experiences are socially interactive and process oriented, giving children time to explore and experiment with varied materials. If, for example, a class is studying dinosaurs, the students talk about them, read about them, write about them, do art projects related to dinosaurs, and sing songs related to the theme. In doing so, they learn about dinosaurs and develop skills in other content areas.

Literacy activities can be integrated into the study of themes and in all content areas throughout the school day. Several are described here to demonstrate how strategies to develop literacy that are discussed in previous chapters can be used in other areas of the curriculum (Pappas, Kiefer, & Levstik, 1995).

Objectives for Art Experiences

In early childhood, art experience should offer children the opportunity to:

1. Be exposed to varied art materials.
2. Explore and experiment with these materials.
3. Express feelings through art.
4. Represent experience through visual art forms.
5. Gain an appreciation for varied art forms.
6. Name and discuss content of art: line, color, texture, form, and shape.
7. Experience literacy learning in art activities.

Art experiences allow children to explore and experiment with interesting materials such as finger paints, watercolors, printing, string painting, sponge painting, colored pencils, felt-tip markers, crayons, colored construction paper, tissue paper, foil, transparent wrap, paste, scissors, yarn, fabric scraps, pipe cleaners, clay, and play dough. If children are encouraged to discuss such materials as they use them, language development flourishes. Children immersed in finger painting, for instance, use such words as *mushy, smushy, gushy,* and *squiggle.* Playing with dough or clay elicits the words *pound, squeeze, roll, press,* and *fold.* Watercolors stimulate such comments as "Oooh, it's drippy," "The paint is running down the page like a stream of water," "Look how the colors all run together. The red is making the blue turn purple," and "My picture looks like a rainbow of colors across the sky." The teacher can take the opportunity to make word lists from the language generated in art activities and to encourage the children to share and talk about what they are doing. The words that individual children generate are a source of Very Own Words.

Children are often eager to exhibit their creations. This practice is likely to result in children's asking each other how they made their projects. The resulting description provides an excellent opportunity for literacy development. Children sometimes ask to dictate or write sentences and stories about their artwork, or write about it themselves. Individual works of art on similar subjects can be bound together in books that include captions, titles, or stories. Art activities also can highlight concepts such as the letter *p*, for example, through the use of purple and pink paint, paper, and play dough.

Objectives for Music Experiences

In early childhood music experiences should include:

1. Having intense involvement in and responding to music.
2. Exposure to different forms of music (instruments, singing, types of music) to be able to discriminate among them and develop an appreciation for varied forms.
3. Music experiences that involve listening, singing, moving, playing, and creating.
4. Expressing feelings through music experiences.
5. Experiencing literacy learning in music activities.

Music provides ample means for literacy development. Children find new words in songs, thus increasing vocabulary. Songs emphasize word patterns and syllabic patterns, which should be brought to the children's attention. Songs can be written on charts and sung, the teacher pointing to the individual words as he or she tracks the print from left to right across the page. Picture storybooks adapted from songs, such as *Old MacDonald Had a Farm* (Quackenbush, 1972), provide predictable reading material for young children. Listening to classical music often creates images and is a rich source for descriptive language. Children can create stories about the music, describe their feelings, or describe the sounds of various instruments.

Objectives for Play Experiences

In early childhood, play experiences include providing opportunities for children to:

1. Problem solve.
2. Acquire new understandings.
3. Role-play real-life experiences.
4. Cope with situations that require sharing and cooperating.
5. Develop language and literacy through play.

Dramatic play provides endless possibilities for literacy development through the use of oral and written language and reading. The materials and activities typical of dramatic-play areas stimulate considerable language, and the addition of new props and materials provides the opportunity for continued growth. Dramatic play provides realistic settings and functional reasons for using print. New units in social studies and science trigger opportunities to add print materials that stimulate reading, writing, and oral language. A unit on community helpers—a topic familiar to early childhood teachers—invariably leads to a discussion of fire fighters, police officers, supermarket clerks, doctors, nurses, mail carriers, and office workers. The mention of any of these community helpers is an opportunity to add literacy materials to the dramatic-play area.

Role-playing supermarket, for instance, is aided by the addition of food and detergent containers, a toy cash register, play money, note pads, a telephone and directory, store signs, a schedule of hours, advertisements, and posters for food and other products. Teachers or aides might visit a nearby supermarket to note for the classroom the print that is there, and to pick up outdated signs and posters. Store managers readily give away such materials when they no longer need them. Definitely include, among materials for dramatic play about supermarkets, a bookshelf full of magazines and books "for sale." All these materials help children engage in conversation as they role-play a store manager, clerk, or shopper. They read posters, books, signs, and magazines and write shopping lists, orders, and new signs when they are needed.

Many topics lend themselves to dramatic play and incorporating literacy materials. A study of health-care personnel can lead to the creation of a doctor's office. A waiting room can be set up with magazines for the patients to read and pamphlets about good health. There can be a *No Smoking* sign, a notice containing the doctor's hours, and posters on the wall concerning good health habits. There should be an appointment book for the nurse, a pad for writing appointment reminders for patients to take with them, a pad for writing prescriptions, patient folders containing forms to be filled out, and a patient address and phone book.

When studying transportation, the class can create a travel agency. Here there would be maps, travel posters, pamphlets about places to visit, and tickets to be issued for planes and trains.

Children enjoy role-playing in these situations because the activity includes meaningful experiences. In dramatic play, children are voluntarily participating in reading and writing.

Dramatic play is considered appropriate in preschools and kindergartens; however, we seldom leave time for it in first and second grades or think of it as an area in which learning can take place. In classrooms that integrate content themes into dramatic play with six- to eight-year-olds, extremely sophisticated productions of reading, writing, and oral language result. It is suggested that first- and second-grade teachers incorporate play into their curriculum. As mentioned earlier in this book, technology has made it more acceptable to engage in dramatic play with second and third graders as they search the Internet for train and plane routes when role-play is about travel. Children also can use the Internet to find other information for any role-playing theme featured.

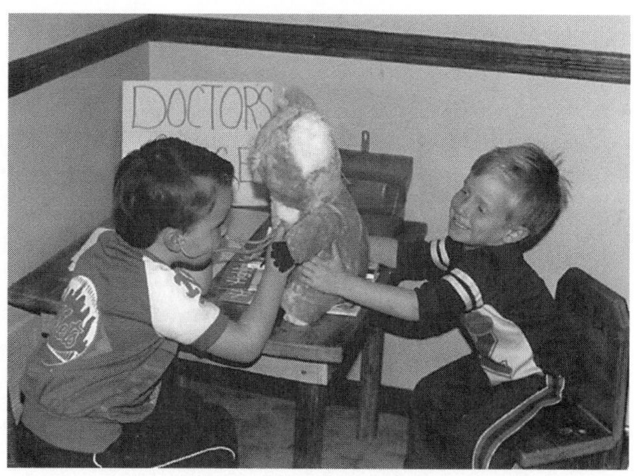

Creative play in the dramatic-play center encourages social interaction, vibrant discussion, and language development.

Objectives for Social Studies and Science Experiences

Social studies and science themes for the most part provide the meaning and function for learning, particularly for literacy learning. Themes provide a reason to read and write about topics of interest. Skills are learned within a context rather than in isolated lessons for skill development.

In early childhood social studies experiences should include:

1. Fostering self-esteem.
2. Learning social skills for functioning, such as sharing, cooperating, and communicating with others.
3. Recognizing and respecting similarities and differences in others.
4. Increasing knowledge of other cultures and ethnic and racial groups.
5. Increasing understanding of the nature of our social world through the study of history, geography, and economics.
6. Using the content of social studies to promote literacy development.

In early childhood science experiences should include activities that involve:

1. Observing, hypothesizing, recording data, summarizing, analyzing, and drawing conclusions.
2. Increasing understanding in
   a. Biological science, the study of living things
   b. Physical science, including the study of
      (1) astronomy—heavenly bodies and their movements
      (2) chemistry—materials found on the earth and the changes that occur in them
      (3) meteorology—weather and air
      (4) physics—the nature of matter and energy
3. Using the content of science to promote literacy development.

Science and social studies are probably the two content areas that provide the greatest opportunities for literacy development. Their contents typically generate enthusiasm, meaning, and a purpose for using literacy strategies. A unit about the farm can lead to oral language development through discussions about farm work, different types of farms, and farm animals. Word lists of farm animals, crops, and jobs on the farm can be made. Pictures of farm scenes, a trip to a farm, or a visit by a farmer generates discussion, reading, and writing. To encourage positive attitudes toward books, the teacher can carefully select good pieces of children's literature about farms to read to the class. The *Petunia* series (Duvoisin, 1950) deals with a delightful goose who lives on a farm. *The Little Red Hen* (Galdone, 1973), *The Tale of Peter Rabbit* (Potter, 1902), *The Little Farm* (Lenski, 1965), and *Charlie Needs a Clock* (dePaola, 1973) are just a few examples of good children's literature that relate to the farm. The teacher should select some international trade books as well. These books will motivate youngsters to pick up the books on their own, retell them, role-play them, and share them with each other. A farm visit can be retold in stories or drawings bound into class books, recaptured in a language experience chart, or reflected in Very Own Words. The teacher can associate letters and sounds in farm words with those in children's names or in environmental print.

Science experiments and food preparation offer opportunities for more discussion, generation of interesting word lists, and reading and writing of recipes.

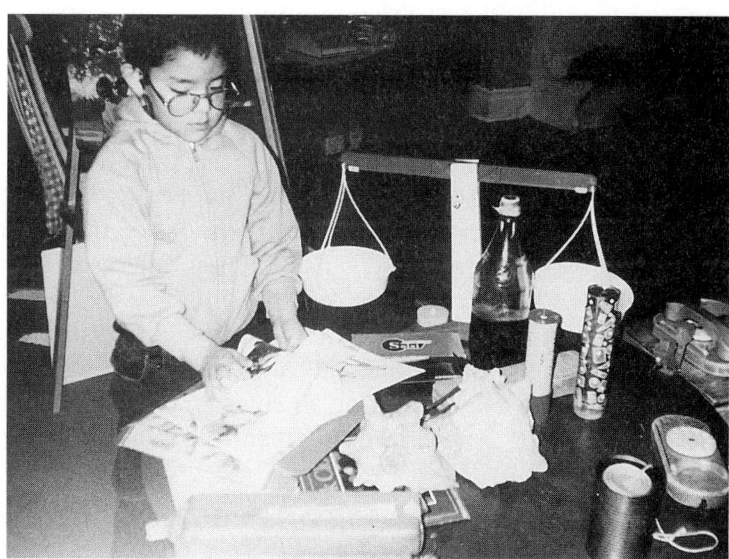
A science theme with experiments and interesting materials to investigate integrates literacy instruction into content-area instruction.

The block center, too, can stimulate literacy activities. For instance, when introducing a unit on transportation, the teacher can add toy trucks, trains, cars, boats, and airplanes to the block corner, along with travel tickets, luggage and freight tags, maps, travel guides, tour brochures, travel posters, and signs common to airports, train stations, and bus depots, such as gate numbers, names of carriers, and arrival and departure signs.

Objectives for Mathematics Experiences

Early childhood mathematics activities should involve:

1. Many opportunities to handle and deal with mathematical materials and ideas.
2. Movement from dependence on the concrete to abstract ideas.
3. Opportunities to classify, compare, seriate, measure, graph, count, identify, and write numbers and perform operations on numbers.
4. Using mathematical vocabulary.
5. Using mathematics to promote literacy development.

In all the other content areas, a teacher can feel confident that he or she is providing a fairly adequate program of study through the themed units used in social studies and science that incorporate music, art, play, and literacy development in early childhood. Math, however, is a specialized area that needs more attention than can be dealt with in a content-area unit. Still, there are many activities that bring meaning to mathematics through unit topics and that include literacy as well. Stories related to numbers can be read; children can count cookies for snack time to make sure there are enough for the class; and children can be in charge of collecting and counting milk money. When studying weather, a chart of daily temperatures can be graphed to observe the variability from day to day.

When literacy skills are developed in an integrated fashion, as in practices and approaches described here, children see purposes and reasons for becoming literate. When we teach literacy skills that do not reflect real-life experience and lack content, children are not likely to perceive their usefulness. When skills are taught in an integrated, interdisciplinary fashion, children ask for the skills they need in order to participate fully in experiences that interest them during their work and play at school and at home (Manning, Manning, & Long, 1994; Walmsley, 1994). During a unit on transportation in a kindergarten class of my own, children asked for even more materials than I had already made available in the several centers. Books on transportation led to requests for books on space travel and various maps of places not in the center. Many children added to their Very Own Words. Children asked for help preparing signs representing places they wanted to visit and highway signs indicating mileage to various destinations. Some dictated travel directions. The need for literacy information was created by preparing an environment that reflected interesting, real-life experiences. In such an environment, learning is to a great extent self-generated.

Preparing a Thematic Unit

Unit themes can be selected by the teacher and the children. Giving students choices concerning what they will learn is important. When a topic is selected, allow the children to brainstorm what they would like to know about. You might begin by suggesting categories to focus on and letting them fill in subheadings (Rand, 1994). In preparation for a unit on nutrition, I asked a class of kindergarten children to help decide what they might like to learn. I used a web to chart their ideas and started it for them with nutrition as the theme and four categories to focus on: Why is food important? What foods are good for you? Where do we get food from? and How are different foods prepared to eat? The web in Figure 10.4 illustrates the children's responses and the content to be studied for the unit.

In planning a unit, the teacher needs to include activities in all content areas. The map in Figure 10.5 will help generate activities related to the unit topic and include each content area. From this map the teacher can select activities to schedule throughout the school day. Following is a mini unit written by Ms. Ngai, a first-grade teacher. As you will see, she integrates activities throughout the content areas as she focuses on her theme.

Thematic Instruction: Good Food

An interesting theme can make learning come alive for children. With food as our theme, and popcorn as our week-long focus, things were really "popping" in our first-grade classroom! Here are some exciting ways to make learning about popcorn fun, while tying in content-area instruction.

Figure 10.4

Curriculum Web for a Thematic Unit on Nutrition

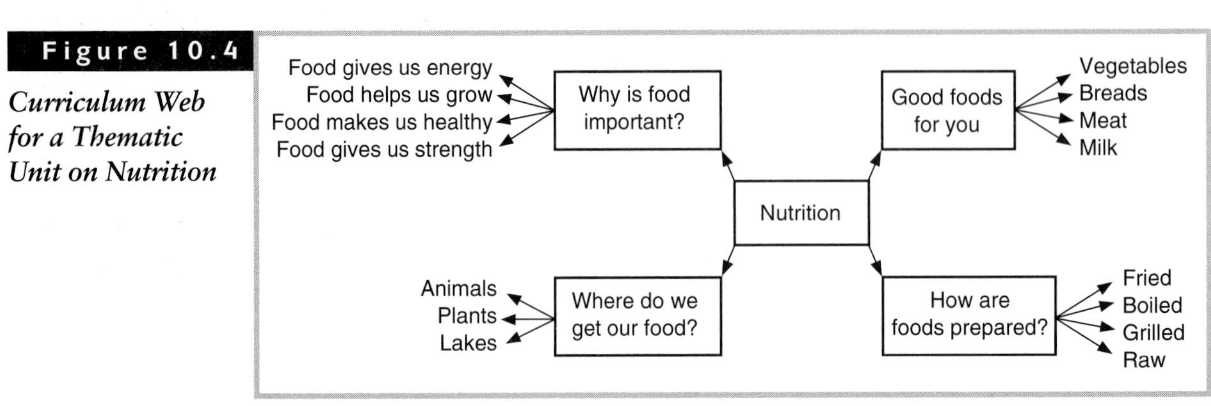

Figure 10.5

Daily Schedule Planning Sheet to Integrate a Theme throughout the Curriculum

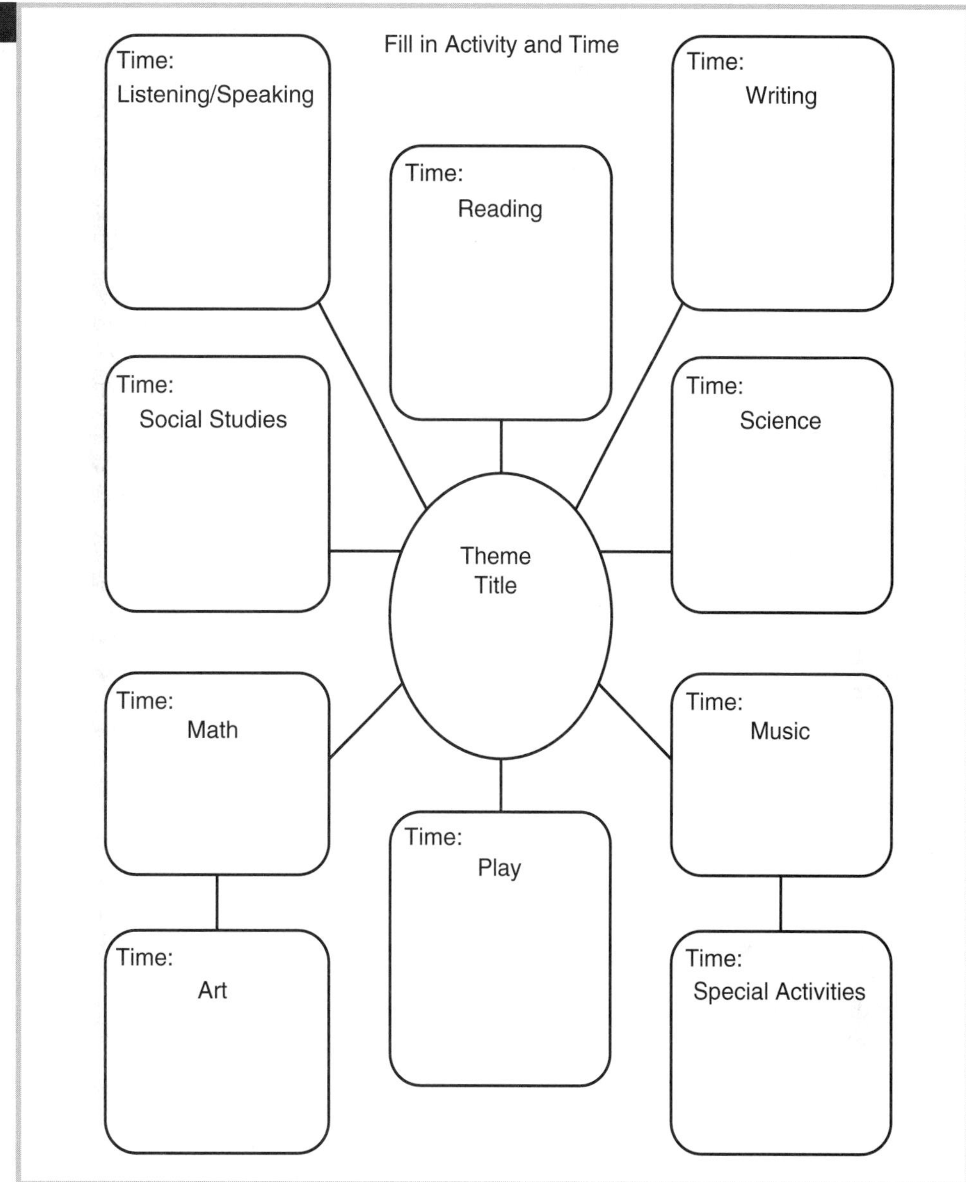

The Friday Before: We planted popcorn kernels in baking tins lined with paper towels. We spread popcorn in the pans, watered the seeds, and covered the pans with plastic wrap. In a few days, the roots began to sprout (*science*).

Monday: Using a log, we recorded the growth of the seedlings over the weekend. We read *The Popcorn Book* by Tomie dePaola. We discussed that the Native Americans introduced popcorn to the colonists. We used the compound word "popcorn" to trigger a list of other food compound words, such as cupcake and milkshake, which we wrote on a chart. Anytime a student thought of or came across a compound word, he or she would write it down on the chart. By the end of the week, the chart paper was full *(science, language arts, social studies).*

Tuesday: We set up an experiment chart for making popcorn. We asked ourselves, "What do I want to find out?" (How does a corn kernel change to popcorn?) "What do I think will happen?" "How will I find out?" "What actually happened?" and "What did I learn?" We answered the first two questions. We used an air popper to pop the corn and then completed the experiment chart, answering the remaining questions. We also enjoyed the popcorn for our *snack*. We planted our seedlings in paper cups filled with soil *(science)*.

Wednesday: We made more popcorn to create an estimation lesson for math. Each child grabbed a handful of popcorn from a large bowl and guessed how many kernels were in his or her hand. After, we used a simple record sheet to log estimations. We then counted to find the actual number. We tried it a second time to see if we arrived at a more accurate estimation *(mathematics)*.

Thursday: One of the ways the Native Americans popped corn was to put an ear of corn on a stick and hold it over a fire until the kernels popped. Another way was to throw kernels into the fire until they popped out all over the place. Still another way was to use clay pots filled with hot sand, in which the kernels were mixed until they eventually popped to the top of the pot. We illustrated the method we thought was the best, and wrote a few sentences as to why we felt that way. We discussed how the Native Americans made necklaces out of popcorn. Using the popcorn from Wednesday, we gave it a try. We used large, blunt needles and heavy thread and created necklaces *(writing, art, social studies)*.

Friday: As a culminating lesson, we had parent volunteers come into our classroom to make popcorn balls. We checked for any growth of our corn plants, and recorded the information in our science logs *(science, cooking)*.

See Appendix D for a complete integrated language arts unit entitled "Healthy Bodies, Healthy Minds" for use in the classroom.

Organizing Instruction to Meet Individual Needs: Guided Reading and Center Activities

There are a variety of strategies for organizing instruction. Children can be taught as a whole class, in small groups, and individually. Children can be grouped homogeneously or heterogeneously by ability, needs, interests, or they can be divided into peer groups for cooperative learning. The use of a variety of organizational strategies is important because some children benefit more in one setting than in another. The use of several different grouping schemes within the same classroom also tends to eliminate the stigmas attached to a single grouping system. Variable grouping makes it likely that children will interact with all others in one group or another.

Whole-Group, Small-Group, and One-to-One Learning Settings

Whole-group instruction is not appropriate until children are almost three years old. Younger children lack the ability to concentrate or to sit in a large-group setting and listen for any period of time. Whole-group lessons, sometimes referred to as shared experiences, are appropriate when information needs to be introduced to all the children and the presentation can be understood by all. In early childhood literacy development, storybook readings by an adult, group singing, class discussions, and brainstorming sessions are appropriate whole-group activities.

Small groups are effective when close interaction with children is necessary for explicit instruction and assessment, as with guided reading and writing instruction. Small groups also are used for cooperative projects with children working independent of the teacher. Teachers should use many types of small-group formations, such as guided reading groups for explicit instruction of skills, groups based on friendships or interests, and independent reading and writing groups. In the description of the language arts block at the end of this chapter, many types of grouping configurations are included. Various group formations is for children to have experiences working with many others, and to avoid the stigma attached to being associated with only one group. In Chapter 2, in which the pros and cons of grouping are discussed, the necessity for participation in many groups and for children's group placement to change from time to time is clear.

Working with children on a one-to-one basis and allowing them to work independently are forms of *individualized instruction.* Although children need to work cooperatively with peers and adults, they also need to problem solve and accomplish tasks on their own. One-to-one instruction provides an opportunity for the teacher to offer personal attention to a child and to learn much about a child. When a teacher works with a child alone, he or she can take running records for assessment and do story retelling instruction and assessment. Children can get help with specific skills they are having difficulty with, and teachers can take story dictations or discuss a new piece of the child's writing.

I learned the value of meeting children one-to-one early in my teaching career. A mother of a child in my class told me that he liked to be absent from school. I was upset by the comment, assuming that her son was unhappy in my class. The mother said that her son liked being absent because when he returned to school he was given "private time with the teacher." I had made a practice of meeting with absentees on their return to school to share work we had accomplished when they were absent. I realized than that children enjoy time alone with their teacher. And, through private conferences, I learned so much about the instructional needs of my children, their emotional needs, and their interests.

Whole-group and small-group settings allow teachers to vary instructional presentation.

During one-to-one instruction, the teacher does frequent running records to determine a child's strengths, needs, and reading level.

Selecting Children for Groups

With such a variety of group formations, many teachers ask, "How do I select children for each type of group?" Children can make decisions about participating in some groups such as those based on friendship and interest. Guided reading and writing groups are selected by the teacher because the instruction in these groups is based on need and instructional level, or ability.

Many pieces of information should be used to determine students' needs and abilities for guided reading and writing group selection. In this book I have discussed several types of assessment that should form a composite picture of the child to help determine group placement. One of the most important pieces of information is teacher judgment. Other types of assessment that will help in group placement include the following:

- Running Records to determine text reading level, types of strengths and weaknesses in word analysis, fluency, and self-monitoring
- Letter-recognition tests
- High-frequency word tests
- Comprehension evaluation
- Standardized test scores

Alternate rank ordering is another way to assign children to groups. This method is mainly based on teacher judgement. List all the children in your class with the child you rank as having the highest literacy ability at the top and the others following to the last child who you rank with the lowest ability. To assign groups, select the top and the bottom child to start two different groups. Place the next child from the top into the group with the top child, and place the next child from the bottom into the group with the child with the lowest ability. Continue this procedure, each time asking yourself if these children are alike enough to be in the same group. When the answer to that question is no, then start a new group. You should end up with four to six groups for your class with about five children per group. After several meetings, if the groups do not seem to be right for certain children, change their placement. As children are evaluated on a regular basis, their grouping placement could change.

Managing Small-Group Instruction during Guided Reading

In Chapter 6, I discussed organizing and managing independent periods for reading and writing, or literacy center time. The purpose of that small-group work is for children to learn to work independent of the teacher and in cooperative social settings with peers. During literacy center time children engage in self-selected independent reading and writing activities and can participate in active hands-on activities. The teacher acts as a facilitator by answering questions and keeping children on task if necessary. During guided reading and writing, the teacher is occupied with small-group instruction and cannot be disturbed, therefore the children not in the guided reading lesson need to know exactly what to do, when to do it, and where. The management plan in Chapter 6 for independent work is

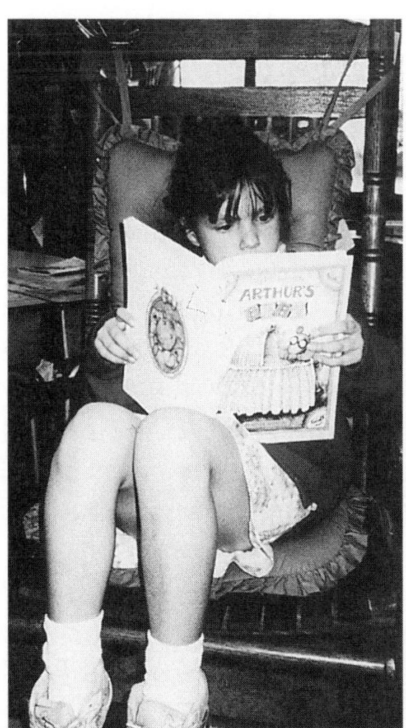

Children work independently and in small groups in productive activities.

a good model for organizing and managing activity choices and rotation systems for working in independent centers to reinforce skills. However, it needs some modifications when children are being instructed in guided reading groups. A visit to Ms. Shea's second-grade classroom provides a look at the organization of independent work to suit the guided reading lesson format.

The activities that Ms. Shea models for her class for independent work are often skill and theme related. In the beginning of the school year, she spends time introducing children to the centers in the room and the types of activities they include. She has her class practice working on the different activities. At this time, Ms. Shea does not work with small groups during independent work; rather, she helps the children so that they eventually will be able to work independently.

The children are assigned some tasks and can select others to do. The tasks engage the children in reading and writing that will help with skill development. Ms. Shea assigns activities 1, 2, 3, and 4 (listed following) to all children. They can select to do activities 5 or 6 (also following) after they finish the required tasks.

1. For *partner reading*, children pair off and read the same book together. They also may read separate books and then tell each other about the story they read. Because the class is studying animals, children are to select books from the open-faced bookshelves that include stories and expository texts about animals. Discussion about what is read is encouraged. Each child must fill out an index card with the name of the book read and one sentence about the story.
2. *The writing activity* requires the children to rewrite the story called *Ask Mr. Bear* that Ms. Shea read at the morning meeting. In their rewritings, children are to include story elements discussed, such as setting, theme, plot episodes, and the resolution. They may consult copies of the book in the classroom if necessary. Each day there is a different writing activity related to the story read.
3. For the *working with words* activity, the children are to find words around the room that have the ***sh*** and ***ch*** digraph in them. They classify these words by writing them on a sheet of paper under appropriate digraph headings. Children also can look through books to find these digraphs.
4. *The listening center* has taped stories about animals. For each story, there is a sheet of paper with a question to answer about the story. Two titles on tape are *Is Your Mama a Lama?* (Kellogg, 1989) and *Arthur's Pet Business* (Brown, 1990).
5. *The art center* has magazines with many photos of animals that children can use to create animal collages.
6. *The computer center* includes software with math and literacy activities.

Ms. Shea has an organizational chart that she uses for assigning children to centers. The rotations occur in coordination with the groups that she meets with for small-group instruction. If children finish before group rotations, they can start one of the optional activities or go on to the next task if there is space at the center. There is a basket for completed work, and every center has sign-in sheets and requires a finished product to be handed in.

In the beginning of the school year, some teachers start center time in a structured fashion. They assign the groups and tasks. As children learn to function independently, they are given opportunities for decision making and select groups to work with or tasks to accomplish.

The management of center time is crucial for its success. Students must know their choices, the activities in which to participate, the rules that guide participation concerning the selection of materials, and what is to happen in groups or when working alone. Children can help generate the guidelines and rules for working independently. Figure 6.3 in Chapter 6 lists rules for children to follow when working independently. Some of the rules that are important for independent work during guided reading are as follows:

Rules for Using Materials and Completing Work

- Do all mandatory tasks before you do the optional tasks.
- Speak in soft voices; people are working.
- Put materials back in their place.
- Take care of the materials so they are in good condition for others.
- Put your completed work in a designated place.
- Record completed work on contract form or in a log.
- If you have questions, use the "Ask Three and then Me," rule. Seek help from other students designated as helpers before asking the teacher when she is in a guided reading group.

Rules for Cooperating and Collaborating

- Share materials in collaborative activities.
- Take turns.
- Listen to your friends when they talk.
- Offer help to others you are working with if they need it.
- When you complete an activity, ask yourself if you were helpful to others, and if you shared materials.

Some teachers provide a list of activities to do during guided reading, as shown in Figure 10.6. This list may indicate that the first few activities are mandatory and the others are optional, if the children have time. Some teachers

Figure 10.6

Things to Do during Guided Reading

Starred activities are done first and are the mandatory activities.

Mandatory Activities*

- Read your guided reading book for review.
- Practice any skills your teacher indicated you need to work on.
- Write an informational piece about hibernating animals, based on the book read during the morning meeting. Include your new high-frequency words in your expository writing.
- Select the material modeled by the teacher from the word-study center that will enable you to practice making words by blending the initial consonants with ending phonograms.
- Listen to the winter story on the headsets and answer the questions posed on a sheet of paper provided.

Optional Activities

- Tell a felt story with the story characters and felt-board.
- Create a roll-story for a book related to the theme being studied.
- Make a winter collage at the art center.

allow children to go from one activity to the next listed on the chart. With this system, children must sign in at a center on a form provided (see Figure 10.7). They can use the center only if there is an empty chair for them, which avoids crowding. When a child finishes an activity, he or she places the product in a designated spot. Accountability for independent work is a necessity. In addition, the child reports the activities completed on his contract (see Figure 10.8 for a student contract agreement and Figure 6.7 in chapter 6 for a student log for readers and nonreaders).

Another way to designate independent work is through the use of a *center chart*. There are many variations on this type of system. The center chart

Figure 10.7

Center Sign-In Sheet

Listening Center

Class List Date: 11/18	Write Your Name Here:
1. Sarah Anders	
2. Barry Duke	
3. Kathleen Carin	
4. Narain Evat	
5. James Gala	
6. Megan Hand	
7. Jovaon Harris	
8. Christine Kim	
9. Dylan Kotter	
10. Kathryn Levin	
11. Irene Lopez	
12. John McNeal	
13. Andrea Penn	
14. Zachary Pierce	
15. Alyx Sax	
16. Gina-Marie Teal	
17. Micah Urani	
18. Max Valley	
19. Brandon Wimbush	

Figure 10.8

Contract Activities

Contract

Name ______________________ **Date** ______________

Things to Do	Specific Activity	Done
	Reading	
	Writing	
	Oral Language	
	Language Arts Manipulatives	
	Listening Station	
	Math Manipulatives 1+4-2	
	Other Activities:	

in Figure 10.9 is an adaptation of the *Work Board* described by Fountas and Pinnell (1996). It designates several choices for three or four different heterogeneously grouped children. The chart is made of tagboard and has a row of figures representing center activities. At the top of each row is a place to attach names of children. The figures are moveable as are the name cards. They can be attached to the chart with velcro, or the chart can have several pockets in it.

Some teachers prefer a more structured approach to assigning independent work, especially early in the school year. A teacher may assign children to the centers then have them rotate from one to the next as the teacher rotates guided reading groups he or she works with. For example, Mrs. Shea's second graders sit in groups of four desks pushed together, which she calls pods. These children are heterogeneously grouped and move together from one center activity to another, or one activity to another as listed on the center chart. From time to time, Mrs. Shea will change the pod groups so children have the opportunity to work with many different others. The groups of children often give themselves names. When Mrs. Shea meets with her first guided reading group, the other children have designated center assignments. When the first guided reading lesson ends, all children move to the next center area with their group to work on a new project. Later in the school year, the children are allowed to select their activities and to do them in whatever order they wish. As they complete one activity, they immediately move to the next.

Figure 10.9 *Center Chart*

Janine, Jen, Keith, Kelly, Rumon	Holly, Michael, Ben, Mat, Alexis	Darren, Tisha, Ivory, Sam, Matt	Sarah, Tim, Yassin, Josh, Kyle
Buddy Reading 	Listening Station	Oral Language	Journal Writing
Journal Writing 	Computer Center 	Word-Study Manipulatives 	Buddy Reading 
Oral Language 	Word-Study Manipulatives 	Buddy Reading 	Listening Station 
Word-Study Manipulatives 	Buddy Reading  	Journal Writing 	Computer Center 
Listening Station 	Oral Language 	Computer Center 	Word-Study Manipulatives 
Computer Center 	Journal Writing 	Listening Station 	Oral Language 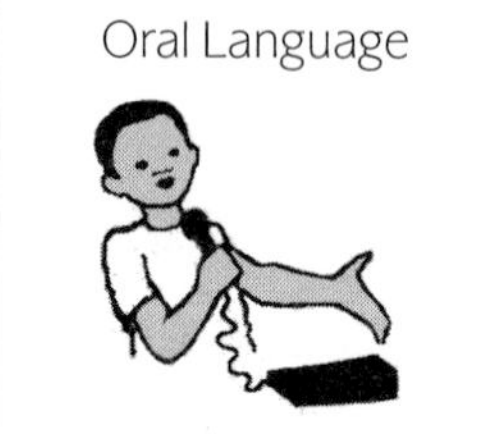

All figures and name cards are removable and can be changed around.

Source: Adapted by permission of Irene Fountas and Gay Su Pinnell: *Guided Reading: Good First Teaching for All Children* (Heinemann, A division of Reed Elsevier, Inc., Portsmouth, NH, 1996).

The teacher arranges her guided reading groups based on need and selects books for them to read based on their level of reading.

Using a Guided Reading Lesson

The guided reading lesson was outlined in Chapter 5. Be sure to refer to it to understand the steps involved. It is important to note that during the guided reading lesson the teacher not only instructs but determines children's strengths and needs. As mentioned, each time there is a guided reading lesson, one child sits next to the teacher for him or her to concentrate on. The teacher can take a running record as the child reads along with the group. Other types of assessment that should be collected and stored in a child's portfolio are frequent writing samples and observation notes about reading behaviors. Teachers should also use the checklists provided in each chapter in this book that deal with different aspects of literacy development. To help you further understand the use of guided reading groups, following is a discussion and description of guided reading in Mrs. Keefe's first-grade classroom.

Although grouping practices based on need and ability are controversial, Mrs. Keefe believes it is the only way she can learn what individual children know and what they need to learn in order to design her instruction. She has organized the class into five groups of four to five children who have similar reading needs, are capable of similar reading skills, and are reading at about the same level. Children frequently move from group to group based on Mrs. Keefe's ongoing assessment of their progress. She meets with each group four to five

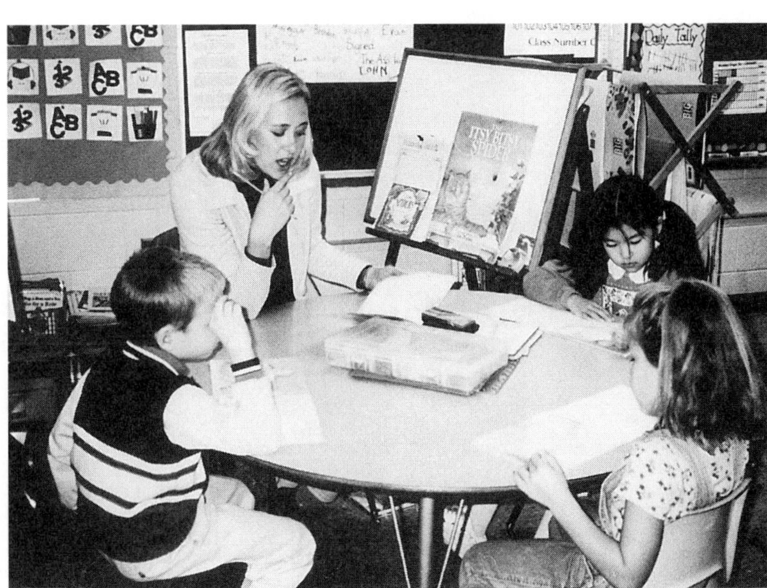

Teachers meet with guided reading groups three to five times a week for direct instruction of skills.

times a week for about 20 minutes. A typical lesson includes (1) reading something familiar for fluency and success, (2) working on a skill involving word analysis, (3) introducing a new book and the decoding or comprehension skills associated with it, (4) reading the new book with the support of the teacher and peers, (5) discussing the story, and (6) doing a writing activity. Mrs. Keefe assesses one or two children's reading development during each reading group by taking a running record of their oral reading and recording errors to determine skill needs and by listening to children's oral retellings of stories to check comprehension.

During a typical day, first Mrs. Keefe engages her children with independent work. When students are working well on their own, she calls on her first group for guided reading instruction. She begins her small-group reading lesson with a familiar text that each child has in his or her baggie. She calls this "a book in a bag," and every day the children bring it to reading group. She uses a familiar text for fluency, to create a feeling of success. The children enjoy the ease with which they can read this old friend.

Next, Mrs. Keefe engages the children in a minilesson, helping them with a skill they need to learn. She wants the children to use the text along with phonic clues to decode unknown words. She writes a sentence on a small white slate, leaving one word blank. She asks the children to predict what word might make sense in the blank. She then asks them to write the word onto their white boards. Mrs. Keefe has prepared a practice sheet with three more sentences that have words missing but that include the first letter of each missing word. She asks the children to work in pairs to figure out the missing words.

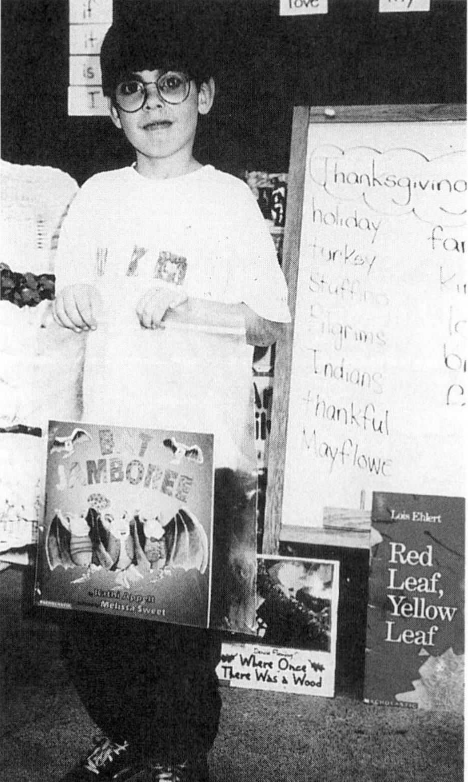

Children read from books at their reading level in guided reading groups. The books are stored in plastic baggies that are often referred to as a "book in a bag."

"Book boxes," one per child, are for storing guided reading materials such as children's "book in a bag."

At this time, a new book about animals is introduced from a set of leveled books selected for the reading ability of the children with whom Mrs. Keefe is working. She introduces some new vocabulary words on 3 x 5 cards. As the children recite the words, she places them in a pocket chart. The children copy the words on their white slates. Mrs. Keefe also has prepared sentence strips that come from the text of the new book, with the new vocabulary words left out. She places the sentence strips in the pocket chart, and the children fill in the blanks with the correct vocabulary word card.

For the first reading of the new book, Mrs. Keefe has the entire group chant the book with her. Following the first reading, she invites the children to read the book independently. Because these are beginning readers, they are to read aloud but in soft voices. She selects a focus child for the day for whom she takes a running record. Tomorrow when she meets with this group again, another child will sit by her side to be assessed.

After the second reading, the children and teacher discuss the story. Mrs. Keefe asks questions that relate to details in the text, and questions that require students to connect the story to circumstances in their own life.

As the lesson ends, Mrs. Keefe writes a short note to all the children's parents about their progress, what they were learning, what they needed help with,

Boxes of books leveled for difficulty are available for children to read and for use during guided reading lessons.

and what their homework is. Homework always requires the reading of the new book with a parent and the parent's signature. When the group finishes its work for the day, all members put their books in their plastic baggies with their homework note. They place their materials in their own box, which sits on the window sill, until it is time to go home.

Mrs. Keefe then meets with another group using books selected for their reading instructional level and carries out an appropriate lesson for them. She meets with three other groups until lunchtime.

The discussion concerning the instruction in these first and second grades includes practices suggested in two documents that have made an important impact on early literacy instruction. Both documents were edited by Snow, Burns, and Guffin. One is entitled *Preventing Reading Difficulties in Young Children* (1988) and the other *Starting Out Right: A Guide to Promoting Children's Reading Success* (1999).

Organizing and Managing Literacy Instruction: Daily Schedules

Scheduling the daily routine in nursery school, kindergarten, first, second, and third grade must take into account the social, emotional, physical, and intellectual levels of the children. It must also reflect the best from theorists' models of early childhood education, including those of Piaget, Froebel, Dewey, Montessori, the behaviorists, and Vygotsky. The environment should be prepared so that learning can take place naturally, but with the guidance and instruction that will help children achieve their fullest potential.

Young children cannot sit for long periods so their schedule needs to vary. Whole-class lessons that require sitting and listening must be few and short. Children need large blocks of time for exploring environments. They need play situations, manipulative materials, learning centers, and outdoor areas. Activities that require sitting and listening need to be followed by ones that allow movement. Quiet times must be followed by noisier times. To nurture literacy, the teacher must allow for rich literacy experiences throughout the day, experiences in using and enjoying language in all its forms and functions.

In scheduling the school day, be sure to include *whole-class, small-group,* and *one-to-one* settings for learning. There need to be *teacher-directed* experiences and activities that children participate in *independently.* Children should have opportunities for *oral reading* and *silent reading* from books and from their own writing. They need to have time for *shared reading* experiences and *shared writing* experiences. Time should be set aside for periods of *guided reading* and *guided writing,* as well as *reading and writing independently.* Children should have the opportunity to *read and write collaboratively* with peers and to *perform* in formal and informal settings the products of their reading and writing. Figure 10.10 provides a self-analysis form concerning the organization of instruction. The form provides space for recording lessons taught. It also asks that lessons be identified as whole-group, small-group, or one-to-one settings, and as teacher-directed or independent. There is a place to record the materials used in the lesson, and where the activity occurred in the classroom. If you record this information for a few days, it will help you analyze the teaching strategies you are using and identify those that you may need to incorporate.

Figure 10.10 *Evaluation Strategies and Organization of Instruction*

Planning Your School Day: Theme Topic ___________________

(TD-Teacher Directed, IN-Independent Activity, WG-Whole Group, SG-Small Group, 1 to 1)

CHANGE TIME SLOTS WHEN USING LONGER OR SHORTER PERIODS OF TIME

9:00 to 9:30 Activity and Content Area: Materials Used: Where Activity Takes Place: TD or IN: WG, SG, 1-to-1:	**9:30 to 10:30** Activity and Content Area: Materials: Where: TD or IN: WG, SG, 1-to-1:
10:30 to 11:30 Activity and Content Area: Materials: Where: TD or IN: WG, SG, 1-to-1:	**11:30 to 12:30** Activity and Content Area: Materials: Where: TD or IN: WG, SG, 1-to-1:
Lunch 12:30 to 1:30	
1:30 to 2:30 Activity and Content Area: Materials: Where: TD or IN: WG, SG, 1-to-1:	**2:30 to 3:00** Activity and Content Area: Materials: Where: TD or IN: WG, SG, 1-to-1:

The sample schedules that follow illustrate where and when specific opportunities to promote literacy can occur. The schedules provide a routine or structure for the day that seems to make children comfortable. Keep in mind there is no one schedule for all classrooms. These are models with content, activities, and organization that should be included. The schedules and descriptions are found in the section, *An Idea for the Classroom form the Classroom* and are presented in the following order:

1. Language program for kindergarten through third grade
2. Full-day preschool and kindergarten
3. Half-day preschool and kindergarten
4. Day-care centers for infants and toddlers.

An Idea for the Classroom from the Classroom

Language Program for Kindergarten through Third Grade

The following is a description of a model for organizing and managing an early literacy language arts block beginning in kindergarten, from a study of exemplary first-grade teachers from the Center for English Language Arts and Achievement at the State University of New York at Albany (Morrow & Asbury, 1999). The teachers in the study were identified by their supervisors as exemplary based on observation of their teaching. The exemplary nature of their teaching also was confirmed by other teachers, parents, students, and the children's scores on literacy tests. The teacher in the description (given the pseudonym Ms. Asbury) is a composite of many we observed when trying to discover a model for exemplary teaching. This description includes many theories and strategies discussed throughout the book.

8:30–9:00: As soon as the children entered Ms. Asbury's class, they began to engage in literacy activities. They located their name and photograph on the attendance chart and turned the picture face up to indicate their attendance. Children who were buying lunch signed their names under their choices on the lunch chart. The children then focused their attention on the daily jobs chart, on which Ms. Asbury changed the children's names every day after school. Those with morning jobs quickly got busy. Damien watered the plants while Angel fed the rabbit. Patty and Ashley worked together to write the date on the calendar and complete the days of the week charts. Kelly was responsible for completing the weather graph and asked Dalton to help her. Stephanie and Justin were the reporters whose job it was to write one or two sentences of daily news, such as what was going to happen during the school day.

The children who were not assigned morning jobs were given a choice of three activities in which they could engage: journal writing, independent or buddy reading, or solving the daily word problem. Angelica chose to write about her upcoming sleepover. Darious finished his journal entry and began reading a book about winter, which was the content-area theme being studied. As they solved the day's theme-based word problem, David and Joel chorused, "Yes!" At 8:55 Ms. Asbury clapped a rhythm that indicated to the students they had five minutes to clean up and join her on the rug for their morning meeting.

9:00–9:40: During the whole-group morning meeting, math and language concepts were integrated in a discussion around the calendar and the weather. The children counted how many days had passed and how many days remained in January. They wrote the date in tallies and represented it in popsicle sticks grouped in tens and ones. Discussion about the calendar was rich with new words learned in the winter thematic unit. The two daily reporters read their news aloud.

Ms. Asbury then began to write a theme-related morning message containing news about an upcoming trip to the ice skating rink. She modeled conventions of print and good penmanship and punctuated her writing with explanations about how print works. Because she was working on punctuation with her students, she included a question and an exclamatory sentence in her message. This prompted discussion and explanation of the question mark and the exclamation point and their appropriate use.

After the message was written and read, Ms. Asbury focused the children's attention to the print by asking them if there was anything in the message they noticed and wanted to point out to the class. The *sh* digraph was a "chunk" they had discussed. David said he noticed the *sh* in "shivers" and circled it in the message. Shanaya noticed the word "ink" in the word "rink." Ms. Asbury took the opportunity to reinforce looking for a little word you know inside of an unknown word as being an excellent strategy to use when reading. She asked the children to see if "rink" was written on their word wall under the "ink" chunk. Shanaya offered to write it on the chart along with an illustration.

Next, two children shared things brought from home with the class. In the biweekly newsletter, Ms. Asbury had explained to the parents that the children were learning about winter. She asked them to help the children choose something related to winter to bring to school and to write three clues about what they chose. The item and the clues were carried to school in a paper bag marked "secret" and "keep out." Each child removed the clues from their bag, being careful not to expose the item they brought. As they read aloud each clue, they called on a classmate to guess the secret item.

Ms. Asbury then read a theme-related piece of children's literature, *The Wild Toboggan Ride* (Reid & Fernandes, 1992), about the last toboggan ride of the day, which becomes a zany adventure for a little boy, his Grandpa, and some surprised toboggan riders. She chose this text because of its sequenced plot episodes and repeated language patterns. Before reading the story, she initiated a discussion about riding down a snow-covered hill. The children brainstormed ways to go down a snowy hill as Ms. Asbury listed their ideas. Using the cover illustration, she then explained a toboggan was a type of sled. The word *toboggan* was added to the posted winter words list.

Next, Ms. Asbury used a directed listening and thinking activity format. She set a purpose for reading by asking the children to listen while she read in order to learn who rides on the toboggan and why the ride is "wild." While reading aloud, she encouraged the children to join in by reading the repeated words and phrases.

After the story, the class talked about who rode on the toboggan and how they became involved in the ride down the hill. As the characters in the story were mentioned, Ms. Asbury wrote what the children said about their role in the story onto sentence strips. She then asked the children to read the strips and put them in the order in which they happened. Then she introduced the words "first," "next," and "last" as a means to express sequence in a story. She explained that the children would be writing about a time they went sledding or played in the snow. She showed the children a graphic organizer or story map they could use to help them sequence their own stories. The story map followed the model of the sentence strip activity. Copies of the map were placed in the writing center for the children's use when writing their own story response.

9:40–9:50: After engaging in shared reading and writing experiences, Ms. Asbury began what she called her Reading Workshop. She explained and modeled center activities for the children to participate in while she met with small groups for guided reading instruction. The following activities were available to the children during Reading Workshop:

Reading Alone or Buddy Reading. Each child had a small basket containing books that were on the child's independent reading level. Books read during guided reading groups were placed in the basket along with self-selected texts from the classroom library. Because theme-related books were featured in the class library and in classroom activities, many children were reading books about winter.

Writing Center. In the writing center, children wrote their responses to the shared book reading of *The Wild Toboggan Ride*. The graphic organizers that were previously modeled were in the center to help the children sequence their stories. The children collaborated with a partner while writing. They conferenced after completing the organizer to check if their stories were clearly sequenced and if their use of sequencing words was appropriate.

Listening Center. In this center, the children listened on headsets to tape-recorded stories. Ms. Asbury had placed several theme-based books of assorted genres in this area. Titles included *The Hat* (Brett, 1997), *Rabbit's Wish For Snow: A Native American Legend* (Tchin, 1997), *When Winter Comes* (Maass, 1993), and *Manatee Winter* (Zoehfeld, 1994). She also had made available two tape recorders for the students to record and listen to their own reading of favorite stories and poems. She found this to be a motivating way for the children to develop fluency and expression.

Word Study. A copy of the winter words list was kept in his area. Today, Ms. Asbury asked the children to choose a word from the list and, using letter tiles, see how many new words they could make from the letters of the selected word. They were to write their new words on a recording sheet. Completed recording sheets were placed in a marked folder. Recording sheets "still in progress" were placed in another folder for later use.

Computer Center. Two computers were used throughout the day. This morning, two children were copying winter poems, which had been learned earlier that week. Ms. Asbury frequently used poems along with children's books in her themed literacy instruction. She found poetry to be a rich context for teaching word chunks, high-frequency words, phonics, and rhyming. She also highly valued the joy of poetry. Many of the children had started their own "Favorite Poems" books. They often used the computers to write and illustrate the poems they wanted to include in their collections.

Science Center. Ms. Asbury was planning to conduct an experiment with the class later in the day. The children would be timing how long it took different frozen items to melt. She wanted the children to think about, write, and explain their estimations before carrying out the experiment. A recording sheet was provided. Their predictions would be tallied and graphed prior to the experiment and confirmed and discussed after the experiment.

Art Center. Materials for making puppets were available to the children in this area. Ms. Asbury had chosen three winter stories with well-defined, sequenced plot episodes for use during shared reading: *The Wild Toboggan Ride* (Reid & Fernandes, 1992), *Do Like Kyla* (Johnson, 1990), and *The Mitten* (Brett, 1989). The children selected characters from the stories to make as puppets, which could be used in retellings of the stories. The class was going to work on the puppet shows and perform them for the kindergarten classes at the end of their winter unit.

The children were reminded they were required to do two of the activities, read alone or with a buddy and the writing response. They had to spend at least 20 minutes on each. They then could choose which center area they wanted to work in for the remainder of Reading Workshop. Because the science experiment was to be done that afternoon, Ms. Asbury reminded those who had not yet made their predictions to do so.

9:50–11:15: While the children engaged in the self-directed activities, Ms. Asbury met with small groups of students for guided reading instruction. She had organized her class into five groups of four to five children who had similar reading behaviors, had control of like reading strategies, and who were reading on the same level. It was common for the children to move frequently from group to group based on Ms. Asbury's ongoing assessment of the children's progress. She met with each group three or four times a week for 20–30 minutes. After each group, she selected one child to focus on and assessed reading development by taking a running record and listening to a story retelling.

This morning's first guided reading group began with a minilesson about attending to print. Ms. Asbury had observed that these children were attending only to the first letter of an unknown word, rather than gleaning all the information found in the print. She also wanted these children to learn to cross-check printed information by checking to see if the word they used made sense in the sentence. She wrote a sentence on a small white board leaving one word blank. She asked the children to predict what word might make sense in the blank. She then asked them to predict what the word would look like by writing it onto their small writing boards. They then worked together to correctly fill in the missing word of the sentence. After doing three sentences this way, the children discussed with Ms. Asbury how this might help them when they are reading.

Then a new book was introduced to the group. Each child had their own copy of the story *The Crazy Quilt* (Avery & McPhail, 1993). Ms. Asbury used a set of leveled books for most of her guided reading instruction. She did, however, use a rubric to level some of her easier to read classroom books about winter. She used the books she leveled for guided reading instruction whenever appropriate. She did a page-by-page "book walk" with the children and discussed necessary background information and vocabulary so the children could read and comprehend the book independently. Following the book walk, she directed the children to begin reading. Because these were beginning readers, they read aloud in quiet voices. Ms. Asbury listened in as they read, guiding children when necessary.

After the children read the story twice, Ms. Asbury praised the use of good reading strategies she had observed in their reading. She particularly reinforced cross-checking behaviors and attending fully to print. The children then composed a sentence that modeled the repetitive pattern of the story. The sentence was cut apart and re-assembled word by word. Ms. Asbury then selected two words from the sentence to be cut apart and re-assembled, again emphasizing the need to attend to all the graphophonemic information in a word. As the group was dismissed, each child placed the book they read into their book basket to be read later during independent or buddy reading time. Ms. Asbury kept records regarding the children's performance during guided reading group on a clipboard. She wrote brief anecdotal notes during and after the group meeting. She also wrote a note to each parent letting them know what had been accomplished in the guided reading lesson, homework the child had to do, and how they could help. This all went in the child's baggie to take home. Reading Workshop ended at 11:20.

11:20–11:30: Cleanup, bathroom.

11:30–12:20: Lunch and recess followed Reading Workshop.

12:20–12:30: When the children returned from recess, Ms. Asbury read aloud from *Little Polar Bear, Take Me Home!* (deBeer, 1996).

12:30–1:15: This afternoon's instruction began with Writing Workshop. Ms. Asbury started the workshop with a 10-minute minilesson about the use of capital letters and punctuation. She noticed during her writing conferences with the students that they needed review about when to use capitals. Though most students were using periods and quotation marks regularly, she wanted them to use question marks and exclamation points consistently.

She had written a paragraph from *Little Polar Bear, Take Me Home!* onto an overhead transparency. She omitted capitals and punctuation from the paragraph. As a class, the children discussed where and why capitals and punctuation needed to be inserted as they edited the paragraph. The children were then dismissed to get their writing folder and worked for the remaining 35 minutes. Many chose to write books related to the winter theme.

Because the children worked independently, they were at different stages in their writing. Some were drafting new stories; others were editing or working on final drafts at the computer. Throughout the workshop, Ms. Asbury conferenced with students individually to discuss their progress and to help them plan the next step in their writing process. Because Ms. Asbury's minilessons often focused on how to peer tutor, the children productively and actively engaged with one another.

1:15–2:00: After Writing Workshop, Ms. Asbury conducted the whole-group science lesson on melting.

2:00–2:45: The science lesson was followed by a 45-minute Math Workshop.

2:45–3:00: The day concluded with a 10-minute whole-class meeting in which two students' accomplishments were applauded: Paul and Linda had completed publishing their books that day and would share them with the class tomorrow. Ms. Asbury then gave last-minute reminders about homework and returning permission slips. Children packed their things for dismissal.

Full-Day Program for Preschool or Kindergarten

(It should be noted that full-day schedules allow for larger blocks of time and more time for learning through exploration and manipulation of materials.)

8:30–9:00: Arrival at school, storage of outdoor clothing. Quiet activities.

9:00–9:30: Whole-group morning meeting, opening exercises, morning message, discussion of unit topic, songs and musical movement activity related to the unit topic, daily news, planning for the school day.

9:30–9:50: Whole-class lesson, either in language arts or mathematics, varying from day to day, with an assignment to complete that flows into the next period.

9:50–10:15: Small-group guided reading instruction. The rest of the class completes work from the whole-class lesson or works on individual contracts from small groups or at centers designated for use during this quiet period (literacy center, math, social studies, science).

10:15–10:45: Free play. All centers open, including dramatic play, blocks, and woodworking. Special art or food-preparation projects are set up in the art center once each week for small groups independent of the teacher.

10:45–11:00: Clean-up and snack.

11:00–11:30: Shared storybook reading, creative storytelling, repeated story readings, role-playing, shared book readings, use of Big Books.

11:30–12:15: Literacy center time. Children use materials in the literacy center (library corner, writing area, oral language area, language arts manipulatives), including Very Own Words.

12:15–1:15: Lunch and outdoor play, if time and weather permit. Otherwise, large-motor activities in the gymnasium.

Afternoon Schedule for Preschool

The morning schedule would be the same for preschool and kindergarten. In preschool, however, the afternoon would differ somewhat and look more like this:

1:00–1:45: Rest period.

1:45–2:10: Center time. All centers open and a special project is in one of the areas. Work in small groups or alone independent of the teacher.

2:10–2:35: Outdoor play, large-motor play in gymnasium, or large-motor musical movement activities.

2:35–2:50: Work-group circle time. Summary of the day's activities, planning for the next day, sharing items brought from home that are related to the unit, sharing work created by children, songs, story reading.

2:50–3:00: Preparation for dismissal. Dismissal.

Afternoon Schedule for Kindergarten

1:15–1:45: Whole-group lesson in science or social studies incorporating language arts, music, or art.

1:45–2:15: Center time (literacy, mathematics, science, social studies). Special projects can be set up in any of these for small groups to rotate through in a given week. The teacher meets with small groups for instruction in math or literacy skills.

2:15–2:50: Whole-group circle time. Summary of the day's activities, planning for the next day, sharing of items brought from home that are related to study units, performance of work created by children, songs, and adult story reading.

2:50–3:00: Preparation for dismissal. Dismissal.

Half-Day Program for Preschool and Kindergarten

8:30–8:50: Arrival at school, storage of outdoor clothing. Quiet activities.

8:50–9:20: Whole-group morning meeting, opening exercises, morning message, discussion of unit topic, songs or musical movement activities related to unit topic, daily news, planning for the school day.

9:20–9:40: Whole-class lesson in language arts, mathematics, social studies, or science, varying from day to day, with an assignment to complete that flows into the next period.

9:40–10:00: Small-group guided reading lessons. The rest of the class completes work from the whole-class lesson; children work on individual contracts in small groups or at designated centers (literacy, social studies, science, or mathematics).

10:00–10:35: Center time. All centers open, including art, music, blocks, dramatic play, literacy, science, and social studies. Special projects may be set up at different centers, such as art or science. Children work alone or in small groups independent of the teacher.

10:35–10:50: Clean-up and snack.

10:50–11:10: Literacy center time. Children use materials from the literacy center (library corner, oral language area, writing area).

11:10–11:30: Outdoor play, if weather permits, or large motor-games in the gymnasium.

11:30–12:00: Whole-group storybook reading with various strategies, including shared book experiences, role-playing, creative storytelling. Summary of the school day. Dismissal.

Day-Care Centers

FULL-DAY PROGRAM FOR INFANTS AND TODDLERS

8:00–9:45: Arrival, caring for infants' needs (diapering, feeding). When involved in these routine activities, caregivers talk to babies, sing nursery rhymes, recite poems, reinforce babies' responses.

Activity period consisting of play (in small groups or one-to-one) with blocks, manipulative toys, books, or paper and crayons. Teacher and aides provide language models by identifying materials and talking about their use and provide positive reenforcement for such literacy activities as attempting oral language, looking at books, and using crayons on sheets of paper.

9:45–10:00: Snack for toddlers, accompanied by song or poetry. (Infants are fed whenever necessary.)

10:00–10:45: Rest or nap. Adults sing a napping song before children lie down.

10:45–11:15: Washing, diapering, caring for babies' needs in preparation for lunch. Adults interact with children verbally through conversation, song, or rhymes.

Activity time focuses on reading stories, looking at pictures, and using taped stories, paper, and crayons.

11:15–12:00: Lunch. Conversation involves the taste, smell, and texture of the food. After lunch, babies are readied for nap time with washing and diapering.

12:00–1:45: Naps, begun with a song and carried through with quiet background music.

1:45–2:00: As children wake, their needs are taken care of again and a small snack is provided.

2:00–3:30: Indoor and outdoor play. In either setting, adults work with small groups, reading stories, encouraging responses from children, pointing out print.

3:30–4:00: Teacher attempts a group session involving singing a song or reading a book aloud. The last 10 minutes of the day are spent preparing the children to leave—toileting, diapering, and general care.

As noted in the introduction to this chapter, day-care centers need to emulate as much as possible homes with rich literacy environments if they are to ensure the natural development of literacy in infants and toddlers.

Activities and Questions

1. Answer the focus questions at the beginning of the chapter.
2. Plan a school day with a balanced perspective in literacy instruction. Select a grade level of your choice from preK to third grade.
   a. Prepare the environment with rich literacy materials and to accommodate the thematic unit studied.
   b. Prepare a letter to send home to parents concerning the activities happening in class and invite them to participate. Chapter 3 dealing with the family has a sample letter.
   c. Include guided reading instruction and independent center activities during guided reading.
3. Observe an early childhood classroom to evaluate the literacy environment. Use the "Checklist: Evaluating and Improving the Literacy Environment" provided in this chapter.
4. Review the sample materials you have collected in the assessment portfolio you began for a child at the beginning of the year. Write a summary concerning the child's literacy development at this time and the progress he or she has made in the months you've been collecting the materials; include suggestions you have for his or her program of instruction.

Case Study Activities

As a recognized professor in the field of early literacy, you have been asked by the editors of *The Reading Teacher* journal to write a review for this book, *Literacy Development in the Early Years: Helping Children Read and Write.* In your review you are to discuss the content of the text, the organization and writing style, and the special features (such as photographs, illustrations, checklists, activities, ideas for the classroom, case studies, bibliographies, and so on). You are reviewing the book for college professors who might adopt it as a text for a course in early literacy development or for practicing teachers who want to broaden their knowledge of early literacy development. Let these individuals know why they should or should not adopt or read this text. Is the book appropriate for undergraduates, graduate students, or both? Is this book appropriate for teachers new to the field or those who have been teaching for some time? Because the book will be revised for a new edition soon, provide suggestions in your review about how the book might be improved. Please send your review and comments to Lesley M. Morrow, Rutgers University, Graduate School of Education, 10 Seminary Place, New Brunswick, NJ 08903. I look forward to hearing from you. *LMM*

Afterword

We must reignite our romance with the written word.

—Steven Spielberg, 1987

This volume has presented a theory- and research-based program for developing literacy in early childhood. It has emphasized the importance of literacy-rich environments; social interaction; peer collaboration; and whole-class, small-group, and individual learning with explicit instruction and problem-solving experiences. The activities suggested underscore the concurrent, integrated nature of learning how to use oral language, reading, and writing. The volume has outlined education that is functional and related to real-life experiences and is thus meaningful and interesting to the child. It has provided for the integration of literacy activities into content areas through units of study that are based on themes that add enthusiasm, motivation, and meaning. It has suggested careful monitoring of individual growth through direct instruction and frequent assessment using multiple measures and allowing ample space for children to learn through play, manipulation, and exploration. Attending to children with special needs has been a concern throughout the volume.

New information about learning is constantly being generated and subsequently changes the strategies we use to help children learn. Teachers must stay abreast of the constant stream of literature that is available after they complete their formal education. Teachers need to be researchers and reflect upon their own teaching to discover their strengths and weaknesses. When teachers are researchers, they will increase their knowledge and skill. To be a teacher–researcher means to formulate questions about teaching strategies, child development, classroom environment, curriculum development, or other relevant topics that will clarify issues or help generate new information. Questions should generate from your daily experiences in the classroom and be of interest to you personally.

When an area of inquiry is decided upon, the teacher should focus on collecting data that will help answer questions posed or clarify issues. Data can be collected in the following ways: Observe and record anecdotes of classroom experiences that are relevant to the question being asked; videotape classroom segments; collect samples of children's daily work over a period of time; interview children, teachers, and parents; administer formal and informal tests; and try new techniques.

As a teacher–researcher, you will always be on the cutting edge of what is current and appropriate. You will always find your teaching interesting because you will be learning about new things on a daily basis. You will enjoy your work more because you have extended your role to include additional professional activities. As a teacher–researcher, you are practicing both the art and science of teaching. The science involves inquiry, reading, observing, and collecting data. The art involves reflecting on findings and making appropriate changes. Teacher–researchers empower themselves to be decision makers and catalysts for making change in their schools. As they study questions for which they have tangible data, they are more likely to be heard when they propose new ideas and change. Rather than having change mandated based on the research by individuals outside your school district or by administrative personnel, take the responsibility for what change will occur by researching issues yourself. Each year that you teach, select another area of inquiry to study. When appropriate, collaborate with your colleagues on research projects. Collaboration with adults, as with children, results in projects that you might not have been able to do alone.

The program described in this volume is meant to be enjoyable for both teachers and children. Enjoyment allows the teacher to work with vigor and enthusiasm. Enjoyment allows the child to associate literacy with a school environment that is pleasurable, positive, and designed to help children succeed. The single most important element in learning to read and write is having a desire to read and write. This desire motivates an interest in learning the skills necessary to become proficient in literary activities. Such an environment ensures a lifelong interest to refine and use literacy skills. The program is designed to help us "reignite our romance with the written word" (Spielberg, 1987).

appendix 

Children's Literature

BOOKS FOR BABIES

Cardboard Concept Books

Brown, M. (1997). *Say the magic word.* New York: Random House.

Crozat, F. (1996). *I am a little hedgehog.* New York: Barron's.

Elgar, R. (1998). *Jack, it's playtime/bathtime/bedtime/Happy Birthday.* New York: Kingfisher.

Lamut, S. (1997). *1 2 Peek a boo.* New York: Grosset & Dunlap.

Sykes, J., & Wyrnes, T. (1997). *I don't want to take a bath.* Waukesha, WI: Little Tiger Press.

Cloth Books

Awdry, W. (1990). *Thomas the tank engine says goodnight.* New York: Random House.

Gleeson, K. (1994). *Yum! Yum!* New York: Western Publishing Company.

Potter, B. (1994). *My Peter Rabbit cloth book/My Tom Kitten cloth book.* London: Penguin Books.

Tong, W. (1996). *Zoo faces/Farm faces.* Santa Monica, CA: Piggy Toes Press.

Tucker, S. (1994). *Toot toot/Quack quack.* New York: Little Simon.

Plastic Books

Barkan, J. (1998). *Splish! Splash!* New York: Random House.

Children's Television Workshop. (1992). *Ernie's bath book.* New York: Random House.

Hoban, T. (1994). *What is it?* New York: Greenwillow Books.

Man-Kong, M. (1999). *Theodore's splash.* New York: Random House.

Yablovsky, B. (1998). *Blue's bubbly tub.* New York: Simon Spotlight.

Touch and Feel

Boynton, S. (1998). *Dinosaur's binkit.* New York: Little Simon.

Campbell, R. (1996). *Cuddle feelies.* New York: Random House.

Hill, E. (1997). *Spot's touch and feel day.* New York: Putnam.

Kunhardt, D. (1984). *Pat the Bunny/Cat/Puppy.* New York: Golden Books.

Milne, A. A., & Shepard, E. H. (1998). *Pooh's touch and feel visit.* New York: Dutton Children's Books

CONCEPT BOOKS

Crimi, C. (1995). *Outside, inside.* New York: Simon & Schuster.

Hoban, T. (1998). *More, fewer, less.* New York: Greenwillow Books.

Kulman, A. (1993). *Red light, stop, green light, go.* New York: Simon & Schuster.

Miller, M. (1998). *Big and little.* New York: Greenwillow Books.

Murphy, C. (1998). *Black cat white cat: A book of opposites.* New York: Little Simon.

ALPHABET BOOKS

Cohen, I. (1998). *ABC discovery.* New York: Dial.

Golding, K. (1998). *Alphababies.* New York: DK Publishing.

Johnson, S. T. (1995). *Alphabet city.* New York: Viking.

Jordan, M., & Jordan, T. (1996). *Amazon alphabet.* New York: Kingfisher.

Kirk, D. (1998). *Miss Spider's ABC.* New York: Scholastic.

NUMBER BOOKS

Baker, A. (1998). *Little rabbit's first number book.* New York: Kingfisher.

Carle, E. (1987). *1, 2, 3 to the zoo.* New York: Paperstar.

Merriam, E. (1993). *12 ways to get to 11.* New York: Aladdin Paperbacks.

Murphy, C. (1991). *My first book of counting.* New York: Scholastic.

Strickland, P. (1997). *Ten terrible dinosaurs.* New York: Dutton Children's Books.

NURSERY RHYMES

dePaola, T. (1985). *Tomie dePaola's Mother Goose.* New York: Putnam.

Hannant, J. S. (1993). *The door knob collection of bedtime rhymes.* New York: Little, Brown.

Rader, L. (1993). *Mother Hubbard's cupboard: A Mother Goose surprise book.* New York: Tambourine Books.

Scarry, R. (1992). *Richard Scarry's Mother Goose and Rhymes and nursery tales.* New York: Golden books.

Sutherland, Z. (1990). *The Orchard book of nursery rhymes.* New York: Orchard.

WORDLESS STORYBOOKS

Aliki. (1995). *Tabby: A story in pictures.* New York: HarperCollins.

Banyai, I. (1995). *Zoom.* New York: Viking.

Hamada, C. (Reteller). (1993). *Fourth question: A Chinese folktale and Kau and the golden fish: A folktale from Thailand.* Danbury, CT: Children's Press.

Jenkins, S. (1995). *Looking down.* Boston, MA: Houghton Mifflin.

Murphy, C. (1995). *One to ten: Pop-up surprises!* New York: Simon & Schuster.

POETRY BOOKS

Bierhorst, J. (Ed.) (1994). *On the road of stars: Native American night poems and sleep charms.* New York: Macmillan.

Brenner, B. (Ed.) (1994). *The Earth is painted green: A garden of poems about our planet.* New York: Scholastic.

Hopkins, L. B. (Selector). (1993). *Extra innings: Baseball poems.* New York: Harcourt Brace.

Kennedy, D. M. (1993). *I thought I'd take my rat to school: Poems for September to June.* New York: Little, Brown.

Silverstein, S. (1974). *Where the sidewalk ends.* New York: Harper & Row.

TRADITIONAL LITERATURE (FAIRY TALES, FABLES, MYTHS, AND FOLKTALES)

Charles, V. M. (1993). *The crane girl.* New York: Orchard.

French, V. (1995). *Red hen and sly fox.* New York: Simon & Schuster.

Grimm Brothers. (1995). *The sleeping beauty: A fairy tale. Little Red-cap. Iron Hans, The golden goose.* New York: North-South.

Harrison, M., & Stuart-Clark, C. (Selectors). (1994). *The Oxford treasury of children's stories.* Andover, MA: Oxford.

Pilling, A. (1993). *Realms of gold: Myths and legends from around the world.* New York: Kingfisher.

EASY-TO READ BOOKS WITH LIMITED VOCABULARY

Eastman, P. D. (1960). *Are you my mother?* New York: Random House.

Miller, M. (1993). *Can you guess?* New York: Greenwillow.

Raschka, C. (1993). *Yo! Yes?* New York: Greenwillow.

Schade, S., & Buller, J. (1996). *Snow bugs.* New York: Random House.

St. Pierre, S. (1998). *It's not easy being big!* New York: CTW/Random House.

BOOKS ABOUT REALISTIC ISSUES

Buehner, C., & Buehner, M. (1997). *I did it, I'm sorry.* New York: Dial.

Davies, S. (1997). *Why did we have to move here?* Minneapolis, MN: Carolrhoda Books.

Hess, D. (1994). *Wilson sat alone.* New York: Simon & Schuster.

Padoan, G. (1987). *Remembering grandad: Facing up to death.* New York: Child's Play.

Vigna, J. (1995). *My two uncles.* Morton Grove, IL: Albert Whitman.

INFORMATIONAL BOOKS

Alexander, H. (1990). *Look inside your brain.* New York: Putnam.

Chermayeff, I. (1994). *Fishy facts.* New York: Harcourt Brace.

Jaspersohn, William. (1994). *My hometown library.* Boston, MA: Houghton Mifflin.

Martin, L. (1994). *Watch them grow.* New York: Dorling Kindersley.

Wu, N. (1993). *Fish faces.* New York: Holt.

BIOGRAPHY

Heslewood, J. (1993). *Introducing Picasso.* New York: Little, Brown.

Greenfield, E. (1995). *Rosa Parks.* New York: Harper Trophy.

Kunhardt, E. (1993). *Honest Abe.* New York: Greenwillow.

Marzollo, J. (1993). *Happy birthday, Martin Luther King.* New York: Scholastic.

Raimondo, L. (1994). *Little Lama of Tibet.* New York: Scholastic.

MAGAZINES FOR CHILDREN

Chickadee. Young Naturalist Foundation, 17th and M Streets NW, Washington, DC 20036 (ages 4–8)

Cricket. Open Court Publishing Co., Box 100, La Salle, IL 61301 (ages 6–12)

The Dinosaur Times. CSK Publications/ B&W Publications, 500 S. Buena Vista Street, Suite 101, Burbank, CA 91521-6018 (all ages)

Highlights for Children. 803 Church Street, Honesdale, PA 18431 (ages 2–12)

Your Big Backyard. National Wildlife Federation, 1412 16th Street NW, Washington, DC 20036 (ages 1–4)

PREDICTABLE BOOKS

Repetitive Phrases

Cameron, A. (1994). *The cat sat on the mat.* Boston, MA: Houghton Mifflin.

Chapman, C. (1994). *Snow on snow on snow.* New York: Dial.

Fox, M. (1993). *Time for bed.* New York: Harcourt Brace.

Lobel, A. (1979). *A treeful of pigs.* New York: Greenwillow.

Sendak, M. (1962). *Chicken soup with rice.* New York: Harper & Row.

Rhyme

Carlstrom, N. W. (1993). *How does the wind walk?* New York: Macmillan.

Kozikowski, R. (1993). *Special street.* Washington, DC: Artists and Writers Guild.

Kuskin, K. (1995). *James and the rain.* New York: Simon & Schuster.

McMillan, B. (1995). *Puffins climb, penguins rhyme.* New York: Harcourt Brace.

Patron, S. (1994). *Dark cloud strong breeze.* New York: Orchard.

Familiar Sequences (days of the week, numbers, letters, months of the year, etc.)

Carle, E. (1969). *The very hungry caterpillar.* New York: Philomel.

Carle, E. (1977). *The grouchy ladybug.* New York: HarperCollins.

Keats, E. J. (1971). *Over in the meadow.* New York: Scholastic.

Roy, R. (1980). *The three ducks went wandering.* New York: Scholastic.

Van Allsburg, C. (1987). *The Z was zapped.* Boston, MA: Houghton Mifflin.

Cumulative Patterns (as the story progresses, the previous line is repeated)

Carle, E. (1990). *The very quiet cricket.* New York: Philomel.

Carle, E. (1994). *The very lonely firefly.* New York: Philomel.

Kharms, D. (translated by J. Gambrell). (1993). *The story of a boy named Will, who went sledding down the hill.* New York: North-South.

Tompert, A. (1993). *Just a little bit.* Boston, MA: Houghton Mifflin.

Wood, A. (1994). *The napping house wakes up.* New York: Harcourt Brace.

Stories with Conversation

Cooper, H. (1997). *The boy who wouldn't go to bed.* New York: Dial.

Johnson, P. B. (1999). *The pig who ran a red light.* New York: Orchard.

Kellog, S. (1971). *Can I keep him?* New York: Dial.

Modarressi, M. (1998). *Monster stew.* New York: Dorling Kindersley.

Polacco, P. (1998). *Thank you, Mr. Falker.* New York: Philomel.

Books that Foster Critical Discussions

Cannon, J. (1993). *Stellaluna.* Orlando, FL: Harcourt Brace.

Curtis, J. L. (1996). *Tell me again about the night I was born.* New York: HarperCollins.

Martin, J. B. (1998). *Snowflake butterfly.* Boston, MA: Houghton Mifflin.

Winn, C. M. with D. Walsh. (1996). *Clover's secret.* Minneapolis, MN: Fairview Press.

Zolotow, C. (1972). *William's doll.* New York: Harper & Row.

BOOKS FOR ENHANCING LISTENING AND DISCRIMINATION OF SOUNDS

Brown, M. W. (1993). *The summer noisy book* and *The winter noisy book.* New York: HarperCollins.

Conrad, P. (1995). *Animal lingo.* New York: HarperCollins.

Kushkin, K. (1994). *City noise.* New York: HarperCollins.

Scammell, R. (1993). *Buster's echo.* New York: HarperCollins.

Serfozo, M. (1993). *Joe Joe.* New York: Macmillan.

FAVORITE WELL-KNOWN PICTURE STORYBOOKS

The following books represent a careful selection of some distinguished authors and excellent children's literature not to be missed.

Barrett, J. (1970). *Animals should definitely not wear clothing.* New York: Atheneum.

Bemelmans, L. (1939). *Madeline.* New York: Viking.

Berenstain, S., & Berenstain, J. (1966). *The bear's picnic.* New York: Random House.

Brown, M. W. (1957). *Goodnight moon.* New York: Harper & Row.

Carle, E. (1969). *The very hungry caterpillar.* New York: Philomel.

dePaola, T. (1975). *Stregna Nona: An old tale.* Englewood Cliffs, NJ: Prentice Hall.

Eastman, P. D. (1960). *Are you my mother?* New York: Random House.

Flack, M. (1932). *Ask Mr. Bear.* New York: Macmillan.

Galdone, P. (1975). *The little red hen.* New York: Scholastic.

Hoban, R. (1969). *Best friends for Frances.* New York: Harper & Row.

Hughes, S. (1979). *Up and up.* New York: Lothrop, Lee & Shepard.

Hutchins, P. (1978). *Don't forget the bacon.* New York: Puffin Books.

Johnson, C. (1955). *Harold and the purple crayon.* New York: Harper.

Keats, E. J. (1962). *The snowy day.* New York: Viking.

Kellogg, S. (1971). *Can I keep him?* New York: Dial.

Kraus, R. (1971). *Leo the late bloomer.* New York: Windmill.

Lionni, L. (1973). *Swimmy.* New York: Random House.

Lobel, A. (1972). *Frog and toad together.* New York: Harper & Row.

Mayer, M. (1974). *One monster after another.* Racine, WI: Western Publishing Co.

McCloskey, R. (1948). *Blueberries for Sal.* New York: Penguin.

Piper, W. (1954). *The little engine that could.* New York: Platt & Munk.

Potter, B. (1902). *The tale of Peter Rabbit.* New York: Scholastic.

Rey, H. A. (1952). *Curious George rides a bike.* Boston: Houghton Mifflin.

Sendak, M. (1963). *Where the wild things are.* New York: Harper & Row.

Seuss, Dr. (1940). *Horton hatches the egg*. New York: Random House.
Shaw, C. (1947). *It looked like spilled milk*. New York: HarperCollins.
Slobodkina, E. (1947). *Caps for sale*. Reading, MA: Addison-Wesley.
Steig, W. (1969). *Sylvester and the magic pebble*. New York: Simon & Schuster.
Viorst, J. (1972). *Alexander and the terrible, horrible, no good, very bad day*. New York: Atheneum.
Waber, B. (1975). *Ira sleeps over*. Boston: Houghton Mifflin.
Wiesner, D. (1988). *FreeFall*. New York: Lothrop, Lee & Shepard.
Wiesner, D. (1992). *Tuesday*. New York: Clarion Books.

BOOKS FOR BUILDING SOUND–SYMBOL RELATIONSHIPS

Consonants

B

Crisp, M. (1995). *Buzzard breath*. New York: Atheneum.
Gregory, V. (1993). *Babysitting for Benjamin*. New York: Little, Brown.
Hadithi, M. (1993). *Baby baboon*. New York: Little, Brown.
Yee, W. H. (1993). *Big black bear*. Boston, MA: Houghton Mifflin.
Yep, L. (1995). *The butterfly boy*. New York: Farrar, Strauss & Giroux.

C (hard)

Berenstain, S., & Berenstain, J. (1972) *C is for clown*. New York: Random House.
Gibbons, G. (1993). *Caves and caverns*. New York: Harcourt Brace.
Hoff, S. (1993). *Captain cat*. New York: HarperCollins.
Owens, M. B. (1993). *Counting cranes*. Boston, MA: Little, Brown.
Scott, A. H. (1993). *Cowboy country*. New York: Clarion.

C (soft)

Duqennoy, J. (1996). *The ghosts in the cellar*. New York: Harcourt Brace.
Ehlert, L. (1992). *Circus*. New York: Greenwillow.
Fowler, S. G., & Catalanotto, P. (1998). *Circle of thanks*. New York: Scholastic.
Kuskin, Karla. (1994). *City noise*. New York: HarperCollins.
Woodman, J. (1986). *Bossy bear at the circus*. London: Brimax Books.

D

Bunting, E. (1995). *Dandelions*. New York: Harcourt Brace.
Carmine, M. (1997). *Daniel's dinosaurs*. New York: Scholastic.
Cole, B. (1994). *Dr. Dog*. New York: Knopf.
Moncure, J. (1984). *My "D" sound*. Elgin, IL: Child's World Publishing.
Steig, W. (1992). *Doctor DeSoto goes to Africa*. New York: HarperCollins.

F

Carlstrom, N. W. (1993). *Fish and flamingo*. Boston: Little, Brown.
Littledale, F. (1987). *The farmer in the soup*. New York: Scholastic.
Lobel, A. (1970). *Frog and toad are friends*. New York: Harper & Row.
San Souci, R. D. (1995). *The faithful friend*. New York: Simon & Schuster.
Silverman, E. (1994). *Don't fidget a feather*. New York: Macmillan.

G (hard)

Grejniec, M. (1993). *Good morning, good night*. New York: North-South.
Grimm, J., & Grimm,W. (1995). *The golden goose*. New York: Farrar, Strauss & Giroux.
Keats, E. J. (1969). *Goggles*. New York: Collier Books.
Kimmel, E. (Reteller). (1995). *The goose girl: A story from the Brothers Grimm*. New York: Holiday House.
Seuss, Dr. (1960). *Green eggs and ham*. New York: Beginner Books.

G (soft)

Galdone, P. (1975). *The gingerbread boy*. New York: Clarion.
Lionni, L. (1979). *Geraldine, the music mouse*. New York: Random House.
Peck, J. (1998). *The giant carrot*. New York: Dial.
Rey, H. A. (1973). *Curious George*. Boston, MA: Houghton Mifflin.
Silverstein, S. (1964). *A giraffe and a half*. New York: HarperCollins.

H

Hadithi, M. (1994). *Hungry hyena*. Boston, MA: Little, Brown.
High, L. O. (1995). *Hound heaven*. New York: Holiday House.
Wormell, M. (1995). *Hilda hen's happy birthday*. New York: Harcourt Brace.
Yolen, J., & Greenberg, M. H. (1995). *The haunted house*. New York: HarperCollins.
Zion, G. (1976). *Harry the dirty dog*. New York: Harper & Row.

J

Grossman, B. (1997). *The bear whose bones were Jezebel Jones*. New York: Dial.
Hennessy, B. G. (1990). *Jake baked the cake*. New York: Viking.
Kalan, R. (1981). *Jump frog jump*. New York: Greenwillow Books.
Ogburn, J. K. (1998). *The jukebox man*. New York: Dial.
Saltzman, D. (1995). *The jester has lost his jingle*. Palos Verdes, CA: The Jester Company.

K

Demi. (1999). *Kites*. New York: Crown Publishing.
Ford, J. G. (1996). *A Kente dress for Kenya*. New York: Scholastic.

Moncure, J. (1984). *My "K" sound.* Elgin, IL: Child's World Publishing.

Senisi, E. (1994). *Kindergarten kids.* New York: Scholastic.

Wood, A. (1985). *King Bidgood's in a bathtub.* New York: Harcourt Brace Jovanovich.

L

Raimondo, L. (1994). *Little Lama of Tibet.* New York: Scholastic.

Scheidl, G. M. (1993). *Loretta and the little fairy.* New York: North-South.

Shepard, A. (1993). *The legend of lightning Larry.* Phoenix, AZ: Scribners.

Yerxa, L. (1994). *Last leaf first snowflake to fall.* New York: Orchard.

Zolotow, C. (1987). *I like to be little.* New York: Thomas Y. Crowell.

M

Allen, J. (1990). *Mucky moose.* New York: Macmillan.

Brennan, H. (1995). *The mystery machine.* New York: Margeret McElderry.

Herman, C. (1993). *Max Malone the magnificent.* New York: Holt.

Lyon, G. E. (1994). *Mama is a miner.* New York: Orchard.

Young, E. (1993). *Moon mother.* New York: HarperCollins.

N

Masner, J. (1989). *Nicholas Cricket.* New York: Harper & Row.

Ryland, C. (1986). *Night in the country.* New York: Bradbury Press.

Wells, R. (1997). *Noisy Nora.* New York: Scholastic.

Wezel, P. (1967). *The naughty bird.* Chicago, IL: Follet.

Wood, A. (1984). *The napping house.* New York: Harcourt Brace.

P

Ehrlich, A. (1993). *Parents in the pig pens, pigs in the tub.* New York: Dial.

Kleven, E. (1994). *The paper princess.* New York: Dutton.

Palatini, M. (1995). *Piggie pie!* New York: Clarion.

Papademetriou, L. (1998). *My pen pal, Pat.* Brookfield, CT: Millbrook Press.

Rockwell, A. (1993). *Pots and pans.* New York: Macmillan.

Q

Good, M. (1999). *Reuben and the quilt.* New York: Good Books.

Harness, C. (1993). *The queen with bees in her hair.* New York: Holt.

Holtzman, C. (1995). *A quarter from the tooth fairy.* New York: Scholastic.

Johnston, T., & dePaola, T. (1996). *The quilt story.* New York: Penguin Putnam.

Wood, A. (1997). *Quick as a cricket.* New York: Scholastic.

R

dePaola, P. (1992). *Rosie and the yellow ribbon.* Boston: Joy Street Books.

Gantos, J. (1994). *Not so rotten Ralph.* Boston, MA: Houghton Mifflin.

Marshall, J. (1993). *Red riding hood.* New York: Scholastic.

Pinkwater, D. (1998). *Rainy morning.* New York: Atheneum.

Weeks, S. (1995). *Red ribbon.* New York: HarperCollins.

S

Burnie, D. (1994). *Seashore.* New York: Dorling Kindersley.

Garland, S. (1995). *The summer sands.* New York: Harcourt Brace.

Robb, L. (Selector). (1995). *Snuffles and snouts.* New York: Dial.

Stolz, M. (1993). *Say something.* New York: HarperCollins.

Thomson, P. (1993). *Siggy's spaghetti works.* New York: William Morrow.

T

Biney, B. G. (1994). *Tyrannosaurus Tex.* Boston, MA: Houghton Mifflin.

Cosgrove, S. (1984). *Tee-tee.* Vero Beach, FL: Rourke Enterprises.

Cocca-Leffler, M. (1999). *Mr. Tannen's ties.* Morton Grove, IL: Albert Whitman.

Gershator, P. (Reteller). (1994). *Tukama tootles the flute: A tale from the Antilles.* New York: Orchard.

Griffing, A. (1999). *Trashy town.* New York: HarperCollins.

V

Bovetz, M. (1993). *Machines.* Bothell, WA: Wright Group.

Cannon, J. (1997). *Verdi.* New York: Harcourt Brace.

Schweninger, A. (1990). *Valentine friends.* New York: Scholastic.

Williams, M. (1981). *The velveteen rabbit.* New York: Scholastic.

Williams, S. (1998). *Let's go visiting.* New York: Harcourt Brace.

W

Brenner, B. (1995). *Wagon wheels.* New York: Scholastic.

Calstrom, N. W. (1993). *How does the wind walk?* New York: Macmillan.

Halpern, S. (1995). *What shall we do when we all go out?* New York: North-South.

Peet, B. (1981). *The wump world.* New York: Scholastic.

Thomas, A. (1993). *Wake up, Wilson Street.* New York: Holt.

X

Langen, A., & Droop, C. (1996). *Felix explores planet earth.* New York: Abbeville Kids Press.

Moncure, J. (1979). *My "X, Y, Z" sound box.* Elgin, IL: Child's World Publishing.

Robbins, J. (1985). *Addie meets Max.* New York: Harper & Row.

Thomas, P. (1979). *There are rocks in my socks said the ox to the fox.* New York: Lee, Lothrop & Shepard.

Y

Kellogg, S. (1996). *Yankee doodle.* New York: Aladdin Paperbacks.

Marshall, J. (1973). *Yummers*. Boston, MA: Houghton Mifflin.

Oram, H. (Reteller). (1997). *Baba Yaga and the wise doll.* New York: Dutton.

Seuss, Dr. (1958). *Yertle the turtle and other stories.* New York: Random House.

Z

McDermontt, G. (1996). *Zomo the rabbit: A trickster tale from West Africa.* New York: Scholastic.

Moss, L. (1995). *Zin! Zin! Zin! A violin.* New York: Simon & Schuster.

Most, B. (1999). *Z—Z—Zoink!* New York: Harcourt Brace.

Steig, W. (1994). *Zeke Pippin.* New York: HarperCollins.

Wynne-Jones, T. (1993). *Zoom at sea.* New York: Harper-Collins.

Vowels (long and short)

A

Berenstein, M. (1998). *That cat!* Brookfield, CT: Millbrook Press.

Cherry, L. (1994). *Armadillo from Amarillo.* New York: Harcourt Brace.

Karlin, N. (1996). *The fat cat sat on the mat.* New York: Harper Trophy.

Lachner, D. (1995). *Andrew's angry words.* New York: North-South.

Ray, M. L. (1994). *Alvah and Arvilla.* New York: Harcourt Brace.

E

Grace, E. S. (1993). *Elephants.* San Francisco, CA: Sierra.

Johnson, S. A. (1994). *A beekeeper's year.* Boston, MA: Little, Brown.

Kent, J. (1975). *The egg book.* New York: Macmillan.

Rockwell, A., & Rockwell, H. (1985). *The emergency room.* New York: Macmillan.

Wood, A. J. (1993). *Egg! A dozen eggs. What will they be?* Boston, MA: Little, Brown.

I

Kinerk, R. (1998). *Slim and Miss Prim.* Flagstaff, AZ: Rising Moon.

Marston, H. I. (1993). *Big rigs.* New York: Dutton.

Moncure, J. (1984). *Short i and long i: Play a game.* Elgin, IL: Child's World Publishing.

Oram, H. (1985). *In the attic.* New York: Holt, Rinehart, & Winston.

Zolotow, C. (1966). *If it weren't for you.* New York: Harper & Row.

O

Frankel, J. (1991). *Oh no, Otis!* Danbury, CT: Children's Press.

George, J. C. (1995). *There's an owl in the shower.* New York: HarperCollins.

Krupp, E. C. (1993). *The moon and you.* New York: Macmillan.

Leonard, M. (1998). *Spots.* Brookfield, CT: Millbrook Press.

Machotka, H. (1993). *Outstanding outsides.* New York: William Morrow.

U

Allen, S. (1995). *The bug and the slug in the rug.* Bridgeport, CT: Green Bark Press.

Anderson, H. C. (1994). *The ugly duckling.* New York: Dorling Kindersley.

Mitchell, M. K. (1993). *Uncle Jed's barbershop.* New York: Simon & Schuster.

Moncure, J. (1984). *Short u and long u: Play a game.* Elgin, IL: Child's World Publishing.

Digraphs

CH

Archambault, J., & Martin, B. Jr. (1989). *Chicka chicka boom boom.* New York: Scholastic.

Hobson, S. (1994). *Chicken little.* New York: Simon & Schuster.

Onyefulu, O. (1994). *Chinye: A West African folk tale.* New York: Viking.

Shen, R. (1993). *Chicken pox!* Boston, MA: Little, Brown.

Tunnel, M. O. (1993). *Chinook!* New York: Tambourine.

PH

Govan, C. (1968). *Phinny's fine summer.* New York: World Publishing.

SH

Brown, M. (1995). *Shadow.* New York: Aladdin Paperbacks.

Cowley, J. (1990). *Mrs. Wishy Washy.* Bothell, WA: Wright Group.

Pfister, M. (1990). *Shaggy.* New York: North-South Books.

Shaw, N. (1994). *Sheep takes a hike.* Boston, MA: Houghton Mifflin.

Simon, S. (1995). *Sharks.* New York: HarperCollins.

TH

Cowley, J. (1987). *One thousand currant buns.* Bothell, WA: Wright Group.

Loedhas, S. (1962). *Thistle and thyme.* Toronto: Alger.

Simms, L. (1998). *Rotten teeth.* Boston, MA: Houghton Mifflin.

Word Families

Brown, M. W. (1984). *Goodnight moon.* New York: Harper & Row.

Butler, A., & Neville, P. (1987). *May I stay home today?* Crystal Lake, IL: Rigby.

Cowley, J. (1990). *Dan the flying man.* Bothell, WA: Wright Group.

Patrick, G. (1974). *A bug in a jug.* New York: Scholastic.

Seuss, Dr. (1957). *The cat in the hat.* New York: Random House.

BOOKS FOR FOLLOWING DIRECTIONS

Benjamin, C. (1982). *Cartooning for kids.* New York: Thomas Y. Crowell.

Carle, E. (1993). *Draw me a star.* New York: Scholastic.

dePaola, T. (1978). *Pancakes for breakfast.* New York: Harcourt Brace Jovanovich.

Gibbons, G. (1990). *How a house is built.* New York: Scholastic.

Vaughan-Ashton, M. (1984). *Wombat stew.* New York: Scholastic.

SERIES BOOKS

Bemelmans, L. (1977). *Madeline.* New York: Puffin Books.

Freeman, D. (1968). *Corduroy.* New York: Viking.

Hangreaves, R. (1980). *The Mr. Men books.* Los Angeles: Price, Stern, & Sloan Publishers.

Lobel, A. (1979). *Frog and toad are friends.* New York: Harper & Row.

Parish, P. (1970). *Amelia Bedelia.* New York: Scholastic.

CHILDREN'S BOOKS RELATED TO THEMES

All about Me Books

Carlson, N. L. (1998). *I like me.* New York: Viking Children's Books.

Hale, I. (1992). *How I found a friend.* New York: Scholastic.

Numuoff, L. J. (1996). *Why a disguise?* New York: Simon & Schuster.

Williams, S. (1996). *Mommy doesn't know my name.* (pet names) Boston, MA: Houghton Mifflin.

Ziefert, H. (1997). *Waiting for baby.* New York: Puffin Books.

Animal Books

Bischoff-Meirsch, A., & Bischoff-Meirsch, B. (1994). *Do you know the difference?* New York: North-South.

Conrad, P. (1995). *Animal lingo.* NewYork: HarperCollins.

Ganeri, A. (1995). *Animals in disguise.* New York: Simon & Schuster.

Riley, L. C. (1995). *Elephants swim.* New York: Houghton Mifflin.

Whayne, S. S. (1993). *Night creatures.* New York: Simon & Schuster.

Dinosaurs

Maynard, C. (1998). *The best book of dinosaurs.* New York: Kingfisher.

Mullins, P. (1993). *Dinosaur encore.* New York: HarperCollins.

Schnetzler, P. L. (1996). *Ten little dinosaurs.* New York: Accord Publishing.

Strickland, H. (1994). *Dinosaur roar!* New York: Dutton.

Wood, A. J. (1998). *Countdown to extinction.* New York: Disney Press.

Ecology

Bash, B. (1989). *Desert giant: The world of the saguaro cactus.* Boston, MA: Little, Brown.

Dunphy, M. (1994). *Here is the tropical rain forest.* New York: Hyperion.

Gilliland, J. H. (1993). *River.* New York: Clarion.

Jordan, T. (1993). *Jungle days jungle nights.* New York: Kingfisher.

Rauzon, M. J., & Bix, C. O. (1994). *Water water everywhere.* San Francisco, CA: Sierra.

Families

Multicultural Books General Books about Families

Anholt, C., et al. (1998). *Catherine and Laurence Anholt's big book of families.* Cambridge, MA: Candlewick Press.

Hausheir, R. (1997). *Celebrating families.* New York: Scholastic.

Yem, S. S. (1997). *All kinds of families.* Birmingham, AL: New Hope Publishing.

Books about African American Families

Kroll, V. (1997). *Masai and I.* New York: Aladdin Paperbacks.

Kroll, V. (1998). *Africa brothers and sisters.* New York: Aladdin Paperbacks.

Strickland, D. S., & Strickland, M. R. (1996). *Families. Poems celebrating the African-American experience.* Honesdale, PA: Boyds Mills Press.

Books about Asian Families

Pomeranc, M. H. (1998). *The American Wei.* New York: Albert Whitman.

Say, A. (1993). *Grandfather's journey.* Boston, MA: Houghton Mifflin.

Young, A. (1989). *Lon Po Po: A red-riding hood story from China.* New York: Philomel.

Books about Latino Families

Garza, C. L. (1996). *In my family.* Danbury, CT: Children's Press.

Morta, P. (1992). *A birthday basket for Tia.* New York: Macmillan.

Pampa, C. M. (1991). *On the Pompas.* New York: Holt.

American Eskimo

Joosse, B. (1991). *Mama, do you love me?* New York: Scholastic.

Ireland

Bailan, L. (1980). *Leprechauns never lie.* Nashville, TN: Abingdon.

Italy

dePaola, T. (1989). *Tony's bread.* New York: Putnam.

Jamaica

Hoffman, M. (1991). *Amazing Grace.* New York: Scholastic.

Jewish Folktale

Gilman. P. (1994). *Something for nothing.* New York: Scholastic.

Native Americans

Goble, P. (1980). *The gift of the sacred dog.* New York: Macmillan.

Miller, J. (1997). *American Indian families* (True book). Danbury, CT: Children's Press.

Russian Family Folktale

Polacco, P. (1990). *Babushka's doll.* New York: Simon & Shuster.

Five Senses

Adolph, A. (1989). *Chocolate dreams.* New York: Lothrop, Lee & Shepard.
Hewitt, S. (1999). *It's science! The five senses.* Danbury, CT: Children's Press.
Miller, M. (1994). *My five senses.* New York: Simon & Schuster.
McMillan, B. (1994). *Sense suspense: A guessing game for the five senses.* New York: Scholastic.
Moncure, J. B. (1997). *Clang, boom, bang: My five senses series.* Elgin, IL: Child's World Publishing.

Insects and Reptiles

Baher, K. (1995). *Hide and snake.* New York: Voyager Picture Books.
Nickle, J. (1999). *The ant bully.* New York: Scholastic.
Petie, H. (1975). *Billions of bugs.* Englewood Cliffs, NJ: Prentice Hall.
Saunders-Smith, G. (1998). *Butterflies.* Danbury, CT: Children's Press.
Simon, S. (1999). *Crocodiles and alligators.* New York: HarperCollins.

Ocean Life

Andreae, G. (1998). *Commotion in the ocean.* Waukesha, WI: Little Tiger Press.
Gibbons, G. (1999). *Exploring the deep dark sea.* Boston, MA: Little, Brown.
Lionni, L. (1973). *Swimmy.* New York: Random House.
Savage, S. (1997). *Animals of the ocean.* Chatham, NJ: Raintree/Steck Vaughn.
Seelig, T. L. (1999). *Ocean.* San Francisco, CA: Chronicle Books.

Seasons and Holidays

Autumn

Hunter, A. (1996). *Possum's harvest moon.* New York: Houghton Mifflin.
Robbins, K. (1998). *Autumn leaves.* New York: Scholastic.
Russel, C. Y. (1997). *Moon festival.* Honesdale, PA: Boyds Mills Press.
Saunders, G. (1998). *Autumn.* Danbury, CT: Children's Press.
Schecter, B. (1993). *When will the snow trees grow?* New York: HarperCollins.

Winter

Blake, R. J. (1997). *Akiak: A take from the Iditarod.* New York: Philomel.
Brown, M. W. (1994). *The winter noisy book.* New York: HarperCollins.
Ehlert, L. (1995). *Snowballs* (Picture book). New York: Harcourt Brace.
Maass, R. (1993). *When winter comes.* New York: Holt.
Schotter, R., & Schotter, R. (1994). *There's a dragon about: A winter's revel.* New York: Orchard.

Spring

Adoff, A. (1997). *In for winter, out for spring.* New York: Harcourt Brace.
Daigneault, S. (1998). *Bruno springs up.* New York: HarperCollins.
Preller, J. (1994). *Wake me in spring.* New York: Scholastic.
Rylant, C. (1996). *Henry and Mudge in puddle trouble.* New York: Aladdin Paperbacks.
Spelter, J. (1999). *Lily and Trooper's spring.* Ashville, NC: Front Street Press.

Summer

Brown, M. W. (1993). *The summer noisy book.* New York: HarperCollins.
Hesse, K. (1999). *Come on, rain!* New York: Scholastic.
Lerner, C. (1996). *Backyard birds of summer.* New York: William Morrow.
Maass, R. (1993). *When summer comes.* New York: Holt.
Sturges, P. (1995). *Rainsong snowsong* (Predictable rhyming text). New York: North-South.

Space

Gaffney, T. R. (1996). *Grandpa takes me to the moon.* New York: William Morrow.
Graham, I. (1998). *The best book of spaceships.* New York: Kingfisher Books.
Hansen, R. (1998). *Astronauts today.* New York: Random House.
Simon, S. (1988). *Galaxies.* New York: Morrow Junior Books.
Sims, L. (1996). *Exploring space.* Chatham, NJ: Raintree/Steck-Vaughn.

■ CHILDREN'S LITERATURE RELATED TO CULTURAL DIVERSITY

African American Books

Cowen-Fletcher, J. (1994). *It takes a village.* New York: Scholastic.
Geraghty, P. (1994). *The hunter.* New York: Crown.
Mendez, P. (1989). *The black snowman.* New York: Scholastic.
San Souci, R. D. (1997). *The hired hand: An African-American folktale.* New York: Dial.
Spetoe, J. (1987). *Mufaro's beautiful daughters.* New York: Lothrop, Lee, & Shepard.

Asian Books

Chang, M., et al. (1997). *The beggar's magic: A Chinese tale.* New York: Margaret McElderry.
Ho, M. (1997). *Brother rabbit: A Cambodian tale.* Lothrop, Lee & Shephard.
Long, J. F. (1996). *The bee and the dream: A Japanese tale.* New York: Dutton.
Martin, R., et al. (1998). *The brave little parrot.* New York: Putnam.
McCarthy, R. F. (1994). *The adventure of Momotaro, the peach boy.* Honolulu, HI: Kodansha International Publisher.

Latino Books

Bunting, E. (1998). *Going home.* New York: Harper Trophy.
Colon-Villa, L. (1998). *Salsa.* Houston, TX: Arte Publico Press.

Dorros, A. (1997). *Abuela* (English with Spanish phrases). New York: Puffin.

Johnston, T. (1997). *Day of the dead.* New York: Harcourt Brace.

Mora, P. (1997). *A birthday basket for Tia.* New York: Aladdin Picture Books.

Native American Books

Bruchac, J. (1998). *The earth under Sky Bear's feet: Native American poems of the land.* New York: Paper Star.

Fisher, L. E. (1997). *Anasazi.* New York: Atheneum.

Goble, P. (1998). *Adopted by the eagles: A Plains Indians story of friendship.* New York: Aladdin Paperbacks.

Goble, P. (1990). *Iktomi and the ducks.* New York: Orchard Books.

McAuliffe, B. (1998). *Chief Joseph of the Nez Perce.* Mankato, MN: Capstone Press.

CHILDREN'S LITERATURE ABOUT CHILDREN'S SPECIAL NEEDS

Communication Problems (speech and language differences)

Butler, D. (1995). *What happens when people talk.* Chatham, NJ: Raintree/Steck-Vaughn.

Dedieu, T. et al. (1997). *The boy who ate words.* New York: Harry N. Abrams.

Flournoy, V. (1985). *The patchwork quilt.* New York: Dial.

Hamilton, V. (1985). *The people could fly.* New York: Knopf.

Lester, H. (1999). *Hooway for Wodney Wat.* New York: Walter Loraine Publisher.

Physical Disabilities (visual, hearing, physical)

Brighton, C. (1984). *My hands, my world.* New York: Macmillan.

Frevert, P. D. (1983). *Its okay to look at Jamie.* Mankato, MN: Creative Education.

Peterson, J. W. (1977). *I have a sister. My sister is deaf.* New York: Harper Trophy.

Rabe, B. (1981). *The balancing girls.* New York: Dutton.

Senisi, E. (1998). *Just kids: visiting a class for children with special needs.* New York: Dutton.

Learning Disabilities

Hermes, P. (1983). *Who will take care of me?* New York: Harcourt Brace Jovanovoch.

Hirsch, K. (1977). *My sister.* Minneapolis, MN: Carolrhoda Books.

Janover, C. (1997). *Josh: A boy with dyslexia.* San Francisco, CA: Waterfront Books.

Ominsky, E. (1977). *Jan O, a special boy.* Englewood Cliffs, NJ: Prentice Hall.

Smith, M. (1997). *Pay attention, Slosh*! New York: Albert Whitman.

appendix 

Quality Television Programs with Associated Children's Books

BLUE'S CLUES

Alexander, L. (1998). *Blue and the color detective.* New York: Simon Spotlight.

Santomero, A. C. (1998). *Blue skidoos to the farm.* New York: Simon & Shuster.

Santomero, A. C. (1998). *Blue's felt friends.* New York: Simon & Schuster.

Yablonsky, B. (1998). *Blue's #1 picnic.* New York: Simon Spotlight.

MADELINE

Bemelmans, L. (1993). *Mad about Madeline: The Complete Tales.* New York: Puffin Books.

Bemelmans, L. (1977). *Madeline.* New York: Puffin Books.

Bemelmans, L. (1977). *Madeline's rescue.* New York: Puffin Books.

Bemelmans, L. (1977). *Madeline and the bad hat.* New York: Puffin Books.

Bemelmans, L. (1977). *Madeline in London.* New York: Puffin Books.

SESAME STREET

Allen, C. (1992). *My name is Big Bird.* New York: Golden Books.

Muntean, M. (1997). *Elmo Can Quack like a duck.* New York: Golden Books.

Roberts, S. (1981). *Ernie's big mess.* New York: Random House.

Sommers, T. (1986). *Big Bird goes to the doctor.* Racine, WI: Western Publishing Company and Children's Television Workshop.

Stone, J. (1996). *Another monster at the end of this book.* New York: Golden Books.

WALT DISNEY

Disney, W. (1994). *Alice in Wonderland.* New York: Disney Press.

Disney, W. (1994). *Snow White and the Seven Dwarfs.* New York: Disney Press.

Lewis, Z. (1995). *Cinderella.* New York: Hyperion Press.

Travers, P. L. (1997). *Mary Poppins.* New York: Buccaneer Books.

WINNIE THE POOH

Camenson, S. (1994). *Winnie the Pooh and Tigger too.* New York: Disney Press.

Milne, A. A. (1994). *The poems and hums of Winnie the Pooh.* New York: Dutton.

Milne, A. A. (1993). *Pooh and Piglet go hunting.* New York: Dutton.

Milne, A. A. (1993). *Pooh goes visiting.* New York: Dutton.

Milne, A. A. (1988). *The world of Pooh.* New York: Dutton.

appendix 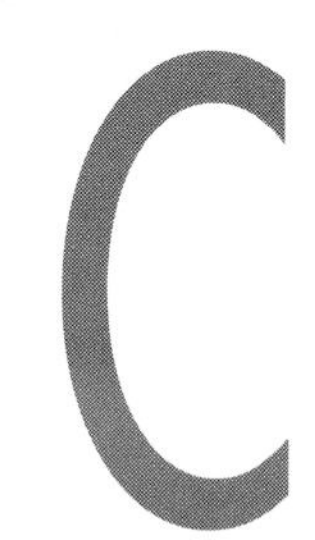

Literacy-Related Computer Software and Web Sites

COMPUTER SOFTWARE

Preschool Parade — Grade: PreK–1

Description: Children work with clowns and animals to learn the alphabet, counting, shapes, and more.

Hardware: MacPlus or higher; 1 MB RAM; System 6.07 or later; hard drive; soundcard recommended; Windows (disk or CD-ROM)

Availability: Nordic Software

Stickybear's Reading Room — Grade: PreK–3

Description: This bilingual program in Spanish and English includes activities in sentence building, word matching, and word finding.

Hardware: Mac DOS System 6.07 with 2MB RAM or System 7 with 4MB RAM; color monitor

Availability: Optimum Resource

Arthur's Birthday — Grade: PreK–2

Description: Children can explore an interactive reading adventure. Focus on reading comprehension, writing, and vocabulary building.

Hardware: Win 3.1, 8MB RAM; CD-ROM; Mac, 6MB RAM; CD-ROM

Availability: Living Books/ Broderbund

Storybook Maker Deluxe — Grade: K–4

Description: Students use this program to create stories, edit work, illustrate, and read.

Hardware: Win 95, Win 3.1; Mac OS or higher; 4MB RAM (5MB recommended); System 7; color monitor; CD-ROM

Availability: Jostens Learning Corporation

Storybook Theatre — Grade: 1–4

Description: Students can create animated stories while experimenting with characters, settings, animation, sound effects, and words.

Hardware: Mac

Availability: Sunburst Communications, Inc.

WEB SITES

Children's Literature Web Guide

Address: http://www.acs.ucalgary.ca/~dkbrown/

Description: An Internet resource related to books for children and young adults. Provides various links for authors; stories; resources for parents, teachers, and children; and children's publishers and booksellers on the Internet.

The Language Arts Pavilion

Address: http://pen.k12.va/us/Anthology/Pav/LangArts/LangArts.html

Description: Students can correspond with well-known book characters, visit literacy giants, publish poetry, and write about their own towns. This site also has great resources, projects, and lesson ideas for teachers.

Online Stories for Students

Address: http://www.ucalgary.ca/~dkbrown/stories.html

Description: This Web page offers illustrated books and stories online for free in a variety of themes.

Kid's Web

Address: http://www.hpac.syr.edu/textbook/kidsweb

Description: This page contains information related to art, drama, computers, literature, music, science, social studies, games, and sports. It is a good page for a novice to begin a Web-based research project.

Intercultural E-mail Classroom Connections

Address: http://www.stolaf.edu/network/iecc

Description: Students can sign up for keypals anywhere in the world. Great way to promote leisure writing.

Big Busy House

Address: http://www.harperchildrens.com

Description: This site explains the process of how a book is made to children. It has links to the Web sites of favorite authors, contains games, features books, and contains book-related activity pages.

appendix 

Suggestions for the Instructors

Literacy Development in the Early Years: Helping Children Read and Write was written for students in graduate and undergraduate classes in courses such as Early Literacy Development and Reading in the Elementary School, or in an Early Childhood Curriculum course that includes literacy development as a major component. The book can also be used for staff development courses for classroom teachers. The book suggests several activities to do with students. I'd like to highlight a few that I have used successfully in class sessions or as assignments. I have also added a complete integrated language arts thematic unit, which teachers can use as a model for beginning literacy programs in their preschool through third-grade classrooms.

ASSIGNMENTS AND IN-CLASS ACTIVITIES

At the beginning of each chapter are focus questions that students should read prior to reading the chapter. At the end of every chapter are activities contributed by classroom teachers that relate to the chapter. In addition, there are activities to engage in and case studies to work out. Read the cases and the activities; you might find that some of them are appropriate for class interaction in small groups and for discussion.

Activities to participate in as you work your way through the book are as follows:

1. Chapter 2 suggests that each student start his or her own portfolio of class work. Included in the portfolio should be the instructor's assignments. As students do assignments, they collect the work in the portfolio and record grades. Teachers should meet with each student once a semester to conference about his or her progress, and review the portfolios.

2. In Chapter 2 it is suggested that students select a child that they can study as they read the book. The child should be between the ages of 2 and 8 years. The student is to begin a portfolio for the child, and meet with him or her from time to time, to try strategies and assess and describe certain behaviors. Specifically, the students should obtain a sample of writing, drawing, oral language, and a story retelling from the child. In addition, several of the measures provided in the book can be used to accumulate data about the child. For example:

   a. When studying the family, interview the child's parents with the form concerning the home literacy environment found in Chapter 3.
   b. When reading Chapter 4 on language development, collect a language sample and analyze it for sentence length and number of different words. To elicit language from a child, ask him or her to tell you about family, pets, TV shows they like, or games they play. Tape record the discussion and transcribe it for analysis.
   c. When reading Chapter 6, interview the child using the form in that chapter that evaluates motivation for reading and writing.
   d. When reading Chapter 7, have the child retell a story that was read to him or her. Tape record the retelling and transcribe it. Analyze it with the retelling instrument in the chapter. Children can also be asked to rewrite the story. The rewriting can be analyzed with the same tool.
   e. In Chapter 8, evaluate the child's knowledge about print with the checklist included.
   f. In Chapter 9, collect a writing sample from the child to determine the stage of writing, and analyze it for sense of story structure, the mechanics of writing, etc. To elicit a writing sample you might have the child draw a picture and write about it. Talk about ideas to write before writing. For emergent writers, assure them that any way they can write is fine. Show them samples of children's writing from the text for them to see that one letter or scribble writing is fine.

3. At least three or four times during the semester, have the class break up into groups to deal with one of the cases presented at the end of the chapters. Have the students solve the problem presented, and have them relate their findings to the group. Compare the differences in solutions. A case that will generate a good deal of discussion is the one in Chapter 7 about Teachers A, B, and C. Have the students respond to the questions posed about the teachers, and discuss which teacher each would wish to be. The students must select one. Discuss the pros and cons of each of the teachers in the case.

4. Have students keep dialogue journals about readings that have made an impression on them. They can also include incidents in class that were particularly interesting, fun, or of concern. Respond to their journals with comments of your own.

5. Have your students take a vocabulary test, using words from the glossary. Teachers need to be aware of the technical language associated with early literacy when talking with peers, interviewing for a job, and explaining issues to parents.

6. Have students bring five genres of children's literature to class to share in groups. This gives them the opportunity to browse through lots of books and see the variety of genres available. Set the books up as if they were going into a classroom. This will give a sense of the numbers and types of books that should be in a literacy center.

7. Ask students to draw a floor plan for their ideal classroom using the philosophy and strategies learned. Pay particular attention to the literacy center. Be sure they create plans to support literacy instruction for whole groups, small groups, and one-to-one settings.

8. Ask each student to be involved in a storytelling project. Give students a list of early literacy skills from those outlined on the checklists provided in the book. Have them select a skill they would like to teach. Ask them to find a picture story book that will enable that skill to be taught. For example, if their skill is to teach sequencing, a story such as *The Old Lady Who Swallowed the Fly* provides a sequence of events that are easily followed. The student then selects a technique for storytelling from those described in Chapter 6, such as a chalk talk, roll story, felt story, or other techniques they create themselves. A lesson plan is developed in which the teacher will present the story and teach the skill through the use of the material created. The material is designed for children to use to practice the skill taught. In Chapter 6 the "Idea from the Classroom for the Classroom" concerning the story *A Bunny Called Nat* illustrates this type of assignment. Students present the storytelling in class.

9. Have the students select a group to work with. Have the group select a topic for a thematic unit. Using the guide for the unit in Chapter 10, divide the sections and prepare a thematic unit for a classroom of children from ages 2 through 8 years.

10. Have students participate in a teacher–researcher project. Each student will select a topic dealing with early literacy, and carry out a ministudy. The study should include a statement of purpose, a short literature review related to the topic, a description of methods and procedures to follow during the study, a discussion of how the data will be analyzed, a report of the results of the data collection, and a discussion concerning the results. This is a large project that is introduced to students early in the semester in order for them to have ample time to carry it out. When writing the literature review, the students should be required to consult a few articles from professional journals. Some topics for study are: literacy and play, computers and early literacy, family literacy, multicultural concerns in early literacy, and early intervention programs.

11. Have students bind their own books based on the directions given in Chapter 9. Have them use the book for their dialogue journal or for writing their storytelling lesson plan.

12. Encourage students to join a professional organization such as the International Reading Association or the National Association of the Education of Young Children.

13. Encourage your students to subscribe to a professional journal and a commercial teacher magazine.

14. For the type of information presented in the course, I think a take-home test is most appropriate. Questions can be selected by the instructor from those asked in the activities at the end of the chapter.

15. One important activity to offer your students is to let them experience what it would be like to be a child learning to read. For this demonstration, I am providing you with materials and a plan for a class experience. This activity should take about 45 minutes of class time and should be done early in the semester when you are teaching theory. The lesson involves learning how to read with an alphabet called the *Confusabet*. Following is a plan for carrying out the Confusabet. Materials needed are provided in this Appendix. You can photocopy them for use in your lesson plan before beginning the lesson or use the pages in the book.

THE CONFUSABET LESSON

Objective: To experience how it feels to learn to read and write for a better understanding of the process and how children feel when they are learning.

Materials

Confusabet Alphabet and translation
Confusabet sight words and their translation
Confusabet worksheets
Confusabet reading book and translation (books must be assembled)

Procedures

1. Before the lesson, ask students to think about and write the following during the experience:
   a. What methods were used to teach reading? Which were good and which were not particularly good?
   b. What emotions did you experience while learning to read and write the Confusabet?
   c. What strategies did you use to teach yourself how to read and write?
2. Hand out or turn to the Confusabet alphabet and pictures that have the names of the Confusabet characters on them.
3. Name the characters and have the students repeat their names.
4. Hand out or turn to worksheet #1. Ask students to find the character's name among other Confusabet words.
5. Hand out or turn to the list of Confusabet words. Provide students with context clues for each word to help them figure out what it says. For example: The color of the traffic light that means you should stop is ______ . Have the students fill in the word and point to the Confusabet word that is red. Context clues are provided in the translations at the end of Appendix D.
6. Do this for all words and provide your own context clues.
7. Repeat the words with the students. You may repeat them all together, call on those who raise their hands, and call on students who do not raise their hands.
8. Turn to or hand out worksheet #2 with the Confusabet words just introduced and ask students to underline and name the word in each list that is the same as the first word at the top of the list.
9. Turn to or distribute the Confusabet primer. Call on students to read a line or a page at a time. Try round robin reading as well.

   During the Confusabet lesson, role-play as if you are a teacher of 6-year-olds. Praise students for doing well. Do some positive reinforcing and use some positive teaching techniques. Try techniques that are often used and words that are often said to students that are punitive, such as: "If you don't get this work correct you won't get to take the book home to your parents" or "You weren't listening; that's why you don't know the words" or "If you don't stop talking, you'll be sent to the principal's office."

   During the Confusabet exercise, students will talk to each other naturally to try and work things out. When this happens, say: "Please do your own work and keep your eyes on your own paper" or " Don't help each other; you have to learn to do it yourself" or "It's too noisy in here" and "We can't wait for you even though you haven't finished your work." When students have answers and are very anxious to give them say: "You've already had your turn; give someone else a chance" or "Please settle down; you are disrupting the rest of the class." When students look ahead to preview materials handed out, say, "Please wait for me to tell you when to turn the page" or "Don't go ahead of me, we aren't up to that yet." This type of role-playing allows students to experience even more how children feel in the classroom, where these types of comments often occur.
10. After reading the Confusabet materials, ask students to write their names and then the sentence: "I like to read and write," with Confusabet symbols.
11. At the end of the lesson ask the questions posed at the beginning:
    a. What methods did I use that were good? What methods did I use that were not very good?
    b. What emotions did you experience?
    c. How did you teach yourself to learn to read?
    d. How did you go about learning to write?

Students will express that they experienced fear, anger, and frustration when they were having trouble. They will suggest that they wanted to tune out and not participate. Those who were succeeding will suggest that they were excited, they wanted to continue, and they wanted to share their excitement. Frequently students who are succeeding will be greeted with remarks such as "You've already had a turn, settle down and let me give someone else a chance." When asked how they felt about this response, they will say that their excitement was drained.

When students discuss the strategies they used to learn to read, they will often make comments similar to the following:

1. I used my past experience with knowledge from our real alphabet to help. For example, the Confusabet words have the same number of symbols as our alphabet. They also resemble some of the letters of our alphabet and I was able to make associations.
2. I used the picture clues.
3. I used surrounding words or the context to figure out the word. (contextual and syntactic clues)
4. I memorized symbols from one page to the next to try and remember.
5. Some words were long or had an unusual shape, which helped me to get a word. (configuration)
6. I looked at the first letter of a word to give me help in figuring it out.

When students are asked some of the things they did to help them read they may say:

1. I pointed to the print to help me find my place.
2. I moved my eyes around the page to try and find clues.
3. I called out words one at a time, the way young children do.

What the students realize as a result of participating in the Confusabet experience is that they look to meaning, past experience, associative strategies, and visual clues to figure out the words, more than they do individual skills such as phonics.

The Confusabet lesson presented here is adapted from materials created by Mildred Letton Wittock from the University of Chicago.

CONFUSABET ALPHABET LETTERS

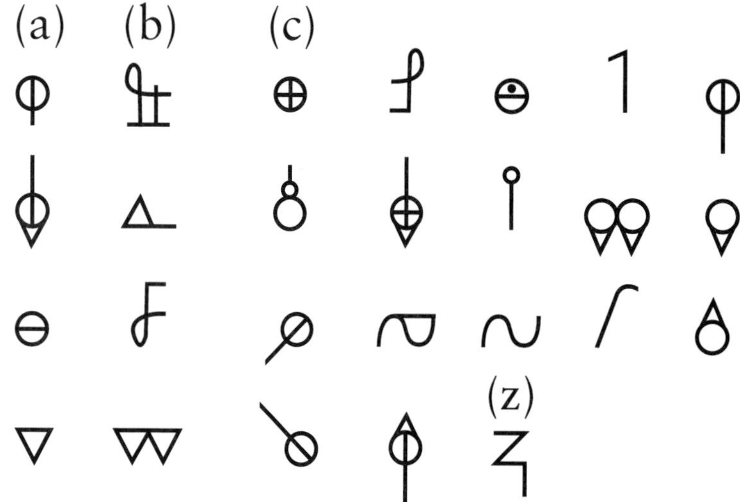

CONFUSABET STORY CHARACTERS

Directions: Instructor names the characters for the students. Students repeat the names.

CONFUSABET VOCABULARY WORDS

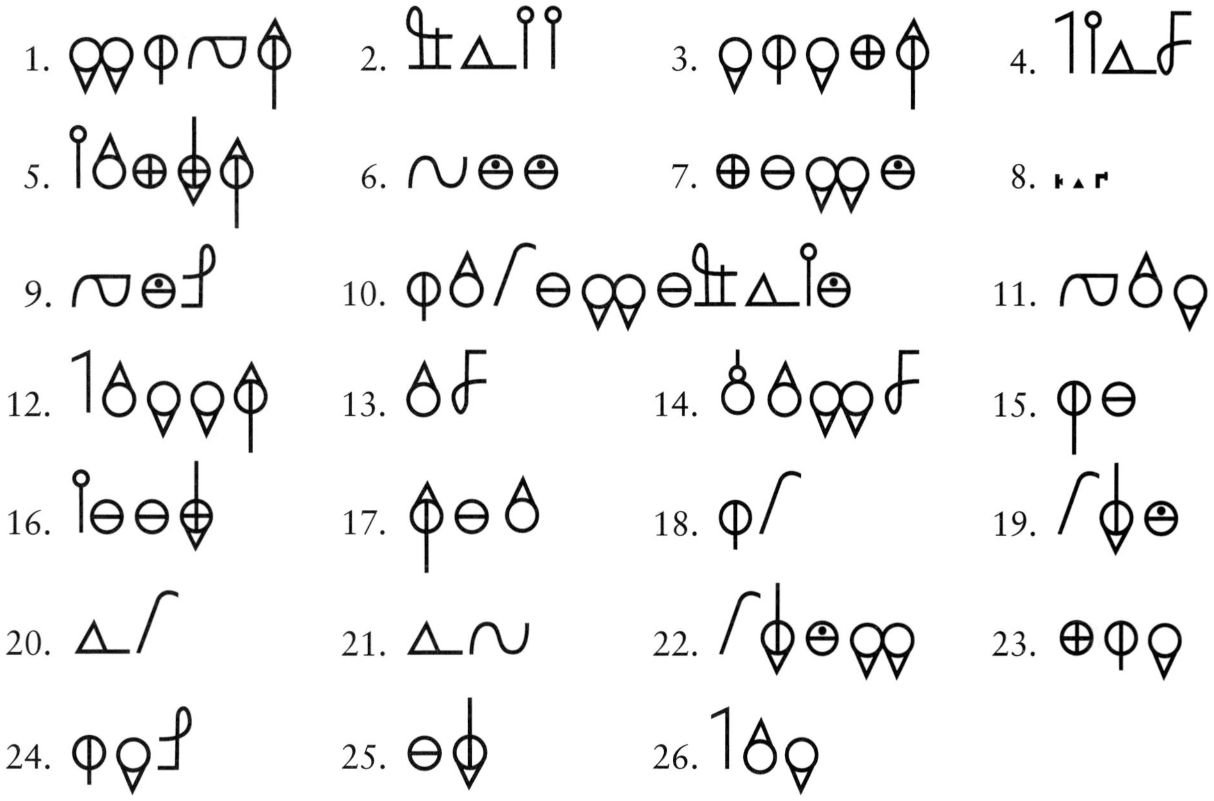

Directions: Instructor gives a context clue for each word to help student to read it. Students repeat the words. Clues are on page 381.

CONFUSABET WORKSHEET 1

Directions: Circle the name of the character in the list of words under his or her name. Say the name as you circle it.

CONFUSABET WORKSHEET 2

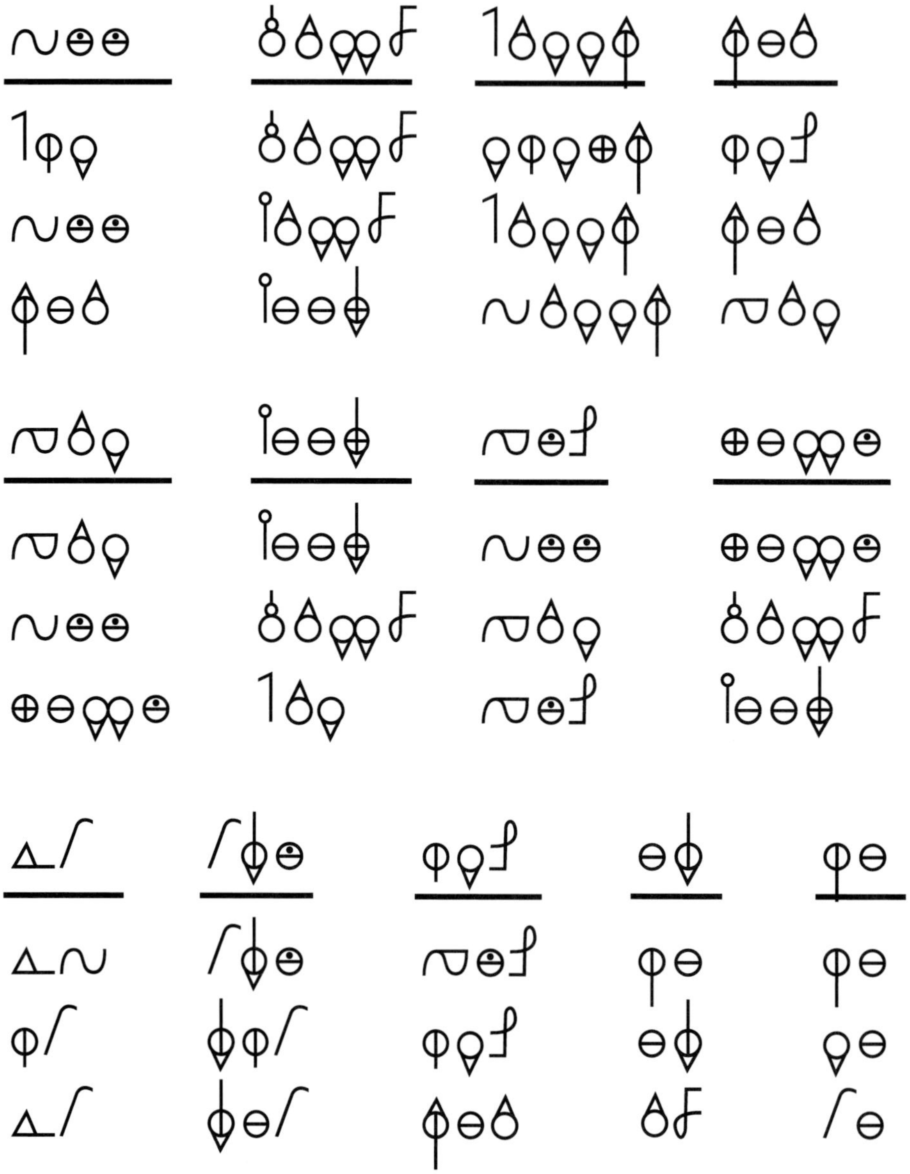

Directions: Circle the underlined word in each column. Say the word as you circle it.

CONFUSABET PRIMER

CONFUSABET STORY #1

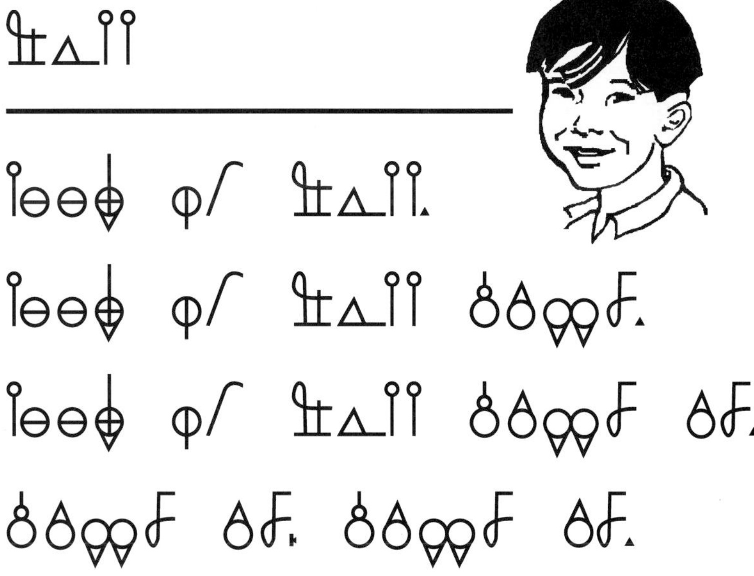

CONFUSABET STORY #2

CONFUSABET STORY #3

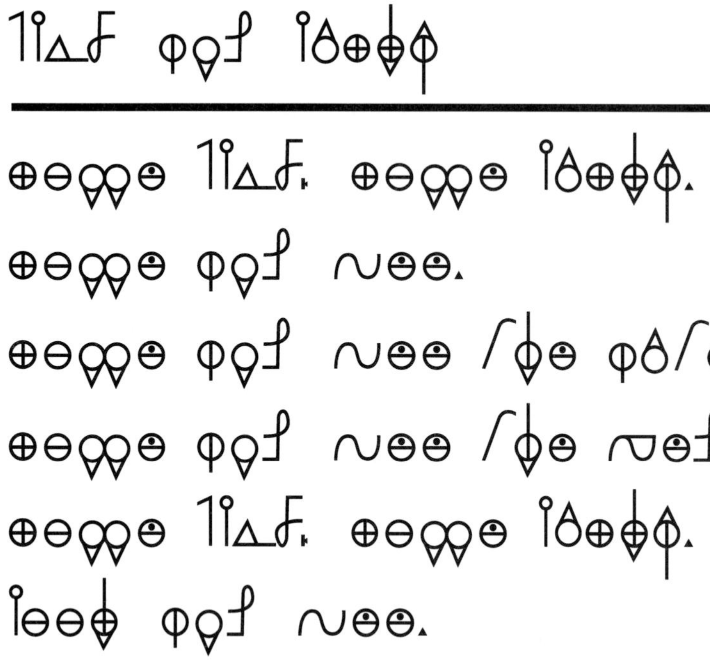

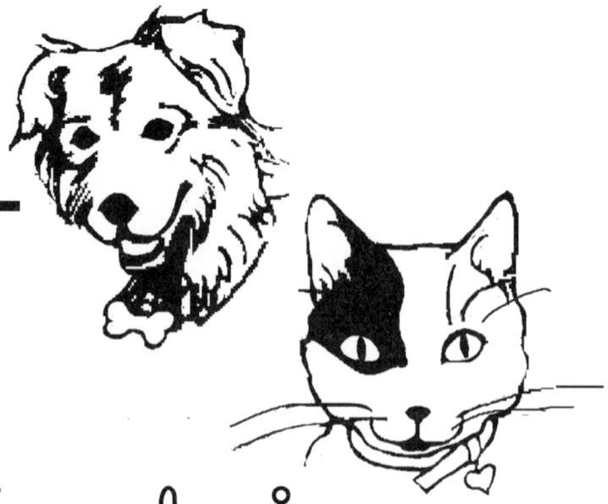

CONFUSABET STORY #4

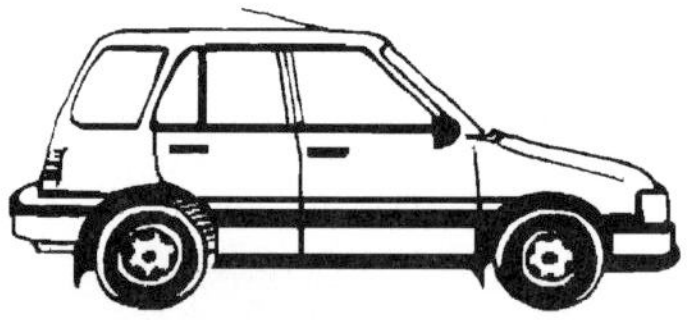

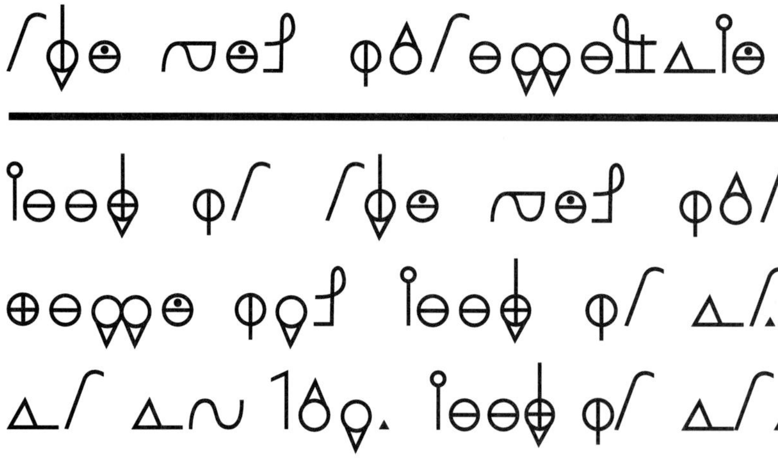

CONFUSABET STORY #5

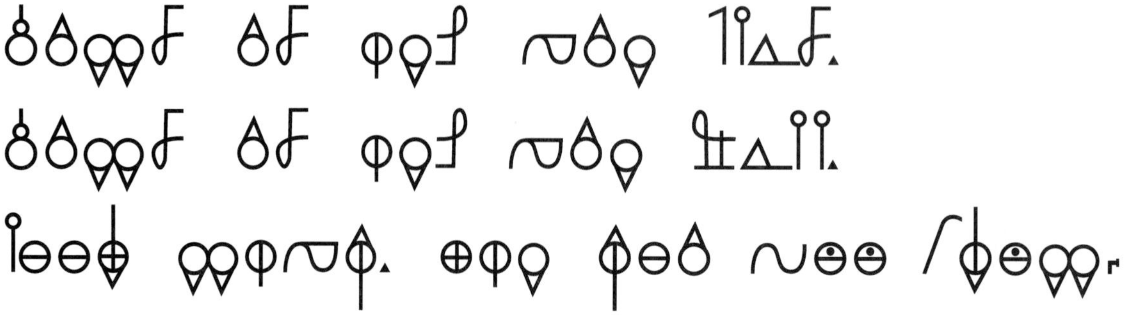

CONFUSABET TRANSLATIONS

STORY CHARACTER NAMES

1. Mary, 2. Bill, 3. Nancy, 4. Flip, 5. Lucky

VOCABULARY TRANSLATIONS WITH CONTEXT CLUE SENTENCES

6. see— With my eyes I ______.
7. come— Please ______ over here.
8. , (comma) . (period) ? (question mark)
9. red— The top color light on a traffic signal is ______.
10. automobile— Another name for a car is an ______.
11. run— When I go fast on my feet I ______.
12. funny— A clown is ______.
13. up— When we take off in a airplane we go ______.
14. jump— When I play with a rope I ______ up.
15. go— The green traffic light means for us to ______.
16. look— A word that rhymes with book and means to see is ______.
17. you— Not me but ______.
18. at— Come and look ______ it.
19. the— ______ red automobile
20. it— Let's get into ______.
21. is— It ______ fun to ride in.
22. them— I'm going over there to be with ______.
23. can— Yes I ______.
24. and— Come ______ play with me.
25. oh— When I am surprised I say ______.
26. fun— When I play with my friend I have ______.

STORY TRANSLATIONS FOR PRIMER

Primer Title — *Look and See*

Story #1 — *Bill*
Look at Bill.
Look at Bill jump.
Look at Bill jump up.
Jump up, jump up.

Story #2 — *Nancy and Bill and Mary*
Look Bill. Look Mary.
See Nancy.
Look and see Nancy.
Funny funny Nancy.

Story #3 — *Flip and Lucky*
Come Flip, come Lucky.
Come and see.
Come and see the automobile.
Come and see the red automobile.
Come Flip, come Lucky.
Look and see.

Story #4 — *The Red Automobile*
Look at the red automobile.
Come and look at it.
It is fun. Look at it.

Story #5 — *(Without pictures)*
Jump up and run Flip.
Jump up and run Bill.
Look Mary. Can you see them?

INTEGRATED LANGUAGE ARTS THEMATIC UNIT: "HEALTHY BODIES, HEALTHY MINDS"

On the following pages, you will find a thematic unit dealing with "Healthy Bodies, Healthy Minds," written for children in preschool through third grade. This unit includes all content areas and weaves literacy instruction throughout. When using the unit, adapt and select the ideas for the children you teach, making sure to repeat activities to reinforce the concepts being taught. When carrying out the unit, samples from each student's work should be gathered through formal and informal assessment measures. This is an excellent way to track the student's progress, and can be used in portfolio assessment. Using this unit as a guide, try your hand at creating another thematic unit for the youngsters in your classroom.

Factual Information

What Does It Mean To Be Healthy in Body and Mind?
Eating nutritious food, exercising regularly, getting enough sleep, keeping ourselves clean, and feeling good about ourselves, are all very important to keeping fit and healthy in body and mind.

Why Should We Eat Healthy Foods?
Good foods are needed to supply your body and mind with the energy it needs to function and grow everyday. All people need food to eat and water to drink to live. Food and water are also necessary for animals and most plants to live. Nutrients are the substances in food that give us the energy and strength we need to grow, work, and play.

What Are the Four Food Groups?
Eating properly, along with plenty of sleep and exercise, will keep a person's body healthy and strong. There are many types of food. Foods are separated into four major groups, and eating a proper amount of each daily will help ensure good health. Foods are categorized in the following manner:

1. *Vegetable-Fruit Group:* Most vitamins and roughage are obtained from fruits and vegetables. A good diet should contain dark green and yellow vegetables and citrus fruits. Some examples include apples, oranges, pears, broccoli, lettuce, carrots, spinach, and squash. It is recommended that four servings be eaten daily from this group.

2. *Bread-Cereal Group:* This group includes breads; rolls; bagels; crackers; cereals, such as oats and rice; and pastas. Carbohydrates, necessary for the energy to work and play, and fiber are the primary benefits of this group. Four daily servings are suggested.

3. *Meat-Poultry Group:* Also included in this group are fish, beans, nuts, and eggs. This group provides minerals and much of the protein in one's diet. Protein is essential for building and maintaining muscles. It is also important for overall growth. Two servings are suggested daily.

4. *Milk-Cheese Group:* This group includes all dairy products, such as milk, cheese, yogurt, and cottage cheese. These products are also high in protein and contain nutrients that build strong bones and teeth. Many products in this group tend to have a high fat content. Three servings are the recommended daily intake.

A proper diet, including ample portions from the four food groups, is essential for a healthy, growing child. However, there are also foods known as "empty calorie foods" or "junk foods." These items provide no vitamins, minerals, or protein and are not necessary for good heath. Foods in this group include soda, candies, potato chips, and some seasonings and spices. On occasion these foods are fine in moderate amounts; however, a well-rounded diet containing items from the four major food groups is best.

People from different cultures eat different food. Because the United States is home to people from many cultures, numerous American dishes have been influenced by Mexican, Asian, French, Italian, and Jamaican cooking, among others. It is fun to try ethnic foods and learn about different multicultural backgrounds.

Why Are Exercise, Rest, and Cleanliness Important?
Exercising by ourselves or with others can be fun. It gives us stronger muscles, healthier hearts, and makes our bodies and minds feel good. It helps circulate our blood and makes us feel refreshed and relaxed.

People around the world exercise regularly to keep healthy. Many of the sports or exercises here in the United States have been influenced by other cultures. For example, baseball was influenced by a British game called cricket, and American football was developed from rugby, a similar contact sport. Regular exercise helps to relieve stress and in getting a good night's sleep.

We spend a third of our lives sleeping. When we sleep, we give our bodies and minds time to rest, during which our heart rate and blood pressure decrease and breathing slows down. This is so our bodies and minds can work hard when we are awake. Getting too little sleep can affect your body and mind's ability to function and grow.

People with clean bodies, hands, faces, teeth, and hair are nice to be around. Clean people are less likely to attract germs and get sick. We can stay clean by washing ourselves and our clothes often.

How Does Self-esteem Affect Your Body and Mind? People who feel good about themselves have self-esteem. They take care of their bodies and minds, and stay away from junk food, drugs, and alcohol. They look healthy and share their energy and good feelings with others around them.

Good mental health is important for coping with the demands of everyday life. Sometimes when you do not feel very good about yourself, it might help to make a list of all the things you can do, for example, ride a bike, read a book, draw a picture, or cook a dish. People can also help us solve our problems and make us feel better. These people include parents, siblings, friends, and teachers. However, it is important to realize that we all have strengths and weaknesses. This kind of self-knowledge helps in our ability to accept ourselves and to relate well with others.

It is healthy to express our feelings in appropriate ways. When someone does not take the time to think about his or her feelings and speak calmly in words, feelings may come out in other ways. People might show anger, feel sick and tired, or might want to be alone. Getting plenty of sleep, eating nutritious meals, exercising outdoors, and keeping up personal hygiene will help you feel better about yourself.

Newsletter to Parents about Healthy Bodies, Healthy Minds

Dear Parents:

Your child will be participating in a unit that explores what it means to be healthy in body and mind. This unit will include study of why we should eat healthy foods, the four food groups, exercise, rest, cleanliness, and the importance of self-esteem.

The good health unit will cover all subject areas—play, art, music, social studies, science, math, and literacy (reading, writing, listening, and oral language) which will be incorporated in the theme. Some of the exciting activities we do here at school may also be carried out at home with your child.

At School and at Home

Art: Art can be a wonderful learning experience for your child. Your child will refine eye-hand coordination and visual discrimination skills and explore and experiment with different art materials as he or she engages in various art activities. At school we will be creating food collages and abstract bean mosaics. At home you can encourage your child to use his or her imagination by providing these and other food-related materials for art activities. Remember that art is for exploring what can be done with different materials, rather than copying an adult model.

Science: Science explorations will be related to meaningful aspects of your child's life. We will be making homemade applesauce, which will give the children an opportunity to listen, follow directions, and learn where apples come from and how they are grown, as well as how food changes as it is cooked. Making healthy snacks at home, such as a fruit or lettuce salad, and involving your child in the preparation by using simple recipes will help to extend listening skills.

Literacy: The letters *H, F,* and *B* associated with *Health, Food,* and *Body* are being highlighted. Please assist at home by labeling healthy food items with these letters or pointing out words that have these and other beginning sounds. Read signs and point out these letters when you are outside the home as well.

Please read stories, poems, informational books, cookbooks, exercise magazines, and other literature related to our theme of good health to your child. Reading to your child, having her or him read to you using illustrations, and retelling a story are all literacy activities that are valuable and enjoyable. Some books that will be featured in the unit include:

Gregory, the Terrible Eater by M. Sharmat, 1984
No More Baths by B. Cole, 1989
Mooncake by F. Asch, 1983
There's a Nightmare in my Closet by M. Mayer, 1968

(continued on next page)

(continued from previous page)

We Need Your Help

We would like your assistance with our multicultural food of the week or your favorite food at home. If you are able to prepare a snack one day and discuss it, please sign your name and tell what type of snack you would like to prepare on the attached sheet.

If you can come in and read your child's favorite bedtime story to the class, please sign your name and tell what date you are available on the attached sheet.

If you have any other materials at home related to our theme, such as empty food containers, seeds, nuts, beans, or exercise or yoga magazines that we may use in our dramatic-play area, please send them in with your child.

Other Activities to Do with Your Child

Go to the supermarket with your child. Prepare a list beforehand of the food you need to purchase. Have your child check the things off as you put them in the cart. Try to purchase food from each food group.

Plant watermelon, avocado, carrot seeds at home. Keep a diary or record of their growth, making comparisons between them.

Make simple, nutritious recipes at home, such as fruit salad, mixed green salad, butter, or peanut butter, to help our lessons carry over from class to home.

Take the time to engage in some exercise with your child each day. A brisk walk or bike ride will help your child learn that exercise is fun and should be done often. It is an activity your family will enjoy together.

Remind your child at bedtime that rest is important for our bodies. Share a special bedtime story each night with your child.

Child's Corner

Ask your child to write or draw something he or she did in school related to our theme.

Help your child keep a journal of what foods he or she eats each day. Keep track of any exercises your child does. Keep track of how many hours of sleep your child gets, writing the number in the journal. Graph the numbers. The journal can be written in a notebook, on a pad, or on pieces of paper stapled together like a book.

If you have any questions about the unit or have any additional ideas, please contact me. If you are in a profession that is related to our theme, such as a nutritionist or any fitness-related career, please consider coming into class and talking to us.

Sincerely,

Lisa Lozak

I would like to prepare the following snack for your healthy bodies, healthy minds unit:

Snack:____________________________ Parent's Name: __________________

I am able to come in on the following date for a storyreading: Date:__________________

Book: ____________________________ Parent's Name: __________________

Preparing Classroom Environment

To begin the unit on healthy bodies, healthy minds, prepare the room so that the theme is evident to those who enter. Begin with some of the following suggestions and continue to add others as the unit progresses. Display environmental signs and labels about nutrition, personal hygiene, exercise, rest, and self-esteem wherever possible. Feature colors that represent the unit, such as white for dairy products, green for vegetables, and yellow and red for fruit.

1. *Dramatic Play:* This center can be turned into either a restaurant or a fitness center. As a restaurant, the center should include menus, receipts, order-taking slips, recipe cards, cookbooks, baking utensils, prop foods, signs commonly seen in restaurants, a cash register, play money, food posters, and waiter and waitress clothing. As a health club, the center could include light weights or dumbbells, jump ropes, balls, a balance beam, mats, gym membership cards, stop watches, heart-rate posters, sign-up sheets for aerobic classes, and towels.

2. *Block Area:* To create places that food comes from such as farms and supermarkets, the following items can be added: farm props (animals and plants), supermarket props (play foods, receipts, money, and bags), environmental print signs and posters displaying food information, and cards for making signs.

3. *Outdoor Play:* A health club/fitness center can be created outside by providing the following items: tables for stands or desks; exercise equipment including jump ropes, balls and a balance beam; play money; cash register; receipts; signs displaying the hours of business; and paper and pencils, so children learn that this is a place to go to keep our bodies healthy.

4. *Music:* Various songs on nutrition, exercise, personal hygiene, and good self-esteem can be added to this center. All tapes should be accompanied by the written lyrics posted on the wall. Props to act out the songs may also be motivating. Students should also be encouraged to write and sing their own songs about good health.

5. *Art:* Include play dough and a poster with play dough recipes to make play foods. Include cooking and health magazines, dry foods to make collages, fruits, vegetables, shaped sponges for printing with paint, and scraps that represent the nutrition colors—white, green, red and yellow.

6. *Science:* Materials for various health and nutrition projects may be added: a stethoscope, a heart-rate chart, blood pressure device, foods to be classified into the four food groups, seed packages, and planting equipment. All of these items should be accompanied with charts and journals to record ongoing progress. Posters of the human body showing the muscles and skeleton and informational books should also be added.

7. *Social Studies:* Pictures of foods and the four food groups, and maps that depict where certain food comes from, as well as where the children's families are from should be included. In addition, posters displaying various athletic events from around the world may appear in the center. Recipe books representing different cultures may also be added.

8. *Math:* Various foods can be used as counters, such as macaroni or dried beans. Charts and graphs to record various activities, such as favorite fruit, laps around the school yard, or number of hours slept per night, should be included. Blank books for children to create their own number books are also needed.

9. *Literacy Center*
   a. *Writing Center:* Materials needed include a recipe box to share favorite recipes, food-shaped blank books, and a message board on which to share the morning message.
   b. *Library Corner:* Include health and fitness magazines, cooking magazines, pamphlets about good nutrition and general health, and a collection of books pertaining to the unit from all genres. (See the following list and the bibliography at the end of the unit.)

Library Corner Booklist with Suggested Activities

Asch, F. (1983). *Mooncake.* Englewood Cliffs, NJ: Prentice Hall.

Brandenberg, F. (1976). *I wish I was sick, too.* NY: Greenwillow.

Carle, E. (1969). *The very hungry caterpillar.* New York: Philomel.

Chambers, W. (1974). *The lip-smackin', joke-crackin' cookbook for kids.* New York: Golden Press.

Cole, J. (1988). *The magic school bus inside the human body.* New York: Scholastic.

dePaola,T. (1975). *Strega Nona: An old tale.* Englewood Cliffs, NJ: Prentice Hall.

dePaola, T. (1978). *The popcorn book.* New York: Holiday House.

Eberts, M. (1984). *Pancakes, crackers, and pizza.* Chicago: Children's Press.

Faulkner, M. (1986). *Jack and the beanstalk.* New York: Scholastic.

Hoban, R. (1976). *Bread and jam for Frances.* New York: Harper & Row.

Hopkins, L. B. (1985). *Munching: Poems about eating.* Boston: Little, Brown.

Irving, W. (1987). *Rip Van Winkle.* New York: Puffin Books.

Izawa, T. (1968). *The little red hen.* New York: Grosset & Dunlap.

Kellogg, S. (1988). *Johnny Appleseed: A tall tale.* New York: Morrow Jr. Books.

Krauss, R. (1945). *The carrot seed.* New York: Scholastic.

Mayer, M. (1968). *There's a nightmare in my closet.* New York: Penguin.

McCloskey, R. (1948). *Blueberries for Sal.* New York: Penguin.

Numeroff-Joffe, L. (1985). *If you give a mouse a cookie.* New York: Scholastic.

Raffi. (1987). *Shake my sillies out.* New York: Random House.

Sharmat, M. (1984). *Gregory, the terrible eater.* New York: Macmillan.

Shaw, C. (1947). *It looked like spilled milk.* New York: HarperCollins.

Suess, Dr. (1960). *Green eggs and ham.* New York: Random House.

Westcott, N. B. (1980). *I know an old lady who swallowed a fly.* Boston: Little, Brown.

Zolotow, C. (1962). *Mr. Rabbit and the lovely present.* New York: Harper & Row.

Introductory Lesson

Objective

A written message will provide for vocabulary development and sound–symbol associations. Print will be recongnized as functional because it relays a message.

Activity: *Morning Message*—Introduce the students to the good health unit by writing a message on the board. Tell them about some of the interesting facts they will be learning during the unit. The message could look something like this: "*Today, we are going to begin learning about how to keep our bodies and our minds healthy. To take care of ourselves we need to eat good food, sleep, exercise, keep our bodies clean, and feel good about ourselves.*" Read the message to the class using a pointer to track the print. Afterwards discuss the content of the message as well as the special words, letters, and sounds. Identify the letters *H, F,* and *B* as letters that will be focused on throughout the unit and associate them with the words *Health, Food* and *Body.* Allow the children to add to the message. Do a morning message daily to inform students of new health facts, as well as any special events or questions that are related to the unit.

Concepts about Print

Objective 1

Increase oral and sight vocabulary through a discussion involving the seeing and writing of Very Own Words. Knowledge of nutrition will be gained.

Activity: *Very Own Words*—Before reading the story *I Know an Old Lady Who Swallowed a Fly,* discuss with the children why it is dangerous to eat inappropriate food. After reading the story, the children will discuss food they should not eat. Then ask them to name foods they like that are also good for them and *The Old Lady.* Write each child's favorite food on a 3 × 5 index card to be stored in their Very Own Word container.

Objective 2

Increase sight vocabulary and the ability to follow directions by using a chart with functional environmental print.

Activity: *Environmental Print*—A helper chart will be made that lists jobs for students to perform. The chart should be located in a visible area and relate directly to the unit. Jobs may include cafeteria monitor, reading the lunch menu, and helping with the daily snack.

Objective 3

The featured letter in a word, story, or song will be identified. The letter's sound–symbol relationship will be made and then copied from a story chart.

Activity: *Featured Letters*—Display pictures of types of exercises that keep a body healthy, using the featured letters: *R—Running, D—Dancing, B—Baseball, W—Walking.* Simple stories and songs with the letters may also be used, e.g., *Barbara plays baseball with Bob in Billy's backyard.* Emphasize the sound the letter makes in each word and have the children write the letter. Students may be encouraged to bring in items from home that begin with the featured letter. Pictures of items that begin with the featured letter may also be made and added to a class book. Do one letter at a time and repeat the activities suggested.

Objective 4

An alphabet book that reviews many nutrition words learned in the unit will be created. Knowledge of letters, both vowels and consonants, and words that are identified with specific letters and sounds will be demonstrated.

Activity: *Nutrition Alphabet Book*—An alphabet book will be made and photocopied for each child in the class. Each letter will relate to nutrition (i.e.,

A—apple, B—bread, C—carrot, D—dairy, E—eggs, F—fish.) and a complete sentence will be written with each letter (i.e., I like ___). The students will read the letters, words, and sentences with the teacher and with each other.

Oral Language

Objective 1
Listening skills will be improved by speaking in complete sentences.

Activity: *Show and Tell*—Have students bring in their favorite foods from home representing different cultural backgrounds. Display and discuss with the class. Another activity would be to have children share a healthy habit they practice at home or at school.

Objective 2
Appropriate vocabulary for the level of maturity will be used when retelling a story.

Activity: *Story Retelling*—Read a story related to nutrition, such as *The Very Hungry Caterpillar*, and allow the class to retell the story using food props that are in the book.

Objective 3
Oral communication skills will be increased, through participation in a literature circle.

Activity: *Literature Circle*—Children will sit in a small group with the teacher and discuss a book that they read related to the healthy bodies, healthy minds theme. Model appropriate book talk and pose questions to facilitate the group discussion. Encourage the children to continue posing questions to each other, without the teacher as a guide.

Objective 4
Language complexity will be increased through the use of adjectives.

Activity: *Webbing and Creating Poetry*—Brainstorm characteristics of nutritious food, such as milk, and provide a graphic presentation with a web (see below). List the characteristics of the food by writing adjectives to describe it. Create a web on the chalkboard. Encourage children to assist in putting together a poem by using the information on the web. Write the poem on the chalkboard. Encourage children to read it with you, tracking print from left to right as you read. Rewrite the poem on chart paper to display.

Developing Positive Attitudes

Objective 1
Develop positive attitudes toward reading through interaction in a well-designed literacy center.

Activity: *The Library Corner*—Include different genres of literature related to the theme of healthy bodies, healthy minds (realistic literature, fairy tales, poetry, informational books, magazines, and newspapers). Provide hand/face/stick puppets, taped stories, felt stories, roll movies, and so on.

Objective 2
A story is read by a class parent to increase family literacy. Using the context of the story, outcomes will be predicted.

Activity: If You Give a Mouse a Cookie, *Prop Story*—A child's family member will read *If You Give a Mouse a Cookie* to the class. Use props such as a mouse doll, a plastic cup, an empty box of cookies, and so on to tell the story again to the class. Encourage participation by having the children use their knowledge of rhyme and context. Place the props in the library corner for the children to use.

Objective 3
A story will be told through the use of a storytelling technique (chalk talk).

Our Poem about Milk

Milk tastes cold and delicious,
Milk is healthy and refreshing,
Milk is a white liquid that is good for you.

Activity: Mr. Rabbit and the Lovely Present, *Chalk Talk*—Read *Mr. Rabbit and the Lovely Present* and discuss the food in the story. Now retell the story and draw the fruit in the story as you come to each part. Use colored chalk for the chalk board. After repeated story readings, encourage children to retell the story themselves.

Objective 4
Enjoy literature while working with a friend.

Activity: Partner Reading—Have children work in pairs in the literacy center. They may retell a story using props, felt-board, hand or face puppets, or a roll movie. They should also be encouraged to take turns reading and discussing a story with their partner.

Concepts about Books

Objective 1
Learn to differentiate print from pictures and know what books are for.

Activity: Big Book—Create a class Big Book that contains pictures and sentences of each child's favorite exercise or sport. When it is completed, read the book together. Place the Big Book in the library corner for repeated readings.

Objective 2
See and understand that print is read from left to right.

Activity: Poetry Reading—Display a poem (such as "Shake My Sillies Out") about movement or exercise on a large chart and read with the class. Use a pointer to show that print is read from left to right. Act out the poem and then create a class poem. Display and read it in the same manner.

Objective 3
Learn that an illustrator draws pictures in a book.

Activity: Illustrators—Read *It Looked Like Spilled Milk* to the class. Discuss the illustrations in the story and allow the students to become illustrators by drawing their own pictures of what they see when they look at a cloud. Create a Big Book of all the pictures.

Objective 4
Learn the function and importance of the title and cover of a book.

Activity: Title Pages—Present several books about health and hygiene (refer to book list if needed) to the class. Read the titles and discuss the picture on the cover. Ask students if they can guess what the book is about just by reading the title and looking at the cover. Explain that the title and picture help the reader know what the story or book is about. Have the students create their own title and cover for a book they would like to someday read or write. Create a class Big Book of title pages.

Comprehension

Objective 1
Learn about story structure by identifying story elements (setting, theme, characters, plot episodes, resolution).

Activity: Story Structure—The story *There's a Nightmare in My Closet,* has been read to the children in the past. Before reading the story a second time, ask the children to try and remember the time that the story takes place, where the story takes place, and who the characters are. After reading the story the second time, have the children identify the three setting elements: *time, place,* and *characters.* Do the same thing with other story elements such as the *theme, plot episodes,* and *resolution.* Have the children prepare a roll movie with five headings: Setting, Theme, Characters, Plot Episodes, and Resolution. Do one section of the roll movie at a time. Encourage them to draw pictures and include narrative for each of the sections. Repeat with other stories.

Objective 2
Demonstrate literal knowledge by acting out a story using stick puppets, as well as identify details of a story by answering literal questions.

Activity: Literal Activity—Before reading *The Little Red Hen,* tell the children to remember the things the hen wanted help with when baking bread. After reading the story, have the children dramatize the episodes with stick puppets of the animals and the hen.

Objective 3
Express feelings, predict, generalize and problem solve.

Activity: Critical Activity—The story of *The Little Red Hen* is repeated. Role play the "Donahue Show" and have a child take the part of Donahue interviewing the animals in *The Little Red Hen* story, asking why they didn't help the hen and what they think about the fact that she didn't share the bread with them. Then interview the hen as well. Video- or audiotape interviews and place copies in an assessment portfolio. With another story such as *Gregory the Terrible Eater,* interview his parents to try and find out why his eating problem exists. Try and extend this activity to other books as well.

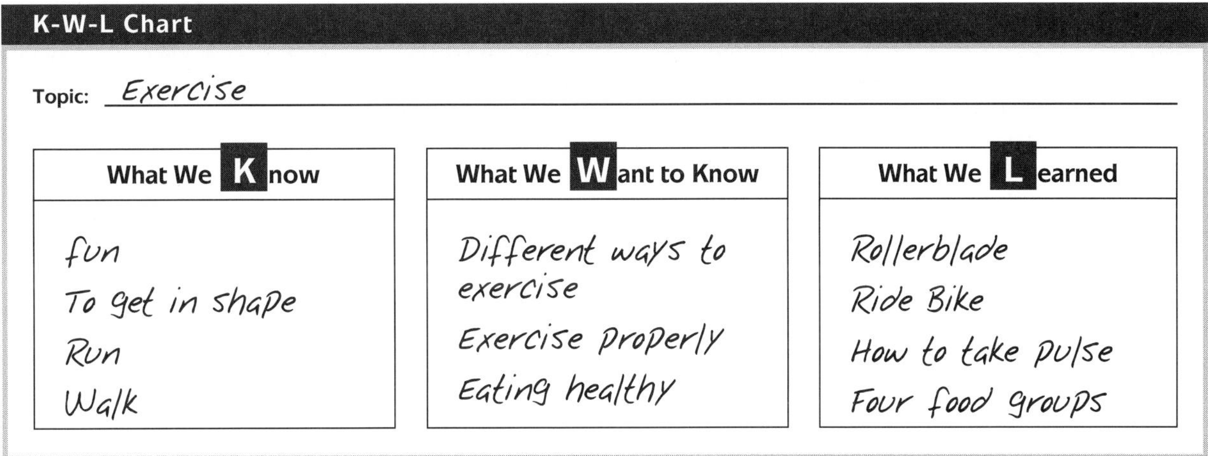

K-W-L Chart
Topic: Exercise
What We Know
fun
To get in shape
Run
Walk
What We Want to Know
Different ways to exercise
Exercise properly
Eating healthy
What We Learned
Rollerblade
Ride Bike
How to take pulse
Four food groups

Objective 4
Create a **KWL** chart (what they **K**now, what they **W**ant to know, and what they have **L**earned).

Activity: *K-W-L Activity*—Begin a discussion about exercise and how it affects the body. Ask what the children know about the importance of exercise. List their responses on chart paper under the heading "What We Know." Ask the students what they might want to learn about the subject and list those responses on chart paper as well under the heading "What We Want To Know." Introduce and read several informational books, posters, pamphlets, and magazines about exercise and a healthy body, such as *Shape* and *Muscle and Fitness*. After several days of discussion and activities in conjunction with these books, refer back to the lists you made at the beginning of the lesson. Create a new heading titled, "What We Learned" and ask the students to share things they learned about exercise over the past several days. Compare this list to the list of what they wanted to know about exercise. Ask questions like: How are they different? What could you do if you didn't learn something you wanted to know? Have the students complete similar charts before and after other lessons.

Writing

Objective 1
Emerging authors and illustrators: Learn that books are written by authors, and that pictures are drawn by illustrators. Children will participate in brainstorming, drafting, conferencing, editing, and revising and engage in an experience chart as a prewriting activity.

Activity: *Bed-shaped book*—Read the book *Mooncake*. Create a story web on experience chart paper as students talk about characteristics of sleep (why it is important, what happens when you sleep). Each child will be writing a story about sleep while teacher conferences take place. Finished products will be written in books shaped like a bed. This activity can be extended to other topics related to the theme. For example, books may also be shaped like a bathtub or bar of soap if the story is about personal hygiene.

Objective 2
Communicate through writing about exercise and nutrition. See and use functional writing.

Activity: *Notice Bulletin Board*—A notice bulletin board with student and teacher sections will be prepared in the classroom. Children may display their work on the board, as well as leave and receive messages in their spaces. Students can share messages, such as what they had for lunch and what food group each item belonged to or what exercise or sport they played in gym or at home. They may also decorate their personal space by drawing pictures related to these topics.

Objective 3
Letter writing as a meaningful form of communication.

Activity: *Healthy Mail Service*—The students will write letters to each other about healthy habits through an in-class mail service. The class as a whole will write to the American Heart Association and other health organizations to request information and pamphlets about good health.

Objective 4
Journal writing as a form of written expression.

Activity: *Journal Writing*—Read *Green Eggs and Ham* to the class. Explain to the children that journal writing will allow them to use writing to convey meaning about things they have learned in the unit. Emphasize that by doing so, they will become authors and illustrators. As in the story, children should be encouraged to write about a food they do or do not like. Throughout the healthy bodies, healthy minds unit, students will periodically write about their experiences. Conventional or invented spelling, scribbling, and pictures are acceptable entries.

Play

Objective 1
Engage in problem solving through dramatic play and environmental print related to the theme of being healthy in body and mind.

Activity: *Dramatic Play. Healthy Food Restaurant*—Turn the dramatic-play area into a health food restaurant by adding menus, cookbooks, recipe charts, receipts, and other signs that would appear in a restaurant. Encourage children to write while taking orders and posting signs.

Objective 2
Block play will be enhanced with theme-related play to acquire new concepts and encourage participation in reading and writing activities.

Activity: *Block Play. Where We Get Food*—Have children create block constructions of the places that our food comes from, such as farms and supermarkets. Provide labels and appropriate props for their construction, as well as paper for children to draw or write about their constructions.

Objective 3
Follow written directions and use print in a functional manner in an outdoor play activity.

Activity: *Outdoor Play. Health Club*—Set up a health club outside with different exercise stations. Have a sign-in sheet at each numbered station. Have children choose roles such as directing an exercise class, pouring water, filling in membership cards, or writing receipts. Encourage the children to name their club and hang posters as advertisements.

Objective 4
Engage in dramatic play while building self-esteem and respect for each other.

Activity: *Dramatic Play. "I'm Glad I'm Me" Kingdom*—Watch Sesame Street's "I'm Glad I'm Me" with Prince Charming Bird. Create an "I'm Glad I'm Me" Kingdom in the dramatic-play area. Hang flags the children have made to represent the things each child is proud of and likes about him- or herself. Supply crowns, robes, scepters, and so on. Place a basket of fairytale books in the center.

Art

Objective 1
Develop perceptual skills and use visual discrimination while copying patterns and colors. Develop concepts about the importance of rest.

Activity: *Body Murals*—Have the children wear their pajamas to school (if possible). Have them listen for rhymes as you read *Rip Van Winkle*. Afterwards, draw the children's body shapes on large paper in a sleeping position. Have children color in the patterns of their pajamas and try to draw their sleeping faces.

Objective 2
Self-esteem and self-assessment will be fostered over the course of the unit.

Activity: *I'm "Thumb" Body Books*—Children will be given blank books to illustrate. On the cover, they will put their thumb print and write the words "I'm (thumb print) Body." Each week, they will draw a picture of something they have accomplished or are proud of. Encourage them to write beginning sounds or engage in invented spelling to accompany their pictures or take dictations in the books. After each entry, collect books and make motivational comments to the children. At the end of the unit, ask children to make a final comment on what they think their biggest accomplishment was.

Objective 3
Learn that parts of most vegetables can be used for print painting as they explore and experiment with these materials.

Activity: *Vegetable Print Painting*—Vegetable printing with ink or tempera paint will be carried out. The ends of discarded vegetables and fruits will be used for print painting. Children will discuss their pictures and describe how they made them. A discussion of conservation and recycling may be conducted.

Objective 4
Gain an appreciation for creativity and ingenuity by designing pictures and jewelry based on different cultures. Increase visual discrimination and enrich vocabulary through observation and discussion.

Activity: *Macaroni Art*—Pictures using macaroni, beans, dried fruits, seeds, and so on can be made. Jewelry can also be made by using macaroni and string. Macaroni can be dyed by placing it in food coloring and water for three minutes. Provide students with pictures, books, or authentic examples of multicultural jewelry, such as Mexican or Native American necklaces, bracelets, or rings. Encourage children to design such types of jewelry. Students will observe and model each other's work and describe their own to the class.

Music

Objective 1
Recall skills will be enhanced, as children relate their own bedtime experiences to the group.

Activity: Bedtime Round—Listen to "Bedtime Round" by Tom Chapin. Post the lyrics and track from left to right as they listen. Talk about bedtime and list other things children say in order to delay going to sleep. After practicing, try to sing the song in rounds as in the recording.

Objective 2

Discuss good health habits. Recognize and create rhymes while acting out a song.

Activity: Brush Your Teeth—Write the lyrics to Raffi's "Brush Your Teeth" and highlight the rhymes. Listen to the song and track the lyrics as you sing. Try to think of lyrics that would rhyme with the numbers 6 through 10.

Objective 3

Increase sight word vocabulary. Talk about feelings and emotions in a supportive environment.

Activity: If You're Happy and You Know It—Sing the song "If You're Happy and You Know It." For each emotion, draw the corresponding face on a paper plate with the emotion written on it. Make a variety of plates, for example, if you're sad and you know it, if you're angry and you know it. Practice the song with the picture cards until the children can recognize the words without the drawings. Talk about each feeling. Make a list of things that make you feel each type of emotion.

Objective 4

Introduce music representative of the Indian culture. Develop an understanding of Yoga as a type of exercise first practiced in India to relax the body and mind.

Activity: Yoga—Children will be asked to sit comfortably on the floor. Lights can be dimmed and Indian music played softly. Children can be asked to close their eyes and concentrate on breathing evenly and deeply. They may engage in simple stretches and poses like the lotus (sitting straight and centered with feet pulled in) or the dead man's pose (lying flat on the back). Later you may want to make Indian food such as hummus and pita bread for snack time. Ask children to describe their feelings and experiences with the activity, or write about it in their journals.

Social Studies

Objective 1

Increase writing and oral language abilities and discuss how following directions is important.

Activity: Strega Nona—Read the story, *Strega Nona*, to the class. Discuss how the story takes place in Italy and note the use of its native food in the story. Discuss how the character in the story should have followed directions. Students may write a similar story, using new characters and food, perhaps from another country they have studied in the unit.

Objective 2

Gain appreciation for other countries' influences on popular sports. Increase knowledge of geography and other cultures.

Activity: Sports Study—Students will work in small groups to research the popular sports of various countries. Each group's contributions can be added to a class Big Book. As an extension activity, students may enjoy playing these sports during outdoor play.

Objective 3

Children are exposed to conflict and resolution, and shown how cooperation and communication are important to developing and maintaining relationships. Cooperation and friendship skills will be increased through role-playing.

Activity: No More Baths—Read *No More Baths*. After reading, discuss the story and note children's feelings about bathing on an experience chart. The students can then take turns role-playing the story.

Objective 4

By introducing foods and customs of different countries, an appreciation for the differences and contributions of other people and cultures will be developed. Oral and written communication skills will be increased.

Activity: Country of the Week—A "Country of the Week" will be focused on. Customs, foods, and major contributions of each will be highlighted. Children will discuss the differences and similarities among the countries, with an emphasis on foods and the healthfulness of each. The students may also write about their favorite food from each country. Different foods will be featured at snack time.

Science

Objective 1

Hypothesize what will happen to a heartbeat during exercise. Record observations of any changes as they occur.

Activity: Heartbeat in Exercise—Demonstrate how to listen to a heartbeat using a stethoscope or by feeling a pulse. Have children listen to a partner's heart before and after doing jumping jacks. Students can then record observations in their journals. Discuss and write a conclusion of the experiment. Older children may record beats per minute and graph their results.

Objective 2
The connection between oral and written language will be made through a discussion about how you catch a cold.

Activity: *I Wish I Was Sick, Too*—Read *I Wish I Was Sick, Too.* Use an experience chart to record what the children know about catching a cold. Discuss the importance of cleanliness and the prevalence of germs in our lives. Allow each child to collect a sample of germs from objects and place on an agar petri dish. Students can then predict which samples will grow faster than others. Children can then record their observations of any significant growth. Provide microscopes and/or magnifying glasses for more detailed observations.

Objective 3
Hypothesize what will happen during the growth of a planted seed. Record observations of the growth as it occurs.

Activity: *Planting*—Allow each student to plant a lima bean seed and keep the plants in the classroom. Have the students write entries in journals each day to record the progress of their plant's growth.

Objective 4
Observe changes that occur in the form of food while following directions in preparing a recipe.

Activity: *Making Applesauce*—Read *Johnny Appleseed* to the class. Discuss the nutritional value of apple products. Make applesauce with the class. Post the recipe and use it as a reference to point out all the steps involved in making applesauce.

Math

Objective 1
The connection between oral and written communication will be made by observing and recording the sleep patterns of animals.

Activity: *Sleep Patterns*—Students will observe and record the sleep patterns of the class pet and graph daily results. Compare any differences on the graphs and discuss how animals need different amounts of sleep at different times of the day.

Objective 2
Compose a nutrition counting book by following oral directions for counting and writing numbers to ten.

Activity: *My Nutrition Counting Book*—Explain to the children that they will be authors and illustrators of their own nutrition counting book. Pass out copies of premade number books and review directions. Children will need to color illustrations and trace or write the number on each page. Each page will feature a number and a food. For example, 3 with 3 carrots.

Objective 3
Relate pictures to text and see that pictures and print go together. Classify objects according to shape (triangles, circles, squares).

Activity: *Sort a Food*—Read *Pancakes, Crackers, and Pizza* to the class. Emphasize the different shapes of food as you read: round pancakes, square crackers, and triangular shaped pieces of pizza. Create a chart with three columns (triangles, circles, squares). Encourage children to classify cut out pictures of food from magazines or newspapers in the appropriate columns on the chart. Provide three shoe boxes labeled with each shape so that children can continue to classify different foods on their own.

Objective 4
Practice counting to twelve and matching the correct number of items to number of words.

Activity: *Counting "Eggsactly"*—Display an egg carton with number words printed on the bottom of each hole. Provide a variety of seeds, nuts, and beans for children to match to the correct number by placing them in the egg holes of the carton.

Culminating Activity

Objective 1
Share the products of the unit with children's family, friends, or other classes in the school.

Activity: Prepare a nutritious food, such as fruit salad and applesauce, for a snack to share with guests.

Activity: Sing a song related to the importance of rest from the unit, such as "Bedtime Round," or related to the importance of personal hygiene, such as "Brush Your Teeth."

Activity: Display art projects related to the unit and describe how they were made.

Activity: Show plants from the science portion of the unit and discuss how they grew.

Lesley Morrow
with Rutgers Graduate Students:
Kathleen Cunningham, Patty DeWitt,
Erica Erlanger, Donna Ngai, Katherine Heiss,
Pam Kelliher, Lisa Lozak, Melody Olsen

Glossary

aesthetic talk A form of conversation revolving around narrative literature in which children interpret and discuss what has been heard or read in relation to themselves.

aliterate An individual who can read but chooses not to.

alphabetic principle Knowing that words are composed of letters.

auditory discrimination The ability to hear, identify, and differentiate among familiar sounds, similar sounds, rhyming words, and letter sounds.

authentic assessment Assessment based on activities that represent and reflect the actual learning and instruction in the classroom.

balanced approach to literacy instruction The selection of theory and strategies to match learning styles of children. Constructivist and explicit strategies are both used.

behaviorist approach A learning theory in which adults provide a model and children learn through imitation encouraged by positive reinforcement.

big books Oversized books designed to allow children to see the print as it is being read.

blend a reader's ability to hear a series of isolated speech sounds then recognize and pronounce them as a complete word.

buddy reading The pairing of a child from an upper grade with a younger child for storybook reading.

chunk Any group of letters within a word that is taught as a whole pattern; a chunk could be phonograms, digraphs, blends, etc.

comprehension An active process whereby a reader interprets and constructs meaning about the text based on prior knowledge and experience.

conference Meeting with the teacher or peer to discuss work in progress.

consonant blends Two or three letters that, when placed together, merge into one sound while retaining representations of each letter sound (e.g., *bl* or *str*).

constructivist theory A theory that views learning as an active process where children construct knowledge to learn by problem solving, guessing, and approximating.

context clues The use of syntax and semantic meaning of text to aid in word identification.

contracts Assignment sheets designating specific activities to be carried out by individual learners based on their needs, interests, and ability levels.

cooperative learning An instructional strategy in which children come together to learn through debate and discussion.

cultural diversity Reference to the wide variety of backgrounds, languages, customs, and environments represented within the larger society or a given classroom.

decoding Identifying words by using letter-sound and structural analysis.

digraph Two letters that, when placed together, make a new sound unlike the sound of either individual letter (e.g., *th* or *ch*).

directed listening and thinking activity (DLTA) and directed reading and thinking activity (DRTA) A framework which offers directions and strategies for organizing and retrieving information from a text that is read by or to a child. The steps in DLTA or DRTA include preparation for listening/reading with prequestions and discussion, setting a purpose for reading, reading the story, and a follow-up postreading discussion based on the purpose set prior to reading.

early intervention Programs, for children with special needs or those who are "at risk," in early childhood education intended to prevent potential problems in literacy development. The focus of the programs is on developmentally appropriate instruction using authentic reading and writing experiences. The program can be a pullout or inclusion setting.

efferent talk A formal mode of conversation about expository text used to inform and persuade.

emergent literacy As coined by Marie Clay, refers to a child's early unconventional attempts at reading, writing, and listening.

engagement perspective A description of readers who have reached their fullest potential; readers who are strategic, social, knowledgeable, and motivated.

environmental print Familiar print found in the surroundings such as logos, food labels, and road signs.

explicit instruction A teacher-directed strategy with emphasis on teaching a task and the specific steps needed to master it.

family literacy Refers to the different ways in which family members initiate and use literacy in their daily living.

fluency Level of reading ease and ability; a fluent reader is able to read on or above level books independently with high comprehension and accuracy.

functional print Print for a purpose such as informational signs, directions, greeting cards, lists, letters to pen pals, and messages for the notice board.

gifted Demonstrating exceptional ability.

graphemes Letters that make up individual sounds.

guided reading Explicit reading instruction usually in small groups based on literacy needs.

high-frequency words Words that are frequently found in reading materials for children.

high-stakes assessment Standardized measures whose scores might determine major decisions about school districts, such as ratings of districts and promotion or retention decisions.

inclusion Special help and enrichment are offered in the regular classroom with the help of resource teachers and regular teachers planning together and teaching all children. This is in place of or in addition to pull out programs for special help.

independent reading and writing periods (IRWP) A socially interactive time wherein children select among books and other literacy-related materials.

informal reading inventory Informal tests to determine a child's independent, instructional, and frustration level of reading.

integrated language arts An approach to literacy instruction that links reading, writing, listening, and language skills.

interdisciplinary literacy instruction Integration of content-area learning with literacy.

intergenerational literacy initiatives Planned, systematic programs specifically designed to improve the literacy development of both adults and children.

invented spelling Improvised spelling for words unknown in conventional spelling wherein one letter often represents an entire syllable.

journal writing Written entries in notebooks by children including: *dialogue,* which is shared with teachers or peers who respond to what they read; *personal,* involving private thoughts related to children's lives or topics of special interest; *reading response,* writing in response to text reading; and *learning log,* a record of information usually involving other content areas.

K-W-L A cognitive strategy that enhances comprehension by assessing with students what they *K*now, what they *W*ant to know, and what they *L*earned before and after reading.

language experience approach (LEA) A reading instruction method aimed at linking oral with written language on the premise that what is thought can be said, what is said can be written, and what is written can be read.

learning centers Spaces in the classroom filled with materials for independent student activity focusing on current topics of study within content areas and including literacy materials as well.

learning disabled Demonstrating significant difficulty in the acquisition and use of reading, writing, listening, speaking, and/or mathematical skills.

literacy center A classroom area composed of a library corner and writing area.

literature-based instruction An approach to teaching reading in which varied genres of children's literature are used as the main source of reading material.

literature circles Discussion groups used to encourage critical discussions about literature among children.

literature genre A specific type of literature such as picture storybook, informational book, or poetry.

mainstreaming Placing children with special needs in regular classroom settings for part or all of the school day to provide social and instructional integration.

mapping and webbing Strategies for understanding text through the use of graphic representations for categorizing and structuring information. Maps deal with more detailed representations.

mental imagery Visualization of readings used to increase comprehension and clarify thought.

metacognition Awareness of one's own mental processes concerning how learning takes place.

morning message A daily message about items of interest to children written by the teacher who points out concepts about print.

narrative writing Writing stories.

nonstandard English A dialectal form of English that differs from the standard form in words, syntax, and language patterns.

onsets Initial letter or letters before the first vowel in a word.

parent-involvement programs Programs designed to involve and inform parents about activities that will promote their children's literacy development in school.

partner reading Peers reading together either simultaneously side by side or taking turns reading to each other.

phonemes Sounds made by individual letters and combinations of letters that make a single sound.

phonemic awareness Knowing that words are composed of a sequence of spoken sounds that have no isolated meaning and being able to hear those sounds. Segmented out of a word and blended together.

phonics A strategy that involves learning the alphabetic principles of language and knowledge of letter-sound relationships. Children learn to associate letters with the phonemes or basic speech sounds of English, to help them break the alphabetic code and become independent readers in the pronunciation of words.

phonogram A series of letters that begin with a vowel and are often found together (for example, *ack, ed, ight, ock, ush, etc.).*

portfolio assessment A strategy for measuring student progress by collecting samples of their work that is placed into a folder called a portfolio. Materials include: samples of student's written work or drawings, anecdotal records, audiotapes, videotapes, checklists, teacher-made and standardized test results, among others.

process approach to writing Steps involved in the production of text including prewriting, drafting, conferencing, revising, editing, and performing.

pull-out programs Students are taken out of their classrooms for special help in literacy instruction or enrichment.

reading readiness Various skills considered prerequisite in learning to read such as auditory discrimination, visual discrimination, and motor skills.

Reading Recovery An early intervention program devised by Marie Clay in which first graders experiencing difficulties with reading receive intensive, one-on-one instruction using developmentally appropriate integrated language arts techniques.

reading workshop A period of time set aside for children to work on reading skills, reading books, and conferencing with the teacher.

response groups A strategy for enhancing comprehension where students exchange or refine ideas and think critically about issues related to what they have listened to or read.

rich literacy environments Environments rich with materials that encourage reading and writing and support instruction.

rimes Ending part of a word that contains the vowel and the remainder of the word. Onsets and rimes make up words.

running record An assessment strategy that involves the close observation and recording of a child's oral reading behavior. Running records may be used for planning instruction.

scaffolding A strategy in which teachers provide children with modeling and support to help them acquire a skill.

segment To divide words into segments based in their sound components; cat is "c-a-t."

self-monitoring A student's ability to read and self-correct words as they are read.

semantics Meaning that language communicates.

shared book experiences Whole- or small-group reading instruction through literature selections, in which Big Books are often used so that children can see the print and pictures. Big Books enable children to listen and participate in actual book readings.

sight words The words that are known immediately by a reader. Once a word becomes a sight word, the reader does not need to use word-attack skills to read it.

standards Achievement goals that are defined at a state or national level and identify what students should know at the end of each grade level.

standardized tests An assessment measure, commercially prepared and norm-referenced, that reports results in terms of grade level scores and percentile ranks.

story retellings The recital of familiar stories, in children's own words, in written or oral form to develop and assess comprehension of story.

story structure The elements of a well-constructed story including setting, theme, plot episodes, and resolution.

sustained silent reading (SSR) A time allocated for children to read silently.

syntax The structure of language or rules that govern how words work together in phrases, clauses, and sentences.

telegraphic language A form of speech used by children at about twelve months of age in which content words, such as nouns and verbs, are used, for example "Mommy cookie," but function words, such as conjunctions and articles, are omitted.

thematic unit A topic of study is learned through explorations across all areas of the curriculum.

thinkaloud A comprehension strategy in which children talk about what they have read or other ideas they have about a story.

think, pair, share A discussion strategy that combines think time with cooperative learning. Following teacher-posed questions, the teacher first has children *think* about their answers; then children *pair* with a partner to discuss their responses; and finally, during *share,* the students share responses with the group.

t-unit An independent clause with all its dependent clauses attached that is helpful in measuring a child's language complexity.

very own words Favorite words generated by children, written on index cards, and kept in a container for them to read and write.

visual discrimination The ability to note similarities and differences visually between objects, including the ability to recognize colors, shapes, and letters.

whole language A philosophy from which strategies are drawn for literacy development. Strategies include the use of real literature, with the concurrent instruction of reading, writing, and oral language in meaningful, functional, and cooperative contexts, to help students become motivated to read and write.

word-study skills Knowledge about print including the use of phonics context and syntax to decipher unknown words; the development of sight vocabulary; and the use of word configuration and structural analysis.

word wall A type of bulletin board or classroom display that features challenging and/or high-frequency words organized alphabetically.

writing mechanics Skills related to writing such as spelling, handwriting, punctuation, and spacing.

writing workshop A period of time set aside for children to practice writing skills, work on writing projects, and conference with the teacher.

zone of proximal development Based on Vygotsky's theory, this term refers to the period of time when a child has been guided by an adult and no longer needs the help. The adult retreats and allows the child to work on his or her own.

The Glossary was composed with the help of Erica Erlanger, Patricia DeWitt, Gina Goble, Katherine Heiss, Pamela Kelliher, Lisa Lozak, Melissa Marley, Monica Saraiya, and Connie Zauderer.

Children's Literature Bibliography

Aliki. (1974). *Go tell Aunt Rhody.* New York: Macmillan.

Avery, K., & McPhail, D. (1993). *The crazy quilt.* Glenview, IL: Scott Foresman.

Base, G. (1987). *Animalia.* New York: Harry N. Abrams.

Bemelmans, L. (1939). *Madeline.* New York: Viking.

Bemelmans, L. (1953). *Madeline's rescue.* New York: Viking.

Berenstain, S., & Berenstain, J. (1987). *The Berenstain bears and too much birthday.* New York: Random House.

Brenner, B. (1972). *The three little pigs.* New York: Random House.

Brett, J. (1989). *The mitten.* New York: Putnam & Grosset.

Brett, J. (1997). *The hat.* New York: Putnam & Grosset.

Brown, M. (1939). *The noisy book.* New York: Harper.

Brown, M. (1947). *Goodnight moon.* New York: HarperCollins.

Brown, M. (1957). *The three billy goats gruff.* New York: Harcourt Brace.

Brown, M. (1990). *Arthur's pet business.* New York: Little, Brown.

Burton, V. L. (1943). *Katy and the big snow.* Boston: Houghton Mifflin.

Carle, E. (1969). *The very hungry caterpillar.* New York: Philomel.

Cole, J. (1987). *The magic school bus inside the earth.* New York: Scholastic.

deBeer, H. (1996). *Little polar bear, Take me home!* New York: North-South Books.

dePaola, T. (1973). *Charlie needs a clock.* Englewood Cliffs, NJ: Prentice Hall.

dePaola, T. (1978). *The popcorn book.* New York: Holiday House.

Duvoisin, R. (1950). *Petunia.* New York: Alfred A. Knopf.

Eastman, P. D. (1960). *Are you my mother?* New York: Random House.

Emberley, B. (1967). *Drummer Hoff.* Englewood Cliffs, NJ: Prentice Hall.

Fujikawa, A. (1980). *Jenny learns a lesson.* New York: Grosset & Dunlap.

Galdone, P. (1973). *The little red hen.* Boston: Houghton Mifflin.

Hazen, B. S. (1983). *Tight times.* New York: Picture Puffins.

Hennessy, B. G. (1991). *The missing tarts.* New York: Puffin Books.

Hennessy, B. G., & Pearson, T. C. (1989). *The queen of hearts.* New York: Picture Puffins.

Hoban, R. (1964). *Bread and jam for Frances.* New York: Harper & Row.

Holdsworth, W. (1968). *The gingerbread boy.* New York: Farrar, Straus & Giroux.

Hurd, E. (1980). *Under the lemon tree.* Boston: Little, Brown.

Hutchins, P. (1968). *Rosie's walk.* New York: Collier Books.

Izawa, T. (1968a). *Goldilocks and the three bears.* New York: Grosset & Dunlap.

Izawa, T. (1968b). *The little red hen.* New York: Grosset & Dunlap.

Johnson, A. (1990). *Do like Kyla.* New York: Scholastic.

Johnson, C. (1955). *Harold and the purple crayon.* New York: Harper & Row.

Kasza, K. (1988). *The pig's picnic.* New York: Putnam.

Keats, E. (1962). *The snowy day.* New York: Viking.

Keats, E. (1966). *Jenny's hat.* New York: Harper & Row.

Keats, E. J. (1967). *Peter's chair.* New York: Harper & Row.

Keats, E. J. (1968). *A letter to Amy.* New York: Puffin.

Keats, E. J. (1971). *Over in the meadow.* New York: Scholastic.

Keats, E. (1974). *Pet show.* New York: Aladdin Books.

Kellogg, S. (1989). *Is your mama a llama?* New York: Scholastic.

Lenski, L. (1965). *The little farm.* New York: Henry Z. Walek.

LeSieg, T. (1961). *Ten apples up on top.* New York: Random House.

Lillegard, D., & McPhail, D. (1993). *Potatoes on Tuesday.* Glenview, IL: Scott Foresman.

Lionni, L. (1963). *Swimmy.* New York: Pantheon.

Livingston, M. C. (1993). *Abraham Lincoln: A man for all people.* New York: Holiday House.

Lobel, A. L. (1979). *Frog and toad are friends.* New York: HarperCollins.

Maass, R. (1993). *When winter comes.* New York: Scholastic.

McCloskey, R. (1948). *Blueberries for Sal.* New York: Viking.

McGovern, A. (1967). *Too much noise.* Boston: Houghton Mifflin.

McNulty, F. (1979). *How to dig a hole to the other side of the world.* New York: Harper & Row.

Parrish, P. (1970). *Amelia Bedelia.* New York: Avon Books.

Piper, W. (1954). *The little engine that could.* New York: Platt and Munk.

Potter, B. (1902). *The tale of Peter Rabbit.* New York: Scholastic.

Quackenbush, R. (1972). *Old MacDonald had a farm.* New York: Lippincott.

Quackenbush, R. (1973). *Go tell Aunt Rhody.* New York: Lippincott.

Reid, S., & Fernandes, E. (1992). *The wild toboggan ride.* New York: Scholastic.

Rey, H. A. (1941). *Curious George.* Boston: Houghton Mifflin.

Sendak, M. (1962). *Chicken soup with rice.* New York: Harper & Row.

Sendak, M. (1963). *Where the wild things are.* New York: Harper & Row.

Sendak, M. (1962). *Pierre.* New York: HarperCollins.

Seuss, Dr. (1940). *Horton hatches the egg.* New York: Random House.

Seuss, Dr. (1957a). *How the Grinch stole Christmas.* New York: Random House.

Seuss, Dr. (1957b). *The cat in the hat.* New York: Random House.

Seuss, Dr. (1960). *Green eggs and ham.* New York: Random House.

Seuss, Dr. (1970). *Mr. Brown can moo! Can you?* New York: Random House.

Slobodkina, E. (1947). *Caps for sale.* Reading, MA: Addison-Wesley.

Tchin (1997). *Rabbits wish for snow: A Native American legend.* New York: Scholastic.

Viorst, J. (1972). *Alexander and the terrible, horrible, no good, very bad day.* New York: Atheneum.

Westcott, N. B. (1980). *I know an old lady.* Boston: Little, Brown.

White, E. B. (1952). *Charlotte's web.* New York: Scholastic.

Zoehfeld, K. W. (1994). *Manatee winter.* Hartford, CT: Trudy Corporation.

Zolotow, C. (1962). *Mr. Rabbit and the lovely present.* New York: Harper & Row.

Bibliography

Adams, M. J. (1990). *Beginning to read: Thinking and learning about print.* Urbana: University of Illinois Center for the Study of Reading.

Allen, R. V. (1976). *Language experience in communication.* Boston: Houghton Mifflin.

Altwerger, A., Diehl-Faxon, J., & Dockstader-Anderson, K. (1985). Reading aloud events as meaning construction. *Language Arts, 62,* 476–484.

Anderson, R. C., Fielding, L. G., & Wilson, P. T. (1988). Growth in reading and how children spend their time outside of school. *Reading Research Quarterly, 23,* 285–303.

Anderson, R. C., Hiebert, E. H., Scott, J. A., & Wilkinson, I. A. G. (1985). *Becoming a nation of readers.* Washington, DC: National Institute of Education.

Anderson, A., & Stokes, S. (1984). Social and institutional influences on the development and practice of literacy. In H. Goelman, A. Oberg, & F. Smith (Eds.), *Awakening to literacy.* Exeter, NH: Heinemann.

Anderson, M., & Anderson, S. (1984). The reading group. An experimental investigation of a labyrinth. *Reading Research Quarterly, 20,* 6–38.

Anderson, R. C., & Pearson, P. D. (1984). A schema-theoretic view of basic processing in reading. In P. D. Pearson (Ed.), *Handbook of reading research.* New York: Longman.

Anderson, R. C., Wilson, P. T., & Fielding, L. G. (1985, December). A new focus on free-reading. Symposium presentation at the National Reading Conference, San Diego.

Andrews, G. (1954). *Creative rhythmic movement for children.* Englewood Cliffs, NJ: Prentice Hall.

Applebee, A. N., & Langer, J. A. (1983). Instructional scaffolding: Reading and writing as natural language activities. *Language Arts, 60,* 168–175.

Applebee, A. N., Langer, J. A., & Mullis, M. (1988). *Who reads best? Factors related to reading achievement in grades 3, 7, and 11.* Princeton, NJ: Educational Testing Service.

Armstrong, T. (1994). *Multiple intelligences in the classroom.* Alexandria, VA: Association for Supervision and Curriculum Development.

Ashton-Warner, S. (1959). *Spinster.* New York: Simon & Schuster.

Ashton-Warner, S. (1963). *Teacher.* New York: Bantam.

Au, T. K., Depretto, M., & Song, Y-K. (1994). Input vs. constraints: Early word acquisition in Korean and English. *Journal of Memory and Language, 33,* 567–582.

Auerbach, E. (1989). Toward a social-contextual approach to family literacy. *Harvard Educational Review, 56,* 165–181.

Baghban, M. (1984). *Our daughter learns to read and write.* Newark, DE: International Reading Association.

Banks, J., & Banks, C. (1993). *Multicultural education: Issues and perspectives* (2nd ed.). Boston: Allyn & Bacon.

Baumann, J. F. (1984). The effectiveness of a direct instruction paradigm for teaching main idea comprehension. *Reading Research Quarterly, 20,* 93–115.

Baumann, J. F. (1992). Effect of think aloud instruction on elementary students' comprehension monitoring abilities. *Journal of Reading Behavior, 24* (2), 143–172.

Bear, D. R., Invernizzi, M., Templeton, S., & Johnston, D. (1996). *Words their way.* Englewood Cliffs, NJ: Prentice Hall.

Bergeron, B. (1990). What does the term whole language mean? A definition from the literature. *Journal of Reading Behavior, 23,* 301–329.

Berk, L. (1997). *Child development.* Boston: Allyn & Bacon.

Birnbaum, J., & Emig, J. (1983). Creating minds: Created texts. In R. Parker & F. Davis (Eds.), *Developing literacy, Young children's use of language.* Newark, DE: International Reading Association.

Bloom, L. (1990). Development in express: Affect and speech. In N. Stein & T. Trabasso (Eds.), *Psychological and biological approaches to emotion* (pp. 215–245). Hillsdale, NJ: Erlbaum.

Bohannan, J. N., III. (1993). Theoretical approaches to language acquisition. In J. Berko Gleason (Ed.), *The development of language* (3rd ed., pp. 239–297). New York: Macmillan.

Boorstin, D. (1984). Letter of transmittal. In *Books in our future: A report from the Librarian of Congress to the Congress.* Washington, DC: U.S. Congress Joint Committee on the Library.

Brandt, D. (1990). *Literacy as involvement: The acts of writers, readers, and texts.* Carbondale, IL: Southern Illinois University Press.

Britton, J. (1982). The spectator role and the beginnings of writing. In M. Nystrand (Ed.), *What writers know: The language, process and structure of written discourse.* New York: Academic Press.

Brown, A. (1975). Recognition, reconstruction, and recall of narrative sequences of preoperational children. *Child Development, 46,* 155–166.

Brown, C. S., & Lytle, S. (1988). Merging assessment and instruction: Protocols in the classroom. In S. M. Glazer, L. W. Searfoss, & L. M. Gentile (Eds.), *Reexamining reading diagnosis: New trends and procedures* (pp. 94–102). Newark, DE: International Reading Association.

Brown, R., Cazden, C., & Bellugi-Klima, U. (1968). The child's grammar from one to three. In J. P. Hill (Ed.), *Minnesota symposium on child development.* Minneapolis: University of Minnesota Press.

Bruner, J. (1975). The ontogenesis of speech acts. *Journal of Child Language, 3,* 1–19.

Bryant, P. (1993). Phonological aspects of learning to read. In R. Beard (Ed.), *Teaching literacy balancing perspectives*. London: Hodder and Stoughton.

Burns, M. S., Snow, C. E., Griffin, P., Alberts, B., & Alberts, B. (Eds.) (1999). *Starting out right: A guide to promoting children's reading success*. Washington, DC: National Academy Press.

Byrne, B., & Fielding-Barnsley, R. (1991). Evaluation of a program to teach phonemic awareness to young children. *Journal of Educational Psychology, 83,* 451–455.

Byrne, B., & Fielding-Barnsley, R. (1993). Evaluation of a program to teach phonemic awareness to young children: A 1-year follow-up. *Journal of Educational Psychology, 85,* 104–111.

Byrne, B., & Fielding-Barnsley, R. (1995). Evaluation of a program to teach phonemic awareness to young children: A 2- and 3-year follow-up and a new preschool trial. *Journal of Educational Psychology, 87,* 488–503.

Calkins, L. M. (1983). *Lessons from a child: On the teaching and learning of writing*. Exeter, NH: Heinemann.

Calkins, L. M. (1986). *The art of teaching writing*. Exeter, NH: Heinemann.

Cambourne, B. (1987). Language, learning and literacy. In A. Butler & J. Turbill (Eds.), *Towards a reading-writing classroom*. Portsmouth, NH: Heinemann.

Cazden, C. B. (1992). Revealing and telling: The socialization of attention in learning to read and write. *Educational Psychology: An International Journal of Experimental Educational Psychology, 12,* 305–313.

Chall, J. S., Conrad, S. S., & Harris-Sharples, S. H. (1983). *Textbooks and challenges: An inquiry into textbook difficulty, reading achievement, and knowledge acquisition*. Final Report to the Spencer Foundation, Chicago, IL.

Chomsky, C. (1965). *Aspects of a theory of syntax*. Cambridge, MA: MIT Press.

Clay, M. M. (1966). *Emergent reading behavior.* Doctoral dissertation, University of Auckland, New Zealand.

Clay, M. M. (1975). *What did I write?* Auckland, New Zealand: Heinemann.

Clay, M. M. (1979). *The early detection of reading difficulties: A diagnostic survey with recovery procedures*. Auckland, New Zealand: Heinemann Educational Books.

Clay, M. M. (1987). Implementing reading recovery: Systematic adaptations to an educational innovation. *New Zealand Journal of Educational Studies, 22,* 35–38.

Clay, M. M. (1991). *Becoming literate: The construction of inner control*. Portsmouth, NH: Heinemann.

Clay, M. M. (1993a). *An observation survey of early literacy achievement*. Portsmouth, NH: Heinemann.

Clay, M. M. (1993b). *Reading Recovery: A guidebook for teachers in training*. Portsmouth, NH: Heinemann.

Cochran-Smith, M. (1984). *The making of a reader.* Norwood, NJ: Ablex.

Cohen, D. (1968). The effects of literature on vocabulary and reading achievement. *Elementary English, 45,* 209–213, 217.

Cohen, M. (1980). *First grade takes a test*. New York: Dell.

Connell, R. W. (1994). Poverty and education. *Harvard Educational Review, 64,* 125–149.

Cox, C. (1999). *Teaching language arts: A student- and response-centered classroom*. Boston: Allyn & Bacon.

Cullinan, B. E. (Ed.). (1987). *Children's literature in the reading program*. Newark, DE: International Reading Association.

Cullinan, B. E. (1989). *Literature and the child* (2nd ed.). Orlando, FL: Harcourt Brace Jovanovich.

Cullinan, B. E. (1992). *Invitation to read: More children's literature in the reading program*. Newark, DE: International Reading Association.

Cummins, J. (1981). The role of primary language development in promoting educational success for language minority students. In J. Cummins (Ed.), *Schooling and language minority students: A theoretical framework*. Los Angeles: Evaluation, Dissemination, and Assessment Center of California State University.

Cummins, J. (1979). Linguistic interdependence and the educational development of bilingual children. *Review of Educational Research, 49,* 222–251.

Cunningham, P., & Hall, D. (1994) *Making words*. Torrance, CA: Good Apple.

Cunningham, P. (1995). *Phonics they use*. New York: HarperCollins.

Delgado-Gaitan, C. (1992). School matters in the Mexican-American home: Socializing children to education. *American Educational Research Journal, 29,* 459.

Delpit, L. (1995, December). *Other People's Children*. Presentation at the National Reading Conference, New Orleans.

Dewey, J. (1966). *Democracy and education*. New York: First Press.

Dickinson, D. K., & Tabors, P. O. (2000). *Early literacy at home and school: The critical role of language development in the preschool years*. Baltimore, MD: Paul H. Brookes.

Durkin, D. (1966). *Children who read early.* New York: Teachers College Press.

Dyson, A. H. (1985). Individual differences in emerging writing. In M. Farr (Ed.), *Advances in writing research. Vol. 1: Children's early writing development.* Norwood, NJ: Ablex.

Dyson, A. H. (1986). Children's early interpretations of writing: Expanding research perspectives. In D. Yoden & S. Templeton (Eds.), *Metalinguistic awareness and beginning literacy.* Exeter, NH: Heinemann.

Dyson, A. H. (1993). *Social worlds of children learning to write in an urban primary school*. New York: Teachers College Press.

Edwards, P. A. (1995). Combining parents' and teachers' thoughts about storybook reading at home and school. In L. M. Morrow (Ed.), *Family literacy connections in schools and communities* (pp. 54–69). Newark, DE: International Reading Association.

Ehri, L. C. (1979). Linguistic insight: Threshold of reading acquisition. In T. G. Waller & G. E. MacKinnon

(Eds.), *Reading research: Advances in theory and practice* (Vol. 1). New York: Academic Press.

Erickson, K. A., & Koppenhaver. (1995). Developing a literacy program for children with severe disabilities. *The Reading Teacher, 48,* 676–684.

Ferreiro, E., & Teberosky, A. (1982). *Literacy before schooling.* Exeter, NH: Heinemann.

Field, T. (1980). Preschool play: Effects of teacher/child ratios and organization of classroom space. *Child Study Journal, 10,* 191–205.

Fitzpatrick, J. (1997). *Phonemic awareness.* Cypress, CA: Creative Teaching Press.

Flood, J. (1977). Parental styles in reading episodes with young children. *The Reading Teacher, 30,* 864–867.

Foorman, B. R., Francis, D. J., Fletcher, J. M., Schatschneider, C. S., & Mehta, P. (1998). The role of instruction in learning to read: Preventing reading failure in at-risk children. *Journal of Educational Psychology, 90*(1), 37–57.

Ford, M. E. (1992). *Motivating humans.* Newbury Park, CA: Sage.

Foster, C. R. (1982). Diffusing the issues in bilingualism and bilingual education. *Phi Delta Kappan, 63,* 338–345.

Fountas, I. C., & Pinnell, G. S. (1996). *Guided reading: Good first teaching for all children.* Portsmouth, NH: Heinemann.

Freeman, D., & Freeman, Y. (1993) Strategies for promoting the primary languages of all students. *The Reading Teacher, 46,* 18–25.

Froebel, F. (1974). *The education of man.* Clifton, NJ: Augustus M. Kelly.

Galda, L., & Cullinan, B. E. (1991). Literature for literacy: What research says about the benefits of using trade books in the classroom. In J. Flood, J. Jensen, D. Lapp, & J. R. Squire (Eds.), *Handbook of research on teaching the English language arts.* New York: Macmillan.

Gambrell, L. B. (1993). The impact of running start on the reading motivation and behavior of first-grade children (Research Report). College Park, MD: University of Maryland, National Reading Research Center.

Gambrell, L. B., & Almasi, J. (1994). Fostering comprehension development through discussion. In L. M. Morrow, J. K. Smith, & L. C. Wilkinson (Eds.), *Integrated language arts: Controversy to consensus* (pp. 71–90). Boston: Allyn & Bacon.

Gambrell, L. B., Almasi, J. F., Xie, Q., & Heland, V. (1995). Helping first graders get off to a running start in reading: A home-school-community program that enhances family literacy. In L. Morrow (Ed.), *Family literacy connections at school and home.* Newark, DE: International Reading Association.

Gambrell, L. B., & Jawitz, P. B. (1993). Mental imagery, text illustrations, and children's story comprehension and recall. *Reading Research Quarterly, 28,* 264–273.

Gambrell, L., Pfeiffer, W., & Wilson, R. (1985). The effect of retelling upon comprehension and recall of text information. *Journal of Educational Research, 78,* 216–220.

Garcia, E., & McLaughlin, B. (Eds.). with Spodek, B., and Soracho, O. (1995). *Meeting the challenge of linguistic and cutural diversity in early childhood education.* New York: Teachers College Press.

Gardner, H. (Ed.). (1993). *Multiple intelligences: The theory in practice.* New York: Basic Books.

Genishi, C., & Dyson, A. (1984). *Language assessment in the early years.* Norwood, NJ: Ablex.

Gesell, A. (1925). *The mental growth of the preschool child.* New York: Macmillan.

Gibson, E., & Levin, H. (1975). *The psychology of reading.* Cambridge, MA: MIT Press.

Gillian, S. (1936). The reading mother. In H. Fellerman (Ed.), *Best loved poems of the American people.* New York: Doubleday.

Gonzales-Mena, J. (1976). English as a second language for preschool children. *Young Children, 32,* 14–20.

Goodman, K. S. (1967). Reading: A psycholinguistic guessing game. *Journal of the Reading Specialist, 4,* 126–135.

Goodman, Y. (1980). The root of literacy. In M. Douglas (Ed.), *Claremont Reading Conference forty-fourth yearbook.* Claremont, CA: Claremont Reading Conference.

Goodman, Y. (1984). The development of initial literacy. In H. Goelman, A. Oberg, & F. Smith (Eds.), *Awakening to literacy.* Exeter, NH: Heinemann.

Goodman, Y. (1986). Children coming to know literacy. In W. H. Teale & E. Sulzby (Eds.), *Emergent literacy: Writing and reading.* Norwood, NJ: Ablex.

Goodman, Y., & Altwerger, B. (1981). *Print awareness in preschool children: A study of the development of literacy in preschool children* (Occasional Paper 4). Tucson: University of Arizona, College of Education, Arizona Center for Research and Development, Program in Language and Literacy.

Graves, D. H. (1983). *Writing: Teachers and children at work.* Exeter, NH: Heinemann.

Graves, D. (1994). *A fresh look at writing.* Portsmouth, NH: Heinemann.

Graves, D., & Hansen, J. (1983). The author's chair. *Language Arts, 60,* 176–183.

Graves, M. F., Juel, C., & Graves, B. B. (1998). *Teaching reading in the 21st century.* Boston: Allyn & Bacon.

Green, J. (1985). Children's writing in an elementary school postal system. In M. Farr (Ed.), *Advances in writing research. Vol. 1: Children's early writing development.* Norwood, NJ: Ablex.

Gundlach, R., McLane, J., Scott, F., & McNamee, G. (1985). The social foundations of early writing development. In M. Farr (Ed.), *Advances in writing research. Vol. 1: Children's early writing development.* Norwood, NJ: Ablex.

Hall, M. A. (1976). *Teaching reading as a language experience.* Columbus, OH: Merrill.

Halliday, M. A. K. (1975). *Learning how to mean: Exploration in the development of language.* London: Edward Arnold.

Hallinan, M. T., & Sorenson, A. B. (1983). The formation and stability of instructional groups. *American Sociological Review, 48,* 838–851.

Hannon, P. (1995). *Literacy, home and school: Research and practice in teaching literacy with parents.* London: Falmer.

Harp, W. (2000). Assessing reading and writing in the early years. In S. Strickland & L. M. Morrow (Eds.), *Beginning reading and writing, kindergarten to grade 2.* New York: Teachers College Press.

Hansen, J. (1987). *When writers read.* Portsmouth, NH: Heinemann.

Harste, J., Woodward, V., & Burke, C. (1984). *Language stories and literacy lessons.* Exeter, NH: Heinemann.

Heath, S. B. (1980). The function and uses of literacy. *Journal of Communication, 30,* 123–133.

Heath, S. B. (1982). What no bedtime story means. *Language in Society, 11,* 49–76.

Heath, S. B. (1993). *Ways with words.* Cambridge, England: Cambridge University Press.

Hiebert, E. H. (1978). Preschool children's understanding of written language. *Child Development, 49,* 1231–1234.

Hiebert, E. H. (1981). Developmental patterns and interrelationships of preschool children's print awareness. *Reading Research Quarterly, 16,* 236–260.

Hiebert, E. H. (1986). Using environmental print in beginning reading instruction. In M. R. Sampson (Ed.), *The pursuit of literacy: Early reading and writing.* Dubuque, IA: Kendall/Hunt.

Hiebert, E. H., & Taylor, B. (1994). *Getting reading right from the start.* Newark, DE: International Reading Association.

Hill, S. (1997). *Reading manipulatives.* Cypress, CA: Creative Teaching Press.

Hoffman, J. V., Roser, N. L., & Farest, C. (1988). Literature sharing strategies in classrooms serving students from economically disadvantaged and language different home environments. In J. E. Readance & R. S. Baldwin (Eds.), *Dialogues in literacy research. 37th Yearbook of the National Reading Conference.* Chicago, IL: National Reading Conference.

Holdaway, D. (1979). *The foundations of literacy.* Sydney: Ashton Scholastic.

Holdaway, D. (1986). The structure of natural learning as a basis for literacy instruction. In M. Sampson (Ed.), *The pursuit of literacy: Early reading and writing.* Dubuque, IA: Kendall/Hunt.

Huck, C. S. (1992). Books for emergent readers. In B. E. Cullinan (Ed.), *Invitation to read: More children's literature in the reading program.* Newark, DE: International Reading Association.

Hunt, K. W. (1970). *Syntactic maturity in children and adults.* Monograph of the Society for Research in Child Development (Vol. 25). Chicago: University of Chicago Press.

International Reading Association. (1998). *Phonemic awareness and the teaching of reading: A position statement of the Board of directors of the International Reading Association* Newark, DE: Author.

International Reading Association. (1999). *Position statement: Using multiple methods of beginning reading instruction.* Newark, DE: Author.

International Reading Association & National Association for the Education of Young Children. (1998). *Learning to read and write: Developmentally appropriate practices for young children.* Newark, DE: International Reading Association.

International Reading Association & National Council of Teachers of English. (1996). *Standards for the English language arts.* Newark, DE: International Reading Association.

Irving, A. (1980). *Promoting voluntary reading for children and young people.* Paris: UNESCO.

Jagger, A. (1985). Allowing for language differences. In G. S. Pinnell (Ed.), *Discovering language with children.* Urbana, IL: National Council of Teachers of English.

Jewell, M., & Zintz, M. (1986). *Learning to read naturally.* Dubuque, IA: Kendall/Hunt.

Johns, J., Lenski, S. D., & Elish-Piper, L. (1999). *Early literacy assessments and teaching strategies.* Dubuque, IA: Kendall/Hunt.

Johnson, D., & Pearson, P. D. (1984). *Teaching reading vocabulary* (2nd ed.). New York: Holt, Rinehart, & Winston.

Juel, C. (1989). The role of decoding in early literacy instruction and assessment. In L. Morrow & J. Smith (Eds.), *Assessment for instruction in early literacy* (pp. 135–154). Englewood Cliffs, NJ: Prentice Hall.

Juel, C. (1991). Beginning reading. In R. Barr, M. Kamil, P. Mosenthal, & P. D. Pearson (Eds.), *Handbook of reading research, Volume II* (pp. 759–788). New York: Longman.

Juel, C. (1994). Teaching phonics in the context of the integrated language arts. In L. Morrow, J. K. Smith, & L. C. Wilkinson (Eds.), *Integrated language arts: Controversy for consensus* (pp. 133–154). Boston: Allyn & Bacon.

Kinzer, C. K., & McKenna, M. C. (1999, May). *Using technology in your classroom literacy program: Current and future possibilities.* Paper presented at the Annual Convention of the International Reading Association, San Diego, CA.

Koch, A., & Peder, W. (Eds.). (1974). The life and selected writings of Thomas Jefferson. New York: Random House.

Labbo, L. D., & Ash, G. E. (1998). What is the role of computer related technology in early literacy? In S. B. Neuman & K. A. Roskos (Eds.), *Children achieving: Best practices in early literacy* (pp. 180–197). Newark, DE: International Reading Association.

Labbo, L. D., Reinking, D., & McKenna, M. (1998). The use of technology in literacy programs. In L. Gambrell, L. M. Morrow, S. B. Neuman, & M. Pressley (Eds.), *Best practices in literacy instruction.* New York: Guilford Press.

Leichter, H. P. (1984). Families as environments for literacy. In H. Goelman, A. Oberg, & F. Smith (Eds.), *Awakening to literacy.* Exeter, NH: Heinemann.

Lennenberg, E. (1967). *Biological foundations of language.* New York: John Wiley.

Lennenberg, E., & Kaplan, E. (1970). Grammatical structures and reading. In H. Levin & J. Williams (Eds.), *Basic studies in reading.* New York: Basic Books.

Lenz, L. (1992). Crossroads of literacy and orality: Reading poetry aloud. *Language Arts, 69,* 597–603.

Lepper, M. R. (1988). Motivational considerations in the study of instruction. *Cognition and Instruction, 5,* 289–309.

Leu, D. J., & Kinzer, C. (1991). *Effective reading instruction, K–8* (2nd ed.). New York: Merrill.

Linden, M., & Wittrock, M. C. (1981). The teaching of reading comprehension according to the model of generative learning. *Reading Research Quarterly, 17,* 44–57.

Lindfors, J. (1989) The classroom: A food environment for language learning. In P. Rigg & V. Allen (Eds.), *When they don't all speak English: Integrating the ESL student into the regular classroom* (pp. 39–54). Urbana, IL: National Council of Teachers of English.

Loughlin, C. E., & Martin, M. D. (1987). *Supporting literacy: Developing effective learning environments.* New York: Teachers College Press.

Lunderberg, I., Frost, J., & Petersen, O. P. (1988). Effects of an extensive program for stimulating phonological awareness in preschool children. *Reading Research Quarterly, 23,* 263–284.

Manning, M., Manning, G., & Long, R. (1994). Theme immersion: Inquiring-based curriculum in elementary and middle schools. Portsmouth, NH: Heinemann.

Marriott, D. (1997). *What are the other kids doing?* Cypress, CA: Creative Teaching Press.

Martinez, M., & Teale, W. (1987). The ins and outs of a kindergarten writing program. *The Reading Teacher, 40,* 444–451.

Martinez, M., & Teale, W. (1988). Reading in a kindergarten classroom library. *The Reading Teacher, 41*(6), 568–572.

Mason, J. (1980). When do children begin to read? An exploration of four-year-old children's letter and word reading competencies. *Reading Research Quarterly, 15,* 203–227.

Mason, J. (1982). *Acquisition of knowledge about reading.* Paper presented at the Annual Meeting of the American Educational Research Association, New York.

Mason, J. (1986). *Reading instruction for today.* Glenview, IL: Scott, Foresman.

Mason, J., & McCormick, C. (1981). *An investigation of pre-reading instruction: A developmental perspective* (Technical Report 224). Urbana: University of Illinois, Center for the Study of Reading.

McCormick, C., & Mason, J. (1981). What happens to kindergarten children's knowledge about reading after summer vacation? *The Reading Teacher, 35,* 164–172.

McCracken, M., & McCracken, J. (1972). *Reading is the only tiger's tail.* San Rafael, CA: Lewsing Press.

McNeil, D. (1970). *The acquisition of language: The study of developmental psycholinguistics.* New York: Harper & Row.

Meers, T. B. (1999) *101 best web sites for kids.* Lincolnwood, IL: Publications International.

Menyuk, P. (1977). *Language and maturation.* Cambridge, MA: MIT Press.

Miramontes, O. B., Nadeau, A., & Commins, N. L. (1997). *Restructuring schools for linguistic diversity: Linking decision making to effective programs.* New York: Teachers College Press.

Moerk, E. L. (1992). *A First Language Taught and Learned.* Baltimore, MD: Paul H. Brookes.

Montessori, M. (1965). *Spontaneous activity in education.* New York: Schocken Books.

Moore, G. (1986). Effects of the spatial definition of behavior settings on children's behavior: A quasi-experimental field study. *Journal of Environmental Psychology, 6*(3), 205–231.

Morphett, M. V., & Washburne, C. (1931). When should children begin to read? *The Elementary School Journal, 31,* 496–508.

Morrow, L. M. (1978). Analysis of syntax in the language of six-, seven-, and eight-year-olds. *Research in the Teaching of English, 12,* 143–148.

Morrow, L. M. (1982). Relationships between literature programs, library corner designs and children's use of literature. *Journal of Educational Research, 75,* 339–344.

Morrow, L. M. (1983). Home and school correlates of early interest in literature. *Journal of Educational Researach, 76,* 221–230.

Morrow, L. M. (1984). Reading stories to young children: Effects of story structure and traditional questioning strategies on comprehension. *Journal of Reading Behavior, 16,* 273–288.

Morrow, L. M. (1985). Retelling stories: A strategy for improving children's comprehension, concept of story structure and oral language complexity. *The Elementary School Journal, 85,* 647–661.

Morrow, L. M. (1986). *Promoting responses to literature: Children's sense of story structure.* Paper presented at the National Reading Conference, Austin, TX.

Morrow, L. M. (1987a). The effects of one-to-one story readings on children's questions and comments. In S. Baldwin & J. Readance (Eds.), *36th yearbook of the National Reading Conference.* Rochester, NY: National Reading conference.

Morrow, L. M. (1987b). Promoting voluntary reading: The effects of an inner city program in summer day care centers. *The Reading Teacher, 41,* 266–274.

Morrow, L. M. (1988). Young children's responses to one-to-one story readings in school settings. *Reading Research Quarterly, 23*(1), 89–107.

Morrow, L. M. (1990). Preparing the classroom environment to promote literacy during play. *Early Childhood Research Quarterly, 5,* 537–554.

Morrow, L. M. (1992). The impact of a literature-based program on literacy achievement, use of literature, and attitudes of children from minority backgrounds. *Reading Research Quarterly, 27,* 250–275.

Morrow, L. M. (1995). *Family literacy connections at school and home.* Newark, DE: International Reading Association.

Morrow, L. M. (1996). Story retelling: A discussion strategy to develop and assess comprehension. In

L. B. Gambrel & J. F. Almasi (Eds.), *Lively discussions: Fostering engaged reading* (pp. 265–285). Newark, DE: International Reading Association.

Morrow, L. M. (1997). *The literacy center: Contexts for reading and writing*. York, ME: Stenhouse.

Morrow, L. M., & Asbury, E. (1999). Best practices for a balanced early literacy program. In L. Gambrell, L. M. Morrow, S. B. Neuman, & M. Pressley (Eds.), *Best practices in literacy instruction* (pp. 49–67). New York: Guilford Publications.

Morrow, L. M., & O'Connor, E. (1995). Literacy partnerships for change with "at risk" kindergartners. In R. Allington & S. Walmsley (Eds.), *No quick fix: Rethinking literacy programs in America's elementary schools* (pp. 97–115). New York: Teachers College Press.

Morrow, L. M., O'Connor, E. M., & Smith, J. (1990). Effects of a story reading program on the literacy development of at-risk kindergarten children. *Journal of Reading Behavior, 20*(2), 104–141.

Morrow, L. M., Paratore, J. R., & Tracey, D. H. (1994). *Family literacy: New perspectives, new opportunities*. Newark, DE: International Reading Association.

Morrow, L. M., Pressley, M., Smith, J., & Smith, M. (1997). The effects of integrating literature-based instruction into literacy and science programs. *Reading Research Quarterly, 32*, 54–77.

Morrow, L. M., & Rand, M. (1991). Promoting literacy during play by designing early childhood classroom environments. *The Reading Teacher, 44*, 396–405.

Morrow, L. M., Scoblionko, J., & Shafer, D. (1995). The family reading and writing appreciation program. In L. M. Morrow (Ed.), *Family literacy connections in schools and communities* (pp. 70–86). Newark, DE: International Reading Association.

Morrow, L. M., Sharkey, E., & Firestone, W. (1994). Collaborative strategies in the integrated language arts. In L. M. Morrow, J. K. Smith, & L. C. Wilkinson (Eds.), *Integrated language arts: Controversy to consensus* (pp. 155–176). Boston: Allyn & Bacon.

Morrow, L. M., & Smith, J. K. (1990). The effect of group setting on interactive storybook reading. *Reading Research Quarterly, 25*, 213–231.

Morrow, L. M., Strickland, D. S., & Woo, D. G. (1998). *Literacy instruction in half- and whole-day kindergarten: Research to practice*. Newark, DE: International Reading Association.

Morrow, L. M., & Tracey, D. H. (1996). Instructional environments for language and learning. Considerations for young children. In J. Flood, S. B. Heath, & D. Lapp (Eds.), *Handbook for literacy educators: Research on teaching the communicative and visual arts*. New York: Macmillan.

Morrow, L. M., & Tracey, D. (1997). Strategies for phonics instruction in early childhood classrooms. *The Reading Teacher, 50*(8), 2–9.

Morrow, L. M., Tracey, D., & Maxwell, C. M. (Eds.). (1995). *A survey of family literacy in the United States*. Newark, DE: International Reading Association.

Morrow, L. M., & Weinstein, C. S. (1986). Encouraging voluntary reading: The impact of a literature program on children's use of library centers. *Reading Reasearch Quarterly, 21*, 330–346.

Morrow, L. M., & Young, J. (1997). A family literacy program connecting school and home: Effects on attitude, motivation, and literacy achievement. *Journal of Educational Psychology, 89*, 736–742.

Moustafa, M. (1997). *Beyond traditional phonics: Research discoveries and reading instruction*. Portsmouth, NH: Heinemann.

Nash, B. (1981). The effects of classroom spatial organization on four- and five-year-old children's learning. *British Journal of Educational Psychology, 51*, 144–155.

National Academy of Sciences Committee on the Prevention of Reading Difficultiers in Young Children. (1998). *Preventing reading difficulties in young children* edited by P. Griffin and M. S. Burns. Washington, DC: National Academy Press.

National Center on Education and Economy & Learning Research and Development Center at the University of Pittsburgh. (1999). *Reading and writing grade by grade: Primary literacy standards for kindergarten through third grade*. Washington, DC: National Center on Education and the Economy.

National Center for Family Literacy. (1993). Parents and children together. In *Creating an upward spiral of success* (pp. 6–8). Louisville, KY: Author.

National Reading Panel Report. (2000). *Teaching children to read*. Washington, DC: National Institute of Child Health and Human Development.

National Reading Research Center. (1991). Conceptual framework: The engagement perspective. In *National Reading Research Center: A Proposal from the University of Maryland and the University of Georgia* (pp. 8–10). Athens, GA and College Park, MD: Author.

Neuman, S., & Roskos, K. (1990). The influence of literacy-enriched play settings on preschoolers' engagement with written language. In J. Zutell & S. McCormick (Eds.), *Literacy theory and research: Analyses from multiple paradigms* (pp. 179–187). *39th yearbook of the National Reading Conference*. Chicago, IL: National Reading Conference.

Neuman, S., & Roskos, K. (1992). Literary objects as cultural tools: Effects on children's literacy behaviors in play. *Reading Research Quarterly*, 27 (3), 202–225.

Neuman, S., & Roskos, K. (1993). *Language and literacy learning in the early years: An integrated approach*. Orlando, FL: Harcourt, Brace.

Neuman, S., & Roskos, K. (1994). Building home and school with a culturally responsive approach. *Childhood Education, 70*, 210–214.

Neuman, S. B. (1997). Guiding your children's participation in early literacy development: A family program for adolescent mothers. *Early Childhood Development and Care*, 119–129.

Neuman, S. B., & Roskos, K. (1997). Knowledge in practice: Contexts of participation for young writers and readers. *Reading Research Quarterly, 32*, 10–32.

Newman, J. (1984). *The craft of children's writing.* Exeter, NH: Heinemann.

Ninio, A. (1980). Picture book reading in mother-infant dyads belonging to two subgroups in Israel. *Child Development, 51,* 587.

Ninio, A., & Bruner, J. (1978). The achievement and antecedents of labeling. *Journal of Child Language, 5,* 1–15.

O'Flahavan, J., Gambrell, L. B., Guthrie, J., Stahl, S., & Alverman, D. (1992, April). Poll results guide activities of research center. *Reading Today,* p. 12.

Ogle, D. (1986). K-W-L: A teaching model that develops active reading of expository text. *The Reading Teacher, 39,* 564–570.

Oldfather, P. (1993). What students say about motivating experiences in a whole language classroom. *The Reading Teacher, 46,* 672–681.

Pappas, C., Kiefer, B., & Levstik, L. (1995). *An integrated language perspective in the elementary school, Theory into action.* New York: Longman.

Parker, R. (1983). Language development and learning to write. In R. Parker & F. Davis (Eds.), *Developing literacy: Young children's use of language.* Newark, DE: International Reading Association.

Pearson, P. D., & Johnson, D. D. (1978). *Teaching reading comprehension.* New York: Holt, Rinehart & Winston.

Pearson, P. D., Roehler, L. R., Dole, J. A., & Duffy, G. G. (1992). Developing expertise in reading comprehension. In S. J. Samuels & A. E. Farsturp (Eds.), *What research has to say about reading instruction* (2nd ed., pp. 145–199), Newark, DE: International Reading Association.

Pedersen, P. P. (1994). *A handbook for developing multicultural awareness.* Alexandria, VA: American Counseling Association.

Pellegrini, A., & Galda, L. (1982). The effects of thematic fantasy play training on the development of children's story comprehension. *American Educational Research Journal, 19,* 443–452.

Pflaum, S. (1986). *The development of language and literacy in young children* (3rd ed.). Columbus, OH: Merrill.

Piaget, J., & Inhelder, B. (1969). *The psychology of the child.* New York: Basic Books.

Pinker, S. (1994). *The language instinct: How the mind creates language.* New York: William Morrow.

Pinnell, G. S., Freid, M. D., & Estice, R. M. (1990). Reading recovery: Learning how to make a difference. *The Reading Teacher, 43*(4), 282–295.

Pittelman, S. D., Heimlich, J. E., Berglund, R. L., & French, M. P. (1991). *Semantic feature analysis: Classroom applications.* Newark, DE: International Reading Association.

Pittelman, S. D., Levin, K. M., & Johnson, D. P. (1985). *An investigation of two instructional settings in the use of semantic mapping with poor readers* (Program Report 85–4). Madison: Wisconsin Center for Educational Research, University of Wisconsin.

Prescott, O. (1965). *A father reads to his child: An anthology of prose and poetry.* New York: Dutton.

Pressley, M. (1998). *Reading instruction that works: The case for balanced teaching.* New York: Guilford Press.

Pressley, M., & Afflerbach, P. (1995). *Verbal protocols of reading: The nature of constructively responsive reading.* Hillsdale, NJ: Erlbaum.

Ramirez, J., Yuen, S., Ramey, D., & Pasta, D. (1991). *Final report: Longitudinal study of immersion strategy, early-exit and late-exit transitional bilingual education programs for language minority children.* San Mateo, CA: Aguire International.

Rand, M. (1993). Using thematic instruction to organize an integrated language arts classroom. In L. M. Morrow, J. K. Smith, & L. C. Wilkinson (Eds.), *Integrated language arts: Controversy to consensus* (pp. 177–192). Boston: Allyn & Bacon.

Read, C. (1975). *Children's categorization of speech sounds in English* (National Research Report 17). Urbana, IL: National Council of Teachers of English.

Reutzel, D. R. (1997, March). Maintaining balance as a teacher of children: Reading instruction for all. In L. M. Morrow (Director), *Rutgers 29th Annual Conference on Reading and Writing,* Rutgers University, New Brunswick, NJ.

Robinson, V., Strickland, D., & Cullinan, B. (1977). The child: Ready or not? In L. Ollila (Ed.), *The kindergarten child and reading.* Newark, DE: International Reading Association.

Rosenblatt, L. M. (1988). *Writing and reading: Transactional theory* (Report No. 13). University of California, Berkeley, CA: Center for the Study of Writing.

Rosencrans, G. (1998). *The spelling book: Teaching children how to spell, not what to spell.* Newark, DE: International Reading Association.

Roser, N., & Martinez, M. (1985). Roles adults play in preschool responses to literature. *Language Arts, 62,* 485–490.

Rossi, R., & Stringfield, S. (1995). What we must do for students placed at risk. *Phi Delta Kappa, 77,* 73–76.

Routman, R. (1991). *Invitations: Changing as teachers and learners K–12.* Portsmouth, NH: Heinemann.

Rousseau, J. (1962). *Emile* (ed. and trans. William Boyd). New York: Columbia University Teachers College. (Original work published 1762)

Ruddell, R., & Ruddell, M. R. (1995). *Teaching children to read and write, Becoming an influential teacher.* Boston: Allyn & Bacon.

Rusk, R., & Scotland, J. (1979). *Doctrines of the great educators.* New York: St. Martin's Press.

Schickedanz, J. A. (1986). *More than ABC's: The early stages of reading and writing.* Washington, DC: National Association for the Education of Young Children.

Schickedanz, J. A. (1993). Designing the early childhood classroom environment to facilitate literacy development. In B. Spodek & O. N. Saracho (Eds.), *Language and literacy in early childhood education: Yearbook in early childhood education* (Vol. 4). New York: Teachers College Press.

Schickedanz, J. A., York, M. E., Stewart, I. S., & White, A. (1990). *Strategies for teaching young children*. Englewood Cliffs, NJ: Prentice Hall.

Seefeldt, C., & Barbour, N. (1986). *Early childhood education: An introduction*. Columbus, OH: Merrill.

Sharon, S. (1980). Cooperative learning in small groups: Recent methods and effects of achievement, attitudes, and ethnic relations. *Review of Educational Research, 50,* 241–271.

Skinner, B. F. (1957). *Verbal behavior.* Boston: Appleton-Century-Crofts.

Slavin, R. E. (1987). Ability grouping and student achievement in elementary schools: A best-evidence synthesis. *Review of Educational Research, 57,* 292–336.

Slavin, R. E., & Madden, N. A. (1989). What works for students at risk: A research synthesis. *Educational Leadership, 46,* 4–13.

Smith, F. (1971). *Understanding reading*. New York: Holt, Rinehart & Winston.

Smith, F. (1978). *Understanding reading* (2nd ed.). New York: Holt, Rinehart & Winston.

Smith, F. (1983). A metaphor for literacy: Creating words or shunting information? In F. Smith (Ed.), *Essays into literacy.* Exeter, NH: Heinemann.

Snow, C., & Perlmann, R. (1985). Assessing children's knowledge about bookreading. In L. Galda & A. Pellegrini (Eds.), *Play, language, and stories*. Norwood, NJ: Ablex.

Snow, C. E. (1991). The theoretical basis for relationships between language and literacy in development source. *Journal of Research in Childhood Education, 6,* pp. 5–10.

Sorenson, A. B., & Hallinan, M. T. (1986). Effects of ability grouping on growth in academic achievement. *American Educational Research Journal, 23,* 519–542.

Spaulding, C. I. (1992). The motivation to read and write. In J. W. Irwin & M. A. Doyle (Eds.), *Reading/writing connections: Learning from research* (pp. 177–201). Newark, DE: International Reading Association.

Spiegel, D. L. (1992). Blending whole language and systematic direct instruction. *The Reading Teacher, 46,* 38–44.

Spielberg, S. (1987). Acceptance speech at the Academy Award Ceremonies, Los Angeles.

Spivak, M. (1973). Archetypal place. *Architectural Forum, 140,* 44–49.

Spodek, B. (1988). Conceptualizing today's kindergarten curriculum. *The Elementary School Journal, 89,* 203–212.

Stanovich, K. E. (1986). Mathew effects in reading: Some consequences of individual differences in the acquisition of literacy. *Reading Research Quarterly, 21,* 360–407.

Stauffer, R. G. (1980). *The language-experience approach to the teaching of reading* (2nd ed.). New York: Harper & Row.

Stewart, J., Benjamin, L., & Mason, L. (1987). *An early literacy program: Putting research into practice.* Paper presented at the University of the Virgin Islands.

Sticht, T. G., & McDonald, B. A. (1989). *Making the nation smarter: The intergenerational transfer of cognitive ability.* San Diego, CA: Applied Behavioral and Cognitive Sciences.

Stine, H. A. (1993). *The effects of CD-ROM interactive software in reading skills instructions with second grade Chapter 1 students.* Doctoral dissertation, The George Washington University. Ann Arbor, MI: University Microfilms International.

Sulzby, E. (1985). Children's emergent reading of favorite storybooks. *Reading Research Quarterly, 20,* 458–481.

Sulzby, E. (1986a). Kindergarteners as writers and readers. In M. Farr (Ed.), *Advances in writing research. Vol. 1: Children's early writing.* Norwood, NJ: Ablex.

Sulzby, E. (1986b). Children's elicitation and use of metalinguistic knowledge about "word" during literacy interactions. In P. Yaden & S. Templeton (Eds.), *Metalinguistic awareness and beginning literacy.* Exeter, NH: Heinemann.

Taylor, B. M., Frye, B. J., & Maruyama, M. (1990). Time spent reading and reading growth. *American Educational Research Journal, 27,* 351–362.

Taylor, B. M., Strait, J., & Medo, M. A. (1994). Early intervention in reading: Supplemental instruction for groups of low-achieving students provided by first-grade teachers. In E. H. Hiebert & B. Taylor (Eds.), *Getting ready right from the start* (pp. 107–123). Newark, DE: International Reading Association.

Taylor, D. (1983). *Family literacy.* Exeter, NH: Heinemann.

Taylor, D., & Dorsey-Gaines, C. (1988). *Growing up literate.* Portsmouth, NH: Heinemann.

Taylor, D., & Strickland, D. (1986). *Family storybook reading.* Exeter, NH: Heinemann.

Teale, W. (1982). Toward a theory of how children learn to read and write naturally. *Language Arts, 59,* 555–570.

Teale, W. (1984). Reading to young children: Its significance for literacy development. In H. Goelman, A. Oberg, & F. Smith (Eds.), *Awakening to literacy.* Exeter, NH: Heinemann.

Teale, W. (1986). The beginning of reading and writing: Written language development during the preschool and kindergarten years. In M. Sampson (Ed.), *The pursuit of literacy: Early reading and writing.* Dubuque, IA: Kendal/Hunt.

Teale, W. (1987). Emergent literacy: Reading and writing development in early childhood. In J. Readance & R. S. Baldwin (Eds.), *36th Yearbook of the National Reading Conference.* Rochester, NY: National Reading Conference.

Teale, W., Hiebert, E., & Chittenden, E. (1987). Assessing young children's literary development. *The Reading Teacher, 40,* 772–778.

Temple, C., Nathan, R., Burris, N., & Temple, F. (1988). *The beginnings of writing.* Boston: Allyn & Bacon.

Templeton, S. (1991). *Teaching the integrated language arts.* Boston: Houghton Mifflin.

Tompkins, G. E., & Koskisson, I. K. (1995). *Language arts content and teaching strategies.* Englewood Cliffs, NJ: Prentice Hall.

Turner, J. D. (1992, April). *Identifying motivation for literacy in first grade: An observational study.* Paper presented at the annual meeting of the American Educational Research Association, San Francisco.

Valencia, S. W., Hiebert, E. H., & Afflerbach, P. (Eds.). (1994). *Authentic reading assessment: Practices and possibilities.* Newark, DE: International Reading Association.

Veatch, J., Sawicki, F., Elliot, G., Barnett, E., & Blackey, J. (1973). *Key words to reading: The language experience approach begins.* Columbus, OH: Merrill.

Vygotsky, L. S. (1978). *Mind in society: The development of psychological processes.* Cambridge, MA: Harvard University Press.

Vygotsky, L. S. (1981). The genesis of higher mental functions. In J. J. Wertsch (Ed.), *The concept of activity.* White Plains, NY: M. E. Sharpe.

Walmsley, S. A. (1994). *Children exploring their world: Theme teaching in elementary school.* Portsmouth, NH: Heinemanan.

Ward, M., & McCormick, S. (1981). Reading instruction for blind and low vision children in the regular classroom. *The Reading Teacher, 34,* 434, 444.

Wepner, S., & Ray, L. (2000). Sign of the times: Technology and early literacy learning. In D. S. Strickland & L. M. Morrow (Eds.), *Beginning reading and writing.* New York: Teachers College Press.

Williams, J. P. (1985). The case for explicit decoding instruction. In J. Osborn, P. T. Wilson, & R. C. Anderson (Eds.), *Reading education: Foundations for a literate America.* Lexington, MA: Heath, Lexington Books.

Wittrock, M. C. (1974). Learning as a generative process. *Educational Psychologist, 11,* 87–95.

Wittrock, M. C. (1986). Students' thought processes. In M. C. Wittrock (Ed.), *Handbook of research on teaching* (pp. 297–314). New York: Macmillan.

Woiwode, L. (1992). Television: The cyclops that eats books. *Imprimis, 21,* 1.

Wylie, R., & Durrell, D. D. (1970). Teaching vowels through phonograms. *Elementary English, 47,* 787–791.

Yaden, D. (1985). *Preschoolers' spontaneous inquiries about print and books.* Paper presented at the Annual Meeting of the National Reading Conference, San Diego.

Yager, S., Johnson, D. W., & Johnson, R. T. (1985). Oral discussion, group to individual transfer, and achievement in cooperative learning groups. *Journal of Educational Psychology, 77,* 60–66.

Yopp, H. (1992). Developing phonemic awareness in young children. *The Reading Teacher, 45,* 696–703.

Index

Note: Page numbers followed by f indicate figures.